JY 2 0

PLAY THE WAY YOU FEEL

PLAY THE WAY YOU FEEL

The Essential Guide to Jazz Stories on Film

Kevin Whitehead

OXFORD
UNIVERSITY PRESS

OXFORD
UNIVERSITY PRESS

Oxford University Press is a department of the University of Oxford. It furthers
the University's objective of excellence in research, scholarship, and education
by publishing worldwide. Oxford is a registered trade mark of Oxford University
Press in the UK and certain other countries.

Published in the United States of America by Oxford University Press
198 Madison Avenue, New York, NY 10016, United States of America.

CIP data is on file at the Library of Congress
ISBN 978–0–19–084757–9

9 8 7 6 5 4 3 2 1

Printed by Sheridan Books, Inc., United States of America

In memory of Sally Whitehead and Paul Wernsdorfer

and

for Lesley Ann

I'd like to play like a bird flies—this way and that, up and down, winging and swinging through the air. No control—whistling, singing, shouting. Just music.

—William Washington as Johnny Williams in *Broken Strings*

But this other music makes you feel like the circus is comin' to town. Kinda turns you loose inside. You can stretch out and play what you feel.

—Ronnie Cosby as young Jeff Lambert in *Birth of the Blues*

You just swing on out and play the way you feel like.

—Kid Ory as himself in *The Benny Goodman Story*

I want to be in one of them bands where you could play free. What? Y'all not even up on two feet yet!

—Jaron Williams as Robert and Wendell Pierce as Antoine Batiste on *Treme*

Suppose it happens great one time and you'd like it to happen exactly the same way, what do you do then?

—Danny Kaye as Red Nichols in *The Five Pennies*

CONTENTS

INTRODUCTION

This book is an extended answer to a short question: How do movies tell stories about jazz and jazz musicians? Not just what they get right, or wrong, but how they tell it: jazzy, or not? And if so, how is that jazziness conveyed? *Play the Way You Feel* is partly about jazz movies as a narrative tradition with recurring plot points and story tropes, and we will trace their spread not just through the best-known films that deal with jazz—the likes of *Young Man with a Horn*, *Lady Sings the Blues*, or *La La Land*—but also overlooked and low-budget features and TV movies: any pertinent commercial release in English we could identify and view. There are also shorter discussions of some nonjazz features and a few television episodes that touch on the music, plus longer looks at jazz-related TV series *Staccato* and *Treme*.

Play the Way You Feel is also a practical guide: a music-loving movie-watcher's companion and reference. Within the text, principal films discussed get a heading with pertinent credits; films dealt with more briefly are identified in boldface. They are discussed chronologically, with occasional swerves for the sake of thematic clarity (and indexed in the back).

Jazz and the movies make natural allies. These signature twentieth-century art forms grew up side by side, building on extant traditions. Jazz slowly coalesced out of blues, ragtime, field hollers, spirituals, and brass band music just after 1900, around the time the spectacle of moving pictures was evolving toward storytelling. Early synchronized sound films in the late 1920s were likewise amalgamated from creative borrowings: part staged theatrical, radio play, and variety show.

Sound recording was around before silent movies geared up, but jazz wasn't caught on record until around 1917. Movies with sound would break through a decade later, with 1927's *The Jazz Singer*, a film famously light on jazz content. And both jazz and the sound film evolved amazingly quickly—the former in the mid-1920s, once jazz recordings become common, no less than the talkies by the early 1930s.

Jazz and film are performance arts that unfold over time. Making that time fly is all about rhythm, and patterns of tension and release. Jazz musicians liken improvising a solo to telling a story (maybe inspired by the story the song's lyric tells). These arts may employ parallel syntax, ways to make that story ebb and flow.

Movies cross-cut between simultaneous scenes to build tension. Jazz orchestras build similar tension via call-and-response: punchy phrases volleyed between brass and saxes, recalling the byplay of preacher and choir. Early talking pictures could resemble filmed plays, every actor on set in a master shot; early jazz was about collective interplay, each musician feeding the overall texture. In either medium, at first the pace might be stodgy as performers got their bearings. Then, quickly, those rickety rhythms faded away. In the 1920s outstanding jazz improvisers like Louis Armstrong developed the individual foregrounded (swinging) solo. Before long, independently, the cinema adopted its parallel to the solo, the close-up.[1] Both devices helped foster greater expression and a star system. Armstrong became the most famous jazz musician ever—in no small part because he appeared in so many films.

Jazz musicians would seem ideal movie heroes: artists whose moment of creation is a public, audible spectacle. Improvising on a bandstand is kinetic, photogenic, and romantic. And for a while anyway, jazz represented a kind of artistic and cultural sophistication. Spotlighting extraordinary individuals, jazz movies occasionally ponder where musical talent comes from. We will meet all kinds in the stories that follow: child prodigies, naturals who pick up the music the first time they hear it, hard workers with a painstaking practice regimen, talented players diverted into soul-killing commercial work, even non-improvisers taught to fake it.

The interactions among jazz musicians, on or off stage, are complex and multifaceted; how do films attempt to portray that dynamic? Jazz champions improvisation, but the old studio system, with its massive support structure and complex production schedules, was inimical to improvisation as a concept (even as a few directors found ways to harness improvisational genius and energy). How does the tension between extemporizing loners and team players work itself out?

Such movies are a key point of intersection between jazz and more broadly popular pop culture. And yet, generally speaking, these films get little respect. Cinephiles balk at the melodrama, recycled plots, and compromised roles for black actors, where they appear at all. Reputable film scholars may mangle plot details or confuse one film for another.

On the jazz side, their reputation is even worse. As a trumpeter friend put it, "Why would I watch a movie about Miles Davis when I can watch the real Miles on film?" Even meticulous biographers breeze past or ignore musicians' screen appearances, and tartly dismiss biopics with their gross fabrications. Jazz folk rue the musical inaccuracies and absurdities, the poor miming of playing instruments, and more importantly—as we'll see—how the movies whitewash jazz history. In film after film, African Americans, who invented the music, get pushed to the margins when white characters don't nudge them off screen altogether.

Musicians who appeared in jazz movies often disliked the experience: too much waiting around to deliver a few lines of dumb dialogue. Billie Holiday acted in one short and one feature, and hated making both. Shooting the first, she was knocked to the ground in take after take. In the second, she played an opera singer's maid.

I was already writing about jazz when I started reviewing films in the early 1980s, and jazz movies naturally drew my attention. I grumbled some myself, but the films I saw all had something to recommend them: elegant form (*New York, New York*); reverent atmosphere and on-screen improvising (*'Round Midnight*); some quirk of storytelling that mirrored improvised music's unpredictability (*Bird*). As a jazz chronicler, I was fascinated by how the larger culture (mis)perceived the music. Trained in close reading of literature, I minded jazz tales' seemingly throwaway details and began seeing patterns. As every filmgoer knows, even so-so pictures may contain transcendent moments, much the way a great solo might erupt during a blah nightclub set. And so in 1947's much-derided *New Orleans*—the one where Holiday plays a maid—there's a scene where a classical conductor/pianist credibly jams with and eloquently praises Louis Armstrong: "You're playing notes between flat and natural. It's like discovering secret scales just made for this type of music!" Exactly.

We look at these films from the perspective of jazz history and culture, and approach them with a glass-half-full generosity of spirit, and good faith, assuming each deserves attentive reading. Of course biographical pictures distort musicians' lives—but how, exactly? What salient facts are left in (or out), what's invented—and what other stories does this one echo? What gets mangled just because, as a writer of several jazz films explained, "It doesn't make any difference"? (That said, most biopics get a surprising amount right.)

We delve deep even when that requires keeping a straight face: Can a 1948 Danny Kaye farce tell us anything about the era's jazz scholarship? (Yes.) And it is often in the details that these stories resonate against each other in sympathetic vibration. Movies can call and respond to each other too.

In charting how movies tell jazz stories, *Play the Way You Feel* connects examples over time, spotlighting a few endlessly varied themes. Black musicians educate white ones, who then play their feelings, expressing themselves in subterranean venues; cats of any color would rather fight than compromise their art. Jazz occasionally clashes with classical music, rock, or pop. Where people or styles are in conflict, a climactic (Carnegie Hall) concert may help sort things out.

Looking at features and a few shorts, spectacles and cheap independents, the good, bad, notorious, and overlooked, we seek to illuminate how jazz and its people are regarded in American culture and how filmmakers depict jazz subculture.

Shorter discussions look at films with jazz musicians (or fans) as characters, although we don't pretend to cite all of those, nor many pictures in which famous bands perform standalone numbers. Neither do we discuss nonjazz films with jazz soundtracks, video-jukebox "Soundies," every film where jazz musicians appear as actors, nor films where a character's jazz connection is incidental to the story—such as, say, the 1944 mystery *Phantom Lady*, where Elisha Cook Jr. plays a leering showband drummer who gets overheated at a basement jam session or 2001's *The Score*, where thief Robert De Niro pulls one last job to pay off his nightclub mortgage. Where a film's plot is the point we annotate it; where it's immaterial we mostly leave details for viewers to discover on their own.

A brief preview of the plan: After a *Jazz Singer* prologue, in chapter 1 we chart early instances of jazz as story element in a few features and shorts, before the first real jazz movies emerge during the swing era, prior to the United States' entry into World War II. By the 1940s jazz-related features were coming fast, and we divide them into two streams. Chapter 2 looks at films that depict the music's formative years, paying particular attention to *New Orleans*. Chapter 3 examines stories of bands whose camaraderie is tested, by analogy with military squads.

The 1950s was an age of jazz biopics and literary adaptations, and in the course of chapter 4 we'll examine some source material and note some true stories that biopics sidestep—making for some longer discussions. By the 1950s there are so many movies (and TV shows) that shed sidelights on jazz, we can cover only a sampling of those in chapter 5. In chapter 6, we look at the influence of low-budget independent filmmaking (and director John Cassavetes in particular) on 1960s jazz tales. The 1970s saw studio spectacles *Lady Sings the Blues* and *New York, New York*, plus a stellar low-budget classic featuring an interplanetary jazz hero, and a couple of thrifty TV biopics—this is all detailed in chapter 7, along with one last spectacle from 1984. The 1980s, per chapter 8, offered a similarly mixed bag of prestige pictures and low-budget indies.

Chapter 9 looks at the generation of younger jazz musicians who came up in the 1980s as represented on film in the 1990s. Here also we see a new trend gathering: stories with unreliable narrators—a "new" rationale for fanciful storylines. That theme carries over into chapter 10, which like chapter 5 surveys how jazz musicians and fans are portrayed in nonjazz movies; there we backtrack to scoop up a few films where jazz musicians perform in unlikely settings. Chapter 11 looks at twenty-first-century jazz tales (including the cable TV series *Treme*) and an outbreak of movies-within-movies. We end with *Bolden* in 2019, rounding off the first century of jazz on record.

In one important area, jazz films do get respect. In recent decades, they've received considerable scholarly attention, and I draw on much of that research, starting with Krin Gabbard's pioneering 1996 *Jammin' at the Margins*. Its viewpoint is more psychological than music-historical, but more than once I found myself retracing his steps. Another valuable book-length study, Morris B. Holbrook's 2011 *Music, Movies, Meanings, and Markets: Cinemajazzmatazz*, should be better known. My hope is to extend the discussion; books too can engage in a kind of dialogue.

I try to relate my findings in plain and lively language, using few specialized terms, the most cited being the verbs *sideline* and *ghost*, and adjectives *diegetic* and *nondiegetic*. Typically, an actor (or musician) on screen will mime playing an instrument to a prerecorded music track. Such miming is called sidelining. The musician heard on the soundtrack is said to be ghosting for that actor or character (by analogy with ghostwriting). Diegetic music exists within a film's action—the characters can hear it. Music on the soundtrack they can't hear is nondiegetic.

All images in the text are screen shots from the films themselves, not publicity stills. Short citations in the chapter endnotes are keyed to the bibliography.

Movies that tell jazz stories cut across diverse genres: biopic, romance, musical, comedy, and science fiction; horror, crime, and comeback stories; "race movies" and modernized Shakespeare. But they also make up a genre of their own, with narrative and stylistic conventions that rise up, recede, and maybe return, even as new ones arise to replace them. It was time someone tried to survey them all—even knowing down deep there's always one more out there.

PROLOGUE: THE "I GOT RHYTHM" OF JAZZ MOVIES, 1927 AND 1946

The Jazz Singer (1927; 88 minutes; director: Alan Crosland; story: Alfred A. Cohn, from a play by Samson Raphaelson). Cast includes: Al Jolson (Jakie Rabinowitz/Jack Robin), Warner Oland (Cantor Rabinowitz), Eugenie Besserer (Sara Rabinowitz), May McAvoy (Mary Dale).
—Jakie Rabinowitz pursues a career as blackface entertainer Jack Robin, to the horror of his cantor father. Jack must choose between family and show business when he's asked to substitute for his dying father at temple, the night of his own Broadway debut.

It's a critical commonplace that entertainment dynamo Al Jolson—a son of Jewish immigrants who was noted for showily emoting as he sang, and who came to prominence performing in blackface, was no jazz singer, despite the title of the Jolson vehicle that brought synchronized dialogue to feature films. And yet *The Jazz Singer*, about a politely rebellious son whose appetite for modern music clashes with Dad's conservative tastes, is a template for a half dozen jazz stories to come: stories that will ring changes on its familiar plot, the way jazz musicians make up their own melodies to the chords of George Gershwin's "I Got Rhythm." The *Jazz Singer* also points the way for other jazz films as the original backstage musical, broadly defined: a story in which the characters are performers who have reasons to break into song—on stage, in rehearsal, sight-reading—and where a performed song's lyric may (often by happenstance) reflect a singer's own emotions. Jolson's Jack Robin sings "Mother of Mine, I Still Have You" on stage, as scheduled, after a surprise visit from mom.

The fact that Jolson was ever tagged as a jazz artist reminds us that in the 1920s, when jazz exploded into American culture, folks who invoked the word weren't always sure what it meant. Was its defining feature improvisation? Syncopation? Was it modern pop, orchestral ragtime, deliberate noisemaking, or stunt work, with drummers bouncing sticks off the floor?

Jolson's conversational emotionalism didn't have the loose, compelling rhythmic momentum jazz folk call "swing," but it wasn't totally unrelated. Famous for rarely singing a song the same way twice, Jolson would alter the melody, phrasing, or lyrics. His half-sung, half-talked routines suggest the influence of one early swinging vocalist, black music-hall comedian Bert Williams, whose line readings jump ahead of or lag behind a written melody with quasi-improvised snap. (Jolson covered Williams specialties "Nobody" and "Why Adam Sinned."[1]) But context matters. Jolson didn't record or associate with players now regarded as jazz musicians (overlooking Cab Calloway's appearances in Jolie's 1936 *The Singing Kid*).

We might think of Jolson, stylistically, as a music-hall performer who'd transitioned halfway to jazz, making him the right star for a technologically transitional part-sound, part-silent film that's about being caught between worlds: between tradition and innovation in music, between religion and the secular life, between the shtetl ways of the hero's parents and his own let's-try-anything attitude, between Jewish family and shiksa girlfriend, between dual identities as the Lower East Side's Jakie Rabinowitz and Broadway's Jack Robin. Of his progressive views, he tells his parents: "If you were born here you'd feel the same as I do."

He's also adrift between black and white visages. Late in the film, the first time he puts on blackface makeup—something Jolson's quick and sure application of burnt cork makes clear he's done many, many times—Jakie looks in the mirror and sees his cantor-father's face. Jack's/Jolson's blackface routines show how a mask can embolden a performer; paradoxically, it makes him more nakedly emotive. As Ted Gioia has noted, Jolson's blackface is divorced from shuck-and-jive racial caricature: "He truly had little knack for the ridicule, irony and sarcasm that racist humor requires for its effect."[2]

In *The Jazz Singer* blackface is one marker of how far Jack has traveled from Eldridge Street. In the most expressive silent scene, he has just blacked up for his Broadway dress rehearsal when his mother comes by his dressing room to talk. She looks at his painted face with utter incomprehension. The gap between their life experiences has grown too great.

Little as it's noted, *The Jazz Singer* does in fact boast one of the movies' earliest jazz solos and some (verbal) improvising. Besides singing and dancing, Jolson did an astonishing whistling bit, demonstrated on "Toot Toot Tootsie," a virtuoso set piece. Using fingers to help manipulate the airstream, he trills and rips like a bird, with piercing tone, and throws in slippery glissandi all his own, even as he paraphrases the melody and chooses pitches that follow the chords. It's a routine, but a real jazz solo just the same.

The verbal improvising comes later. Years after fleeing home to make his way in the world, Jakie returns to New York to rehearse for a Broadway revue and stops by his parents' flat where he finds his mother. (She's played by Eugenie Besserer, a virtuoso of reaction shots after making hundreds of silents.) Jakie leads her to the parlor where—as we switch from silence to sound—he previews one of his featured numbers from the show, Irving Berlin's "Blue Skies." Jolson inexpertly mimes the piano part; he strides across the keyboard with his right hand instead of his left.

He sings one chorus, then breaks off to ad lib dialogue for the microphone, telling Mama how much he loves her, and how great life's going to be once he makes it and they

FIGURE 0.1 Al Jolson, jazz whistler, in *The Jazz Singer*.

move to the Bronx. Besserer makes a feeble attempt to keep up, seemingly as knocked out by his prattling as the movie audience was going to be. Then he returns to an even more frenetic "Blue Skies"—"I'm gonna sing it jazzy," he says, throwing in a few scatlike *do-do-dos*—brought to an abrupt end when his father appears in the doorway, and yells "Stop!" to end the sound sequence. The cantor's command to halt progress turns back the clock: it returns us to the silent era, depriving the son of his voice. In that moment the film's form and content become one.

The Jazz Singer anticipates later jazz films in another way, by promoting the notion that for a performance to be valid, the artist has to really mean it—has to sing the way he feels with no faking. At the climax, when Jack debates blowing off his Broadway debut to sub for his dying father at temple on Yom Kippur, Mama advises, "Do what is in your heart, Jakie. If you sing and God is not in your voice—your father will know."

The Jolson Story (**1946; 129 minutes; director: Alfred E. Green** [**musical numbers directed by uncredited Joseph H. Lewis**]**; screenplay: Stephen Longstreet; adaptation: Harry Chandlee, Andrew Solt). Cast includes: Larry Parks (Al Jolson), William Demarest (Steve Martin), Ludwig Donath (Cantor Yoelson), Tamara Shayne (Mrs. Yoelson), John Alexander (Lew Dockstader), Evelyn Keyes (Julie Benson), Scotty Beckett (young Asa Yoelson).**

—Asa Yoelson pursues a career as (blackface) entertainer Al Jolson, to the delight of his cantor father. But the compulsive performer must choose between family and show business when his wife wishes he'd spend more time at home.

Two decades later, the fanciful Technicolor *Jolson Story* would invent a rationale for *The Jazz Singer's* title. Jolson (Larry Parks), a young apprentice with Dockstader's blackface minstrels, wanders out of a New Orleans theater before the show one evening, sans makeup, and into a black neighborhood where he discovers a spirited (and uncredited) early jazz band, playing for themselves and the neighbors in an outdoor carriageway. He is welcomed and watches them spellbound. Al returns to the theater eager to spread the news: "I heard some music tonight—something they call jazz. Some fellas just make it up as they go along—they pick it out of the air." He always describes it in race-blind terms.

Jazz gives Jolson fresh ideas about modernizing his own and the troupe's music, and finding ways out of the trap of singing songs the same way every time. Back at the minstrel show his ideas are curtly rebuffed—the real Lew Dockstader was in fact anti-syncopation, though he gave Jolson more exposure and creative leeway than he does here. Shortly thereafter, movie-Al describes working with songwriters to put that jazz feeling into the material he sings. But he never goes out to hear such music again or to seek out its performers. He takes their idea and runs in his own direction.

This fabricated origin myth is as old as minstrelsy itself. It's a retelling of how, in the 1830s, traveling entertainer from up north Thomas D. Rice observed a black singer/dancer performing for his own amusement at a Louisville livery stable. From that model (the story goes) Rice created the blackface caricature Jim Crow, the template for a zillion white minstrels into the twentieth century.

Like most biopics, *The Jolson Story* takes broad liberties with the truth. It also tweaks the *Jazz Singer* plot for the amusement of a knowing audience. To strengthen the parallels to Jack Robin's story, it eliminates young Asa Yoelson's siblings, and has his mother survive into his adulthood. *The Jolson Story* begins in a burlesque house, and is partly a burlesque of the earlier film itself. In *The Jazz Singer*, Jakie is discovered singing in a saloon by a tattling member of his father's congregation; in *The Jolson Story*, Asa's discovered in the showbiz sense, while singing along from the balcony, by vaudeville performer/composite character Steve Martin (*Jazz Singer* bit player William Demarest, exhaling greasepaint). That becomes their act. Steve and Asa replicate that balcony discovery in theater after theater: shtick masquerading as spontaneity. Cantor Rabinowitz renounced his entertainer son; in *The Jolson Story*, Al's cantor father reads *Variety* to track Jolie's success, decoding the lingo for his wife. "Sockeroo, mama? That's double socko!" (The real Papa Yoelson leaned more toward Cantor Rabinowitz.) And both films end with scenes where Jolson sings an ode to Mammy (here it's "Rockabye Your Baby") with his mother in the house.

Larry Parks is a sort of hyper-real Jolson, with better looks and more hair, doing an extended solo on the Jolson persona—much the way any biopic takes a few motifs from its subject's life, works variations on it, and cribs from existing material, developing the story in a manner akin to a jazz improvisation. Parks is a virtuoso lip-syncher in close-up; he's ghosted by Jolson, singing his old hits with his later, lower, more leathery, and ever-so-slightly jazzier voice. So even the singing is hyper-real. (There's a self-reflexive 1949 sequel, *Jolson Sings Again*, where during a USO-tour montage Al briefly sings a jazzy chorus of "Chinatown, My Chinatown" with jamming GIs, and where Jolson, again played by Larry Parks, meets Larry Parks and goes to see *The Jolson Story*.)

In *The Jolson Story*, Al first blacks up to cover for a drunken colleague who can't go on, backing into the practice. He's never rueful or apologetic about it, though he phases it out as he gets more successful. Parks's blackface routines, also devoid of shamblin' stereotypes, are weirdly, creepily seductive, more than Jolson's own. Parks makes you see the appeal of late-phase minstrelsy to earlier generations of white (and black) Americans. The blackface signifier seems to float free of any meaningful relationship to actual black America, and thus free of racial animus. The sinister minstrel becomes just an eager-to-please white man in harlequin makeup.

There's a glimmer of some other possibility there, a less absurd and sordid marriage of black and white aesthetics. Something like jazz.

/// 1 /// DUKE'S DAY AND FIRST FEATURES 1929–1940

Jazz Singer knockoffs came quickly. The sobbing Jolson of the clarinet, Ted Lewis, starred in the (mostly) lost 1929 feature *Is Everybody Happy?* as Ted Todd, who trades in his violin for saxophone and starts a jazz band, alienating his Hungarian immigrant folks. The film mainstreams the *Jazz Singer* paradigm: the family reconciles on Christmas Day.

The fictitious Four Seasons in director Wesley Ruggles's **Street Girl** (1929), penned by prolific screenwriter Jane Murfin, demonstrate that period definitions of jazz could be squishy. This quartet of multi-instrumentalists play their bread-and-butter song "Lovable and Sweet" hotsy-totsy and also sing it in bland harmony. But the hot music gets deemphasized when they fall in with schmaltzy Mitteleuropean violinist Frederika Joyzell (Utah-born Betty Compson, who played violin). She makes them a hit, if only because the papers link her to a dashing prince from the old country. Yet Fredi only has eyes for the band's sulky, jealous trumpeter/pianist. At the end, she begins to assimilate, fiddling along with the boys on one last boisterous "Lovable and Sweet." That number and the Gershwin knockoff "Broken Up Tune," both by Gershwin chum Oscar Levant, inject what little spark and momentum *Street Girl* has. Even comics Jack Oakie and Ned Sparks come off as starchy.

The coming of synchronized dialogue actually made some early talkies less visually dynamic. As silent star Mary Pickford said, "Looking at the artistic evolution of pictures, you would think the talkies had come *first*."[1] To record live dialogue on set, directors might arrange actors in fixed positions around hidden microphones. A scene might resemble a tableau with sound more than a moving picture.

So it goes in 1929's **The Vagabond Lover**, directed by Marshall Neilan, whose silent comedies were admired by Howard Hawks. It starred crooner and saxophonist Rudy Vallee, a post-Jolson singing sensation who occasionally hinted at hot rhythm. Hubert Vallée had gotten his nickname because he idolized reed virtuoso Rudy Wiedoeft. Vallee

FIGURE 1.1 Immigrant violinist Frederika (Betty Compson) tries on jazz in *Street Girl*.

was no great saxophonist, but he did get a pleasant sound. His alto playing on radio—that other medium that came of age in the late 1920s, and the one that made him a star—allegedly inspired 11-year-old Charlie Parker in Kansas City.[2]

The Vagabond Lover namechecks jazz, but fails to evoke its hectic innovations; it's the rare jazz-free jazz film. Fronting his own sweet octet, the Connecticut Yankees (plus a couple of actor ringers), Vallee plays amateur bandleader Rudy Bronson. He has recently stepped up his (modest) saxophone chops via mail-order lessons and a mail-order horn, both endorsed by Ted Grant (Malcolm Waite), "the greatest living bandleader—the man who made America jazz-minded," and "the greatest saxophone player in the world," in Grant's own estimation.

Bronson and company seek out this paragon at his posh Long Island rental and Rudy's band is mistaken for Grant's. They wind up playing under his name on a neighboring dowager's musical evening. Despite Grant's massive radio presence, no one notices till later that Bronson's an imposter—not even when he sings the new song "If You Were the Only Girl in the World" like a simpering Rudy Vallee.

There are dim glimmers of the star's biography in James Ashmore Creelman's script. Young Vallee had briefly corresponded with Wiedoeft, who'd given him some tips, and later they became friendly in New York. Around the time they corresponded, Vallee had bought a mail-order saxophone. And Bronson, like Vallee, breaks through via radio.[3]

We don't hear Ted Grant perform, but Rudy Bronson is no improviser, playing the same mildly variational alto chorus on "Nobody's Sweetheart" twice, minutes apart. Vallee always insisted he was no jazz musician, and there's no jazzy momentum in Bronson's music, or the movie, save for a brief dance interlude.

Perhaps a lack of jazziness is the film's point: snobby commentary on the music's ephemeral value. Everyone's into jazz for the wrong reasons. Ted Grant is a vain, touchy cynic, who sneers at fans and fakes interest in his nominal students—though he likes Rudy when he finally hears him, recognizing a monetizable success story. The dowager swears "I just adore jazz" but drafts the band in hopes of besting a social rival who champions opera singers. Bronson uses his saxophone mostly as a prop, like a sixties rock singer's tambourine.

It would take a director with more sensitivity to timing and the gumption to move the camera a little, or fill the frame (and soundtrack) with activity, to do justice to the music—preferably better music. The proper jazz film gets off to a stronger start with a pair of 1929 two-reelers spotlighting Bessie Smith and Duke Ellington, written and directed by an early maverick of American cinema, Dudley Murphy. Born in 1897, Murphy started working as an extra in the fledgling Los Angeles movie business. Before long he started making his own arty shorts featuring scantily clad women in seaside locales. By 1923 he was in jazz-crazed Paris, where along with his new friends Ezra Pound and Man Ray he began work on an abstract, playful art film with jazzy energy. Painter Fernand Léger later became involved, and 1924's *Ballet mécanique* is often credited to him, but Murphy was the only real filmmaker among the four and the only one involved throughout. That 16-minute film makes conspicuous use of rhythm and repetition, recurring sequences, mirrored, inverted, or upside-down images, kaleidoscopic fragmentation, and double-vision effects.

Murphy made his own edit of *Ballet mécanique*, which he brought back to New York. For its first American run in 1926, some (unidentified) Harlem drummer improvised to the film every night, a reminder that some early meetings of jazz and movies occurred when improvisers like Fats Waller accompanied silents in theaters. (Jazz musicians had also appeared in silent films, going back to the Original Dixieland Jazz Band in a 1917 comedy.[4] And Eubie Blake and others had appeared in pre–*Jazz Singer* phonofilm sound shorts.) The post–*Jazz Singer* transitional period created demand for performance-oriented sound shorts to fill out theater programs. Murphy's were among the more ambitious, fusing story and song—anticipating the video-jukebox Soundies he'd make with African American talent in the 1940s.

St. Louis Blues (1929; 16 minutes; director/writer: Dudley Murphy). Cast includes: Bessie Smith (Bessie), Jimmy Mordecai (Jimmy), Alec Lovejoy (building supervisor), Hall Johnson Choir.
—Wronged by her two-timing gambling man, Bessie sings the blues, and a barroom full of onlookers joins in.

St. Louis Blues showcased W. C. Handy's song of the same name, by 1929 one of the great hits of the century. (Today there are literally thousands of jazz recordings.) Handy and Murphy would each claim to have come up with the idea for the film and for casting as its star the Empress of the Blues, Bessie Smith.[5] She had recorded a memorable "St. Louis Blues" in 1925, with Louis Armstrong tartly answering her voice on cornet over Fred Longshaw's country-church harmonium.

African American blues compiler, composer, and publisher Handy made liberal use of melodies and lyrics he heard in his travels, incorporating them into his copyrighted tunes; he was among the first of countless composers to lay claim to traditional blues. That practice—and calling his 1941 autobiography *Father of the Blues*—made him easy to denigrate. (We return to him in chapter 4.) But this 1914 song is a marvel of construction, with the formal variety of ragtime, the heartfelt quality of downhome blues, and three memorable melodies.

"St. Louis Blues" figures in several jazz films, and is itself a three-scene short subject in rhythm, with contrasting slow and fast blues themes in G major flanking a G minor tango. Handy said later he put in that interlude ("St. Louis woman, with her diamond rings") because the tango was all the rage in the 'teens and for the sheer pleasure of breaking out of straight 4/4 into Latin syncopation. (Technically, with its delayed second-beat rhythmic hiccup, that tango is a Cuban habanera as heard in countless Chicago blues mambos and booting rock-and-roll sax riffs.)

The third-section blues is jumpier than the opening strain, the chords sometimes changing with every beat. It draws on sources sacred and profane. The insistent rising-falling three-note pattern—"Got the *Saint*/Lou-ie *blues*"—came from the chant of an Alabama preacher, rattling the collection plate. And Handy had overheard one line of the lyric—"My man's got a heart like a rock cast in the sea"—muttered by a woman on a St. Louis street in 1893. The song's story is a template for the cry-in-your-beer brand of blues. The singer's man has left her, his head turned by a hussy's diamond ring and off-the-shelf wig. And the pain gets worse at sunset.

Though Bessie Smith was by all accounts magnetic on stage, *St. Louis Blues* is her only film, despite the range she demonstrates in it. Her first two minutes on screen are a virtual demo reel. As the character Bessie arrives at her rooming house to find another woman with her scornful man, she's by turns happy, puzzled, anxious, anguished, belligerent, violent, pleading, and desperate. That's all before she sings a note—before the grand symphonic "St. Louis Blues" that makes up the second half.

Like Handy's blues, the story unfolds in three scenes and settings. *St. Louis Blues* begins in an upstairs boarding-house hallway where a crap game is in progress. Bessie's peacock of a boyfriend Jimmy makes a typically grand entrance. He knows he cuts a fine figure: a trim handsome man in a flashy three-piece suit, tan shoes, and perfect fedora. His nameless outside woman, with her store-bought mop of hair and a flashing ring containing what may not be a real diamond, rubs the dice for luck, to good effect.

But that's just the foreground action. Director Murphy values texture both visual and sonic. Down the hallway, straight behind the crap game, women come and go, busying themselves for the camera. The soundtrack has a similar deep focus—a stunning aspect of the film seldom noted. Behind the dialogue, fragments of music are heard: a primitive blues wail played on a reedy harmonica, what sounds like Bessie Smith singing unaccompanied, a few scattered notes of guitar.

That reedy mouth harp continues in the background when Jimmy and his mistress adjourn to Bessie's room and the dialogue starts moving toward song. Speaking of his woman's way with the dice, Jimmy tells her, "Whatever you did it was tight like that"—singing the last three words, as in the current hit "It's Tight Like That." They start messing around, and Bessie bursts in, halfway through that gamut of emotions that began in the hallway when she arrived and was advised to check her room. She and the woman squabble; the building super comes in to evict Bessie over the ruckus.

Bessie begs Jimmy not to leave in spite of it all, but he's already packed: "Woman, I'll be gone before the evening sun goes down." And as he delivers that paraphrase of Handy's opening lyric, that same harmonica whines and a few guitar notes are plucked in the background, as if a performer were checking the tuning before a song. These scraps of background blues appear to be diegetic—music of the boarding-house environment. The soundtrack subtly introduces some of the raw materials Bessie is about to put into her musical cry of pain.

Jimmy knocks her down, primps in the mirror, and laughs on his way out the door, shaking her off as she grabs at his leg. Alone, on the floor, she starts to moan a line that takes her a few tries (and a shot of gin from a nearby bottle) to get all the way out: "My man's got a heart like a rock cast in the sea"—the very line Handy had heard in St. Louis when *he* was absorbing the song's raw materials. It's as if Bessie reenacts its creation.

We cut from a medium shot to a close-up and she sings the complete line four times, shaping the melody into two abbreviated blues choruses. As she sings, between those choruses the scene shifts to a barroom. Bessie's at the rail by the service area with a mug of beer, mulling over her predicament. She worries that lyric and melody, as if musing how to develop them further—how to turn her hurt into music: how to sing the way she feels.

This saloon is the film's grand set, a Harlem nightspot re-created on a midtown Manhattan soundstage, with real beer on the tables. There's a bandstand against the left wall, opposite the bar; in back, right-angled stairs lead up to the street. (Jazz movies have loved subterranean venues from the first.) As a traveling camera walks us past the 10-piece band, the pianist (esteemed James P. Johnson) strikes up a proper intro at a slow drag tempo. Bessie at the bar sings how she hates to see that evening sun go down, and all the folks sitting sedately at tables join in—they're the Hall Johnson Choir, including Handy's daughter Katherine. Their answerbacks variously echo Bessie's line, exhort her to continue, or wordlessly fill in the texture with stringlike chromatic runs as the band plays softly. The choir is so worked up by the second strain they all but drown out the rhythm section's bumping tango. By the third strain the singers are more percussive and abstract—rebels in the amen corner. But they never look her way.

The film slices the blues several ways. Bessie ostensibly spins her lyric off Jimmy's exit line, and then the choir takes it up. So the blues is both an utterance from the

FIGURE 1.2 Bessie Smith feels a song coming on in *St. Louis Blues*.

heart and a collective composition, a lone voice amplified and refined by everyone who has a go at the same material. On the one hand, the collective wisdom of the community gives the music its cumulative power. On the other hand, all the instrumentalists have sheet music in front of them; this particular blues is available for sale from Handy Brothers Music Co.

After Bessie sings the third strain, something curious happens—the choir goes off book, taking the lead—and now Bessie answers them, the only time she acknowledges their presence. They sing one of those floating blues verses that seems to have been around forever and that turns up in countless songs (like Carl Perkins's "Matchbox"), though not in "St. Louis Blues": "Let me be your little dog till your big dog comes (2x)/ Then tell your big dog what your little dog done."

Extraneous verses with no connection to the rest of the song are a venerable blues and folk tradition; they're often used as placeholders when a performer can't think of anything better. But what to make of this interjection? It's not as if the choir were coming on to her. (They've barely turned their heads in her direction.) Are they taunting her with some past indiscretion? Whatever the reason, it marks a radical change of tone, with another directly ahead. As soon as that verse is finished, the trumpets take the lead, the band modulates to a brighter key and tempo, and the players swing into a disarmingly merry "St. Louis Blues" as heard under the opening credits.

The room's mood instantly shifts from commiseration to mockery, as folks jump out of their chairs to start dancing—as if Bessie's anguish had become too much to bear without release. The blues laughs at miseries, and 1920s horn players who accompanied blues singers like Smith could take a heckling stance. That mockery turns explicit when Jimmy enters, dressed as before and reacting as if all this jubilation were on his account. The crowd greets him as if he were right.

Jimmy preens for the room and does a self-congratulatory two-step, a few feet from Bessie who fails to notice till he hails her by name. She turns, and her face lights up for the only time in this long sequence—her smile is a blinding flash of warmth. They embrace, the band goes into a slow-drag version of the second blues theme, and they start a clasping, slow reunion dance. But it's all a sham, an opportunity for Jimmy to filch the money secreted in her stocking-top. Once he's got it, he flings her away and she lands back at her spot at the bar. (This cad who puts on airs, takes Bessie's money, and keeps a flashier woman on the side is a stand-in for Smith's no-good husband Jack Gee; they'd split up only months before.) Jimmy grandly exits with her cash in hand as the band sarcastically quotes the grand opening of Gershwin's *Rhapsody in Blue*. Bessie all but literally cries in her beer as the choir takes up Handy's blues with a vengeance, a meanness to it now. Bessie joins in for the ending, still crying over the lout.

Murphy's visual scheme reinforces this emotionally messy dynamic. Bessie's deep connection to the song is at the heart of the sequence, but while singing she stands at the bar, in profile. Aside from staggering a little to signal she's drunk, she barely moves; her singing conveys it all.

Murphy used four cameras synchronized to music recorded live on set (a feat in itself), and photographed Smith from 20 feet out, using a long lens, so as not to distract her. But she's not always alone in the frame. A bartender steps in and out of view, his face a series of reactions—pity, worry she might be trouble, amusement at Jimmy's antics, an all-business demeanor. His silent obbligatos are in counterpoint to the often off-screen choir. Customers and waiters sometimes pass between Bessie and the camera, reminding us that her isolation is public. A waiter tries to amuse her, twirling a tray. *St. Louis Blues* is a male director's woman's picture; the heroine suffers for our entertainment. And so the bar's carefree crowd mirrors the one in the movie theater. The only person who displays any sympathy? That disapproving bartender, ruefully shaking his head at her low condition, if not the way she's been treated.

The film refines the *Jazz Singer*'s authenticity principle: A performer's (improvised) music is a display of untempered emotion. In the movies, jazz artists play or sing the way they feel—unlike, say, actors, who know how to fake it. You've got to suffer if you want to sing the blues—in contrast to Smith's records, where she might keep more aesthetic distance. Hear how pitilessly she handled a similarly worthless man on "Aggravatin' Papa (Don't You Try to Two-Time Me)" back in 1923.

When all's done, the real star of *St. Louis Blues* is Handy's song itself. We hear it as vehicle for sorrow, joy, derision, and dancing pleasure: a composition suitable for all occasions. Also in 1929, it turns up in King Vidor's dynamic black-cast musical melodrama *Hallelujah*; backsliding reformed woman Nina Mae McKinney sings it shortly before her demise.

> ***Black and Tan* (1929; 19 minutes; director/writer: Dudley Murphy). Cast includes: Duke Ellington, Fredi Washington, Arthur Whetsol (themselves), Alec Lovejoy (piano mover), Irving Mills (stage announcer), Five Blazers (dancers), Hall Johnson Choir.**
>
> **—Duke Ellington rehearses his new "Black and Tan Fantasy." His girlfriend Fredi pursues a dancing career, despite a weak heart, and collapses on stage. Her dying wish is to hear Duke's new composition in toto.**

Bessie Smith enjoyed making *St. Louis Blues*—when shooting was finished, she dropped by Murphy's place with a celebratory case of gin. But her singing aside, she didn't exert creative control. The director's follow-up *Black and Tan* was a very different case; Duke Ellington's fingerprints are all over it.

Starting in the late 1920s, when Ellington was making his reputation at Harlem's Cotton Club, he, manager Irving Mills, and their press agents effectively shaped Duke's image as a serious American composer not to be lumped in with mere jazz bandleaders or entertainers. Every aspect of Ellington's presentation underscored it: the focus on original and highly distinctive material, his impeccable dress and aristocratic manner. (Edward Kennedy Ellington had picked up the nickname Duke early.) Putting him on film in the right vehicle fit the publicity plan. Most likely Mills made the deal; he handled all the business decisions.[6]

As Murphy biographer Susan Delson points out, the director's penchant for African American themes didn't stem from passion for social justice or racial equality.[7] He was attracted to the music's excitement and the stylish people. The high degree of stylization in his own art made a good fit with Ellington's. The 1927 composition "Black and Tan Fantasy" by Duke and his pioneering wah-wah trumpeter Bubber Miley is a case in point. Its first theme, played over a blues chord sequence, paraphrases the chorus of the Protestant hymn "The Holy City." Twice during that theme, a single pitch is sounded four times in a lightly syncopated *dum-dum-da-dum* rhythm, as in the signature motif of Chopin's "Funeral March." That allusion sets up a quotation from the same work at the end of the piece, a dramatic finale that earned the composition much acclaim and a key spot in Ellington's repertoire.

The film *Black and Tan* is built around that very piece. As it opens, Ellington is playing (a fictionalized version of) himself at an upright piano in his boarding-house room. Dressed for work in vest and shirtsleeves, he runs down the first two strains of his new "Black and Tan Fantasy" for visiting bandsman Arthur Whetsol—he's still got his hat on—who reads the wah-wah muted trumpet line off the page. That the song was two years old makes *Black and Tan* a biographical picture, which in classic biopic fashion invents dramatic situations and writes a key figure out of the story. By 1929, co-composer Miley was out of the band, and is unmentioned here; Whetsol hadn't yet joined when it was first recorded. (Duke probably picked Whetsol for the role, finding him presentable and reliable.)[8]

Whetsol and Ellington play live on camera. The composer is portrayed throughout as a dignified figure, in stark contrast to two comically illiterate movers who arrive to repossess Duke's piano until girlfriend Fredi Washington gets home and buys them off with a bottle of gin. (Washington also plays a fictionalized self; she and Ellington were involved for a time.) Ellington's body language during this transaction is revealing; one gathers he was directed to look at these piano-moving buffoons with amusement. In a medium shot he plants a placid smile on his face but leans away like a Pisan tower, managing to look both amused and askance. (The chatty mover is Alec Lovejoy, the building super in *St. Louis Blues*.) As they're leaving, we see where Whetsol disappeared to; he sits in a corner, reading a magazine, occupying his mind. The contrast between musicians and movers highlights the film's internal contradictions.

Fredi announces she's secured a featured dance spot at a club, with Duke's band in support. He reminds her of her doctor's warning—her heart is too weak. But she's determined, and changes the subject by asking to hear that new tune they're working up; she steps on Duke's line, but he rolls with it. Duke and Art reprise the opening of "Black and Tan Fantasy" before the fade.

In the next scene Ellington's orchestra is on that job, playing "The Duke Steps Out" at a fancy (but not Cotton Club–like) venue with a mirrored dance floor in front of the stage, playing for a quintet of male dancers, the Cotton Club's Five Blazers. When the band goes into the lovely "Black Beauty," the Blazers go into their "one man dance," a soft shoe in unison and close formation, one in front of another, a tightly packed queue, quintupled. Even the loose drape of their trousers falls in unison. We see this spectacle from all angles as the formation rotates on stage. The effect is made doubly bizarre by that mirrored floor; all those visual repetitions suggest trick photography. It's a visual analogue to what Ellington does in "Black and Tan Fantasy," superimposing "The Holy City," Chopin, and the blues.

But Murphy is just getting started, as he cuts away to a skimpily clad Fredi in the wings, looking wan and unsteady as she waits to go on. The director gives the viewer no cues to signal a leap back in time, but what we see next is those same two Blazers numbers (almost three minutes of action) repeated from what is and isn't Fredi's point of view: a doubling of the action in time, and also in space. There are a few shots of Duke and the orchestra from her sidestage perspective, and cutaways to Fredi, but mostly we see the Blazers from the audience's viewpoint, with one crucial difference. To convey her fragile state, they're refracted through a quasi-kaleidoscopic fly's-eye lens, repeating the basic image as many as seven times, so that at one point during the one-man dance 35 Blazers (and four Ellingtons) crowd the frame. Murphy has replicated *Ballet mécanique*'s avant-garde flourishes—rhythm and repetition, recurring sequences, inverted or upside-down images, kaleidoscopic fragmentation, and double-vision effects—in a naturalistic story setting.

FIGURE 1.3 Duke Ellington and the unison-dancing Five Blazers, in kaleidoscopic view, in *Black and Tan*.

Ellington later performed "Black Beauty" as "Portrait of Florence Mills." The 1920s stage dancer had died of tuberculosis in 1927 at 31, weakened by an exhausting work schedule. She may have inspired the character Fredi. Soon after, Fredi comes on doing her shimmy-shake-hula-strut high-kicking routine to an uptempo "Cotton Club Stomp"— some of it shot from below, as if through the mirrored floor. Fredi collapses; a trouper, she holds on till the song's final bar.

The emcee (Duke's manager Irving Mills) instantly tells some stagehands to drag her off. "Sit down Duke and play something," he directs the alarmed bandleader. "Play the girls' number. Get the show on. Keep the show on." Ellington takes his orders, and a line of feathered Cotton Club chorines hit the stage to the tune of "Hot Feet." But when Duke overhears Mills tell a stagehand, "Don't tell him now, wait till after the show," the bandleader cuts the music off and walks out in anger. (There's also a 15-minute edit of the film that eliminates the sequence after Fredi's collapse—everything that reflects badly on the Irving Mills character.)

Finally we are back in Duke's and Fredi's room where she lies in bed. The Hall Johnson Choir has gathered, vainly attempting to sing Fredi back to health. Dying, she asks to hear the assembled Ellington band play "Black and Tan Fantasy"—the first and only time we hear it complete, with the choir chiming in as best they can. Fredi expires just as the orchestra gets to that Chopin funeral-march ending. She gazes at Duke, who slides out of focus. But then (as the music winds down), Murphy briefly doubles down on that earlier doubled-time gambit. We now see Fredi's death once more, from her subjective point of view. In a lingering reprise, Duke's sad face again goes out of focus and then fades to black, fleetingly resembling a death's head.

Give Murphy credit for the striking images and the weird unsignaled turns—he makes up his own grammar and syntax. The mix of the refined and the vulgar, along with striking effects, is avant-garde art Ellington could relate to. (The real Fredi Washington kept dancing, and came back to the movies with Murphy's 1933 Eugene O'Neill adaptation *The Emperor Jones* with Paul Robeson.)

When artistic genres are young, when rules aren't set and forms are in flux, you get such oddities: novels like *Tristram Shandy*, silent films like Georges Méliès's *A Trip to the Moon*, and jazz like Jelly Roll Morton's "Dead Man Blues," low and stately at once. So it went with some early talkies. Their crude, uneven quality contributed to their invigorating effect. Filmmakers would soon polish away such rough edges.

> **King of Jazz** (1930; 98 minutes; director: John Murray Anderson; writer—comedy sketches: Harry Ruskin). **Cast includes: Paul Whiteman, Bing Crosby, Harry Barris, Joe Venuti, Eddie Lang. New songs: "Music Hath Charms," "A Bench in the Park," "I Like to Do Things for You," "Happy Feet," "Song of the Dawn," "Has Anybody Seen Our Nellie?" (words Jack Yellen/music Milton Ager), "My Bridal Veil" (Yellen and Anderson/Ager).**
> **—Paul Whiteman and members of his orchestra appear in a series of musical and comic vignettes.**

Paul Whiteman (like W. C. Handy) might be remembered more favorably now if he'd had a different publicist. The first successful big-bandleader of the 1920s, Whiteman commissioned *Rhapsody in Blue* from George Gershwin and later scooped up top white musicians including Bing Crosby, Bix Beiderbecke, Joe Venuti, and Jack Teagarden. Yes, but: Whiteman's band was a sometimes lumbering behemoth where such talents got limited exposure. His promotional moniker "King of Jazz" helped business in the short term but has plagued his posthumous reputation. How could this betuxed white man with a baton wear the crown in the same decade that Armstrong and Ellington emerged?

Calling Whiteman's 1930 early Technicolor revue film *King of Jazz* exacerbated the problem, as did its infamous (and seemingly interminable) "melting pot" finale, introduced this way: "America is a melting pot of music, wherein the melodies of all nations are fused into one great new rhythm—jazz!" Dwarfed by what looks like an enormous copper fondue cauldron, or perhaps steaming toilet bowl, musical hordes assemble: Scottish pipers, Spanish guitarists, Viennese violinists, Russian balalaika players. No one from the continent south of Europe appears, tacitly acknowledging that melting-pot metaphors often exclude African Americans. The cheesy musical goop we hear extends the fondue metaphor, and makes the absence of African pepper more glaring.

We get this monstrous whiteout despite the curious introduction Whiteman has already given to (an eight-minute abridgement of) *Rhapsody in Blue*, which the orchestra premiered at New York's Aeolian Hall in 1924—an event that echoes through numerous jazz films. "The most primitive and the most modern musical elements are combined in this *Rhapsody*, for jazz was born in the African jungle, to the beating of the voodoo drum." (Whiteman had put it more bluntly in the opening to his 1926 book *Jazz*: "Jazz came to America three hundred years ago in chains.")[9] This spoken intro leads not directly into the Gershwin but to a solo "African" dance performed on a giant drumhead; hoofer Jacques Cartier wears a fanciful headpiece, short shorts, and glistening, full-body black makeup.

Rhapsody aside, there isn't much jazz in the *King of Jazz*—mostly short vignettes from violinist Joe Venuti and guitarist Eddie Lang, along with limber singing by the Rhythm Boys: Bing Crosby, Harry Barris, and Al Rinker. The film was originally conceived as a biopic, with Whiteman playing himself. But he was no actor, and the writers came up empty. For want of a better idea, they settled on an episodic cavalcade of free-standing vaudeville-ish episodes: music, dance, comedy, and sentimental numbers, and bizarre digressions like that African dance. It's united mostly by a few recurring melodies and a fascination with oversize props. The episodes themselves ostensibly derive from the pages of Whiteman's 20-foot-tall journal; the orchestra emerges to play *Rhapsody* from under the lid of a giant grand piano. The gigantist motif helps give the film the air of a hallucination (and anticipates *Batman* comics' preoccupation with oversize objects, starting a decade later).

As the skits accumulate, that dreamlike effect is reinforced by double-exposed spectral presences; a singing painting; a living rag doll; giant dancers overrunning (a Lilliputian) Times Square; Wilbur Hall following up his double-take–inducing trick violin work by squeaking out "Stars and Stripes Forever" on a bicycle pump; a smirking mustachioed infant in a cradle who delivers a naughty punchline; Whiteman himself confronting his own dance double. The film's early use of Technicolor—where the blues are decidedly greenish—might have helped suggest a dream state to viewers, as when *The Wizard of Oz* shifts out of black-and-white Kansas.

A rationale for all that soundstage surrealism may lie in *King of Jazz*'s opening sequence, which confronts its/Whiteman's presumptuous title head on. A short cartoon (produced by animator Walter Lantz, pre–Woody Woodpecker) is presented to explain how Paul came to wear the jazz crown. (Portly and jowly, with a widow's peak and comic mustache, Whiteman was ripe for caricature.)

Tired of big city living, Paul goes big-game hunting "in darkest Africa." On the veldt, our great hunter pursues and is then pursued by a fearsome loping lion, who's closing in fast when Whiteman pulls out a fiddle. His hot playing (well, Venuti's, on the on-the-nose "Music Hath Charms") instantly soothes the beast's savage breast. The lion starts dancing to the tune (interjecting a Jolson "Mammy"), as do a pair of stealthy natives, a derby-wearing snake, and cartoon-franchise star Oswald the Lucky Rabbit. Even a coconut tree breaks into a hula. This outbreak of dance fever sets the butterfly wings of chaos into motion. An elephant drawing water, moved by the music, lets loose a mighty spray that alarms a gyrating monkey, who launches a retaliatory coconut. But his wild pitch strikes Whiteman in the head, where he promptly grows a crown-shaped lump, and the bandleader sees stars.

So Whiteman's reign as monarch of syncopation is a delusion—he's King of Jazz the way a cartoon mental patient is Napoleon. Even as the film's title confirms his royal status, he gracefully slides out from under the crown. That concussive coronation raises doubts about the reality of all that follows. As in David Cronenberg's *Videodrome* or *Naked Lunch* a half-century later, you can't tell what's real and what's the projection of a disordered brain.

In the early 1930s, Duke Ellington appeared in three nonjazz features. They include *Check and Double Check* of 1930 with Amos 'n' Andy (comic taxicab entrepreneurs, played by the white team who created them for radio, blacked up). After arriving by our heroes' fresh air taxi, Duke and his orchestra briefly perform at a dance, insulated from the unabashedly racist main action and a tedious society subplot.

The Ellingtonians' appearance in director Mitchell Leisen's theater revue–mystery **Murder at the Vanities** (1934) is similarly silly but thematically richer. The orchestra functions as a collective trickster imp, in a sequence that begins as pure kitsch. A genteel soloist sits at the piano and sings "Hungarian Rhapsody," in the persona of Franz Liszt himself: "Some day/The finest orchestra will play my rhapsody." That travesty gives way

FIGURE 1.4 Paul Whiteman wears the crown in *King of Jazz*.

to a symphonic version of the piece, disrupted (to the conductor's dismay) as Duke's brassmen abruptly pop out from behind the longhairs to interject wah-wah commentary. More of Ellington's men emerge; there's a brief sonic tussle between swingers and squares till the latter yield the bandstand to the rebels, who toss the no-longer-needed sheet music in the air. (It's all part of the show—the Ellington orchestra is listed in the program, for what's called "The Rape of the Rhapsody.") As the band jazzes up the Liszt, showgirl Gertrude Michael steps forth to sing the limbered-up "Ebony Rhapsody" (adapted by Sam Coslow and Arthur Johnston): "Instead of playing music like you do/They supply a little classical voodoo." The lyric anticipates Hoagy Carmichael and Johnny Mercer's "Old Music Master" and Chuck Berry's "Roll Over Beethoven."

The band then gets two minutes to themselves, with close-ups taking in Johnny Hodges on alto sax beside Barney Bigard on tenor, Sonny Greer at the traps, Wellman Braud twirling his bass, and Duke working the keys, looking twice as dapper as that ersatz Liszt. His piano lines dance more energetically than the black chorines who emerge, dressed in bandanas and aprons. To cue the curtain, the classical conductor returns to tommy-gun them all down, using blanks—that's listed in the program too. This episode is an early skirmish in the war between jazz and classical music at the movies, and not the last time Ellington would find himself in the crosshairs. He didn't really buy into the 1930s fad for jazzing the classics, but (like other bandleaders who introduced new songs on film) he did record a spirited version of "Ebony Rhapsody," with Ivie Anderson on vocals.

> **Symphony in Black: A Rhapsody of Negro Life (1935; 10 minutes; director: Fred Waller). Cast includes: Duke Ellington and the Orchestra (themselves), Billie Holiday (spurned woman).**
> **—Duke Ellington composes, and his orchestra performs, a suite inspired by African American culture.**

In 1935 Ellington made a (short) film fully worthy of his talents. The classic *Symphony in Black: A Rhapsody of Negro Life* contains a bit of manufactured drama, but not enough to upstage the music. As it begins, a letter arrives for Duke, from an official at the National Concert Bureau: "Just a reminder that the world premiere of your new symphony of Negro Moods takes place two weeks from today. I trust that work on the manuscript is nearing completion so that you may soon start rehearsals." There is a whiff of panic in this request, understandably. Ellington was notorious for working best under the gun: "I scarcely do anything without a tight deadline. I work to the last minute."[10]

So here, for the first time on film, is the real Ellington—not one who falls behind on his piano payments, or piles his players onto Amos 'n' Andy's taxi to go to Westchester. Instead, this screen-Ellington realizes two already stated goals: to present an ambitious suite depicting scenes from African American life and to perform at a major New York concert hall.[11]

FIGURE 1.5 Duke Ellington composes on deadline in *Symphony in Black*.

As in *Black and Tan*, we first see Ellington at work, at the piano—though now he has a grand. Duke makes pencil corrections to a manuscript, and then reads through the first section of the suite. We see a purported score from his viewpoint; the opening movement is called "The Laborers." (The bars of "dummy" music seen in inserts come from Brahms's Fourth Symphony, second movement.) After a four-bar intro, we crossfade to the concert stage, where the full orchestra (padded out with extra players in some shots) takes up the music, for a white audience in a hall often shot from the balcony. A heavy, co-ordinated, recurring beat suggests a work song—taking us back before the birth of jazz, to the synchronized hits used to focus the muscle power of longshoremen, railroad builders, and stone-hauling slaves. (We think of such heavy accents in African American music as falling on even-numbered offbeats—the backbeat—but this one falls on the first beat of every other bar.) The work-song effect is reinforced by Joe Nanton's trombone in field-holler mode and moaning commentary from Johnny Hodges's alto. Now as the music continues the scene shifts again, to industrial-age laboring in rhythm: Olive-skinned men in short sleeves or stripped to the waist (but wearing snakeskin boots or loafers) shovel coal into the maw of a giant furnace. One wonders if Duke supplied even this music at the last minute, because the tempo of the filmed action doesn't match the tune; the discrepancy calls for artful, mostly unobtrusive film edits between those heavy slams. We also see workers straining under what look like sandbags.

As "The Laborers" concludes with a Hodges flourish, we're back with Duke in his studio, moving on to Part Two: "Dance/Jealousy/Blues," and then to the concert stage again. With deadline pressure looming, the real Ellington sometimes recycled previously written material into a new piece, as he does here. For the first section of this movement Duke has rearranged his dance number "Ducky Wucky"; the new version has more drive and spirit than the lone 1932 Brunswick recording. (The band had been playing it on the road; its title is a term of endearment from the *Amos 'n' Andy* radio show, invoked in *Check and Double Check*.)

Then the scene shifts again, to show what such music is made for and what inspired it: dancing. Duke said that after a concert tour, the band was rejuvenated by playing for dancers again, feeding off their energy.[12] We see a small apartment where a man and woman dance to the gramophone—spinning "Ducky Wucky," presumably—and cast shadows on the curtains. Their undulating silhouettes are observed by a woman in the street below, leaning against an el-train stanchion. It's Billie Holiday, 19 when the film was made, who'd barely recorded at that point.

Primed for a night out, the man and woman bolt down the stairs. In the street Billie confronts the man, who knocks her to the pavement before moving on. (Holiday said in her autobiography *Lady Sings the Blues* that she got badly bruised from multiple retakes, and you can see her dead-cat bounce off the studio floor.)[13] For a moment, we are back with Ellington in his garret, playing a stormy rubato intro—and then with the band on stage as Barney Bigard picks up the theme on clarinet, before we return to Holiday. Sprawled on the sidewalk, propped up on her elbows, she sings the rewritten vocal couplet from Duke's decorated blues "Saddest Tale": the fanfare that gets them in and out of the original. She sings, "The saddest tale on land or sea / Is when my man walked out on me"—losing the 1934 original's Gertrude Steiny bite: "Is the tale they told when they told the truth on me." (Duke had stage whispered that one himself.)

Then Billie collapses, and back on the concert stage Nanton's wah-wah trombone picks up the story, as (in faint double exposure) she gathers her strength to stand up to sing a proper, newly added blues chorus. You'd think the tune was called "Lost My Man Blues," the way the lyric harps on the phrase. Never content to leave his sources exactly as he found them, Ellington adds a twist. The form is a 12-bar blues frame, but the stanza squeezes in six short lines rather than the usual three, though it doesn't feel rushed. This early film appearance helped feed the misconception that Billie Holiday, who sang dozens of standards and very few blues, was really a blues singer—even in the title of her book.

Holiday doesn't look at the camera as she sings that stanza, her eyes closed in concentration. The setting and some particulars differ, but we've encountered this scenario before, in *St. Louis Blues* where Bessie starts singing from floor-level. That film portrayed blues performance as a spurned woman's spontaneous utterance even as the musicians backing her played from sheet music. *Symphony in Black* teases those layers apart, shifting as it does among three levels of time, two specific—Duke at work in his studio, the orchestra performing on stage—and one more general: the quotidian world in which hard

FIGURE 1.6 Billie Holiday, bounced to the pavement in *Symphony in Black*.

labor and heartbreak (and, as the suite continues, death and celebration) are eternal verities.

When Ellington writes his songs of Negro Moods, he gives voice to the feelings of his people and at the same time gives them vehicles to express those feelings. In those conjoined levels, Ellington the man is fused with his music and his community. *Symphony in Black* is a vivid portrait of Duke sketched in nine minutes—a sort of biopic in pantomime. Lovely as his voice is, he doesn't speak.

That trifurcated action continues in the last two segments as well. "A Hymn of Sorrow" is a plaintive melody for straight-muted trumpet, over a cushion of reeds. It takes us to a dimly lighted, plain church, where a leonine patriarch presides over a small child's funeral—there's an open coffin draped in a sheet before the lectern—and leads the congregation in somber prayer. From Sonny Greer's rack of orchestral chimes, a church bell tolls. (It's a shorter segment, under two minutes, and a lovely, overlooked Ellington melody.)

In Duke's vision, this was the conclusion of the suite—echoing the funereal ending of *Black and Tan*. But in the editing it was decided to flip the order of the final movements and go out with a bang on the even shorter "Harlem Rhythm," actually the floor-show flagwaver "Merry-Go-Round" from the year before, tightened up a bit. That melody sets off an uptown montage: dancer Earl "Snakehips" Tucker (whose image is briefly doubled and superimposed, in a faint echo of *Black and Tan*), grass-skirted chorus girls walking the bar, barflies in silhouette, flashing electric signs. Musically, the suite plays well in either order.

Ellington never performed *Symphony in Black* as heard in the film, and the score was lost. Eight years later, in January 1943, Duke presented his "tone parallel to the history of the American Negro," the 40-minute suite *Black, Brown and Beige*, at Carnegie Hall. It began with "Work Song" with its grunting accent on the first beat, and moved on (via Greer's churchbell chimes) to the solemn hymn "Come Sunday." The "Brown" movement started with a Harlem-festive "West Indian Dance" and included a (Betty Roché) vocal on "The Blues" that isn't a straight blues, expanding the stanza form. This monumental suite Ellington had planned for years was written on deadline, ready at the last minute, and included a bit of recycled material.

So we might look at *Symphony in Black* as Duke's prospectus for *Black, Brown and Beige*. Prospectus, and maybe prediction too: With this film, he steps up to the plate and points his bat at the center-field fence. Many jazz films draw on incidents from real life; this time the movie version came first, with Ellington visualizing his goals.

Sweet Music **(1935; 100 minutes; director: Alfred E. Green; screenplay: Jerry Wald, Carl Erickson, Warren Duff; story: Wald). Cast includes: Rudy Vallee (Skip Houston), Ann Dvorak (Bonnie Haydon), Allen Jenkins (Barney Cowan), Ned Sparks (Bill "Ten Percent" Nelson), Joseph Cawthorn (Sidney Selzer), Al Shean (Sigmund Selzer), Helen Morgan (herself). New songs: "Sweet Music" (words Al Dubin/music Harry Warren), "Ev'ry Day," "There's a Diff'rent You in Your Heart," "The Good Green Acres of Home," "Selzer's Cigars" (Irving Kahal/ Sammy Fain), "I See Two Lovers," "Fare Thee Well, Annabelle" (Mort Dixon/ Allie Wrubel).**
—Squabbling entertainers Bonnie and Skip develop warm feelings for each other and find success on radio, despite anarchistic outbursts from his combative band.

Duke Ellington's African American rhapsody wasn't the only forward-looking movie music of 1935. It isn't exactly a jazz film, but the Rudy Vallee vehicle *Sweet Music* boasts some shockingly dissonant music integrated into the story, even if played only for laughs. It's worlds more kinetic than *The Vagabond Lover* six years earlier, a sign of how quickly filmmaking had evolved. Vallee (as singer and violinist Skip Houston) again fronts his (ever larger) Connecticut Yankees on the lugubrious ballads.

But in some scenes, Skip's Merry Mad Men aka Mad Merrymakers are played by a forgotten late-period vaudeville act, the Frank and Milt Britton Orchestra—musical Dadaists of the first order, and precursors to gag bandleaders Spike Jones and Willem Breuker. Frank Wenzel and Milt Levy had teamed up (and changed their names) in the 'teens, and were still on the road two decades later. The band's level of interpersonal violence makes the Three Stooges look sedate. They smack each other's faces, squirt one another with seltzer bottles, and dump pails of water on heads or smash violins over them. (Their props budget must have been staggering.) Charles Ives's gleeful cacophony is in there too; when Skip plays the sentimental "Souvenir" on violin, the band drowns him out with eight bars of "Stars and Stripes Forever."

The Brittons were then featuring trick trombonist Walter Powell, doing things that would be considered avant-garde 30 years later. It's a quirk of music history that vaudeville and early jazz shock effects—such as a percussive, slap-tongue saxophone attack—would be revived decades later as progressive "extended techniques" in jazz and concert music. In *Sweet Music* Powell plays plosive pitchless gasps, and sings through the horn as he plays—getting the thick multiphonic burr that Germany's Albert Mangelsdorff would later be acclaimed for. Powell swings the bell around in the air to exploit the pitch-shifting Doppler effect, and uses his hand as a mute to shape the tone quality. But he's not trying to be avant-garde: He's doing impressions of a steam engine pulling out or a plane taking off. There's a fine line between comic and subversive noise music. (In comedians Conlin & Glass's 1928 Vitaphone short *Sharps and Flats*, future character actor Jimmy Conlin's keyboard clusters and rolling-hand attack anticipate 1960s and 1970s free jazz.) In the late 1920s, Vallee himself would imitate a droning airplane on saxophone during a stage skit. He wasn't avant-garde either, but he sometimes cued key changes with a system of hand signals during performances or played two saxes at once, long before Rahsaan Roland Kirk did.[14]

The Brittons/Merrymakers intervene in the nonjazzy story, which is about singing tap dancer Bonnie who can't stand Skip's (Vallee's) blandly toothy persona, at least not until they fall for each other. When Bonnie, Skip, and his publicist Barney spar at a rehearsal, the band punctuates their barbed repartee—like a drummer backing a comedian—with trombone raspberries or a free-jazzy hubbub. When the musicians rehearse with a toneless out-of-tune singer, his violin accompanist responds in kind.

The Merrymakers antagonize Skip, but also do his bidding. When Houston lands a weekly radio show, its (stereotypically Jewish) squabbling-brother sponsors keep making contradictory demands: Make the music more hot *and* more sweet! So Skip unleashes the band to push back against the meddling money men. Their blaring overture pulls out all the stops: They fire pistols and tear each other's clothes, the pianist lunges at the keys from across the room for a fat atonal cluster, there's more smashing of violins—and guitar, and drums, and music stands—and finally a swan-dive onto a grand piano that brings it and the music to a crashing finish. "The boys are very temperamental, they can't stand business talk," Skip explains. Nothing in teen-rebel pics like *Blackboard Jungle* tops this tantrum.

This conventional story with radical details anticipates a couple of films a half-century later. Dissonant music as anticapitalist weapon returns in 1988's *Stormy Monday*. And the finale—an impossibly elaborate, barely coherent train-station number with dancing red caps (and a blackface gag), prelude to Skip's and Bonnie's actual departure for Hollywood—looks ahead to 1984's *The Cotton Club*. Director Alfred E. Green would edge closer to jazz in the 1940s, with *The Jolson Story* and *The Fabulous Dorseys*.

Nineteen thirty-five was also the year Benny Goodman's success begat the swing era, when hot and sweet big bands came to dominate popular music. Before long, such bands started making brief film appearances. Goodman pops up as himself to play with his orchestra in 1936's *Big Broadcast of 1937*, for example, and with that band and his racially mixed quartet in Busby Berkeley's *Hollywood Hotel* in 1937. Musicals such as Raoul Walsh's 1938 *College Swing*, with songs by Frank Loesser, began incorporating jazz rhythms. Some featured a bandleader hero—like James Cagney, who helms a New York swing-and-strings ensemble until Hollywood comes calling in 1937's *Something to Sing About*. Mickey Rooney leads a similarly mixed high-school outfit in *Strike Up the Band* in 1940—in which Paul Whiteman cameos as an arbiter of taste, hosting a nationwide band contest. But jazz rarely figures in the storyline.

> **Champagne Waltz (1937; 89 minutes; director: A. Edward Sutherland; screenplay: Don Hartman, Frank Butler; story: Billy Wilder, H. S. Kraft). Cast includes: Fred MacMurray (Buzzy Bellew), Gladys Swarthout (Elsa Strauss), Fritz Leiber (Franz Strauss), Jack Oakie (Happy Gallagher). New songs: "Paradise in Waltz Time" (words Sam Coslow/music Frederick Hollander), "When Is a Kiss Not a Kiss" (Ralph Freed/Burton Lane), "The Merry Go-Round" (Ann Ronnell).**
>
> **—American bandleader Buzzy Bellew brings jazz to a Vienna dancehall, dooming business at the adjoining waltz palace. Buzzy falls in love with the waltz king's granddaughter, who doesn't know he's the enemy.**

Fred MacMurray plays a bandleader hero in 1937's *Champagne Waltz*, where jazz invades the main plot. Mostly set in Vienna, it isn't all that good, stiff with languorous interludes when top-billed mezzo-soprano Gladys Swarthout sings or ballroom dancers Veloz and Yolanda hold the floor. There's also some business about the scarcity of chewing gum in Vienna, a flashback to Johann Strauss's day, and a comic B-plot about an aristocratic con woman preying on gullible Americans.

But it sowed seeds for jazz films to come, with narrative turns we'll see again. A welcoming committee turns out to greet a jazz musician at a European train station; an empty dance floor shows that a style of music has lost its audience; the venue where musicians play conveys their social status. The ending is the template for a stock jazz-film finale: a big New York concert that brings estranged lovers and/or seemingly incompatible musics together. That finish declares a temporary truce in the war between jazz and classical that broke out in *Murder at the Vanities*. The germ story was cowritten by jazz fan and ex-Viennese Billy Wilder, seven years before he'd direct MacMurray in *Double Indemnity*.

Champagne Waltz acknowledges the impact jazz had in Europe, where the music had been welcome from the moment it showed up in the late 'teens and where black musicians got more respect than they did in the States. The filmed record supports this last assertion. The 1934 Danish revue *København, Kalundborg Og -?* presents Louis Armstrong as a jazz musician and dynamic, funny stage performer. The "Dinah," "Tiger Rag," and "I Cover the Waterfront" he performs with a jazz orchestra are much-anthologized classics—our first real look at Armstrong the artist on film. Meanwhile, Hollywood treated him more like a clown. In an infamous 1932 cartoon he's a giant cannibal head chasing Betty Boop through the jungle, as he sings "I'll Be Glad When You're Dead You Rascal You."

In *Champagne Waltz*, clarinetist and alto saxophonist Buzzy Bellew (MacMurray) becomes a fixture at Vienna's Jazz Palace after a successful run in Paris. The Austrian city started going jazz crazy as soon as he arrived, when his band played a roaring "Tiger Rag" in a swing-era arrangement that defrosted and then thrilled the dignitaries pressed into meeting his train. (Armstrong had been getting used to warm train-station receptions himself, starting in Copenhagen in 1933.) That smashing first impression puts Buzzy over locally, and four months later he's still packing in crowds at the Jazz Palace, although— or maybe because—he often plays more sweet than hot. Buzzy/MacMurray also sings a little, notably the ballad "When Is a Kiss Not a Kiss." The band sounds not so very modern, playing 1923's "Charleston."

Before breaking into movies Fred MacMurray had played saxophone with the horns-and-strings California Collegians, some of whom appear as members of Buzzy's band. (Shades of Rudy Vallee.) They re-create a bit of their stage shtick; the violinists do tricks with their instruments and five players flop around the floor like trained seals.

The raucous sounds leak through to the companion Waltz Palace next door, where jazzmania is killing business for violinist and legacy hire Franz Strauss of *the* Strausses. But his protests are rudely ignored. Franz's singing granddaughter Elsa (Swarthout) soon meets and is charmed by Buzzy, who keeps her from discovering he's the jazzman next door. (Like other jazz heroes he has a character flaw: Buzzy's a breezy liar.)

Desperate to win back listeners, Franz has his waltz-estra rehearse "Tiger Rag," from dubious sheet music. But their ensemble work is a mess; they can't master the language, the rhythms, or the flashy gestures. The drummer keeps dropping a stick he tries to toss and the bassist falters, twirling the bull fiddle on its endpin. "Hours we've practiced, but it's nothing like next door," Franz laments. He learns the hard way that jazz calls for entirely different skills that aren't so easy to master.

Over Buzzy's objections, the landlord shutters the Waltz Palace to expand the Jazz Palace, throwing the Strausses out of work. Elsa recoils when she discovers her suitor's true identity. Bellew breaks his contract and goes back to New York, where he scuffles, now working a dump named Tony's, playing a corny two-beat version of "When Is a Kiss Not a Kiss" in a two horns/two rhythm quartet. (New York doesn't care who's big in Vienna.) Despite his own fallen state, he convinces Viennese allies to back the Strausses in New York, where the waltzes that had lost their home audience are a novel sensation.

Elsa and still-scuffling Buzzy reconcile, and she has a brainstorm: a combined Jazz and Waltz Palace, which is where our story ends. Franz and Buzzy lead absurdly over-sized string and swing orchestras on risers at opposite sides of the Palace stage. (Franz commands about 20 basses alone; Buzzy's band includes five percussionists and around 15 banjos, 8 tubas, and 60 more horns.) At first the orchestras alternate "Blue Danube"

FIGURE 1.7 Jazz and classical intersect in *Champagne Waltz*.

and "Tiger Rag." Then the opposing forces merge those tunes—swinging the waltz over the "Hold that tiger" riff—as both outfits (on rolling platforms) intermesh at center stage. There Elsa joins in, singing Strauss with English lyrics. It's pure musical kitsch, but crystal-clear storytelling. For a coda, Buzzy plays a few legit bars on Franz's violin, and Franz takes a break on Buzzy's tenor with a classical saxophonist's prim timbre. Just before they do, Elsa quips, "E pluribus unum," a callback to earlier dialogue. Jazz and classical stand as equals. The gap between them can be bridged.

Later in 1937, Fred MacMurray played another horn player, Skid Johnson, in Mitchell Leisen's **Swing High, Swing Low**. Johnson is a trumpeter in the Panama Canal Zone trying to woo Carole Lombard's stranded Maggie. She doesn't like the trumpet, finding it loud and boorish, but she melts when she hears Skid's sultry wah-wahs and deft double-tonguing in showy Whiteman novelty style. (Ghosted with gusto by studio pro Frank Zinzer, he comes off like a danceband trumpeter who wants to sound racy, but lacks an Ellingtonian's bluesy bite.) This won't be the last movie where a man's commanding manner on trumpet wins a woman over, as if the way he handles his horn portends confidence and skill in other areas.

Skid and Maggie wed, but then he ships out to New York where he's billed as "King of Trumpeters" and backs singer Anita Alvarez (Dorothy Lamour), who's out to seduce him. In their act, Skid milks his Armstrong-style high-note endings, pushing himself up the scale to a final high C (not so dazzling, for 1937), as Anita and the crowd chant, "Higher, higher." (Drained of erotic subtext, that bit comes back in the 1939 short *Artie Shaw's Class in Swing*.) By and by, Skid overindulges, hits the skids, and wanders around Manhattan in a daze, anticipating Kirk Douglas in *Young Man with a Horn*. But then, with Maggie's help, his lost chops come back just in time, during a last-chance radio guest shot.

> *Alexander's Ragtime Band* (1938; 106 minutes; director: Henry King; screenplay: Kathryn Scola, Lamar Trotti; story: Irving Berlin, Richard Sherman). Cast includes: Tyrone Power (Roger Grant/Alexander), Alice Faye (Stella Kirby), Don Ameche (Charlie Dwyer), Jack Haley (Davey Lane), Ethel Merman (Jerry Allen), Helen Westley (Aunt Sophie), Jean Hersholt (Prof. Heinrich), John Carradine (taxi driver). New songs: "Now It Can Be Told," "Walking Stick" "Marching Along with Time" [cut from release print] (Irving Berlin).
> —Starting in 1911, bandleader Alexander and singer Stella enjoy great success performing Irving Berlin songs, together and separately. Quick tempers and bad timing keep these would-be lovers apart, until a big New York concert brings them together.

By 1936, when composer and lyricist Irving Berlin had belatedly established himself in Hollywood, 20th-Century Fox producer Daryl Zanuck had the (obvious) idea to do a biopic, stuffed with as many Berlin classics as would fit. That latter point was the one unchanging element in the film that resulted two years later, *Alexander's Ragtime Band*. (Director Henry King's previous film *In Old Chicago* had also starred Tyrone Power, Alice Faye, and Don Ameche.) Twenty-five Berlin tunes are heard at least in part; sometimes as little as eight bars.[15] Berlin's life story was a biopic ready-made, the story of an East European immigrant who'd attained great popular success—a story many Hollywood moguls could identify with (Nebraska-born Zanuck not included).

For once a biopic might have been drawn straight from life. Berlin had spent his hardscrabble toddler years in rural Russia before growing up in ethnic New York (with a cantor father). He sang for pennies in Bowery saloons; as a singing waiter at a Chinatown cafe, he observed which tunes grabbed people. He became a songplugger before he started writing his own modest hits. Then came his 1911 smash "Alexander's Ragtime Band." The sheet music sold over a million copies in a couple of months, and kept selling. Soon after, he met his first wife (the story goes) when she came to his office looking for fresh Berlin to sing and had a knockdown fight with another singer on the same mission. After a whirlwind courtship they honeymooned in Havana—where she contracted the typhoid fever that helped kill her mere months after they'd met. Drafted into the army in World War I, Berlin wrote a show for singing dancing GIs including his own vocal feature "Oh! How I Hate to Get Up in the Morning." In the 1920s he wooed a silver-and-telegraph heiress whose disapproving father whisked her off to Europe; Irving romanced her long distance with ballads "Remember" and "All Alone." (They'd later elope.) He built his own Broadway theater and mounted shows around his songs, and had a habit of reaching into his trunk for abandoned tunes he'd turn into hits like "Blue Skies" and "Easter Parade." He never put on airs or lost the common touch—though he might worry he was losing his songwriter mojo. Berlin's first foray in Hollywood was a flop—one movie had almost every song cut—but he came back to triumph, writing for Fred Astaire and Ginger Rogers in the mid-1930s.

Berlin had no interest in such a biopic; he wasn't about to turn his first wife's death into entertainment (although it did prompt his first hit ballad "When I Lost You"). But he was all for a film stocked with his hits, so he and Zanuck came up with an ingenious solution. The story treated fictitious ragtime bandleader Alexander as if he were a real person, one with a weakness for Irving Berlin songs. Berlin recognized that the evolution of his composing—from ragtimey ditties to jazz-age fodder to elegant movie ballads—could mark the passage of time as the story trotted across decades. (He'd pitched a similar tale in 1928.)[16] Perhaps with *Champagne Waltz* in mind, he proposed ending the story with a reconciliation between Alexander and his estranged singer/soulmate at a Carnegie Hall concert—refining the template for the stock jazz-film ending.

As written, Alexander resembles Paul Whiteman more than Berlin: a trained violinist from out west who played the classics at San Francisco's Fairmont Hotel and discovered the new syncopated music at a Barbary Coast beerhall, who waved his baton for show in front of increasingly gargantuan orchestras that mixed strings and jazz instruments, and who had a notable success at a New York concert hall, where he played (besides *Rhapsody in Blue*) "Alexander's Ragtime Band." (Whiteman, 1926: "We first met—jazz and I—at a dance dive on the Barbary Coast. It screeched and bellowed at me from a trick platform in the middle of a smoke-hazed, beer-fumed room. . . . It was like coming out of blackness into bright light."[17]) In early drafts of the script, Alexander crossed paths with Berlin himself. In the final story, Irving's unmentioned, except for two inserts that show his composer credit on sheet music and a record label. But the film's on-screen title is *Irving Berlin's Alexander's Ragtime Band*, and it's all about the ennobling effects of his music. Without it, there would be no Alexander. The song creates the man and his band.

Circa 1911 in old San Francisco, classical violinist Roger Grant (Tyrone Power) sneaks out after hours to play popular airs with a two-horn quintet, including songwriting pianist Charlie Dwyer (Don Ameche) and drummer Davey Lane (Jack Haley). Drummers are sometimes depicted as hypermasculine, but Davey shatters that stereotype, a gentle soul with a light touch at the traps. For Nob Hill's Roger it's a step down to audition at Dirty Eddie's—even the fog outside looks cheap—although it's practically a step up for a saloon singer angling for the same job, brassy Stella Kirby (Alice Faye). But Roger's band has misplaced its sheet music, and winds up on stage with Stella's audition piece: something new and novel sent to her from New York—"Alexander's Ragtime Band." At first the players stumble, thrown off by the timing. "What kind of time is this?" Charlie whines, squinting at the music. (Alexander points out the tricky quarter rest at the front of every bar—but that's mostly on the verse, while they play only the chorus.) But then at once it comes together, in a peppier tempo. Roger: "That's it boys—swing into it."

FIGURE 1.8 The original formation hits a syncopated groove for the first time, in *Alexander's Ragtime Band*: Jack Haley (drums), Tyrone Power (violin), Don Ameche (piano).

The song breathes life into the musicians—opens a window onto a whole different kind of rhythm. Their initial disorientation suggests they're unfamiliar with ragtime more than a decade after syncopation became a craze. The harmony is simple enough, with long stretches over one chord, although it changes key going into the chorus. The melody was maddeningly catchy, the chorus leading off with a four-notes-on-two-pitches hook ("Come on and hear"), a little sequence that repeats and then (after the tune's title is sung) moves up a fourth, mimicking a blues chorus. The song is not a blues in form, but the two notes in that signature phrase are the alternating major and minor thirds of the underlying chord, suggesting the sliding blue third that falls in the crack between major and minor. The opening phrase of the introductory verse likewise deploys alternating quasi-blue thirds. The blues is in the air.

Like other period songs, "Alexander's Ragtime Band" had a couple of built-in melodic quotations, both flagged by the lyric. The first is from a bugle call, the second from Stephen Foster's 1851 "Old Folks at Home" aka "Swanee River," "played in rag-time" by Alexander and company. This pop-song quotation culture echoes in jazz musicians' habit of working bits of familiar songs into their solos. Berlin's lyric describes the man Roger Grant will become: leader of "the best band in the land . . . the bestest band what am." The song taught singers modern style too, with a quasi-spontaneous aside slipped in after "band what am": "Oh, my honey lamb." Learn to sing an interjection from sheet music, and you can start doing such things on your own. No wonder singers fought over Berlin's songs—they pointed the way.

Back at Dirty Eddie's, when Stella realizes they've swiped the tune she's been rehearsing right down to the hand gestures, she starts singing along as she makes her way to the stage. Violinist Roger immediately drops the melody to play a counter-line—a proper arranger knows not to double voice with an instrument. They harmonize instantly—but as soon as the song is over, they start squabbling over who's muscled in on whom. These hotheads' mutual dislike is so intense, any moviegoer knows they'll be together by the end.

For the moment, they're stuck with each other—the proprietor wants all or none, and dubs them Alexander's Ragtime Band. Now Roger is no longer Roger—he's Alexander, one name only (aka Alex, Alec, or Mr. Alexander). Berlin's ragtime-inflected popular music is a welcome alternative to the starchy string quartets he's been playing. The same music that loosens him up refines Stella, who starts dressing and acting more ladylike. Highbrow and lowbrow meet in the middle—as in Berlin's lyrics, with their celebrated mix of elevated diction and au courant slang: "And I trust that you'll excuse / My dust when I step on the gas."[18]

The band moves up and expands as it gets more successful, from Dirty Eddie's (quintet) to the Ship Cafe (nine pieces—two violins, three horns, four rhythm, Alexander conducting with a fiddle under his arm, Stella touted as "the queen of ragtime") to the Sunset Inn (13 players) to Cliff House overlooking the ocean (15). The unstated reason for their rise: they've sent to New York for more Berlin tunes like "Everybody's Doin' It Now" and "Ragtime Violin" (from 1911) and "The International Rag" (1913).

Everything's going great musically until (Berlin's) Broadway producer George Dillingham offers Stella alone a job in New York. The US enters World War I (making it 1917), and some of the musicians get drafted. It's Alexander and not Irving Berlin who writes and stages that soldier show on Broadway, and it's Davey who sings "Oh! How I Hate to Get Up in the Morning" (with its own bugle call quote, from "Reveille"). Postwar, Alex and Stella still can't get together—one or the other is always off somewhere or spoken for. Alex and Davey assemble a new version of the band with dynamic, thundering singer Jerry Allen (a grinning, pleasantly restrained Ethel Merman), who catches Alex on the rebound. Those three go hear (an unseen by us) Paul Whiteman, whose orchestra plays "Say It with Music" (1921) and "A Pretty Girl Is Like a Melody" (1919), as Jerry sings along from her seat. It's not Whiteman on the soundtrack—the diverse arrangements are by Alfred Newman—but the rippling saxes sound authentic enough.

"It's swell music," says Davey. "It sure has changed though. It's got a new rhythm, nice and slow." Alex, in a foul mood: "Like syrup—kind of sweet and sticky."

Later, when Stella seeks out Alex at the Greenwich Village speakeasy where he's based, she and Jerry are mutually gracious, like adults. Jerry sings "Blue Skies" (1927) at Stella's request (in front of a black band), then brings her up to finish it, with Jerry among the background singers: a rare case of women making music together in a jazz film, however briefly.

Then Alexander's Ragtime Band is off to Europe, where le jazz is all the rage. (Whiteman went over in 1923.) There Jerry performs a tune that mocks those who'd decried jazz as satanic, 1922's "Pack Up Your Sins and Go to the Devil," about how much livelier the afterlife is down below, with better music. Berlin's ability to compose in various styles helps sell the idea his songs come from many pens: from Charlie ("Now It Can Be Told"), or hack songwriters ("You Bring Out the Gypsy in Me," which sounds like Irving wrote it on a coffee break), or Alex himself, presumably responsible for "My Walking Stick," which pokes fun at an affectation he picked up on the continent and quickly drops back home. (That new tune was actually a Fred Astaire reject.)

Years pass before Alex returns—that Village speakeasy is now a post-Prohibition cocktail lounge—and lands a sponsored national radio show, à la Benny Goodman at NBC in 1934. It's more than 20 years since our story began, though no one looks much older, not even two disapproving elders from Alexander's past, his aunt and his old-world teacher Prof. Heinrich, who've since come around to the value of his music.

The film illustrates, without comment, the symbiosis between composers and musicians in the early twentieth century. Ragtime pianists influenced songwriters like Berlin whose tunes provided material to jazz musicians whose rhythmic refinements influenced songwriters whose sophisticated harmonies fed jazz. By the 1930s we are a long way from ragtime. Now newspapers talk about Alexander's swing music. Perversely enough the new song that spells out this theme of artistic progress was cut late in the editing, though an instrumental version serves as the opening and closing theme. In "Marching Along with Time," performed in a radio studio, Jerry sings about staying in step, as surely as folks once traded in horses for cars: "There'll be a change in music / A change in rhythm / A change in dancing / But I'll be right with 'em."[19]

Finally Alexander's band gets the ultimate validation: a "swing concert" at Carnegie Hall. We find out from a newspaper headline, and the two paragraphs under it (which flashed by far too quickly to be read by a movie audience, but are readable in freeze-frame) that "the popular leader has developed a style that is strictly his own"—bad history, but this isn't that kind of historical picture. In the paper Alexander calls his material "a new type of American folk music" comparable to the polka or Hungarian or Russian dances—dipping into King of Jazz's fondue pot. Even when you stop to read the fine print, in Alexander's Ragtime Band, only that anonymous orchestra on "Blue Skies" suggests that African Americans are connected to any of this.

Filming began on Alexander's Ragtime Band in late January 1938, two weeks after Benny Goodman played Carnegie to much fanfare. On Alexander's big night, we hear swing-band riffing on "Marie" (with a few squiggles of Goodmanesque clarinet), "Cheek to Cheek," and "Heat Wave"—one last stylistic change for the film (and music director Newman) to track. Alexander's band has kept expanding, and is now gargantuan. A conventional jazz big band is around 16 pieces; Whiteman's orchestras topped out at 35 players.[20] Alexander at Carnegie has 11 violins and as many reeds, 12 trumpets, 10 trombones, and a 16-piece rhythm section with paired pianos, harps, tubas, and rhythm guitars, 6 basses, tympani, and Davey's drums, plus Jerry on vocals and 20 backup singers. There are far fewer players on the soundtrack, but visually, bigger means better. Alexander's financial success is revealed at a glance, in a Veblenesque display of conspicuous consumption of musical resources. Anyone who can afford so many superfluous musicians clearly has money to burn. No wonder his auntie is thrilled.

Stella, meanwhile, has dropped out of the big time, working tank-town cafes and beer gardens under a name reflecting her fallen status, Lily Lamont. But she doesn't compromise on material, singing "All Alone." She happens to be passing through New York the night of Alex's concert, and with help from a vaguely sinister, slightly pushy taxi driver whose motives aren't immediately clear (John Carradine, stealing the last act), she arrives at Carnegie Hall before the end of the show, which is sold out, even standing room, despite a live radio broadcast. She talks her way backstage in time for the encore folks have been yelling for, which Alexander introduces as "the first and best of all swing songs." When it's already in progress, he spies Stella in the wings, and coaxes her out to sing "Alexander's Ragtime Band" one more time—a callback to her mid-song walk-on back at Dirty Eddie's—to cinch their happy reunion with loving glances, and remind us how much they and their music owe to never-mentioned Irving Berlin.

The songwriter is the ultimate behind-the-scenes fixer; the artists get the glory, but the royalty checks come to the composer. Still, much of *Alexander's* feels like an elegy for music whose day has passed. By the swing era, early Berlin sounded like another age.

Second Chorus (1940; 84 minutes; director: H.C. Potter; screenplay: Elaine Ryan, Ian McLellan Hunter; story: Frank Cavett, with input from Johnny Mercer). Cast includes: Fred Astaire (Danny O'Neill), Burgess Meredith (Hank Taylor), Paulette Goddard (Ellen Miller), Artie Shaw (himself), Charles Butterworth (J. Lester Chisholm). New songs: "Dig It" (words Mercer/music Hal Borne), "Would You Like to Be the Love of My Life?" (Mercer/Artie Shaw), "Poor Mr. Chisholm"/"Hoe Down the Bayou" (Mercer/Bernie Hanighen).
—Trumpeters and friendly rivals Danny and Hank compete for the affection of their band's ex-manager Ellen, now working for Artie Shaw. Danny gets the edge when he earns a spot on a big Shaw concert.

In the late 1930s, Benny Goodman was the nominal King of Swing, despite a notably frosty personality. His rival Artie Shaw was more Hollywood's type, cheekbone-handsome and well-spoken, and he took to the place, developing a weakness for (marrying) screen goddesses. He'd relocated from New York to Beverly Hills even before landing a part as himself, fronting his band, in *Dancing Co-Ed*, shot in 1939. Early in 1940 he'd impulsively marry its star Lana Turner. That same year he signed on for a more substantial role as a version of himself in *Second Chorus*, with the proviso he could rewrite his dialogue. He'd also write most of its music and collaborate with top lyricist Johnny Mercer. It was to be a serious film about a trumpeter played by John Garfield, torn between jazz and the family business—another riff on *The Jazz Singer*, but with a downer ending: by the time he returns to music, jazz has passed him by. When Garfield proved unavailable it morphed into a Fred Astaire frolic, involving constant last-minute rewrites. Shaw said later that this circus soured him on making movies.[21]

And yet *Second Chorus* is light and funny, among the most purely entertaining jazz films, more straight comedy than typical Astaire vehicles; he sings only three songs and dances three numbers. (H.C. Potter—who'd previously directed Astaire in *The Story of Vernon and Irene Castle*—would crank up the crazy with his follow-up *Hellzapoppin'*.) On the jazz side, the story deals with musicians' rivalries and practical jokes, the importance of good management, the trade-offs that come with financial patronage, the jobs struggling musicians take in a pinch—and how sexist language is a tool of economic exploitation. Shaw blends jazz and highbrow strings on the soundtrack, and also on the film's concert stage, more ably than Buzzy Bellew or Alexander at Carnegie Hall; such unions were becoming a jazz-movie staple. And *Second Chorus* like *Sweet Music* looks ahead to the jazz avant-garde: in this case, to the practice of conducted improvisation.

At the outset, Danny O'Neill (Astaire) has been leading a New England college band, O'Neill's University Perennials, for the seven years since he's been a freshman; the Perennials do so well he and trickster sidekick and foil Hank Taylor (Burgess Meredith) can't afford to graduate. (They must have matriculated late: Astaire had just turned 40; Meredith was 32.) The group's founding predates the swing era, but they're up on the latest trends; Danny and Hank are superb trumpeters—ghosted, respectively, by Bobby Hackett and Shaw sideman Billy Butterfield, who's seen soloing on Shaw's first number, "Everything Is Jumpin'," and on "Concerto for Clarinet."

Perennials business has been even better since they hired Ellen Miller (Paulette Goddard), nominally a secretary but their de facto manager and booking agent, for $36 a week, double her previous pay. Ellen has a rare way of talking anybody's language—old ladies' tea societies, Broadway swells, country clubbers, frat boys—to get the orchestra a gig. The band even starts poaching engagements from Artie Shaw, which gets the star clarinetist's attention: "Either they've got a great band, or a fine manager." He goes to one of their dances, casually inquires about the terms of the contract, and hears enough of the music to hire Ellen away on the spot, just as the boys' college careers are crashing to a close. Shaw pays no mind to Danny and Hank as they trade fours on "Sweet Sue," striving to catch his ear. They're thinking only of themselves, not the music—it's every man for himself. (Hackett and Butterfield—who steps on Danny's/Hackett's phrase endings—act the characters here more conscientiously than Astaire and Meredith, who barely pretend to look like they're playing.)

Ellen gets right to work procuring gigs for Artie, and is far too professional to flirt with her new boss. Besides, Danny's in love with her, and she's starting to fall for him. They've already shared a two-minute, one-shot (and one take) dance duet on "Dig It"—pull your feet together, then skid to the side. (That long take is followed almost immediately by another: a 90-second reverse tracking shot, Danny and Hank taking a last prop-and-dialogue–heavy stroll across campus.)

Hank pursues Ellen too, though she never gives him a word of encouragement. Burgess Meredith looks at her like a literal wolf, eyeing his lunch. At her urging, Shaw agrees to let the two trumpeters sit in one night to see if they have the skills to play with him, no promises. (He's not short on brass talent, but Ellen is a good manager.) Getting hired by Shaw would let the winner court her on the boss's dime, and play in an excellent swing band. Besides, neither trumpeter wants to go into the family business: concrete or textiles.

Jazz soloists can be highly competitive. For some cornet and trumpet players going back to Buddy Bolden, the written or improvised solo statement has been part display of plumage and part pure male swaggering. Even before they'd met Ellen, Danny and Hank were using their horns to catch women's attention. All's fair in love and economic warfare; the friends compete for Artie's approval. On a band break before they audition, Danny agrees to play the ballad "I'm Yours," without bothering to look it over first—"I can play anything on the page," he tells Artie. So Hank secretly revises Danny's part, writing in clams—wrong pitches—including a long held high note that's painfully out of the key and resolves to another note just as bad. Which is exactly what Danny dutifully plays—he knows something's wrong, but it's on the paper, no matter how crudely scrawled in, and he can't help himself. That would seem to reflect poorly on his jazz skills, although bebop drummer and studio percussionist Stan Levey told a similar story, of playing a note he knew to be wrong on a record date: "It's what's there on the paper, and that's what I have to play."[22] Danny's may be the worst jazz audition until *The Man with the Golden Arm*.

When it's Hank's turn to solo, Danny simply yanks him off the platform from behind. They're both bounced from the joint, and once word gets around—and Artie sees that it does—no name leader will touch them. Hank takes a job at the racetrack, playing First Call with bluesy bends at post time ("I never had such a big audience," he tells Danny of his new job: "strictly solo stuff.") Danny plays his horn in a Russian balalaika band at a borscht house, and does a Cossack dance. (I had to quit Whiteman, he tells Hank: "If I'd've stayed with him I'd have lost my individuality. Same thing happened to Bix.")

Ellen, meanwhile, has been cultivating a new resource: Cincinnati bottlecap tycoon J. Lester Chisholm (character actor and virtuoso babbler Charles Butterworth, who liked to improvise dialogue). He's a Dickensian specter of what the boys might have become if they'd abandoned music for the family business—a musician-wannabe nursing lifelong regrets. He fingers air-mandolin at Shaw's dances, tries to talk like a hepcat, and thinks he hears better than he does. Chisholm finds Danny's mock-Russian singing of the ballad "Would You Like to Be the Love of My Life" soul-stirringly authentic, a chill wind off the steppes. He even liked Danny's audition solo. (And maybe he was right—one listener's clam is another's piquant minor ninth.)

Chisholm's as sweet and harmless as he is clueless, and everyone exploits him without qualm. Shaw has been itching to do a major concert, rather like Ellington's in *Symphony in Black*, but with a mixed jazz-classical ensemble. (As with Duke, this was a real ambition of Shaw's.) Ellen tells J. Lester he'd be privileged to bankroll it. It'll run you about 15 grand, says Artie. Better make it 20, says Ellen. Danny, with a little help from Hank, has written

FIGURE 1.9 Danny (Fred Astaire) smells a rat, sight-reading a doctored part in *Second Chorus*; trumpeter Billy Butterfield is at right.

a song mocking Chisholm ("He tried to swing and he broke a string every time"). But Danny convinces the financier the melody is an old folk tune, "Hoe Down the Bayou"—Chisholm smells the authenticity here too. Pressed by his backer, Shaw gives it a listen. Tickled by the lyric, he green-lights an instrumental version for the concert, arranged by Danny for swing band and strings, with a little input from Artie.

Shaw meantime rehearses his "Concerto for Clarinet," as it was named when he recorded it soon after. He'd say later, "I didn't really write anything, I just dictated a frame."[23] A pastiche of clarinet blues, boogie-woogie, Krupa-style tom-tom beating (from Nick Fatool), and soothing strings, it's the kind of gilded mish-mash a few jazz movies build to, if better than most. But then Shaw was mixing jazz and strings with taste in 1936, before recording as a leader.

At the concert, Shaw introduces Danny as the composer of "Hoe Down the Bayou" and then hands him the baton, to Danny's evident surprise. (He must have missed the newspaper preview revealing the concert would introduce an "interesting newcomer." Ellen had surely alerted Artie that Danny can dance.) He turns to the orchestra and starts conducting in pantomime—arms up for high notes, baton down for lows, acting out drum parts, punctuating the action with his taps. The scene was Astaire's idea—his reason for making the picture. He shares the climactic dance sequence not with his love interest, but Shaw's expanded band.

Danny's graphic display looks forward to any number of spontaneous conductors of postwar improvising orchestras, from Sun Ra to Butch Morris to Astaire's beanpole doppelgänger, Tristan Honsinger of Amsterdam's ICP Orchestra: the conductor as mime, dancer, and action painter. Danny doesn't cue the change-ups for the musicians as much as he sets the jubilant tone. And finally he takes a tap solo, over a stoptime chorus so soft, one might assume he'd planned to jump in there anyway. (It would explain the tap shoes.) Someone in the wings throws him a trumpet so he can play a few bars at the close.

He has reason to act jubilant. Ellen sees that Danny is changing. He'd tried his best to get Hank on the concert, and "Hoe Down the Bayou" shows that he can channel his energy into something constructive—that he can see past the end of his horn. Just before he went on, she'd said, "You're improving so amazingly, Danny, I think I'll make you my manager." (It's a jazz musician's fantasy ending: marrying a booking agent.) Backstage afterwards, Shaw tells him, "Looks like I'm gonna have to hire you after all. But only because I don't want to lose a good secretary."

Say what now Shaw? You sought Ellen out as your manager, but now that she's pulling in the great gigs and big money, you want to pay her a secretary's wage instead of a commission? Given that Shaw had liberty to rework his own dialogue, the credit for that snub may be his.

In the end, J. Lester Chisholm, who paid for the concert, misses the show. He was so determined to play mandolin on it, Hank slipped him sleeping pills. But the old fellow got something for his trouble: Charles Butterworth just about steals the picture.

Postscript: In the real world Paulette Goddard became friends with Artie Shaw that season. Four years later, she married Burgess Meredith.

> ***Broken Strings*** **(1940; 60 minutes; director: Bernard B. Ray; story: Ray, Carl Krusada, with input from Clarence Muse, David Arlen). Cast includes: Clarence Muse (Arthur Williams), William Washington (Johnny Williams), Sybil Lewis (Grace Williams), Tommie Moore (Mary), Matthew Beard (Dickey Morley), Darby Jones (Stringbean Johnson), Elliott Carpenter (himself).**
> **—Injured in an accident, classical violinist Arthur Williams can no long support his children, and is enraged when son Johnny plays swing fiddle to earn their keep. Johnny plans to play a classical piece in a talent contest, but necessity pushes him back toward swing—with unforeseen consequences.**

Another 1940 production looks at the tension between jazz and classical music, this time within the African American community: the one-hour low-budget *Broken Strings*, with a nearly all-black cast. In the independent black American cinema that evolved in the 1930s, jazz was less of a subject than part of the cultural atmosphere. A black band, like Lucky Millinder's in 1939's *Paradise in Harlem*, might punctuate the action or back a singer, much like a white swing band in a Hollywood picture. Despite its promising title, black cinema pioneer Oscar Micheaux's 1938 *Swing!* is a ho-hum backstage musical where a theatrical producer frantically looks for a dazzling headliner, when he's already auditioned little-known Doli Armena (aka Dolly Jones), who plays dynamic trumpet in the Louis Armstrong style. But somehow she fails to land that featured spot.

Broken Strings takes the music more seriously. It was directed by Russia-born B-movie vet Bernard Ray, from a script credited to him and an equally prolific screenwriter from Vienna, Carl Krusada. Each had dozens of quickie westerns to his credit. (The director squeezed in *Broken Strings* between *Daughter of the Tong* and *The Cheyenne Kid*.) But star Clarence Muse has an additional dialogue credit, and music director Elliot Carpenter may have written his own lines. There's a sense the film speaks from as well as to the black community.[24]

As it opens, Muse's Arthur Williams is finishing a violin recital at the Lyric Theater in an unnamed city for an enthusiastic black audience that brings him back for two curtain calls. "I'm overjoyed, playing for my folks," he tells them, as adult daughter Grace and 12-year-old Johnny wait in the wings. "It matters not, if I shall play for the people of the world. There's a kinship tonight, that strikes here," holding his left fist to his heart, "that will live forever in my memory. Something that only you and I can understand."

Backstage, he's greeted by well-wishers. A church lady who'd nodded off at the concert wants him to play a benefit—until she hears about his $1,000 fee. Next comes a huge fan in more ways than one, a very tall, untutored banjo player who later identifies himself as Stringbean Johnson. "You sure swings a wicked bow," he says, praise Williams politely gives the weight it merits. As the man departs, Arthur's manager jokes they should play a joint concert sometime—a comment Stringbean apparently overhears, as the idea becomes his own *idée fixe*: he brings it up often.

Arthur Williams is at the peak of his career, on the verge of a cross-country tour, when a stock-footage auto crash cripples his fingering hand; that left fist once held over his heart as a sign of love is now frozen in place (at least when Muse remembers it's paralyzed). Over the course of a year, he depletes his savings, consulting specialists in vain. He still teaches, but unable to finger his instrument, he's embittered, lashing out at pupils he's ill-equipped to help. "You are not a musician here," he scolds an adult student, hand to heart again. "You have no soul for music."

After that lesson Arthur steps out to take a call, ceding the action to two heretofore peripheral figures, son Johnny, an aspiring violinist himself, and Dad's young lesson pianist Mary. Now Arthur's down to two students: snooty, uninspired but diligent Dickey Morley (Matthew Beard, ex-Stymie in the *Our Gang* comedies) and Johnny, who has the right spirit—you can hear it when he plays his Dvořák—but lacks discipline.

"I've got to learn control, repose"—or so says his father. "It's awful hard, Mary," Johnny admits, as he finally gets a close-up. "I'd like to play like a bird flies—this way and that, up and down, winging and swinging through the air. No control—whistling, singing, shouting. Just music." He is the first of several jazz heroes to give some version of that speech.

And just like that, the peripheral son moves to the center of the story, and *Broken Strings* is revealed as a *Jazz Singer* variant. One reason you might not see it coming: Clarence Muse's baritone gravitas and commanding presence (and a decade in front of the camera) overwhelm the raw sincerity of William Washington as Johnny, who hits his marks in his big speech, throwing his shoulders into *this* and *that*, delivering those improbable mouthfuls as if ready to break into song. From now on father and son share center stage, in a conflict between two musics. (One thing the movie does right—Washington and Beard both look reasonably convincing playing violin in near-identical tightly framed close-ups. One suspects a third party's left hand on the fingerboard.)

Arthur is a black musician in love with European concert music, and he gives his son hell when he returns to find Johnny swinging away, over Mary's surprisingly limber stride piano. "You're desecrating a classic!" But not just any classic. Dvořák wrote his "Humoresque" no. 7 while the Czech composer was living in New York in the 1890s, championing American music in general and African American in particular. "Humoresque," with its plain harmonies, free rhythmic feeling, and (almost entirely) pentatonic catchy melody, suggests black influence and made it inviting material for jazz musicians. (It was a minor hit in 1937, recorded by Glenn Miller, Tommy Dorsey, and Red Nichols. Pianist Art Tatum made a showpiece of it, first recording it in 1939. Violinists Stuff Smith, Joe Venuti, and Eddie South recorded it after *Broken Strings* came out.) Arthur has enabled his son's defection to jazz just by assigning it. And in truth, from what we hear of their playing, Johnny is a better jazz fiddler than Arthur is classical recitalist. That's got to smart.

Broken Strings is set in the world of the black bourgeoisie—office clerks, people who pack classical concerts, church ladies, teenage boys who wear business suits while listening to the radio (and, in real life, pious people who thought jazz was devil music or a surrender to primitive stereotypes). Add to those African Americans one more neurospecialist, who gives Arthur's hand a careful visual inspection and determines the problem is "displacement of the nerve adhesions." It's treatable, and he'll even defer his fee for now, but that still leaves hospital expenses. Grace loses her white-collar job, worn down by the boss's son's sexual harassment, but Johnny runs a solution past Mary (Tommie Moore, playing 12 at 22). We'll go into clubs and play for tips when the band's on break: "We'll play a few bars straight, and then we'll swing on out."

Early jazz lore is full of musicians who took to jazz as teenagers: Louis Armstrong, Bix Beiderbecke, Benny Goodman, the Austin High Gang in the Chicago suburbs. Johnny's sister Grace and her beau, a decade or so older, don't feel what these youngsters feel—for them, popular music is just for dancing and talking over. Johnny and Mary are avatars of a later generation, swing kids who grew up with jazz in the air. But being so young makes it hard to break in. At the Mellow Cafe, the boss puts the kibosh on their plan using circular logic. Oh yes, I'm sure you can play what you learned in your classical lessons. No no, we play jazz and such—we make it up as we go along. "Now I know it's no good. You kids have nothing to sell."

They bluff their way on stage anyway, and swing "Humoresque" one more time—they are considerably hipper than the house band—and are showered with cash. (So some grown-ups do dig swing.) Next time we see them at the same venue, they're again sitting in with that strings-and-trumpet group, which only slows Johnny and Mary down.

The kids are creating their own little scene; Stringbean dances in the aisle—and steps up to defend Johnny when Arthur (tipped off by Dickey) arrives to drag the boy away, in a *Jazz Singer* callback.

"I'll drill the skill of the masters into you, and drive out the spirit of jazz," Arthur vows—and makes Johnny practice fingering exercises until he collapses, just as Grace arrives to set her father straight about who's supporting the family. "I'll never forgive myself," Arthur tells his son. "I'll never do it again," Johnny pledges in return.

There's one last hope to raise those hospital fees: the $250 first prize in a radio amateur-hour contest, hosted by Elliott Carpenter as himself. Little remembered now, the pianist had played with ragtime-to-jazz bandleaders James Reese Europe and Will Marion Cook in the 'teens, and in the 1920s went to Paris and then London, where he recorded with the Red Devils quintet. Carpenter was also a latter-day member of the Clef Club, the now-waning fraternity of New York's African American musical elite. Classically trained, Carpenter preferred pop—so in a way, *Broken Strings* is his story too. He played nightclub piano in a jazzy, stride-inflected style—and two years later would play off camera for *Casablanca*'s sidelining Dooley Wilson. Carpenter and Clarence Muse had shared music credits for the 1938 Joe Louis boxing picture *Spirit of Youth*, in which Muse costarred. (Muse had also cowritten Louis Armstrong's theme "When It's Sleepy Time Down South.")

At the talent show, Carpenter addresses a little speech to the African American audience in the seats and at home. It sounds impromptu, like his interviews with the contestants. "As you know, music is the international language, expressing sorrow, joy, laughter, tears, love." His face makes all the right expressions in turn. "We are considered one of the most musical people, because we have suffered." Music expresses the soul of the people; you'd expect Arthur, in the audience, to sign off on that. But when Carpenter sits at the piano to make his point that "there's beauty in all music, classic, swing or jazz," Arthur sits on his hands, despite the pianist's deft James P. Johnson blue thirds.

Not all the snobs are so resistant. Snooty young Dickey may diss jazz to Arthur, but he listens to Carpenter's radio show—it's how he'd learned about the contest. And even Arthur's antiswing feeling weakens when an adorable sister act sings and taps to Carpenter's piano syncopations—tap being the only dancing that works on radio.

Next up is Stringbean, doing a Mutt and Jeff routine with the diminutive Carpenter as they attempt to share a microphone, chatting before the big man performs. Stringbean's participation is a puzzle on the face of it; the way he keeps popping up—grooming himself for success by straightening his hair, talking up his own talents, telling Arthur he wants to split a concert with him, and now telling the radio audience he's as good on banjo as Williams on violin (with Arthur in the house no less)—it's a surprise he's still an amateur, or passing for one. "I want to play Mr. Arthur Williams' favorite concert number in swing," he says, and we're all ears—save Carpenter, he's the only adult we've heard defend the music. But then Stringbean happily strums out what might sound like jazz to a jazz-hater's ear: a tuneless, repetitive, moronic din. The contrast between his string music and Johnny's highlights the virtues of improvisation rooted in the best technique, and inspiring material.

So jazz isn't just about playing the way you feel, with no control—you need talent and training too. Stringbean is like Robert De Niro's aspiring comic in Martin Scorsese's *The King of Comedy*: an amateur who wants to go straight to the top without working his way up, who has too little stage experience to know what he lacks. "If the composer could hear that, he'd turn over in his grave," Arthur mutters, not naming said composer—because really, who can tell what Stringbean thinks he's playing?

Johnny and Mary go on last; Carpenter has in fact seen them perform at the Mellow Cafe, but keeps it to himself as he brings them on. They begin the mazurka they've selected, but earlier, backstage, rival contestant Dickey had tipped the odds, partly filing through the bottom strings on Johnny's violin. One phrase into the somber melody, Johnny's low string snaps, and the audience breaks into laughter. He begins again, an octave higher. The next string breaks, the crowd re-erupts, and we see the pain on Arthur's face, witnessing his son's humiliation.

So Johnny takes the only course left. He improvises his way out of trouble: cues Mary to cut loose, as he swings on out on two strings. The house bassist immediately jumps in, followed by the rest of the band. (They appear to be the Mellow Cafe players, unleashed at last—the trumpeter glisses and plays obbligatos, the drummer plays Baby Dodds

FIGURE 1.10 Down to two strings, Johnny (William Washington) improvises his way to success in *Broken Strings*.

"nerve beats" and twirls his sticks.) The applause makes it obvious these underdogs have clinched the win. Even Arthur is moved. He begins clapping so forcefully, his fingers uncurl; relaxing his antijazz fist, he gets his own musicality back. The soulful invention in his son's music reaches him right down to the nerve adhesions.

It's not the only indication that jazz can make you a better person. Backstage, Dickey owns up to being responsible for those broken strings, and he and Johnny patch up their differences. When Arthur approaches, Johnny blurts out in anguish, "I just couldn't help playing swing! It was the onliest way out!" But Dad is all forgiveness, taking the maimed fiddle from his son to show off his revitalized digits. "My heart still belongs to the masters. But look what swing has done for me!" And then Arthur resumes his (unswinging) classical career.

/// 2 /// ORIGIN STORIES 1941–1947

By the late 1930s, as streamlined swing bands evolved ever farther from New Orleans–style free-for-alls, some jazz fans became curious about the music's early days. Collectors analyzed rare records and sought out early performers who were still around, bugging them with questions about who'd played with whom and when, reviving a few moribund careers in the process. Frederic Ramsey and Charles Edward Smith's 1939 essay bundle *Jazzmen* helped to spur nostalgia for those early days, to inspire bands who harked back to jazz before it became industrialized, and to prompt reissues of classic recordings. As jazz movies began to proliferate, filmmakers too turned to origin stories. Where did this music come from? And where did it go from there?

> ***Birth of the Blues* (1941; 86 minutes; director: Victor Schertzinger; screenplay: Harry Tugend, Walter DeLeon; story: Tugend). Cast includes: Bing Crosby (Jeff Lambert), Eddie "Rochester" Anderson (Louey), Mary Martin (Betty Lou Cobb), Brian Donlevy (Memphis), Jack Teagarden (Pepper), Harry Barris (Suds), Ruby Elzy (Ruby), Ronnie Cosby (Jeff as a child), Minor Watson (Henri Lambert), Mantan Moreland (Basin Street cornet), Sam McDaniel (Basin Street clarinet), Bud Scott (Basin Street banjo), J. Carroll Naish (Blackie), Ernest Whitman (doorman). New song: "The Waiter and the Porter and the Upstairs Maid" (Johnny Mercer).**
> —**In old New Orleans, clarinetist Jeff Lambert puts together a jazz band, intent on introducing this new black music to white listeners.**

The first major Hollywood film to look at jazz origins is 1941's cheery Bing Crosby vehicle *Birth of the Blues*. Like other 1940s jazz films it's historically spotty, racially problematic, and poorly regarded; Krin Gabbard denounces its "startling naïveté and unrepressed racism."[1] It begins after all with a white child casually out-improvising African American adults, and ends with a triumphant image of Paul Whiteman. In *Birth of the Blues*, New Orleans in the 'teens is curiously bereft of black musicians. Even its 1926 theme song, which Whiteman had popularized, offers a deracialized fantasy of how the blues began, emerging not from slave-era hollers and spirituals, but "the breeze in the trees singing weird melodies" and "the wail of a down hearted frail." (The lyric's by one of the film's producers, Buddy DeSylva, one of several songwriters who became studio execs.)

Even so, *Birth of the Blues* aims for something vaguely high-minded, dedicated as it is to "those early jazz men who took American music out of the rut and put it '*in the groove*.'" It's less about the birth of jazz than its introduction to white audiences as something worth their attention: the story of how jazz became, as Bing puts it in the final scene, "everybody's blue music."

African American musicians do appear in the problematic prologue, set "on the levee at the foot of Basin street," by the river—suggesting journeyman screenwriters Harry Tugend and Walter DeLeon hadn't consulted a city map. (It was shot at Paramount.) A locator card establishes this is "New Orleans in the Nineties"—the late 1890s, as a band sitting on crates and cotton bales, and playing for cakewalking dancers, has struck up a loose "At a Georgia Camp Meeting," copyright 1897. The instrumentation is fairly typical of early New Orleans bands—cornet, clarinet, and trombone; banjo, bass, and drums— and their syncopations are rooted in folk music. The tune recalls "those over-and-over strains" with no clear beginning or end, such as W. C. Handy heard in his travels around then, a lively ragtime number with built-in breaks—moments when everything stops to let a soloist play some little quip, before the thicket closes back in. The band sounds fine, not least for the 1890s. Their boisterousness conveys that this is new music—that the players are still in the act of discovering or inventing the language.

Tonight they are sounding even more animated than usual; the clarinetist (Sam McDaniel, brother of Hattie) and cornetist are a little unnerved by the disembodied sound of a second clarinet, till the banjo player (Bud Scott, an early jazz recording artist and bonafide Orleanian) spots an interloper. Young Jeff Lambert, looking all of 12, plays a student-model clarinet from a secluded spot nearby, weaving his own variations around their parts. Found out, Jeff tries to bolt, but the musicians call him back. I was just practicing, he explains—having no one else to play with. The cornetist: "Why, you sure was flying high. Where did you learn that hot stuff?" Jeff: "I just picked it up hanging around Basin Street." The clarinetist: "White boy, come set beside me. There's a few things I want to pick up!" And then they get right back to playing.

The traditional reading of this scene is that these African American adults bow before the white child's musical superiority, but there's a more generous interpretation: Established musicians graciously extend a hand to a cocky newcomer, encouraging his own voice, recognizing in his bratty bravado a familiar need to play. (Jeff's brattiness will pass; as an adult his persona will be so cool, he'll be played by Bing Crosby.) The musicians accept him in a spirit of fellowship that transcends race and age.

Jeff has learned from them, eavesdropping on Basin, and now, as the clarinetist implies, it's time to give something back. This meeting of their spasm-band earthiness and his well-honed technique restages the blending that resulted (in one tidy formulation of jazz history) when black musicians from the country, accustomed to working informal rhythmic and melodic variations on (or "ragging") old tunes, moved to New Orleans and

FIGURE 2.1 Young Jeff (Ronnie Cosby) is welcomed by musicians played by Sam McDaniel (clarinet), Mantan Moreland (cornet) and Bud Scott (banjo), in *Birth of the Blues*.

gradually intermingled with urban, mixed-race Creoles who read music well and were drilled in the fundamentals. From the former, classic New Orleans jazz got its blues and grit and improvisational spirit; the Creoles brought high instrumental standards, and ways of weaving horns together derived from Sousa-style concert bands. Young Jeff is the Creole in this scenario.

"Creoles of color" preserved French culture in nineteenth-century New Orleans, but in the twentieth century, this mixed-raced bourgeoisie lost status as segregationism intensified, and they got lumped in with poorer African Americans. A few such Creoles quietly passed into white society and white bands—notably clarinetist Achille Baquet. The name Lambert looks more French than it is, but Jeff's father's name is Henri, suggesting the family is (white) Creole. That Creole families traditionally regarded as white/pure European might be suspected of harboring black blood may explain Henri's aversion to jazz. Coming from a line of musicians, he seeks to protect the Lambert brand. On the other hand, the surname gets an English not French pronunciation, as if the Lamberts were quietly stepping away from Creole associations. We don't hear how "Henri" is pronounced.

In any case, Henri is not happy when he arrives at the levee, reluctantly guided by family retainer Louey (Eddie Anderson), and finds his son sitting in, going 'round and 'round "Georgia Camp Meeting" one more time (and repeating many of his precocious licks—he is just a kid after all). "What is that, a jungle dance?" the judge bluntly asks, eyeing the high-kicking dancers. Louey, drily: "Ain't no minuet." As punishment Jeff is sentenced to practicing music exactly as written, over and over. But when Dad's away he starts swinging Paderewski's "Minuet in G"—a callback to Louey's zinger. Jeff uses his classical technique to enliven the material, varying his timbre and pitch as well as rhythm, giving the music a blue tinge.

Father catches him, and ups the penance: Now play it 200 times—Henri turned antijazz tyrant like *Broken Strings'* Arthur Williams. "Honestly, Jeff, you got me worried. Did you ever hear any white folks play that low-down drivel?" Just me, Jeff confesses: "But this other music makes you feel like the circus is comin' to town. Kinda turns you loose inside. You can stretch out and play what you feel." Henri takes off his belt to give him something else to feel, but before the leather descends, he offers Jeff an out: Pledge you'll never play that "vulgar darkey music" again. Taking that deal would turn this picture into another *Jazz Singer*, but it's a feint; Jeff considers it, then bends over Henri's knee to take his punishment.

In the next scene he's grown up into Bing Crosby, hustling suckers at a pool hall where he and a couple of musician buddies hang out, playing situational licks between shots. Jeff even improvises a blues chorus over the felt—"I'm gonna finish this game / Fast as I know how"—as his trombonist and pianist back him up. Louey, now balding but still on retainer, has brought word that a hot white cornetist from Memphis has turned up at the jail. This is the break they've been waiting for. Jeff and his fellow New Orleans Hot-Shots—the only white jazz band, as far as they know—have been hustling for change or working day jobs because they lack a lead horn. Jeff's squad includes trombonist Pepper (laconic jazz giant Jack Teagarden, who has natural screen presence) and bassist Suds (Harry Barris, once one of the singing Rhythm Boys with Crosby). These Hot-Shots have the right spirit; they drop everything at the rumor of a chance to play, and use what little cash they have to bail out that cornetist.

In *Birth of the Blues*, it's a given that a racially mixed band isn't an option (those black Creoles who passed for white aside). No blatantly mixed band could work in New Orleans in whatever year this is supposed to be. By now it should be the mid or late 'teens, to judge by the music we hear. That would make Jeff about 30, almost a decade younger than Crosby—but there's nary a motorcar amid the horse-drawn vehicles, and at one point someone calls the 1907 hit "Waiting at the Church" a new song. The label "jazz" only caught on around 1916, and no one in the story uses that term.

Whenever it is, Jeff has been looking for a white cornet player for rather a long time. Perhaps his band has been rehearsing with one of New Orleans' many hot black cornetists in secret—because when they do get a lead horn, he fits right into the ensemble fabric. Outside the jail, Jeff's band calls out for the horn man, who appears at a window and gets nicknamed Memphis so fast we never do learn his name. Memphis (jaded Brian Donlevy) talks big, telling the other musicians he'd actually invented this (still) new music they all play. But his bluster doesn't faze them. "Puttin' us on, puttin' us on," Pepper mildly observes. The cornetist shows he's got chops to back up the bravado, as he leads the band into Handy's 1912 "Memphis Blues." Every African American in sight appears to dig it—clothesline ladies, bootblacks, fellow prisoners—but it befuddles some white hayseeds and scares a horse, right there at the corner of Basin and Customhouse streets. (There was no city lockup there, for the record.) A carriage driver calls the musicians "low white trash."

From this point there is much business that scarcely concerns us, regarding destitute transient Betty Lou Cobb (Mary Martin), saddled with a cute kid who's really her aunt. Betty Lou and Jeff will duly fall in love, though Memphis will make a play for her first, seemingly more out of habit than genuine interest.

Adult Jeff has grown out of playing hot solos; he barely struts his stuff on clarinet anymore. Now having a band comes first—that and promoting jazz: "Up till now folks never had Tabasco in their music. We're gonna improve their taste." Memphis can play but lacks Jeff's ideals; for him blue improvising is about making a buck. He's too cynical to play what he feels, yet his music sounds fine.

Most of the band were ghosted by members of Jack Teagarden's orchestra—Jeff by Danny Polo, Memphis by Pokey Carriere—and the music bears the trombonist's amiable stamp and compelling swing. Teagarden's participation lends the picture jazz credibility, and makes a subtler point than the opening scene does about what white players can bring to (and take from) black music. His phrasing like Crosby's bore the unmistakable influence of Louis Armstrong, but his singing and playing blended blues with a cowboy drawl, reflecting Texas and Oklahoma roots.

African American musicians may be largely absent, but white folks like Henri know perfectly well where jazz comes from. Memphis: "You know this blue music is darkey stuff." (So much for his inventing it.) "How do you know that the white folks are gonna like it?" Jeff reminds him they're white. But when the Hot Shots debut as an added attraction at a white movie house, playing "Tiger Rag," patrons rush the exits. "They're playing darkey music!"

Since Betty Lou/Mary Martin is hanging around, they work her into the act. (Part of Martin's youthful shtick growing up in Texas was imitating Crosby.) But Betty Lou has no jazz feeling, as we hear when she sings "Waiting at the Church," the kind of mildly naughty music-hall song that jazz would help kill off. *Birth of the Blues* contains several reminders of what prejazz pop sounded like: Jeff's "By the Light of the Silvery Moon," Betty Lou's "Cuddle Up a Little Closer," a staid "After the Ball." Early in the picture a Sousa-type cornetist plays "Carnival of Venice," a virtuoso display of brass technique with no rhythm to sell it, minutes before Memphis blows his horn through the jail bars—showing what his bravura style owes to that older tradition and how jazz breaks with it.

Wanting "to sing like the colored folks," Betty Lou asks Louey to teach her "noodling," which he defines as "singing a song exactly the way it ain't been written." But his advice is too abstract for her to follow: "You take a note . . . the one you're gonna sing. But don't sing it. Then you take another note, bring it around from the other way—and ignore it." It's played for laughs, but composer Will Marion Cook had given young Duke Ellington similar advice: "First you find the logical way, and when you find it, avoid it, and let your inner self break through and guide you."[2]

Jeff steps in to offer Betty Lou more concrete lessons, unwitnessed by us. But we hear the results at their next gig, opening night at gangster Blackie's café. In tandem with Jeff, Betty Lou swings 1905's creaky "Wait 'til the Sun Shines, Nellie" employing call-and-response, rudimentary counterpoint, quasi-improvised vocal breaks, and a round of whistled trades. (When the bassist's bow breaks, he hits on the expedient of plucking/slapping the strings, jazz-style.) As Jeff mostly sings nowadays, the Hot-Shots have quietly acquired a second clarinetist; this barely acknowledged shadow clarinetist faintly calls back to the prologue.

Two months later they've already made a 10-inch disc recording of the instrumentals "Shine" and "St. James Infirmary" (both recorded by Teagarden in 1940). It's unclear when all this is happening, but this would be among the very earliest jazz records, made who knows how, as there were then no recording studios in New Orleans. The band may have intended the disc only as a calling card; they've sent a stack to Chicago venues in hopes of finding work there. (In the film, the record mostly exists to hang a hokey plot device on; later the Hot-Shots will put it on to sneak away from Blackie's goons, while ostensibly rehearsing in the next room.)

There are plain parallels to the Original Dixieland Jazz Band: a white New Orleans outfit that played "Tiger Rag," beat the black bands who influenced them onto record, and left town for Chicago to take a gig there, and whose cornetist Nick LaRocca was a braggart who credited himself with inventing the music. But the ODJB didn't record either tune the Hot-Shots do.

"Shine" from 1910 has music by Ford Dabney, African American composer and transitional figure between ragtime and jazz. Louis Armstrong later popularized it, singing a lyric that pushes back against odious coon songs—don't think you know me 'cause you know my skin tone—where coon songs are all about reinforcing stereotypes. The Hot-Shots' version has no vocal, so any identification of its white performers with black role models is barely implied.

But that identification becomes more explicit in the big number that follows, when the band jumps to a new, swanky spot with a tonier clientele. There, Crosby, Martin, and Teagarden—or Jeff, Betty Lou, and Pepper—perform the patter-song "The Waiter and the Porter and the Upstairs Maid." It's by Johnny Mercer, white son of Savannah whose laconic relaxation as a singer gave listeners the (correct) impression he'd spent a lot of time on the black side of town growing up.

The lyric's elaborate narrative makes for a short talking picture within the movie. It's mostly Jeff's first-person tale of a bored guest at a posh private dinner, who wanders into the kitchen to see what's cooking, and discovers a much livelier scene at the back of the house. The domestic staff are having their own party between service calls, dancing to the music drifting in from out front, and jamming on impromptu instruments. The vocal trio briefly shows us how it's done: a washboard rhythm, a basin-and-spoon backbeat, and Teagarden doing a pet trick, getting a braying, bluesy sound by blowing through the U-shaped trombone slide into a drinking glass he holds by his cheek.

The dinner guest, liking what he discovers and finding a warm welcome, repeats the pattern at other stuffy affairs (and maybe brings friends along). He moves so easily between the front and back of the house, he comes to identify with the help; by the middle of the song, the singers take on the personas of waiter, porter, and maid, addressing members of the nightclub audience in dignified character: "Pardon me, folks / The roast is carved / The wine is served / You must be starved."

Nothing in the lyric identifies these gracious domestics as African Americans, although the trio's eight-bar jug-band blues break is suggestive, as is the setting. The Hot-Shots perform the song for a room full of white New Orleans swells, including a big-spending "old colonel" Jeff hails during the introductory verse. Race and class issues can be hard to tease apart, but in any case, Jeff, Betty Lou, and Pepper implicitly offer themselves as role models to their listeners. They're welcome around back precisely because they pay proper respect and don't embarrass themselves—just as Crosby and Teagarden found convincing ways to bridge white crooning and the blues. And of course singing this hip song to the moneyed class validates the audience's hipness too. A flattered old colonel is a better tipper.

To be sure, the lyric's confident white dinner guest is privileged to move between worlds as African Americans were not. He never wonders if he's genuinely welcome—or if he, too, is being flattered, like the servants' employers. In a pointed prelude to that song, Louey is sent around to the nightclub's back entrance by the black doorman—who, as a bonus, disses the Hot-Shots' white jazz and maybe black solidarity too. Louey, hearing the band from outside: "Our music sure is gone highbrow." Doorman, dubious: "*Our* music?"

The "Waiter and Porter" set-piece is almost immediately followed—via a fugue for battling stunt doubles, when Blackie's men bust up the joint—by the movie's other big number, one where black music trumps white. Louey, beaned in the brawl, lies comatose at home, an enclosed carriageway downstairs from Jeff's place. Louey's wife Ruby asks the Hot-Shots to play him back to consciousness, and they go into a soft "St. Louis Blues." Jeff tries to sing but chokes up. So Ruby (Ruby Elzy, who introduced "My Man's Gone Now" as Serena in *Porgy and Bess*) picks up the tune, with help from a choir of friends and neighbors keeping vigil in the doorway—and their more potent/soulful ministrations bring Louey around. Where it really counts, black music has a restorative power beyond Jeff's/Bing's abilities.

This scene contains strong echoes of the 1929 *St. Louis Blues* with Bessie Smith—an anguished African American woman sings Handy's classic with the aid of a Greek chorus of onlookers—and also *Black and Tan* where band and choir minister to bedridden Fredi, with similar expressionist shadows on the wall. It also looks ahead: Eddie Anderson would have a more protracted near-death experience in *Cabin in the Sky* two years later. And a young singer in search of musical inspiration would find it in a New Orleans carriageway in *The Jolson Story* in 1946.

With Louey recovered and an offer from Chicago in hand, the Hot-Shots need only escape Blackie's thugs and hasten down to the docks. There they await a riverboat to start their journey north—all except Louey and Ruby, to be sent for later. Once they're aboard, Jeff finally confesses his love to Betty Lou. "But are you as crazy about me as your blue music?" she asks. He ducks the question. "That ain't mine. That's gonna be everybody's blue music." (It's not his, but he gives it away anyway.) This declaration cues Jeff/Bing to reprise the theme song, over a stock-footage montage of luminaries and a pastiche of their musical styles: Ted Lewis, Ellington, Armstrong, Tommy and then Jimmy Dorsey, Benny Goodman, Gershwin, and finally (Crosby's, Barris's, Teagarden's, and Mercer's old boss) Paul Whiteman.

To build that montage toward the most grandiose music makes dramatic sense, even as it contravenes the play-what-you-feel spontaneity the movie ostensibly espouses. (Ostensibly, because Betty Lou learned to fake it.) The order of that montage suggests that jazz greats like Armstrong serve to feed composers like Gershwin. Rough black music gets gentrified by whites, who bring that back-of-house music out into the ballroom—which is just where we see Whiteman conducting for a throng of dancers, as that montage nears its close.

> ***Syncopation*** **(1942; 88 minutes; director: William Dieterle; screenplay: Philip Yordan, Frank Cavett; story: Valentine Davies). Cast includes: Bonita Granville (Kit Latimer), Jackie Cooper (Johnny Schumacher), Todd Duncan (Reggie/Rex Tearbone), Adolphe Menjou (George Latimer), Frank Jenks (Smiley Jackson), Jessica Grayson (Ella Tearbone), Leith Stevens (Ted Browning), Rex Stewart (King Jeffers), Clinton Rosemond (Prof. Elia Topeka), Ted North (Paul), Peggy McIntyre (Kit as a child), Jack Thompson (Reggie as a child), Bob Stebbins (page), Connee Boswell (herself). New song: "Under a Falling Star" (words Rich Hall/music Leith Stevens).**
>
> **—In a story that sweeps through several decades, pianist and jazz fan Kit Latimer moves from New Orleans to Chicago to New York. As a girl she grows up alongside cornetist Reggie Tearbone, whose talent is nurtured by the great King Jeffers. In Chicago, Kit meets trumpeter Johnny Schumacher, who gets sidetracked playing symphonic jazz before bringing a new swing feeling to New York's Fifty-Second Street.**

Birth of the Blues plays loose with the facts about early jazz, all in fun. By comparison *Syncopation* is a crash course in jazz history. The story's by Valentine Davies, who was to be involved with several more jazz films; cowriter Frank Cavett had worked on *Second Chorus.* Journeyman director William Dieterle, who started out acting in German silents, squeezed in this assignment between *The Devil and Daniel Webster* and *Tennessee Johnson.*

Syncopation establishes that jazz has roots in West Africa and its line of derivation came through slave songs and spirituals. It also lays out that whites learned to play it listening to black singers and musicians, that it was linked to dancing—the motion like the music evolving over time—and that some whites see their own take on jazz as the next evolutionary step. *Syncopation* also acknowledges women as agents of musical conservation and change, and gives us characters modeled on Louis Armstrong (a precocious New Orleans cornetist who goes on to greater fame) and Bix Beiderbecke (a white cornetist who gets stuck in an orchestra that stifles his creativity).

Beyond that, grander still, it situates jazz as the latest manifestation of an old communal impulse: people working out their troubles through social ritual. *Syncopation* has a central pattern of sonic and visual imagery that fuses the themes of music, dance, custom, and evolution: the sound (and look) of feet on the dance floor—a pattern prefigured by the film's first image, of a West African ring dance to drum-choir music. But there are problems too, that it shares with later tales like *New Orleans*. At a certain point, the black characters disappear.

Syncopation opens with a wallop: on the West African coast during the slave trade, at the start of a montage that speeds through several centuries. We hear that first scene before we see it. Under stylish, scrolling opening credits, we hear not a jazzy theme but a pounding accent-on-the-one tom-tom beat more stereotypically Native American than sub-Saharan—a beat that (shifting into double-time as the credits end) accompanies that aforementioned ring dance, errantly moving clockwise, in the background. In the foreground, slave traders buy off a local chieftain with luxury items: a parasol and top hat, totems to reinforce his exalted status. Then in quick succession we see slaves in a ship's hold (the Middle Passage), and laborers in a cotton field (slavery), and then a song of jubilee (Emancipation) even as an on-screen title tells us it's 1906 already. We find ourselves in New Orleans, where African Americans are finding jobs—longshoreman, bootblack, laundress, rail porter, white family's nanny, barber. There's also a banker, looking peacock-proud, smoking a cigar, and sporting a top hat that calls back to that complicit African potentate—as if the old-world social order had been reconstituted, with the top man still looking out for number one. There is something a little off about that last note. The montage gives African Americans credit for rising up and then knocks them down a little—like the story to come.

That working-folks montage is capped by an educator: Elia Topeka who runs his own music school, where his star pupil is playing for the class. Reggie Tearbone, a lad of maybe 10, blows a syncopated line on battered cornet like he can hear a band behind him—swinging his phrases with a singing tone, and moving up to a high-note finish. Any jazz fan knows how to read this: Reggie stands in for young Louis Armstrong, taken under a band director's wing at a tender age. The dialogue that follows is touching. After the other students file out, Topeka sits to talk to Reggie, who's still standing, so his teacher is looking up at him—the effect is that he addresses Reggie as an equal. You play better than any student we've ever had, the professor says, but there's nothing more we can do for you if you can't read music.

"Mis' Topeka—music on paper don't mean nothin' to me." Reggie looks crestfallen, and Topeka tells him not to be ashamed. "I ain't exactly ashamed. Was just thinkin' how I's gonna tell my mammy Ella. She wants me to be a teacher." Topeka: Should I break the news to her, gently? "Nobody breaks no news to my mammy gently like. I'll tell her myself—slow and easy." There's a disconnect, between the fineness of the sentiment and the forced dialect.

Ella is the next person we see, sweeping a sidewalk. She is easy to underestimate, as movie domestic and expository character, who clues us that her proud employer, architect George Latimer from a grand old New Orleans family, is markedly short on cash. Quietly, Ella's the engine behind much of the music in the film, as first teacher to Reggie and his playmate, George's daughter Kit. The children are tight; they banter. Reggie: I'm gonna practice this horn till I can blow the stars from the sky. Kit: Then blow out that bright one for me.

The Latimers live a couple of blocks behind Jackson Square, in the heart of the French Quarter, and tiny Kit can play some credible (and believably unfancy) blues on piano. Her father tells a visitor he has designed a church for Ella's congregation, and when we follow Ella and Reggie to a fundraiser—promising a special appearance by the angel Gabriel, a great come-on—we see the sad state of their present one. Their Gabriel is local cornet legend King Jeffers, a proxy for Armstrong mentor Joe (later King) Oliver, who's to play from outside a dormer window, as if direct from heaven. But he's late; Reggie climbs up on the roof to cover for him, and accidentally pokes a hole in it. He starts blowing his horn through the hole—a hymn, slow and easy—and the congregation first hums along, then jumps to life. (They're the Hall Johnson Choir, who'd been in many films since *St. Louis Blues* and *Black and Tan*.) King Jeffers turns up and starts blowing through that high window: two trumpets in the sky. (Jeffers is played by Ellington cornetist Rex Stewart, but reportedly ghosted by white swing star Bunny Berigan.) Now that the congregation's singing is self-sustaining, on the roof King and Reggie start trading phrases, blasting their horns to the surrounding area—both to advertise the fundraiser and for their mutual pleasure.

This scene demonstrates two aspects of Armstrong's development that the parallel film *New Orleans* misses: his apprenticeship with Joe Oliver and the influence of loose congregational singing on jazz phraseology. It's not just that Reggie ignites the singers; they in turn spark him and King Jeffers. It's the film's wildest scene.

Jeffers hears immediately that Reggie has talent, and drafts the youth into his limber four horn/four rhythm band down at a dancehall, the Mississippi Cafe. There Jeffers gives Reggie a lesson in ensemble dynamics, recreating a scene out of New Orleans jazz lore (and the book *Jazzmen*), when original cornet king Buddy Bolden would instruct his band, "Simmer down, let me hear the sound of them feet." Other bands like Kid Ory's did it too: played at a whisper to let that shuffle come through. It would "sound like sandpaper," musician Manuel Manetta recalled.[3] On a brash blues, when King Jeffers cuts off the horns and the rhythm section plays softly, we can hear (and see) the dancers' slow and sandpapery two-beat drag on wood planking. The horn players groove to it, eyes closed, blissed out, the sides of their heads touching: Jeffers has become Reggie's surrogate dad.

Ella's not happy when she turns up—shades of *The Jazz Singer*, *Broken Strings*, and *Birth of the Blues*—not due to any aesthetic objection, but because she doesn't want Reggie

FIGURE 2.2 Reggie Tearbone (Jack Thompson) and mentor King Jeffers (Rex Stewart) play for dancers in *Syncopation*.

distracted from his formal music studies. (Evidently he's put off manfully giving her that bad news.) But silver-tongued Jeffers convinces her to leave the boy in his care: "Reggie got something that no teacher can give no one, no how. Every once in a great while the Lord takes a tiny little spark and drops it inside of someone. . . . Let Reggie be with me, and I'll watch after that spark of his."

It's a persuasive plea, and Ella does know Jeffers from church. His offer is also fortuitously timed because her employer Latimer is moving to Chicago to secure new business. He plans to bring Ella along to look after the house and Kit, who's even less happy than Ella to leave the city she loves. To console the child at bedtime, Ella sings her a slow blues, revealing the source of Kit's precocious blues sense. "The same boat that takes us," Ella sings, "Can bring us back some day," before we segue to the riverboat they'll leave town on, as Reggie on cornet plays them off from the dock—finishing his mother's blues. She gave him his head start too. Ella, George, and Kit make their way up the Mississippi, to the tune of "Memphis Blues" and "St. Louis Blues," before a train takes them to the city of stockyards.

Now it's 1916, and Kit's seventeenth birthday. She's grown up to be played by Bonita Granville, but she's still homesick as she listens to a New Orleans jazz record (although none existed yet, unless it's the *Birth of the Blues* band). Tonight of all nights, Dad and her boyfriend Paul are tied up with business. Restless, with one of Ella's blues in her ears, she wanders out of the family home near the Water Tower on North Michigan Avenue— George's local contacts have paid off—and wanders some miles down to the South Side, where she meets rough teen Johnny Schumacher (Jackie Cooper). They quickly discover a shared love of hot music.

Johnny takes her to a rent party thrown by smooth-talking vaudeville performer and passable ragtime pianist Smiley Jackson, and Kit sits down at the piano to show 'em all some lowdown New Orleans blues, though she almost instantly slides into Chicago-style boogie-woogie. (She's more assimilated than she knows.) The joint is jumping, some neighbor calls the cops, and before you know it, Kit's on trial for disturbing the peace.

The first rough cut of *Syncopation* ran almost a full hour longer than the 88-minute re-lease version, and while the story speeds along with admirable efficiency, in the trial sequence some heavy cutting is apparent. We get a bare glimpse of the prosecution's case, but enough to hear it rests on the immorality of young women playing disreputable music. Indeed, when defense witness Ella concedes she'd taught young Kit songs of the street and the riverfront, the prosecution seeks to damn the girl with that admission. Ella protests, agitated: "It's trouble music"—music from the soul that brings relief to the afflicted, as we've already seen. And you hear such songs everywhere, Ella reminds the court, through her tears—even in Chicago. Acquittal is assured when Kit re-creates the music that got her busted (her lawyer having trucked in a piano), and judge and jury foreman start moving to the beat. Spectators start dancing in place, and we see and hear their feet do a tap-dancer's eighth-note shuffle, in contrast to that slower King Jeffers groove. The music's jumpier—more like Chicago. The foreman delivers a wordless not-guilty verdict in the form of a shave-and-a-haircut tap-dance step, before two strikes of the judge's gavel finish the phrase—an atypically farcical touch.

Kit's trial garners a lot of local publicity—in an insert we see a newspaper story that gets the facts wrong, placing the party at her South Side apartment. Post-verdict, Smiley Jackson approaches her father about booking her some gigs. But George, who's always encouraged Kit's piano playing, is aristocrat enough to bristle at Smiley's breezy familiarity and the idea that his daughter should cash in on notoriety. He tosses Smiley out, leaving Kit in tears. It is the last we will hear of her playing professionally. In black Chicago jazz of the early 1920s, pianists Lil Hardin (who would play with King Oliver and marry Armstrong) and Lovie Austin (who backed many blues singers and recorded in trio) would play pivotal roles. That life is barred to Kit.

But she still loves her father, and the music. She and beau Paul check out Johnny's dixie-ish sextet, an ex–high school band that stuck together, an echo of the (later) clique of talented white suburban Chicagoans known as the Austin High Gang. (We'll return to them.) The band sounds rather good, playing "Copenhagen," a tune from 1924. But it's 1917; before the scene's over a newsboy announces that the US has entered the World War.

By now, the viewer longs to know how Reggie Tearbone is faring. We soon find out, when Smiley Jackson travels to New Orleans in search of talent, perhaps on a tip from Kit. He hits the Mississippi Cafe, where Reggie still holds forth. King Jeffers had fanned that spark well: Reggie is now Rex Tearbone, the personable and well-spoken king of the cornet (played by Todd Duncan, Gershwin's original Porgy, fingering expressively). Smiley's visit is well-timed. New Orleans was forced to close its open prostitution district Storyville during the war. Here, in a scaled-down version of that upheaval, Basin Street will shut down at midnight. As the last minutes tick away Rex says a farewell to the old times and declares he's off to Chicago. With scant time remaining he goes into a triumphant and vaguely military blues. The neighborhood's white beat cop likes the music so much, he pushes the hands on the clock back an hour.

Syncopation was shot early in 1942, shortly after the US declared war on Germany for the second time. The World War sequence would have been poignant for contemporary viewers, especially when Kit's sweetheart Paul ships out for France—more audible feet, loudly tramping off to the troop trains—and doesn't return. On the home front, everyone pitches in. Johnny's in an army band, Kit volunteers at a canteen where there's a piano she maybe gets to play, and Chicago newcomer Rex plays a war-bond parade from the back of a wagon. What kind of music is that, a lady in the crowd asks a stranger, and slaps his face when he answers, "Jazz"—a word then also employed as a euphemism for copulation. When the parade passes the Latimer place, Rex's mother sees her son for the first time in a decade, and faints at the sight. That's the last we see of the film's secret hero, Ella's fate presumably consigned to the cutting-room floor.

The night Kit learns Paul was killed in action, she runs to the cafe where Rex is playing; as they talk by an open window, he tries to blow out a star for her, honoring the request she'd made when they were kids. Johnny arrives, and is knocked out by the band. Rex invites him to sit in. "You can't learn this music with no book, soldier," Rex says, putting a spin on what Prof. Topeka had once told him. They jam till the next morning, trading phrases on the blues, the student copying the master and adding a little of his own, much the way Rex did with Jeffers way back when—a realistic depiction of the jazz oral tradition. Come back any time, Rex tells Johnny—the experienced (black) musician generously sharing his knowledge with the (white) admirer. Johnny doesn't get to return, locked up for going AWOL, but he'll nurture that spark.

Postwar, Johnny starts touring and recording, and he and Kit get together. His expanded band gets hired at a mob joint, sounding okay on "That's A-Plenty." But he knows he's no Rex. "You shouldn't be. You've got a style of your own," says Kit, who's been keeping tabs on new developments, working in a record store. "Rex is New Orleans: Basin Street. And you're Chicago. You pick up where Basin Street leaves off." That scene is the last time Kit mentions the Crescent City she once missed so badly.

They marry (in 1923—a license plate tags the year), and that very day Johnny gets a break. Smiley Jackson is producing a big concert piece, *American Rhapsodie*, by orchestra leader Ted Browning (played by *Syncopation*'s music director, longtime Hollywood composer just moving over from jazzy radio work, Leith Stevens, looking like the young Citizen Kane). Browning's a stand-in for Paul Whiteman, specifically the Whiteman who'd premiered *Rhapsody in Blue* (working title: *American Rhapsody*) and then employed and stifled cornetist Bix Beiderbecke.[4]

As time marches on in *Syncopation*, jazzy music gets more formalized. At the theater where *American Rhapsodie* will premier, Kit runs into Rex, on his way out of town and out of the movie: "We're gonna hit that open road. There must be some spot 'round here where they still like it hot—where a man don't have to beat his brains out on set routine music—where a man can play just what he feels." Kit says stay in touch, but Rex explains he's not one for writing—unlike Armstrong, a tireless and colorful correspondent.

Johnny will soon learn what Rex was fleeing. Browning hires Johnny's group as "the old-fashioned jazz section of his orchestra" (just as Whiteman had a dixieland segment on his 1924 Aeolian Hall concert). In a way Browning's symphonic kitsch picks up where Basin Street left off, but not in a good way. From what we see, Johnny's crew is just reading parts, drowning in a musical soup including brassy fanfares, galloping strings, riffing bassoons, sentimental melody, and every once in a great while a bluesy lick in syncopated rhythm. (Life follows art: Leith Stevens's *Rhapsodie* got some actual concert performances.)[5] After a few nights Johnny's men have had enough. But Smiley's booked the orchestra for a yearlong tour, and Johnny elects to go along because (after years of scuffling) the money's too good to refuse.

The only time he and Kit fight is over this. She can see what it'll do to him, playing the same written music every night with no chance for self-expression. He'll be a "monkey on a stick," she tells him, as if they'd seen *Blues in the Night,* which had come out while *Syncopation* was being shot late in 1941. (That film's in the next chapter.) Johnny thinks he can change Browning's thinking, and besides, he tells her, "The kind of jazz we know is dead."

Sure enough, a montage confirms that all the repetition quickly drives Johnny crazy; to hammer home the point, we keep hearing the same zippy passage for strings replayed verbatim. Johnny keeps begging Browning to let him swing his parts, to no avail. The notes on the page taunt him until they swim before his eyes. (There's a brief, blurry, surreal image of Johnny clawing his way through musical staves that resemble cornet tubing.)

The heroes of later jazz films would know what to do: play the way he feels, and get honorably fired. Less bold, Johnny follows the score till he collapses on stage, missing a cue, and gets fired anyway. (Beiderbecke, as some tell it, was done in less by sheer repetition than by too few moments to shine. He left Whiteman when his drinking got too bad for him to continue.) Then, like Stella in *Alexander's Ragtime Band*, Johnny drops out and takes off to see America. One scene that was cut would have shown him drawing musical inspiration in a hobo camp.[6]

When he and Kit reunite, years later, the ease of their reconciliation underlines the allegory-thin characterizations. But he has much to report. On the road, even the most downtrodden folks would gather in the evening to sing "music made up by guys in a jam—songs about broken lives and busted dreams." (There's a speech like this in *Blues in the Night* too.) It's an echo of Ella defending "trouble music" in court. "It made me see what brings people together," Johnny continues, tying a ribbon around the film's themes. "They want to get rid of their troubles—talk 'em, sing 'em, or dance 'em away."

Smiley, now a big New York talent booker, reminds his aide Kit that he's known her for 10 years. That would make it 1926, but those hoboes and Johnny's new Bunny Berigan mustache suggest the 1930s. Also the slang: One of Johnny's men wants "a root-toot suit with an alreet pleat." Listening to the new record by Johnny's reunited and now expanded band, Kit tells Smiley, "It's more than just jazz. It's got kind of a swing. It's new." (In the 1930s, opinion was divided whether swing was jazz's next phase or something new altogether.) Smiley: "It's too new for me."

But in truth there's nothing confounding about it. For the first time in *Syncopation*, we have a disconnect between music as heard and described. What we hear is 1940s dixieland, a blues with light, loosely coordinated riffing behind Johnny's cornet (on which you can hear traces of Rex's declamatory style; Rex and Johnny were ghosted by Bunny Berigan, sometimes at least). Johnny's four-horn octet can't evoke the massed power and precision of great swing bands like Benny Goodman's—although the record's flipside gets closer to the mark. The tenor saxophonist sounds like he's in the swing era for sure.

Smiley starts representing Johnny's band but they bomb in Buffalo, where folks can't dance to it, and they lose their choice midtown Manhattan booking to Ted Browning's snoozy orchestra. Johnny and company land at the new and nearby Jive Club on Fity-Second Street. (A booming strip of nightclubs there had made that location jazz central from the mid-1930s.) The band catches on, with help from a jazz-loving page at the ball-room Browning plays who all but drags the patrons over to the Jive Club. There the page (mugging Bob Stebbins, 13 looking 11) installs himself as a sidewalk shill—"It's the miracle of Fifty-Second Street!"—like a miniature doppelgänger for Swing Street's legendary barker and freelance doorman Gilbert Pincus, who turned up around the time the movie came out.

This unnamed page is hip enough to recognize a special guest sitting at the bar: singer Connee Boswell, who's come down to help launch the club right. She sings a new number the band has rehearsed, one Kit might have written herself, given two references to "trouble music" during the bridge: "Under a Falling Star." If Rex couldn't knock that star from the sky for her in life, Kit can do it in art—can make that star fall on its own. Kit digs Boswell's vocal so much she nudges the band's pianist off the bench to grab a solo in her usual bluesy style, lightly modernized, winning a blink of approval from Connee. (In the same scene there are winking reaction shots from Johnny, Smiley, and the page, as if there are cinders in the midtown air.)

This is one of the rare moments in jazz films where women make music together, although Boswell, who always performed seated, remains at the bar. One hopes the band has noticed Kit sounds better than their regular pianist. That young page dreams of getting a horn like Johnny's, and Kit's dad, George (who's turned up from somewhere), says that he will—as if he'll buy it for him.

Johnny strikes up a riff tune, with Kit still on piano, and then he shuts the rhythm section down so they can listen to the shuffling feet, at the new style's brisker tempo. There's one last ankle-high shot of a dance floor, as the horns play a cappella breaks to keep the tune going, soft and easy. "Rex must have had such nights in New Orleans," Johnny says, righter than he can know.

The couple take a break as the band plays on. Look at the crowd, Kit says—this time the music's here to stay. "They're not dancing just to forget their troubles—they're getting something they can carry away. They're dancing to music that comes from the heart, music that's American born"—a rare instance of flagwaving in a jazz movie. And then very abruptly, we shift from jazz fiction to jazz fact: a studio blues jam with (white) stars chosen through a *Saturday Evening Post* poll. Harry James is on trumpet, Jack Jenney on trombone, Benny Goodman on clarinet, Charlie Barnet on tenor, Alvino Rey on guitar and steel guitar, Joe Venuti on violin, and Gene Krupa on drums, most of them assembled in one room. (We hear but don't see bass player Bob Haggart.) As an ending it's dramatically incoherent, but an honest finish to a didactic tale: Real jazz beats the made-up kind. *Syncopation* sends you home with both in your ears.

Director Andrew L. Stone's ridiculously entertaining backstager **Stormy Weather** (1943) is another biographical fantasia, this one very loosely inspired by the lives of its African American stars, champion hoofer Bill (aka Bojangles) Robinson and ex–Cotton Club chorine Lena Horne, both at peak charm. (Ted Koehler, who'd written the lyrics to the 1933 Cotton Club song "Stormy Weather," shares a story credit.) A secondary character in a long early sequence is Lt. Jim Europe (played by *Birth of the Blues*'s snarky doorman Ernest Whitman): James Reese Europe, an important figure from the 'teens when jazz was taking shape. As shown, Europe led the band for the decorated Fifteenth Infantry black regiment (of New York's National Guard) during World War I. The film doesn't mention that his transitional ragtime-to-jazz military band alerted the French to new developments in the States, but does show his musicians playing for the parade up Fifth Avenue that greeted those troops when they returned, and playing soon after for civilian audiences. (Not this soon though; the lead couple meet at a Europe gig hours after the parade.) Appropriately enough, Jim Europe exits the story early; he died within months of his return. The character's appearance here makes amends for his absence from 1939's *The Story of Vernon and Irene Castle*; he'd been that dance team's indispensable bandleader before the war.

Stormy Weather barely has a story, the better to make way for one stellar performance after another. The stars each sing a few tunes; Robinson's feet on a sandy riverboat deck make rhythm like a drummer's wire brushes. Cab Calloway brays "Geechy Joe" and "Jumpin' Jive," and his supercharged band backs the acrobatic Nicholas Brothers on a definitive stair dance. Ada Brown sings the blues and Mae Johnson a "St. Louis Blues"-y "I Lost My Sugar in Salt Lake City." Fats Waller (quintessential New Yorker awaiting discovery in Memphis, for some reason) mugs and wisecracks through an "Ain't Misbehavin'" where Zutty Singleton takes a double-time drum solo. With little plot to slow it down, *Stormy Weather* swings harder than jazz films that do tell a tale.

Rhapsody in Blue (1945; 141 minutes; director: Irving Rapper; screenplay: Howard Koch, Elliot Paul; story: Sonya Levien). Cast includes: Robert Alda (George Gershwin), Joan Leslie (Julie Adams), Alexis Smith (Christine Gilbert), Charles Coburn (Max Dreyfus), Albert Basserman (Prof. Franck), Herbert Rudley (Ira Gershwin), Morris Carnovsky (Morris Gershwin), Rosemary DeCamp (Rose Gershwin), Hazel Scott (Paris entertainer), Oscar Loraine (Maurice Ravel), Mickey Roth (George as a child), Oscar Levant, Paul Whiteman, George White, Anne Brown, Al Jolson (themselves).

—Gifted composer George Gershwin grapples with conflicting goals—to write serious concert music and Broadway hits—and puts blues feeling into his classical music. But how much time will he have to do it all?

How did jazz come to influence George Gershwin so profoundly? You wouldn't know from the black-and-white epic *Rhapsody in Blue*, which came late in a cycle of (European) composer biopics that had begun in the 1930s. It was more serious than the star-studded greatest-hits songwriter biopics MGM would soon produce: 1946's *Till the Clouds Roll By* (Jerome Kern) and 1948's *Words and Music* (Rodgers and Hart).

The real Gershwin, born in 1898, like other white musicians of his time picked up African American syncopation at least partly from the source. While still a boy, his family lived briefly in a Jewish enclave in Harlem; at some point, a young George would stand outside Barron Wilkins's club, eavesdropping on James Reese Europe's orchestra. By 1920 Gershwin was crossing paths with uptown pianists like James P. Johnson, Willie the Lion Smith, and Fats Waller, and would hear them play in Harlem. Their colleague Luckey Roberts claimed to have given Gershwin piano lessons. "When you hear *Rhapsody in Blue* you hear me," the not-always-credible Roberts once boasted. "He had all of my tricks in that."[7]

We hear movie-George play enough hot piano to know he learned some fancy licks someplace. But the transfer is all indirect. He picks up hot rhythm as a kid of 11 or so, by following player piano rolls, putting his fingers down where the mechanism depresses the keys (which is how young Edward Ellington learned to play James P.'s "Carolina Shout"). It's a raggy version of Anton Rubinstein's "Melody in F," to which George appears to add embellishments of his own—thinking like a composer already, before his family gets a piano. Later he continues his education by sight-reading populist ditties as a vaudeville pianist and publisher's songplugger. It's as if, in the years leading up to 1919 when Gershwin wrote "Swanee"—his syncopated takeoff on "The Old Folks at Home," sung and whistled here by blackface Jolson as himself—jazz had already so permeated musical culture, in New York at least, that a young musician could be well versed in post-ragtime black music without contact with African Americans.

This is not so plausible a scenario for the 'teens. But all period pieces are about when they're made as much as when they're set; think of the look and aesthetic of Robin Hood movies from any decade. By 1943, when *Rhapsody in Blue* was shot, many white musicians who'd never met a black person were playing jazz or showing its influence.

There are faint echoes of the *Jazz Singer* early in this Jewish New Yorker's story: George picks up and performs the new music in vulgar venues, and a parent disapproves—but this time it's mother, worried music may not be a steady profession. (She'll come around—and then son Ira's writing lyrics.) George's Mr. Fixit father admires the music's craftsmanship. He listens attentively in concert halls, stopwatch in hand, duration his proxy for quality. "Fourteen minutes and five—a very important piece!" (In contrast, *Variety*-addicted Papa Yoelson in the following year's *Jolson Story* knows the value of a brisk show: "Running time is everything!") Morris Gershwin's fixit skills extend to "S'Wonderful"—he whistles a workingman's phrase that unblocks the songwriter's process, when George had been striving for something more arty. The Gershwins' rise is measured by Morris's successive businesses—tobacco shop, bakery, grocery, stationery store, Turkish bath—the last a telling comment on the New York melting pot. (The real Morris had one.) As father betters himself, and then as George becomes successful, the Gershwins move on up: Lower East Side to the Bronx to Riverside Drive, hopping right over Harlem.

George also acquires a mentor who challenges him to stay true to old world musical traditions and to spurn jazz: bearded Prof. Franck (Albert Basserman, who once played Beethoven), who knew Brahms, stands in for Gershwin's several European-born teachers. His objections to George's new musical ways are more practical than those of Cantor Rabinowitz or *Broken Strings'* Arthur Williams. Yes, it's nice you're writing hits: "But is your work the best—as good as you can do?" He challenges George to see himself as extending the great European tradition into American music.

Franck's foil on George's other shoulder, the composer's (real) manager/publisher Dreyfus (gruff Charles Coburn), says the boy's got a gift for writing whole hit shows, that's not nothing. He writes for America. Franck: "He will write American music, yes, but great American music, not just little tunes that jingle like coins in your pocket." Franck talks of American sources in the same race-blind terms as everyone else here. Dvořák had been more frank about the African American source of the national music's power.

Those opposing elders are doubled by two women George dallies with, personifying Entertainment and Art. Either would be a catch, if music didn't come first: sweet show-girl Julie, who introduces his songs in New York, and a refreshingly unneurotic blocked painter in Paris, Christine, who digs cubism and introduces him to Ravel. (The French composer asks what inspires Gershwin's rhythm, but we don't hear the answer.) "In time, I'll write the way I feel," George tells Franck. He takes his teacher's challenge to heart, but George has so much to do in such a hurry, only jittery jazzy rhythms can keep pace. Gershwin would die of a brain tumor at 38, and there are many foreshadowings: "I'm afraid you'll burn yourself out," Julie frets when he's only 20; Franck compares his gift to (dead at 32) Schubert's; a fellow songplugger compares him to a fizzy drink casting off bubbles.

Rhapsody in Blue echoes *Symphony in Black* (and *Second Chorus*) by proposing a big concert piece as the epitome of (jazz) success—with this movie's title, how could it not? A Gershwin biopic called *I Got Rhythm* would be a different kind of picture, one where

George goes to Harlem. In *Symphony in Black*, Ellington's commission from the National Concert Bureau was for his jazz orchestra, but in other movies, you need to give jazz that symphonic treatment that signals good taste and high culture both. But before that triumph, George has a setback: his first dark operetta, called here *Blue Monday*, a minishow within Broadway producer George White's *Scandals of 1924*. In reality *Blue Monday Blues* was staged in the 1922 edition, and White was for it; here, he resists, seconded by Dreyfus: "Harlem. Dame shoots a guy. That's not for the *Scandals*." But the show's (actual) bandleader Paul Whiteman defends it, and conducts it from the pit.

The film restages an abbreviated *Blue Monday Blues*, mostly using tan-toned white actors—a classier brand of blackface. The exception is the lead, Anne Brown, who (on stage) sings a song of lament in a club with a bar, tables, and a dance floor, and a sympathetic crowd. Her wayward man makes a strutting entrance, and they embrace, but then things go south. Described like that, *Blue Monday* sounds like the template for the Bessie Smith *St. Louis Blues* (though many particulars differ—the heroine kills her man, wrongly believing him unfaithful, and he dies singing about going home to mother). W. C. Handy had attended the premiere of *Rhapsody in Blue*; might he or director Dudley Murphy have seen *Blue Monday Blues* (then or in a 1925 revival), planting the idea for *St. Louis Blues*?[8]

As presented, *Blue Monday* is earnest but a bit preposterous, and the white audience gives it a frosty reception. But in a cutaway we see a raptly attentive, uniformed black couple in the rear—an usher and coatroom attendant? The woman weeps. They are offered as (presumptuous) evidence that Gershwin gave voice to African American experience even before *Porgy and Bess*. We'll see this trope repeatedly in films to come, as we had in *Birth of the Blues*: a white artist's authenticity is validated by approving black listeners.

Backstage, dejected, Whiteman tells Ira Gershwin, "All we've got to do is get the public blues-conscious," as if the blues were some novelty they'd just dreamed up. On the spot, Whiteman invites George to write "a serious concert piece based on the blues." George: "A serious piece that's blue too. Blue themes and jazz rhythms—of course." (We've already heard him play a few licks from it, years earlier.) Say this for Whiteman: Duke Ellington didn't land movie parts that presented him as an arbiter of culture.

But the pivotal as-himself player here is pianist, wit, and Gershwin friend Oscar Levant, adding some authentic eastern wiseacre sarcasm. (He's from Pittsburgh.) Oscar the character has a proprietary interest in George's big piano pieces—keeps referring to "our concerto"—but he also plays the king's truth-telling fool. He gets to repeat at least one actual Levant bon mot: "If you had it to do all over again, would you still fall in love with yourself?"[9]

Whiteman's commission leads us to Manhattan's Aeolian Hall, one snowy night in 1924, for the famous concert that supposedly made a lady out of jazz. *Rhapsody in Blue* the composition is lightly abridged (to a still lengthy 13:35) but superbly staged, with German-expressionist lighting that changes from shot to shot without being too obtrusive—timpani casting giant shadows on the wall—and with close-ups that call attention to Ferde Grofé's instrumentation: that memorable trombone blues line; an ascending motif passed from clarinet to Harmon-muted trumpet; the French horns; the trembling bass clarinet. There's a little in-joke: Oscar, in the front of the balcony, is as nervous as if he's on stage, fingering the right-hand parts on the railing; Levant ghosted some of Gershwin's piano, and it's his hands in keyboard close-ups. Prof. Franck, on his deathbed, listens over the radio, hanging on every bar, rather like Cantor Rabinowitz at his end. George's synthesis of high art and folk sources is complete. The classical critics agree.

Later on, *An American in Paris* is presented in contrasting style—from the composer's vantage point, as it takes shape. George at the piano, in his garret with a Seine view, turns that car horn sounding in the street below into a winsome melodic figure. (This follows 1938's *The Great Waltz*, where Johann Strauss constructs "Tales from the Vienna Woods" out of birdsongs, carriage horns, and clopping hooves.) We listen to the finished product as we see what inspired Gershwin: the ballet, nights at the Folies where everyone knows him, street cafes, and stock-footage scenery. The town feeds a musician's inspiration, looking ahead to *Paris Blues*. George: "Over here I feel more American than I do when I'm home," a perception any traveler or expatriate might recognize.

George trots off to Paris a couple of times (as the real Gershwin did, in 1926 and 1928); these fond visits would have been bittersweet for wartime audiences to watch. (*Rhapsody in Blue* opened in New York shortly before World War II ended, and nationally shortly after.) It's on his first visit that we find out what African Americans really make of Gershwin's music: They make jazz of it. New in town, he goes to an elegant nightery where singer/pianist Hazel Scott performs, wearing a tiara. She gives the visiting composer a gracious introduction in French, and does "The Man I Love" slow, in two languages. Her very lively "Fascinatin' Rhythm" segues via an outbreak of Harlem stride piano into "I Got Rhythm," and finally the rare "Yankee Doodle Blues" with the house orchestra—that last number the aural backdrop for some dance-floor chit-chat. Musical arrangements have been discreetly modernized, to make them unobtrusive (or at least not fusty), much the way westerns track contemporary trends in sideburns.

Trinidad-born Scott was well cast; she'd played jazz and classical music separately and blended. Charming and gorgeous, she'd been a fixture at New York's Café Society a few years earlier, before she hit Hollywood, where pushing back against racist stereotypes scotched her film career. Her early benefactors overlapped Gershwin's, including conductor Walter Damrosch and Fats Waller. Piano king Art Tatum was another Scott mentor—hence her mean left hand.

Scott at the keys delivers the picture's peppiest Gershwin. Her selections pinpoint why jazz musicians love his tunes: the subtle blues undercurrents, the internal drive, and the ways strong motifs in the melody ("The Man I Love") or the syncopated beats ("Fascinatin' Rhythm") lend themselves to free paraphrase or improvised development, in which you can still discern the original tune. Those songs come from 1924; the anachronistic "I Got Rhythm" is from 1929, post-*American in Paris*, but its inclusion makes sense. Its challenging harmonic structure is the template for a jillion jazz contrafacts: new (copyrightable) melodies built on existing (noncopyrightable) chord sequences. Jazz is

FIGURE 2.3 Hazel Scott performs Gershwin for Gershwin, in *Rhapsody in Blue*.

inside Gershwin's tunes, waiting to break out, and the currency jazz musicians give his songs is a main reason we collectively remember so many now.

Hazel Scott performing Gershwin in his honor doesn't stop an entitled fat cat from dragging George over to his table for a little party, just as the music grows most intense. This is where George meets painter Christine. (Hollywood often put black entertainers into superfluous scenes that could be excised in the South; this scene is an exception.) We'd rather George had dallied to chat up Scott's character, an early jazz expat on screen (and apparent stand-in for racier toast-of-Paris Josephine Baker, who arrived in 1925). The film forecasts the future: Hazel Scott would move to Paris in the late 1950s, where she'd welcome visiting musicians. And in movies ever since *Rhapsody*, Paris is the token foreign location where jazz is dug.

Back in the States, George strides from triumph to triumph—the *Cuban Overture*, a Pulitzer for the show *Of Thee I Sing*—and hatches a plan for a new opera: "I'd like to use a folk theme—something American, if I can find it." If this were a radio play, you might not know *Porgy and Bess* had anything to do with African America. On screen it's represented only by "Summertime," sung by the returning Anne Brown, the original Bess. The opera gets less screen time than *Blue Monday*—as if, after that early flopera and two symphonic triumphs, the filmmakers were ready to wrap up. At least this *Porgy*'s cast is African American. Again, Gershwin's music isn't seen to come from black America; it's a gift to it.

His occasional headaches get worse; George, Ira, and Oscar decamp for Los Angeles. The composer plays a concert where his hand freezes up, foretelling doom. (This actually happened.) In the final minutes there's a musical recapitulation, a callback to the passing of Prof. Franck: Gershwin dies out west as Levant plays *Concerto in F* on a radio broadcast from New York. Word arrives via telegram, handed to and read aloud by the conductor minutes before the finale, letting Oscar slam out the final bars, railing against either Gershwin's fate or the conductor's crass interruption.

Then follows the world's biggest outdoor memorial concert, where Levant gets to play *Rhapsody* as himself, for what looks, in process shots, like the entire American population. The concert's held at some Albert Speer fever dream of the City College of New York's old Lewisohn Stadium—it's identified on the concert program, in an insert— at Amsterdam Avenue and 136th Street. Gershwin had come to Harlem at last.

> **New Orleans (1947; 90 minutes; director: Arthur Lubin; screenplay: Elliot Paul, Dick Irving Hyland; story: Paul, Herbert J. Biberman.) Cast includes: Louis Armstrong (Satchmo), Billie Holiday (Endie), Arturo de Córdova (Nick Duquesne), Dorothy Patrick (Miralee Smith), Richard Hageman (Prof. Ferber), Jack Lambert (Biff Lewis), Irene Rich (Mrs. Smith), Barney Bigard, Kid Ory, Bud Scott, Red Callender, Zutty Singleton, Meade Lux Lewis, Woody Herman (themselves). Original songs: "The Blues are Brewin'," "Endie," "Do You Know What It Means to Miss New Orleans?" (words Eddie De Lange/music Louis Alter), "Where the Blues were Born in New Orleans" (Cliff Dixon/Bob Carleton), "Farewell to Storyville" (Spencer Williams).**
>
> **—In a story that sweeps through several decades, and takes us from New Orleans to Chicago to Paris to New York, the early development of jazz is traced, chiefly through the career of Satchmo aka Louis Armstrong. Also, a casino owner turned jazz promoter is attracted to an opera singer.**

Generations of jazz fans have found *New Orleans* easy to dismiss, but it began with good intentions similar to *Syncopation*'s: an earnest attempt to tell the story of jazz from 1917 on. The original story by Elliot Paul, who'd worked on *Rhapsody in Blue*, salvaged elements from his prospective script for a jazz segment in Orson Welles's never-completed anthology film *It's All True*, from the early 1940s. That segment was to follow Louis Armstrong, playing himself, from early apprenticeship with King Oliver in New Orleans through to Chicago, New York, and Paris. (That segment got scrapped early in preproduction. An early version of *Syncopation*'s script turned up in Welles's files, but any connection to *It's All True* is unclear.)[10] In *New Orleans* Armstrong as himself follows the same trajectory, save that Oliver has been erased, maybe because *Syncopation* had already depicted that mentorship. *New Orleans* shadows that film rather closely as it is: a story spanning decades that takes its New Orleans cornetist to Chicago after Storyville closes, from which said cornetist disappears as we follow white characters to New York, where a once-disreputable fellow has become a jazz impresario and lovers reunite.

Producer Jules Levey ordered rewrites, fearing too many black ticket buyers would scare off skittish whites.[11] The final script essentially split *New Orleans* into two movies, only one of which is ridiculous. Black musicians are squarely at the center of the jazz plot, with Armstrong and Billie Holiday in prominent roles. But they're eclipsed by the wrong-side-of-tracks romance between classical soprano Miralee Smith and Storyville casino owner Nick Duquesne.

Armstrong's and Holiday's biographers mangle plot details—it's the most misremembered jazz movie. James Lincoln Collier gave Bing Crosby the lead role, conflating it with *Birth of the Blues*, and John Chilton claimed Armstrong played a butler. Clarinetist Barney Bigard recalled it ending with a symphonic "St. Louis Blues," confusing it with another film he made.[12] But it's not all bad, for one thing because there's so much Armstrong in it. *New Orleans* was his first real jazz feature, one loaded with his music—including his only (brief) pass at "Buddy Bolden's Blues." And like *Syncopation* it catches some of the epic sweep of the music's history.

What else it gets right: The important pioneers were primarily New Orleans blacks, many of whom left town in the late 'teens; most landed in Chicago where the music found a substantial white audience and broke through commercially. The breakout star was Armstrong, (later) nicknamed Satchmo, which is short for Satchelmouth, who graduated from small groups to big bands and went on to triumphantly tour Europe. By then the jazz capital had shifted to New York, and white swing bands began attracting more attention than the black originators.

New Orleans also features one of the great jazz-movie scenes. We're behind the scenes at Nick's Orpheum Casino, in a spacious kitchen and storeroom that serves as an ad hoc saloon and performance space for black musicians and friends—the province of waiters, porters, and upstairs maids. (The Orpheum is on the same corner as the jail in *Birth of the Blues*: Basin and Iberville, formerly Customhouse—on the border between Storyville and the more respectable French Quarter.) Right now all is quiet, and Satchmo, as everyone calls him, sits and warms up his cornet. He plays a short out-of-tempo intro, then launches into the opening tattoo of "Mahogany Hall Stomp" (not yet written in 1917, but let it pass). The tune's title hints at why a Storyville address poses a respectability problem for Nick Duquesne. Lulu White's mansion Mahogany Hall was one of the most elegant bordellos in that district.

In Armstrong's opening fanfare, you can hear the bugle calls that inform New Orleans brass playing; the melody is rooted in the ragtime in vogue when Storyville thrived. In the movie as in life, the early New Orleans jazzers still call their music ragtime. As Louis begins to play, eyes closed, a slight older white man in conservative attire furtively slips in. We know him: Mr. Ferber, the European music master who'll be conducting Miralee's debut recital.

Ferber tiptoes to the piano and joins Louis in mid-chorus, riffing on the melody with his right hand and tightening up the beat: the professor knows his stuff. Satchmo, unfazed, opens his eyes, nods a greeting and picks up the pace, until he winds up to a couple of high notes and slithers down a long glissando.

FIGURE 2.4 Prof. Ferber (Richard Hageman) and Satchmo (Louis Armstrong) jam in *New Orleans*.

Ferber: [breaking off, waving excitedly] Stop it! Stop it! That note isn't even in the diatonic scale!

Satchmo: Diatonic? [looks at his horn, wide-eyed] Did I do something wrong?

Ferber: Something extraordinary! You're playing notes between flat and natural. It's like discovering secret scales just made for this type of music!

Satchmo: Horn, did you hear what the gentleman said?

Armstrong appears to play the fool—talking to his horn was an old gag—but his character's delight is genuine. It's as if Ferber had given him the password, or passed a language exam: the prof hears the blues scale! They go back to playing companionably. Ferber's easy dotted rhythms suggest he's been studying ragtime scores, in addition to sneaking into the back room of the pointedly titled Orpheum: where lofty folk descend into the underworld. New Orleans doesn't have basements, but this room looks like one. Sturdy dark wooden pillars in this black workers' sanctuary support the rest of a building devoted to white commerce, suggesting a metaphor.

Ferber is turned to watch Armstrong as they play a full chorus, ending with a call-and-response volley, and a mock-Tchaikovskian flourish. Nick Duquesne, who's just come in, recognizes Ferber: "I've seen you conduct at the concerts but I never thought I'd see you conduct ragtime."

Ferber: Frankly, it leaves me a little mixed-up.

Satchmo: He never get mixed up when he play with us. . . .

Nick [a bit testy]:   I suppose you think ragtime is all right as long as it's locked up down here.

Ferber: No, that's the trouble, you can't lock it up. It leaks through everywhere. It's as though I had caught some virus, except that a virus makes one ill and this music doesn't make me ill, it makes me feel very well. But—mixed-up.

Nick: I see. So while Dr. Jekyll conducts the classics in the concerts, Mr. Hyde comes down to Basin Street to play ragtime . . . as if to get away from something.

Ferber [standing to leave]:   Maybe it's to come back to something.

New Orleans eventually works up to a cathedral wedding of jazz and classical. But here we have that union more quietly arrived at, 15 minutes into the picture: a classical-music authority hails jazz for specific musical advances and gut appeal.

Even so, in white New Orleans, here as in *Birth of the Blues*, jazz is tainted stuff, even if early jazz bands rarely worked the brothels, playing more often in the open air, or in bars where they might throw open the windows to draw customers. Some of those bars were in Storyville, just north of the French Quarter and Canal Street, with many more in nearby neighborhoods. Later on, Nick will give high-society Miralee a reality-check auto tour of the sordid side of the district, which is teeming with white reprobates, including sailors on the prowl, a streetwalker who calls to Nick by name, and a crazed alkie who's thrown her life away on a heel long gone. And indeed, by 1917 Storyville was on the skids; business was way down, and many of the sporting mansions had closed.

Nick Duquesne (Arturo de Córdova, Mexican star who had a short run in Hollywood) and Prof. Ferber (conductor Richard Hageman, with his clipped Dutch accent) may be open to jazz as cultural outsiders themselves. Ferber's given name is Henri, like Jeff Lambert's father in *Birth of the Blues*, but to some locals he's "Henry." (Hageman mimes expertly to Arthur Schutt's jazz piano on "Mahogany Hall Stomp," and appears to play his own florid Chopin in a scene that demonstrates that Storyville musicians also appreciate highbrow stuff.) Nick's hard vowels and consonants make him hard to place. Duquesne appears to have a shady past, but now strives for respectability; a string trio plus harp plays in the casino, as Satchmo and friends cavort in the back. Nick helps police the district. Early on he heads down to the docks to meet the Mississippi steamer *Dixie Belle*— the name of the riverboat the real Armstrong apprenticed on, starting in 1918—and run off Memphis gambler Biff Lewis, who'd hoped to set up shop in town.

A white dixieland sextet in a bandwagon is there to greet the boat, rushing "There'll Be a Hot Time in the Old Town Tonight" and looking very pleased with themselves. But they're struck dumb when Satchmo's Orpheum septet strikes up a swaggering "Maryland, My Maryland." His cornet catches the ear of Marylander Miralee Smith (dewy blonde Dorothy Patrick), apparently arriving by riverboat from Baltimore to join her patrician mother, who gambles at Nick's. Miralee's done her New Orleans homework, recognizing Nick's name when he's introduced: "The King of Basin Street Duquesne?"

At the Smith manse, Miralee hears her lady's maid Endie before she sees her: "She sings like an angel!" Mrs. Smith: "There's more devil than angel in that music." Endie is the regal Billie Holiday, last seen in *Symphony in Black*. A chapter in her autobiography *Lady Sings the Blues* details her unhappy experience making *New Orleans*, starting when she learned she'd play a maid. Holiday and Dorothy Patrick didn't get on—it didn't help that Billie showed up on set 12 days late—though the tension doesn't show on screen. Holiday would demur, "I was no actress, never had been one, never pretended to be one." She gives herself too little credit. Lady Day can make her face light up, cock an eyebrow, and bring the sparkle. One reason she looks great: she knew who to befriend on set—the cameramen.[13]

She also has that angel/devil voice. Another singer might feel threatened by a maid who sings like Billie Holiday, but Miralee is all questions. What were you just singing? "A kind of little old blues tune." (Actually, a pop song with a bluesy undercurrent written for the film by Eddie De Lange and Louis Alter, the instant standard "Do You Know What It Means to Miss New Orleans?") Do you only sing the blues when you're blue? Endie: When you're blue, or happy, or in love—like I am with my Satchmo. The scene ends with Endie finishing the tune for her new boss, sotto voce—and in the next, Miralee sings bel canto at a little classical soirée, forcing a comparison between Endie's heart tones and her employer's head tones.

Miralee soon persuades a reluctant Endie to take her to the Orpheum to hear hot music. (Proper young ladies don't do such things.) Endie sits in with Louis's band to sing "New Orleans" again. Miralee discovers Ferber's clandestine visits, and confesses her instant love of jazz to Nick, peppering him with questions about its sources. "Work song, the Gold Coast of West Africa, little Christian churches, riverboats," he tells her. "They made up the music as they went along."

She's worked hard to make old European music hers, Miralee says. "But this—this music's mine already!" Sherrie Tucker's feminist reading of *New Orleans* justly slams Miralee's entitled air, but her intentions are good; like *Birth of the Blues'* Jeff Lambert, she wants to help the music find a wider (whiter) audience.[14] But she's blind to racist realities holding it back. "There's a wall around it," Nick tells her: "A big invisible wall you can't climb over." Jazz is like prostitution—tolerated only within boundaries.

To her credit, at the Orpheum Miralee has been listening more than talking, not that Endie's style will rub off on her. In the same scene, Satchmo has been holding forth, introducing his band with the patter song "Where the Blues were Born"—Louis sings "was"—in which everyone plays a little break. The septet boasts other distinguished Orleanians: trombonist Kid Ory, drummer Zutty Singleton, clarinetist Barney Bigard—the Zelig of jazz films from *Black and Tan* to 1958's *St. Louis Blues*—and guitarist Bud Scott, last seen on banjo in the prologue to *Birth of the Blues*, connecting the films' universes. Two musicians are ringers from Los Angeles where most of *New Orleans* was shot, pianist Charlie Beal (who'd recorded with Armstrong in 1933) and 30-year-old bass modernist Red Callender, who with a sly wink quotes a bebop lick on his four-bar break.

As we've seen, historical films often feature anachronistic music. This rhythm section's smoothly flowing beat is far from the stricter syncopations of 1917. But 1940s dixieland revivalists like Kid Ory carried on as if they were still playing the way they had back when, as if stylistic evolution had been too gradual for practitioners to notice. "Where the Blues were Born" has an anachronistic lyric to match, touching on a mid-1940s controversy. "Now I know some people call it corn," Satchmo sings, of his own music. No one would have claimed that in 1917, but it was a common charge in the 1940s when traditionalists feuded with bebop progressives. With his bop lick Red Callender was showing his colors on rival turf.

There is another weird disconnect, in Armstrong playing himself. In 1917 he was no confident leader, but a 16-year-old getting started as a professional. *New Orleans'* Satchmo is unstuck in time, ditto Billie Holiday, who sings with slinky 1946 phrasing; in 1917, the ascendant African American singers were big-voiced shouters like Ma Rainey. Holiday—who'd never set foot in the Crescent City, and never would—was cast mostly because she and Louis shared the same manager, Joe Glaser, a tough-talking Chicagoan with rumored mob connections.[15]

Unintended consequences: *New Orleans* helped alter jazz history. For a decade and a half, Armstrong had been fronting high-overhead big bands. His small group here put him among peers and gave him more elbow room. To tie in with the movie's release, Glaser booked him with a similar group, which evolved into Louis's All-Stars, a sextet with Bigard originally on clarinet (and Jack Teagarden on trombone). Armstrong stuck with that format the rest of his career.

In the real world, the secretary of the navy forced the Storyville brothels closed. No one here mentions it, but in April, the US had entered the World War and the district was now perpetually flooded with sailors on shore leave. In the movie, it closes when a wayward socialite stumbles drunk out of the Orpheum and into traffic. Open corruption? Tolerable. Dead white woman? Time to act!

In *New Orleans*, the closing of Storyville, at midnight on November 12, 1917, is a biblical Exodus, in which the neighborhood's residents are evicted. As the hour approaches, musicians and friends gather in the Orpheum's back room, for a glum last meal and a sermonette from brother Satchmo, who calls for one last tune for the road. Pianist Beal strikes up a scrap of sad slow melody, and a lady calls out to Endie to put words to it, something about goodbye to Storyville. Endie steps up, gets a faraway look in her eyes, and joins in the band's farewell dirge, speaking for her peers, and riffing on Satchmo's little talk: "The law stepped in / And called it sin / To have a little fun." She takes away the sting of impending exile, even as the beat of the bass drum evokes tramping off into an uncertain future. When she gets to the refrain, her listeners echo her, then take up that refrain for themselves. It's the only sequence in *New Orleans* that approaches a conventional musical: a spontaneous outpouring of heartfelt song.

This collective lament continues as we cut to outside. Cops in military formation march into the zone and line the streets. At midnight one blows a whistle, lights begin to blink out, and the area's stunned residents emerge from their lairs with bedrolls and baggage. The Orpheum crowd joins them, continuing their dirge. Endie impulsively races off to say goodbye to her family as they're being swept along. She and Satchmo are separated.

The scene is freely adapted from the aforementioned book *Jazzmen*: "As the evening wore on the musicians came out of the houses, one band after another, and formed into line. . . . Slowly it marched down the streets, Iberville, Conti, Customhouse. As it made its solemn stand it played 'Nearer My God to Thee'—plaintively, like the brass band on the way to the graveyard. On Franklin Street, prostitutes moved out of the long-shuttered cribs, mattresses on their shoulders. The brasses moaned, while the clarinets sung shrilly above them."[16]

(This wouldn't be the last time Pops—to use Armstrong's hipper nickname—would help stage the exodus from Storyville. He did it again on the quasi-documentary TV series *You Are There* in 1954, except that time he played King Oliver—serving up some Oliver licks—and did an anachronistic "When the Saints Go Marching In." His All-Stars portrayed Oliver's band and white drummer Barrett Deems performed in blackface.)

Uptown, that same night, Miralee's debut concert must have started very late; it's still going on past midnight when Nick arrives. Miralee's determined to run off with him after the show. Equally determined to save her reputation, Nick plays the cad to her mother backstage, discrediting himself—an operatic deception, underscored by Miralee's on-stage aria. When she finishes to great applause, Nick requests an encore, giving him time to slip away. So she steps back out, and with Ferber's reluctant acquiescence and crushed-interval piano intro, kicks off "Do You Know What It Means to Miss New Orleans?" A few members of the orchestra join in, infected by the jazz virus. Others look embarrassed.

In the movie's universe, her performance is courageous and open-minded. But it's dreadful, and not just compared to the Holiday versions already heard: she's out of tune, unswinging, and very self-satisfied. There's no trace of work song or little Christian churches, let alone the Gold Coast of West Africa, with all that implies. (She's ghosted by socialite soprano "Teddy" Lynch, wife of oil tycoon J. Paul Getty.)[17] The concert audience is divided. Some give her a standing ovation. The snobs show better taste, booing and walking out. In the aftermath, Miralee and Ferber are equally disgraced. Her jazz taint is on him.

Before long, the Smiths set sail for Europe (apparently on the *Dixie Belle*, which would make for a rough ride across), in hopes Miralee can outrun scandal, restart her career, and forget Nick. At the last minute, Ferber joins them at the dock. "Are you sure now just which side your heart is on, musically speaking?" asks Mrs. Smith. "Musically speaking, there's only one side left," he replies cryptically. Ferber returns to his own side of the Atlantic, home to music that's his already, perhaps hoping to shake off that jazz virus. That scene at the dock aside, an hour into *New Orleans*, we flee town for good. Nick and Satchmo and a stream of exiled musicians—everyone but Endie, whereabouts unknown—regroup in Chicago. Never mind that Armstrong didn't leave New Orleans until 1922—and didn't start playing with Ory regularly until after Storyville closed.

The movie's last half hour hurtles along with northern efficiency. In Chicago, Nick wants to open a casino in a burned-out restaurant; one of the painters is Meade Lux Lewis, who on finding a piano plays his boogie-woogie classic "Honky Tonk Train Blues." But Nick soon realizes Satchmo's music is a bigger draw than roulette wheels. Collegiate white kids want to dance to it—in droves. (No black listeners come around.) A drunk who wanders in one night gives the band's modernized ragtime a new name: "Jass it up, boys, jass it up!" "Jass" was a common spelling/pronunciation of "jazz" early on.

Satchmo's music at Nick's new Club Orleans sketches Armstrong's early Chicago career without squandering a line of dialogue. The real Louis had come north to join King Oliver's two-cornet band; here Satchmo's expanded Chicago outfit has New Orleans' Mutt Carey on second cornet. When they play Oliver's "Dipper Mouth Blues," Louis re-creates his mentor's muted solo from the original recording, unmuted. (He'd been doing that in various settings since the 1920s.) Then guitarist Bud Scott yells a falsetto "Oh play that thing!" exactly as on one early version, confirming his disputed presence on Oliver's record: lagniappe for discographers. Oliver and Armstrong recorded "Dipper Mouth Blues" (twice) in 1923, more than five years after Storyville closed. By now the whole narrative has come unstuck in time. Adding to the confusion, a copy of *Billboard* proclaiming ragtime's sweep of Chicago is dated September 14, 1946.

As displaced New Orleans musicians keep arriving, and demand for jazz grows, Nick becomes a talent booker. A bigwig in Chicago music who has underworld contacts (Biff Lewis is around) and who manages Satchmo, Nick effectively becomes Joe Glaser, the manager whose approval the film's producers needed to snag Armstrong.

Now comes a heady montage sequence, over another new De Lange and Alter tune, "The Blues Are Brewing." This montage does more heavy lifting than the pillars in the Orpheum's back room, squeezing an act's worth of transcontinental/transoceanic action into just over three minutes. We see that Satchmo, still at (an ever swanker) Club Orleans, has graduated from stubby cornet to noble trumpet, and now fronts a full orchestra (like Armstrong in the 1930s). He's just swinging the tune's intro when the missing Endie suddenly appears to take the vocal, somehow knowing the song already. She is looking fine with Holiday's signature gardenias in her hair. As Endie comes out of the song's bridge, a succession of shipping-trunk destination tags tells us Pops is now hitting the rails, from Denver to Salt Lake, from San Fran to Spokane. In a sleight-of-hand transition, in Minneapolis his baggage jostles Woody Herman's, and we now pick up that swing bandleader's trail, as the music segues (via choo-choo saxophones, still present when Woody rerecorded "The Blues Are Brewing" weeks later) into Ralph Burns's Herman arrangement. Woody on alto takes a stylized melody chorus in front of his big band, back at Nick's club, where the increasingly upscale crowd now sits instead of crowding the stand. Then—we're still in the montage—Herman's band heads east on the baggage-tag express, as trumpeter Sonny Berman takes the bridge, his declamatory style showing how Armstrong affected all who came after him. Herman's trunks make their way, stop by stop, to New York where they again bump Armstrong's luggage, which is bound for the Opera Trianon in Paris (cue stock footage of a steamship and the Tour Eiffel) where—a poster in French informs us—Miralee Smith has been appearing in Gounod's *Faust* as Marguerite: the fallen ingénue who goes to heaven in the end.

You'd expect a breather after that bicontinental sprint, but as we crossfade to another poster announcing the appearance of Louis Armstrong et son American Hot Jazz Band (in this picture only the French don't call him Satchmo), he's already launched a new number, the joyful "Endie"—"Hooraytion! Endie's out of circulation!"—which tells us all we need to know about the resolution of that plotline. (There was also the radiant look on his face when she suddenly turned up—never underestimate Armstrong's acting.) We'll shortly learn they are now married, though we don't see Endie again.

In Paris, Louis is a hit; even royals in a private box head-bob to his tuxedoed and elegant swing orchestra. (He is soon invited to give a command performance at Buckingham Palace.) Backstage at the Trianon, he greets a well-wisher: Miralee, toting a copy of Armstrong's autobiography, *Swing That Music*. One suspects Joe Glaser's hand in this product placement. The moment acknowledges Armstrong's parallel life as a stylish prose writer as no other film does. This seeming naïf who'd asked Ferber if reading music gets in the way of his feelings when he plays? He also writes (very good) books.

Miralee now looks slightly older and more self-possessed. But she's still stung by Nick's betrayal, and Satchmo has to straighten her out—he did it to save your reputation, he's still pining—and to update her: "He's a very important music man . . . trying to educate New York for jazz." As in, respectable enough for a woman like you. Mutually elated, they go out on a literal high note—his played, hers sung—that brings stagehands scurrying. It's the only time these two make music together (or interact at all). It's also our last sighting of Satchmo. But we'll see Armstrong in that city again, in another film that gives him credit as a literate musician, *Paris Blues*.

How long has it been, since Miralee left New Orleans? In the real world Armstrong showed up to play Paris's Salle Pleyel in 1934; *Swing That Music* was published in 1936. Down the rabbit hole: in the book Miralee carries, Armstrong describes the very tour that took him to Paris.

New Orleans ends with Miralee mauling "Do You Know What It Means to Miss New Orleans?" again, this time at "Manhattan Symphony Hall." Other endings were contemplated. Red Callender says they shot an unused concert finale featuring Armstrong's and Woody Herman's bands. In an early script, the film ends more modestly at New York's integrated Café Society Downtown. There Endie performs (as Holiday had, in the late 1930s) with an integrated band, and Miralee, in a callback to Endie's spontaneous Storyville send-off, improvises her own reading of jazz genesis: "Born in the land of cotton / Born in Africa, too / Born in the brass of a noisy parade / Born in a gamblin' house, too."[18]

The actual ending is more spectacular, and silly. By now Nick works out of the New York office of his national booking agency. He's so big, shady Biff Lewis begs him to get Woody Herman into one of his joints. In the early reels, jazz was seen as a corrupting influence; now it's turning gangsters into entrepreneurs. Not that Biff recognizes Woody when he runs into him at Nick's office—and Herman auditions for him like a nervous kid, in a comic bit. (He's funnier than Artie Shaw.) These days Satchmo's always touring, staying in touch by telegram. Woody is Nick's new confidant; he knows all about Miralee.

For Woody's sake and his own, Nick has become obsessed with getting Herman's big band into Symphony Hall, to validate jazz before a high-art audience. (Never mind Pops is playing opera houses and command performances in Europe.) Miralee's New York debut next week is at that same august venue, where Nick can't even get a meeting with the manager. "I've waited a long time for Miralee to come back. But it will never work out until our music can stand where she stands, as equals."

Woody Herman is well cast: a swing bandleader still going in 1946 when big bands were running aground. (He'd temporarily disband at the end of the year.) His postwar First Herd was studded with Stravinsky lovers who'd quote from his works in solos and scores. The Herd had recently recorded the homage "Igor" and Stravinsky's own *Ebony Concerto*, which they'd played at Carnegie with the composer conducting—all of which informs the final scene.

The end of *New Orleans* works variations on Miralee's New Orleans recital: another concert where she's introduced to a city and sings "New Orleans" for Nick who appears backstage at the last minute, exploiting his knack for getting past stage doormen. "An encore just for you," Miralee tells him, stepping into the wings as her conductor Henri Ferber slips over to the piano and vamps an intro. The raised platform on which she stands rotates her back onto the stage. As she goes into "Do You Know What It Means to Miss New Orleans?" a matching platform across from her, stage left, turns to reveal an *ooh-aah* wordless choir. Two additional pianos move into view on a riser in the back, and the cocktail tinkling intensifies: "New Orleans" arranged for three pianos, soprano, and choir.

FIGURE 2.5 Woody Herman and his big band (top right) make up a small fraction of the mixed orchestra at the end of *New Orleans*.

After 32 bars, another platform rolls out at the rear: Woody Herman's First Herd, with vibist Red Norvo out front, takes over the tune, on the very stage where Nick has failed to book them. The symphonic musicians now pitch in, percussionists rat-a-tatting on snare drums, the strings zinging away. This assembly makes the Carnegie finale of *Alexander's Ragtime Band* look tastefully understated. We get one close-up of Ferber, nodding at Mrs. Smith out front: nice, eh? She thinks so. So does the Hall's jazz-hating manager, once he sees the highbrows swaying in their seats. Woody takes eight bars on alto, and everybody chimes in on the main melody, before Miralee comes in on the bridge to take the tune out. From the piano, the score propped in front of him, Ferber conducts a ritard for the ending; the movie ends as the song does.

Miralee sings with a little more seasoning than last time, but living in Europe hasn't enhanced her jazz feel. The arrangement is rubbish, a good song crushed by kitsch. Who in the movie is responsible for that chart? This orchestral bloat is so far from "Igor" or *Ebony Concerto*, we can safely absolve Woody from blame. The culprit can only be Prof. Ferber. In New Orleans, he never got lost playing with Satchmo. But after years in Europe, he's lost his way back.

New Orleans is often criticized because Armstrong and Holiday miss the finish, but who'd involve them in this mess? The music's quality is beside the point. This marriage of jazz and classical is only a proxy for Miralee's and Nick's nuptials. The finale is a big vulgar wedding cake.

/// 3 /// BANDS OF BROTHERS
1941–1948

Japan's attack on Pearl Harbor in December 1941 finally drew the US into World War II, and at least one wartime film would draw parallels between jazz bands and military units. Conflicts between musicians, played for laughs in 1940's *Second Chorus*, became serious business—now when everyone needed to pull together.

> ***Blues in the Night*** (1941; 88 minutes; director: Anatole Litvak; screenplay: Robert Rossen, after a play by Edwin Gilbert). Cast includes: Richard Whorf (Jigger Pine), Priscilla Lane (Character Powell), Betty Field (Kay Grant), Jack Carson (Leo Powell), Elia Kazan (Nickie), Peter Whitney (Pete), Billy Halop (Peppi), Lloyd Nolan (Del Davis), William Gillespie (jailhouse singer), Will Osborne (Guy Heiser), Jimmie Lunceford (New Orleans bandleader), Herbert Heywood (railyard guard). New Songs: "Blues in the Night," "Hang on to Your Lids, Kids," "This Time the Dream's on Me," "Wait Till It Happens to You," "Says Who, Says You, Says I" (words Johnny Mercer/music Harold Arlen).
> —In a St. Louis jail, pianist Jigger Pine and friends overhear a striking bluesy tune, and make it their own. Their co-op jazz band plays a seedy club just outside New York; Jigger quits and goes commercial, with dire psychological consequences.

Songwriter Johnny Mercer had two new movies out in November 1941. Just after *Birth of the Blues* with "The Waiter and the Porter and the Upstairs Maid," a film opened for which he'd cowritten four new songs, a movie retitled after the best of them: *Blues in the Night*, originally to be called *Hot Nocturne*. Those Mercer films have curious parallels. In both, an uninvited white soloist jams with a black band; a jailed jazzman is drafted into a white unit whose leader learned about the real stuff from black musicians; a band rescues a braggarty horn-hocking trumpeter in New Orleans, then they all go to work for gangsters; a square singer gets some remedial education; and in the end everyone hits the road to spread the music around.

But where *Birth of the Blues* is a vanilla froth, *Blues in the Night* is dark. (Anatole Litvak directed on a modest budget for Warner Bros.) Nearly every scene is set at night, in an uncertain universe where men make dubious choices. It's practically a jazz film noir, rich with conscious and unconscious subtext—about capitalism versus the commune, and whites plundering black music. And in its way it's another jazz origin story.

In the opening scene, a barnstorming piano-drums duo pound out lowdown boogie-woogie at the St. Louis Café, where they'd rather fight than play "I'm Forever Blowing Bubbles" for an abusive drunk who compares them to organ-grinder monkeys. Tossed in the city lock-up as troublemakers, pianist Jigger Pine (Richard Whorf), rheumatic drummer Peppi, and their jazz aficionado pal Nickie (Elia Kazan, before he was a director), a clarinetist from a family of lawyers, run into bass player Pete. On the spot they resolve to form a band. "It's gotta be our kind of music, our kind of band," Jigger insists, playing songs they've heard while knocking around the country: "Blues, real blues, the kind that come out of people, real people, their hopes and their dreams . . . the whole USA in one chorus."

And to play it all? "That's five guys, no more, who feel, play, live, even think the same way. That ain't a band, it's a unit . . . It's got a kick all its own and a style that's theirs and nobody else's. It's like a hand in a glove—five fingers, each that fits, slick and quick." Peppi gets so excited he has a coughing fit and blacks out.

Across the way in the black inmates' cell, a prisoner (Ernest Whitman of *Birth of the Blues* and *Stormy Weather*) calls out: "What's the matter with that white boy, has he got the miseries?" We all have them in here. And then one of his cellmates begins to sing softly, "My mama done told me / When I was in knee pants . . ." and a couple of other voices join in, either because they know the tune or are improvising along. It's "Blues in the Night," introduced in grandly understated fashion. The scene hums in sympathetic vibration with Jelly Roll Morton's account of being struck by the sound of prisoners singing when he passed through a New Orleans jail as a boy, or white clarinetist Mezz Mezzrow first hearing the blues sung by black inmates at a reformatory. It's also part of a movie tradition, dating back to 1930, in which black prisoners' "plaintive song served as an editorial," per film historian Thomas Cripps.[1]

Jigger, agog: "Boy that's the blues—the real lowdown New Orleans blues." But not really. The memorable tune is by Harold Arlen, a sort of real life Jack Robin/Jakie Rabinowitz: Hyman Arluck, the son of a Buffalo cantor who brought genuine blues feeling to popular songs, some of which (like "Stormy Weather") he'd cowritten as in-house composer at Harlem's Duke Ellington–era Cotton Club. More recently he'd composed the music for *The Wizard of Oz*. The plot demands the tune must sound like an authentic oral-tradition blues, but also lend itself to classical-style thematic development. Arlen's musical solutions were elegant. The opening theme is a 12-bar blues on a lightly modified chord pattern, and the way Mercer's lyric repeats "My mama done told me" in the second line (and in this rendering, as the cellmates' answerback in the second section) suggests a conventional blues stanza where the first line is sung twice.

But that first theme's main melody sidesteps blues practice as much as it mimics it. That rising opening figure involves a jazzy major seventh of the scale, not a bluesy dominant seventh. There are a few of those in there too, along with major and minor thirds—Arlen mixing them up to suggest the blues scale's ambiguities, rather like Gershwin in *Rhapsody in Blue*. That theme ends with a downward tumble of an octave over the title phrase, plunging by a fifth to the melody's low note. It lands on the final "night" like darkness falling.

The 12-bar "Now the rain's a-fallin'" refrain that follows mostly juggles the same chords in a looser sequence, abstracting further from the blues, and Arlen more aggressively juggles major and minor thirds and sevenths, the way blues pianists do, to hint at and signify blue notes in the cracks between flat and natural. (The song also has a lyrical conventional bridge that wanders far afield harmonically, which is never sung in the film, and is first heard when Jigger's tickling the ivories, later. In the world of the movie, it's the only part of the song Jigger composed himself.) Arlen's poignant harmonic motion and chiseled-profile melodic contours are grist for thematic development. The song unfolds like a story. When the prisoners get to Mercer's unforgettable if easily mangled bluesman's itinerary—"From Natchez to Mobile, from Memphis to St. Joe"—their stark rendition is buried under a not-quite-gospelly choral version, as visually we're whisked out of the jailhouse and into a short montage sequence to take the song out.

Litvak's direction is stodgy, but the film's numerous stock-footage–enriched montages, directed by Don Siegel before he started making his own crime and action films, inject jazzy energy. This sequence tracks the band's travel south via train, riverboat, and oversized map, as black workers pick cotton, tote bales, and unload watermelons. In post-montage New Orleans the players run into ne'er-do-well trumpeter Leo (reliably insincere Jack Carson), who over the band's protests convinces Jigger to get his horn out of hock. "Give him the four bucks. The guy's a musician, he needs his horn."

But can he play? They soon get their answer, over a communal rice bowl purchased with their last buck at a white-folks' cafe with no cover charge, where Jimmie Lunceford's great African American swing band is blasting away. (Future Armstrong All-Star Trummy Young solos on trombone.) Our friends are all suitably knocked out, except Leo: "I could step into the middle of that, pick up the beat and blow them all right out of the joint." On a dare, he stands up at their table in back, and takes an impromptu solo just as Trummy is rising to take another of his own; Lunceford, conducting, overlooks this breach of sitting-in protocol and signals the trombonist to cool it, curious if this nervy guy can pull it off. White appropriation of black music: Leo uses the Lunceford orchestra as his audition band. Leo doesn't lift the bandstand as promised, but he does sound good, dubbed by Lunceford ace Snooky Young; Jimmie even cues in the horns to answer one of Leo's shapelier licks. When he's done Leo gives them a cursory wave of thanks; gracious as Lunceford has been to the intruder, he seems to enjoy watching him get threatened with a punch in the nose a minute later.

Jigger's band hits the road in another montage; eight months pass. Leo's wife, known only as Character (ex–Fred Waring bandsinger Priscilla Lane), has also joined up and does the cooking, and under that montage we hear them working up their version of what Jigger calls "our blues"—the one they lifted from those now conveniently forgotten St. Louis jailbirds. Sometimes they ride the freights, setting up shop in a boxcar that serves as rehearsal hall, dorm, and kitchen. When passing hobo Del Davis holds them up somewhere near Pittsburgh, they fork over their $5.60 nest egg without resisting and don't rat him out to the world's friendliest railroad goon, who digs the band. "You probably need it more than we do." From each according to his ability, to each according to his needs.

Blues in the Night was based on an Edwin Gilbert stageplay that Elia Kazan optioned but couldn't get filmed; the role of Nickie was his consolation prize.[2] (Gilbert also wrote that year's anti-Nazi Bogart comedy *All Through the Night* for Warner Bros.) The screenplay was by Robert Rossen, then an idealistic member of the American Communist Party, later a target of Congressional red-hunters as well as director of *All the King's Men* and *The Hustler*. Rossen's political sympathies are all over the script: the band succeeds because they all pull together, everything for the collective. Character: "Now for the first time we belong to something." *Blues in the Night* posits the jazz band as microcommunity: as a model for a larger society long before free improvisers started looking at their interactions in a comparable way. Even skirt-chasing unserious Leo straightens out on learning Character is pregnant; he opts for the greater good.

But all that class solidarity makes the tone-deafness to racial issues more vexing: the band never thinks twice about appropriating "Blues in the Night" because it's presumed to be folk material—the collective wisdom of the masses, available to all, for free. (As someone says to Jigger later, "Cowboys used to make up songs about themselves, about their work—*real* songs. The kind of songs you'd've like to've played.") From each according to their ability: It's not like the prisoners are aware Jigger lifted it. And just who would he assign copyright to? But the band never acknowledges where "our song" came from.

Del the thieving hobo gets them a gig at a New Jersey roadhouse run by some ex-cronies he's headed east to muscle in on. The place is appropriately named the Jungle, a cesspool of predatory capitalism. In an inspired touch, it's located directly across the Hudson River from what by 1941 had become jazz's capital, Manhattan. Our heroes are Moses on the threshold of the Promised Land, represented by a painted-scenery George Washington Bridge and illuminated uptown skyline. (A couple of real clubs occupied similar locations, the Riviera in Fort Lee and the Rustic Cabin in Englewood Cliffs, which burned down shortly before *Blues in the Night* opened.)

By the time it's all over, the Jungle's principals will have killed each other or themselves, in a frenzy of greed, pure selfish id, and pathetic self-loathing; the crooks are the band's dark doppelgängers, always at odds. Even so, Jigger somehow falls for gun moll Kay who sings a little (very little) herself; she's supposed to be a shrew and an irresistible seductress both, a plot-serving contortionist. Betty Field plays the shrew so well the seductress hasn't a chance. Jigger takes up with Kay because he's really in love with

Character—Leo's wife—as she is with him. (He's written "This Time the Dream's on Me" for her, a covert love letter—"Someday we'll be close together, wait and see.") But being true to the collective, they never discuss or even acknowledge how they feel. Only Kay picks up on it.

Character's doctor says she should give up performing in a month, till after her baby is born. (He's right to be concerned: she's not gaining an ounce.) But who could sub for her in the meantime? Nickie says he heard a girl up in Harlem, but she wasn't as good. Character's the only one who supports Jigger when he proposes swapping Kay in as a sub. The others are aghast; the greater good is obviously not one of Kay's priorities. Plus, they've heard her sing. (Trudy Erwin ghosts her, in brassy character.) In another Don Siegel montage, Jigger rehearses Kay on "This Time the Dream's on Me," a lovely Arlen tune with tricky leaping octaves and sixths for a singer to navigate before arriving at a trickier bridge. Kay's failure to nail it is credibly underplayed. Even after she gets the notes, the timing's missing—the feeling. Her timbre is a wailing cat scraping a blackboard.

Kay's shortcomings sour everything and drive a wedge between Jigger and his crew. He quits, moves out, and gets a job across the river in Manhattan, hired by a name band. "Monkey on a stick," Pete predicts (alluding to the opening scene he hadn't been around for), and the Promised Land indeed turns out to be hell with a bright marquee.

Jigger's musical nadir provides some comic relief: a brutal send-up of the smiling face of an entertainment industry that grinds gold into pyrite powder. At the midtown Pal'o'mine Ballroom, "discovery of the year" Jigger Pine joins radio's Guy Heiser and His Band, "starring the Musical Knights, the Five Heiser Highlights, the four turbulent trombones" and vocalist Baby Beth Barton. This is a bandleader who understands branding. Heiser's a stand-in for Kay Kyser (who made his own wholesome unjazzy movies), and is played by Will Obsorne, sweet-band leader who could poke fun at other outfits and himself. (When his band plays straight, you can hear they're pretty good, if a long way from Lunceford.)

They play Heiser's current hit, "Says You, Says I" (actually "Says Who, Says You, Says I"). Again Arlen and Mercer were called on to write in character—in this case as Tin Pan Alley hacks. It's expertly crass: "And way up high / The moon's an apple pie / The clouds are egg frappés." Baby Beth Barton (Mabel Todd) delivers this dross with help from a singing, dancing quartet who double on clarinets and piccolos; she's a grown woman carrying on like a little girl playing dress-up as a bride. She sings a little in baby talk, and there's a bit where she tries and fails to replicate a spiraling piccolo line in a perverse echo of the Jigger/Kay rehearsal montage. Baby Beth perches herself on the closed piano lid, on which one of the Highlights does a tap dance as the piano rocks in place and Jigger keeps playing, looking more alienated by the second. His old band buddies have come out to see him, and stand watching nearby. They are too horrified to try to hide it. Jigger quits Heiser the same night, a shame in a way—you'd love to know what Beth Barton would have to say backstage, out of character. Jigger's public humiliation has nothing on hers.

Jigger nosedives, for months, and the band loses track of him. The guys finally find him in a Times Square musician's bar where he's begging for a drink. They regale him with tales of smiting the competition at Harlem jam sessions. Jigger claims he's been composing: "working on our blues—trying to build it up and make something big out of it." But when he sits at the piano to show them, the notes won't come, and he collapses, with a keyboard bang.

Don Siegel's final montage is his big solo, as Jigger hallucinates his way through his "neuropsychiatric disorder." The whole movie flashes before his eyes in fractured form: Jigger as organ-grinder Heiser's monkey; black prisoner laughing about the miseries; the whole USA in one chorus, five fingers, thick and quick. He hallucinates an orchestra where Kay fills every chair. He slams piano keys that turn to taffy under his fingers.

Then his three-month ordeal is abruptly over, and he's back with the band at the Jungle. He plays a gussied-up solo rhapsody on "Blues in the Night" to rapt young people, exploiting the Beethoveneseque potential in Arlen's insistently repeated phrases (and losing his place at the finish). Character: "That's everything we've been talking about!" But it isn't—has nothing to do with the band, or a beat. He's just in it for himself now. Jigger's been out of bed four days, during which time he hasn't asked after Leo and Character's kid (who had died). The breezier version of "Blues in the Night" the band plays next is better, but Jigger turns the piano over to Character. He's got Kay-related business to wrap up.

In the end the band hits the road again. The unit is slightly modernized, Nickie now on alto saxophone. We last see them playing "Blues in the Night" in the doorway of a

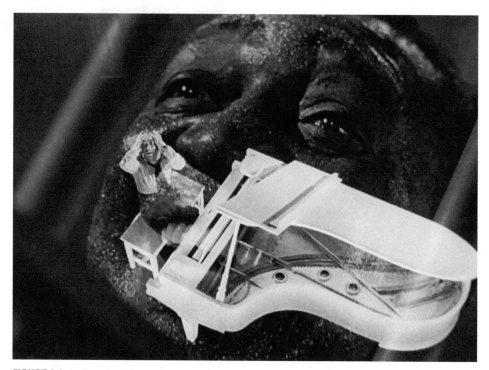

FIGURE 3.1 A disturbed Jigger (Richard Whorf, with Ernest Whitman) is haunted by the memory of black prisoners he lifted a song from, in *Blues in the Night*'s final montage.

retreating boxcar, for that friendly brakeman they used to run into—playing for the working man. But Jigger on guitar looks dazed, narcotized, smiling but not quite all there. It's gonna take a lot of barnstorming to bring him all the way back. And maybe in some town they'll play for African Americans who'll think that song they're so proud of sounds awfully familiar.

Blues in the Night came out three weeks before the attack on Pearl Harbor, but its "unit" is a war-movie squad already: Jigger the natural leader everyone looks up to, Peppi the emotional Italian-American, the apparently Armenian Nickie (the end credits give the surname Haroyan), Pete who looks like a hayseed, and selfish Leo who steps up when his crew really needs him. There's even a casualty who's too young to die: character's stillborn son.

> ***Orchestra Wives*** **(1942; 98 minutes; director: Archie Mayo; screenplay: Karl Tunberg, Darrell Ware; story: James Prindle). Cast includes: Ann Rutherford (Connie Ward), George Montgomery (Bill Abbot), Glenn Miller (Gene Morrison), Lynn Bari (Jaynie Stevens), Carole Landis (Natalie Mercer), Virginia Gilmore (Elsie), Mary Beth Hughes (Caroline Steele), Cesar Romero (Sinjin Smith), Jackie Gleason (Ben Beck), Tamara Geva (Mrs. Beck), Tex Beneke (Phil Mercer), Moe Purtill (Buddy Steele), Harry Morgan (Cully), Ray Eberle, Marion Hutton, the Modernaires, the Nicholas Brothers (themselves). New songs: "People Like You and Me," "At Last," "Serenade in Blue," "(I've Got a Gal in) Kalamazoo" (words Mack Gordon/music Harry Warren).**
> **—A small-town woman elopes with a trumpeter in a touring big band and is thrown in with the duplicitous wives who travel along. Interpersonal frictions drive the newlyweds and the musicians apart until a New York engagement brings them all back together.**

US troops were already in Europe and the Pacific when Archie Mayo's *Orchestra Wives* began filming in March 1942, and Hollywood was already doing its bit. (Mayo's many films after *Is Everybody Happy?* include 1936's *The Petrified Forest*, which had made Humphrey Bogart a star.) *Orchestra Wives* is a two-worlds romance and a cautionary tale about not seeing beneath surfaces—and incidentally a look at commercial big band practices in the later swing era. But it's also a wartime propaganda film. More than one musician has compared working in big bands to serving in the army: uniforms, precision drills, a hierarchy with strictly defined roles, and too little free expression. And the big band led by Gene Morrison faces wartime platoon problems: constant relocation, loose lips, sabotage, and failure to recognize the enemies within.

Morrison is played by top bandleader Glenn Miller (who's pretty good, with a cranky edge), and his musicians play themselves—or, in the case of tenorist Tex Beneke and drummer Moe Purtill, henpecked versions of themselves. The names are changed, but the Modernaires still call Beneke "Tex" in "I've Got a Gal in Kalamazoo," one of four new Harry Warren/Mack Gordon songs. The Hollywood ringers include George

Montgomery as sweet trumpet soloist Bill Abbot (ghosted by Miller's Johnny Best), in thrall to Harry James.

As we open, Morrison is in a New York studio recording "People Like You and Me," an innocuous ode to homespun pleasures, sung by Miller regulars Marion Hutton, Ray Eberle, and the four Modernaires. The lyric celebrates the little things anyone can enjoy—moonlight and birdies and corny songs like this. But after Bill's trumpet solo, tenor man Phil (Beneke) comes down front to sing a chorus with Hutton that takes a new tack: "Hey get a load of those guys / High in the skies / Wingin' to victory / Up and at 'em in the fight for / People like you and me"). The song makes the only direct references to the war in the film as released, save perhaps a frantic "Bugle Call Rag." But another Hutton song dropped in the editing spelled out the parallels between this unit and the military, "That's Sabotage" ("I can't sleep, I've got to keep my Eff Bee Eye on you / 'Cause if you've been untrue that's sabotage").

It's not their comrades the musicians need to be wary of, but the camp followers: a handful of wives who join them on the tedious tours they undertake for the regular folks who buy their records. (A few wives toured with swing musicians, if seldom in a gaggle as here. Miller-band wives did in fact socialize and were in Hollywood while the picture was being shot.)[3]

Orchestra Wives presents swing tunes as music for young people: vehicles for blowing off steam, and for vicarious thrills. One such fan will soon join the tour herself—Connie Ward (Ann Rutherford), wide-eyed small-town Illinois gal who's fallen in love with Abbot from listening to his dreamy solos on a soda-fountain jukebox. (This is independent thinking on Connie's part; Abbot doesn't inspire mass adulation, and Morrison doesn't promote him like a star.) Harry Morgan plays a squeaky-voiced soda jerk who's kind of a jerk, who takes Connie to an outdoor dance where Abbot spots her and puts the moves on in four seconds flat.

It's a fact of jazz life that some (married or unmarried) musicians misbehave on the road, hitting on women whenever they can. Abbot and running buddy St. John 'Sinjin' Smith (Caesar Romero, an indifferent mime at the piano, ghosted by Chummy MacGregor) are their early representatives on screen, cheerful predators. Ah, but this time it's different. After spending less than 15 minutes with Connie over two evenings, as she's about to slip away, Bill impetuously proposes. They cab to Indiana and marry. Suddenly Connie's thrown in with the other traveling wives, most with nothing better to do than gossip, backstab, and make (discreet, off-screen) passes at each other's husbands. They're the women-on-a-ship of military taboo. No good can come of their presence.

The only sympathetic frau is married to bass player Ben Beck (young Jackie Gleason, trying to inject a little humor). She has a backstory we never get to hear. The Becks are devoted to each other, though she's a little old for him and has an unidentified East European accent. (She's played by George Balanchine's ex-wife, Russian dancer Tamara Geva, nine years older than Gleason.) We never get her first name—she's always Mrs. Beck, or Becksie, or Mom—and she's a little too domestic, tugging around a vacuum

FIGURE 3.2 Trumpeter Bill Abbott (George Montgomery) mesmerizes Connie Ward (Ann Rutherford) in *Orchestra Wives*, perturbing her date (Harry Morgan).

cleaner. The alpha wives condescend to her but she's unfazed, as if she's seen far worse in her time. (Geva seems equally uninterested in playing to the camera, refusing to compete on any level.) We gather she's a war refugee; it may be telling that one catty wife who hasn't yet met Connie inquires if she's Japanese.

The younger wives are comically vacuous, spouting malapropisms—soliciful, slavoir faire, inn-genue. The characterizations are shamelessly sexist (though Carole Landis, Virginia Gilmore, and Mary Beth Hughes gamely give them life), but there is a subtle point to it. These women need something constructive to occupy their time.

Their compatriot in malice is the only single woman aboard, ballad singer Jaynie Stevens (Lynn Bari with her marionette eyebrows, ghosted by Pat Friday), fresh off a yearlong affair with Bill and scheming to get him back. She acts like Connie's new best friend. In a wicked twist, she lends the new bride a negligée Bill might recognize. We see how Connie can't penetrate surfaces; her reaction to Jaynie's frosty initial greeting is, "Isn't she lovely?" At that point she still perceives Jaynie as she'd seen her on the bandstand, warm and engaged, singing "At Last" with Eberle. (But even then eagle-eyed Jaynie had spotted Connie in the crowd, mooning at Bill.) The contrast between Jaynie's inner and outer nature confirms that jazz performing isn't always about expressing the way you feel. Sometimes it's more like acting.

Marion Hutton is also on the tour, and for story purposes is married to fellow vocalist Eberle. But she stays well clear of the other wives. The only evidence we have she's along at all (after "That's Sabotage" got cut) are two quick sightings in a travel montage.

Orchestra Wives is breezily cynical about the morals of jazz musicians and company, though (owing to the Hollywood production code) all their transgressions take place off screen—raising the possibility some alleged hanky-panky is just rumor or idle boasting. No one ever admits to anything. On the road the men and women barely intermingle; we never learn which musician wife Elsie is married to.

Morrison's musicians are busy playing every night. They were promised a (grueling) month-long tour before they left New York, but due to new bookings or a continuity glitch, five weeks after Bill's marriage mid-tour they're in Iowa, working their way back east. The frequent band numbers work like the cetological chapters in *Moby Dick*, interrupting the narrative to suggest the slow passage of time on a long trip. There's an early instance of one of jazz moviedom's pet licks, segueing from one performance of a tune to another: a seamless transition from Connie listening to the rave-up "Boom Shot" at the soda shoppe to a high boom shot of the band playing it on stage the same night, before a jitterbugging crowd. (*Blues in the Night* had a similar segue, from a rehearsal to a performance.)

We see and hear Morrison's stagecraft: a section of four muted trombones huddle together, the tips of their slides almost touching, playing pianissimo to introduce the future Etta James hit "At Last"—the lovely timbral effect and attention to dynamics both worthy of Ellington. The brass players fan their bells with derby mutes, then wear them like helmets—Guy Heiser hokum with a military twist. Bill is so proud of the way he twirls his trumpet away from his mouth at the end of a solo, he even does it in the studio.

As in other movies, during musical numbers the players' positions on stage are discreetly rearranged to meet the demands of the moment or the composition of a shot. (Phil moves from one end of the sax section to the other, between close-ups and long shots.) At a dance where we hear ballads, drums are in the back. The next night, when the band plays a frantic "Bugle Call Rag," drums are down front and Morrison messes with Buddy using his slide. (Buddy keels over in mock-exhaustion at the end, like he's Gene Krupa.)

The songs resonate with the plot, just as songwriters' corny musings describe the emotions of countless listeners, and sometimes the singers too. The night after meeting Bill, Connie takes a bus to the next town where the band's appearing. When she gets off in front of the hall, inside the horns are quoting "The Girl I Left Behind Me"—wartime tune of the previous century—during "American Patrol." Jaynie performs "Serenade in Blue" while scheming to seduce Bill, who's seen in close-up as she sings, "Tell me darling is there still a spark?" (The Modernaires appear from nowhere to harmonize the close.) "I've Got a Gal in Kalamazoo," about a romance between a band musician and a Midwestern civilian, is so on-the-nose you'd think it was about the Abbots, but it's on a list of the band's new tunes in the opening scene.

Connie falls in with the witchy wives for lack of other company—even she finds Becksie dull—but finally their malevolence is too much for her. One of them blabs about

Jaynie's history with Bill, just before Jaynie maneuvers the big dummy into a compromising situation to give Connie the wrong idea. These women are a fifth column, eroding the whole rolling battalion from within. (Glenn Miller would never have permitted what Gene Morrison does.)

Connie snaps: she spills all the gossip to turn the selfish wives against each other, with unintended ship-sinking consequences. Phil and Buddy quit to save their marriages, and also because how can you play with a guy who might be two-timing you? Morrison tells Bill to keep his wife in line so he quits as well. Unable to replace them on the road—good musicians were scarce in wartime—Morrison breaks up the band. "The best trumpet man in the business, and the best drummer too," Morrison laments. "And where am I going to get a saxophone player that can sing like Phil?" Sinjin pays Phil/Beneke a similarly backhanded compliment. In *Second Chorus*, trumpeters Danny and Hank compete for the same woman, let it wreak havoc with the music, and couldn't care less. They wouldn't have lasted three days with these crybabies. Connie goes back to her hometown to find gossips there too, among the people like you and me.

A symmetrical resolution must have occurred to someone involved in the production: Divisions among the wives broke up the band, so they must put differences aside to bring the men back together. They might even form the band's new tour support staff, part of the greater campaign like *Second Chorus*'s ultra-competent Ellen Miller. Alas, that was a feminist step too far for *Orchestra Wives*. It's left to Connie alone, with a little help from Sinjin, to trick the scattered musicians into regrouping—everyone but Jaynie. The players, all apparently unemployed, are summoned to a New York hotel, each thinking he's been hired by a different name band. There they find the warring wives have okayed a reunion, bought off with diamonds and a mink coat charged to Morrison's account. The reunited band goes into the Glen Island Casino—swing-central dance hall in New Rochelle where Glenn Miller had broken through in 1939—for a big "Kalamazoo" finale.

Actually it's a double finale, because after the Miller/Morrison band has its way with the song, the African American Nicholas Brothers come out to sing it again during a typically acrobatic dance routine. Their duet blows away everything we've heard (or seen) so far, in terms of rhythmic snap, dynamism, and sheer charisma. Fayard and Harold Nicholas sing in call and response, slide as on ice, do tap routines in unison, somersault off pillars, bound up steps, and bounce off mini-trampolines. It's an Endie versus Miralee reality check, and one of those sequences easily excised for white southern audiences who'd get no pleasure from watching gravity-defying black hoofers best the band. Their appearance, just before the film ends, in effect pulls back to a wider perspective, takes us out of Morrison's little world and into a larger musical universe where more interesting things are afoot.

Orchestra Wives came out in September 1942—the month Glenn Miller broke up his band for real, voluntarily, on accepting a commission with the US Army Air Force. When his plane disappeared over the English Channel in 1944, he became jazz and pop's most conspicuous war casualty.

Orchestra Wives' footnote and evil twin is H. Bruce Humberstone's **Sun Valley Serenade** released 13 months earlier, a vehicle for Norwegian figure-skating champ and tireless twirler Sonja Henie as a grinning, unstoppable sociopath: a stalker film told as a fizzy romance. Henie plays a scheming war refugee who takes one look at her luck-of-the-draw sponsor (John Payne as Glenn Miller's pianist) and resolves to bulldoze his fiancée and all other obstacles aside to get him. She follows him from New York to Idaho, where she courts him via a long ski chase for stunt doubles. The aggressively cheerful Henie is downright creepy in close-up—it doesn't help to know she'd been friends with Hitler—but aside from that frisson the film is a dud, although Hitler was rumored to love it. It's an icy warmup for *Orchestra Wives*, which would put many of the same elements to better use: the Miller band as its meta-self, surpassed on stage by the singing/dancing Nicholas Brothers (assisted here by Dorothy Dandridge); Lynn Bari ghosted by Pat Friday (and Lorraine Elliott) as the band's jilted singer; a comic ringer (Milton Berle, tiresome); and some Harry Warren/Mack Gordon songs—including "At Last," heard only as skating music. Bari's duo version was cut, to be restaged the following year in *Orchestra Wives, Sun Valley Serenade*'s instant better retread.

Even before *Orchestra Wives* opened, another bandleader was called up to (fictional) active duty. In Tay Garnett's **My Favorite Spy** (1942), Kay Kyser gets drafted into the army as a lieutenant, but quickly demonstrates his military incompetence and is just as quickly discharged. But then the feds enlist him in a plot to draw out Nazi spies. The Germans plant an arranger in Kyser's radio band—they killed the old one—who encodes dots-and-dashes secret messages into scored passages heard over the air (a scheme reprised from the 1939 British spy farce *Let George Do It*). We only hear one example, for a fluttering trumpet trio. A Morse-codey piano modulation alerts the viewer (and the Nazis) when it's coming.

> ***Sweet and Low-Down*** **(1944; 76 minutes; director: Archie Mayo; screenplay: Richard English; story: English, Edward Haldeman). Cast includes: James Cardwell (Johnny Birch), Benny Goodman (himself), Lynn Bari (Pat Stirling), Linda Darnell (Trudy Wilson), Jack Oakie (Popsy), Dickie Moore (Gen. Carmichael), Allyn Joslyn (Lester Barnes). New songs: "I'm Making Believe," "Ten Days with Baby," "Chug Chug Choo-Choo Chug," "Hey Bub! Let's Have a Ball" (words Mack Gordon/music James Monaco).**
> **—Benny Goodman takes on a protégé, trombonist Johnny Birch from his old Chicago neighborhood. But then Johnny is goaded into taking over Benny's band.**

As epochs go, the Swing Era was brief. It began in 1935 when Benny Goodman's big band caught on, and was pretty much over by 1946. World War II was tough on the bands. With US involvement on the horizon, in October 1940 the Selective Service began drafting men, musicians included. That November, Goodman formed a new outfit that lasted 20 months. He went through over 60 musicians, including 23 saxophonists and 10 drummers, not counting guest appearances by Gene Krupa—one of several Goodman stars who'd left to form his own band, like trumpeters Harry James and Bunny Berigan.

Lesser-known sidemen had always been drifters; Goodman's bassist in 1944's *Sweet and Low-Down*, Sid Weiss, had urged the clarinetist's rival to play higher and higher in the 1939 short *Artie Shaw's Class in Swing*; in between, Weiss had worked for Tommy Dorsey. The draft increased that turnover, and younger, less experienced players passed through name orchestras, and salaries increased. Goodman had always been a tough boss, but now he might sack new hires the week they arrived, and he began taking more solos as seasoned men dropped out. Thanks to a 1942 strike called by the American Federation of Musicians, no bands made commercial recordings for a couple of years. (That strike sent a bunch of bandleaders and musicians to Hollywood, seeking movie appearances.) It was not a good time to work for Goodman—except on film.[4]

Sweet and Low-Down grew out of a proposed Goodman biopic. Fox had purchased his life rights but the movie is barely biographical, although Goodman had input into the story, which reflects wartime realities in the big band business. In Archie Mayo's *Orchestra Wives*, a band's wartime problem is sabotage. In his *Sweet and Low-Down* it's mutiny. (In the interim, Mayo directed *Crash Dive*, one of those progressive Hollywood war films featuring a racially integrated squad at a time when real combat units remained segregated. Meanwhile jazz bands on screen mostly remained all-white, in a period when a few leaders including Goodman hired black soloists.)

As a poor kid from Chicago's tough Near West Side, Benny Goodman got early musical training at Hull House on South Halsted Street, a so-called settlement house—one of those neighborhood institutions that helped urban immigrants assimilate into mainstream America. As the story begins, locally revered Benny (playing himself) is doing his annual concert for the old neighborhood at the fictional Dearborn Settlement House. One kid tells him he's got a trombonist brother he should hear, and Benny realistically blows him off—so the boy grabs the star's clarinet case and leads Benny on a slow chase to his apartment, where brother Johnny is blowing his horn, crafting a melody. Johnny Birch sounds good—he's ghosted by Goodman trombonist and future Woody Herman star Bill Harris—and Benny decides to hire him on the spot. He's been looking for a way to do something more for the folks back home, and Johnny had trained at the settlement house, and supports his family. Plus, Benny has been thinking of adding a third trombone to the band. (And trombone makes a good faking horn for actors.)

So Johnny Birch hits the road with a big band during wartime in a train car less fancy than Gene Morrison's in *Orchestra Wives*. Players may be drafted at any time, and sidemen come and go. Sometimes that's because singer Pat Stirling (*Orchestra Wives* villain Lynn Bari, ghosted by Lorraine Elliot) has a habit of dating fellow musicians. To Benny's dismay, she quickly sets her sights on Johnny.

Benny checks out Johnny's reading skills, and assigns him a couple of solos on his first night with the band—16 bars on "Jersey Bounce," 8 on a vocal-jive tune—at a military school dance where the officers debate the merits of Art Tatum and Basie (pronounced like "Maisie") in hipster slang. The general in charge is an imperious teenager with a riding crop who tries to order around his date—his aunt Trudy Wilson, who's five years older and a friend of Benny's. Her father is a classical-music bigwig in New York, and Benny loves playing chamber music. Trudy is enough of a fan to spot Goodman's new trombonist right off. Benny more or less throws her at Johnny, hoping to save him from Pat. "He's got a lot of rough talent but the wrong kind of confidence."

By and by Trudy and Johnny will fall in love, but he can't picture being with someone as rich as she is until he makes it big. (Trudy doesn't care—she volunteers at a settlement house herself. There's a hint here of Goodman's own society romance, discussed when we get to *The Benny Goodman Story*.) That trombone melody Johnny was tinkering with when Benny discovered him becomes the band's latest hit "I'm Making Believe"—never mind that the real-world recording ban was still in effect—and Johnny becomes Goodman's latest star sideman. The record's on track to sell a million copies, and Johnny makes the cover of *Down Beat*.

Benny works hard to build the kid up, but Johnny nurses grudges from when Benny told him to practice when he wanted to go drinking with the guys, or wouldn't let him sit in at what was billed as a jam session but was really a performance by Benny's quartet (with the only real Goodman musicians on hand, bassist Weiss, pianist Jess Stacy, and drummer Morey Feld; the rest are portrayed by actors). "He's done nothing for me," Johnny tells his mom, "except try to keep me back since I clicked on 'I'm Making Believe.'" Johnny Birch isn't the only one put off by Goodman's manner; so is Pat Stirling's officious agent Lester, and he and Pat start urging Johnny to go out on his own, just months into his professional career.

Jealous of Trudy, Pat helps the cause by making some mischief of her own. When Johnny's working-class family shows up in New York on a surprise visit, she sends them over to the Wilson mansion, where Johnny's gone to hear Benny play Mozart with a string quartet. When they arrive, some snob makes a smart remark. Johnny loses his temper and tells Benny off when he tries to intervene, shocking Trudy.

Apparently other sidemen have been nursing grievances. When Johnny quits to go out on his own, agent Lester—with a secure ballroom booking in his pocket—convinces the rest of the band, and Benny's vocal quartet The Pied Pipers, to jump with him. (This coup is only remotely plausible if the Goodman band is on hiatus, but that's never established.) Johnny says he's got his own ideas. But aside from singing a bit himself and getting Weiss to double on tuba, his ideas mostly consist of copying Goodman; they're even doing his new novelty "Hey Bub! Let's Have a Ball." Birch is a good-looking kid coasting on his looks (that must be what Trudy sees in this jerk); you couldn't say that about plain, bespectacled Benny.

Opening night, the Tivoli Ballroom is packed, and they sound all right. But by week three there are five lonely couples on the dance floor. You can see the players' flop-sweat and the leader isn't rallying the troops. Now we see the point of that military-school sequence: Johnny's no more ready to lead than a teenage general. The Tivoli's owner gives them their notice: Next week I'll put a name band in here. Hearing that, Johnny can't even pretend to be an independent force: "If Goodman's band isn't the best in the business . . ." "You mean with Goodman it is," the owner interrupts.

Johnny's men have seen it coming, and have already decided to go back to Benny, hats in hand—including Pat who helped instigate the mutiny. "There's been something missing ever since the night we opened," one player says. "We're just not in there. Without Benny we're just a bunch of musicians, period." (In fact, they still sound fine— it's still Goodman's band on the soundtrack.) Let this be a warning to sidemen who are contemplating going out on their own: Stick with a winner—at least till you're ready. And Benny takes them all back! But he does so off-screen; we never see his reaction to the mass defection.

Too proud to beg, Johnny goes back to Chicago and his old factory job, working the swing shift. Benny returns to the road, still featuring "I'm Making Believe." (Oddly, Johnny isn't living on the publishing royalties; he must be listed as co-composer at least.) Given the wartime talent shortage, Benny's reduced to using loyal gofer and assistant road manager Popsy (Jack Oakie) on third trombone, clearly a temporary measure. Eager, long-frustrated Popsy plays too loud and not very well. When he messes up, Benny looks away with a frown—instead of subjecting the offender to the withering Goodman stare musicians dubbed "the ray."

A year after our story began, Benny is back in Chicago to play the settlement house again, and Popsy brings a reluctant Johnny down to the hall. (Actually, Popsy has to throw him down a flight of stairs and carry him there, unconscious.) Backstage Johnny reunites with Trudy, still pining for some reason. Now even scheming Pat pushes them together. In the end, all's well. As the band answers a request for "I'm Making Believe," Johnny saunters out on stage, playing his solo part—his pride showing again—and Benny welcomes him back. They play together at center stage for the close, reconciled and exchanging warm glances.

Something similar to Johnny's experience had actually happened to Count Basie in Kansas City in the mid-1930s. The members of Bennie Moten's band had deposed its leader and appointed Basie in his stead. But he wasn't ready to lead, and when bookings fell off, one by one the players crawled back to Moten, who'd started a new band. Moten, who had a warmer reputation than Goodman, would eventually welcome Basie back too.[5] The clarinetist's musicians may have roared laughing at the nurturing, generous Benny of *Sweet and Low-Down*. Those laughs would have been bittersweet. Before the film finished shooting in March 1944, Goodman had broken up his orchestra. When he regrouped the following year, he started using three trombones for real.

The Fabulous Dorseys (1947, 88 minutes; director: Alfred E. Green; writers: Richard English, Art Arthur, Curtis Kenyon). Cast includes: Jimmy Dorsey, Tommy Dorsey, Paul Whiteman, Bob Eberly, Helen O'Connell, Art Tatum, Charlie Barnet, Ziggy Elman, Ray Bauduc (themselves), Janet Blair (Jane

FIGURE 3.3 Trombonist Johnny (James Cardwell) and clarinetist Benny Goodman reconcile to end *Sweet and Low-Down*.

Howard), William Lundigan (Bob Burton), Arthur Shields (Pop Dorsey), Sara Allgood (Ma Dorsey), Buz Buckley (Jimmy as a child), Bobby Warde (Tommy as a child). New song: "To Me" (words Don George/music Allie Wrubel).
—Squabbling brothers Jimmy and Tommy Dorsey come out of Pennsylvania coal country and co-lead a successful band. They quarrel, split up, and go on to independent fame. Might a big New York concert reunite them?

The 1950s would see a rash of swing-era biopics, but first came *The Fabulous Dorseys*, low-budget and full of malarkey, about battling brother bandleaders Jimmy and Tommy. Directed by Alfred E. Green, coming off the more lavish *Jolson Story*, it was released in February 1947, two months ahead of *New Orleans*. (Green, like Archie Mayo, Henry King, William Dieterle, and so many other prolific generalists, had been directing since the silents.) Cowriter Richard English had worked on *Sweet and Low-Down*.

The Fabulous Dorseys gets almost everything wrong except the Dorseys' hardscrabble coal-country upbringing and toxic mutual antagonism. With Jimmy and Tommy playing themselves, it's a wonder it got made at all. (An earlier attempt fell through at the talking stage.)[6] It is also Paul Whiteman's last feature; the age when his imprimatur carried weight was ending.

Discussing *Rhapsody in Blue* in chapter 2, we mentioned white jazz musicians with only tenuous connections to black culture who still learned to play improvised syncopated music from records, or fellow whites, or on their own. The Dorseys were early in that wave. Born in 1904 and 1905, a half-decade after Gershwin, they grew up in Shenandoah, Pennsylvania, between Scranton and Harrisburg. Tommy's biographer Peter Levinson, generally dismissive of the film, praises its depiction of their early years, and his own description of their childhood echoes the biopic in various particulars.[7]

The boys' music-teacher father is played by Arthur Shields (brother of Barry Fitzgerald) with a brogue so think you'd think he'd just stepped off the boat, though Pop Dorsey was born in Pennsylvania. As depicted, Pop was a coal miner subject to frequent layoffs, who taught music at home and saw it as his kids' ticket out of the mines. He made elder Jimmy practice saxophone and Tommy the trombone for hours a day, when they'd rather be playing ball. They made their first professional appearances as teens in their father's ensembles, one of which played at Gorman's Hall in nearby Lansford.

Everything else is fictive embellishment. Proprietor Gorman has never even heard of the saxophone. "Something new for dance bands," Pop explains. "Like the callin' of angels." The band gets a welcome lift when Tommy, bored by the over and over strains they've been playing (like Irving Berlin's "Everybody's Doin' It Now"), starts swinging off book on a waltz, and with a tilt of the head calls Jimmy in to join him. (The real Tommy had an enviably gorgeous trombone tone, but disparaged his own improvising skills.) The band eagerly joins in. Pop's about to clamp down, till he sees everyone's charmed, even grumpy Gorman. The Dorseys' jazz doesn't come from absorbing late-period ragtime; it springs from within.

"They do well side by side, they really balance," Ma marvels. Pop agrees: "If they just stick together they can lick the world." Ah, but the boys are not always so cooperative: Irish, you see, and therefore combative by nature. As kids, they get into fistfights for just about no reason, but that doesn't mean they don't love each other. Their real-life sister has been replaced by neighbor girl Jane Howard, who helps referee. She's so much like a sister they don't even hit on her when she grows up to be played by pretty, pouty Janet Blair (an ex-bandsinger from Altoona). Jane sings with and does laundry for their barnstorming sextet the Wild Canaries. (Women bandsingers often got stuck with such domestic chores.)[8]

Now Jimmy and Tommy Dorsey start playing their squabbling selves, and 15 seconds after they first share a frame, they're ready to throw punches. Work is scarce, and their Model A Ford often breaks down. When their pianist defects in some little town, they get a line on a tickler who plays for silent movies down the street. (That's how we know it's the 1920s.) Using Jane as bait they lure him into the band, the wholly fictitious Bob Burton. Jane's skeptical of his talents until she hears his tune "To Me" (a new one, whose title plays on Tommy's 1937 hit "To You"). They start making love eyes at each other. Everything happens fast.

The brothers get a job playing on newfangled radio, but their dixieland is too much for the microphones and chaos ensues. Jimmy: "Who told you you could take a solo?"

Tommy: "I felt like it!" The brothers are ready to fight, but when a fracas with station staff breaks out, they stick together. The Wild Canaries break up, and the Dorseys go to work for Whiteman, prominently billed as the King of Jazz and looking far too old to pass for his 1920s self. In his orchestra they play Walter Donaldson's "At Sundown," sharing pocket solos with Whiteman trumpeter Henry Busse and banjo wiz Mike Pingitore. But that's just till the brothers land the Sands Point gig that gets the Dorsey band back on its feet. They actually secured their engagement at that Long Island club (from which they broadcast on NBC) in 1934, 13 years after their radio debut and seven after joining Whiteman. But in biopics, years vanish just as collaborators do.

While they're off with Whiteman, Jane, Bob, and two other ex-Canaries work in a Nat Cole-esque saloon combo, featuring "To Me." The lyric refers to an unfinished symphony, and it turns out Bob has been writing a concerto.

Jane says, "I didn't know you were interested in . . ."

Bob: "Serious music? Janie, don't you know that every comedian has a hankering to play Hamlet?"

Still, he's had a mild case of composer's block. Bob has been stuck searching for a phrase for days, till Jane plays just what he's been looking for, absent-mindedly tapping glassware with a table knife. He goes straight to the piano and extrapolates a four-chord sequence that unblocks his process. It's less a Cage-ian lesson in the music of everyday life than a B knockoff of the "S'Wonderful" and Parisian car-horn bits in the film *Rhapsody in Blue*. Bob sketches out one theme at the piano for Jane. "I wrote this part for trombone and sax. It's modern and thoroughly American."

"You do beautiful things with music, Bob. And there's no reason you shouldn't continue to do them on a higher plane." For these two, jazz is not serious enough.

But now that the Dorsey brothers' band is getting back together, Bob and Jane can't be happy as long as she's dousing brushfires. The lovebirds even chaperone, just in case, when the boys head out to jam with piano god Art Tatum. (Bob proposes to her during a skittering Tatum ballad—he might be talking over one of the all-time jazz greats, but isn't wasting the mood Art sets.) The Dorseys sit in on a slow blues, along with fellow bandleader Charlie Barnet on tenor, Tommy sideman Ziggy Elman on trumpet, and drummer Ray Bauduc. This jam is often cited as the highlight of the picture. Less noted is that Tatum, a famously busy and scene-stealing accompanist, becomes quite remarkably inaudible when Bauduc kicks up the tempo and the Dorseys solo. Tatum wasn't going to steal this movie the way the Nicholas Brothers stole *Orchestra Wives*.

For all the hokum, the bickering seems authentic. To their credit the Dorseys don't seem self-conscious playing their ageless Dorian Grey selves. Their actual dynamic comes through: Tommy the controlling martinet, the younger brother who acts older; Jimmy the needler who cuts little brother down to size. TD leads the rehearsals, JD disputes fine points of interpretation. As in life, they argue about proper tempos. The film re-creates their actual break over the jaunty "I'll Never 'Say Never' Again"—the title a little too on-the-nose, given the plot. They quarrel when Tommy counts it off too fast at the (Glen) Island Casino—the Dorsey Brothers Orchestra ends the same place *Orchestra Wives* does—before the trombonist storms off stage. (Embellishment: Ma and Pop are in the house.) Jimmy: "If you walk out now, it's for good." "Okay, for good!"

From there the narrative rushes along two tracks, following the rise of the siblings' individual bands. Jane goes with Tommy's new orchestra, Bob sticks with Jimmy, and Bob's concerto gets filed away along with his wedding plans. A hits-and-headlines montage cross-cuts between brothers, filling us in on parallel triumphs. Box office smash! Pollwinner! Tied for #1! (In the great montage tradition, no publication bears a date.)

A record sleeve hails Tommy as a "starmaker" but *The Fabulous Dorseys* doesn't name names. Every biopic streamlines gnarly life stories, but not always so aggressively. This one writes out Glenn Miller, who helped shape the brothers' sound before the split; Tommy's breakout sidemen Frank Sinatra and Buddy Rich; and the brothers' wives. (By the time the film was made Tommy had alienated Sinatra and Rich and had moved on to wife number two.) Jimmy's former singers Helen O'Connell (who's absorbed her Billie Holiday) and Bob Eberly (a little more of a song stylist than younger brother Ray Eberle) reprise their 1941 hit "Green Eyes."

Tommy's band does their famous syncopated sing-along version of "Marie," but there's no hint of where the arrangement comes from, bought cheap off the black Sunset Royal Orchestra the brothers had encountered at a battle of the bands. (Now there's a movie scene: when Dorsey's men later went back to the Royals to buy their similar arrangement of "Who?" they were run off, but copied it anyway.)[9]

In reality the brothers patched up their feud enough to be in the same room from time to time; in the movie even that's impossible. Ma and Pop are heartbroken, but Jane devises a plan to reunite them, with help from Paul Whiteman. She quietly filches a copy of Bob's *American Concerto* for jazz band and strings, and Whiteman invites each Dorsey to be the principal soloist at its premier. Neither knows it's a double concerto until the rehearsal. Each stomps out on seeing the other, but then word arrives that Pop is on his deathbed. They hurry together to his side, then agree to perform the concerto in posthumous tribute.

As in *New Orleans* the big concert that marries jazz and classical also reunites the lovebirds. In the audience, Bob finds himself seated next to Jane, and it slowly—rather too slowly—dawns on him that the music he's listening to is his own. And that this is his big break. Paul Whiteman's star was fading, but on screen he was a starmaker to the end. The *American Concerto* is a proxy for *The Fabulous Dorseys* itself: the brothers put aside their differences to make a not-so-grand statement.

The concerto, by Hollywood orchestrator Leo Shuken: sentimental blues, swelling strings, a clarinet and pizzicato holiday, and finally the brothers side by side, trading phrases with each other and orchestra. Jimmy's on clarinet, not saxophone as Bob Burton had envisioned it; the pair in a tight shot echo the reunited trombone/clarinet duo capping *Sweet and Low-Down*, except these guys look less delighted. Maybe that's because the concerto is a trifle, too perfunctory musically or dramatically to sustain the finish of even this modest picture—a failed soufflé beside *New Orleans*'s grotesque layer cake.

FIGURE 3.4 Trombonist Tommy and clarinetist Jimmy reconcile to end *The Fabulous Dorseys*.

Tommy Dorsey played himself again the following year in *A Song Is Born*, Howard Hawks's superfluous remake of his own screwball comedy *Ball of Fire*, itself a variation on Snow White and the Seven Dwarfs. But first we need to back up a little. In ***Ball of Fire*** (1942) those fairy-tale archetypes had been transformed into a nightclub singer and a brother-hood of sheltered encyclopedia scribes, whose Prof. Potts (Gary Cooper) is researching contemporary slang. Barbara Stanwyck plays Sugarpuss O'Shea, currently singing with Gene Krupa. Her moniker suggests she's a knockoff of current Krupa thrush Anita O'Day, who like O'Shea was a hip kitty who challenged you to take her on her own terms and who (in O'Day's words) "could play the hard-boiled dame."[10]

Worried that he's out of touch when he meets a slang-talking trash man and can barely suss a word, Potts goes out among the people to catch up on today's lingo. At a club, he hears Sugarpuss (ghosted by Martha Tilton) sing "Drum Boogie" with the Krupa band—trumpet star Roy Eldridge takes a short solo. (So that's one integrated jazz band on screen.) Then O'Shea reprises it as a quiet encore, with Krupa playing the striking surface of a matchbox, using matchsticks like wire brushes. Sugarpuss talks fluent jive, so Potts tries to enlist her help with his research. Needing to lay low for a few days—there's a criminal boyfriend—she hides out with the scholars and brightens their lives, Potts's above all. (Brightens and disrupts—as in *A Song Is Born* the professor invokes the super-stition that women aboard ship are bad luck.)

It gradually becomes clear O'Shea is not a Krupa regular but an entertainer at the club where he was performing. The cops are looking for her, but there's no indication anyone from the club is, let alone Gene or his men. Easy come easy go, where (women) singers are concerned. Would they all be so blasé if Roy Eldridge disappeared?

Krupa again plays himself in the flimsy backstage revue *George White's Scandals* (1945), where women entertainers suffer other indignities. When a bevy of beauties sign up to audition for producer White's girly show, Gene and his men eavesdrop to jot down select phone numbers; Krupa writes them on a drumhead. Meeting a couple of the chorines later, he rattles off their info from memory. In fairness, he also jams (on too-tall fake bongos) with all-but-forgotten Hammond organ wiz Ethel Smith, of radio's *Your Hit Parade*, a swinger who's all over the dual keyboards and bass-register pedal board—wearing heels.

Smith isn't the only woman keyboardist playing with a handicap. A star's housemaid—African American nightclub entertainer Rose Murphy—plays grooving piano in cleaning gloves, as she sings a quick lively "Wishing Will Make It So." Like Smith she's entertaining enough to be in the movie, but not young and beautiful enough for White's stage show. The only black performers in that production are three small boys in turbans, though in a stage montage we glimpse a blackface dance routine.

Gene Krupa was a dynamic showman, as his numbers here demonstrate—including a weird one where he plays small drums, bells, and cymbals affixed to dancers' dresses, ears, or garters, 11 years before Ellington's problematic title *A Drum Is a Woman*. From a high angle above the orchestra pit, we also see Krupa rehearse a "Leave Us Leap" where he conducts the band, away from the drums—jumping from huddled saxes over to solo trumpet, and from solo tenor to trombones, grooving, clapping, finger-popping, and dancing to the beat. As conductor he's no Fred Astaire, but it's good theater, and the band has a terrific late-swing-era snap akin to Woody Herman's First Herd, despite Krupa's unit having a few violins (and here, two pianos). But Gene's on-screen gyrations may have undercut the (true) assertion that his notorious 1943 marijuana bust was a frame-up. More on that when we get to *The Gene Krupa Story*.

> *A Song Is Born* (1948; 113 minutes; director: Howard Hawks; story: Billy Wilder, Thomas Monroe). Cast includes: Danny Kaye (Prof. Hobart Frisbee), Virginia Mayo (Honey Swanson), Benny Goodman (Prof. Magenbruch), Buck and Bubbles, Louis Armstrong, Tommy Dorsey, Lionel Hampton, Charlie Barnet, Mel Powell, Louie Bellson, the Golden Gate Quartette (themselves), J. Edward Bromberg (Prof. Elfini), Mary Field (Miss Totten). New songs: "Daddy-o," "A Song Is Born" (words Don Raye/music Gene de Paul).
> —A team of reclusive musicologists learns about jazz from a panel of experts, while one scholar falls for a nightclub singer with mob connections.

A Song Is Born isn't half the picture *Ball of Fire* is, and it's a film nobody really wanted to make. Howard Hawks had suggested a remake of his earlier hit to Sam Goldwyn, who'd been looking for a Danny Kaye vehicle. Hawks didn't want to redo his own picture, until Goldwyn offered him so much money the producer soon became resentful. Danny Kaye was in the dumps, separated from his wife/creative director/personal songwriter Sylvia Fine, who was barely involved. He looks glum throughout, and doesn't sing. Virginia Mayo was tired of Danny Kaye pictures—this was her fourth—and Hawks didn't want her. (She got so little direction, she watched *Ball of Fire* to copy Barbara Stanwyck's mannerisms.) The many writers involved all turned down screenplay credit, after Hawks recycled abundant dialogue (and linguistics jokes) from *Ball of Fire*.[11]

But in the remake the scholarly subplot is a jazz story, which features a surprisingly funny Benny Goodman in a character role. The shut-in scholars are now musicologists, writing an encyclopedia-sized history of music with recorded examples for the same Totten Foundation that paid the bills in *Ball of Fire*. (Mary Field again plays cost-conscious but flirty spinster Miss Totten, as if she's sponsoring research all over town—which would make *A Song is Born* a copycat sequel, not a remake.) The sweetly named singer played by Mayo (ghosted by Jeri Sullivan) is Honey Swanson.

This time the academics' wake-up call comes from hip window washers played by venerable comedians Buck and Bubbles, using their own names. Buck Washington—a serious pianist who'd recorded with Louis Armstrong and Bessie Smith—sits down to jazz up a couple of classical melodies the professors demonstrate, boogie-woogiefying a little Bach and Grieg's "Anitra's Dance." (Once more, black musicians freely share knowledge with whites.) This syncopated wonderment astonishes the profs, unaware of every style Buck and Bubbles name—swing, jive, jump, blues, two-beat dixie or rebop (as still-new bebop was sometimes known). These dwarfs have been sequestered (only) nine years, without a radio.

Two of these recluses get at least a glimmer of what jazz is about. Prof. Magenbruch (Goodman, with slicked back hair and a waxed mustache, playing to his absent-minded professor reputation) can't follow the action well enough to play along on his clarinet, but he scribbles down a few notes he hears.[12] Pianist Dr. Elfini discerns parallels to the classical chaconne (improvising over fixed chords) and passacaglia (improvising over a fixed bassline) "except that the amazing variations on the melody depend so much on the peculiar passing tones and leading notes."

Either of those sharp-eared fellows might have written a good monograph on jazz, but the topic is consigned to Hobart Frisbee (Kaye) who covers folk music, which is how the profs classify this brace of new styles, without discussion. Frisbee heads out to nightclubs to corral a panel of informants: Louis Armstrong, Tommy Dorsey, saxophonist Charlie Barnet, vibist Lionel Hampton (seen guesting with Armstrong's All-Stars with Zutty Singleton, Barney Bigard, and saxophone ringer Benny Carter), Goodman pianist Mel Powell, the Golden Gate gospel quartet, the guitars-and-percussion Samba Kings, and Honey Swanson. While making his rounds Frisbee must have caught a Spike Jones set too, reporting he'd heard "Rimsky-Korsakov played on a washboard, a bicycle pump, a plunger of some sort, and pots and pans."

Jazz is not Prof. Magenbruch's field, but he procures a copy of Winthrop Sargeant's book *Jazz: Hot and Hybrid*, whose recent second edition gets strong product placement. Frisbee reads out the title, he and Magenbruch are seen carrying it around, and it's used as a prop in a quick gag. The book is in fact an ideal introduction to jazz for academics: a musicological study by a classical critic, with abundant musical examples. (Those chaconne and passacaglia comparisons are in there.) It gets way down in the weeds in discussing the mechanics of jazz syncopation. Magenbruch asks Frisbee if in his travels he'd heard any music where an eighth-note melody got recast in *umpateedle* rhythm. It's not a musician's term, and sounds like Danny Kaye-ish doubletalk, but Sargeant goes on about it for pages.[13] *Umpateedle* is an onomatapoeticism meant to mimic the rhythm of straight eighths swung as a sequence of dotted eighths and sixteenths. Sargeant cites two Benny Goodman solos as examples—although Magenbruch later claims he's never heard of this Goodman fellow. Even so, the professor confesses that hot rhythm "holds a strange fascination for me." It's a little dust-devil of in-jokes.

Magenbruch may be bad with names, but he's a quick study. Consultants Hampton and Mel Powell would demonstrate some Goodman-style small group swing—"a small combo doing jump with a head arrangement"—if only they had a clarinetist. So Frisbee drags in Magenbruch, clutching his *Jazz: Hot and Hybrid*. The cats are skeptical, and the prof's intimidated by the idea of playing without a score. But once Hamp dives into Fats Waller's riffing "Stealin' Apples," a Goodman favorite, Magenbruch knows just what to do. He plays one warm-up line in simple imitation, and then he's off and running—respecting the form, adding to what the others are doing, not hogging the spotlight, and playing very well. When he whips off a two-octave run, Armstrong, Barnet, and Dorsey sit up in their chairs. Magenbruch can't figure out quite when to stomp his foot like Hampton, but that doesn't affect his clarinet timing. The author once witnessed a similar epiphany: a classical musician sitting in suddenly realizes she can improvise, and instantly takes to it.

Frisbee has been reading Sargeant too. On a blackboard he reproduces a flow-chart from the book that tracks whirlpools of influence among African and various European and American musics (though Frisbee purges "Jewish" from the list of Eastern European strains). And to cap and supplement his recent studies, Frisbee assembles his cast of consultants to record, in one epic take, a lecture-demonstration on jazz history (jazz roots, really): a travesty that exposes his woeful musicology. Earlier he'd asserted he and his colleagues weren't "the slapping together kind," mentioning their lofty goal of "bringing the peoples of the world closer together through the universal language of music." But we've already seen one campy reconstruction they'd worked up, of a mating chant from Polynesia, or was it the West Indies? Days later, they're unsure. One of the brethren had sung the woman's part on their recording—close enough for these scholars.

Frisbee narrates his jazz primer: First there was the African drum—and Louie Bellson plays a very un–(West) African isorhythm on tom-tom. To which was added the voice, Frisbee continues, as behind him the Samba Kings start singing long notes like no African choral music ever. Then came the shepherd's flute, says Frisbee—and we hear an Eastern

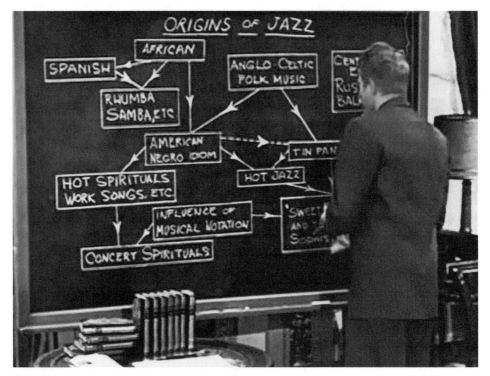

FIGURE 3.5 In *A Song Is Born*, a musicologist (Danny Kaye) copies a flow chart from critic Winthrop Sargeant.

mode from concert flute, very un-shepherdy. By now the cumulative effect of drum, voices, and flute bears scant relation to music of West Africa, Cuba, Manhattan, or anywhere but Hollywood.

He continues, ungrammatically: "The basic beat of the tom-tom and the same thematic strain of the chant that was carried across oceans, and contained in early Spanish music after the invention of the guitar." And we hear flamenco and then samba strumming and a stiff Bellson *clavé*. This mish-mash is a disgrace, and not just for Frisbee's demure circumlocution about the slave trade. He goes on. "The ever widening cycle finally reached the shores of southern United States, where the beat was momentarily lost." Has folk scholar Frisbee never heard a work song? He couldn't have finished reading *Jazz: Hot and Hybrid*; Winthrop Sargeant knows better.

Cue the Golden Gate Quartet singing what Frisbee calls "pure Negro spiritual": the original number, "A Song Is Born." Its melody is derived from the hymn "Goin' Home," itself lifted from the largo movement of Dvořák's *New World Symphony*, which was inspired by African American music. It's not exactly a folk tune, but it does stir those whirlpools of influence. And then the gospel quartet start swinging its rhythm, and the jazz musicians, including a now-confident Magenbruch, jump in. Honey Swanson and then Armstrong take over the vocal, the lyric a not-so-scholarly riff on "Birth of the Blues": "They took a reet jungle beat / Brought it to Basin Street / And that's how jazz was born." The musicians must have helped Frisbee with the lingo and the arrangement. It's a catchy number and a spirited performance, overlooking all the bad history.

The choice of a Dvořákian melody may be explained by Frisbee's limited exposure to the music he presents. After hearing pianist Buck's jazzed-up Bach and Grieg and that noise-band Rimsky-Korsakov, he thinks jazz musicians turn to classical themes more often than they do. He mistakes a minor tendency for a jazz essential.

Throughout *A Song Is Born* the professors face the loss of institutional funding, and in a just world this shoddy display would seal their fate. One can only imagine what Frisbee's projected eight chapters on jazz will look like, should that history ever be completed. Perhaps his work would have been more conscientious had he not been so distracted by Honey Swanson.

/// 4 /// YOUNG MEN WITH HORNS: THE JAZZ BIOPIC'S GOLDEN AGE 1950–1959

The 1950s jazz-biopic fad was sparked by the box-office success of *The Glenn Miller Story*. Although the trend lasted only five years, the target audience for such films shifted between 1954 and 1959. Evidently the time was ripe for jazz lives on screen. The decade's first big successful jazz picture was a near-biopic: the life story of a fictional musician loosely based on a real one.

> *Young Man with a Horn* (1950; 112 minutes; director: Michael Curtiz; screen-play: Carl Foreman, Edmund H. North, from the novel by Dorothy Baker). Cast includes: Kirk Douglas (Rick Martin), Lauren Bacall (Amy North), Juano Hernandez (Art Hazzard), Doris Day (Jo Jordan), Hoagy Carmichael (Smoke Willoughby), Jerome Cowan (Phil Morrison), Nestor Paiva (Louis Galba), Walter Reed (Jack Chandler), Orley Lindgren (Rick as a child).
> —Mentored by early jazzman Art Hazzard, young Rick Martin grows up to be a trumpet star. But when he marries badly, his world begins to crumble.

Casablanca director and virtuoso of the studio system Michael Curtiz helmed *Young Man with a Horn*, a rare screen adaptation of a jazz novel. Dorothy Baker's 1938 book had been inspired by the music, but not the life, of gifted, doomed 1920s white cornetist Bix Beiderbecke. The novel retains the barest outline of Bix's story: a horn man who also plays piano is too gifted for the commercial band that employs him and drinks himself to an early death. The nugget of the plot comes from critic Otis Ferguson's 1936 *New Republic* paean of the same title: "Bix appears to have struck too fast a pace in the years after he was brought to New York by Jean Goldkette . . . drinking himself gradually out of the picture in the last years with Whiteman, becoming less and less productive, and worrying his friends."[1]

From that outline, Baker goes her own way, inventing another life. Bix never wed; Rick had a bad marriage. Bix was from riverfront Iowa; Martin grows up in Los Angeles and plays with black musicians early on, unlike Beiderbecke. That wrinkle was Baker's way of acknowledging the music's African American roots, though her black characters may be thinly drawn—notably Rick's buddy, slow-talking easygoing drummer Smoke Jordan. Smoke's sister Jo grows up to have a career like the young Billie Holiday's, recording with her pick of musicians. Smoke introduces teenage Rick to pianist Jeff Williams who becomes his mentor.

In time Rick arrives in New York, where singer Jo introduces him to Amy North, psychiatry student with her own glaring hang-ups. Rick and Amy meet and marry and drift apart in 20 pages, but it's enough to propel him into an alcoholic haze. After a fevered all-night session with Smoke over in Jersey, Rick reaches for and botches a big ending on Jo's record date. (Jeff: "That note he was going for, that thing he was trying for—there ain't any such thing. Not on a horn.")[2] From there he slides downhill, with a stop at a seedy sanitarium where no one has the sense to call an ambulance for a patient with pneumonia.

Like other jazz authors, Baker can be musicologically vague about just what musicians are up to. In one conversation, Rick goes off on an extended, not-quite coherent discussion of a supposed bane of trumpet players, "getting a roll." It reads like something Baker jotted down from memory after a night in a club. "It comes from dropping the mouthpiece too low on the lower lip. . . . Say your lips are a hose; if you close the nozzle, the water, which is your air, in comparison, see, backs up or swells up in the back of the hose, which is really your throat, see? . . . That's what puts so many brassmen in the nut house." The film makes even more of this woeful habit; the roll comes up over and over, as if trumpeters obsess on it. (They don't.) Jazz for Baker is at once humble, orderly, and exotic. The difference between what she calls Memphis style (where musicians solo in turn) and New Orleans style (where everyone blows at once) "is something like the difference between two styles of chow mein: in one you get the noodles and the sauce served separately, in the other sauce and noodles are mixed before they are served."[3]

The book isn't that good, but it furthered Bix's mythic status and was about the only jazz novel anyone could name, then or later. Warner Bros. had been developing an adaptation for years. Composer, jazz pianist, and Beiderbecke friend Hoagy Carmichael had signed on early, as had Lauren Bacall, to play twisted Amy. Warners had obtained the rights for star John Garfield, who'd since left the studio. (He had already sidestepped *Second Chorus* and *Blues in the Night*; later he'd be in contention for *The Man with the Golden Arm*.) Other actors were considered—James Stewart, Ronald Reagan, Dane Clark—before rising star Kirk Douglas got the nod.[4]

As with any big studio picture, many cooks pass through the kitchen. Warners commissioned a script from Stephen Longstreet, then another from Edmund North (which got Baker's okay), and a third from Carl Foreman, told by honcho Jack Warner to tack on a happy ending and play down all that black stuff. North and Foreman shared screenplay credit; Carmichael and Kirk Douglas had a little input. And there are a couple of interpolations from *Really the Blues*, the 1946 autobiography of Mezz Mezzrow, white clarinetist who identified strongly with African American musicians and had a comically inflated opinion of himself.

With all that crosstalk, there's barely a shred of Bix left—the death knell coming when bravura high-note trumpeter Harry James was signed to ghost Rick. Bix's playing was subtle, rhythmically and harmonically—he liked odd melody notes that seemed to float over the underlying chords. Harry James liked to plant high notes on the ceiling—as in the film's Max Steiner theme.

The end result affirms the capricious nature of screen adaptations. Some dialogue comes almost straight from the book, if seemingly chosen at random. Characters were broadly reconfigured: Hoagy Carmichael plays Smoke (whose nickname, now that he's white, is explained by his tobacco habit), with some aspects of pianist Jeff Williams's character folded in. Singer Jo Jordan, no longer Smoke's sister, is played by blonde ex-bandsinger Doris Day. To make up for that double whitewash, trumpeter Art Hazard, barely present in the book, gets an extra jazzy z added to his last name, and Hazzard becomes Rick's new mentor, played with teary-eyed sentiment by Puerto Rico–born Juano Hernandez: the first of four memorable performances he'd give in jazz tales.

As jazz movies go, it's very well made—the New York nightclub sets are improbably lavish—and it's well acted by the leads. Bacall's Amy simmers with hostility and self-hatred under a cool veneer. Kirk Douglas conjures the right intensity and anguish.

The film's main bid for jazz credibility comes from casting Carmichael, the singer and composer of "Star Dust" and dozens of other jazz-inflected songs, previously seen as a hero's pianist pal in *To Have and Have Not* (with Bacall) and *The Best Years of Our Lives*. Smoke and Rick play together in a couple of bands and barnstorm around the country early on—but Smoke is also the narrator, directly addressing the viewer as he sits at an upright piano in some deserted cafe; his bookend segments and occasional expository voiceovers recount the story of his old friend. (As Krin Gabbard has pointed out, Smoke talks of Rick in the past tense, like he's dead.) Carmichael biographer Richard Sudhalter observed how un-Hollywood Carmichael's slow Indiana speech cadences are—indeed, his talking has a jazzier feel than anything else in the story. Rick, Smoke tells us, "was cut out to be a jazzman the way the righteous are chosen for the church"—a line lifted verbatim from the first page of Mezzrow's book.[5]

Like Baker's novel, the movie follows Rick from unsupervised boyhood, as he learns to play piano watching a pianist chord "In the Sweet By and By" down at a homeless mission. He gets a job setting pins at a bowling alley. From here the movie veers off. Across the back alley is the Club Dixie (black staff, white patrons) where Art Hazzard and His Dixie Pickers perform. Rick is drawn to their sound—a mournful "Moanin' Low" in particular. After Art spots him eavesdropping from a transom, he invites him in, offers him a sandwich and a friendly ear, and takes a liking to the kid. In time he helps Rick pick out a pawnshop horn, gives him lessons, and warns him against getting a roll. Presumably it's the 1920s, although Curtiz doesn't strive for authenticity; modern cars roll through the streets. Art Hazzard's music sounds less like 1920s jazz than the modernized unmixed-chow-mein version you'd hear at Nick's or Eddie Condon's in New York in the 1940s.

Art's band, like one of those later outfits, even has a tenor saxophone, relatively rare in such settings in the 1920s (though common in 1920s-era scenes in jazz movies).

Hazzard plays in a sort of sub-Armstrong style (ghosted by white trumpeter Jimmy Zito, veteran of the same Les Brown band as Doris Day). The early jazz musicians in Los Angeles mostly came from New Orleans or Texas, and the name Dixie Pickers is suggestive, but all we learn about Hazzard's background is that after decades in the business, he has no family and nothing to show for it all. He exists only in relation to Rick, his very name a warning: art may be hazardous to your health.

In no time young Rick grows up to be Kirk Douglas, consumed by music-making, living for the horn. Before Art leaves town for New York, he cautions the young man: Don't get too obsessive about it. Live a little. Later Jo Jordan, the singer in the first band Rick joins, gives him similar advice; you need a hobby to get your mind off music a minute—collect stamps, or get a dog. She's attracted to him immediately, but just as quickly rules him out as a prospect; she can't compete with that horn. Or his nebulous aspirations: "I'm gonna hit a note that nobody ever heard before." But it's not clear what that means: either a harmony no one ever hit on (highly improbable, but a Bixian ambition) or a high note beyond his horn's range (a more Harry Jamesian urge).

Rick's early work experience echoes the free-spirit-versus-regimentation conflicts of other jazz protagonists like *Syncopation*'s Johnny Schumacher. Rick meets Smoke and Jo when he joins them as a member of Jack Chandler's Collegians at the Aragon Ballroom on Santa Monica's Lick Pier.

Smoke's piano parts were mostly ghosted by Buddy Cole, who'd worked with Carmichael in radio and by Hoagy's estimation could imitate him well.[6] Smoke is at the piano, in an empty hall and a contemplative mood, when he meets and first hears Rick play—the only moment in the film when Rick/Harry James evokes Beiderbecke. Smoke immediately falls in with a few glossy chords recalling Beiderbecke's piano set piece "In a Mist"—a wordless editorial comment. (When Rick had walked in, the pianist had been musing over another melody—the movie's Max Steiner main theme, previously heard over the opening credits. It's as if Hoagy/Smoke, half in and half out of the story, can hear the nondiegetic soundtrack.) But after hours, later that evening, when Jo overhears Rick play "Moanin' Low" alone in a dressing room, she pegs him as a Hazzard disciple.

Despite his impeccable influences, Rick has already run afoul of the boss. At his first rehearsal, he gets called out for improvising flashy obbligatos behind Jo on "The Very Thought of You," not having the sheet music ready. These arrangements cost money, Chandler lectures Rick, so play what's written. (We'll see this scene repeated in *Bix* and *Giant Steps*.) And remember, everybody, we're a dance band, so mind those tempos.

But when Chandler steps out one night and leaves Smoke in charge for the last set, Rick goads the pianist into letting a few of the men play some real jazz. The dancers crowd the bandstand, digging it, but when Chandler returns, he pulls the plug, and instigator Rick gets sacked. In the novel, when the leader sees the crowd likes hot music, he has the sense to leave it in the act, letting Rick shine. The film version more closely follows an incident in Mezzrow's *Really the Blues*, when Red Nichols came back from a break to find his sidefolk had chucked his arrangements to swing out on "Sweet Sue," and fired them all.[7]

Smoke also leaves Chandler's band, and he and the trumpeter hit the road, living day to day and playing where they can. In the book there's a whiff of homoerotic tension, when Rick calls Smoke "honey," like Twain's Jim coaxing Huck back to the raft. (Baker delicately notes Rick's "wrong terminology.")[8] In the movie, the buddies sing "Sam from Alabam" together—the only time Carmichael sings—to pass the time as they drive rear-projected back roads, in a convertible older than cars Rick saw as a kid. To fit both into a tight two-shot, the actors huddle together in the front seat, one shoulder in front of another, like sweethearts. Neither character ever looks happier.

One snowy evening in Chicago, they cross a Capone-like scarface who doesn't dig their morose "Silent Night." A little brawl breaks out when a thug slams the piano lid on Smoke's hands. Scarface sits Rick down, asks him to play a little, and tips the bell of the horn back, much as Art Hazzard would, when worried the kid would get a roll. Then the thug pours beer into the bell—waterboards him, in effect. The whole episode breaks our vagabond heroes' spirit. Smoke departs for Hoagy's native Indiana, and in the next scene, Rick hits New York.

By now it must be years since Santa Monica, in something like the present day: 1949's *Sword of the Desert* plays in Times Square. Everyone's moved on: Jo is now a theater headliner fronting a mixed jazz-and-strings orchestra, and Art Hazzard has a steady gig downtown at Galba's ritzy below-street-level nightclub; but he's gone gray, wears old-man specs, and plays with less fire. (He now favors a straight mute, for a quieter sound, and his sextet includes accordion.) His old protégé sits in with him, and magically, Rick's horn creates its own reverb, making him sound even more like Harry James. "I taught him how to hold that trumpet," Art tells the audience. "But I didn't teach him how to play it—not the way he does. That's something that you can't learn." Slick bandleader Phil Morrison, in the house, scoops Rick up for his strings-encrusted dance band, which will soon bring in Smoke on piano.

Rick quickly makes his name, getting featured billing with Morrison. After hours, to his employer's displeasure, Rick sits in at Galba's, helping out his old mentor by drawing in the customers. (Kirk Douglas had argued that Galba's should be dowdy, but sleek visuals trumped story logic.)[9]

And then one night Jo walks in with Amy North, and the jazz story mostly goes on hiatus. Rick's and Amy's doomed, enervating romance takes up 40 minutes of screen time, a sign Hollywood folk are more fascinated by failed marriages than music. Neither book nor movie explains the attraction; as Beiderbecke friend Eddie Condon said of the novel's Amy, "Bix would have outrun sound getting away from her."[10] Bacall's Amy is insufferable, a rich psychiatry student who think she sees right through everybody, but she's the one with (daddy) issues. Amy is fox to Rick's hedgehog. He only knows one thing. She's tried on a few roles already: writer, interior decorator, student pilot, cabaret singer. Why not wife?

FIGURE 4.1 Rick Martin (Kirk Douglas) plays for mentor Art Hazzard (Juano Hernandez) in *Young Man with a Horn*.

Amy: "Tell me about jazz. You think it's purely African?" Amy asks.

"I don't know. I don't do much thinking about it, I just like to play it. If you listen to it enough—"

"I didn't come here to listen to it. I came to study the people. . . There's something about jazz that releases inhibitions, it's a sort of cheap mass-produced narcotic."

Their relationship simultaneously heats up and goes downhill from there. Their quickie marriage lands in the crapper just as fast. They keep different hours and live in different worlds. She starts dallying with an intense lady painter who wants Amy to come up and see her sketches—one more experience she can find wanting. It's no wonder Amy flunks her psych classes; her insights are puddle-shallow and are of no help to anyone. In the book she's almost amusingly awful; Bacall's Amy sucks the oxygen off the screen. She's worse than all the *Orchestra Wives*.

Maybe she dislikes jazz because she only knows it from other movies. "Oh I know it's supposed to be our native art: cotton fields, the levees, old New Orleans and blues in the night," she says—echoing Nick Duquesne educating Miralee Smith in *New Orleans*, and namechecking an earlier Warners jazz film. Later she quotes a line of Leo's from *Blues in the Night*: "The situation as it's presently constituted stinks." Art Hazzard also talks like he's seen it: "I heard you had the misery." A barroom disagreement over repertoire, a brush with a gangster, and a tormented hero's mental collapse all echo that earlier film.

Even Warners set decorators pay (accidental) homage to that earlier movie: a photograph of a trombonist that hangs inside the door of the Manhattan dive where Jigger collapses occupies the same spot at the Club Dixie. But there's a crucial difference between these films: Jigger and his men appropriate black music without crediting the originators, or giving it a thought. Art Hazzard (like Rex Tearbone in *Syncopation*) gives freely, for the sheer love of sharing his knowledge.

Young Man with a Horn shows its Warner Bros. pedigree another way. The studio's cartoon composer Carl Stalling peppered his scores with in-jokes, quoting tunes whose titles comment on passing action. The selections here do likewise. Rick plays for kooch dancers: "Pretty Baby." Rick and Smoke jam while Chandler's away: "Get Happy." Jo becomes a star: "Too Marvelous for Words." When Rick first enters Galba's, the place where his life will begin to unravel, aging Art is playing "Blue Room." When Rick sits in, "With a Song in My Heart" is his New York calling card. When we first see Amy, Rick's already playing "You Took Advantage of Me." When they meet, and she shares her fascinating views on jazz, Art plays "Love for Sale" in the background, and then Jo sings "I May Be Wrong (But I Think You're Wonderful)." (Later she'll try to warn Rick less subtly, too late.) Amy dolled up in mink leaves Rick's no-frills pad very late, and the elevator boy whistles "If I Could Be with You One Hour Tonight." She and Rick impulsively marry, then dance to "What Is This Thing Called Love." She's bored when he puts on his old Art Hazzard collectibles: "Can't We Be Friends?" They drift apart; he plays "Someone to Watch Over Me." Jamming to forget her: "There'll Be Some Changes Made" and "I Gotta Right to Sing the Blues."

If *Young Man with a Horn* is a Warners cartoon, it's a Freudian one. The horn, Amy helpfully points out twice, is Rick's alter ego. "That trumpet's part of me," he agrees: "It's the best part." Earlier Jo had told him, "The way you baby that thing, you'd think it was alive." At the end of an all-night jam, another player says he's too tired to hold his horn. Rick: "That's funny. I got just the other trouble. This keeps sticking to my hand, I can't shake it off." (That bit is from the book.) He even takes it with him on a late date, like a real New York musician who knows not to leave instruments in the car.

Young man and horn are joined not at the hip, but near it. It's like the writers are baiting Freudian critics: Rick keeps giving Art Hazzard cigars. That round dimple on Kirk Douglas's protruding chin doesn't just resemble a trumpet mouthpiece. Psychoanalytic-minded Krin Gabbard has a field day with this picture (and those cigars).[11] When Rick's chops deteriorate, he smashes his trumpet in frustration. Soon he's hit skid row, and goes into a pawnshop to buy a busted-up 75-cent horn, just to clutch it under his arm—in a crumpled brown bag, like a wino's bottle. (It's also a callback to his original pawnshop horn.) But when he stumbles in the street a taxi runs it over. Tragic self-mutilation is replayed as farce.

The Art Hazzard plot has an Oedipal payoff. The collapse of Rick's marriage should have him doing cartwheels. But he's in a long-term funk, and no longer makes it down to Galba's, where crowds dwindle and a failing Hazzard's future is uncertain. When Art finds him in a bar one day, Rick, in a foul mood, unloads on his mentor: "You did a lot for me. I try to pay you back. But—well, if you're through you're through! I can't hold you up forever." At that moment, Rick stands in for every white swing star who made way more money than his black role models, and accepted it as the natural order of things.

Art's/Juano Hernandez's reaction is heartbreaking—he won't call out Rick on his cruelty. (You wish Jo or Smoke would tell him to quit being a jerk, instead of babying him like he's special.) No problem, Art tells him, I get it—and then staggers out, so brokenhearted he jaywalks into the path of a car, and dies before remorseful Rick reaches his bedside.

Despite Hazzard's long residency at Galba's, his funeral is sparsely attended—even Jo, Smoke, and club owner Louis Galba skip it. It's the only time we see Hazzard draw a black crowd: his church congregation. Art's band joins the choir for "Nobody Knows the Troubles I've Seen." Rick impulsively joins in, on Art's horn, playing the melody straight. (Jack Warner wanted that scene cut: too black.)

Rick and Amy's marriage is really kaput when she smashes his stack of precious Hazzard 78s. She leeches from Rick like Rick from his mentor: she breaks Art's records, but Rick broke Hazzard's heart. Rick's drinking starts to get in the way of his playing. No one says it, but it sounds like he's getting a roll, blocking his nozzle. He loses his money gig, and after that all-nighter where the horn won't leave his hand, screws up his big ending on Jo's perfect record of "With a Song in My Heart." That failure is more overwrought than in the book (where he's looking for some perfect note he can't find). The movie version is more like Mezzrow's operatic account of Armstrong, with shredded lips, building toward a heroically self-destructive high-note ending.[12] This is when Rick smashes his horn, losing the best part of himself.

He wanders around town in a New York montage, often in the shadow of the Third Avenue El, till he winds up in that crummy sanitarium where Smoke and Jo gather at what appears to be his deathbed. Finally Rick hears that clean sweet note he's been searching for all these years—the siren of the ambulance coming to take him to a real hospital. He sits up in bed, looking at something far off . . . and just before he collapses and dies, we cut away.

Curtiz had obviously shot two endings, and then we get the other one that Jack Warner ordered: a reprise of Jo's record date, where a fully recovered Rick now nails that fancy ending. (Some viewers insist he and Jo are now a couple, but that's conjecture.) Smoke's final address to the audience tries to smooth over that final cadence's abrupt modulation from minor to major: "The desire to live is a great teacher, and I think it taught Rick a lot of things. He learned that you can't say everything through the end of a trumpet, and a man doesn't destroy himself just because he can't hit some high note that he dreamed up. Maybe that's why Rick went on to be a success as a human being first, and an artist second." It's such gibberish, Amy North might've said it. These peppermint chords are an unconvincing resolution to the film's stormy last act. If Rick Martin had been a real person, the movie would have eased his fall. The biopics just ahead would never get so bleak—though that would change later.

The Glenn Miller Story (1954; 115 minutes; director: Anthony Mann; writers: Valentine Davies, Oscar Brodney). Cast includes: James Stewart (Glenn Miller), June Allyson (Helen Burger Miller), Harry Morgan (Chummy MacGregor), Charles Drake (Don Haynes), George Tobias (Si Shribman), Nino Tempo (Willie Schwartz), Barton MacLane (Gen. Arnold), Leo Mostovoy (Joseph Schillinger), Louis Armstrong, Gene Krupa, Frances Langford, Ben Pollack, Babe Russin, the Modernaires (themselves).
—Arranger and trombonist Glenn Miller searches for a distinctive sound, which helps make him a successful bandleader, ably supported by his loving wife. During World War II, Miller leads service bands and disappears over the English Channel.

The Technicolor *Glenn Miller Story* was another major studio picture. Star James Stewart and director Anthony Mann were both under contract at Universal, and this was their fifth collaboration since 1950's *Winchester '73*. Mann's westerns can get gritty, and Stewart's characters complicated; perhaps only Hitchcock was better at luring the actor down into the sweaty depths. *The Glenn Miller Story* is far lighter fare. As jazz films go, it's refreshingly free of intergenerational conflict or dangerous women.

It also marks the graying of the swing-band audience. In 1942's *Orchestra Wives*, Miller's/Gene Morrison's band entertained young people like heroine Connie, still living at home before she eloped. The lyrics the band's singers delivered helped articulate young folks' romantic yearnings. At one point in the *Miller Story* 12 years later, the band plays at a ballroom for "those kids," as they're identified, but almost everyone on the dance floor looks middle-aged or on the verge, as if a call had gone out to Miller fan clubs for extras—surrogates for the film's audience who still think of themselves as youngsters, digging Miller's late 1930s hits. Movies had often featured musicians appearing as themselves, but as jazz's early days receded, these as-themselves players had begun to look improbably long in the tooth; here they include drummers Ben Pollack, Gene Krupa, and the ubiquitous Louis Armstrong.

By the 1950s, big-band swing was already nostalgia music. *The Glenn Miller Story* was rife with hits, to recall the old days for aging jitterbugs. The story's themes make that target audience even more obvious. Unlike *Orchestra Wives* it involves real grown-ups' problems: making the rent and the payroll; taking drudge jobs to make your nut until you barely notice you're in a rut; putting a little money aside for the future, and selling off assets when things go bust; cutting through bureaucratic red tape when one's superiors are content to do things the same old way; replacing crucial personnel on short notice, scheduling wardrobe fittings, and coming up with a strong marketable brand. Stewart's Glenn Miller is the organization man.

Other jazz heroes express themselves/their feelings on their instruments. Not Miller, who was always an indifferent trombonist—no Teagarden or Tommy Dorsey. Even so, in the film, Glenn holds his own with Armstrong (and His All-Stars) in a jam session, but on that occasion he has reason to act feisty; he'd just gotten married. For Krin Gabbard, it's "as if Armstrong were preparing him for the sexual initiation of his wedding night."[13] To put that another way: Pops is the jazz family elder or tribal chief, presiding over an informal wedding reception.

Glenn's passion is for arranging: the orchestration of parts for a jazz band, the fleshing out of a basic composition. Early on, Miller and sidekick Chummy MacGregor (Harry Morgan, making up for being a jerk in *Orchestra Wives*) try out for Ben Pollack's band in Los Angeles, and Glenn brings a stack of sheet music instead of his trombone. (At the same audition, Pollack tries out clarinetist Willie Schwartz—played by reedman Nino Tempo—though in real life the bandleader had just hired teenager Benny Goodman. The real Schwartz plays on the soundtrack, where Miller's hits are faithfully rendered.) As Miller tells the pawnbroker to whom he's always hocking his horn, "To me, music is more than one instrument; it's a whole orchestra playing together. And the only way I can express myself is to work out an arrangement." There's even a scene that shows why arrangements matter: a crass floor show turns "Moonlight Serenade" into a boom-boom burlesque number. (There's a similar scene in the Sigmund Romberg biopic *Deep in My Heart* later that year, involving his "Softly, As in a Morning Sunrise.")

Like *Young Man with a Horn*'s Rick, Glenn talks a lot about chasing some nebulous sound that no one's heard before—one it appears he can neither describe to himself, hear in his head, nor hunt for on piano. Nor does he use the commercial arrangements he writes to search for it. He seems to forget his quest entirely for years on end.

The Glenn Miller Story manages to get a fair amount right, like most jazz biopics. He was indeed living in Los Angeles when Ben Pollack hired him to play and arrange for a new band, which was then appearing at the Venice Ballroom overlooking the water—just down the beach from *Young Man with a Horn*'s Lick Pier. In the film as in life, Miller leaves Pollack in New York so he can freelance, rather than move on to Atlantic City. (We get a brief glimpse of what must be the Fifty-Second Street nightclub district, a few years too early.) After two years of scuffling Miller lands in the pit band for the (Gershwin) show *Girl Crazy*, along with Krupa, Goodman, and Red Nichols. He also sends to Boulder for his getting-tired-of-waiting college sweetheart Helen Burger. With her encouragement, Glenn eventually starts a band of his own, but during a punishing midwinter tour, he pulls the plug. As in life, this happens just after Helen loses a baby and any chance of having another. The symbolism is too perfect; the band's all but stillborn. Later, the Millers will adopt two kids, one of each, just as Glenn would lead two famous bands, civilian and military.

As in life, Stewart's Miller gets help from manager Don Haynes and a financial backer, Boston ballroom operator Si Shribman, as he's listed in the credits. (The animated speech patterns and glitchy syntax of affable George Tobias suggest old-country origins, where the real Cy Shribman was quiet and refined.)[14] Trying again, Glenn launches a successful band with a signature sound: a clarinet lead over tightly harmonized saxes.

The movie also gets a few things out of sequence, and compresses chronological time, as biopics do. Miller joined Pollack in 1926, and formed his second band in 1938; here the passage of time is mostly conveyed by Chummy's cars getting more modern, and men giving up boxy suits and bow ties. As in any biopic, folks important to the hero's tale (Tommy Dorsey, Tex Beneke) aren't even mentioned. The real Chummy wasn't the hot pianist we hear audition for Pollack, and he and Miller met years later. And there's a bit of gleeful biopic hokum, planting song titles in the dialogue. When Glenn calls Helen to coax her to New York, they keep yelling back and forth his hotel's phone number, Pennsylvania 6-5000. And he keeps talking about giving her a string of pearls.

The screenplay and Anthony Mann's direction hit all the dramatic beats on time. The movie is a low-friction machine that's made to move—like a trombone or barnstorming band. In the opening scenes, the Los Angeles pawnshop Miller frequents is on a hillside corner, below the funicular railway Angel's Flight—we get several views of the cable car ascending, possibly with mannequins aboard; the out-of-focus passengers never stir. Does the tram car in motion stand for a trombone slide reaching for the heavens, or is it a metaphor for the Miller band itself: showy contraption with little room for self-expression (it's about the arrangements) on a mechanized trip to the top?

June Allyson's portrayal of Helen is as cheerfully, briskly efficient and as brimming with goodwill as a Glenn Miller tune. She always emotes toward the camera, and even when she pouts, waiting for Glenn to hem and haw through their slow-motion long-distance courtship, she just wants to move things along. Miller's friend and biographer George T. Simon once wrote, "The tender rapport projected in the film by June Allyson, who reminded me so much of Helen, and by Jimmy Stewart, who reminded me so very much of Jimmy Stewart, was entirely authentic."[15]

Simon was not wrong about Stewart. Glenn Miller's own performance as Gene Morrison in *Orchestra Wives* suggests the steely resolve a bandleader needs, just to get his troops mobilized. Stewart plays him squarely in his own shambling comfort zone; his characterization is three-fifths putting on the Miller rimless glasses, and learning the trombone slide positions. (He mimes better than most faking actors, looking plausible in the same shot with real trombonists.) Miller wasn't a stammering shillyshallier in the Stewart mold; the real Glenn didn't need much pushing.

The movie is hagiography, and given Miller's wartime disappearance—leaving Helen to carry on—it's at least partly a woman's picture. The real Helen Miller was often on the set. There's a publicity shot of the stars and the family, Stewart holding a trombone mouthpiece out to young Stevie Miller, as if handing it down from his father by Hollywood proxy.[16]

Still, only a handful of women have speaking roles, and the film flunks the Bechdel-Wallace test. (Don Haynes's wife Polly hovers in several scenes, never saying a word.) But Helen is the best woman behind a Hollywood jazzman since Ellen Miller in *Second Chorus*. She's the film's moral arbiter and aesthetic authority: when the music is right, she gets a tingle on the back of her neck. Helen tells Glenn on their wedding night she's the kind of wife who'd take money from a husband's pockets and put it in the bank, and when he finally starts his own band, she's got the $1,800 nut ready in a dedicated account. Even before that, when he'd gotten complacent about pays-the-bills Broadway pit work, she was nudging him—why don't you go back to studying with that Dr. Schillinger? The film gives Helen more than her due. He writes a pretty tune for Schillinger homework, which catches her ear, and she and Glenn cook up a title on the spot: "Moonlight Serenade." In fact that tune had had three earlier titles, with lyrics to match.[17]

A long sequence in the middle of the film dramatizes how Miller found "The Sound"—one of those rare moments when a jazz movie tackles musical particulars. The night before his reorganized band's Boston opening—this would be 1938—the players are rehearsing Glenn's arrangement of "I Know Why (and So Do You)." That tune hadn't been written yet—it's from 1941's *Sun Valley Serenade*—but never mind. Miller has scored it with a trumpet lead over saxophones, but at the run-through, high-notey lead trumpeter Joe accidentally cuts his lip, and can't continue. (Joe will pop up again later, just for a second—in Army khakis, to remind us war is coming.) Miller has to improvise a fix, and hits on the idea of substituting clarinet for lead trumpet. It didn't happen quite like that in real life; Miller had written for a high-note trumpeter in another band, and when he left Miller assigned the lead to a clarinetist, who could read off the same B-flat chart. He had hit on his signature effect some time before he realized its value.

In the film, now that Glenn's had his (as yet untested) inspiration, he has to put his idea into practice—and the band needs his finished charts in time for tomorrow's State Ballroom opening. In the real world he wouldn't need to rewrite them all just to change the lead instrument, but Glenn says he wants to adjust the saxophone voicings, bunch 'em all in one octave. The artfully edited set piece that follows, built around "Moonlight Serenade," plays variations on the rehearsal-to-performance segues we've seen before. It's late that same night, and Glenn works in Shribman's plush, dimly lit office, drinking coffee, and sitting on a stool between desk and piano. He's writing out the very bass and piano quarter-note intro we're hearing on the soundtrack. (You can just see faint guide marks for Stewart on the staff paper.) The camera moves back and up as Miller keeps writing, and his band arrangement of "Moonlight Serenade" continues on the sound-track; he pauses on occasion to check his work, leaning over to the piano to hit a chord or rippling arpeggio at just the right moments, the piano heard over (and also as part of) the band; the sound is diegetic and nondiegetic at the same time.

Now as "Moonlight Serenade" continues we are back with the band in its rehearsal room, in tight close-up on a clarinet bell. The camera pulls back to reveal Willie Schwartz, playing lead from the middle of the saxophone section, and now we see the whole band, Miller conducting. We slowly dolly in to a close-up of Stewart, having his Anthony Mann moment of doubt. He looks haggard and a little Hollywood-scruffy from lack of sleep, breathing a little too deeply and fast, gulping once, and listening critically. Glenn looks less like he's convinced his new idea will work than like he knows what's at stake if it doesn't. For a moment Stewart looks like *Vertigo*'s Scottie Ferguson staring into the abyss—and then he smiles ever so faintly.

"Moonlight Serenade" keeps playing as we dissolve to that State Ballroom opening in progress, with all those aging Miller fans out front. Glenn sneaks a shy smile at Helen, who's sitting at a side table with Haynes and Shribman, and she rubs her neck, the sign

FIGURE 4.2 Glenn Miller (James Stewart) rewrites music on deadline in *The Glenn Miller Story*.

she's getting that tingle of artistic excellence. Now the fans do something that only happens in movies: they start applauding all at once, in the middle of the tune for no apparent reason except that the trombones have stood up—presumably the extras' cue to clap. Miller turns around, surprised and a little stunned. Shribman: "Looks like he's got it maybe. Listen to those kids!" Helen: "There's no maybe about it, Mr. Shribman. That's The Sound."

Oddly, after Miller discovers The Sound—fueling a headlines and bobby-soxers montage that establishes the band's rise to the top—we don't hear much of that signature effect on the hits that follow: "Pennsylvania 6-5000," "Tuxedo Junction," "In the Mood," "Chattanooga Choo-Choo," "American Patrol"—or "String of Pearls," dutifully announced as a Jerry Gray composition, which prompts Glenn to give Helen a pearl necklace. (We do hear the clarinet lead, barely, on "At Last" and "Adios," behind dialogue.)

One more front-page insert skips us ahead three years in one headline. The Millers have moved into a Clampett-style mansion. Glenn's two feature films get conflated into one, which is unnamed, though the one scene we see of it at a dubbing session tacitly acknowledges the best parts of Miller's real movies: a standalone number for African American hoofers (the Archie Savage Dancers), on "Tuxedo Junction," which wasn't in either *Sun Valley Serenade* or *Orchestra Wives*. Absurdly, the musicians fit the music to the filmed dancing, not the other way around. By now it's wartime, and Miller, as in life, jumps from Hollywood into the service, joining the Army Air Forces as a captain. (Stewart, a pilot, had served in the Air Corps, leading bombing runs over Germany.)

The war-years story is told pretty straight, a ready-made third act. Miller's given an army band, but bristles that higher-ups only want them to play Sousa marches. When he impulsively has the band play a martial but jaunty "St. Louis Blues" during a field parade for a visiting general, the GIs march with a little more spring in their step—not least a few black soldiers who pepper the white platoons, although the real army was then still segregated. (Miller's service bands were all white, as shown.) He's about to be disciplined for it—he cut through the parade to get to the band, a breach of military protocol—when Gen. Arnold pops in to commend him on his musical initiative. Now with the general's support Glenn can play music his way: the sound of home, to soothe the homesick. Miller and Don Haynes and the musicians ship out for England, where they do broadcasts and a big USO show in an airplane hangar, with special guests the Modernaires (in uniform) and film star Frances Langford. As they play "In the Mood" for troops at an outdoor concert, stock-footage Nazi buzz bombs fly over and explode nearby, magically complementing the tune's terraced dynamics. And then one fogbound December day, Miller gets on a plane bound for liberated Paris, and somewhere over the English Channel he vanishes forever.

The tearjerk final scene, at the Miller home on Christmas, is effectively handled: June Allyson, famous for her screen crying, knew not to overdo. But it's mostly balderdash. The band plays a holiday broadcast as scheduled, announcer Haynes mentioning only that Miller couldn't be there, though his loved ones know the truth: Gen. Arnold had called personally. As they'd waited for the show to start, Si and Chummy had told Helen that the band continuing on without Glenn would validate his whole concept—it'd prove the music's an institution, bigger than one man. It's blatant justification for the several Miller tribute bands, official or unofficial, which were operating when *The Glenn Miller Story* was made (and which would get a boost from the picture).

In that final scene, a hokey little subplot pays off. All through the movie, it's a running gag that Helen's favorite tune is "Little Brown Jug," which Glenn had always disparaged. But for that Christmas show beamed back to the States, he'd planned a special surprise: his swinging new arrangement of that very song. Helen listening to it in close-up is Allyson's big solo in pantomime. (She fingers a toy brown jug he'd given her as a gag present—another doubling, like her strings of pearls and "String of Pearls.") Hearing it gives Helen that back-of-the-neck tingle—thereby validating the posthumous so-called ghost-band concept—and brings a faint smile to her face for the fade.

The script plays a little too fast and loose here. "Little Brown Jug" had been a hit for Miller in 1939, and what real fan wouldn't know that? (The arrangement isn't even his; it's by Bill Finegan.) The story resolves on a dissonant note. It's as if a respectful John Lennon biopic ended with him getting shot right after writing "Yesterday" for Yoko.

Pete Kelly's Blues (1955; 95 minutes; director: Jack Webb; writer: Richard L. Breen). Cast includes: Jack Webb (Pete Kelly), Peggy Lee (Rose Hopkins), Edmond O'Brien (Fran McCarg), Lee Marvin (Al Gannaway), Martin Milner (Joey Firestone), Ella Fitzgerald (Maggie Jackson), Janet Leigh (Ivy), Andy Devine (George Tenell), Jayne Mansfield (cigarette girl). New songs: "Sing a Rainbow" (Arthur Hamilton), "Pete Kelly's Blues" (words Sammy Cahn/music Ray Heindorf).

—In 1920s Kansas City, a gangster leans on bandleader Pete Kelly, and forces him to hire a singer he doesn't want. As mob rule over the music trade turns increasingly violent, Kelly fights back.

Pete Kelly's Blues isn't a biopic, but cornetist Kelly was another fictional character with history. Actor/producer Jack Webb's picture had its origins in NBC radio's 1951 summer-replacement show of the same name, starring Webb who already had a radio hit with his signature rat-a-tat–dialogue show *Dragnet*, soon to expand to TV. On radio Kelly and his dixieland Big 7 play at an unnamed speakeasy where, as Kelly/Webb quips in Joe Fridayesque voiceover, "The whiskey was cut more times than a chin at a barber college." Kelly would mind his own business if he could, but with Kansas City being run by gangsters, he's regularly bullied or cajoled into trying to solve other people's mob-related problems, not always successfully.

It's good radio, a crime drama with jazz interludes. Kelly's trips out to the back alley to meet with or take beatings from thugs are interspersed with a couple of compact, complete hot performances, ring-led by cornetist Dick Cathcart (whose torrid style on the theme is out of *Young Man with a Horn* Harry James) and arranger and clarinetist Matty Matlock. Nick Fatool manned the drums. As *Dragnet* demonstrated, Webb loved the particulars of a working person's daily routine; on radio Kelly describes how records are cut in the studio, and sometimes he talks down a number's flight plan before the band takes off. ("Everybody goin' in. Nick, flood those breaks solid. . . . I'll take it for 16, Matlock you take 16, then everybody out.") The Big 7's sound is 1951-style dixieland. The action is set circa 1922, but they play "Singin' the Blues" like 1927 Bix and Frank Trumbauer. There's often a road trip out to Fat Annie's across the river in Kansas, where Maggie Jackson (Meredith Howard) sings blues and ballads and dispenses timely information. She's obviously African American, and some members of Pete's band might be too, with their not-too-hammy downhome accents (though they were voiced by white actors).

In the 1955 widescreen Technicolor version, it's 1927, and the speakeasy, one flight below street level, has moved a few blocks north from 417 to 17 Cherry—an address that would put it on a hillside near the riverfront, although exteriors were shot on Warners' New York–style brownstone street. But the film does a good job of putting everyone in the right clothes. Webb was meticulous about period details, like the vintage of the compositions Kelly plays—everything except that picture of Jean Harlow on his rooming-house wall.[18] And we see that his Big 7 is all white. (The actors were ghosted by the reunited radio band.)

In the late 1920s, Kansas City's leading black bandleader Bennie Moten played some lightly orchestrated blues, laying groundwork for the swing era. Moten's band and the Oklahoma Blue Devils would beget the mid-1930s Count Basie orchestra whose example made the swing era swing harder.

The big white bands playing KC ballrooms in the 1920s were out of Paul Whiteman and Jean Goldkette. A few small groups spun off of big ones like the Coon-Saunders Orchestra, but those little bands didn't record, and rate scant mention in the histories. That lack of documentation affords the (eight-piece) Big 7 some stylistic leeway. Cathcart and Matlock's mid-1950s dixieland (like the 1940s version) didn't really sound like 1920s jazz. The rhythm is too limber, the arrangements too modern. Still, Kansas City's African American scene was ground zero for a looser kind of swing, and Kelly's band strives to be up to date. Its four-piece rhythm section includes guitar, not banjo, the four horns include tenor saxophone, and they're debating adding a baritone. It's a small band evolving into a big one. Who's to say these white Kansas Citians might not have come up with a streamlined collective style, with some of that springy hometown flavor, thereby anticipating the modernized dixieland of later decades? In the movie Kelly's Big 7 does cut a record, apparently somewhere in the Ozarks, to judge by the painted scenery, but we don't hear of it getting released. (As Kelly tells it in radio episode "Zelda," his 1922 outfit cut so many records under so many pseudonyms, he'd forgotten one that figures in the case. That would make the fictional Big 7 one of the most recorded early jazz bands.)

Admittedly, this charitable reading would be more credible if Kelly expressed any interest when the speakeasy's cigarette girl (Jayne Mansfield, no less) asks him out to go hear Moten. Black and white Kansas City barely intersect in *Pete Kelly*. During an argument, the Big 7's hotheaded drummer Joey Firestone (Martin Milner) threatens to defect to the Blue Devils, laughably; that black Oklahoma City band still had its founding drummer Edward McNeil.

The only black musician Kelly interacts with is Maggie Jackson (Ella Fitzgerald), who sings "Hard Hearted Hannah" at Fat Annie's roadhouse and illegal distillery over in Kansas. Pete and Maggie aren't as close as they were on radio, but they're still friendly; when he's really jammed up she'll sing a "Pete Kelly's Blues" (as a nondiegetic orchestra swells up behind her trio). But when a meeting of bandleaders is called at Fat Annie's to address gangster trouble, only whites are represented. Kansas City was in fact a wide-open town where booze flowed freely during Prohibition, and musicians could generally play what they pleased. But black musicians also knew the downside of working for the mob. The white leaders buckle under, but they'd have had more clout if they'd reached across the color line.

Even so, Kelly is more connected to African American sources than he knows. A prologue begins at a New Orleans funeral in 1915 (shot on location downriver in Lafitte, with a NOLA church choir and a band led by cornetist Teddy Buckner—which plays slow at the graveside and in celebration heading back to town). The deceased is an (unnamed) early jazz master, whose cornet Pete will later win in a crap game.

Radio-Kelly looked into other people's problems, but in the movie the trouble is his own. Hood Fran McCarg muscles his way into the job of band manager, taking a criminal 25 percent cut. Even worse, he installs his singer girlfriend with the band. Rose Hopkins is played by Peggy Lee, so the character can sing. She does the 1926 hit "Sugar," Arthur Hamilton's "He Needs Me" (first performed by Meredith Howard as Maggie on radio), and a bit of 1924's "Somebody Loves Me," but Rose has a drinking problem and doesn't even want the gig. Loud audiences rattle her. Peggy Lee's fragile flat-affect singing style is perfect for the character, presumably why Webb sought her out. (His pitch: "It's not glamorous and we'll deliberately light you poorly.")[19] Her only previous screen role was in a jazzless 1953 remake of *The Jazz Singer*. Webb shot her scenes in sequence, to help her stay in character, and Lee is convincingly zonky. She taps into her own struggle with performance anxiety, and she'd seen the effects of alcoholism up close, in her first marriage.

Real jazz musicians had gangster problems. Earl Hines got stalled in Chicago after the scene had shifted to New York because he couldn't break a contract; Al Capone wanted him around. Musicians in similar binds computed the odds and gave in. So, reluctantly, do Kelly and most of his men—all except clarinetist Al Gannaway (Lee Marvin), who heads East to work for ex-KC leader Jean Goldkette, and drummer Joey, who stands up to them with fatal consequences. (His unnamed replacement is a true innovator for 1927; sitting in before joining the band, he keeps time on his ride cymbal, ahead of his time.) The gunmen who nail Joey are a credit to their profession. Pulling up at the end of the alley behind the club, they instantly recognize him, at night, in the rain, while his back is turned. Maybe Pete shouldn't have yelled "Joey! Look out!"

McCarg's out of control, smashing glassware and abusing Rose. But Kelly doesn't take action until Al Gannaway comes back to town—he swings by after a gig in Wichita, 200 miles away—and shames him for not seeking justice for Joey. As Al reminds him, we were soldiers once. We learn Pete's mouthpiece has an origin story too; it belonged to a felled World War bugler. The law is of no use, so Pete resolves to gather evidence against the bad men. (Federal agents can't even locate Fat Annie's, despite its flashing electric sign. An ostensibly honest local cop—wheezing Andy Devine—expects Kelly to do his job for him.) Pete starts asking too many questions, and the bad guys set a (pointlessly elaborate) trap for him at a darkened downtown ballroom—complicated by the arrival of spoiled flapper Ivy, who's been chasing Pete all through the picture. McCarg gets shot, order is restored, and Kelly goes back to gigging with the Big 7, now blissfully singer-free. (Rose has lost her mind, sits in a madhouse, binking on a toy piano, and clutching a faceless ragdoll. It's

FIGURE 4.3 A rowdy crowd rattles singer Rose (Peggy Lee) in *Pete Kelly's Blues.*

Lee's big scene, in which she also introduces the new song "Sing a Rainbow" in a faraway voice. She got an Oscar nomination for Best Supporting Actress.)

Anyone who's seen *Dragnet*'s Joe Friday lecture a hippie knows Jack Webb's screen persona could be a humorless scold, but there are moments when Webb signals via a pleasant grimace that Kelly may occasionally be enjoying himself. It's as if jazz fan Webb took his trademark staccato delivery and swung it just a little. What's missing, for a Webb production, is that quotidian workaday detail—unless you count an early scene that shows (under dialogue) what goes into a bottle when a flush customer orders bootleg champagne, or a scene where drunks drown out the band, spooking Rose. We never see the Big 7 rehearse, and Kelly doesn't talk through any solo routines before they play.

Four years later a TV version lasted half a season, recycling some radio scripts. William Reynolds played Kelly, still ghosted by Dick Cathcart. It aired in spring 1959, a few months before the show that brought the crime-fighting jazzman up to date, *Johnny Staccato* (discussed in chapter 5).

The Benny Goodman Story (1956; 156 minutes; director/writer: Valentine Davies). Cast includes: Steve Allen (Benny Goodman), Donna Reed (Alice Hammond), Herbert Anderson (John Hammond), Hy Averback (Willard Alexander), Sammy Davis, Sr. (Fletcher Henderson), Berta Gersten (Dora Goodman), Robert F. Simon (Dave Goodman), Shepard Menken (Harry Goodman), Douglas Evans (Kel Murray), Fred Essler (Prof. Schoepp), Jack Kruschen (Murph Podolsky), Dick Winslow (Gil Rodin), Wilton Graff (John Hammond, Sr.), Barry Truex (Benny as a teen), Buck Clayton, Ziggy Elman, Lionel Hampton, Harry James, Gene Krupa, Helen O'Connell, Kid Ory, Ben Pollack, Teddy Wilson (themselves).

—Benny Goodman learns to play clarinet in Chicago, puts together a band in New York, and scores his first major success in Los Angeles. His music thrills the public, but he has trouble connecting with the woman he loves.

After the success of *The Glenn Miller Story*, Universal bought the lapsed rights to Benny Goodman's life. Since *Sweet and Low-Down* days, Goodman had hoped for a biopic, and he'd enjoyed *Glenn Miller* even as he marveled at its making dramatic hay out of voicing a clarinet lead over saxophones. "They could build a whole movie around a stupid little saxophone sound," Goodman imperfectly recalled. "I wouldn't have believed it if you had shown me the script, but they did it very well."[20]

Goodman's own romanticized story, shot in 1955, came at an opportune moment for the clarinetist. He had no regular band at that time, and the year before had embarked on an ill-fated tour where he and co-headliner Louis Armstrong had butted heads. Comedian Steve Allen (then the pioneering host of late-night's *Tonight!* show) was cast in the lead. Goodman would ghost his character's many solos, a chance to show he still had it. The soundtrack re-created more than a dozen of his orchestra, trio, and quartet performances. The star-studded studio band included Gene Krupa, Teddy Wilson, Lionel Hampton,

Harry James, Buck Clayton, and guitarist Allen Reuss, who'd sideline to their own prerecorded parts.

For his screenplay, director Valentine Davies (who'd cowritten the *Miller Story*) drew heavily on *The Kingdom of Swing*, Goodman's 1939 autobiography written with Irving Kolodin, the source for almost everything in the script about his early life, music, and career. The script isn't exactly accurate, but does tick off a lot of real details. We see that Benny came from a large, struggling family living on Chicago's Francisco Avenue. Father Dave, a tailor, did the food shopping, and couldn't afford fresh milk for his large brood. But he obtained musical instruction and instruments for three of his boys, including tubist Harry and clarinetist Benny, who'd go on to study with eminent Franz Schoepp, formerly of the Chicago Musical College; movie-Schoepp even assigns Benny the right Baermann and Klosé practice exercises.

The parallels between book and screenplay continue. While still in knee pants, Benny gets his union card and does his first gigs for promoter Murph Podolsky. He's so young that when he shows up early, another musician tries to kick him off stage, thinking he's a kid messing around. (In the book it's Bix; in the film, saxophonist Gil Rodin.) A Podolsky outfit splits a bill with a prominent African American jazz musician, whose band catches young Benny's ear. He works so often that when mama gets pregnant yet again, Benny can contribute to the family fund.

Through Podolsky sideman Rodin, Goodman gets drafted into a new band Ben Pollack is organizing in Los Angeles. (It's the Pollack band Glenn Miller joined—and on screen, its lone trombonist is a Jimmy-Stewart–skinny guy with wire-rim glasses, two cinematic worlds converging.) Teenage Benny is still growing, and grows out of his stage clothes; a montage marks the passing of time by how far his shirt cuffs stick out. And while he's building his rep with Pollack, Dave Goodman dies, struck by a car.

In time (in book and film), Pollack's band works a gangster joint in Chicago from which they extricate themselves, bound for New York. There Goodman does studio gigs, and hangs out at the Trombone Club with other proponents of "hot music." (The word "jazz" barely comes up in the movie.) He meets wealthy go-anywhere jazz advocate John Hammond, who'll later coax Goodman into playing the Mozart clarinet concerto at a soirée at the Hammond family manse, inviting a few jazz musicians to make Benny feel more at home.

In the film as in life, Goodman has a nebulous dream of leading his own band, and (in 1934) he assembles an outfit to pursue and win a spot on NBC's Saturday night radio show *Let's Dance*, opposite (sweet) Kel Murray and (Latin) Xavier Cugat; as Krupa points out in the movie, they have to pre-audition just to land an audition. Very soon after, Goodman gets a boost when the great if sporadically successful black bandleader Fletcher Henderson starts arranging for the band, which includes Rodin, Harry Goodman now on string bass, and Krupa on drums.

When that radio gig ends, with help from agent Willard Alexander, Goodman's band embarks on a cross-country tour, where they meet some resistance from audiences and promoters. At Elitch's in Denver, they aren't even allowed to play their own repertoire, and (fictional embellishment) they get the same injunction at the Palomar Ballroom in Los Angeles. But there the band's fortunes turn. (The film doesn't give the date—August 21, 1935—of one of the most famous engagements in jazz history, the symbolic birth of the swing era.) If we're gonna flop, says Benny, let's do it playing our own stuff. Their hot music captivates the crowd. The dancers gravitate to the bandstand, just listening, and wanting to get a look.

As the movie shows, that Palomar booking is so successful it's extended, and is followed by a long residency at the Congress Hotel in Chicago. Other triumphs follow: an enormously successful stand at the Paramount theater in New York, where fans pack the place from the first morning show (Stan Getz takes a solo), and jitterbug in the aisles; movie appearances; a major concert at Carnegie Hall with Goodman's band and selected guests. At Carnegie (in the film as in life), the orchestra opens with Edgar Sampson's "Don't Be That Way," and plays the Harry James feature "Shine"; there's a lighthearted throwback to jazz's early days on a dixieish "Sensation Rag"; and a long "Sing, Sing, Sing" featuring a Goodman-Krupa duet. That concert ends the film, and arrives late in *The Kingdom of Swing*, which was written later that same year, 1938.

Also, somewhere in there (as in the book), Goodman brings his immigrant ma Dora and one of his brothers east. He also plays at a party with pianist Teddy Wilson, which leads to the formation of the Goodman trio with Krupa, which sometimes appears on the same bill as the orchestra. That trio then spawns a quartet with Lionel Hampton, after Benny hears him at a Los Angeles sailors' dive, the Sunset Cafe, where Hamp held down a few jobs.

The movie gets all that right, plus a few things not in the book—chiefly, that Benny courted Hammond's sister Alice, despite mother Goodman's reservations. John had first introduced the couple in 1934, but then Goodman had forgotten all about it by the time they met again five years on. (In the movie he's forgotten her two scenes later—they have the same conversation twice, a Beckett touch.)

Yet for all that, Goodman biographers call it "a travesty" (James Lincoln Collier) and "absolutely dreadful" (Ross Firestone). "The story is patently false," Firestone adds, and indeed, like most any biopic, this one botches or blithely disregards umpteen details, while shuffling the chronology. *The Benny Goodman Story* braids two stories—his rise from the old neighborhood to landmark success, and his mismatch romance with socialite Alice—as if they'd happened at the same time. But the real Benny and Alice became involved in 1939, a year after Carnegie Hall. That was when she'd returned to the States from England, where she'd been married to a peer and had had three kids—all airbrushed out of the film. She isn't mentioned in *The Kingdom of Swing*.

Davies's screenplay ingeniously/brazenly layers one timeline over the other, thereby replicating the romantic trajectory of *New Orleans*, but with a better concert at the end: the lovers can't get together until his music is vindicated on her stage. The obstacle here is mostly in Benny's head. Neither Alice nor her aristocratic dad care—they never even allude to Benny being Jewish. But Goodman can't forget what her brother John had once told him: Alice's idea of a real musician is someone who plays Carnegie Hall. And indeed father Hammond's reservations about how swing music whips up young people will melt away at that big concert, where he'll tap his feet to Krupa's beat.

The romance plot lets Davies face and defuse a problematic aspect of the Goodman story: his personality, or lack of one. "I never was much of a hand for talking about things I like," Goodman says in his book, telling how Jack Teagarden thought Benny hated him, the way he'd stare at him on stage: giving him what sidemen dubbed "the Goodman ray." (Sometimes, but not always, he was just absentmindedly looking in their direction.) He'd also bristle when lesser musicians tried to give him direction: "I got to be known as a difficult guy to handle in some circles." That's fair self-criticism. Musicians told many stories at his expense. Zoot Sims was once asked what it was like playing with Benny in Russia: "Every gig with Benny is like playing in Russia."[21]

In the film he gets along fine with his musicians; Gil Rodin sticks with him through the whole picture. Goodman's poor communication skills let the screenwriter (and Steve Allen) off the hook—no big speeches about finding some elusive sound. "I have a few ideas, I don't know if they're crazy," Benny says. "They're musical ideas, I can't put them into words."

Davies transfers the socially awkward, even chilly side of Goodman's personality onto the love story. Growing up so fast as a musician, he never learns how to talk to girls; we barely glimpse his sisters. When Rodin fixes up teenage Benny (Barry Truex) with a blind date between sets, she laughs at his knee pants and he storms off, less embarrassed than indignant. In the previous scene, on a bandstand for the first time, we had just seen how calm he can be under pressure. Rodin: "Just take it easy, don't let it worry you." "It doesn't." Later, when he's about to play Mozart, Alice tells Dora he doesn't seem nervous. "No, he isn't." But soon after that, when Alice criticizes Benny for taking a schlocky waltz gig, he storms away—from her and then the band, when leader Kel Murray gets high-handed with him.

When Benny first meets Alice, and they're alone a minute, he gazes at the ceiling and puffs out his cheeks, unable to make small talk. When they repeat some of the same dialogue at their second meeting—Alice consciously, Benny unaware—it barely goes better. Much later, after Alice travels cross-country to his Palomar opening, she waves to him from her table. From his reaction shot you can't tell if he's even seen her. But that same night he blows off a bunch of autograph-seekers to hang with her, telling them he'll see them outside in a minute. (He doesn't.) Still later, back in New York, Benny and Alice meet for a drink, and he tries to muster the nerve to propose—but he has a rehearsal in 10 minutes.

Critics knock Steve Allen's performance—he'd had little acting experience—but he effectively channels his own awkwardness into the character, making Benny almost likeable. (And he gets to do a little nervous comic shtick, dealing with a Chicago gangster who turns out to be from the old neighborhood.) Allen even learned to play clarinet, coached by Goodman-freak Sol Yaged, who also ghosted Benny in spots; Allen looks pretty authentic, fingering the Mozart.

The film is better than most at catching styles of earlier eras. The re-created Ben Pollack music is far more faithful in rhythmic feeling than, say, Vince Giordano's 1920s jazz on HBO's 2010–2014 *Boardwalk Empire*. (That's understandable; Giordano is six decades farther from the source.) But ghosting his younger self on clarinet, Goodman makes no attempt to be historically accurate. Rather than re-create his comparatively rough early style, he shows what he can still do now. In the film—improbably, for a Chicago musician circa 1926—Goodman has no inkling of jazz until he plays opposite trombonist Kid Ory's outfit. In life, Benny's Podolsky band once split a bill with Lil Armstrong, Louis's wife, who was available to play herself. But Ory was an early jazz hero who'd been living in Chicago in 1926, and the most prominent New Orleans revivalist in Los Angeles, a favorite of Orson Welles. And the filmmakers may have balked at giving a woman this initiating role.

Young Benny is mesmerized when he hears Kid's take on "Original Dixieland One-Step," especially, oddly, the third strain where Ory plays straight melody. Benny stands transfixed, close enough to risk getting thocked by Kid's slide. As the band continues, Benny asks, "That solo, did you make that up as you went along?" Yes, Ory tells him, about playing that written passage—because he's an actor reciting his lines, no matter how dumb, or because Ory the character is pulling Benny's leg. A moment later, Kid will identify Georgia-reared Fletcher Henderson as a New Orleans baby like himself. Much later, Ory will pop up (with Fletcher) to tell Benny, "You have the best band I've ever heard anyplace." It's like a scene in a western when a real Indian tells a white actor "You beat us fair and square."

The 1926 Ory makes jazz sound simple: "You just swing on out and play the way you feel like." "Playing the way you feel," Benny muses, already streamlining what he gets from black musicians. It's all new to him, so Kid fills him in on New Orleans, Fletch, Louis, and Joe Oliver. That seems to clarify everything, somehow. "Say, do you mind if I sit in?" Benny asks, already talking like a jazz musician. And then he's magically playing like one: in the idiom, rhythmically fluent, swerving around the other horns, intuiting his way into the whole elaborate instrumental vocabulary, like Goodman's own Prof. Magenbruch in *A Song Is Born*. At the fade, Ory elbows him gently—not bad, son. (On "Sensation Rag" at Carnegie later, Benny will flash back to this epiphany, still drawing on it.)

In life, Goodman didn't sit in with Lil Armstrong that night and doesn't seem to have played with Ory or any African Americans so early. Where 1945's *Rhapsody in Blue* eliminated Gershwin's Harlem contacts, *Goodman* writes in Ory to clarify the music's black roots—a sign perhaps of a postwar shift in Hollywood's/white America's thinking about African Americans, and a better understanding of jazz roots. As enabler, Kid is like an uncomplicated Art Hazzard.

Not that Ory teaches Benny anything else. As Franz Schoepp had said (like Hazzard or *Syncopation*'s King Jeffers), "To play like that, no one teaches you. You come born with this." Benny had the gift. But before turning pro, the real Goodman had come up listening to jazz on record and jamming with other young musicians after picnics or parades. He was learning the grammar of melody and rhythm and embellishment even before he met the Austin High Gang, those young white Chicagoans obsessed with the new black music. The Austinites are represented here only by their ally Krupa, who first turns up in New York, chewing gum and cracking wise like an overgrown Dead End Kid. (With the aging Krupa and Ben Pollack playing themselves, you miss how young these players were when they arrived.)

As in most any biopic or literary adaptation, characters get combined or eliminated, not always for purely narrative reasons. To head off potential lawsuits, living people had to sign off on being portrayed—a process sometimes colored by their current opinion of a film's subject. By the mid-1950s Benny had strained relations with old ally and now brother-in-law John Hammond, who rightly objected to his role in Goodman's career being minimized—there's nothing about him producing the clarinetist's early records or getting Fletcher Henderson to write for the band. In the film, Henderson volunteers his services after hearing Benny on the radio.

As the love story heats up, Hammond (Herbert Anderson, who has the right lean look) is around just to keep Alice company while she listens to Benny. (Donna Reed spends a lot of screen time seated, all ears as he sends her romantic messages through his clarinet.) Goodman's agent Willard Alexander (Hy Averback) mostly delivers chunks of exposition: "The deal is closed for the Congress Hotel, and it looks like you're booked solid with one-night stands all the way from here to Chicago." And: "Say Benny, just ran into Wynn Nathanson, he's come up with a great idea. How would you like to give a concert at Carnegie Hall?" (His diffident reaction: "I don't think so. We're doing all right." Goodman had in fact been initially cool to the proposal; Nathanson had worked for impresario Sol Hurok.)

Neither Hammond nor Alexander cared for early scripts in which they'd been merged into a composite character (under either name). They signed off, Hammond wrote later, only after the screenwriters managed to sketch "barely recognizable versions" of them.[22] John and Alice's mother, a Vanderbilt, still alive in the 1950s, is never referred to; their father had died so his character was fair game. On screen, father Hammond squires around his cousin Mrs. Vanderbilt. Many musicians who were key to Goodman's success are never mentioned, and like *Glenn Miller*, the *Goodman Story* all but writes singers out of the big-band story; we sometimes hear only the instrumental beginnings or endings of vocal numbers. Goodman's old pianist Jess Stacy was to appear and play in the Carnegie sequence at least—he would have been the only returnee from *Sweet and Low-Down*— but when he reported for duty Benny ticked him off, and the money wasn't that great. So Stacy quit, to be replaced on screen and soundtrack by Teddy Wilson—exposure that resparked the latter's slumping career.

In life, the African American Wilson played only in Goodman's trio and quartet. Those combos helped break the color barrier for performing jazz bands, which were racially segregated in the mid-1930s. But Goodman's big band was then still all white. The film even gives his orchestra a second black member, Basie trumpeter Buck Clayton, originally brought in to play on the soundtrack. (He'd been on that Carnegie concert.) Deep-dimpled Clayton was ridiculously handsome, so Davies inserted him into Benny's band on screen and threw him a line or two of dialogue. Buck asked the director why he hadn't hired, say, Cootie Williams, the black trumpeter who'd passed through Benny's band in the early 1940s. "Ah, what the hell," Davies told him. "It doesn't make any difference."[23] Davies took that credo to heart; in *The Benny Goodman Story*, jazz capital New York isn't much of a jazz town. For Davies like other biopic writers, if you get the broad strokes right, you can fudge the rest. He weaves variations around themes and incidents from *The Kingdom of Swing*, with knowing glances at *New Orleans* and *The Jazz Singer*.

The most fanciful distortion: In his book Goodman tells of going (on a tip from Hammond) to see Lionel Hampton at the Sunset Cafe, a rundown sailors' hangout where Hamp was "director of the orchestra, producer for the show, arranger for the band, M.C. for the floor show, and general handyman" as well as drummer and vibraphonist.[24] Goodman liked what he heard, and brought Krupa and Wilson down the next night to jam. In the movie, this landlocked South Central joint is relocated 18 miles south to the San Pedro waterfront, and Benny's entourage, just off the boat from a benefit at Avalon on Catalina Island, has stopped in for a bite. Hamp (playing himself) is the bartender, waiter, chili chef, emcee, and the entertainment—it's a bit demeaning to Hampton, who seems not to mind. Goodman, Wilson, and Krupa all sit in before the vibist can finish a tune, spontaneously creating the quartet's classic arrangement of "Avalon."

FIGURE 4.4 In *The Benny Goodman Story*, vibraphonist Lionel Hampton gets acquainted with pianist Teddy Wilson and Benny (Steve Allen).

The list of details unimportant to Valentine Davies is a long one: The Goodman boys got their first instruments at the local synagogue, not Hull House (where they studied a bit later); brother Freddy was given a trumpet, not the more photogenic French horn. (The elder brothers, testing tuba and horn, briefly and unwittingly free improvise together.) Benny's sister, not father, got him his first tux; it was Pollack, not Goodman, who got the band out of their Chicago contract; Benny's mother didn't live with him in New York; of the musicians depicted in the film, the only one at that Mozart recital was Fletcher Henderson, absent here because in the movie he hadn't met Benny yet; the trio didn't start splitting bills with the big band till later than depicted, and so on. Just typing this list feels nitpicky. Davies may be right that none of it matters.

And yet the screenplay takes time to acknowledge (twice) how Dean Kincaide's and George Bassman's early arrangements helped set the band's style, and it credits Edgar Sampson with writing "Don't Be That Way." But it gives the impression that Eubie Blake's "Memories of You" and Gordon Jenkins's mournful "Goodbye"—Goodman's closing theme—were both Benny's creations. The latter is depicted as a spontaneous outpouring from his teenage heart. He plays it on Chicago and New York rooftops, when he needs to be alone.

Davies can be deft, showing rather than telling, and staging big sequences. When the Goodman band headed west toward the Palomar Ballroom, after tepid receptions at a few (but in reality, not all) of its stops coming across the country, the band clicked in Los Angeles, apparently because the hot stuff they'd played on radio late at night in New York hit West Coast college students in prime time. Davies illustrates the point in a montage that precedes Palomar triumph. It's Goodman's last set of the night in the radio studio in New York, just before one a.m., and four clocks on a wall cue us to the time zones we crossfade to. On the East Coast a kid listens while turning in for the night; in the Midwest where it's almost midnight, a couple cuddle on the couch to the music; out in Mountain time, a mere three couples dance at a ski lodge, as if things wrap up early out there; but on a California campus it's barely 10, and party time. The kids are all dancing to "Stomping at the Savoy," announced as a new Fletcher Henderson arrangement (because he's just entered the story), though it's by Edgar Sampson.

When the band finally reaches the Palomar, and Benny resolves to play their hot stuff no matter what, Davies doesn't have the crowd erupt (that comes later, at the Paramount). He gives the sequence a slow build; it's mostly shot from behind the band, the camera facing the dance floor, which is empty as they start their first hot number. A few couples straggle out, and as the players take their solos, the floor slowly begins to fill. It's about two-thirds full when Buck Clayton takes a chorus. (It's all proper ballroom dancing—no crazy jitterbugging.) There's a cutaway, and when we come back, the floor's packed. And then, a little less slowly, folks stop dancing and converge on the bandstand like ants on a picnic—just as Goodman had described it in his book. Even so, Benny doesn't grasp what it all means till he hears the cheers at the end.

It's nicely done. Except that the tune that gets everybody's juices flowing, that night in 1935, is Count Basie's "One O'Clock Jump" as arranged by Basie in his characteristic style, two years before its first recording, before Count's band had broken out of the Midwest, before Goodman—or pianist Wilson, here channeling Basie—knew that fleeter Kansas City style even existed. In the story, Benny's already recorded it. So it goes in biopics. As in his *Glenn Miller* script, Valentine Davies pokes fun at genre conventions. "I'm only Dave Goodman," Dad helpfully declares in the opening scene. And: "What am I? A cutter in a pants factory." Benny's so headstrong, people keep telling him, "Don't be that way"—Schoepp, Teddy, brother Harry (twice). What else could he name that new Edgar Sampson tune? (Never mind that Chick Webb had been playing it under that name for years.)

Removing the synagogue from the young Benny's history plays down his Jewish background, but the film doesn't completely erase it: Dora tells Alice, "You don't mix caviar with bagels." Krin Gabbard rather overstates the parallels with *The Jazz Singer*—it was Dave Goodman who pointed Benny and his brothers toward secular music, after all.[25] But then the parallels pertain more to the hero's mother love. Gabbard misses one explicit callback, to the scene where Mama Rabinowitz visits her son backstage in New York, and is bewildered by his blackface visage—a cultural leap too far for mom. Here, when Dora visits Benny backstage at the Paramount, where he's a smash, she doubts his cultural loyalties. She fears losing him not to black culture but to the Protestant upper crust—like Goodman's real mother, apprehensive about her own fate as Benny began moving in different circles.

The real Goodman was not quite so hopeless with women; he'd had a string of girlfriends, and might have proposed to his singer Helen Ward if he hadn't thought marriage a bad career move. Movie-Benny would be lost if his horn didn't demonstrate his capacity for human emotion. "My poor Benny," Alice says, when he's typically flummoxed. "So many things he wants to say—and no clarinet to say them." When she'd complimented him for putting so much feeling into that concerto, he'd told her "That wasn't me, that was Mozart." But when he plays "Memories of You" as a love song to her, and she tells him it sounds like spontaneous Mozart (it doesn't), he says, "That wasn't Mozart, that was me." Not Eubie Blake? But even this hash is the screenwriter riffing on Goodman, in *The Kingdom of Swing*, commenting on how jazz and classical make different demands on players. In the latter, "All the time you're trying to get back to what Mozart had in mind, while in the music we play, when someone plays a solo, he tries to put his own ideas across."[26]

The Carnegie Hall finale ties up the loose ends. Besides the recreations of tunes from the actual concert mentioned earlier, including that "Shine" where band star Harry James (seen only at this concert) shows off what he learned from Armstrong, the film includes three numbers not heard that night, notably "And the Angels Sing," actually from the following year. It's the only appearance by a Goodman singer—Martha Tilton, who sang it on record—and by trumpeter Ziggy Elman, whose celebrated solo was based on an old Jewish freilach (though due to lip trouble he was ghosted by Mannie Klein). Its inclusion tacitly but pointedly asserts Benny's Jewishness.

You'd think his mother in the fourth row would appreciate this declaration of cultural loyalty in the home of WASPy high culture, but she seems not to notice. She's always turning around to see if Alice is going to show up before the show's over, because now Dora wants her for Benny. As Goodman spies the newly arrived Alice hugging his mother, he starts playing "Memories of You." Don't worry, Dora tells her, now he'll propose. "He's asking me now," says Alice. Goodman's music has rescued him from his awkward self.

St. Louis Blues (1958; 105 minutes; director: Allen Reisner; writers: Robert Smith, Ted Sherdeman). Cast includes: Nat King Cole (Will Handy), Juano Hernandez (Rev. Charles Handy), Eartha Kitt (Gogo Germaine), Pearl Bailey (Aunt Hagar), Ruby Dee (Elizabeth), Cab Calloway (Blade), Mahalia Jackson (Bessie May), Billy Preston (Will as a child), Ella Fitzgerald, Constantin Bakaleinikoff (themselves).
—W. C. Handy's fiancée and preacher father take a dim view of the bluesy songs he writes, and the sultry singer who performs them. Will flees Memphis, leaving them all behind—until a big New York concert reunites everybody.

Paramount's 1958 W. C. Handy biopic *St. Louis Blues* flips the music-born-in-a-bawdyhouse script of Handy's own 1929 Bessie Smith short of the same name. Here Handy gets his first inkling of booty rhythm in church. Its star, singing pianist Nat King Cole, had made a few films, and had won praise for his performance in Samuel Fuller's recent Vietnam drama *China Gate*. Beyond that, he radiated warmth as a stage performer, the biopic would be packed with good and great songs for him to sing, and Cole knew Handy casually.[27] But starring him in a feature was a gamble. In 1957 when the film was shot Cole was preoccupied with his acclaimed but struggling weekly TV variety show— where he was more animated than he'd get as Will Handy.

In truth, his acting range was narrow. Cole had even given a wooden performance as himself in *The Nat 'King' Cole Musical Story* (1955). An 18-minute wide-screen color short with Jeff Chandler's narration bridging the narrative gaps, it's a condensed biopic; a few historical incidents are encrusted in fanciful detail. The opening scene set in 1940 dramatizes a press agent's canard that Nat had started singing when a barroom drunk badgered him into crooning "Sweet Lorraine." In fact he'd sung a bit from the start of his professional career, and began doing more when the public responded. (He first sang on record in 1938.)

In the short, manager Carlos Gastel (Ray Walker) happens to be in the house that fateful evening, and the next night he brings along the head of the biggest label on the West Coast, one Ben Evans—a stand-in for Capitol exec Johnny Mercer. Both scouts declare their intention to sign Cole on the spot. A different drunk wandering by dubs him "King Cole," a nickname his new partners run with; Nat gets his best career advice from barflies. He then records "Straighten Up and Fly Right" for his new label—it was in fact his breakthrough at Capitol, in 1943, shortly after signing with Gastel and Mercer. (In life Cole had known both for years; he'd recorded two Mercer songs in 1938.)

A hits-and-headlines montage whisks us along. When we drop back in, Evans has no time to listen to Cole's new recording "Pretend"— "Pretend you're happy when you're blue"—because he's too preoccupied with all the paperwork Nat's success generates. (This inattentiveness may be meant to shed light on the singer's well-publicized tax troubles.) The label exec quashes any talk of Nat taking a vacation while the dough rolls in—especially now that Cole's booked into Carnegie Hall for Easter. But the non-stop pace has given Nat ulcers, and after a backstage physical, his doctor forces him to cancel. Nat himself informs the audience before going to the hospital. (All that is pretty accurate—he was headlining a 1953 package tour, and had done the first show before offering apologies at the second). Laid up, Nat's down, but "Pretend" is released while he recuperates, and its positive message proves a tonic to its singer. (In fact it was already on the charts when he got sick.) Cole comes back bigger than ever. The narrator praises him for staying humble, and on stage Nat thanks the public for its "warmth and gracious acceptance"—as close as the *Musical Story* tiptoes to racial issues. (There's nothing, say, about resistance to his family breaking the color line in LA's Hancock Park.) In the final scene Cole's quartet is joined by an orchestra, and the tuxedoed singer performs his 1955 hit "Darling Je Vous Aime Beaucoup" standing up, away from the piano, the one-time jazz musician transformed into a pop star.

Cole is no natural on camera, but Handy had a rather stiff demeanor himself for the father of the blues, and in *St. Louis Blues* the character's/star's unease feels utterly authentic. It's the chintziest-looking 1950s jazz biopic. Director Allen Reisner mostly worked in TV, and that pedigree shows in the uncrisp black and white photography and all-too-familiar backlot streets. It was shot in 22 days.[28]

The script discards the arc of Handy's life to revive the outmoded *Jazz Singer* paradigm: A son who's gotta make his own music defies a stern religious father. There's a direct callback when a member of Dad's congregation (Mahalia Jackson) rats him out for working at a music hall. The script is credited to journeyman Ted Sherdeman (whose other biopics include *The Eddie Cantor Story*) and producer Robert Smith (who'd written an early draft of a long-gestating Red Nichols biopic).

They had plenty to work with. Handy's 1941 autobiography *Father of the Blues* is thick with filmable vignettes, as Will makes his way from barnstorming minstrel to Memphis songwriter to New York industry mogul. In St. Louis in 1893, down and out and hungry, he spied the prettiest women he ever saw, and (as recounted earlier) heard another mutter, "My man's got a heart like a rock cast in de sea." Many years later, on a deadline, he rents a room down by Beale Street and composes "St. Louis Blues" in 24 hours—drawing on that muttered line, the three-line stanzas he'd been hearing in Mississippi blues country, and that habanera rhythm he'd heard in Cuba, on the trip when his wife Elizabeth told him she was pregnant. Later there's a fracas at a parade when some rebellious musicians try to hijack his Memphis band. The threat of violence is ever-present as Handy crisscrosses the Deep South, encountering a few colorful (often racist) maniacs, including one who kidnaps the band so they can play "The Last Shot Got Him" as he shoots a foe—a plan ultimately thwarted.

Father of the Blues is best remembered for a vivid origin story cited in umpteen blues histories, a key musical anecdote of the twentieth century: the moment when a schooled musician discovers the power of the unschooled. It's 1903, and 30-year-old cornetist and budding composer Handy has already been all over North America and is now running a band out of Clarksdale, deep in Mississippi's blues-soaked Delta. Waiting for a train one night in Tutwiler, Handy dozes off and awakens to the sound of a slide guitarist playing "the weirdest music I have ever heard" and singing a three-line chorus about "Goin' where the Southern cross the Dog"—meaning the place, 40 miles south, where the Southern railroad intersected the Yazoo Delta line, aka the Yellow Dog.[29] It was the moment the blues caught Handy's ear, though it had been at the periphery of his notice for years. He'd use that enigmatic line in "Yellow Dog Blues" a decade later.

Two pages farther along, Handy gets another music lesson. His nonet is playing a dance in the Delta when the locals inquire if a hometown string trio might play a set. "They struck up one of those over-and-over strains that seem to have no very clear beginning and certainly no ending at all"—music Handy thought beneath his own more Europeanized stuff. But then the trio was showered with more money than Handy's band was making all night. "Then I saw the beauty of primitive music," he'd write with disarming candor. "That night a composer was born—an *American* composer."[30] He'd learned to follow the money.

That movie practically writes itself, but there's barely a whiff of it in the actual *St. Louis Blues*. A more faithful version would have cost much more, and would confront racial issues this film ducks. Instead the screenwriters deploy *The Jazz Singer* as an enduring template to weave a tale upon, a useful form rather like the blues itself. But by 1958 that 1920s plot was played out, whereas the blues endures.

Krin Gabbard has argued that the parallels to Jolson's Jackie Rabinowitz render movie-Handy in *St. Louis Blues* functionally white. (Not Jewish?) It's misguided criticism, like the notion that *The Cosby Show*'s Huxtables were functionally white because they were well-off, well-spoken, and owned many sweaters. *St. Louis Blues* places Handy squarely in an early twentieth-century black community where, as in life, preachers exerted great moral authority over those whose lives revolved around the church, and where (as in *Broken Strings*) some middle-class folk abhorred jazz and blues as raunchy symbols of what they'd risen above or put behind. There are only five white actors with (mostly brief) speaking parts in the film.

The story in a nutshell: Will Handy wants to write songs drawn from working-class vernacular, but his preacher father believes them to be the work of the devil. Eventually those songs find a wide audience with the help of (fictitious) singer Gogo Germaine. But Rev. Handy is unyielding—and Will's fiancée Elizabeth has her own reservations—until Gogo conspires to get Handy's people to New York's Aeolian Hall where a symphonic "St. Louis Blues" caps a program of orchestral classics for a highbrow white crowd. In life, Handy's father did take a dim view of his son's secular music until he heard Will with a touring band. Dad liked the music, and that ended their rift—in the 1890s, over a decade before Handy wrote his early hits.

We've seen biopics fudge chronology, streamline stories, invent characters, get little things right and big ones wrong, but few do all of the above as aggressively as *St. Louis Blues*. Even so it's very entertaining, not least because there's so much great music. This composer's biopic features many of Handy's blues hits and a lesser-known ballad (1931's "Chantez les Bas," plucked from obscurity by Louis Armstrong for his 1954 album *Plays W. C. Handy*), plus the lovely hymn "Morning Star," with Mack David's new secular lyric. The diverse singers on camera include comic entertainer Pearl Bailey, slithery Eartha Kitt (as Gogo), and gospel star Mahalia Jackson; Harlem's Ella Fitzgerald turns up in Memphis singing "Beale Street Blues" as herself. As actors, Bailey and Kitt also hold their own beside Juano Hernandez (as Handy's peevish unyielding pa) and Ruby Dee (as Will's fretful fiancée Elizabeth), leaving Nat Cole little heavy lifting to do. The cast is so overstuffed with singers that big band shouter Cab Calloway (as a shady club owner) and future pop star Billy Preston (at age 11, as young Will) don't get to sing a note. (Cole, Bailey, and Kitt all recorded Handy tie-in albums.)

A locator card establishes that our story begins in Memphis, "near the turn of the century," with Will as a boy. The real Handy turned 27 in 1900, by which time he'd made up with his father, married, and toured North America and Cuba with Mahara's Minstrels. He'd actually grown up in Alabama and hadn't yet moved to Memphis. The opening scene is a quasi-improvised soliloquy by Pearl Bailey in the role of Will's (fictitious) Aunt Hagar, as she makes her way down the street on a Sunday morning, bound for church. She volubly reacts to everything she sees, including a couple of tipsy gents belatedly concluding Saturday night services at P. Wee's saloon; Hagar recognizes one as the husband of a fellow churchgoer. On this Sunday, the choices are clear—God's work or worldly mischief. Hagar's searching for nephew Will, and finds him on the street: Will blows softly on a cornet (bought secretly for $2.50), accompanying a work song grunted out by sack-hauling laborers. They sing an abbreviated version of "Goin' to See My Sarah," which Handy had heard roustabouts and coal miners do in his travels, and had transcribed from memory for a 1926 folio he edited, *Blues: An Anthology*. The original is 16 bars, here truncated to 12 to better approximate a blues chorus—not that anyone in this movie stops to analyze blues form. The word "blues" barely comes up except in song titles.

Hagar confiscates the boy's cornet, and they head to the Rev. Charles Handy's Methodist Episcopal church, where Will plays organ. Hagar and Mahalia Jackson's Bessie May sing a spirited "Heist the Window, Noah," rocking in place to (and helping inspire) Will's spontaneous syncopated fills, till the reverend, who can't find the beat, shuts them down, accusing them of turning a hymn into an occasion for "evil jigging." He glares down from the pulpit at Will, who looks back through the lattice of the organ's ornate music holder. As they're walking home Rev. Handy exhorts him to aim higher, but even at that moment, Will is distracted by vulgar street music. Then father discovers the cornet—"There's only two kinds of horns, Gabriel's and the devil's"—and tosses it under a wagon's wheels, which crush it the way a taxi crushed Rick Martin's horn. And then (lest the symbolism escape you) young Will shrieks, and shrinks into a fetal position, doubled over in psychic pain, clutching the damaged pipe.

FIGURE 4.5 Young Will Handy (Billy Preston) jazzes up his church organ in *St. Louis Blues*.

Something vaguely like this happened, minus the symbolic emasculation. Young William saved up for a guitar, which his father made him return, and a few years later he secretly bought a $2.50 cornet. And Charles Handy did tell his son something very like what he tells him here: "I will follow your coffin to the grave, before I see you become a maker of music for the devil!"[31]

Years pass—12, maybe? Even for a biopic, *St. Louis Blues* is slippery with elapsed time. Only one scene's date can be fixed, to 1920, courtesy of a headline proclaiming the arrival of Prohibition, but that's later. For now, cars have replaced horses, and the adult Handy has completed his schooling and entered into a seemingly endless engagement. (The real Will and Elizabeth married not long after they met.) He mentions having traveled with a minstrel show on summer vacation and making it to San Francisco.

And yet little else has changed; Will is back on the organ bench on Sundays, haunted by that squashed cornet. Rev. Charles Handy still despises secular music, and Aunt Hagar still runs his house, mediating between father and son. The real Handy had no Aunt Hagar—his mother died after he left home—but he did write "Aunt Hagar's Children," which acquired a lyric about a blues-loving church lady. Here churchgoing Hagar gets to preview "St. Louis Blues" as Will plays it for her. Hagar sings from the sheet music, dancing around the room, and adding some Pearl Bailey running commentary.

In life, Handy was a professional musician for many years before he got his first break. On screen he gets it the summer he returns to Memphis from teacher's college—the real Handy had no such schooling—when he's asked to write an election campaign song. The

1909 melody the real Handy wrote for Edward Crump's Memphis mayoral campaign was so catchy, folks made up their own ribald words, so he wrote an official lyric. He published it three years later as "Memphis Blues," his first sheet-music hit.

On screen, the reform candidate Handy backs is one Sheriff John Baile, and Will is asked to write both words and music for a campaign song. (This happens at P. Wee's saloon, where Handy stashes his horn—the real Pee Wee's was an informal musicians' hiring hall, and Handy did in fact begin work on "Mr. Crump" there.) Yet no one bothers to sing his lyric when Handy's brass band takes the tune to the street, where it attracts dancing, second-lining fans who follow them to a political rally. His on-screen band includes some jazz-film familiars: Red Callender on tuba or bass, Teddy Buckner on cornet, and clarinetist Barney Bigard. The drummer is sometime Cole sideman Lee Young, Lester's brother. We hear but don't see a rhythm guitar.

When movie-Will writes new noncampaign lyrics for that song, the tune is revealed as Handy's 1914 "Yellow Dog Blues." In the story, Will lifts its opening phrase from a rising and falling five-note work song he overhears—found art, like Gershwin's car horns. That borrowing is almost the only reference to appropriated (folk) material in Handy's works, aside from this declaration: "The music I play is the music of our people; it's not mine, it's theirs." The substitution of one Handy tune for another does let us hear that line about "goin' where the Southern cross the Yellow Dog," albeit devoid of context. But the real reason for the swap-out is that Handy had been conned into signing away the rights to "Memphis Blues," which acquired new lyrics after he'd sold it. It was a sore point ever after.

Will rewrote Baile's campaign song at the instigation of imperious Gogo, who's looking for good tunes and knows one when she hears it. She's based at the Big Rooster cafe, where she can barely draw flies with what she's singing now—although the number she sings so drearily before meeting him is in fact Handy's 1926 "Friendless Blues." Gogo is a modern woman, defying convention. Eartha Kitt oozes surly, dangerous sex appeal, and Gogo isn't above using it to get what she wants from Handy or the Big Rooster's chiseling owner (Cab Calloway). But she doesn't lead Will on. Don't fall in love with me, I can only love myself, she tells him when they duet on "Careless Love." (In the film he wrote this nineteenth-century song, instead of just copyrighting an arrangement.) Gogo tells Will she's from St. Louis, where there are lots of pretty girls. "They lost one when you went away," he drily observes. It's Cole's only suave moment when he's not singing.

In Handy's song the St. Louis woman is a tart, and in any other movie Gogo would lead him astray. But in the end she engineers Handy's reconciliation with his estranged people. Gogo just wants Will to be the best songwriter he can be—for his sake and for hers. Her honorable behavior is a defense of show folk: that flashy woman may look like she's flirting with your man—that's certainly how it looks to prim Elizabeth—but that's just the crazy business they're in. It's Gogo who brings Handy's songs to New York, who records them and spreads the word. Her billing as "Queen of Jazz" (according to one poster) suggests the character owes something to the Empress of the Blues who'd recorded "Yellow Dog Blues" and "Careless Love" as well as "St. Louis Blues." But Eartha Kitt doesn't shout like Bessie Smith; she purrs.

"Yellow Dog Blues" is a hit at the Big Rooster. We segue from a run through with the campaign lyrics to a performance with Handy's actual words, save that his "easy rider" becomes a more chaste "easy timer." The audience at the black-run Rooster is white; Handy often played for white audiences in Memphis. But this early triumph turns to ashes. When the song gets recorded, he doesn't get a dime. *Father of the Blues* tells a long convoluted tale of how Handy got conned into signing away the rights to "Memphis Blues." It was decades before he knew the full story, and any sane screenwriter would bypass that mess. Here Will sells "Yellow Dog Blues" in a straight deal when approached by a white lawyer, but fails to read the contract. The film gets this right: he made $50. When money starts rolling in for songs he does hold on to, Will like the real Handy is surprised how big the checks are. He tries to reason with his father once more: "My music can't be all evil if a big company will sell so many records, they pay me $900."

Will tries to pacify his father by using royalty money to buy the family a piano, like mother had always wanted. He warms it up playing "Morning Star" for surrogate mom Hagar, but the reverend, returning home mid-song, rebuffs him anyway, like Cantor Rabinowitz stopping the celestial "Blue Skies" in *The Jazz Singer*.

In *St. Louis Blues*, once Will turns to full-time songwriting he never touches the cornet again, and turns into a singing pianist very like Nat Cole. (Handy had sung in a vocal quartet and played organ when young, but was never a singing pianist.) Like Handy, Cole was the Alabama-born son of a minister who hated jazz and the idea that his son might become a musician instead of preacher or teacher, but who later made peace with his success. Cole, like Handy, had dealt with numerous racist indignities, and had impetuously sold the rights to his first smash ("Straighten Up and Fly Right").

The film highlights those parallels, blending actor and subject—it was the young Cole, not Handy, who got called out by his father for jazzing up his church organ and who played hot music on the sly while living at home. Late in the film, when Handy leaves Memphis to hit the road in a song montage, he starts out solo, then plays with a lithe combo before moving on to an orchestra, attracting larger and larger crowds as he does—recapitulating Cole's trajectory after *he* left home in 1937. And as in life and *The Nat 'King' Cole Musical Story*, he has a medical setback. Like the real Handy at age 49, Will goes temporarily blind—in reality from an infected tooth, in the movie because he can't bear his father's disapproving glare. (Juano Hernandez is as implacable as he was forgiving in *Young Man with a Horn*.) Will gets his vision back when he returns to playing in church and starts writing hymns—just as Handy wrote that his blindness turned him back toward spirituals (though he started writing them in earnest only in his sixties). In *St. Louis Blues*, when Will's vision comes back in church, it's a miracle. The first person he sees is his father, through the organ's lacy music rack, a callback to the film's opening sequence. That's as close as Allen Reisner gets to a directorial flourish.

But Will can't be happy giving 25-cent piano lessons to bored students—shades of *Broken Strings'* frustrated Arthur Williams. That's when he reluctantly hits the road, leaving his father, Hagar, and Elizabeth behind. When the real Handy left Memphis, in 1918 at age 44, he settled in New York. There, he would write in his autobiography, he was welcomed by the fraternity of African American composers, fended off new swindlers using old tricks, and built up his music publishing house (with a couple of partners unmentioned in the film). Then it all collapsed when Handy went blind. He slowly recovered two years later, and rebuilt his business.

One night, and not for the first time, Handy recounts in his autobiography, he treated a slumming white man to a Harlem tour. This one turned out to be an investor, one Robert Clairmont, who went on to finance a Handy evening at Carnegie Hall. That 1927 concert featured 60 voices, 30 musicians, and organist Fats Waller on "Beale Street Blues." (When Clairmont lost everything in the Crash, Handy sought him out and helped him.) Paul Whiteman and many others worked up symphonic treatments of "St. Louis Blues," arrangements Handy likened to a fieldhand plowing in a tux. He heard reports that the song was played all over the world. Those symphonic evenings point the screenwriters toward a version of the stock jazz-film ending: a big concert for a white audience legitimizes the hero's music as it brings estranged lovers together. In jazz movies, white audiences validate black performers, and vice versa.

Gogo swings through Memphis on her way to an engagement in St. Louis, looking for Will. When she finds out he's vanished, she sneers at proper Elizabeth for fixating on his new hymns: "Unless he's free to love his kind of music, he's not going to be free to love you or anyone else." Religion is not a force for good in *St. Louis Blues*. Before it's over, Gogo will call out the reverend for being an anti-blues bigot, when they finally meet and he looks her up and down. "That's right, reverend, stick to your guns," she advises, "because prejudice is a time-saver." The word stings him, but she presses on: "A busy man like you, you can form an opinion without wasting time bothering about facts."

She tells him this in New York. Charles, Elizabeth, and Hagar have journeyed to Manhattan's Aeolian Hall—where *Rhapsody in Blue* premiered—in hopes of finding still-missing Will. The evening's Haydn, Mozart, Mendelssohn, and Handy concert is sold out, so the family sits in the wings. Hagar doesn't know how to behave in this world and keeps getting shushed. Before the "St. Louis Blues" finale, Russia-born Hollywood conductor Constantin Bakaleinikoff gives it a warm introduction, testifying to its international reputation—and throwing in the old chestnut that jazz and blues are America's only true art form, while everything else comes from Europe. (You'd think Hollywood would know better—what about the western?) When we played Handy's song abroad, Bakaleinikoff says, the audience stood up, mistaking it for our national anthem.

These are the facts Gogo spoke to Charles about, and now he and Elizabeth get the picture: not only are the blues respectable, but Will is the reason why. Then Gogo walks on stage to emote the title tune, heard in a modern horns-and-strings arrangement by Cole ally Nelson Riddle; the sleek backgrounds on the tango section anticipate his *Route 66* theme. As she's wrapping it up, the concert's surprise guest—Will, of course—emerges from his dressing room, straightening his black tie, too blasé or nervous to catch the whole number. Will and family are mutually surprised. Charles and Elizabeth embrace him, now that Will's art has been approved by Bakaleinikoff. There's nothing left but for the composer to step on stage to sing an abbreviated reprise of his most famous song in yet another orchestral version, with lots of brass shakes. Handy vows in verse that he'll love his baby till the day he dies, and for once looks like he means it.

The real Handy died at 84, 10 days before the movie premiered.

The Five Pennies (1959; 117 minutes; director: Melville Shavelson; screenplay: Jack Rose, Shavelson; story: Robert Smith). Cast includes: Danny Kaye (Red Nichols), Barbara Bel Geddes (Bobbie Meredith/Willa Stutsman Nichols), Tuesday Weld (Dorothy Nichols), Susan Gordon (Dorothy as a child), Harry Guardino (Tony Valani), Bobby Troup (Artie Schutt), Ray Anthony (Jimmy Dorsey), Shelly Manne (Dave Tough), Ray Daley (Glenn Miller), Bob Crosby (Wil Paradise), Louis Armstrong (himself). New songs: "Follow the Leader," "Lullaby in Ragtime," "Good Night—Sleep Tight" (Sylvia Fine), "The Five Pennies" (words Fine/music Salve d'Esposito, adapted by Fine).

—Cornet player Red Nichols builds a highly successful band, and tours so much he neglects his young daughter. But when she contracts polio, Nichols gives up his career to care for her. Years later, can he mount a successful comeback?

For all their nonsense, biopics offer some remedial education; the Miller and Goodman stories, for example, did credit the largely forgotten Ben Pollack for giving our heroes an early break. And casting Ben as himself reminded folks he was still around—though neither film sparked a Pollack revival. Late in 1954, in the wake of *Glenn Miller* and with the *Goodman Story* in the works, the biopic of an increasingly forgotten pioneer was announced: cornetist and bandleader Red Nichols.

In the 1920s, Nichols had been one of the most recorded jazz musicians, an expert sight reader who played on (and organized) hundreds of record dates under a blizzard of pseudonyms (Midnight Airdales, Charleston Chasers, Six Hottentots . . .), giving early employment to, among many others, Goodman, Miller, the Dorseys, Krupa—all the white biopic bandleaders. He's namechecked in the *Glenn Miller Story*. But by the 1930s Nichols's fame had faded as fashion passed him by. He'd attracted little attention since, though in the mid-1950s he started recording for Capitol. His band the Five Pennies was on screen all of six seconds in the 1950 Mickey Rooney noir *Quicksand*.

One reason Nichols had fallen off the radar: Even old associates had little use for him. Eddie Condon, Mezz Mezzrow and Max Kaminski all dinged him in their memoirs. Red was a martinet and didn't like it when the playing got too rowdy. Kaminski (whose book came after the film) describes a brief New England tour: "Nichols loathed us and we returned the compliment." Condon disparaged his playing. "I know a dozen guys who can play twice as good," he recalled claiming in 1927. The main problem, for Condon: "The music is planned. Jazz can't be scored."[32]

True, Nichols liked to arrange what other New Orleans or Chicago style bands might prefer to work out without discussion, or on the spot—but so did Jelly Roll Morton on his Hot Peppers classics. Nichols combined novelty and lightly skipping rhythm on tunes such as "Delirium." And he and trombonist Miff Mole, his partner in many formations, had a ready bond. On cornet Red was no Bix Beiderbecke, but was still pretty hot. He had no signature hits, but the film would work around that with a (mostly) fictitious repertoire, though we do briefly hear his theme "Wail of the Winds" a couple of times.

The project got rolling when Paramount commissioned a 10-page treatment, called "Intermission," from *Quicksand* screenwriter Robert Smith. Reporting on the fledgling production in her newspaper column, Hedda Hopper (mis)informs us, "Red was top of the heap when his little girl contracted polio and he gave it all up to spend his time nursing her back to health." She touted William Holden for the role. Nichols had in fact dropped out in 1941, when gigs were few, to work Bay Area shipyards and to tend to his daughter, before returning to music in 1944.[33]

The kid-versus-career melodrama was at the heart of *The Five Pennies* when it came out five years and as many scripts later, but by then it had been transformed into a star vehicle for irrepressible Danny Kaye—a redhead, like the film's subject. In the end Robert Smith got a story credit. The screenplay was by director Melville Shavelson and producer Jack Rose, but to a great extent the film's guiding light was Kaye's wife and creative director Sylvia Fine, who bent the story toward his strengths and wrote a few songs that had little connection to Nichols's actual music: workmanlike vehicles for the singing, mugging, dancing star, flawlessly playing the role of compulsive extrovert Danny Kaye. (Three of those songs have the same chords, so they can be superimposed, including the title tune, whose melody resembled the Italian pop song "Anema e core" enough to invite a lawsuit; Fine settled.)[34]

The most lightly tedious 1950s jazz biopic, *The Five Pennies* gets some things right, starting with the size of Red's ego. He was indeed from Utah and his real name was Ernest Loring Nichols. He did play cornet—Nichols ghosted Kaye—which his father had taught him to play. He did move to New York in 1924 (when the film begins) and before too long met Louis Armstrong, who preferred a looser style. (But Red didn't meet Louis, or his future wife, the night he arrived.) Nichols did lead small bands and then bigger ones, sometimes employing Miller, Jimmy Dorsey, Artie Schutt, and Dave Tough. Red's wife, stage name Bobbie Meredith, really was born Willa Stutsman. (She was a dancer; in the film she sings too.) Nichols was riding high in the 1920s, but later when Miller and Dorsey were big, few remembered him. He and Willa had a daughter, Dorothy, who was stricken with polio (as a teenager, not a small girl). Red dropped out, worked in a shipyard, then made a comeback with his own band. At the comeback gig, Dorothy hit the dance floor without a cane, to her father's surprise. That is about it for accuracy—or Red Nichols appreciation.

The jazz plot, such as it is, is mostly recycled, from *The Glenn Miller Story* especially. There's the first boss's hostility to his young hire's new ideas, a trip to the pawnshop in lean times, tires spinning in mud as the band goes from gig to gig (who maps these ill-advised shortcuts?), an obsession with arrangements, and an encounter with Louis Armstrong in a luridly lit Harlem juke joint. Red's bills-paying commercial gigs include a Russian Cossack act, as in *Second Chorus*—that other story radically rewritten for its musical-comedy star. Even the daddy-I-can-walk final scene, at Red's comeback gig, echoes Arthur's miraculous recovery in *Broken Strings*.

In its way, *The Five Pennies* champions the arranger's art even more than Miller's tale. Although many jazz movies declare the imperative to play the way you feel, in jazz as in the movies there's a countervailing tendency: to nail down something elusive when you get it right. Jazz thrives on that tension, between freedom and form, the spontaneous and the fixed, and on the inspirational feedback loop between improvisers and composers. But classic studio movies were rarely improvisation-friendly; here Kaye created continuity problems by improvising new details in different takes of the same scene.

The Five Pennies itself makes a bold case against improvisation. Early on, Red, new in New York and newly, vocally drunk in a nightclub, tries to sit in with Louis Armstrong. But once Pops warily assents, Nichols asks, where's the sheet music?

Armstrong: "Man, nobody writes down dixieland. You just let it happen."

"Suppose it happens great one time and you'd like it to happen exactly the same way, what do you do then?"

"It's like tapping a nightingale on the shoulder, saying, 'How's that again, dickie bird?'"

Undeterred, Nichols passes out his arrangement of "The Battle Hymn of the Republic," a refreshing alternative to "Dixie." He just happens to have the written parts in his pocket, including one for himself, but he proves too snockered to play. He retreats in disgrace, to the men's room, apparently for a restorative purge. Then, not least to prove his abilities to his skeptical date Willa (Barbara Bel Geddes, in a plummeting follow-up to *Vertigo*), Red mounts his second assault. In a lull between numbers, he blows a solo chorus of "Battle Hymn" from the back of the room, softly at first, with some blue notes thrown in—the black ladies at a nearby table pay heed. While Red was in the john the musicians must have speed-read his chart. They don't have the music in front of them, but as he makes his way to the bandstand, they fall into playing what seems to be Nichols's now vindicated arrangement; there's a corny/dramatic upward modulation in the middle. Pops improvises some "Glory Glory" vocal obbligatos behind Red's solo before they swap phrases, Red on his father's silver cornet—the horn passed down, generation to generation, like Pete Kelly's—and Pops on shiny trumpet. Selmer instruments get a plug in the opening credits. (In 1924 Armstrong was in fact in New York playing with Fletcher Henderson, whose big band is hinted at only by the presence of alto saxophonist Bill Greene—last seen on clarinet with Ella Fitzgerald in *St. Louis Blues*—added to Armstrong's usual All-Stars sextet.)

By the time the tune's over, the two face each other, Pops all the way on stage, Red with one foot still on the steps: not quite Armstrong's equal, but (in his own mind at least) getting there. Red gets the ultimate jazz movie accolade: a white improviser is validated by approving black listeners. (White ones like him too.) As he scoops up a now-willing Willa on his way out, Armstrong quips, in a callback, "He caught the nightingale."

FIGURE 4.6 Trumpeter Louis Armstrong welcomes cornet newcomer Red Nichols (Danny Kaye) in *The Five Pennies*.

You would think, from context, "Battle Hymn" was one of Nichols's early hits. He did in fact record it a few times, starting in 1946, 22 years after this scene is set. (For the film, most jazz numbers were arranged by Nichols saxophonist Heinie Beau, who plays on the soundtrack.)

The next time we see Armstrong at least six years have passed and probably more, making it the 1930s. In that decade Pops fronted orchestras, but in the movie he sticks with his dixieish All-Stars. By now he and Red are friends, and Louis has to twist Red's arm to get him to sit in on the last set of a night. (Nichols has brought his young daughter along—Mom's away and Dorothy can't sleep.) The primacy of the composed over the improvised is once again asserted, as they scat-sing and perform some Sylvia Fine patter over "When the Saints"—transparently imitating a big Armstrong–Bing Crosby number in *High Society*. (We will get to that.) The saintly doggerel honors the greats who've gone before: not improvisers but classical composers—the guys who want it to sound the same way every time.

"Do you dig Rachmaninoff?"

"On and off."

"Rimsky?"

"Of course-akov!" There's a nod to Fats Waller, but only to rhyme with Mahler. Say this for *The Five Pennies*: the soundtrack sessions occasioned the only recordings to feature Nichols and Armstrong together.

When that number is done, Pops gives his guest a warm endorsement: "The greatest horn in the country, Loring Red Nichols!" Having him make this claim is not quite as demeaning to himself as it seems. In fact Armstrong did lavish exorbitant praise on other musicians; in the 1930s he'd called several horn men "the best trumpet player in Europe."[35] Red tells Willa later, "I'm not the greatest horn in the country, he is. But in a little while, maybe I could be."　⸰

He never was, though. By the 1930s competition would be too stiff, and more modern. But that aspiration spotlights movie-Red's constant need to keep his ego fed (sweeping his family along or aside as necessary). His pet saying: "Pretty soon you'll all be working for me." Even in that early sequence, when Armstrong is singing on stage, drunk new-in-town nobody Red does a loud bad Pops impersonation from his seat, and won't be shushed—everything's all about him. Later he even lies to Willa about Dorothy beating him at poker; he claims she cheated, but she'd bluffed him.

The real Nichols's active recording schedule and engagements in Broadway pit bands mostly kept him close to New York. But the movie's Five Pennies is a barnstorming band on a perpetual college tour. (Subheadline in a montage: "Five Years on Road and Still Climbing.") Despite the hellish schedule the lineup is remarkably stable, including Glenn Miller, Jimmy Dorsey, Artie Schutt, and Dave Tough—the last three played by trumpeter Ray Anthony, pianist Bobby Troup, and drummer Shelly Manne. No one mentions Miff Mole. These Pennies are a song-and-dance troupe, not an arranger's jazz band. Their set piece is Sylvia Fine's "Follow the Leader," sung by Red, Willa (ghosted by Eileen Wilson), and the Pennies' fictitious tenor saxist turned manager, the very New York–Italian Tony Valani. He, Red, and Willa had all been together since early in the picture, when they worked for soft-spoken but privately nasty crooner Wil Paradise (Bob Crosby, doing a malicious take-off on brother Bing, cut with a little Jolson).

When Willa mulls leaving the act to raise Dorothy in a proper home, Red says, "What, and leave me alone on the road for 10 months?" So they put the tot in boarding school, and resume touring. In a follow-the-map montage sequence, in Denver Red now has a larger 12-piece band, with Tough/Manne all over the drums on "Out of Nowhere," about the only indication that the swing era is upon us. But by the time they reach Nashville, they're back to playing dixie warhorse "That's A-Plenty," and the band seems to have lost two trumpeters. Perhaps they'd been fired for upstaging Red, same reason Wil Paradise had sacked him. While Mr. and Mrs. Nichols see the country, missing Dorothy's birthday and major holidays, she goes out in a cold rain when she's already sneezing and subsequently starts showing symptoms of polio—an illness not caused (as the movie seems to imply) by pregnant Willa's over-enthusiastic dance-floor bouncing, or by Dorothy riding buses, staying out late, skipping breakfast, or getting rained on.

The film's tone is perversely inconsistent. It's a sick-kid melodrama, but also a family frolic, with lots of cute stuff between Kaye and nine-year-old Susan Gordon as little Dorothy. But it's not all kid stuff. The night Red meets Willa, she's all over him in the taxi when they leave the club after "Battle Hymn," prelude to Red's lewd toothpaste squirting on their soon-to-follow wedding night. (In that early nightclub scene Armstrong arrives on stage bathed in sweat, as if he'd just rolled out of a hot bed, but that wasn't an attempt to sex him up; the crew had given up drying him off between takes.) At times, you may sense a more serious picture buried several script revisions below this one: a dark tale of a driven career couple wracked by guilt. (*Was* it the dance-floor bouncing?) But Red and Willa are not plagued by introspection. When Red suffers, it's because little Dorothy blames him, not because he blames himself.

An obvious biopic rule: when the hero is played by a stylish entertainer, the subject takes on attributes of the actor. Cornetist Nichols becomes manic, singing, dancing, double-talking, mugging Danny Kaye just as cornetist Will Handy became silky singing pianist Nat Cole. Even little Dorothy, stuck in the sick kids' ward, gets worn down by her father's need to be the center of attention, leading the other kids in song. (Subtext: Danny and Sylvia's daughter plays one of those kids.) It's as if Danny Kaye is as deaf as his character to how overbearing the guy is.

But Red has already decided to give it all up. In a scene echoed three decades later in *Bird*, he chucks his Selmer horn off the Golden Gate Bridge. (This never happened.) Then Hitler invades Czechoslovakia (that makes it 1939), and Red takes a job in a wartime shipyard. Little Susan Gordon grows up to be Tuesday Weld (at 15 playing 14) for the last act.

When that takes place is hard to say. Glenn Miller keeps turning up in civilian clothes, and he enlisted in 1942 (and disappeared in 1944). Adding to the confusion, Dorothy's friends come off like 1950s teenagers, who find their parents' music hopeless or comically out of date. When their ringleader checks out Red's old records and asks, "Is he hip enough to have some Benny Goodman or Jimmy Dorsey here?" he might not be paying those guys a compliment.

It's so long since Dorothy was a cute kid, she no longer remembers why her father quit music, or how good or famous he was, or who his sidemen were, and her friends have never even heard of the Five Pennies. Red, incensed, tries to set them straight: "There was Bix, and there was Louie, and there was me," he yells. "And that was it!" He picks up his horn to show them, but he's out of practice, blows clams, and gives up in defeat. The kids shuffle out: "Is he always like this?" Oh my, yes.

In the end, Red has to be talked into a comeback, starting all over on his horn. It looks like no one's gonna show up opening night. But wait! There's Armstrong, Jimmy Dorsey, Glenn Miller, Artie Schutt, and Dave Tough arriving en masse to sit in and launch this comeback right. (Only Jimmy was among the actual celebrity well-wishers that night.) And Red dances with Dorothy, as mom looks on, reprising the sappy title song. Then Red and Pops and company reprise "Battle Hymn" in the modulating Nichols arrangement, vindicating his repeatability concept.

It's all a bit of a mess. When a friend grumbled to Nichols later, Red replied, "It's Hollywood—what did you expect?"[36] Even so, *The Five Pennies* prompted a real Nichols comeback—he was busy in his final five years. And he landed a brief movie appearance as himself later in 1959, in the decade's final jazz biopic.

The Gene Krupa Story (1959; 101 minutes; director: Don Weis; writer: Orin Jannings). Cast includes: Sal Mineo (Gene Krupa), Susan Kohner (Ethel Maguire), Susan Oliver (Dorissa Dinell), James Darren (Eddie Sirota), Celia

Lovsky (Mother Krupa), Shelly Manne (Dave Tough), Bobby Troup (Tommy Dorsey), Red Nichols, Anita O'Day (themselves).
—Swing drummer Gene Krupa lets success go to his head, and lets the woman who loves him slip away. But after he's framed on a marijuana charge and hits rock bottom, she's there to help him climb back to the top.

By the late 1950s, Hollywood was eyeing a new audience. *The Glenn Miller Story* had catered to nostalgic swing fans. Five years later the black-and-white *Gene Krupa Story* targeted teenagers. Star Sal Mineo had been James Dean's pal in *Rebel Without a Cause*; Gene's made-up sidekick Eddie Sirota is played by new heartthrob James Darren—the love interest in *Gidget* earlier in the year. He sings the 1939 ballad "Let There Be Love" a couple of times, the first ostensibly in 1927, when our story begins. (The song had no apparent connection to Krupa; Darren would rerecord it in a mildly swinging version.)

Selling this biopic of a 1930s jazz star to teens made crazy sense. Rock music was about a big beat, and Goodman's flashy, good-looking gum-chewing drummer had pointed the way. You can trace later arena-rock drum solos straight back to "Sing, Sing, Sing." And Krupa had had teen-idol problems: too many women, success that went to his head, a media-circus drug bust—problems Hollywood could relate to.[37]

Director Don Weis mostly worked in TV, but made a minor specialty of youth pictures. He'd already done *The Affairs of Dobie Gillis* and would go on to *The Ghost in the Invisible Bikini*. Still, the story bears vestigial traces of the hoary *Jazz Singer*, though the callbacks feel halfhearted, as if everyone's seen that one enough. Pa rejects Gene's modern music, and wants his son to be a priest—but then dies almost immediately; he only speaks in the opening scene. Mama doesn't like Gene's drumming either—and objects to his playing a speakeasy, opposite a black blues singer. But Gene's biggest battles are internal.

The real Krupa had been a teenage prodigy. In the movie, his whole poverty-stricken family tells him to get real. Dad punches holes in his drumheads. How can you be so frivolous, he asks Gene: "There are men walking the streets, begging for work," as if the Depression had hit Chicago years early. By 1927, when Krupa turned 18, he'd hooked up with the so-called Austin High Gang, those precocious white musicians including cornetist Jimmy McPartland, who'd closely studied Chicago's best black and white bands. They got to record with visiting banjoist Eddie Condon that year, when many engineers still believed you couldn't record a full drum set without making the disk-cutting needle jump. But when they muffled Krupa's kit that day, it worked. The sides they cut won him attention as far away as New York.

By the time Krupa started hanging out, the Austinites had been out of school for years, working musicians with road experience. In the movie they're a quiet, youthful student band. Their eventual leader Sirota bears no resemblance to hard-drinking McPartland (who'd replaced Bix in the Wolverines). As in life, Krupa spends a year at a Catholic seminary, studying for the priesthood to mollify his mom, but he can't get his mind off the traps: "I hear an 'Ave Maria,' and my mind takes off on a syncopated version of it." So he drops out and goes back to the gang. But even by 1928, as we see, jobs for musicians were drying up—partly because talking pictures were squeezing out theater orchestras—and the migration of Chicago musicians to New York was beginning. In the movie Austin High drummer Dave Tough ("Davey" here, invariably) has already moved to New York to join Paul Whiteman. (Actually, Tough spent two years in Europe before landing in New York, and didn't work for Whiteman.) So Gene and Eddie resolve to try their luck in Manhattan too.

Tagging along is Ethel Maguire (Susan Kohner), who's always had a thing for Gene, though she started dating Eddie while Gene was in the seminary. Ethel is both drawn to and scared by his ability to tap into the primal. "It's like drums must have been when they began back there in the jungle," she'd told him: "voodoo drums making black magic, getting everybody all shook up like." You can see how he excites her—the crazy drum talk gushes out of her. (Kohner does what she can, but had a much juicier role in tearjerker supreme *Imitation of Life* that year.) Ethel even gives up her dreams of attending Juilliard and composing; she takes a job as a switchboard operator to support the boys when they can't find work in New York. But whenever she and Gene get close, some rich tramp intervenes.

The real Gene and Ethel met cute in Manhattan. He knew her voice before laying eyes on her. She was the hotel operator who placed his morning wake-up call. When someone pointed her out in the lobby, he immediately asked her out. In reality they married and divorced, and then remarried in the 1940s. In the movie, to keep things moral, they're only engaged (though clearly sleeping together: he buttons her up one morning in this most sexually frank 1950s biopic).

After months of scuffling, the musicians get a break. Davey Tough (played, as in *The Five Pennies*, by his admirer Shelly Manne) invites them to a jam session at the luxury pad of spoiled socialite Dorissa Dinell (Susan Oliver), known as DD. There Gene plays with the real Red Nichols (who's not very Danny Kaye–like) and the Dorsey brothers (the younger played by Bobby Troup, a little nicer and more soft-spoken than the real Tommy). Krupa catches their ears with a tom-tom solo that looks ahead to "Sing, Sing, Sing." On the spot, Nichols hires him for the pit band for Gershwin's (1930) musical *Strike Up the Band*.

Since she knows so many musicians, DD decides to make her own jazz record with a band that includes Eddie Sirota, Nichols, Tommy Dorsey, and a bow-tied wisecracking guitarist obviously modeled on Eddie Condon. The real Condon liked liquor, but this guy tries to slip Gene a reefer, thinking anyone who plays drums like that has got to indulge. Krupa has never even seen a joint before, and declines. On bass and saxophone are two anonymous black musicians from that earlier jam session, who never interact with the white characters off the bandstand. In 1950s movies, jazz bands are depicted, without comment, as integrating earlier and with much less fuss than in life. (The movies have yet to deal with that particular jazz story—save in *Lady Sings the Blues*.) But white musicians are always in the foreground. We never hear about Krupa's African American inspirations Baby Dodds and Chick Webb.

At DD's rehearsal, the nonet sounds all right, the singer so-so, as they run down "On the Sunny Side of the Street." But DD is all complaints, focusing her ire on (a commendably discreet) Gene: "We're not doing the zombies' mating call." She frets that "all that boom boom would knock the needle to hell and gone." So she drapes her fur coat over the bass drum. "There—now you can bang your pretty head off." The practical muffling of the drums at that 1927 Chicago session here becomes an insulting gesture—the princess kicking the commoner. They growl at each other so fiercely, it's no surprise when they fall into bed the same night, Gene standing up Ethel on her birthday. To make amends, soon after he takes Ethel to the club he's working, then blows her off to schmooze up his soon-to-be manager and the entertainment columnist Mark Hellinger. The lovers drift apart.

Biopics smooth away character flaws, especially when their subjects are alive, but movie-Gene is a heel. He's an exhibitionist on stage and off, and soon the toast of debutantes and gossip columns. He feeds on the attention, because he didn't get enough love at home. Krupa himself could look manic on stage, and Mineo worked hard to master his casual stick twirling and hunched-over, gum-chewing, grimacing theatricality. But Mineo adds an extra layer of queasy feverishness to it all, as if Krupa were fighting the flu.

There is some adolescent acting-out involved for Gene. "Who are you beating on those drums?" Ethel had once asked—it's like you're beating some devil out of them. On the bandstand, the night of the Mark Hellinger incident, we get one answer. In real life, after Krupa left the seminary, his mother supported his choices, and died not long after he landed in New York. In the film she lives on to torment him. At the nightclub, Gene is working with an integrated Sirota octet; its layered, riffing style suggests the advent of the swing era (and that trumpeter Eddie has been digging Roy Eldridge). Gene has just received a letter from mom, spurning his invitation to come east to see how well he's doing.

FIGURE 4.7 In *The Gene Krupa Story*, Gene (Sal Mineo) works out his frustrations on a letter from home.

When Eddie calls the jazz workhorse "Cherokee" (from 1938), Krupa sets mama's letter on his snare drum, and plays it to shreds—his solo so animated that a crowd gathers and chants "Go, Gene, Go!" (In some shots his crash cymbals are mounted way high, so they don't block his face from the cameras—like the real Krupa's cymbals in other movies.)

"Can you hear that, mama?" he mutters. "They're yelling for your boy. Mama, *they* approve!"

The rising-star montage soon to follow confirms it. We don't see Gene hire a publicist, but he must have a great one, judging by how often he makes the papers. An item in *Down Beat* (fine print: copyright 1942) screams "KRUPA ON WAX: FATS WALLER signs KRUPA to cut two sides this week, featuring solo drums." In fact Waller and Krupa did cut two sides together, in 1929, backing vocal quartet The Four Wanderers, sans solo drums. (No one was cutting drum solos in 1929, five years before *Down Beat* started publishing.) Here we see how jazz stories get retold in Hollywood terms—as if details of upcoming recording dates are announced in the press, covered like movie productions. The idea that Waller would have a record date mapped out far enough in advance to make a print deadline is absurd. Six months before that Four Wanderers session, Waller's label had hired Eddie Condon to get Fats to a recording date, prepared and on time. Condon did his best (he'd claim), but two hours beforehand, they still didn't know who'd play on it, or what music they'd play.[38]

Other montage items: records by Bix and Mal Hallett (misspelled) with Gene's name right on the label. (He recorded under Beiderbecke's name in 1930; he played with but didn't record with Hallett, a Krupa friend all but forgotten by 1959.) Another news item: "Latest Krupa Recordings Top Sales List." These two sides are described as "practically drum solos." Only at montage's end does he join Benny Goodman, the band that actually made the drummer a star; here it's just one more stepping stone to the top. Goodman isn't depicted (the production couldn't afford him), and we don't hear his music. But we see what playing with him does for Gene's wallet. Before long Krupa's got his own big pad with a Central Park view, hosting jam sessions like DD, living large.

Once more, the character takes on attributes of the actor. This biopic was Mineo's pet project, a chance to break out of teenage roles. He lobbied for it, learned to play drums (Krupa gave him a set), and had input into casting and script: this Hollywood star who had trouble getting his head around early success, whose self-indulgent behavior and cavorting with starlets put him in gossip columns, and who smoked marijuana. (Sal grew his own at his Laurel Canyon rental.) Depicting Krupa's growing pains was a way of working through his own.

Krupa stayed with Goodman for three years; here he's in and out of the band in no time. At one of Gene's parties, DD drops in with special guests: saxophonist Frankie Trumbauer, trumpeter Bunny Berigan, and Bix Beiderbecke, which she pronounces with a long "e" on the end, DD/Susan Oliver not knowing any better. You'd think Gene would be more surprised to see Bix, who'd been dead for seven years. We can date this scene to 1938, because it's the night Krupa decides to start his own band, immediately after hearing party guest Anita O'Day sing a languorous "Memories of You." ("Not bad, if you like talent," DD concedes.) But when Gene asks DD for a cigarette, she passes him a joint instead. He draws on it before he knows what it is. And then has a couple more hits when he does. That pot must be powerful—he starts acting like a boisterous drunk, or the hyper Krupa of *George White's Scandals*. And its effects must have lingered, because he then hires DD instead of O'Day, the real Krupa band's signature singer. (Like Dinell, O'Day had short hair and sometimes wore slacks; her cameo establishes that evil DD's not supposed to be her.)

Gene takes his 17-piece band on a long break-in tour, headed across the country. Conspicuously absent and unmentioned: its star instrumentalist, black trumpeter Roy Eldridge. (This screen band is all white.) You might think it's a movie gimmick, the players having little tom-toms by their music stands, but that was for real. (You can see them in *Ball of Fire*.) Ever the showman, Gene walks around the drum kit while playing a melodic cymbal break on "Indiana." There's a bit when he strikes the bass strings—but then he drops a stick, which gets him the fish-eye from Eddie. Backstage, Sirota tells him to rein in the partying. They argue and Eddie quits (but—editing glitch—he's back in the brass section later in the tour). Gene has in fact kicked marijuana, and thought he'd helped DD quit too, but she's relapsed.

Then, in San Francisco, a couple of narcotics cops search his dressing room and find (oddly small) envelopes containing 38 and a half reefers in his overcoat. (His valet is looking very guilty, won't meet his eye.) The real Krupa was busted in 1943, so apparently it's taken the band five years to reach the Coast. As he told it later, the weed wasn't his, but a gift from his outgoing band boy, who'd bragged about it. In the film it's strongly suggested Gene has been set up.

Sure I tried pot, but it was poison, he tells his lawyer. "That stuff not only threw my timing off, but it made my, m–my sticks kind of slippery"—a little-noted side effect. But who'd want to frame him? Could be anyone, the lawyer replies—maybe a jealous woman. Now DD's the one looking guilty. She was supposed to be the key defense witness, somehow, but now she declines to help and slinks out of the lawyer's office—and town, and the film. While Gene's still there conferring, his mother reaches him by phone. Now she's behind him—too little, too late. The movie (sensibly) simplifies the bust and legal wrangles, but Krupa did indeed serve about 90 days. Among his visitors, in life: Benny Goodman, who offered support, and ex-wife Ethel, who offered to return the $100,000 alimony she'd never spent.

In wake of the bust, Krupa disbanded and got over trying to live like a movie star. In life rehabilitation was quick: Goodman rehired him to play a two-month residency in New York, and within a month of release, the drummer headlined a successful war-bond rally. In the movie, he's a pariah, his arrest unleashing a wave of antipot hysteria. (He and cannabis did get some bad press.) He's reduced to playing out of town gigs under an assumed name—the kind of play-what's-written-or-you're-out gigs other heroes endure early in their movies/careers. Bottoming out, playing a Philly strip club, Gene looks more drugged than ever. It doesn't help his morale when the pianist who wears sunglasses indoors offers him a joint, curtly declined. "How else you gonna stand it," the guy asks. "Look at those hands—shaking like they were waving goodbye."

But just when things are darkest, there's Ethel in the audience; she's tracked him down, and still loves him, and persuades him to finally learn to read music (something the real Krupa had done a decade before, though he did study harmony in this period). On a tip from Ethel, back in New York he approaches Tommy Dorsey, who's putting together a new band—including Eddie, reviving "Let There Be Love." (Must be a while since he sang it—he needs sheet music.) Tommy digs Gene but has just hired Davey Tough, who'd in fact worked for Dorsey in the late 1930s (though the real Tough was currently in the Navy). But then Eddie has an idea. In the real world, after Krupa's stint with Goodman in 1943, Dorsey hired him for his band, unveiling him at the Paramount. When the band rose from the pit and the audience saw who was on drums, Krupa got "the greatest standing ovation of my life," which went on for minutes.[39]

In the movie, Gene's an advertised added attraction, and nervous as a cat backstage. A page hands him an envelope with his name on it, and he smells another set-up—but it's half a stick of gum: a little token of support from Ethel, literally waiting in the wings. The band's already in mid-set when he rises from the pit, pounding those tom-toms, to take his place at the front of the stage. But he's greeted by stone silence, then jeers not cheers. "Hey, Krupa, got a reefer?" "Smoke one for me!" And when Gene takes a solo on an uptempo blues—"Hey, jailbird!"—he drops a stick, and has to go crawling after it. (In jazz movies, no drummer who drops a stick ever has a spare within reach.) There's tittering from the house. He returns to the drums, defeated, silent.

But all is not lost. On his riser at the back of the stage, Davey Tough plays a little drum fill, trying to jump-start Gene. When he doesn't respond, Davey keeps going— more like Shelly Manne than the real Tough, who disliked solos and flashy technique— till Krupa dives in at last. They start trading drum breaks, with a little punctuation from the band, which eventually takes them into "Cherokee." Gene takes another solo on that, and now the fickle fans are all "Go, Gene, Go!" (Mineo did his homework—he tracks Krupa's prerecorded drums very well, while impersonating his expressions.) Gene and Davey trade two-bar phrases to take the tune out. In the 1950s Krupa played staged drum battles with the highly competitive Buddy Rich, but as this scene confirms, such faceoffs are usually about mutual respect. Davey Tough saves the day, for the kid who'd been following in his footsteps since Chicago—Austin High Gang to DD's jam session to the Dorsey band.

Backstage, when everyone's glad-handing Gene just like old times, Ethel slips away. But he follows right after her.

Someone asks him, "Hey where you goin' man, ain't you comin' to our party?"

"Thanks man, I've been to that party." One more big New York concert brings estranged lovers together.

/// 5 /// THE JAZZ MUSICIAN (AND FAN) AS CHARACTER 1951–1961

There have been jazz musician characters in many more movies than we have mentioned; Hollywood loves their colorfully seedy demimonde, and all the feeling that jazz folk put into the music, practitioners and fans alike. There are jazz haters on screen too, some of whom might be expected to know better. In their sixth and last adventure, 1947's *Song of the Thin Man*, bon vivant crime solvers Nick and Nora Charles (William Powell and Myrna Loy) land in the midst of a bunch of jazz musicians, whose slang they find impenetrable and customs ridiculous, and who keep hours too extreme even for these seasoned night owls. By now the Charleses have a child—they've entered their middle years, and put kid stuff like jazz behind them. In the 1950s, jazz folk turned up in all sorts of pictures: in film noir, musical, sex comedy, cartoon, problem picture, or rock-and-roll movie, and on TV. This chapter presents a sampling.

Drummers (like singers) are the butt of a thousand musicians' japes, and director Leslie Kardos's **The Strip** (1951) is a sort of protracted joke about a drummer's obliviousness. Mickey Rooney is Stanley Maxton, a shell-shocked veteran who only wants to play. But the brand-new drum kit he's given when he leaves a VA hospital gets trashed in a car wreck as he makes his way to Los Angeles. He never gets around to replacing it, after going to work in a bookie joint for the guy who ran him off the road. It pays better than drumming. A meet-cute with ambitious dancer and nightclub cigarette girl Janey (Sally Forrest) leads Stanley to her workplace, Fluff's Dixie Land, a smallish club on Sunset Strip where the staff all get into the act. The house band that backs up the dancing waiters features Louis Armstrong, Jack Teagarden, Barney Bigard, and Earl Hines, appearing under their own names: two-thirds of Armstrong's post–*New Orleans* All-Stars. Armstrong and Teagarden sing a bit: "Shadrack" and "Basin Street Blues." (In movies, real musicians often perform at fictional venues far below their professional standing—a topic we'll address in chapter 10.) Earl Hines needed no help, but Fluff often joins in on second piano.

Stanley's hot for Janey, who's out of his league and tells him so. She's only into guys who can help her get a studio contract. But Armstrong's drummer is leaving, and Fluff (cranky avuncular William Demarest) hears enough of Stanley trying out the house kit to offer him the gig. (Rooney, who could play, sidelines pretty well to All-Star Cozy Cole's drumming.) Fluff encourages Janey to lure him in, but then when Stanley takes the job, the proprietor warns him not to be swayed by a self-absorbed dame. Such a woman once broke Fluff's heart, which is how he came to write the ballad "A Kiss to Build a Dream On," heard in a few versions. (It's actually by Harry Ruby and lyricists Bert Kalmar and Oscar Hammerstein, from 1934.) After *The Strip* it became an Armstrong hit and a staple of his live shows.

Fluff isn't the only one who doesn't know his own mind. Or maybe Stanley's just a dope, a drummer stereotype. To curry favor with Janey, he introduces her to someone with better contacts, his ex-boss Sonny, the one guy Stanley knows who is sure to steal her away. And Stanley's all but oblivious to Fluff's sweet hatcheck girl, who throws herself at him whenever she can. Worse, it never dawns on Stanley he's landed a potentially career-making gig with Louis Armstrong. He doesn't bother to hang with or chat up any of the musicians, ignoring a peerless networking opportunity. Janey and Sonny get shot—he's dead, she's in a coma—and the cops are liking Stanley for it, till Janey regains consciousness long enough to clear him before dying. Down in the dumps, Stanley heads over to Fluff's and sits in with the band. Within eight bars he seems fully recovered; one hi-hat beat is worth months of mourning. He'll be making it with that hatcheck any minute.

Stanley wasn't the only drummer with issues. In Otto Preminger's 1955 **The Man with the Golden Arm**, adapted from Nelson Algren's novel, Frank Sinatra is Frankie Machine, Chicago jazzman who can't stay off heroin. ("I thought I could take it or leave it alone.") He learned to play during a six-month stint at a prison hospital—like Stanley in *The Strip*, he's given a drum set on release—and thinks he's ready to put dealing cards behind him and get hired by a big-time orchestra. He joins the musician's union, full of hope. (How he paid the initial dues when always short of cash is unexplained.) But he also thinks he can stay clean.

He doesn't. Eventually, strung out and in need of sleep and a shave, Machine auditions for Shorty Rogers's Los Angeles big band, which for some reason is looking to replace rhythm ace Shelly Manne in Chicago. (The real reason: the film was shot in Hollywood.) But once behind the drums to sight-read a wailing chart with the band, Frankie's a mess. He holds his sticks backwards, misses a cue to come in, drops a stick while Rogers counts off the tempo a second time, moves his lips as he counts through the beats of a six-and-a-half-bar rest, and then loses control of his hi-hat, splashing like a waiter spilling soup. (Drummers love this scene, as comedy: slippery sticks had indicated a drug problem four years before *The Gene Krupa Story*.) After that, Frankie skulks out in disgrace, not saying a word—he's in and out of the rehearsal room in under two minutes. As he's leaving, Manne replaces him at the traps and kicks off the same tune at a faster tempo, as if annoyed he had to listen to this clown.

FIGURE 5.1 Drummer Frankie Machine (Frank Sinatra) bungles an audition in *The Man with the Golden Arm*.

If only Frankie's unhinged wife had let him practice more in their dingy apartment (or he'd had a practice pad to work out on, as in the book). "There must be a million drummers play better than you do," she'd told him, only a little unfairly. Even the guy hammering the beat at the strip club down the corner sounds better.

Later on the day of that failed audition, Frankie's ex-squeeze Kim Novak persuades him to go cold turkey, and she locks him in her room. This scene is Oscar-bait for Sinatra (who got nominated for Best Actor). Frankie gulps water, scurries like a caged rat, breaks the bed, shakes himself off the mattress to roll around the floor, pounds on the door, smashes a chair . . . When Novak comes to check up on him, she turns on the radio to drown out the noise, and by chance the very piece he'd flubbed at the audition is playing. In his autobiography *Straight Life*, saxophonist and longtime junkie Art Pepper testified, "The agony of kicking is beyond words. It's nothing like the movies, *The Man with the Golden Arm*, or things you read: how they scream and bat their heads against the wall. . . . That's ridiculous. It's awful but it's quiet. You just lie there and suffer."[1]

High Society (1956; 112 minutes including overture; director: Charles Walters; screenplay: John Patrick, from Philip Barry's play *The Philadelphia Story*). Cast includes: Bing Crosby (C. K. Dexter Haven), Grace Kelly (Tracy Samantha Lord), Frank Sinatra (Mike Connor), Lydia Reed (Caroline Lord), Louis Armstrong (himself). New songs: "High Society Calypso," "Little One," "True Love," "You're Sensational," "I Love You, Samantha," "Now You Has Jazz," "Mind If I Make Love to You," "Who Wants to Be a Millionaire?" (Cole Porter).

—Rhode Island songwriter Dexter Haven aims to prevent his ex-wife from remarrying, the same weekend his houseguest Louis Armstrong is to perform at Newport's jazz festival.

Frank Sinatra stuck to singing in the following year's *High Society*, MGM's glossy musical remake of 1940's *The Philadelphia Story*, about a guy who wins back his ex-wife just as she's about to marry again. (The main characters aren't even renamed.) While it was brewing, MGM had also been developing a film about the Newport Jazz Festival, the event, started in 1954, that would spawn myriad outdoor summer shindigs from the Monterey Jazz Festival to Woodstock. Folding that abortive film into the remake, the setting was changed to Rhode Island's summer playground of the idle rich. Dexter Haven (Bing Crosby) is one of the sponsors of Newport's unnamed jazz festival (which unlike the real one lasts only one night), and is putting up friend Louis Armstrong's band while they're in town to headline. Dexter's icily regal ex-wife Tracy (Grace Kelly) lives next door and is remarrying the next day—a plan Dex intends to thwart. Sinatra plays a gossip-sheet reporter, in town to cover the wedding, who further complicates matters.

Dexter comes from money (grandpa's) but is a professional songwriter. When his marriage fell through he wrote the hit ballad "I Love You, Samantha"—that's Tracy's middle name, what he always calls her. He wears his heart on his sleeve like Irving Berlin with his lovelorn lyrics. (Dexter also wrote the piano opus "Choo Choo Mama," sadly unheard.) The songs are actually by Cole Porter, writing for the three most influential male singers in twentieth-century pop. Crosby and Sinatra sing two love ballads each to Kelly, and Sinatra and Crosby have a patter-song duet ("Did You Evah," the lone Porter oldie), but Louis doesn't sing with Sinatra. (They had done so before, reading blues lyrics from cue cards on a 1952 *Frank Sinatra Show*.)

Armstrong and band function as a Greek chorus, laying the plot exposition on us at the top, by singing "High Society Calypso" as their band bus rolls into Newport. "End of song, beginning of story," a very red-eyed Pops tells the camera. He's smoking a conspicuous cigarette. His All-Stars joke about how they're out of place in this tony setting. Like Smoke in *Young Man with a Horn*, Armstrong is both inside and outside the story, addressing the audience directly. The band provides romantic background music within the narrative. When Dex on his patio starts making up the love song "Little One" for Tracy's smitten kid sister, Pops and company, rehearsing nearby, softly pick up the tune. When it's over, Pops mutters, "Right song, but the wrong girl." His occasional comments suggest he's watching the movie along with us; he knows things his character doesn't witness. Tracy's heart softens toward Dex when she hears Armstrong's version of "I Love You, Samantha" floating over from next door; he's played it to prime the pump. "Now we're gettin' warm," Louis says afterward. MGM house director Charles Walters had wanted to make more of Armstrong playing Cupid—to make him the kind of character later tagged a "Magic Negro"—and the lyric to that opening calypso hints at such a role. But Walters didn't get his way.[2]

That evening, there's a long, ultimately drunken pre-nup party, where Dexter and Louis—his name properly pronounced, with a sibilant *s*—do a little special material. In "Now You Has Jazz," the film's golden moment, Dex introduces the members of the band in rhyme—shades of Satchmo's band at Nick's in *New Orleans*. Armstrong, clarinetist Edmond Hall, and trombonist Trummy Young play some short breaks on the blues, and there's plenty of byplay between Dexter and Pops, trading bon mots about how jazz has conquered the world: "The Frenchmans all prefer what they call *les jazz hot*," Louis sings, mangling two languages as he mugs. "*Formidab'*," replies Dex *en français*. "Why don't you write cute songs like that," asks Tracy, in her cups. Dexter: "I wrote that one." (Porter was no jazz expert, and Bing, Pops, and arranger Saul Chaplin pitched in on the lyric.)[3]

In the end, Tracy impulse-remarries Dex, who's been pressing his case right along. It makes some sense, in light of her options. (The film's sexual politics are creepy. She's beset by much older men, and her fiancé wants her on a pedestal.) At least with a songwriter who hangs out with jazz musicians, a woman might have some fun. She doesn't even mind when Armstrong's men appear from nowhere to hijack the wedding march and show the audience out. Dexter may not be fully focused on his festival duties tonight. But you can bet he and Louis will reprise "Now You Has Jazz," after the way it went over at the party.

One reason moviegoers might have smelled a rat in that marijuana bust in *The Gene Krupa Story*: they'd seen a similar frame-up in Alexander Mackendrick's 1957 **Sweet Smell of Success**. Making Martin Milner's character Steve Dallas a jazz musician is enough to explain why mighty showbiz columnist J. J. Hunsecker (Burt Lancaster) might consider him a poor match for his sister Susie. J. J. instructs his equally loathsome errand boy, publicist Sidney Falco (Tony Curtis), to drive a wedge between the couple. One thing Hunsecker may hold against Dallas: he talks like a jazz musician in a movie. To Susie: "Just don't leave me in a minor key."

In truth, Dallas does have a chip on his shoulder where J. J. and Sidney are concerned. (He might give Hunsecker credit for living at 1619 Broadway—songwriter central, the Brill Building.) The guitarist is slightly more polite in a club, when he blows off an intellectual jazz fan (glasses, hair up) who wants to talk about the group's fusion of traditional and progressive elements and to know how Dallas formed the band. "Well, we just sort of got together," he tells her. "Look, why don't you ask Fred Katz, he writes all the stuff"— leaving cellist Katz looking unhappy at the handoff.

Dallas was being disingenuous about their just getting together. As Katz might explain to that fan, Dallas has hired four-fifths of drummer Chico Hamilton's lightly swinging Los Angeles combo, with Paul Horn on flute, Carson Smith on bass, and Katz with his charts. Fronting this polished, established outfit on the opposite coast buffs Dallas's reputation. Hamilton runs the band when the nominal leader is off the bandstand, and minds the clock on their breaks—his players know who the real boss is. (Exteriors were shot in

New York, and interiors in Hollywood—hence the LA musicians.) Still, there's disappointingly little jazz in the film. Martin Milner didn't play guitar; in a couple of bandstand close-ups, we see the left hand of Hamilton guitarist John Pisano on the frets, reaching around Milner who blocks him from the camera.[4]

As shot by James Wong Howe, midtown Manhattan looks terrific—one club Dallas plays is on the south side of East Fifty-Ninth Street between two approaches to the Queensborough Bridge—but the world of Apple nightlife has never seemed sleazier. As in real 1950s New York, the cops see jazz musicians as easy prey; they're only too happy to bust (and rough up) Steve for the marijuana Falco plants in his topcoat. (After planting it Falco learns Steve and Susie have already broken up, but he can't be bothered to retrieve the dope.) Back then a drug conviction could wipe out a musician's livelihood; it might cost them the police-issued, so-called cabaret card needed to work any place in New York City that sold alcohol. Knowing this makes Falco's last-reel downfall all the sweeter.

Tony Curtis doesn't look much like a jazz musician, but he got cast as a horn player in three films over the next three years. In Delmer Daves's 1958 World War II drama **Kings Go Forth**, Curtis is Britt Harris, a charming, insincere Army sergeant in Southern France, who lives it up on the Riviera whenever he can get leave. The many things that come easily to Harris include the ability to play hot jazz trumpet, as we discover at Nice nightclub Le Chat Noir—an arched stone cellar, no mere new-world basement—when he sits in with the local sextet. Its bearded vibraphonist in a peasant cap is obviously jazz great Red Norvo, energetically comping to get our attention. On a fast riff blues, Britt rips out four solo choruses in the trumpet voice of bopper Pete Candoli (who hands him the horn), and blows the second out-chorus an octave up. The scene is out of character with the rest of the movie, but it's a fulcrum of the plot—the moment when mixed-race gamine Natalie Wood turns her attention away from gentleman lieutenant Frank Sinatra.

Britt strings her along—tells her he has every record Bessie Smith ever made—but in a sordid turnabout reveals himself to be a slumming racist. As in life, playing African American music doesn't guarantee a player's progressive views. Britt acknowledges his essential lack of character before dying, in an unforgiving Sinatra's arms, during a mission behind enemy lines where he doesn't even pretend to play the hero. (He wasn't the only young mess of contradictions with a horn: in Britain's drab kitchen-sink drama *Look Back in Anger* of 1959, Richard Burton's testy amateur dixielander blasts his trumpet to be obnoxious at home, but his quieter playing reveals hidden sensitivity.)

Jazz lover Billy Wilder's celebrated farce **Some Like It Hot** (1959) concerns two new members of a traveling orchestra in 1929: men passing as women. Tenor saxophonist Tony Curtis and bass player Jack Lemmon, broke and needing to flee Chicago in a hurry, borrow clothes from showgirls and take a three-week booking in Miami with an all-woman band. The singer with Sweet Sue and Her Society Syncopators, Sugar Kane, is played by Marilyn Monroe. Hilarity ensues, or at least men lurching around in women's clothes and some dumb-blond humor. As in other movies, men who walk a mile in women's pumps learn about sexism, being treated like a piece of meat, and comfort-versus-fashion in shoe design. But their education only goes so far.

Sugar Kane has given up singing with bands staffed by men, not because she's tired of being hit on, but because she can't resist tenor saxophonists, no matter how worthless. A couple of times she disparages "this crummy girls' band" she sings with, and it appears the viewer is supposed to accept her appraisal.

Fair to say all-woman bands have never gotten their due. Even the punchy International Sweethearts of Rhythm, part of a wave of "all-girl" bands that cropped up during the World War II manpower shortage, might get dismissed (by male critics) as inferior players or mere eye candy. There had been real women's jazz bands in the late 1920s— or at least bands that played jazz among other styles. A 1927 photograph of Indiana's Parisian Redheads shows a group much like Sweet Sue's, with brass, reeds, and strings. Multi-instrumentalists The Ingenues made a pair of one-reelers for Vitaphone in 1928; their *The Band Beautiful* ends with a rousing "Tiger Rag." The Debutantes fronted by violinist Harry Wayman also made a Vitaphone short that same year, followed in 1929 by Green's Twentieth Century Faydetts.[5]

Like other women's bands, Sweet Sue's has a male manager who lacks high ideals: he seeks only blondes under 25. We don't hear so much of the Syncopators, but they're remarkably good for 1929. Rehearsing "Runnin' Wild" while crowded together in a moving train carriage, they play hot riffs with spirit and varied dynamics. On stage, Sugar is a fine sultry singer; behind her kewpie-doll vocal on "I Want to Be Loved by You," the Syncopators show they can play sweet as well as hot. The arranging is good, the violins are in tune, the brass blend smoothly, and the rhythm section has a light touch. "I'm Through with Love" shows off a very lilting beat for the period—never mind that the song's from

FIGURE 5.2 Sweet Sue and Her Society Syncopators rehearse in *Some Like It Hot*: Marilyn Monroe as Sugar Kane, center, with ringers Tony Curtis (tenor sax) and Jack Lemmon (bass).

1931 (or that it's studio jazzmen on the soundtrack; saxophonist Gene Cipriano and bassist Red Callender ghost the male leads). In truth the Syncopators do lack memorable soloists. That new tenor saxophonist with the low Eve Arden voice plays in a somewhat corny sub-Bud Freeman style, and that new bassist with a throaty laugh seems eternally distracted, fingers barely moving on the fingerboard.

The other Syncopators aren't so well-differentiated. We see them up close mostly when they stuff themselves into a sleeper-car berth for an impromptu party—Billy Wilder riffing on the Marx Brothers. These movie women talk about something besides men—booze—and enjoy each other's company; no *Orchestra Wives* bitchiness on this train. They do grumble about Sweet Sue's strict rules, though Sue turns a deaf ear to that Pullman-car party. But then grousing about the boss is one way musicians bond. Women rarely make music together in jazz films. Here they do it en masse.

Tony Curtis helped make New York rough for musicians in *Sweet Smell of Success*, but he's on the receiving end in Richard Mulligan's **The Rat Race** (1960), one of those wearying period sex comedies that involve fretting over a woman's reputation. (Don Rickles plays the horny heavy; Jack Oakie's a bartender.) Curtis is Pete Hammond Jr., a reed player who's come to Manhattan hoping to get established as a freelance musician, only to discover a surfeit of them scrounging for work. He's come prepared with baritone, tenor, alto, and soprano saxes, clarinet, and three flutes.

Pete's shy about admitting he's from Milwaukee, lest New Yorkers think he's a hick. Not that they intimidate him. "I heard some of these local cats blow. You know what they do? They steal a little Brubeck, they clip a little of Charlie Parker, and these cats, they think they're really making it." He is moved to editorialize: "Some of the best progressive jazz in America today comes from the Midwest"—according to this musician whose baritone solos are ghosted by Queens-born Gerry Mulligan. An occasional actor himself—he has a cameo as a shipboard bandleader—Mulligan ghosts Pete in character; he's good but no Gerry Mulligan, with a less sturdy tone.

Pete moves into a musician-heavy neighborhood between Eighth and Ninth Avenues around Fifty-First Street—the rehearsals and casual performances we hear through his open window are a nice touch. (A lot of musicians did live in Hell's Kitchen, convenient to Broadway theaters.) At one point he plays along with a quartet jamming in the building across the way, who may not even notice his participation. Finally, Pete's invited to audition for a name band, the Red Peppers, represented at his tryout by their pianist (jazzman Joe Bushkin) and a couple of reedmen (including tenor saxist Sam Butera). Things seem to be going well, until the Peppers send Pete out for beer and steal all his horns (though they leave a note that compliments his alto playing and states they're not really the Red Peppers). But there's a happy resolution; Pete gets a cruise ship job from a contractor neighbor who's heard him practicing. Love interest Debbie Reynolds puts her virtue in peril to finance a couple of new horns she buys on her own initiative. Before sailing, we gather, Pete swaps the tenor she'd bought him for the alto he was told to bring.

Richard Brooks's **Blackboard Jungle** (1955) brought rock-and-roll to the movies; its opening and closing theme is Bill Haley's howl "Rock Around the Clock." But there's more jazz than rock in it, and its most notorious scene takes aim at jazz itself. This problem picture is about new high-school teacher Rick (Glenn Ford) who teaches at an inner-city hellhole where the worst students are violent bullies, joy-riders, truck hijackers, an attempted rapist, and a poison-pen letter writer. Rick's fellow newbie, idealistic Josh Edwards (Richard Kiley)—"Two first names, like Harry James"—is a big jazz fan and lets you know it. He plays Stan Kenton on a bar jukebox when he and Rick unwind after work. "Stan the man," Josh enthuses. "Terrific stuff; very educated gentleman." (The tune is Bill Holman's "Invention for Guitar and Trumpet" from 1952, not actually available on a 45 until an English single followed the film.)

One day Josh unwisely hauls to school the precious collection of 78-rpm jazz records he's spent 15 years assembling, a collection he's quite proud of. Lead delinquent Vic Morrow goads him into playing his gang something, and Josh picks Bix Beiderbecke's 1927 "Jazz Me Blues"—though one kid protests, "Ahh—how about some bop?" Edwards drops the needle two minutes into the record, which seems careless for a collector, though he pinpoints the beginning of Bix's cornet solo; Josh must play it often. But vicious Vic then smashes Josh's records, calling out the names of some first—"Cow Cow Boogie," "Cherokee," "Clap Hands, Here Comes Charlie." Edwards gets roughed up when he tries to intervene. The incident breaks his spirit, and he quits his job. Maybe he should have spun "Cherokee" for that bop fan. The destruction is nihilistic, and we don't blame the victim. But Josh comes off as weak, naive, and effete; his fetishization of his 78s seems a little pathetic, as if, by 1955, jazz fans lived only in the past. At least that broken Bix would be easy to replace; Columbia had reissued it on LP.

Teacher Rick begins to break through to promising student Sidney Poitier when he and five harmonizing friends rehearse the spiritual "Go Down, Moses," hoping for a slot on the school Christmas show. Music really can help reach the kids.

This was only an opening skirmish between the jazz and rock generations on screen, a sign of things to come. A new front had opened in the war between jazz and other musics. By the late 1950s, rock-and-roll was for the kids and jazz was for Dad, who got old and didn't know it, like Danny Kaye's Red Nichols or those graying ballroom extras in *The Glenn Miller Story*.

There's a notorious scene in the 1957 Elvis Presley vehicle **Jailhouse Rock**, in which his date Peggy Van Alden—a low-level record industry flack who's advised him to sing "like how you feel it"—takes him to a faculty party hosted by her parents. Presley, as ex-con Vince Everett, is ostensibly alienated by the hifalutin' commentary of a bunch of jazz fans as they listen to the latest side by Stubby Wrightmeyer. Stubby's cool West Coast pastels confirm he's a stand-in for trumpeter Shorty Rogers, who'd auditioned Sinatra in *Man with the Golden Arm*.

Some of these jazz lovers don't dig innovation. "I think Stubby's gone overboard with those altered chords," someone comments, when the (totally inoffensive) record has barely begun. One lady longs for the return of dixieland. Another confesses that

(Dave) Brubeck and (his saxophonist Paul) Desmond have taken dissonance as far as she can follow. Someone else: "Oh nonsense! Have you heard Lennie Tristano's latest recording? He reached outer space!" As Tristano didn't record much, the man can only be referring to the pianist's eccentric 1956 LP for Atlantic, where he manipulated the tapes and overdubbed several pianos for a dense contrapuntal texture: futuristic music on the cusp of the space age.

When Vince is asked for his views, he curtly responds, "Lady, I don't know what the hell you talking about," and bolts for the door. To Peggy, outside: "I'm not even sure they were talkin' English." But Vince was in a sour mood before Stubby's record came on, having failed to get a rise out of Peggy's unflappable dad when Vince told him he'd been in show business "about a week," having just got sprung from the state pen. "Oh is that so? What was the rap?" Vince is thrown off by the man's pleasant equanimity. That's when Peggy's mom, possibly a little rattled, suggests putting on that new Wrightmeyer side: "After all I'm sure Mr. Everett is interested in jazz music. It's his profession." She may be baiting Vince right back. His bad-boy routine doesn't faze these open-minded intellectuals any more than talking about his prison time did—as Peggy points out: "That bomb kind of laid an egg, didn't it?"

Still, Vince may get in a dig at these highbrows later. When he does a "Jailhouse Rock" production number on a TV special, the band includes a braying tenor sax, the antithesis of Stubby's reticent sound. Vince pours his jailhouse and jazz humiliations into his art—singing like how he feels it.

The Cry of Jazz (1959; 34 minutes; director: Edward O. Bland; writers: Bland, Nelam Hill, Mark Kennedy, Eugene Titus). Cast includes: George Waller (Alex Johnson), Linda Dillon (Faye), Dorothea Horton (Natalie), Andrew Duncan (John), Leroy Inman (Louis).
—After a meeting of a jazz-appreciation society, arranger Alex explains that jazz is African American music, to a few (mostly skeptical) white fans.

Jailhouse Rock's Prof. Van Alden compares favorably to the defensive white fans in the dramatized frame story to *The Cry of Jazz*, writer/director/disc jockey Edward O. Bland's didactic, low-budget half-hour documentary from Chicago—a precursor to the low-budget independent jazz films of the 1960s. In an apartment adorned with African sculpture, a meeting of the Parkwood Jazz Club has just broken up. This friendly interracial group has stationery and keeps meeting minutes. Just last night they went out to hear some dixieland.

But a conversation among a few dawdlers grows tense when pushy white newcomer Natalie and can't-believe-what-I'm-hearing hothead John take exception to the unexceptional idea, expressed by three black members, that jazz is distinctly African American: "the Negro's cry of joy and suffering." Point man is society recording secretary Alex (George Waller, like the rest of the amateurish cast otherwise unknown), who's introduced as an arranger for the Paul Severson group—an oddly dissonant detail nothing is made of. (Severson was a white Chicago trombonist who wrote the Doublemint gum jingle. But it's a courtesy mention; Severson contributed a little music to the film.) Natalie and John would seem like straw figures if their objections weren't still heard 60 years later. But there have been good white jazz musicians, right? Why don't they get more attention? (As if that were ever a problem—look at jazz movies.) And somebody besides blacks could have invented jazz even if they didn't, right? You say you've suffered, but hasn't everybody?

John: "Jazz is American. You guys are trying to make a racial distinction where there isn't one." Alex: "The white musicians you speak of are merely playing follow-the-leader." Tell me more about jazz history, says Faye, the most sympathetic white fan—plumping down next to Alex and tilting her head invitingly.

We break away from that playlet as Alex's voiceover takes us into documentary footage of black neighborhood life and poverty—stylish walking, club dancing, cockroaches on a stove—and he lays out his (or rather filmmaker Bland's) interpretive theories, illustrated by the background music. Almost all of it is by Chicago bandleader Sun Ra, before he became jazz-famous. We see pianist Ra and some of his bandmembers, filmed in nightclubs, often faceless or in shadow or silhouette. They are anonymous by necessity, representing practitioners of most of the styles Alex refers to. Scenes of white life—a snowy lawn, commuter trains, poodle-grooming—get Severson's pastel cool jazz to match.

As Alex tells it, jazz represents black America's ongoing oppression and resistance. Circular song forms are structurally and harmonically restrictive, but improvising over same with swinging rhythm and an individual sound makes for freedom on the

FIGURE 5.3 Alex (George Waller) delivers some hard truths to receptive Faye (Linda Dillon) and resistant John (Andrew Duncan) in *The Cry of Jazz*.

fly—makes for the living in the present that defines African American life. On the sound-track, John Gilmore running fast blues changes on tenor saxophone makes Alex's case. "Then the history of jazz is the story of the fantastic ingenuity of the Negro in America," Faye says, quick on the uptake. Say what you will about *The Cry of Jazz*'s narrative creaki-ness, no one in Hollywood jazz movies makes that point.

Tell me more, Faye implores Alex, leading him by the hand to a loveseat. Undistracted, he lays out the short version of the music's development in a way jazz movies seldom do. Original New Orleans jazz was good; white dixieland was a pale imitation. (*New Orleans* concurs.) Swing, with its massed riffs and diminished solo opportunities, reflected the greater conformity and constraint brought on when southern blacks moved to northern cities. Bebop was complex and made no concessions to entertainment; cool jazz was a faint white reaction, greatly influenced by saxophonist Lester Young. The apotheosis of all this evolution, Alex tells them, is bandleader Le Sun Ra, endorsed as we hear his "A Call for All Demons"—typically inventive, harmonically tangy, melodic and richly col-orful mid-1950s Ra.

Then Alex drops the real bombshell, when asked where jazz is headed: "Jazz is dead." Poor John looks like he'll pop a blood vessel. Alex explains: All those old cycles have been exhausted, with no way forward—a maddening, fragmented piano loop underscores his point. But a new kind of music will arise that retains jazz's spirit. A loop of Sun Ra music, tied to images of fire and ruin, suggests that this new form to come is the turbulent, con-troversial stuff soon dubbed free jazz (or "fire music")—part of jazz, not its successor. Alex's potted history isn't too bad overall; he's too hard on cool jazz, but right about its Lester Young strain. Yet like other (jazz) commentators he goes awry when predicting the future. End-of-history arguments are invariably premature.

By film's end, even Natalie and John seem to be coming around to Alex's thinking (or else they're just sick of arguing a losing side). Alex eventually concludes by reminding the white folks they too can benefit from blacks' hard-won wisdom. In the end, Faye again does the summing up: "Then America needs the Negro to teach us how to be American, right?"

Warner Bros. cartoons had jazzified a couple of fairy tales in the 1940s war years. In *Goldilox and the Jivin' Bears*, the playing's so hot a piano catches fire, while the Carl Stalling score to *Coal Black and De Sebben Dwarfs* is laced with allusions to "Blues in the Night." But both films trafficked in racial stereotypes and were rarely seen in later decades. And neither tells a jazz story, unlike the seven-minute Looney Tune **Three Little Bops** (1957), directed by top Warners animator Friz Freleng, a recasting of The Three Little Pigs. As in *Alexander's Ragtime Band*, a group plays increasingly upscale venues. But the titular por-cine trio is plagued by an interloper, in the tradition of enthusiastic but clueless *Broken Strings* banjo man Stringbean Johnson.

The pigs have a lithe jump-blues trio with piano, a snare drummer who doubles (once) on string bass, and an electric guitarist doubling (once) on saxophone; they are quick with those instrument swaps. (The music is by trumpeter Shorty Rogers. It's narrated in sung rhyming couplets by lyricist and radio comedian Stan Freberg.) All is well till a Big Bad Wolf "with red-rimmed eyes"—a druggie—shows up at the House of Straw where the Bops are performing, and announces he's joining the band. But he's a terrible trumpeter, with poor breath control—although when they eject him, he manages to work up enough ire and wind to flatten the place with a blast of his horn.

At the Dew Drop Inn, made of sticks: same deal. The piggy-boppers obligingly set up the Wolf's solo with a fat D-flat blues riff, which he swings for and misses, out of key, out of tune, out of breath and ideas. But again, he finds the lungpower to level the place when given the bum's rush at the crowd's insistence. The Little Bops' next engagement is in a more secure brick structure, in some eastern town—a sign the combo's moving up. (The building dates from 1776: "High-class place with a high-class crowd / Sign on the door 'No Wolves Allowed.'") The wolf tries disguising himself, comes in playing James P. Johnson's "Charleston" on ukulele, wearing a raccoon coat like it's 1926. He's ejected yet again, but when bricks prove impervious to his Jericho horn-blasts, he tries to dynamite the place. Given the no-wolves policy, you feel his rage. But he blows himself up before completing his mission.

There's a supernatural coda. The Wolf goes to hell, condemned to a stewpot over a roaring fire—but he's still got his horn, and the sound that seeps up to the bandstand from the netherworld is a revelation. It's the only moment when Shorty Rogers gets to show off on trumpet, with shapely lines and full round tone, deftly riding the chord changes. (He dug Sweets Edison.) The pigs approve, and their pianist delivers the moral: "You gotta get hot to play real cool." Jazz really is the devil's music. Lionized in death, like other difficult jazz musicians unrecognized in their time, Big Bad Wolf is posthumously admitted to a band now billed as "The Three Little Bops Plus One." His spectral sound is a marketable if macabre gimmick giving new meaning to the term "ghost band."

The ending reminds us that great musicians—trumpeters in particular—aren't always model citizens. And that dead musicians may be subject to cynical exploitation.

> ***All the Fine Young Cannibals*** **(1960; 112 minutes; director: Michael Anderson; screenplay: Robert Thom, from Rosamond Marshall's novel *The Bixby Girls*). Cast includes: Robert Wagner (Chad Bixby), Natalie Wood (Sarah/Salome Davis), Susan Kohner (Catherine MacDowall Bixby), George Hamilton (Tony MacDowall), Pearl Bailey (Ruby Jones), Louise Beavers (Rose), Mabel Albertson (Mrs. MacDowall).**
>
> **—High-born and low-born young Texans pair off across class lines in the Northeast. Poor boy Chad Bixby becomes a star trumpeter who tries to get an ailing singer back on her feet.**

Big Bad Wolf wasn't the only trumpet player from the sticks leaving disaster in his wake. Another turns up in tawdry 1960 big-screen soap opera *All the Fine Young Cannibals*. A jazz subplot, introduced with a classic set piece, is easily the best thing in this dreary tale

FIGURE 5.4 A now-ghostly Wolf sits in with *The Three Little Bops*.

of trashy but yearning North Texans (married stars Robert Wagner and Natalie Wood) who split up and marry spoiled oil-money siblings (George Hamilton and *The Gene Krupa Story*'s Susan Kohner). These sexually frustrated, self-pitying, scenery-chewing narcissists are generally awful to each other; the one who seems nicest is merely too dim to keep up. As Wagner's Chad Bixby tells the woman he loves, "If I can't have ya, then I wanna hurt ya, and I will." Each of the leads sports an atrocious come-and-go "southern" accent—inscrutable code-switching.

Chad's ticket out of gully-low Pine Alley is an empathetic skill he's been honing since he was a kid sneaking down to black Deep Ellum. "All of Chad's tunes are original, heart-breaking, and composed on the spot," explains jukejoint owner Rose, when he drops by one night. "He's gonna tell us what he feels, and then he's gonna play us what he feels, just like he's been doin' down here since he was seven." Which Chad duly does on trumpet, with plenty of feeling to express, having just skipped his harsh preacher father's funeral. "This is how strong my father was," he says—and plays a steely stately line, delivered like all of Chad's musical pronouncements, with plenty of body English. (He's ghosted by sultry-sounding Hollywood regular Uan Rasey.) And this is the love I had for him I couldn't express, Chad continues—tender and quiet in the low register, like he's playing "Taps." "And these are my tears"—putting a little slow-bend blues into his ending. When the crowd approves, Rose protests. "You don't applaud this kind of playing. You weep." Amen to that.

Soon after Chad meets Rose's sister, celebrated singer Ruby Jones (Pearl Bailey, doing the best acting by a mile), whose horn-playing man has left her, and who's using the bottle to hurry death from a broken heart. (We hear her only in decline.) She and Chad appear to fall into bed—the second time we see them, they're in her bedroom, Ruby in a robe, though she claims, "I don't carry on with no white boys." Thereafter their relationship grows more ambiguous; Hollywood's Production Code office demanded rewrites. Ruby is beyond caring by the time Chad takes up with that oil brat. (Subtext, for what it's worth: Bailey was famously and happily married to white drummer Louie Bellson.)

Whatever their relationship, Ruby takes a liking to Chad—though it takes her awhile to stop addressing him as "white boy"—and helps him realize he can monetize his gift. She brings him to New York and gets him established, talking her agent Sammy into taking him on when Chad is still raw as a turnip. In improbably little time, Bixby becomes a slick recording and supper-club sensation. He'll improvise solo intros that paint one of his emotional portraits, before the band comes in for the rest of the tune; his music is no longer quite so spontaneous. Now Chad is more like a standup comic, who riffs on the day's headlines before going into prepared material. (A rumor persists that the role was tailored for emotive pretty-boy trumpeter Chet Baker, who'd sprung from Oklahoma soil, but whose drug problems nixed the deal. No evidence has confirmed this. Robert Wagner later recalled the story had been developed for Elvis.)[6]

Chad and Ruby move in together in a black neighborhood. If she'd only sing again, he's convinced, she could climb out of the deep hole of depression—channeling other people's pain to expunge her own. When he goads her onto stage one night, she stumbles through a middle fragment of "Happiness Is Just a Thing Called Joe," and then picks up Billie Holiday's 1947 weeper "Deep Song" in mid-tune, as Chad backs her. Then—getting into it now—Ruby goes into Holiday's signature "God Bless the Child." A mysterious male choir (plus strings) joins in; perhaps those voices are the posh patrons spontaneously testifying, guided by familiarity with Billie's lush 1950 version.

But the cure doesn't take: "I sung for you Chad, and I still want to die." More subtext: Billie Holiday, whose troubles with men and substance abuse were well-known, had wasted away the year before, at 44. And the lyric to "God Bless the Child" concerns friends who leave you flat when you're broke. So it goes: Chad still pays lip service to Ruby—you're the only person I love that I don't hate, too—but he's living on Park Avenue by the time she dies alone. He takes her body back to Deep Ellum where a black swing band plays her off at an abbreviated mournful-then-joyous jazz funeral. Chad doesn't join in.

Making Bixby a jazz musician lets him emote all over. The different ways the music is perceived culturally also serve the rags-and-riches plot. It's a respectable enough occupation for the film audience to appreciate Chad's rise in the world, but not respectable enough for his wealthy new mother-in-law. "A bugler, no less—a nightclub personality," she sniffs. "What did I do to deserve this?"

Staccato/Johnny Staccato (TV series, 1959–1960; 27 half-hour episodes; producer: Everett Chambers; directors include: John Cassavetes, Richard Whorf, Boris Sagal, John Brahm, Bernard Girard, Jeffrey Hayden, Sidney Lanfield; writers include: Richard Carr, Jameson Brewer, Sam Gilman, Laurence E. Mascott, Stanford Whitmire. Regular cast: John Cassavetes (John Staccato), Eduardo Ciannelli (Waldo).

—In this TV series, a New York jazz pianist pays the bills by working as a private detective.

After *The Strip, Pete Kelly's Blues*, and *Man with the Golden Arm*, the link between jazz and crime on screen only intensified. In the 1958 feature *I Want to Live!* Susan Hayward played a Gerry Mulligan fan on death row. Count Basie wrote the theme to *M Squad*, and Henry Mancini penned one for jazz-loving private eye Peter Gunn. Then came the first modern-day musician detective, in NBC's half-hour drama *Staccato* aka *Johnny Staccato*. (It aired under both titles.) It starred intense and nervous John Cassavetes, a New Yorker who'd started on stage and moved into semi-steady work in television in the 1950s before breaking into feature films. He'd reluctantly signed on to pay off debts he'd incurred while making his directorial debut, the low-budget art film *Shadows*, which was billed as "an improvisation" (though mostly scripted by the director) and had a jazz score.[7] (More on *Shadows* in the next chapter.) Cassavetes also saw *Staccato* as a chance to hone his directing and writing chops. He and the producer he'd brought on, Everett Chambers, rewrote many of the scripts and tangled with the network. Once he was out of debt, Cassavetes openly groused about commercial pressures in a successful effort to break his contract. The show lasted 27 episodes, short of a full TV season. (In spring 1959, *Pete Kelly's Blues* made it only to episode 13.)

John Staccato, we gradually learn, is a (Korean?) war veteran who knows karate, and admits to a habit of poking his nose into other people's business. A New Yorker through and through—Cassavetes conveys the native impatience—Staccato grew up on Mulberry Street, lives near the Holland Tunnel, and talks in jazzy metaphors: "You play at your tempo, I'll play at mine." He likes to walk the streets to clear his head, but will tell you the subway's the quickest way to get around. He tells a date he'd wanted to be a classical pianist, and tells us, in one of his frequent voiceovers, that his ambition outstripped his jazz talent.

So to pay the rent he does a little light detective work, doing business out of a nightclub, like Peter Gunn. Clients seek him out or cases fall in his lap at Greenwich Village basement joint Waldo's, where he plays a little piano between jobs. (Interiors were shot in Los Angeles, and the musicians in the house band are all Angelinos, including jazz stars Barney Kessel, Red Mitchell, and Shelly Manne in the pilot, and mostly studio musicians thereafter. Future film composer John Williams ghosted Staccato's piano and is often seen on the bandstand.)

As mentioned earlier, Johnny's character—a war vet whose cases came to him, who worked in a subterranean club, and spoke to the audience in voiceover—owes more than a little to Jack Webb's Pete Kelly. In a *Staccato* episode that echoes the movie *Pete Kelly's Blues*, a mobster installs his daughter (Susan Oliver, pre-*Krupa Story*) as Waldo's house singer: "I want all of this—but I've got to earn it on my own." Like Kelly, Staccato does the best he can in a chaotic world. In another episode, wily Elizabeth Montgomery tries to draw him into a stolen-gem scam. He's tempted, but worries if he turns corrupt, it'll pollute his music—the very thing that lets him slough off the violence at the end of the day. When he sits in at Waldo's, his musings may reflect tonight's case: Latin octaves after helping a Spanish Harlem boxer, a pentatonic folk tune after an adventure in New York's obscure Little Tokyo.

Many exteriors for the black-and-white series were shot in New York, with a dark, gritty, noiry look, and the film-noir effect is enhanced by Johnny's expository narration and the moral quagmires he wades into. (Three episodes were directed by Richard Whorf, *Blues in the Night*'s Jigger.) In "Poet's Touch," a beatnik poet hangs with stevedores to be authentic, till they beat a guy to death for kicks. Cassavetes wanted his character to be complex, and sometimes Staccato doesn't save his client or solve his case. He also occasionally gets a little too drunk and stumbles through Waldo's, or boorishly throws himself at a pretty stranger.

A few episodes take up jazz themes. The second to air, and the first of five directed by Cassavetes, was "Murder for Credit," a juicy roman à clef about a glad-handing big-band leader with a powerful piano attack, who's beloved though some say past his prime. Lester Prince, played by Charles McGraw, is a gaudy white Duke Ellington knockoff, a mean-spirited caricature. (The series debut had fictionalized Elvis and his shady manager Col. Parker.) Like Duke, Prince had been in a career slump till a recent upswing. The fictional pianist has high hopes for his schmaltzy new single "Life." (Paul Gonsalves's marathon crowd-whipping saxophone solo at the 1956 Newport festival had sparked an Ellington revival.)

The Prince hires Staccato to find out who's been slowly poisoning him: his estranged wife and ex-singer? His new singer? His business manager? His sensitive behind-the-curtain arranger and orchestrator Jerry Lindstrom (Martin Landau)? The poison kills Prince before Staccato IDs the killer. It was Jerry, frustrated that the Prince claimed authorship over his own heartfelt music, "Life" very much included. ("He wanted to put his name on my 'Life'!") That's how Staccato cracked the case; Prince was too much of a lout to write such a pretty tune. So it's a roman à clef where Billy Strayhorn murders Ellington—Strayhorn who in the late 1950s was just beginning to get overdue credit for co-composing much Ellington music from the 1940s on.

That urge to kill the bad father resurfaces in the episode "The Man in the Pit." A young hothead comes into Waldo's one night—we hear a big band brass section, with only a quintet on stage—and impulsively slugs trumpeter Pete Candoli, mistaking him for Shank Millikan, the father he's never laid eyes on, who may be trying to blackmail the kid's mom. I know Shank, Staccato says, trying to cool the kid down; Johnny testifies to Shank's good character and attests he was one of the greats who played with "Bird Parker," Kenny Clarke, and Dexter Gordon. Either Johnny's memory is off or he's testing the kid, because his old friend and one-time idol Shank despises those bebop modernists as a traditionalist of the old school. Johnny looks him up, and moments after they greet each other, Shank's badmouthing those cats. "They flat their fifths, we drink ours," he says, recycling Eddie Condon's old jibe. Shank swears he's no blackmailer—"I'd rather play bop than sink that low!"—and is despondent that his son is studying progressive jazz in college. Alas, the real blackmailer kills Millikan before Staccato arranges a family reunion.

In "The Wild Reed," Harry Guardino plays Johnny's old friend Frank Aspen, manic tenor saxophonist bouncing back from a nervous breakdown and currently playing in a dive bar fronting a nothing piano-drums duo. Aspen thinks he's at the peak of his game, playing new sounds that leave Charlie Parker in the dust. But Johnny hears only squawks and squeaks, failures of imagination and technique—though the soundtrack musicians who ghost the trio resist the temptation to camp it up, perhaps out of professional pride. From a dramatic standpoint, Aspen's musical shortcomings are rather understated.

"How can a guy who was so good a few years ago be so lousy now?" Johnny wonders, and soon gets his answer: Frank's sidemen deal heroin, using his out-of-town bookings to distribute junk around the country, and they've got him on the needle. Frank's obsessed with his horn—he walks around town with it slung around his neck, ready for sudden inspiration—but can't hear how low he's sunk. Oblivious, he plays right through the

FIGURE 5.5 Saxophonist Harry Guardino reminisces with private eye John Cassavetes on an episode of *Johnny Staccato*.

climactic showdown between John and the pushers in the dive's back room, showing a dedication to practicing during intermission surpassing even John Coltrane's.

Reliably long-suffering Juano Hernandez stars in "Collector's Item" as Romeo Jefferson, a New Orleans pianist making a comeback at swanky Basin Street East, thanks to admirer Johnny, after 30 years off the scene. (Playing the blues, Romeo sounds more like he hails from Red Garland's Dallas.) Alas, Jefferson is being blackmailed, having stumbled into someone else's murder ballad, the story of blues singer Hannah Green and her jilted lover Redtop (Rupert Crosse of *Shadows*, later in *Too Late Blues*). Romeo didn't kill her, but there's a *Perry Mason*–sized stack of circumstantial evidence against him, including a disc recording of an after-hours session where Romeo and Hannah argued just before she was shot. (Recordings are threaded all through; Staccato tells Romeo, when I heard you on record, I knew you had heart; Romeo tells Johnny he was drawn to Hannah when he heard her on disc.) Johnny deals with blackmailing killer Redtop at the Polo Grounds baseball stadium—an unlikely but photogenic spot for a 2:30 a.m. rendezvous.

Later episodes wander far from Waldo's and any music connection. Everything's gone sour, on screen and off. In his penultimate case, in a small town full of anticommunist vigilantes, Staccato can't stop the death of the man he's trying to protect, or the friend who hired him. The final installment brings it all back home, "Swinging Long Hair" with George Voskovec as Stanley Kaytner, classical pianist who defected from the Eastern bloc during a concert tour. He's been on the lam ever since, and has now taken an apartment across the street from Waldo's. Foreign agents are everywhere, it seems—they find him in a piano warehouse he sneaks into so he can practice, and outside Waldo's after he auditions for a job. Immigrant Waldo is only too happy to give it to him—turns out the club owner doesn't even like jazz, and would rather feature classical music.

Stanley, appearing under the transparent *nom de keys* Stanley Kay, splits the difference; his solo music amalgamates blues, ballads, and nineteenth-century classics both airy and thundering, like a Soviet Oscar Peterson. When cellist Fred Katz, flutist Paul Horn, and guitarist John Pisano from Chico Hamilton's band drop by for an after-hours jam, they play a little Bach, swinging it Modern Jazz Quartet–style: jazz meets classical without drama or 100 violins. Their one-world art music suggests everybody can get along. But no: those spies arrive to shoot up Waldo's. Staccato pops them, but not before they gun down Stanley in the street in front of his wife (Celia Lovsky, last seen as Gene Krupa's mother). "Killing: I kill, they kill. It seems it never ends," Johnny says in his final voiceover. "I've had it." And the man who liked to walk the town to ponder it all walks away and keeps walking. How can the music wash away violence, when it winds up bringing it on?

Staccato was a high-water mark for the jazz musician as TV character, but there were other sightings ahead. On a 1961 episode of *Route 66*, "Goodnight Sweet Blues," wandering heroes Buz and Tod (George Maharis and Martin Milner) are just leaving Pittsburgh when they encounter ailing but sassy retired blues singer Jenny Henderson: Ethel Waters in her beaming, beatific late period. (It garnered her an Emmy nomination.) Waters's own 1926 record of "I'm Coming Virginia" is presented as an example of Jenny's art. With mere weeks to live, she commissions the boys to chase down some leads and reunite her

1920s band at her bedside: the sextet the Memphis Naturals. They're the closest thing to family Jenny has: all very different people, but man did they sound good together. Three of them are played by jazz giants: tenor saxophonist Coleman Hawkins, trumpeter Roy Eldridge, and drummer Jo Jones.

Musically it's all semicoherent—jazz fan Buz improbably recognizes the style of Count Basie saxophonist Snooze Mobley (Hawkins) in the New Orleans–style clarinet on the dixieland flipside of Jenny's record. (Hawkins wasn't with Basie, who is, however, a bandleader TV viewers might have heard of.) Ex-Basie drummer Jo Jones had the meatiest role as ladies-man trumpeter Lover Brown, having charmed the producers into swapping his original minor role for a bigger one. The part of drummer A. C. then went to trumpeter Roy Eldridge, who knew his way around the traps.

Buz tracks down Snooze playing in a San Francisco club, and starts yelling to him about his mission while Mobley is in the middle of a solo (a Coleman Hawkins solo, no less). You'd think that takes creative license too far, Buz being a jazz buff and all, but Von Freeman swore that Chicago bar patrons would try to engage him in conversation while he was blowing. Scouring the East Coast, Tod nabs A. C. at New York's A&R Studios. He agrees to come to Pittsburgh but first gets another drummer to cover his dates, a little sign of professionalism from those much maligned jazz percussionists. The bass player, now a lawyer, clears his court calendar; Lover Brown, jailed for bigamy, talks his way into compassionate leave. The band's worthless banjo man is dead, but his grown son steps in on guitar. Jenny had been more a mother to him than anyone, singing him to sleep with the bawdily inappropriate "Goodnight Sweet Blues"—the closest thing she knew to a lullaby. (It's credited to episode writers and future *Hawaii Five-0* masterminds Leonard Freeman and Will Lorin).

Everybody's on board except proud trombonist King Loomis, played by that staunch friend of the jazz drama Juano Hernandez, in one last heart-tugging performance. (He kept acting through the 1960s, but not in jazz tales.) Buz finds Loomis shining shoes alongside young boys, a shaky, scared, reformed alcoholic hanging on one day at a time. King hocked his horn and walks the long way to work so he doesn't have to see it in a pawnshop window. Buz retrieves his trombone, and in the phoniest moment in a show with a few, leaves it unattended on Loomis's East St. Louis front stoop as neighbors look on.

When all but King Loomis arrive at Jenny's, Snooze restricts himself to monosyllables, but then Coleman Hawkins wasn't much for small talk. Lover turns on Jo Jones's considerable charm. They have a little session. We see Eldridge on drums, and Hawkins presumably sidelining on clarinet. Outside the windows, a spontaneous street party breaks out. The band plays a last reprise of "Goodnight Sweet Blues" before bedridden Jenny slumps on her pillow and eases off to gloryland.

King Loomis had arrived in time for a tender reunion. He brought his trombone but didn't try to play, afraid to. But now that Jenny's gone, and the reconstituted Memphis Naturals play her home, Loomis's horn leads them off, singing out like the voice of God—like Art Hazzard and Rev. Handy and Romeo Jefferson all rolled into one. Juano Hernandez: he gets you every time.

INDEPENDENTS IN BLACK AND WHITE 1961–1967

When jazz was popular music, in the swing era, it turned up in pop movies like *Second Chorus* and *Orchestra Wives*. Twenty years later, jazz was more and more viewed as art music, something for sophisticated listeners, and now it inspired art movies: a 1960s wave of low-budget independent films in black and white. Despite *Johnny Staccato*, and his 1962 film *Too Late Blues*, writer/director John Cassavetes wasn't that much of a jazz fan. But his presence hovered over or near a few jazz-related movies in the 1960s, when a new scrappier filmmaking aesthetic took hold—an antidote to Hollywood's widescreen color spectacles. *Too Late Blues* came out the same year as *Lawrence of Arabia* and *How the West Was Won*.

The improvisational first draft of **Shadows**, which Cassavetes had screened in New York in 1958, had been a local sensation, even more than the 1961 release version shown at European festivals the year before. *Shadows* posited a new American film movement, one that gloried in its roughhewn nature. The splinters in the grain were proof of authenticity. In either version, *Shadows* had a jazzy aura, billed (misleadingly) as an improvisation, and boasting a mostly improvised score by bassist Charles Mingus and (for the revised version) his saxophonist/flutist Shafi Hadi.[1] *Shadows* follows three African American siblings and their circles. Light-skinned Lelia (Lelia Goldoni) dates a white creep who assumes she's white. Bennie (Ben Carruthers) is a trumpet player—he handles a horn in one scene as a prop—but nothing is made of it, though he tells a dubious (and forgettable) Charlie Parker anecdote. Early on, he and friends visit a jazz bar in search of women. We don't see a bandstand, but hear tenor saxophone and drums (Hadi and Dannie Richmond) trading phrases, as if at the end of a bebop tune. (That's followed by solo tenor mood music, in a gray zone between diegetic and nondiegetic.)

Older brother Hugh (Hugh Hurd) tries to maintain his integrity as a nightclub pop singer employed by crass club owners: Can't he introduce the girly act and tell a joke or two? He also endures unsolicited do-it-like-this advice from a proudly slicker vocalist: "It's an up tune, man. You got to go and *swing.*" At least Hugh has an aggressive (if quick to compromise) manager, played by jiving scene-stealer Rupert Crosse.

Weak as those jazz connections are, *Shadows* reinforced period links between that music and other modern or avant-garde art forms. Jazz musicians improvised behind poets, live and on record; painters painted to jazz records and maybe played a little them-selves, like amateur saxophonist Larry Rivers. In the new decade, scrappy improvisational music fit scrappy independent filmmaking. One sign of how such films broke the jazz-movie mold: suddenly more black musicians are represented on screen. That 1960s jazz films were mostly low-budget also speaks to the music's diminished popularity and vis-ibility. *All the Fine Young Cannibals* aside, there were no Technicolor romances like the previous decade's Miller and Goodman biopics. Post-Elvis rock's increasing dominance of popular music, even before the Beatles hit, socked jazz on the chin.

The new film aesthetic could be easily imitated: the grainy black-and-white images, the long scenes that take their sweet time paying off. French contemporaries like Godard knew something about those in-the-air methods too, and before them, the postwar Italian neorealists who helped inspire experimental New York director Shirley Clarke.[2]

The Connection (1961; 112 minutes; director: Shirley Clarke; writer: Jack Gelber, from his play). Cast: Warren Finnerty (Leach), Jerome Raphael (Solly), Garry Goodrow (Ernie), Jim Anderson (Sam), William Redfield (Jim Dunn), Roscoe Lee Browne (J. J. Burden), Carl Lee (Cowboy), Barbara Winchester (Sister Salvation), Henry Proach (Harry), Jackie McLean (Jackie), Freddie Redd (Freddie), Michael Mattos (Mike), Larry Richie (Larry).
—In a grungy New York loft, a director and cameraman film a group of heroin addicts—including a jazz quartet—awaiting their drug connection.

The direct and indirect influence of *Shadows* is all over Shirley Clarke's black-and-white *The Connection*, a hit at Cannes in 1961 that opened in the US the following year, delayed by its controversial content. The germ of *Shadows* had grown out of improvisational exercises run by Cassavetes's friend, acting coach Burt Lane. *The Connection* was likewise shaped by the actors' performances. It was based on Jack Gelber's stageplay of that name, which opened in 1959 and ran for years at the forward-looking Living Theatre.

The play is about eight heroin addicts waiting around for Cowboy—the guy who took their money and went to score—to come back with their dope. And it's also about a theater producer and playwright hoping to sculpt the junkies' experience into the very play they're appearing in. At the Living Theater four of the addicts were played by pianist Freddie Redd's quartet with Jackie McLean on alto sax. They played live jazz on stage— ostensibly rehearsing as they waited around—and interacted with the four principals, their nonplaying counterparts. The parallel is plain: One quartet talks, the other expresses itself in music. Each talker gets a solo—has at least one confessional monologue. These lowlifes are at the fringe of the jazz scene. Host Leach can handle a pair of drumsticks. Ernie is a saxophone player who squeaks a little on a mouthpiece, though his horn is in hock. (Actor Garry Goodrow did play some, and had put Gelber and Freddie Redd together.)

Jack Gelber also scripted the film, where the meta-story is a better fit: the producer and playwright have become documentary filmmaker Jim Dunn and second camera operator J. J. Burden, the latter more heard than seen. J. J. is Dunn's connection to this crowd: he and Jackie McLean supposedly went to school together in Harlem, and each tells the other he's changed for the worse since then. Jackie: "I'm my own man. Is your name gonna be on this film?" Yes, as it turns out. The film itself purports to be Burden's edit of the footage shot that day, and plays like a rough cut, with a few whited-out exposures and abrupt edits. Jim Dunn says, "I'm not interested in making a Hollywood picture," after cuing a preconceived monologue. Dunn wants the addicts to be honest and truthful and spontaneous, but for the camera: fair exchange for the drug buy he's just bankrolled. We know about Dunn's manipulations because Burden (perhaps goaded by Jackie) has his own agenda, undercutting his employer. He keeps his camera rolling when Dunn tells him to cut, before he coaches the junkies to liven things up. J. J.'s version is different from what Dunn was aiming at, because it adds Dunn as a character.

On stage, over 700 performances, the play could get loose and improvisational, with the balance shifting between actors and musicians from night to night. Jackie McLean: "By the time we stopped playing it, we had forgotten what the original lines were, and I know it was better then than in the beginning." The film version is inevitably fixed, less fluid— although as director Clarke pointed out, the words were less important than "the images, the voices, the faces, the movements—the cinema."[3] The music of it, she might have said. The Redd quartet's (sometimes) live-on-camera jazz aside, *The Connection* the film is a simulacrum of an improvisation, like *Shadows*. (There's an arresting moment when a camera moves off an actor in close-up, to track a cockroach crawling up a wall.) J. J. Burden's version critiques ginned-up quasi-documentary material—the kind of fabricated "real life" later associated with so-called reality television.

Gelber wrote jazz musicians into the script because so many were known to be addicts—he specified the music should be in the tradition of alto saxophonist Charlie Parker, who'd famously died too young in 1955. We see Parker's photo on the wall of the grimy top-floor loft where all the action takes place. (Designer Richard Sylbert's set is marvelously realistic, down to the cigarette butts on the floor. And that wrangled cockroach.) A mysterious character named Harry wanders in twice, plugs in his portable record player, drops the needle on Parker's 1948 "Marmaduke"—everyone listens, heads bowed, receiving a sacrament—then unplugs and wanders out without a word. The film in effect "samples" Parker in the hip-hop sense, squeezing a bundle of subtext out of a few borrowed bars—samples and loops him, actually, because one time Harry drops by, the record skips. Bird's voice at the end of that particular take—"Okay, play that back please"—is the last voice heard in a film bursting with talk.

Freddie Redd had hired altoist Jackie McLean because he'd absorbed so much of Parker's language and had idolized the man (though Bird was not above borrowing and then hocking Jackie's horn). The jazz musicians on stage underlined, facilitated, and added

FIGURE 6.1 A shadowy filmmaker observes Freddie Redd (piano), Michael Mattos (bass), Larry Ritchie (drums), and Jackie McLean (alto saxophone) rehearse in *The Connection*.

to the play's improvised content. Their music broke up the action and accompanied the monologues. For an authentic vibe, the musicians—including bassist Michael Mattos and drummer Larry Ritchie—were called by their own first names, like the actors in *Shadows*. (As Freddie Redd explained, it got their names out there: no such thing as bad publicity.)[4]

The jazz musicians imbued *The Connection* with authenticity another way. Most of the stage actors (many of whom re-created their roles on screen) had no personal knowledge of heroin addiction, which the musicians had observed up close or knew first hand. The play gave McLean the steady work he was denied in New York clubs; because of his own busts, he'd lost his cabaret card. In the movie, reflecting the musicians' tutelage, the actors have the rhythms of addiction down, starting with the waiting. Being a junkie isn't just expensive, it can be absurdly time-consuming; the dope is never there soon enough. Between fixes, there's sleep, quiet misery, and then extended whining: Where is it, when's it coming, and hey Jim could you spare five bucks in the meantime? Ernie, after a six-and-a-half–minute monologue: "I talked for 20 minutes, man!"

Cowboy is so long in coming, viewers who know their Samuel Beckett may be surprised when he does arrive, halfway through, with the dope. Carl Lee's Cowboy talks with the exaggerated delivery of a stereotypical jazz poet. He is accompanied, for cover on the way over, by a naive older street evangelist, Sister Salvation—not affiliated with the Salvation Army, she carefully notes—who eventually determines that all the men who visit the bathroom with Cowboy, one after another, and come out acting funny, must be drinking wine in there. (The band plays as the line forms, and each musician ducks into the toilet in turn, reducing the quartet to a series of round-robin trios.)

More junkie realism: When they emerge from the washroom, the principals are each temporarily euphoric, riding the high. A few minutes later they start to nod out. They fall on the floor, curl into a fetal position, or trail off in the middle of a story. Then the whining begins anew: I didn't get enough! It is all too realistic—maybe even tediously so. Less plausibly, the addicts goad Jim Dunn into shooting up, to see what it's really like. (Sharing means less for them.) And a half hour after the heroin floods Jim's system, he decides to abandon his film—either because he now realizes how phony it is, or because he's surrendered to instant addiction.

After complaining his first hit was weak, Leach shoots up a second time, after tying off and cooking the dope in a spoon, on camera (without a needle-push money shot), and he overdoses. He'll survive, but realistically enough, as soon as it looks like there's real trouble, the musicians quickly split—Freddie Redd's men and Ernie too. Jackie asks if he can help, but he's already headed for the door.

The grubby behavior of *The Connection*'s junkies contrasts with Frank Sinatra's epic scenery-chewing in *The Man with the Golden Arm*. Heroin use figures in a handful of later jazz films, but seldom with such dreary quotidian realism. In its modest way *The Connection* helped cement the impression that a jazz musician might be a junkie. In one sense it's a romantic choice: embracing heroin is a way to express a commitment to live in the moment, the way jazz musicians improvise in the moment. "Jazz musicians don't want success," John Cassavetes would later comment. "The jazz musician doesn't deal with the structured life—he just wants *that night*, like a kid."[5]

The Connection was striking enough to make Shirley Clarke's reputation as a filmmaker, and she would draw on jazz again. Pianist Mal Waldron composed the jazz and rhythm-and-blues score for her 1963 follow-up *The Cool World*, partly shot on Harlem streets, and she made a 1985 documentary about saxophonist Ornette Coleman, *Ornette: Made In America*.

Paris Blues (1961; 98 minutes; director: Martin Ritt; screenplay: Jack Sher, Irene Camp, Walter Bernstein; adaptation: Lulla Rosenfeld, from the novel by Harold Flender). Cast includes: Paul Newman (Ram Bowen), Sidney Poitier (Eddie Cook), Diahann Carroll (Connie Lampson), Joanne Woodward (Lillian Corning), Barbara Laage (Marie Séoul), Louis Armstrong (Wild Man Moore), Serge Reggiani (Michel "Gypsy" Devigne), André Luguet (René Bernard).
—Living the good life in Paris, black and white American jazzmen—one an aspiring composer—romance a pair of tourists from the States. This prompts the expatriates to weigh the relative advantages of staying or leaving.

Compared to *The Connection, Paris Blues* looks tame, and its reputation as a film that ran from controversy makes it easy to underestimate. It gets judged by what it isn't. Harold Flender's 1957 novel *Paris Blues* is about a black American saxophonist living in Paris who has an affair with a schoolteacher visiting from the US. As initially developed for the screen, the story became a tale of two musicians, black and white—Sidney Poitier and Paul Newman—who have cross-racial romances with tourists Joanne Woodward and Diahann Carroll.

The race-mixing intrigued Duke Ellington enough to agree to write the music, in conjunction with compositional alter ego Billy Strayhorn. But then distributor United Artists nixed the interracial angle. As Poitier would later say of that decision, "It took the spark out of it." Ellington, already committed, felt the same. It cut the heart from what *Paris Blues* was intended to be. Director Martin Ritt would later claim, "We had no script on that picture." Instead, the story goes, the filmmakers made the most of a picturesque location—Paris in overcast winter—and a first-rate cast with sexual chemistry. Newman and Woodward were married and often worked together; Poitier and Carroll had a long-simmering mutual attraction.[6]

Beyond shying away from interracial romance, *Paris Blues* scrapped most of Flender's story. It became a movie about something else, the education of a jazz composer, a theme the novel doesn't even hint at. There's a residual trace of that transgressive romance plot early on, when trombonist Ram Bowen (Newman) meets vacationing friends Connie Lampson (Carroll) and Lillian Corning (Woodward). The latter is a jazz fan who knows Ram's music, and is eager to have a Parisian fling, but he makes his play for Connie, who's younger and prettier, and looks like she's waiting for someone to muss her perfect hair. Ram's cool, diffident manner works on the French woman he's casually involved with— more on her later—but African American Connie is not intrigued by a white man with an automatic come-on.

When Connie meets tenor saxophonist Eddie Cook (Poitier), however, they click, and as these small-town vacationers will only be in Paris 12 days, things happen fast. A few walking tours of Paris into their relationship, Connie and Eddie want to stay together. But Connie is involved in the Civil Rights Movement, fighting the good fight for herself and her people, as that fight heats up back home; Eddie had come to Europe five years earlier to sidestep American racism—to be somewhere he can just be Eddie Cook. To him, Paris means freedom. To her, he's running away, and ducking a fight.

As they hash it all out, he does his best to show her the town the way an expatriate knows it: the little hillside streets and scenic overlooks, Notre-Dame seen from the back. Expatriates in Europe love the off-season, when tourists are thin on the ground. I speak from experience: That's when you most feel like you yourself belong, embracing the short days and damp weather casual visitors shun. *Paris Blues* captures that dimension of expat life, though the filmmakers hadn't gone looking for it. Ritt hadn't known Paris in the winter would be so gray, but he ran with the look.

For once, black characters aren't pushed to the sidelines; Connie and Eddie talk about things that matter, albeit in generalities. "We do need our roots, don't we?" she asks. "And where our roots are, our home is, wouldn't you say?" Eddie calls her "a swinger for the cause." In the end he will resolve to go home, to be with her.

The issues they argue about were real concerns for black expats, who'd typically escaped to Europe after years of battling racial oppression at home. "When I first came back," said pianist Hazel Scott after her decade in Europe, "people would say to me, 'You went away from the fight.'" Her tart reply: Before that, "I was down South desegregating audiences in town after town and getting out one jump ahead of the sheriff. So don't be telling me I ran away from the fight."[7]

Once Lillian throws herself at Ram hard enough to get his attention, they grow closer too, though they see less of Paris, lolling around his room with a rooftop view, in various states of undress. We only see the white characters in such intimate circumstances, but the black couple get all the sexy kisses. In the film's final scene, Eddie and Connie exchange one last long one, through the window of her train compartment, as the train begins to move. Partings don't get much more romantic. (And this one's only temporary.)

Ram's cool manner might have turned Lillian off, after her first flush of infatuation, but she perceives another, more vulnerable side of him, in his trombone playing. Martin Ritt had requested Ellington give Ram a sound like Tommy Dorsey's, clean and romantic, unlike Duke's eccentric sliphorn players; Bowen's horn was ghosted by both white Murray McEachern and black Billy Byers. (Eddie Cook's tenor is ghosted by Ellington steamer Paul Gonsalves.) Lillian's instincts are confirmed when Ram plays her a preliminary demo record of "Paris Blues." She had tried to plunk it out on piano, finding his sketches there—"You think that melody's heavy?" he'd asked, ever defensive—but she doesn't read music well.

Billy Strayhorn loved Paris and was glad to be working there, and the "Paris Blues" theme and that demo arrangement are almost certainly his. (Ellington, busy on the road in the States, arrived later.) The early 1960s was a very good period for Duke and his orchestra, and that demo is in the classic Ellington manner of the time, with countermelodies, surging backgrounds, lush saxophones, and a lovely wayward melody—it's classic Strayhorn too. Between them Strayhorn and Ellington composed one of the greatest jazz-film scores. Within the story, it makes sense that Ram Bowen's music resembles theirs. At the club he features their tunes like a diehard fan: "Take the 'A' Train," a three-minute "Mood Indigo," both unspoiled by dialogue, and "Sophisticated Lady."

Lillian's faltering piano version is not our first taste of the film's grand main theme "Paris Blues." Directly after the opening credits, way after hours in the subterranean club where Ram and Eddie are in residence, the trombonist had played his friend that very melody. (Newman studied trombone to prepare, and mimes well.) Eddie arranges Ram's music, and when he muses about scoring that melody for oboe against trombone, to lighten the texture, Ram assumes he's knocking it—that Eddie thinks the line is too heavy. (Hence that question to Lillian.) They get testy in a hurry, like brothers who spend too much time together. "All right," Eddie says sarcastically, "You're Gershwin—you're Ravel and Debussy." "What's wrong with that?" Ram wants to know. Eddie tells him what Lillian will: It sounds like you—and isn't that the idea? But Ram is not reassured.

The timeline in *Paris Blues* is built around the arrival and departure of the visitors, and of one other American: jazz great Wild Man Moore, who's a character from Flender's novel, though the film might as well have just called him Louis Armstrong. (Louis shot his part on a break from a marathon African tour.) The character Armstrong plays is closer to his real self than in any other film: the international celebrity and respected figure in the music world, the jazz elder and ambassador he'd become by 1960. Posters all over town announce (but give no date for) Wild Man's upcoming Nuit du Jazz concert. When he arrives at Gare Saint-Lazare on the train from seaport Le Havre, a cheering crowd and a celebratory jazz band are there to greet him. He blows trumpet out the train window at the folks on the platform, trading phrases with the French band—the kind of welcome Pops had enjoyed more than once.

Among those who've come to greet him is Ram Bowen, on a mission. After an exchange of compliments—Wild Man hears nothing but good about Ram's playing these days—Bowen produces a "Paris Blues" piano score that Wild Man looks over; he pledges to pass it on to his friend René Bernard, apparently the arbiter of musical high culture in Paris. In *New Orleans* 14 years earlier, Satchmo worried that sheet music was an obstacle to expressing one's feelings; Wild Man has a fuller skill set, and prestigious connections.

That same train also carries Connie and Lillian, who bump into Ram, who promptly starts flirting with Connie, and invites them to the club. Trains turn up in numerous jazz movies—this film also ends with one, returning Lillian and Connie to Le Havre. In life, bands depended on trains to get around; in Europe, musicians still rely on them to go medium distances. This is why jazz composers pen train songs. (Blues composers too; W. C. Handy, you'll recall, first met the blues at a depot.) Ellington's 1924 debut recording was

FIGURE 6.2 Wild Man Moore (Louis Armstrong) examines a score by Ram Bowen (Paul Newman) in *Paris Blues*.

called "Choo Choo," and that hard-traveling composer would go on to write numerous locomotive numbers, including "Daybreak Express" and "Happy-Go-Lucky Local." Ram Bowen has trains on his mind too. The first sound in the picture, at the fade in, is a long high note like a European locomotive's steam whistle: Ram's trombone, kicking off Strayhorn's "Take the 'A' Train."

At Club 33, also known as Marie's Cave, Ram and Eddie have a close-knit sextet, with Strayhorn pal Aaron Bridgers on piano (ghosted by Ellington), and guitarist Michel "Gypsy" Devigne (future French star chanteur Serge Reggiani), an addict modeled neither personally nor stylistically on Parisian Manouche picker Django Reinhardt. (Gypsy is around to carry a dispensable anti-narcotic subplot; the only interesting twists are that his pusher is a twinkle-eyed grandmotherly type, and that he neither kicks dope nor dies.) Occasionally, the band adds a lowkey but effective ballad and scat singer—the club's French owner Marie Séoul, perhaps inspired by Marie-Thèrése Ricard who ran the basement jazz club Chat Qui Peche. (In Flender's novel Michel is a wealthy, mentally ill black Frenchman, and Marie is a bitter black American expat.)

We don't get quietly glamorous Marie's back story, only clues. Her name and likeness are prominently displayed inside the club and out (where she gets bigger billing than Bowen or Devigne)—as if she'd had a pop hit or two, or had sung with a name band. (Barbara Laage who plays her was 40—old enough for Marie to have had a previous career.) But now she prefers a quieter life, arranged to her liking. She sings when the mood strikes, or maybe because customers expect it. She may stroll the room while performing, very much at home. The lively cavern she runs is a testament to Parisian/European devotion to jazz. As with real clubs in Europe or elsewhere, some nights it's packed, with a colorfully varied crowd (including interracial and gay couples) and plenty of dancing—as under the opening credits. And sometimes things are a little sedate and the couples more plain vanilla.

Marie is also Ram's casual lover. The lack of commitment suits them. His moodiness rolls off her. She knows how to defuse his little flare-ups, and she reads him well. "Why do you need me today?" she asks, when he gets amorous, not long after grousing at Eddie over that oboe. "Because you feel you're wonderful, or because you feel you're worth nothing?" Marie doesn't get huffy when Lillian starts hanging around, even though the new arrival threatens their comfortable arrangement.

Lillian wants Ram to come back to the States, to live with her and her two kids in their never-named small town, where she'll keep the world at bay while he composes. She seems not to share friend Connie's political commitment. When Lillian brings Ram the *International Herald Tribune* one morning, they don't discuss the headline story, though it elicits his throwaway "Well whaddya know?": John F. Kennedy has been sworn in as president. (That fixes the date of the action: mid-January 1961.)

The white couple's dynamic is like a negative image of the black one's. Connie persuades Eddie to repatriate to get into the thick of what really matters. Lillian wants to cut Ram off from the city and the artistic whirl that stimulate his music, like Franz Liszt's mistress in 1960's *Song Without End*—even though Lillian started falling for Ram when she heard him play, and the one time he looks truly happy is when Wild Man Moore makes good on a pledge to come down to Marie's and blow him out of the joint. (But Lillian's not there that night.)

Wild Man's drop-in may be the most raucous, joyous cutting contest in any movie. It's a lively evening, with lots of dancing, and Ram and Eddie have just finished a riff blues, when they hear a clarion call from the back of the room: Wild Man, at the foot of the stairs, followed by what must be his big band's entire brass section, plus reinforcements, soon setting background riffs. The crowd reacts realistically: instant pandemonium, not least because they know they'll be talking about this night forever. (And it's going to be great for Club 33—a night to make the Paris guidebooks; when it's all over, the first thing we'll see is Marie ringing up the cash register.) "You ready, man?" Wild Man asks Bowen, and then kicks off a fast line on "I Got Rhythm" chords, as the guest horns fall in with another Ellingtonian riff. Wild Man's trumpet solos challenge Eddie and then Gypsy, who give him their best shots in response, and then Moore engages in some call and response with his own troops, before slowly turning toward Ram: Wild Man merrily throws down the challenge, one brass player to another. Their exchange culminates in a series of fast trades. A snare tattoo from the drummer breaks the tension, as if he couldn't take any more, and leads to a messy, attenuated, higher-and-higher ending. It rams home the point that such lockhorn battles are about mutual respect: love not war.

(This scene echoes a real incident: just before the short-lived 1954 Armstrong–Benny Goodman tour, Louis and company had crashed a Goodman rehearsal, barging in with "When the Saints Go Marching In," which led to 20 minutes of bedlam, according to witness John Hammond. Goodman being Goodman, he asked Louis to leave so he could keep rehearsing.)[8]

This is the life Lillian wants to pry Ram away from—the life jazz composers thrive on. The excellent 1967 TV documentary *On the Road with Duke Ellington* shows how composing is part of his daily routine: something he works on in the pauses between other obligations. More than once we see Duke's road manager and tired stagehands all but drag him away from the piano, long after a gig has ended; he's working in installments on a trio piece he'll premier when he accepts an honorary degree. Ellington learned, and loved, to compose amid the bustle of the real world that inspired him, folding birdcalls and rail rhythms into his melodies. In that same doc, Ellington marvels at classical composers who invest untold time, writing pieces they never got to hear—the fate awaiting Ram in Lillian's little town.

Ram Bowen keeps his ear on his composing too, even during his idyll with Lillian; he grumbles that he and Eddie aren't getting any work done. The film's underscore, its Ellington-Strayhorn soundtrack, isn't exactly nondiegetic, I'd argue (echoing Krin Gabbard), because one character can hear it in his head: At least part of that underscore is "Paris Blues" as it takes shape in Ram's imagination. At one point we even hear the oboe Eddie had suggested, as if Ram were considering it after all.

While Bowen shapes his big piece, his artistic crisis arrives. René Bernard has studied his score, and shall render a verdict. Ram's meeting in the great man's office—adorned with a big Wild Man Moore poster and collage-y modern art—takes less than three minutes of real time/screen time, but seems excruciatingly longer. "I have a long been an admirer," Bernard begins, later circling back to that point: "Every time you put a horn to your mouth you are composing." But, he explains, there's big difference between that spontaneous composing and the "important piece of serious music" Ram aspires to, something to be played in concert (by a symphony orchestra, presumably). "Paris Blues," Bernard says, is merely "a jazz piece of a certain charm and melody." But maybe if Bowen decided to commit himself to serious study of theory, harmony, and counterpoint (here in Paris), he could really make something of himself. Maybe then he could become a real composer, says Bernard. Duke Ellington had been given similar advice, after the premier of *Black, Brown and Beige* in 1943.[9]

The condescension fairly drips off René Bernard—as Gabbard says, by dissing Bowen's theme, he's really dissing Billy Strayhorn who composed it. Reluctantly, we must defend this French snob a little. Bernard has judged "Paris Blues" only by the piano score, not that demo record which better demonstrates Ram's intentions and talents. Much of the celebrated "Ellington effect" is in the scoring. He/Strayhorn had acute ears for fusing harmony and timbre; Duke cultivated individual players and then combined them, typically in ways that sounded more striking and singular than notes on the page might suggest.

Ram's friends tell him to pay no mind, but he can't shake the idea that René Bernard is right. His first impulse is to run away; Ram tells Lillian he'll tag along when she leaves tomorrow. But then he has second thoughts. For an evening he goes full Europhile. He gushes over Gypsy's not so dazzling flamenco guitar at a going-away party, then muses on piano over a de-bluesified, Europeanized version of his theme. Finally Ram resolves to take Bernard's advice.

It's not clear how the filmmakers view René Bernard's recommendations. Hadn't Eddie already pointed out Ram's better off sounding like himself than Debussy? But there is a big fat clue, in the final scene, back at Gare Saint-Lazare, where Eddie is seeing off Connie till he can follow along and Ram tells Lillian he's staying. At the station, a billboard for Wild Man's concert—which our friends had skipped without comment, by the way—is being papered over by an ad for Larousse, publisher of literary masterworks. The classics blot out jazz.

But Ellington gets the last word, in more ways than one. The music is usually the last major element of a film to be completed, after principal editing. Duke did his final scoring back in the States, and the music he wrote for this final scene, in Gabbard's astute reading, lets us glimpse the future: Ram's final development of his theme. But also, as we plainly hear, he has written it not for a symphonic ensemble, but for an Ellingtonian jazz orchestra. In the end Ram Bowen rejects René Bernard's values and embraces his own tradition. He takes a key lesson from Duke's example. If you want to write for an orchestra and the culture industry is indifferent, assemble one of your own.

Saying goodbye at the station, Lillian tells him, you'll never forget me, and our time together; you'll see me on the street everywhere, and know I was the one. (It's Woodward's big scene; she has the most thankless part, and does the most with it.) The music swells as she walks off to board her train. (One thing has been settled: that thin oboe sonority has been transferred to high brass.) As Ram watches the train pull out, the music changes to a train's rhythm and surging power, with steamwhistle phrases in the brass. Lillian is right—he will remember. He's composing in his head even now, and the train section of "Paris Blues" will evoke that mix of loss and elation he feels at this very moment—elation, because now he can grapple with those musical challenges in earnest, undistracted. Like Eddie, Ram will stride out of the station like a man with places to go: He hears the future calling. The music's buoyancy confirms he's made the right choice. Ellington's last word continues, after the final image of Wild Man being papered over fades to black.

At the end of *Paris Blues*, Ellington's band does what it did in *Murder at the Vanities*: rebels against the Euro-classical establishment with a blast of his own idiosyncratic style. Soundtrack composers manipulate audience responses all the time, of course: that's their job. But this is a rare example of a composer effectively rewriting a film's ending.

Ram Bowen, we assume, will go back to Club 33 and his comfortable relationship with Marie Séoul; he'll patch things up with unreliable Gypsy and let his jazz experience feed his composing. But something fundamental will have changed. Easy as it is to overlook, Ram faces two partings at the finish. He and Eddie have come to an ending too; the composer won't have his arranger to lean on anymore. "If you have the right partner, you can correct each other's faults, go further," Parisian expat saxophonist Steve Lacy once said.[10] But as Lacy knew, even great partnerships may run their course. When Ram tells Lillian, "I gotta find out how far I can go—and I guess that means alone," he's talking about Eddie as well.

> ***Too Late Blues*** **(1962; 103 minutes; director: John Cassavetes; writers: Richard Carr, Cassavetes). Cast includes: Bobby Darin (Ghost Wakefield), Stella Stevens (Jess Polanski), Everett Chambers (Benny Flowers), Cliff Carnell (Charlie), Richard Chambers (Pete), Seymour Cassel (Red), Dan Stafford (Shelley), Nick Dennis (Nick Bubalinas), Vince Edwards (Tommy Sheehan), Val Avery (Milt Frielobe), Mario Gallo (recording engineer), Rupert Crosse (Baby Jackson), Marilyn Clark (Countess). New song: "A Song After Sundown" (David Raksin).**
> **—Ghost Wakefield's quintet plays his moody jazz in parks and orphanages instead of nightclubs. When Ghost poaches his manager's woman and makes her the band's singer, trouble ensues. Ghost dissolves the group and goes commercial, till he can't live with himself. Is it too late to get the old crew back together?**

Jazz movies aren't always about jazz. Sometimes the music is a more kinetic and photogenic proxy for a less dramatizable creative process: writing, say. Or low-budget filmmaking. John Cassavetes said his dramas about maladjusted people coping with life were really about himself, and his Boswell, scholar Ray Carney, has limned how *Too Late*

Blues concerns the director's own recent career: shooting (and extensively reshooting) the quasi-improvised *Shadows*—and alienating cast members by promising them bigger profit shares than they got—before starring in TV's *Johnny Staccato* for the money and then fighting his way back toward more personal projects.

Too Late Blues is nominally about a composer-leader "on the outer fringes of the jazz world" in Cassavetes's words, who alienates the improvisers who give life to his composing. In a rash moment he dumps them to go commercial, and winds up playing functional piano in a nightclub where there are many distractions—which could be Johnny Staccato's job description. And then he tries to get that old independent spirit back, by reuniting the old gang. The cast and crew of *Too Late Blues* includes a few veterans of *Shadows*. That film had slowly brought Cassavetes recognition—it played in London on a bill with *The Cry of Jazz*—and prompted Paramount to greenlight one of several scripts he'd pitched, a low-budget jazz story. For a split-second after *Staccato*, he was Hollywood's jazz guy. He'd even been up for the lead in *Paris Blues*, whose producer Sam Shaw was an old friend and patron (and his own future producer); Cassavetes had already made two films with friend Sidney Poitier.[11]

Cassavetes and *Staccato* writer Dick Carr had hammered out the script for *Too Late Blues*. Paramount let Cassavetes direct, but boxed him in. He wanted to shoot on location in New York; he got Los Angeles. He liked to work slowly, rewriting as things developed on set—improvising a little—but he was locked into a six-week shoot, and the original script. He wanted Montgomery Clift and Gena Rowlands; he got Bobby Darin in his first nonsinging role, and recent Elvis costar Stella Stevens. Darin is not very good, no Cassavetes—you can picture the director delivering the dialogue far better. Stevens is surprisingly fine, playing an underestimated woman, with pathos, like Rowlands in the director's later films.

Cassavetes shot this studio picture like an independent, in rough and ready black and white, and with rambling sequences that run very long. (Much would be made of that tic in 1970's *Husbands*, but he hones the practice here.) That said, as shot by seasoned cinematographer and *Staccato* holdover Lionel Lindon, it looks like a real movie, not shady like *Shadows*. Cassavetes shot it on the cheap, partly because he mistakenly thought the studio would then respect him more, not less.

Like a shoestring indie filmmaker, *Too Late Blues*' Ghost Wakefield—he gave himself the nickname—relies on unconventional funding. (Cassavetes raised money for *Shadows* with an on-air appeal during a radio interview.) Ghost's quintet doesn't do nightclubs, instead playing orphans' and old folks' homes, city festivals, and parks. As such they may be the screen's first publicly subsidized jazz band. Which means this jazz film that isn't a jazz film looks ahead to a hot jazz topic of the 1970s and beyond, in Europe especially: Should the government subsidize unpopular music? (Dutch saxophonist Peter van Bergen's rejoinder: Why would you subsidize popular music?)[12]

It's one thing to play at a home for children who like your sound enough that one kid will impulsively grab a saxophone so he can honk on it. (Now that's an honest response—and more believable kid music than Jeff Lambert down on Basin Street in *Birth of the*

Blues.) But it's another thing to play for union scale in a picnic grove for exactly one person—evidently a park employee—and a bunch of empty tables. There's way more action on a ballfield in the distance.

Ghost is happy just to hear his compositions the way he wants to hear them. But his most seasoned and independent sideman, alto saxophonist Charlie (*Shadows* street brawler and crew member Cliff Carnell, ghosted by the great Benny Carter) pushes him to try to line up some real gigs—like, at night. What good is honing Ghost's repertoire if only they get to hear it? Put the music before a paying audience and let's see how it measures up, as skeptics would comment about subsidized music, later.

The others go along with playing for kids and trees because they like Ghost's music and the way they all interact: drummer Shelley (one-time Cassavetes roommate Dan Stafford, who played some drums, ghosted by Shelly Manne), bassist Red (Cassavetes sidekick Seymour Cassel, another *Shadows* vet, ghosted by Red Mitchell), and trumpeter Pete (Richard Chambers, ghosted by studio mainstay Uan Rasey; the character's name suggests Cassavetes had hoped he'd be ghosted by *Staccato* day player Pete Candoli). At the gig in the park, after the others start packing up in disgust, Pete keeps playing, providing a little diegetic background music. Then there's foreshadowing: as they're leaving they get lured onto the baseball field, where the musicians show team spirit, but Ghost strikes out swinging with bases loaded.

Ghost's music is okay, a little dreamy. The score is by Hollywood composer David Raksin, who'd played clarinet and saxophone in jazz bands as a teenager and once recorded with Buck and Bubbles. Raksin had already written the jazz-friendly movie themes "Laura" and "The Bad and the Beautiful." The big number he Ghost-writes, "A Song After Sundown," is never named—it's only referred to as an "untitled blues," though

FIGURE 6.3 Ghost Wakefield's quintet plays for the trees in *Too Late Blues*.

it isn't a blues. It has a rangy but haunting quality: something out of the ordinary but not forbidding. (Stan Getz would record it with the Boston Pops.) Some complain Raksin's score sounds little like circa-1960 jazz, but that's the point: Ghost goes his own way.

"A Song After Sundown" sounds even better when Ghost hooks the band up with singer Jess Polanski. Stella Stevens breathes real life into this beauty with zero self-esteem: she doesn't think anyone's interested in her mind or personality, but she has the urge to sing. (It's not clear who ghosted her wordless "no-singing singing," as someone dubs it.) Ghost hears her at a party hosted by Baby Jackson (the imposing light-skinned African American actor Rupert Crosse, *Shadows*' jivey talent agent and *Staccato*'s Redtop), a jazz musician who has a jocular but sometimes slightly aggressive manner, and stands up to white folks (a waiter, his agent) when he thinks they don't show proper respect. Those attributes suggest he's a stand-in for imposing light-skinned African American bassist Charles Mingus, who'd worked on *Shadows*. (We don't see Baby perform, but in Stuart James's novelization of the screenplay, he's a bass player.)

The party scene is where Ghost first hears Jess deftly show what she's got as a singer, and what she lacks. A pianist (Slim Gaillard) and friends encourage her to join him, and whatever figure he plays at the keyboard, no matter how beboppy or complex, she imme-diately sings it back, accurately and in tune: she has a phonographic memory. But when he leaves space for her to improvise she freezes up. And when he plunks out a note a few times, to give her the pitch to start a song on after he plays an intro, she immediately repeats it verbatim, misreading the cue. It's an efficient, musical character sketch: she's got plenty of raw talent but no experience.

She's at the party with Ghost's on-and-off agent Benny Flowers (*Staccato* producer Everett Chambers). He and Jess are dating, and she's hoping he'll find her work, but Benny is more interested in denigrating her talents, to keep her dependent. Ghost encourages her, and winds up taking her home—she makes a pass at him, thinking it's the only way to be sure she'll see him again—and the next day he brings her to that gig in the park. And the day after that she joins the band in the studio, when (with Benny's help) they cut a demo of "A Song After Sundown" for Gold Star Records. Jess knows the melody from hearing it the day before.

By that demo session she and Ghost are already an item. She tries to tell him she's been around the block, after he starts calling her Princess. Jess Polanski is the flipside of *Some Like It Hot*'s Sugar Kane: a blond singer with a reputation as a dummy who feels the sting of sexism every day. (You can see it in Stevens's face, in every demoralized close-up.) Safe to say she assumes Ghost never would have put her on the recording date if they weren't involved.

That said, she gives the music its tang. Her wordless vocal makes the number mem-orable and gives the band a distinctive sound. Not that the session producer can hear it. Cassavetes has some meta-fun here with know-nothing producers. Gold Star's Milt Frielobe hates the tune on first hearing, but when Ghost barges into the booth to argue, Frielobe decides he prefers the number the band's now playing: the same tune. Later on Ghost will say, very Cassavetes-like, "Name me one guy in this business knows anything about music. . . . There's nobody, I don't care who it is, man, knows anything good from anything bad. It's all a matter of opinion."

Ghost and Benny didn't get along even before Ghost stole his woman, and as Benny explains to Jess, in a moment worthy of *All the Fine Young Cannibals*' Chad Bixby, "You know I'm the sensitive type. You hurt my feelings, you've got yourself an enemy for life." So Ghost exercises poor judgment when he leaves the Gold Star negotiations to Benny, who sabotages the deal. The band will be paid union scale for four sides, and he's sold Ghost's publishing rights cheap—then tries to convince his client the money's so bad, he should pull his potential hit song from the date. And then Benny brings in another of his clients to sing on the recording. "That other girl had a foggy voice," he tells Frielobe. "This girl has a clean voice." (Frielobe, not trusting his own ears, like some real producers defers to his engineer, who hates everything, even the studio itself.) With this forced substitution of one singer for another, *Too Late Blues* becomes a film about its own production: the artist wanted his own woman on it—Cassavetes was married to Gena Rowlands—but was outmaneuvered. (At another point, story and meta-story collide when Ghost addresses Charlie as "Clifford"—calling the character by the actor's name, *Shadows*–style.)

The second record date is a disaster, but things had already fallen apart. After the previous day's demo session, they'd unwound at their clubhouse, Nick's pool room. This 18-minute scene, with much heavy drinking, slowly builds to a brawl (encouraged by scheming Benny) between the band and working-class tough Tommy who dislikes jazz musicians. When Tommy suddenly turns violent the musicians all jump him—all except Ghost, who freezes. (He acts like a pacifist, actually—resists but doesn't retaliate.) But when it's over, and a badly shaken Jess reaches out to Ghost, his shame gets the better of him—he pushes her toward Charlie, and when the dust settles she decides she's done with music and these musicians.

At the recording session the next day, Ghost tells Frielobe he's not giving away his big number for peanuts. The band turns on Ghost; they're invested in this material too, having whipped it into shape on their low-money gigs, and this record could put them over. Ghost calls them a bunch of talentless phonies, nothing without him. Pete, Red, and Shelley fire right back, and in an instant, the band is over. Only Charlie, the money player, says it's cool, call me anytime: "These cats don't understand tough scenes."

With everything in ruins, Ghost tells Benny to book him anywhere the money is, and Benny hooks him up with "the Countess" (*Shadows* bit player and *Staccato* guest star Marilyn Clark), who doesn't care about the music, but does "subsidize" (Ghost's term) young musicians in exchange for sex. She's a malicious caricature of "jazz baroness" Nica De Koenigswarter, an eccentric but genuine and generous friend and patron to numerous jazz musicians. (Cassavetes had met Nica when Mingus brought her to a *Shadows* scoring session.)

A year passes; Ghost has been playing in a trio in a loud lounge. He's making good money and doesn't see the old gang anymore. But we hear just enough of his piano (ghosted here by Jimmy Rowles) to know the music he's playing is more forgettable (and easy to ignore) than his old stuff. "I never played better in my life," he tells Benny, trying to leverage a better gig, but Benny for once tells the truth: "A hundred guys can play what you're playing out there and 99 of them can play it better."

"I play what I like with no compromises," Ghost insists, but Benny again sets him straight: "When an idealist sells himself out, everybody passes judgment. The bigger the idealist, the bigger the bum." In the novelization, the last word is "whore."[13] That point will soon be underscored when Ghost breaks with the Countess, and Benny, and seeks out Jess. He finds her working as a bar girl, getting lecherous guys to buy her drinks and making a few more bucks if they take her home. (This parallel between prostitution and playing commercial music will come back in *The Fabulous Baker Boys*.) When Ghost walks in, two eager guys are trying to arrange a package deal. Now he gets violent—throws them out, makes a scene, and tells her he'll take her home. Jess, shakier than ever, smashes the mirror in the bar bathroom, as if intent on suicide. She'd threatened it before.

But instead of home Ghost takes her to a bar where the members of his old band, and a couple of ringers, play nondescript music in matching spangled jackets. Jess freaks out when they arrive—it had ended badly between her and Charlie—and when Ghost approaches the bandstand to apologize, Red and Shelley don't want to hear it.

Drummer Shelley kicks off a tune with a Latin beat to cut Ghost off. And then Jess, slumped in a corner, all but catatonic, starts wordlessly cooing "A Song After Sundown." There's a short Ivesian collision of her tune and Shelley's, and then the horns cluster around to join her—starting with Charlie, perhaps feeling guilty. (The tune must be in the band's repertoire; even the new guys know it.) For one fragile minute, Ghost's band is reunited. It's the most downbeat musical-reunion ending in jazz movies. Jess drops out before they finish. And there *Too Late Blues* ends, before we find out whether the reunion will take. In Cassavetes's cut, Jess walks out when the tune's over.

Too Late Blues (like the original script for *Second Chorus*) is about a guy who misses his moment; Ghost becomes a shadow of what he might have been. He wrecks his own career by being an easily manipulated, impulsive, self-important jerk. Such characters are as familiar in jazz as in Hollywood. Cassavetes himself didn't think it was very good, and reviewers agreed. It may be the least memorable film he wrote and directed—a training exercise. But his taste for long sequences and personal psychodrama would pay off in films like *Faces* and *A Woman Under the Influence*.

All Night Long (1962; 91 minutes; director: Basil Dearden; writers: Paul Jarrico, Nel King). Cast includes: Patrick McGoohan (Johnny Cousin), Paul Harris (Aurelius Rex), Marti Stevens (Delia Lane), Keith Michell (Cass Michaels), Richard Attenborough (Rod Hamilton), Betsy Blair (Emily Cousin), Maria Velasco (Benny), Charles Mingus, Dave Brubeck, Johnny Dankworth, Allan Ganley, Tubby Hayes (themselves). New song: "All Night Long" (words Sonny Miller/music Philip Green).
—Bandleader Aurelius Rex's drummer Johnny wants to starts his own band, featuring singer Delia Lane, who'd retired when she'd married Rex. Over the

course of a long late-night party, Johnny schemes to convince Rex that Delia is unfaithful, hoping that breaking them up will clear the way for her comeback.

On one level *All Night Long* is like a more presentable *Connection*: a drama spun out over a few hours, in one location, with real musicians playing jazz interludes. It's also one in a line of offbeat Shakespeare adaptations: a jazz *Forbidden Planet*. *All Night Long* streamlines the plot of *Othello* to take place over one endless surprise party and jam session. (Director Basil Dearden knew his genre pictures; in the 1960s he made a few hot-topic dramas and international escapades.)

It's not the craziest idea: *Othello* calls for the blowing of trumpets and woodwinds, and includes a wise, diplomatic and well-spoken Duke. There is in fact an Ellington figure in *All Night Long*: Othello has become regal, successful African American bandleader Aurelius Rex, who strikes up Ellington's "Mood Indigo" and "In a Sentimental Mood" when he sits at the piano, and who like Duke has sidemen who can be a headache. The portrait of this quasi-Duke is in the end not so flattering, but then Shakespeare blithely disregarded historical accuracy too.

Rex's Iago is his drummer of six years, loquacious, scheming, pot-smoking Johnny Cousin (Patrick McGoohan), who's ready to give notice and launch his own band, like an evil Gene Krupa. But Cousin has gotten ahead of himself by promising potential backers he's obtained the services of pop singer Delia Lane, who'd retired when she married Rex a year ago. (As she'll ambiguously put it, "It was my own idea to quit. Rex wouldn't marry me till I did.") So if Johnny can break that happy couple up, Delia will be free to sing again. And he's hoping to make that happen tonight, at Rex and Delia's anniversary party, thrown by rich, glad-handing jazz fan Rod Hamilton.

The screenplay came from the States—from blacklisted screenwriter Paul Jarrico, and Nel King who'd later edit Charles Mingus's rollicking autobiographical novel *Beneath the Underdog*. *All Night Long* was shot in the UK and set in London, but the principal characters remain American—so Rex is dislocated, like Othello in Cyprus. That dislocation is reinforced by New York–born Irishman McGoohan's not-so-American–sounding mid-Atlantic accent, and by his bandmate and saxophonist Cass being played by Australia's Keith Michell.[14]

For what it's worth, *All Night Long* depicts the interracial American couples abroad we didn't get in *Paris Blues*: Rex and Delia, and also Cass and his good woman Benny, played by Maria Velasco, who'd briefly appeared at the going-away party in *Paris Blues*—as if these stories share the same universe.

Jarrico's and King's Shakespeare revamp can be audacious: in place of Desdemona's lost handkerchief, Delia's purloined cigarette case; in place of Othello misinterpreting an overheard conversation, a doctored audio tape. The party is held at Rod's converted loft in a Southwark warehouse just south of the river, with exteriors shot along winding narrow Shad Thames with its exposed catwalks over the street. Despite the unity of place, *All Night Long* uses more sets than you need to stage *Othello*: a stairwell, Rod's bedroom

FIGURE 6.4 A jazz Othello and his Iago: Aurelius Rex (Paul Harris) and Johnny Cousin (Patrick McGoohan) in *All Night Long*.

and conversation den, a vast space for entertaining, internal and external walkways and balconies, and a roof with a view of Tower Bridge. Interior windows on several sides overlook the river.

Time is compressed, and with all the action crammed into a few hours, this *Othello* approaches a door-slamming farce. The whole Shakespearean plot is Johnny's frantic cannabis-fueled improvisation, making *All Night Long* another shaggy-dog drummer's joke, like *The Strip*—or maybe just a pothead's crazy dream.

Follow Johnny's logic. Delia's told him she doesn't want to join his band. But if she and Rex break up, why wouldn't she? And since Rex's road manager Cass is an old friend of Delia's, all Johnny has to do is make Rex think there's something between the two. So if Johnny can persuade Cass, who's recovering from a nervous breakdown, to get high and act up—goading him into picking a fight with Rex's booking agent—then Delia will have to intervene on Cass's behalf, making Rex doubt her fidelity. Ever alert for an angle he can exploit, Johnny impulsively tapes a couple of upstairs conversations on Rod's reel-to-reel recorder, in hopes of catching something incriminating (or something he can make sound that way—this clown is a fast, deft tape editor).

Give Johnny his due: wherever he sees a crack, he drives in a wedge. Delia does miss singing. True, she'd tired of her old bread-and-butter ballad "All Night Long"—she groans a little when someone requests it—but being married to Rex has stimulated her creativity. With this surprise party for her husband in the works, she and Cass have quietly cooked up a surprise for Rex, something new for her: a jazzy arrangement of "I Never Knew," where she'll scat sing. (This bit of music ties a cross-cultural knot; blonde American Marti Stevens is ghosted by black English singer Cleo Laine.) You can imagine how Johnny spins Delia's and Cass's secret rehearsals to her husband, who does indeed confess to a jealous streak; Rex is flattered she gave it all up to be with him, even as he reminds folks it was her idea.

This speed-read *Othello* would be too transparently hectic if the jazz numbers didn't offer relief. Rod isn't just throwing a party, it's a session, with frequent, credibly casual performances giving the plot twists time to sink in (and Johnny time to scheme and edit tape). The basic set-up is plausible enough. Musicians abroad do encounter superfans who like to socialize with them and pour the drinks, and whose attention isn't always entirely welcome. (Some just talk about how many other musicians they know.) After a while Rex and Delia are like party guests in a Buñuel film, having no fun but unable to leave.

Still, the music is good: circa 1960 London bop, a little light and polite. The characters who perform include Rex, Delia, Johnny, and Cass, and (apparently) other members of Rex's band; plus a percussionist who plays bongos and timbales in Cuban style, but is nonetheless identified as Brazilian, maybe because boss nova was big in 1962. London luminaries appearing as themselves include tenor saxist and vibraphonist Tubby Hayes, saxophonist Johnny Dankworth (whose wife, Cleo Laine, sends regrets), and drummer Allan Ganley (who coached and ghosted McGoohan). Also attending, as themselves, are two American stars in town at the moment, pianist Dave Brubeck—his presence a tribute to noble Rex—and bassist Charles Mingus. Some music seen and heard was recorded live on camera, in particular the Brubeck-Mingus duet later issued as "Non-Sectarian Blues."

Mingus is such an imposing figure on screen—almost Falstaffian—you can't help but notice how little he's around. He was reportedly a pest on set, making mostly unwelcome suggestions about the story, music, and camera angles. When West Indian trumpeter Harry Beckett came in to sideline, Mingus drafted him into a band that they'd rehearse on the side.

In the story, Mingus is the first musician to arrive at the warehouse, and may have broken in. He's the only person there when Rod arrives around 11:20, to find the door hanging open, and Mingus upstairs warming up his bass. "Hope you don't mind—I just walked in," Mingus greets him. "Liberty Hall," Rod quips. He calls him "Chas." Mingus's main contribution to the story is dispensed within the opening minutes, as he and Rod share a drink and expository dialogue.

As more musicians arrive, Rod thoughtfully greets each by name. Ganley kids Mingus about getting there early. "Yeah baby and I'll be the last one to leave," he pledges—his last line of dialogue, about four minutes in, and an inaccurate prediction. He does play bass on a couple of numbers with Tubby on vibes, until Johnny Cousin arrives, with some instantly ditched flunkies carrying his drums. Mingus vacates the performance area immediately, without a word. After that he vanishes for long stretches—perhaps prowling the neighborhood, looking for a pub.

Between real bassists and drummers, failure to connect isn't always personal—sometimes they fail to mesh despite best efforts. But one can see why Mingus would avoid devious blustering Johnny. Among his other faults, Johnny's a whiner. He tells the Brazilian, "I belong to that new minority group: white American jazz musicians." (He lifted that zinger from Stan Kenton.)[15] Rex politely laughs, without pointing out that he employs a few.

Mingus returns unannounced sometime after Rex arrives, as if the bassist's main reason for attending was to play with this Ellington figure. Mingus loved Duke's music, and early in his career called himself Baron Mingus; he imitated Ellington's piano playing, wrote several tributes, and echoed his distinctive instrumental effects. ("That's what *he* says," was Duke's acid appraisal.)[16]

They had a little history. In 1953 Duke had hired the bassist as a temporary sub, but Mingus quickly clashed with trombonist Juan Tizol and just as quickly exited (pursued by Tizol, with a knife). But the bassist still longed to record with Ellington, and the year after shooting *All Night Long* they made the trio album *Money Jungle* with drummer Max Roach. It was a contentious session, partly because the pianist declined to play any Mingus music.

Fictional Rex is more cooperative. The tune he and Mingus play together, joined in progress, turns out to be Mingus's "Peggy's Blue Skylight." For once, Rex's thick jabbing chords sound convincingly Ellingtonian—because on this number Mingus, overdubbing, supplied the piano as well as bass part: he got to play alongside and be the Ellington figure at the same time. In any event, by the time Johnny's sinister plot bubbles over in the last reel, both Mingus and Brubeck are long gone.

As the night wears on, Rex knows that Johnny's up to something, the way he's always pulling him aside with some more distressing news. Ellington, who dealt with more than his share of shifty characters, would not have been fooled by this cluck. But Johnny does fool Rex, whose long simmer of jealousy and misunderstanding boils into rage. He chokes Delia and throws Cass over a balcony before Johnny is at last exposed, by his own abused, devoted, and horrified wife Emily: My Johnny never told the truth in his life. (She's played by Betsy Blair, blacklisted American in English exile, looking perpetually blinded by headlights.)

Othello racks up the bodies, but in this Shakespeare skit, everyone lives: Delia was only unconscious, Cass just got some scrapes and the wind knocked out of him, and Delia stops Rex from strangling Johnny. (Hard to imagine Mingus standing by while all that transpires; Tubby Hayes is no help at all.) In the end everyone is forgiven or forgiving—we last see Rex and Delia arm in arm, walking away as dawn breaks—all except for Johnny, who spurns Emily's attempt at reconciliation. Last to leave, Johnny plays one final cathartic drum solo to an abandoned room: the kind of victimless improvising he should stick to. He's smart to get in the practice, as he'll be needing a new job. And he'll be lugging those drums home himself.

Dr. Terror's House of Horrors (1965; 93 minutes; director: Freddie Francis; writer: Milton Subotski). **Cast includes: Roy Castle (Biff Bailey), Kenny Lynch (Sammy Coin), Tubby Hayes (himself), Peter Cushing (Dr. Schreck). New songs: "Everybody's Got Love," "Give Me Love" (Kenny Lynch).**
—In one segment of this horror anthology, a London trumpeter ignores warnings not to insert sacred voodoo themes into his jazz.

In oral traditions like jazz, "found" material is borrowed and reworked all the time—that's the story of *Blues in the Night*. W. C. Handy, as we've seen, folded overheard blues lyrics and tunes into his copyrighted music. Jelly Roll Morton once demonstrated how the New Orleans staple "Tiger Rag" derived from an old French quadrille. Needing an ending for a jam tune, Count Basie's band tacked on a riffing line from the Chocolate Dandies' "Six or Seven Times," and Count's theme "One O'Clock Jump" was born. Via ex–King Oliver saxophonist Rudy Jackson, bits and pieces of Oliver's "Camp Meeting Blues" crept into Ellington's "Creole Love Call"—and within months of its release, Oliver wrote Duke's label demanding royalties.

Such borrowings/pilferings occur all over. In 1920s Cuba, musicologist Alejo Carpentier and a composer friend were observing a ritual celebration of the Abakuá secret men's society when the friend began jotting down musical phrases. This brought the marathon ceremony to a halt.

"What are you writing down there?"

"The music."

"Why?"

"To make some dance tunes out of it."

"If you don't want a tragedy to occur, put away the notebook and the pencil. . . . This is not a thing for making fun of. . . . Nobody called you here."[17]

Such borrowings reach across cultures: Cuban rhythms had influenced Stateside music before the Civil War. A mid-twentieth-century boom in ethnic-music records spurred Western composers and also made their far-flung influences easier to spot. Listeners could connect, say, timbre-rich patterned variations in Steve Reich or Anthony Davis music with Indonesian gamelans and West African percussion choirs. In jazz movies, such appropriations typically pass without comment or debate; again, think *Blues in the Night*. A rare big-screen consideration of the ethics of appropriation is tucked into a low-budget color English horror anthology, *Dr. Terror's House of Horrors* (1965). The semi-comic segment, fittingly enough, brazenly borrows and reworks crime writer Cornell Woolrich's 1935 short story "Dark Melody of Madness," adapted for radio's *Escape* in 1948 and for US television's one-hour anthology series *Thriller* in 1961.

The *Thriller* episode "Papa Benjamin" was directed by Ted Post and shot in noirish black and white by Cassavetes collaborator Lionel Lindon. It concerns New York's Eddie Wilson (John Ireland), whose dance band has been booked at a hotel on Santa Isabela, a small English-speaking island nation 60 miles south of Puerto Rico. (Eddie mostly tells the tale in flashback, to the police; the short story and radio version were set in New Orleans.) Wilson's music is bland, but the tropics have whet his ambition: he wants to write "a rhapsody based on Afro-Cuban themes." Intrigued by a chant and its accompanying beat he overhears his biracial drummer Statts (Henry Scott) sing and play with a faraway air—a musical theme Statts won't talk about or reproduce—Eddie tails Statts to a mansion where he eavesdrops on that music in context, as part of a voodoo rite. When Eddie's found out, high priest Papa Benjamin (Jester Hairston) would execute him on the spot, but Statts vouches for his boss, claims he wants to convert to their religion. Wilson swears on his life it's true, and that he'll keep their secrets.

But he lies. Composing around the clock like a man possessed, Eddie turns that sacred music into his "Voodoo Rhapsody," and then has the chutzpah to premier it with much hubbub at the hotel down the beach. (Statts has quit after trying to warn him off.) Wilson's duplicity has certainly helped the music; his blah orchestra sounds amazingly better, playing a chart by Hollywood jazz composer Pete Rugolo, echoing Cuba's Benny Moré. The cavernous low saxophones sound like 1950s Sun Ra, the trombone solo like Ellington's Juan Tizol, the rhythms alternately Latin and swinging. But during the performance Eddie collapses with a stabbing pain: attack by voodoo doll.

Pain persists back in New York, even after he retires the rhapsody. (He's reluctant to explain his ailment, since it involves plagiarism.) Folks tell him it's all in his head. In desperation he returns to Santa Isabela and shoots a defiant Papa Benjamin, though there's no body when Eddie leads the cops to the scene; they think he's squirrely too. Now recovered, he's rebooked into that beachfront hotel, where he plays "Voodoo Rhapsody" in response to many requests—it's still in the band's book, #22—and he's fatally stricken at the piano.

As TV voodoo tales go, "Papa Benjamin" is notable for portraying (generic) African religion with respect; the ring dance for once moves properly counterclockwise. Still, at 50 minutes including host Boris Karloff's bumper segments, it's way longer than necessary, padded out in Woolrich's paid-by-the-word pulp style.

Dr. Terror's House of Horrors doesn't credit Woolrich or John Kneubuhl's TV adaptation, but tells the same basic story, with more focus, economy, and wit, in less than half the time. In the film's narrative frame, Peter Cushing's ominous Dr. Schreck, consulting his tarot deck, tells the fortunes of five strangers who share a train compartment, giving each (and us) a vision of a possible supernatural fate: one's house is consumed by a killer vine, another is pursued by a severed hand.

The assembly's compulsive joker is Biff Bailey, London jazz trumpeter and entitled wiseacre. In Biff's segment his sextet includes *All Night Long* sessioneers Tubby Hayes on tenor and flute and Allan Ganley on drums. (On screen and soundtrack Biff fronts Hayes's band, with Jimmy Deuchar on mellophonium, which looks like a French horn partly unwound to resemble an oversize trumpet.) We get a glimpse of what a nitwit Biff is when he learns the band's been booked at a hotel on the West Indian isle of Paiti (pronounced with three syllables, the way much of the world pronounces Haiti), and he starts babbling in a mock India-Indian accent.

Bailey has no sense of boundaries when it comes to other people's cultures. Or much of an ear. In Paiti, he praises the authentic calypsos of singer Sammy Coin, who's a Cockney Londoner barely faking an island accent. (He's played by black English pop singer Kenny Lynch, who performs his own tunes.) Sitting at a table, Biff grabs a cigarette girl's hand, so he can examine her ring bearing the image of voodoo god Dambala: "Look at that monster." This effrontery shocks his fellow patrons, black and white; Dambala has many followers hereabouts. At night there are jungle rituals, exotic and alluring, Sammy tells Biff: Stay away from those.

Of course he doesn't, sneaking out after hours to spy from the bushes. As the chanting and drumming and dancing go on, Biff takes out a notepad, draws a quick staff, and starts notating the music (very inexactly: no dotted notes or triplets). Comic relief: Every time we cut from the rite to Biff writing, one more native stands behind him. He's brought forward, and his conversation with the head priest parallels the one Alejo Carpentier had witnessed. But the screen version is more crass.

Biff: "I was listening to your music, so I wrote it down. . . . It could be a hit—make a fortune." Conspiratorially: "If you wrote it, we could go 50–50."

"This is music known only to Dambala's own people, for centuries!"

"Well, if it's that old, then it's out of copyright."

"Do not steal from the god Dambala!"

But even before he's back in London, Biff resolves to do just that, over the objections of his new singer Sammy Coin (who'll perform another Kenny Lynch song, this one with an American accent). At his manager's new club Biff unveils "an ancient voodoo tune . . . in his own special arrangement," with plenty of drums, and Bailey's scorching trumpet. In another cross-cultural pile-up, he's ghosted by black West Indian Shake Keane—so the islands sneak into Biff's playing as well as writing. Biff's placed an image of Dambala on the wall behind the bandstand, and kisses it for a laugh.

The weakest aspect of the efficient storytelling is that Biff's tune (Tubby Hayes's "Voodoo") doesn't sound much like Dambala's sacred music. Still, Tubby supplies a helpful gloss on cross-racial musical pilferage, with a flute solo that appropriates the shrieking, singing-while-playing style of African American jazzman Rahsaan Roland Kirk.

That flute rustle is foreshadowing: While Biff's band plays to a packed room, a mighty wind blows through from the garden, flapping the swinging doors and blowing around sheet music and tablecloths. The patrons flee, but the musicians finish the number anyway: professionals. The place is a shambles, but the owner's insured. I could redo it Moroccan-style, he muses: one more culture to pluck like a chicken. Undaunted, Biff vows to revise the music, but later that night a Dambalan in loincloth and face paint will retrieve the chart, as Biff falls dead at his feet. Back in the frame story, a less dim Biff Bailey grasps the moral: "That'll teach me not to steal tunes." He spells it out so plainly there's nothing to add. Even oblivious choices have consequences.

Movies parallel life: Ghanian drummer Guy Warren, who wrote a number of pieces that drew on West and Central African sacred music, complained that British saxophonist Kenny Graham had ripped off and retitled his composition "The Haitian Ritual."[18]

A Man Called Adam (1966; 109 minutes; director: Leo Penn; writers: Les Pine, Tina Rome). Cast includes: Sammy Davis Jr. (Adam Johnson), Cicely Tyson (Claudia Ferguson), Ossie Davis (Nelson), Louis Armstrong (Willie "Sweet Daddy" Ferguson), Frank Sinatra Jr. (Vincent), Peter Lawford (Manny), Michael Lipton (Bobby Gales), Ja'net Dubois (Martha), Lola Falana (Theo), Johnny Brown (Les), Gerald S. O'Loughlin (policeman), Kenneth Tobey (tour manager), Mel Tormé, Kai Winding (themselves). New song: "All That Jazz" (words Al Stillman/music Benny Carter).

—Sensitive/abrasive cornetist Adam is ground down by racism and personal tragedy. He mentors a protégé, but alienates his longtime band. Meanwhile, a Civil Rights activist who's fallen for Adam only wants to help.

Unforeseen consequences also figure in *A Man Called Adam*, in which entertainer and occasional jazz singer Sammy Davis Jr. plays a temperamental, alternately obnoxious and charming cornet player lightly modeled on the similarly moody, no-relation Miles Davis. The project had been developed for Nat King Cole, who'd died of lung cancer in February 1965. Producer Ike Jones brought the property to Davis, and shooting began that November. Davis had plenty to keep him busy already. He'd just begun shooting a weekly TV variety show. And for the better part of a year and a half, he'd been starring in the Broadway boxing musical *Golden Boy*, an athletic role in which he sang, danced, skipped rope, threw punches, and took a few.[19]

A movie about a jazz musician indifferent to public approval was an offbeat choice for a performer who craved it. Sammy Davis Jr. occupied a weird place in American culture for decades. He was a lifelong, high-energy entertainer who did a few things very well. (From age four he'd worked in a flashy dance trio with his father, who'd played Fletcher Henderson in *The Benny Goodman Story*.) Sammy frequently appeared in clubs and ballrooms, on TV, in movies, and in the gossip columns. He'd been scarred and had lost an eye in a road accident. He was a convert to Judaism, a black man married to a Scandinavian blond, and a member of Hollywood's Rat Pack, openly courting the approval of ringleader Frank Sinatra, who used to be warmly supportive, but now treated him with increasing disdain. Davis was short and the frequent butt of his buddies' (often racial) jokes.

On the other hand, Davis wouldn't perform before segregated audiences—and had criticized Cole and Armstrong for doing so—and he'd marched on Washington and Alabama with Martin Luther King. Davis could sing ballads and swing tunes, scat a bit, and play a few instruments, and he'd recently recorded with Count Basie. Yet as Gerald Early has pointed out, black and white intellectuals gave him no respect, and it wasn't just them.[20] Two decades later Bruno Kirby would deliver a memorable anti-Sammy screed in the mockumentary *This Is Spinal Tap*.

Adam was, on one level, an attempt to upgrade his image. The actor's public persona enhances his performance as a talented artist who can be hard to like. It's a role an actor can dig into, and Davis brings his customary intensity. It's not a great performance but he's not in over his head like Bobby Darin in *Too Late Blues*.

A Man Called Adam is about an artist on the way out, one badly bruised by the world's disrespect, playing a music portrayed as suffering similar affronts. "There are only six decent jazz joints in the whole country," Adam's road manager Bobby tells him—a bit overstated (he must mean outside New York) but a sign of the times, like the low budgets for 1960s jazz movies. *Adam* catches that air of jazz in decline. Adam Johnson shares a few traits with the mercurial Miles Davis, who could be an irresistible seducer and utter cad. Like Miles, Adam is a sharp dresser who can be arrogant but may also betray great sensitivity, who'll turn his back on an audience as it gives him a standing ovation (in the middle of a set, no less). The name Adam Johnson says it all: the original dick. He leaves a string of discarded women in his wake.

Sammy Davis was a talented mimic—he did hilarious impressions of other singers—and he knew the trumpeter; he'd tried to persuade Miles to let wife Frances Taylor take a prominent role in *Golden Boy*. But aside from turning his back on applause, he doesn't copy Miles's mannerisms, nor his sandpaper voice. There's more than a little Sammy Davis in Adam however. Lifelong friend Nelson (Ossie Davis) explains Adam's appeal: "What makes an actor, a performer, a star: that excitement—that quality of personal danger, like any moment he might explode." (*Golden Boy*'s star had sustained several well-publicized injuries on stage.) In an early scene, Adam enters a saloon where he's a regular—that's the star's mother Elvera Davis tending bar—and immediately unplugs the jukebox a couple of guys are grooving to, because he's not in the mood for rhythm-and-blues, and because he's looking for trouble. When those larger guys start razzing him—"He coulda been white, but he turned it down"—Adam responds by flattening them both, with a quick jab, a pointed elbow, and a double ear-slap. One of his chastened victims (Carl Lee, *The Connection*'s Cowboy) then clues in the other: "When a guy's little . . . and he thinks that you're thinking he's little—look out!"

A Man Called Adam was mostly shot late at night, after the curtain fell on *Golden Boy*. Davis knew that could work—he'd had a similar experience in Vegas, shooting the Rat Pack opus *Oceans 11*. He would nap in his limo on the way to locations; the production shot at a few of Davis's regular haunts. Some Broadway costars turn up: Johnny Brown as Adam's blind pianist Les, Kenneth Tobey as a tour manager, Ja'net (then Jeannette) DuBois and Lola Falana as women he unceremoniously dumps.

With few daylight sequences. *Adam* brings out the black in black and white. Much of it is set in the middle of the night, and the film has an almost palpable nocturnal feel. To helm it, Davis hired Leo Penn, who'd clicked with Sammy when directing his guest shot on TV's *Ben Casey*. Penn worked almost exclusively in television—he should not be confused with filmmaker Arthur Penn, coincidentally the director of *Golden Boy* on Broadway—and the film has the somewhat hasty feel that commercial TV location shoots sometimes share with independent films. *A Man Called Adam* unites those seemingly disparate aesthetics. Things look a little chintzy. The album covers that adorn his hotel flat—*Adam's Genesis, Lonely Night, Adam in Eden*—look like bargain-bin anthologies, beneath his status as a jazzman who's been on the covers of *TIME* and *Life*. (The one LP sleeve that looks plausibly slick, *If I Ruled the World*, is Sammy's own recent release, with Adam's name covering his.)

At times connective scenes seem missing—like one that introduces Ken Tobey's character—and people may behave inconsistently. But much of that inconsistency is deliberate. Almost everyone here has two faces, and not just in the way that performing artists have public and private selves. (Miles Davis's Janus-like qualities get further attention in 2016's *Miles Ahead*.)

Adam's dualities are firmly established in the opening scenes, not least through his music, which comes in two distinct flavors. His cornet is ghosted by hardbop spitfire Nat Adderley, and Adam's band plays roaring, swinging in-the-pocket soul jazz, a style that cropped up in the 1950s—a hamhocks-and-blackeyed-peas shout of black pride, readable as an East Coast riposte to the bleached white Los Angeles jazz heard in Hollywood pictures. But Adam also sings downbeat ballads in a studiously unshowy, emotionally naked manner, not unlike California's Chet Baker.

In the opening scene Adam does the 1960 torch song "I Want to be Wanted"—"Not tomorrow, but right now." That lyric is a tell—he just wants *that night*, like a kid, as Cassavetes would say—a point underscored by handler Bobby minutes later, after Adam throws a tantrum when he's heckled: "Musicians. You're all children." That happens during an abbreviated week in Cincinnati, where Adam has convinced local woman Theo to leave her family, job, and home to follow him to New York, even though he keeps calling her Cleo. Once there, he quickly stashes her in a hotel across town, and soon forgets her.

Two faces: Adam's rudeness drives his friend Nelson crazy, but Nelson is more apt to grumble to others than confront him. After Adam pursues the woman he knows Nelson wants: "You're mad at me, right?" "Who, me?" Adam's white protégé Vincent (Frank Sinatra Jr.) tries to copy his trumpet licks and hey-baby manner with chicks, but the facade cracks when he's challenged.

Inconsistency may signify complexity. Adam's new woman, Claudia Ferguson (Cicely Tyson), is a proud Civil Rights activist who'd been jailed for taking part in a sit-in, but she gives Adam a brief version of the Talk black parents give kids: Don't provoke the cops, even when they're obnoxious. Don't give them an excuse to hurt you; your life is too valuable. (It may be part of her commitment to passive resistance.) Proud Claudia had laughed at his loutish arrogance when they'd met: "I have all your albums, Mr. Johnson, because I dig you the most, really I do." But then she falls for him, for real.

Two faces: Martha, the woman Claudia displaces in Adam's life, bonds with her after they meet (in a traditional way—a visit to the ladies' room). But next time Martha sees her, she's out for blood. Adam hates Manny, the head of the Amalgamated booking agency, so much so he threatens him with a broken bottle. (Manny is so loathsome, Davis cast his public friend Peter Lawford to soften the blow.) But when Sammy comes crawling back to him—literally, across a restaurant floor during lunch—Manny takes him back as a client, because business is business. Indeed: right after debasing himself, on the spot Adam negotiates a pretty good deal for a tour—$1,250 a week. Even the small-town cop who runs Adam in for Being Upstate While Black turns up at a New York bar to check out his music (unless character actor Gerald S. O'Loughlin was just moonlighting as an extra).

Louis Armstrong, in a rare (and last) dramatic role, plays Claudia's grandfather, veteran trumpeter Sweet Daddy Willie Ferguson: a sort of alternate-universe Pops who never became a star. Now thanks to Nelson, Sweet Daddy is mounting a comeback, and sings a blues onstage with an All-Stars-like sextet including drummer Jo Jones as himself. But even Willie, who goes on about the old days and forgotten old-timers, hangs out at a club where modernists play, chatting up a young waitress.

Sweet Daddy's character echoes 1940s phenom Bunk Johnson, the early jazz cornetist who'd been living in Louisiana rice country and who was brought to New York as an exemplar of Pure Jazz and enjoyed a temporary vogue. Adam worries Willie will just get his hopes up and then the world will move on—which is more or less what happened to Bunk. Willie himself can see he makes younger people nervous; they don't know how to talk to him. Armstrong doesn't overmilk it. He's quietly effective, as Davis would acknowledge: "I'm there to give it my all, because I'm the star, and then they show a close-up of Louis and suddenly it turns into a Louis Armstrong movie."[21]

Screenwriters Les Pine and Tina Rome went out on the road with jazz musicians, hoping to catch the authentic flavor of their milieu. Adam sits in at a jam session, where lesser musicians line up to play. He borrows a flugelhorn, but correctly uses his own mouthpiece, like Jimmy Stewart's Glenn Miller at his jam session. (But Adam's is magic: makes the bigger horn sound like a cornet—it puts the Johnson into the sound.) He goes to an industry party where Mel Tormé as himself sings the film's swinging theme, "All That Jazz," and blustery comedian Jack E. Leonard, kibitzing and trying to get with it, comes off as sadly square.

Promoting this film, producer Ike Jones denigrated the stereotypical story lines of other jazz movies, but *Adam* recalls a few nonetheless. The opening scene—in which a drunk nightclub patron demands Adam honor a request—echoes *Blues in the Night*. Late in the film, driven to find something he can't reach on his instrument, Adam smashes it, à la *Young Man with a Horn*. During a tutorial, Adam encourages Vincent to look past what he's studied, to play his soul, like black cats do. (They play with more soul, Adam explains, because they had to figure everything out for themselves, and their soul was all they had to express—as if there hadn't always been plenty of reading and schooled black jazz musicians.) "You sure you ain't colored?" Adam flatters him after Vincent testifies on his horn, Chad Bixby–style. The screenwriters may also have peeked at a recent jazz novel. The car accident that cost Adam's family their lives—with Adam drunk at the wheel—and his encounter with a racist upstate cop parallel John A. Williams's 1961 *Night Song* (and the film based on it, discussed next).

In memory of his son, Adam has hung a kid's mobile from his bedroom ceiling: a collection of model rocket ships. (They're highlighted a few times, even in close up.) One, horizontal, looks tumescently penile; the others are pointed straight down, bad omens. Adam has developed a cough that comes over him from time to time on the bandstand,

FIGURE 6.5 Adam (Sammy Davis Jr.) is arrested for defying racist cops in *A Man Called Adam*.

which Claudia takes as a sign he's dying of ... something. Unless he destroys himself first. He quarrels with his band, including pianist Les—blinded in the same car accident— and trombonist Kai Winding who plays himself. Adam alienates them again after they're persuaded to welcome him back—walking out like a jerk without explaining that the cops made the boss fire him.

To make Adam earn that $1,250 a week, wicked Manny has booked him on a punitive tour of the South—where, Adam reminds him, a guy with his outspoken views puts himself in danger just showing up. He takes a new band, a septet with four horns, Vincent included. We are prepared for the worst, but the southern swing goes pretty well. The band plays for integrated audiences—save for one house, where they point their horns toward the black balcony. When a couple of crackers throw bottles after the trumpeters hug on stage, breaking a racial taboo, cops quickly roust the troublemakers. Times have changed in the decade since a racist incident down south contributed to Adam's car crash—a change partly due to crusaders like Claudia.

It's only when the tour is back up north that they encounter real trouble. Vincent is attacked after a show, for no apparent reason—a missing scene?—and Adam freezes up, useless, like Ghost in *Too Late Blues*, and a character in *Night Song* in a similar spot. Claudia blames herself: by warning Adam not to risk his own safety, maybe she'd emasculated him.

Now Adam's rocket is really pointed down. Just as Sweet Daddy echoes Bunk Johnson, Adam's demise harks back to original jazz hero Buddy Bolden, believed by some to have scrambled his brains by playing too hard. (He spent his last decades in a mental hospital.) Like Bolden, Adam plays cornet, the early jazz horn largely supplanted by trumpet after Armstrong switched. The Bolden echoes appear deliberate; making an announcement at a Sweet Daddy gig, Nelson invokes "the good old bad old days back in Tintype Hall"—the apocryphal New Orleans venue Bolden was said to have played.

Back in New York after Vincent's beating, and sick over it, Adam sits in with his old Les-and-Kai band one night, and as his friends watch in horror, he blows increasingly strangulated high notes, more porpoise-song than jazz. He pours his hurt through his horn, before smashing it against the piano. Then he howls in pain, collapses and dies. In effect he plays the sound of his own death from exhaustion and terminal frustration.

According to (allegorical) legend, the day Bolden cracked up a raggedy white kid in the crowd made off with his horn.[22] Vincent takes the mouthpiece from Adam's battered cornet—as if, after the beating he'd endured, his mentor owed him that much. Vincent fondles it like a talisman, a sign of a handoff. Or maybe he's just hoping that mouthpiece will make him sound like Adam. "Blow what's in you," Adam had advised Vincent: stock jazz-movie advice. But Adam's feelings were so intense and contradictory, that imperative led to disaster. Blowing what was in him, he blew up.

Postscript: Not long after, Cicely Tyson became involved with (and much later married and divorced) Miles Davis. She imitated his gravel voice, playing the title character as an old woman, in 1974's *The Autobiography of Miss Jane Pittman*.

Sweet Love, Bitter (1967; 91 minutes; director: Herbert Danska; screenplay: Danska, Lewis Jacobs, from the John A. Williams novel *Night Song*; additional dialogue, Martin Kroll). Cast includes: Dick Gregory (Richie "Eagle" Stokes), Don Murray (David Hillary), Robert Hooks (Keel Robinson), Diane Varsi (Della), Jeri Archer (Candy), John Randolph (Big Rod Nolan).
—A college professor drinking away his pain falls in with a trio of New Yorkers: an interracial couple, and jazz great and dope fiend Eagle Stokes. But Eagle plummets when his new friend lets him down when it counts.

"We took the camera out onto the streets," Sammy Davis would later boast about *A Man Called Adam*, "with believable people and real traffic noises, daring and experimental for its time." But by 1966 that style had already become mannered, maybe even expected. There was one more such jazz picture to come, based on African American novelist John A. Williams's *Night Song*. Although released in 1967, it was shot months earlier than *Adam*. During production, in March 1965, comedian and Civil Rights activist Dick Gregory had taken time off to march on Selma with Dr. King.[23]

Sweet Love, Bitter is at heart a four-character drama. Gregory plays alto saxophonist Richie Stokes, aka Eagle, transparently based on Charlie Parker, nicknamed Bird. The other principals include David Hillary, a white college professor on the skids in lower Manhattan, grieving for a wife who died in a car crash when he was at the wheel. We don't get the details, but David's a heavy drinker. There is also—in a faint echo of *Shadows*—an interracial couple worn down by everyday racism, Della and Keel. The latter is Eagle's protector, and now David's employer at Sadik's coffeehouse, a hangout for hipsters and jazz musicians with a believably filthy kitchen.

Shot mostly in Philadelphia doubling for New York (and for a town upstate), *Sweet Love, Bitter* has many of the now-familiar tics of the modestly budgeted post-*Shadows* indie: grainy black-and-white images (one bedroom scene takes place in daring near-darkness); handheld-camera jiggling; guerrilla street-shooting where actors in long shots blend with unwitting pedestrians; some garbled or unintelligible talk, clunky transitions, and awkward scenes. Much of the dialogue comes straight from *Night Song*. The screenplay is an efficient adaptation, tightening up the story where it needs it, and trimming away minor characters (including, mercifully, a musician-hating white critic) and a melodramatic mafia subplot. Eagle is the catalyst. The story begins when he and David meet. Realism: When Stokes starts talking to him in a bar, the white man blows this chatty black dude off, until he recognizes him. Then his attitude abruptly changes. David's a jazz record collector, specializing in saxophonists.

As we've seen, characters modeled on real people fill myriad story functions all the time. But Stokes resembles Charlie Parker more than the story requires, in the film even more than the novel. Like Bird, Eagle is a bebop pioneer, brilliant but not always consistent, who's got a good beat but plays weird harmonies, and has played in Europe. He's a heroin addict and dedicated drinker, a sometimes very funny man whose humor can be vulgar but who may adopt lofty speech as a put-on. Like Bird he enjoys the movies, gets around in taxis, wears shades indoors, has had his cabaret card revoked, and hits up fans for money; he carries his horn in a paper bag, as Bird was rumored to do. He'll borrow a saxophone from another player when his own is in hock, and maybe crib money from a friend only to give it to someone else he thinks needs it more. Like Bird, Eagle listens to modern classical music, has learned good lessons about harmony working with guitarists, and knows where to score dope in every town he's played (once he gives the slip to the fellow musician assigned to watch him), but cautions others to stay off heroin. Parker played Birdland and the Royal Roost; Eagle plays Chicken-in-the-Basket. Bird might address a white stranger as "Jim" (as in "Crow"). Eagle calls white guys "Jimsey."

For Parker lore, the novelist and screenwriters draw heavily on the writings of Robert Reisner, who'd known Bird and had penned a series of articles about him in the late 1950s. Then in 1962—after *Night Song*, but before the movie—Reisner collected his biographical material and extracts from interviews as *Bird: The Legend of Charlie Parker*. Williams put a few of Parker's lines preserved in that book into Stokes's mouth, almost verbatim: the adage "Bread—that's your only friend," the assertion that as a Muslim he always sits facing east (though neither Bird nor Eagle was doing so when he said it), a comment to a white groupie propositioning him: "It ain't gonna rub off, baby." On screen as in the novel, Eagle wears specific clothes Reisner mentions: a beret and Bermuda shorts for comic effect; a tan topcoat with oversize buttons.[24]

Stokes sits in at a club one night, playing Parker licks. (He's ghosted by Bird disciple Charles McPherson; the sidelining band includes trumpeter Dave Burns and drummer Al Dreares—who played on pianist Mal Waldron's moody, evocative, overlooked jazz score—and young Chick Corea on piano and Steve Swallow on bass.) Richie also talks a little jazz, in two scenes ripped from the book: "Get your own style, and say what you feel, what you think," Richie advises a young white tenor player who emulates Lester Young. (The film adds this grace note: "I don't try to sound like Pres," the kid objects. "I mean, not anymore.")

"Tell me about jazz," Richie challenges David, "The only *true* American art. And how *we* did it," he says, pointing to himself. But Richie himself does the telling: I don't make money even though I'm famous. But: "You paddy-boys pick up a horn and go *bloo-bloop, bloop-bloop*, and right away, man, you playin' jazz. . . . Understand? It's your world. You won't let me make it in it." We are a long way from *Birth of the Blues, Young Man with a Horn*, or even *A Man Called Adam*, where black musicians freely pass knowledge to admiring whites. Eagle pays heavier dues than his white admirers, as a run-in with a cop makes plain.

The screenplay gleans one or two additional scraps from Reisner. Disc jockey Big Rod Nolan thinks that musicians like him because he gets them low-paying gigs. He's based (as the novel makes clearer) on deejay Symphony Sid Torin, who'd host broadcasts from clubs Parker played. Reisner mentions Sid's show carried ads for zoot suits; in the movie Eagle asks, "How in the eff are those zoot suits sellin', you mutha?" (That catches the dialogue's timid naturalism.)

In the book Eagle has a love-hate relationship with white Candy, who on film becomes another malicious portrait of the jazz baroness Nica de Koenigswarter, worse than Countess in *Too Late Blues*. Like the baroness, Candy speaks aristocratically, tools around Manhattan in a Rolls Royce convertible, and was with the saxophonist the night he died. Unlike Nica, Candy is sexually involved with Eagle, and calls his friends to haul him away when he suffers a (nonfatal) overdose. She's generally preposterous: an older woman in inch-thick makeup, preening in a peignoir at her doorman-building duplex. Candy doesn't resemble Nica physically—the baroness was far more presentable—and is inspired not by the real woman but by the femme fatale portrayed by scandal sheets like *Exposé* after Bird died.

The irony was cruel. Born in England into the mega-rich Rothschild family, Nica was no dilettante. During World War II she'd been a translator, decoder, and ambulance driver for the French resistance, and when this friendly unpretentious aristocrat moved to New York in 1953, she proved a reliable and undemanding patron of various jazz musicians, Thelonious Monk above all. But her flamboyance and flagrant race-mixing drew ire from busybodies like gossip columnist Walter Winchell. When an ailing Parker died in her apartment while watching TV in 1955, the news made the New York papers. There was talk in the musicians' community that she was somehow culpable—when in fact she had placed Bird under a doctor's care—and even allies like Mingus grumbled. These baseless rumors reached Paris, where Julio Cortázar wrote a 1959 story, translated as "The Pursuer," about a Parker-like saxophonist who's manipulated and fed drugs by self-indulgent marquesa Tica. More irony: Nica had known Parker only about a year, and not very well. But their names are forever linked.[25] (The 1988 biopic *Bird* would do better by her.)

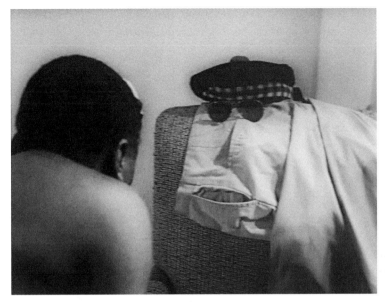

FIGURE 6.6 After a beating from a policeman, an addled Eagle (Dick Gregory) talks to his pants in *Sweet Love, Bitter*.

In the movie, Eagle, like bebop pianist Bud Powell, acts erratically after being beaten by a policeman while out of town. (Bud's beating had occurred in North Philadelphia, a few miles from where the scene was filmed). That's when he calls Big Rod on the phone, giggling, to ask about those zoot suits. In his addled condition he also has a conversation with his pants.

David and Keel grow as people by helping Richie Stokes, and they bond over it. For a 1960s film—for an American film—the racial dynamics are handled pretty well, and whites don't squeeze everyone else off screen. Every character has their say and has an interior life. Della gets a long scene where she talks about the indignities she and Keel suffer as a mixed couple (although Diane Varsi looks like she might be reading off cue cards). Keel gets a (low-budget) dream sequence, set in a movie theater, incorporating a brief art-film-within-the-film, in which Eagle blowing fleet alto turns into Keel himself, sputtering feebly. (Keel's having sputter issues: "Dammit! How come Eagle don't have trouble making out with a white chick?") Eagle horses around with his musician pals out behind Sadik's, and while on tour visits with a drug connection and a young prostitute.

After David helps Eagle recover from an overdose, Keel says to him, "Must be the light—you're looking a shade darker." It's as ridiculous as the parallel moment in *A Man Called Adam*. But it flatters David. In the real world there are some white jazz devotees who believe their love of African American music and musicians renders them virtually black—thereby granting themselves outsider cachet with no loss of white privilege. Keel's quip aside, he and Eagle see that side of David. When Stokes tells him, you don't have to live like this, being white, David weakly replies, "Can't we forget the Outer Man sometimes?" His delivery and gestures are so exaggerated, it's as if even whitebread Don Murray is laughing at his character. His new friends assume David will go back to his old life after he straightens out.

Which is just what happens. He interviews for his old job at (made-up) Onondaga College, the same day Eagle hits town on an upstate tour, and they've arranged a rendezvous. But David is 20 minutes late, and while Eagle waits for him on the street, he's hassled by a local cop for Loitering While Black. Eagle stands up for himself, and the cop winds up giving him a beatdown—just as David ambles along with his department chair, and freezes at the sight. (For a second he fantasizes coming to the rescue, like a silent movie hero, an odd grace note.)

Once they're back in New York, a guilt-ridden David confesses to Eagle, to make himself feel better—it certainly doesn't help the victim. The betrayal triggers Eagle's final tailspin. Acting crazy, and crazy high, he disappears. By the time Keel and David find him, he's dead of an overdose. Keel says a few words over the body, mangling a bit of Zechariah 11, like someone who'd learned and forgotten his Bible verses: "For the forest of vintage is come down. Pride of Jordan is spoiled." (In the novel, Keel had gone to Harvard Divinity School.) Still, it's almost apropos; the same chapter has a verse about a holy man betrayed.

In the last scene, David leaves for upstate, and the film ends with Della and Keel, whose relationship is looking sturdier. "He's a nice guy," Della says of David. Keel gets the last word: "Yeah. You're a nice guy, I'm a nice guy. The whole motherin' world is full of nice guys." For all the good that did Eagle.

In the 1980s in particular, suffering nonwhite movie characters often had a sympathetic white friend, as if white viewers needed to identify with same in order to care at all. You see this trope in *The Killing Fields, Cry Freedom*, and jazz epics *'Round Midnight* and *Bird*. John A. Williams pointed the way when he created David Hillary, but the African American novelist also cautioned the befriended: Your white buddy may not be there when you need him.

/// 7 /// SPECTACLES 1972–1984

The 1970s was a good decade for the movies, when young directors with bold ideas were ascendant: Francis Ford Coppola, Martin Scorsese, Steven Spielberg, George Lucas. By contrast, for some observers, it was jazz's worst decade. Bop-based headliners like drummer Art Blakey were working far less, and record companies were more enamored of jazz-rock fusion bands like the Mahavishnu Orchestra and Return to Forever, or musicians who'd come up in the 1960s avant-garde like Anthony Braxton and the Art Ensemble of Chicago. But the eclipse of mainstream jazz in the 1970s has been greatly overstated. Dozens of bop-based musicians continued to record (many on small, independent labels that sprang up when the majors lost interest), and there was still an audience out there. In Baltimore, for instance, hundreds attended weekly Left Bank Jazz Society concerts, hearing name acts perform—like saxophonist Dexter Gordon, whose mid-decade late-career renaissance led to his starring in 1986's 'Round Midnight.

Seventies jazz films were scattered stylistically, thematically, and budget-wise. First up, in 1972, was an old-fashioned fanciful biopic, lavishly produced, much-hailed, and very popular—but as jazz pictures go, a dud.

> **Lady Sings the Blues (1972; 144 minutes; director: Sidney J. Furie; writers: Terence McCloy, Suzanne de Passe, Chris Clark, from the book by Billie Holiday and William Dufty). Cast includes: Diana Ross (Billie Holiday), Billy Dee Williams (Louis McKay), Richard Pryor (Piano Man), James T. Callahan (Reg Hanley), Paul Hampton (Harry), Sid Melton (Jerry), Ned Glass (Bernie), Virginia Capers (Mama Holiday), Scatman Crothers (Big Ben).**
> **—Singer Billie Holiday uses heroin to blot out pain that stems from racism and sexual abuse, the same pain that gives her music its power. Through it all, a devoted man stands by her**.

The road to *Lady Sings the Blues* had begun in the mid-1950s, when Billie Holiday and journalist William Dufty fashioned her autobiography of the same name, which was published in 1956. As critics dutifully point out, she wasn't really a blues singer—she recorded many more pop songs—and the book's title might be read as a comment on its tone. (She'd wanted to call it *Bitter Crop*, quoting from a song she'd popularized, the coolly ironic portrait of lynching as a Southern tradition, "Strange Fruit.") Holiday had led a hard life, starting from her childhood in Baltimore. She got hooked on narcotics in an age when celebrity addicts made easy marks for law enforcement, and she had some well-publicized drug busts—the last while on her deathbed in 1959. She'd also been mired in several long-term abusive relationships.

Dufty did the writing, based on conversations with Billie and old interviews. The book created a sensation with its lurid tales, and it was adorned with a few biopic-ready scenes in which comments Billie makes in conversation—"Don't explain" (to a lover) or "God bless the child that's got his own" (to her mother)—inspire her to write on-point songs. Even before the book came out, Holiday was hoping for a movie adaptation. The rights were sold, Dufty worked on a couple of scripts—one with songwriter Ann Ronnell—and Holiday made plans to record songs its still-unnamed star would lip-sync to. *The Glenn Miller Story*'s Anthony Mann would direct. Top contenders for the lead were African American beauty Dorothy Dandridge and a white star with a dark complexion, Ava Gardner. Nothing came of it.

Producer Jay Weston revived the idea in the late 1960s, as a vehicle for Abbey Lincoln, a jazz singer with big-screen presence who could act; she'd just starred opposite Sidney Poitier in Weston's *For the Love of Ivy*. Lincoln sang in a Holiday-influenced style, and like Billie was striking-looking if not a conventional beauty. But Lincoln was having problems in her marriage (to drummer Max Roach), and passed. Eventually talk turned to a pop singer whose acting experience was mostly limited to comic sketches on stage and TV, and playing a singing nun on an episode of TV's *Daktari*: Motown star and ex-Supremes front woman Diana Ross. In a certain way, it made sense: to make a biopic of an African American with crossover appeal to whites, cast a pop singer whites already love. The producers approached Ross via Motown mogul Berry Gordy, her paramour who guided her career and who had been looking to break into movie producing himself.[1]

To help land the deal, Gordy baited the hook. Ross was slated to appear on a Bob Hope TV special; Gordy told her to learn Holiday's "My Man" and perform it on the show in Billie's style. You can find the clip online; she sounds very little like Billie. Ross's clear soprano is pitched about an octave higher than Holiday's port-wine contralto, and she's no swinger. (Ross later said that when she first heard Holiday she didn't get what the fuss was about.)[2] Holiday was a big woman; Ross a waif. She was a genuine talent, but wrong for the part.

As coproducer, Berry Gordy invested heavily and took a hands-on role. He nixed the initial script by Terence McCloy and Toronto-born director Sidney J. Furie (who'd made the stylishly gritty 1960s spy drama *The Ipcress File*), and brought on two Motown associates to give it "more blackness": production aide Suzanne de Passe and (white) singer Chris Clark.[3] (It's McCloy's, de Passe's, and Clark's only screenplay credit.) Their avowed source was the autobiography; Holiday's last husband Louis McKay was billed as a technical advisor.

As the script developed, Diana Ross objected that they were drifting far from the life of this African American icon—specifically, when all her ne'er-do-well men got rolled into saintly, devoted Louis McKay (Billy Dee Williams). Gordy told her, "White people don't worry about changing the facts to make good movies. Why should we be saddled with it just because we're black?" It's a fair point. Furie had always been candid this was to be a commercial venture, putting its star in eye-popping clothes. (Auteurist critic Andrew Sarris had already flagged the director's "fabric fetishism" in *The Leather Boys* and *The Appaloosa*.)[4]

Lady Sings the Blues is a hit on its own terms: a classic African American date movie. And to be fair, its writers didn't throw the source book away. Not that the autobiography itself is always accurate; much about Holiday's personal life remains unclear. Even responsible biographers sift through rumor and conjecture.

In life, or either version of *Lady Sings the Blues*, young Eleanora Fagan comes from Baltimore. She runs errands for a neighborhood cathouse and is fascinated by records she hears there. She lives with a relative named Ida after her mother moves away to work. After being raped as a young girl, Eleanora comes to New York to be reunited with mom, who innocently installs her in a Harlem boarding house Eleanora quickly recognizes as another brothel. There she begins turning tricks, only to quit when confronted by a patron who makes much of his manly endowment: Big Blue in the book, Big Ben in the film.

Still in her mid-teens, she auditions as a dancer at a neighborhood club run by a man named Jerry. (The real club was Pods' and Jerry's, called Dean's and Dean's here.) Her dancing is so bad the rehearsal pianist asks, can you sing? She can, and gets hired. Her stage name is partly inspired by Hollywood star Billie Dove. (The film never names her father, guitarist Clarence Holiday.) Where other singers at the club collect their tips by picking folded bills off tables using their upper thighs or a nearby body part, Billie declines—earning her the arch nickname Lady. Men started handing her tips out of respect. And in those early days she first sees the man who will become her (second) husband, handsome Louis McKay, though in life they wouldn't get together for another 15 years.

Billie sings with a white swing band that's just getting started whose tours take them south, where she suffers numerous racist indignities. When the band finally clicks and gets a New York radio show, she's squeezed out in favor of a white singer, though she stays on good terms with her ex-boss. That would be Artie Shaw in life—the first white bandleader to hire a black singer—and in the movie, farm boy–looking Reg Hanley, who never notices his unctuous pianist Harry has hooked Billie on heroin. The real Holiday was already recording regularly—and had filmed *Symphony in Black*—by the time she went with Shaw. Movie-Billie still hopes to break out of Harlem.

Now comes that drifting away from the particulars of her life to the vaguely accurate, in scrambled order. Following the facts, she becomes successful. She uses salty language. She is called to the phone at a club one night, to learn that a parent has died. (Her father in life, her mother here.) She might wield a razor in a dispute with her man. She tours the country and visits Los Angeles. Billie works with a pianist who's a good and loyal friend, but who has his own heroin problem. (That's not in the book: Carl Drinkard, who worked with her in the 1950s.) She takes a cure, and gets arrested for heroin possession. Holiday gets locked up for a while, and then can't play New York clubs because her bust cost her her cabaret card, called a license here. She is sometimes heard with violins behind her (only on record, in reality). The film ends with her successful 1948 concert at Carnegie Hall. Billie sings over a looking-to-the-future headline montage that reveals that in the years ahead she didn't get her license back and died at 44.

With real events reshuffled, chronology goes haywire. Billie sings 1946's "Good Morning Heartache," post Hanley tour, just after an emcee establishes it's 1935. The film begins in medias res, with Holiday being booked on a drug charge in 1936—the darkest opening of any jazz film since *Syncopation*'s slave trade. The real Holiday started using heroin in the early 1940s and she didn't get involved with Louis McKay until about three years after the concert that ends the movie.

The real McKay was no angel. He beat her, spent her money, ran whores on the side, and had other women; he propositioned Corky Hale during her brief spell as Billie's pianist. Movie-McKay is steadfast, for years and years, and gives Billie the first gardenia she sticks in her hair, helping to define her look. He's only stern when she's out of control, and he does his best to wean her off drugs. The real McKay snorted heroin himself. They did eventually marry—so they couldn't testify against each other—but in 1957 they separated, and she filed for a never-finalized divorce. When she was dying of cirrhosis two years later, he tried to persuade her to sign over her book's movie rights.

But in a date movie, you don't make the love interest a heel—the heel's the guy who gets dumped. Holiday genuinely loved McKay, but it insults her memory to have her rescued by a good man—that is not the Billie Holiday story. As Farah Jasmine Griffin has written, "*Lady Sings the Blues* is not about Holiday. It is a post–Black Power fantasy of a beautiful, talented, but weak and childish woman who is rescued time and again by a strong, supportive, wealthy, handsome black man."[5] William Dufty saw it too: it's Berry Gordy's version of the story of Gordy and Diana Ross, the singer from a poor

FIGURE 7.1 Even at a triumphant Carnegie Hall concert, a headline montage foretells more trouble for Billie Holiday (Diana Ross) in *Lady Sings the Blues*.

urban background he'd groomed into a major star. In the movie, when Holiday first sets eyes on the much-older McKay, she goes literally weak at the knees at the beautiful sight of him. (The real Holiday and McKay were born five years apart.) When Diana Ross, auditioning for Motown at 16, first laid eyes on Berry Gordy, 31, she started flirting with him immediately.

McKay to Billie, in the film: "Everything I do, all that I plan for you, is done with you in mind." Gordy to an unsure Ross, while making the film: "Haven't I always told you I'll take care of you?"[6] Billie keeps it together on the road only when Louis is there to prop her up. "See, we can't do everything by ourselves," she sniffles, explaining why musicians keep messing up. When she wants to quit the business to be a housewife, Louis convinces her to resume singing.

We've seen all this before: biopics that turn their subject into a version of their star, wreak havoc on chronology, feature anachronistic music, and invent a fictitious life where the real one would serve. Building a film around a romance that didn't even begin until after the big Carnegie Hall ending? That's *The Benny Goodman Story*. But 1950s biopics always give you a taste of authentic music, some idea why viewers might care about the film's subject: we get Glenn Miller's mellow reed voicings, W. C. Handy's compositions, and the actual sound of Benny Goodman, Gene Krupa, and even Red Nichols. What made Billie Holiday great was her way of putting over a tune. *Lady Sings the Blues* rarely gets within a mile of that.

Even writers who dislike it praise Ross's performance, somehow. She was nominated for an Academy Award, but the Oscars had a weakness for showy cold-turkey performances; Sinatra got nominated for *The Man with the Golden Arm. Lady Sings the Blues* is heavy on junkie-porn. After the opening credits montage, Billie suffers from withdrawal in lock-up. (Those credits themselves set the tone for what follows, identifying actors by role: . . . as the Rapist; . . . as the 1st Madam; . . . as the 1st Whore; . . . as the Detective.) Ross flings herself around, screams, pounds the padded walls, bounces her head off walls and floor, and finally writhes in a straitjacket. It's as if withdrawal gives sufferers a burst of energy— and frizzes their hair.

Withdrawal also triggers an hour-and-45-minute flashback of her life up to that moment, starting at age 14, when Ross conveys youth by bouncing on her heels and swinging her arms, like a sketch comedienne. (Holiday was actually assaulted at 11.) Life is movie-gritty. Holiday had lived in a narrow East Baltimore rowhouse on an alley where her front door was three steps from the sidewalk; in the movie, a flight of two dozen steps sweeps up a shrubbery-lined yard, leading to Billie's big if shabby free-standing home.

At the brothel where she does chores, Billie first hears a record she fixates on, a faux-1920s version of "T'Ain't Nobody's Business" (sung by obscure Motowner Blinky Williams), starting with the oft-omitted opening verse. We hear from that record six times, three in the first 10 minutes. When young Billie sings along, we hear that even at a tender age, she already sounded like Diana Ross. Billie loves that record so, it's surprising she never notices that another entertainer (played by Yvonne Fair) at Dean's in Harlem sings in the same voice.

The screenplay gives Ross opportunities to chew scenery even when Billie's not strung out or high as a kite. There's a fictitious sequence where Reg Hanley's band bus rolls up on a Ku Klux Klan rally down south. The musicians try to hide Billie but she lashes out, cursing at high volume, unrestrainable. It's the one moment that hints at a new trend in early 1970s cinema: the blaxploitation film, where African American heroes confront the oppressor. (Nothing like this happened, but Holiday didn't suffer racists gladly.)

Also while deep in the South, Billie gets out of the bus to pee and stumbles on the scene of a lynching—another fiction. Apparently she then composes one of her signature tunes, "Strange Fruit," in response. (It was actually by New York schoolteacher Abel Meeropol, under the name Lewis Allen. Her book wrongly suggests she had a hand in writing it.) The grisly scene that inspires her song also breaks her spirit, pushing her toward the numbing effects of heroin—thereby making a direct connection between racism and drug addiction.

So some big thoughts creep in, but it's mostly a love story. As Gordy would tell it, the dialogue for Billie's and Louis's first date at a classy nightspot wasn't working, so Ross and Williams improvised "one of the cutest scenes I've ever seen."[7] But fledgling improvisers often falter. A verbatim taste:

Billie: I've been to a whole lot of places like this before.
Louis: [clears throat] Ah—is that so. Right. Uh, how well—where?
Billie: [pause] Huh?
Louis: Uh—where?
Billie: Where what?
Louis: You said you, you've been to a lot places like this before. Dah, where?
Billie: Did I say that?

This isn't the only scene that runs too long; the film is almost two-and-a-half hours. There is in fact some jazzy verbal improvising in it: Richard Pryor's riffing as Billie's loyal (as in only) accompanist, who's funny and trash-mouthed in a very 1970s Richard Pryor way—totally anachronistic but welcome relief. Pryor had been brought in to do a one-scene bit, but once he started improvising on set, his part was radically expanded. His character is called "Piano Man"—that's not a generic description, that's his actual name: an indicator of the depth of characterizations here. Musically, the real Holiday bonded with horn men who'd answer her phrases on records, especially the elliptical, fog-toned tenor saxophonist Lester Young, who had the same nonchalant, behind-the-beat swing feel. There is no complementary horn man and little rhythmic relaxation in *Lady Sings the Blues*. Lester Young is never alluded to.

As usual, the film's music was prerecorded, with Ross singing in character. Gordy would claim her first pass at some Holiday classics sounded so eerily like Billie, he instructed music director Gil Askey to pull her back—to put more Diana in it, to protect her own brand. It is hard to credit the notion that Ross could perfectly imitate Holiday, after that televised "My Man." In the film, only a few tunes suggest she'd ever heard her; "Don't Explain" and a brief a cappella "Lady Sings the Blues" come closest. Ross will occasionally alight on a note from above, but she doesn't glide down to it Holiday-style. The gap between the movie's "Lover Man" and Holiday's heartbreaking version is wide.

The screenwriters take a pass on those helpful prompts from the book, where "Don't Explain" and "God Bless the Child" sprout from conversation. From the movie, you'd think Holiday's artistry lay in putting together pertinent or prescient set lists, the lyrics reflecting what she's going through at the moment. Just before she meets Louis McKay, she sings ("Some day he'll come along") "The Man I Love." Just after, the band tees up ("I fell in love with you the first time I looked into") "Them There Eyes." Louis leaves her on the road to tend to business in New York: "You've Changed." When Piano Man is severely beaten, drug-addled Billie sings him "God Bless the Child" instead of summoning an ambulance.

Billie Holiday was peerless at infusing lyrics with feeling. She made you hear joy or loss or longing as something she knew first hand. She had a narrow vocal range, but could smooth out a melodic line to her advantage, with teasing variations, swinging like a jazz horn. Diana Ross doesn't touch on those emotional depths or musical heights (though she'd sung standards with the Supremes). She sings mostly straight, with occasional hints at jazzy timing, emoting visibly. Songs are abbreviated, in the movie manner, blunting their impact; she goes from the first two lines of "Strange Fruit" straight to the top of the final verse, cutting half the lyrics and distending the form.

In fairness, the music that accompanies Ross makes it hard to conjure the right feeling. Jazz saxophonist turned Hollywood composer Oliver Nelson had signed on to do the score but was quickly replaced by Frenchman Michel Legrand, sometime jazz pianist and writer of sweeping romantic movie themes. At Carnegie Hall in 1948, the real Holiday had a piano-guitar-bass-drums quartet; in the movie she gets a jazz orchestra plus string section. Reg Hanley's mid-1930s band sounds like slick and driving late-1950s Count Basie.

We recall what director Valentine Davies said of inaccuracies in *The Benny Goodman Story*: "It doesn't make any difference." This Billie Holiday never visits a recording studio, let alone a movie studio. In *Lady Sings the Blues*, the only Holiday on record is Reg Hanley's instrumental version of "Don't Explain," with strings, years too early. It appears no jazz or historical consultant was on hand to point out absurdities. In the movie, a New York swing band tries to secure a New York broadcast contract by touring the country, to "build up your name in the sticks," hoping "Mr. Network Radio Scout" will discover them in some backwater—which is just what happens. Later in her career, when she's barred from Manhattan clubs, her agent Bernie explains, "If you're not working in New York, you're nothing." His solution is for Billie to build up demand there, by touring the country, accruing good reviews—as if New Yorkers cared what clicks in Oklahoma City. Bernie says a couple of months should do it, but the road stretches on and on. A montage larded with archival photos suggests it is a very long tour; on one theater marquee she's on a bill with the 1937 picture *There Goes My Girl*; on another she's appearing opposite 1951's *The Company She Keeps*. She's a time traveler: one newspaper review appears under the headline, "Billie Holiday Opens Tonight."

There's a goal at the end of that endless road. Bernie: "Did you ever hear of any agent in the world booking a jazz singer into Carnegie Hall?" (Holiday first sang there in 1946 on a Jazz at the Philharmonic show.) At Carnegie, our troubled heroine goes out on a sugar high, singing "My Man" (its ending anyway) and "God Bless the Child" as Louis watches from the wings. That's fair play: Holiday's book ends with her invoking McKay and "My Man." The film makes no attempt to convey how strikingly Holiday's voice changed between the mid-1930s and her later years, reflecting the ravages of her life—an essential part of any real Billie Holiday story.

We probably shouldn't be too critical of Diana Ross for failing to impersonate Holiday. Berry Gordy was right, in a way: there are downsides. Holiday's mannerisms, especially toward the end, when her voice was reduced to a creaky croak, lend themselves to caricature. Other singers would imitate her as a stunt.

Consider the 2016 HBO version of Lanie Robertson's 1986 stageplay *Lady Day at Emerson's Bar & Grill*, revived in 2014 starring Broadway favorite Audra McDonald. It depicts a white-gowned Holiday four months before her death in 1959, doing a sloppy long last set in Philadelphia with a trio. She strolls or stumbles across the stage (or behind the bar) and rambles on about her life, usually if not always accurately. Billie explains herself at length—"I got to sing the way I feel"—as protective pianist Jimmy Powers (Shelton Becton) does his best to keep her moving through the set list. (Her actual accompanist then, Mal Waldron, found her less vexing than nursemaid Jimmy does; Holiday treated her pianists well.) She's drinking heavily, and at one point leaves the stage to shoot up in her dressing room. She is often funny, and briefly brings out her beloved chihuahua Pepi, but this is the tragic Holiday, with no redemption ahead.

Audra McDonald looks the part—she's closer to Billie's body type than Diana Ross—and evokes more than she replicates Holiday's public body language: the swaying arms, raised eyebrows, and head tilts. She obviously studied tapes of the singer talking and rehearsing in the 1950s, and reduces the melodic contours of Lady's speaking voice to a limited set of specific gestures. Singing, McDonald nails the late-period signifiers: the woozy, constricted-throat timbre, the swelling notes or pinched round vowels, a tiny falsetto grace note tucked into a phrase, the occasionally wayward (and quickly corrected) pitch, the heavy terminal vibrato, and the audible expulsion of air at the end of a (sung or spoken) line: "Darling please-uh." Billie's swing feel is more elusive—but then the real Holiday was said to have (rare) nights when her timing was off. McDonald's performance is technically impressive, more faithful and entertaining than Diana Ross's. But you're always aware it's an impersonation: the animatronic Billie Holiday.

> *Space Is the Place* (1974; 63 minutes; director: John Coney; writers: Joshua Smith, Sun Ra). Cast includes: Sun Ra (himself/Sunny Ray), Ray Johnson (the Overseer), Christopher Brooks (Jimmy Fay/Chicago emcee), Clarence Brewer (Bernard), Jack Baker (Bubbles), Tiny Parker (Tiny), Walter Burns, Gordon Upton (government agents).

—After a few years traveling in space, bandleader Sun Ra returns to Earth. He spreads his message of interplanetary salvation to Oakland's black community, and he and the satanic Overseer draw cards to determine the fate of the world.

When it comes to the living inimitables, better they should play themselves. It worked for Louis Armstrong, as it did for bandleader Sun Ra, who (in his personal mythology at least) traveled the spaceways from planet to planet. In *The Cry of Jazz*, he'd been kept in the shadows. But he's front and center in *Space Is the Place*: the first jazz superhero.

When *Space Is the Place* was shot in 1972–73, Sun Ra was a portly, haggard-looking man in his late fifties. And yet he was movie-ready. No one in 1970s jazz was half so colorful. He and the members of his alternately screeching and swinging big band/Arkestra wore ornate headgear and flowing costumes; the 12-piece version in the movie was billed as his Intergalactic Myth Science Solar Arkestra. Ra played all manner of electronic keyboards, and he and vocalist June Tyson led the band in sing-along chants that posed brain-teasers, illuminated his cosmic philosophy, and charted their interplanetary treks. Arkestra concerts were part carnival, part revival meeting, and part free-jazz blowout.[8]

In a similar way, John Coney's 1974 epic is part low-budget science fiction movie and part underground film—it was collectively written, with much input from Ra, who'd often go off script. It's also a blaxploitation pic, taking white oppression of the black community as a given and featuring a cross-section of neighborhood characters. In addition, it's easily the most apocalyptic jazz film. The biggest spoiler in this book: in the end, planet Earth blows up, which in context does not seem like much of a loss.

Shot mostly in Oakland, *Space Is the Place* came about after Ra taught an Afro American Studies course at UC Berkeley in 1971, in which he'd lectured about religion, permutative wordplay and hidden meanings, and occasionally about jazz. His didactic tone on screen suggests carryover from the lecture hall. He was a great talker.

The story is episodic and elliptical, but there are clues to decoding its mysteries, starting with the first words we hear, before the credits. June Tyson and the band intone one of Ra's familiar chants—"It's after the end of the world / Don't you know that yet?"—as the tail end of a spaceship recedes into the void. The film loops back on itself. Chronologically, its beginning directly follows the ending, when Ra departs a crumbling Earth. Under the opening credits, Sun Ra inspects his new home: a fecund pink-sky planet where plant stalks are topped by human hands, or wine goblets. Floating about are what appear to be helmet-protected brains trailing exposed spinal columns. (Also soap bubbles.) "The music is different here, the vibrations are different, not like planet Earth," Ra says. He's wearing a helmet with two vertical horns, suggesting both a set-top TV antenna and a prop from a sitcom lodge meeting. "We'll set up a colony for black people here, see what they can do on a planet all their own, without any white people there." So *Space Is the Place* also retells the story of Moses leading his people out of captivity, bound for a land of their own.

The film has a place of honor in the annals of black science fiction and Afrofuturism. Greg Tate may have had it in mind, describing how being black in America "parallels the kind of alienation that science fiction writers try to explore through various genre devices—transporting someone from the past into the future, thrusting someone into an alien culture, on another planet, where he has to confront alien ways of being."[9] Sun Ra always said he was not of this Earth, that on the whole he'd rather be elsewhere. His loyalties to our world were weak.

From that unnamed planet we shift to the story's earliest scene: to Chicago 1943, where "Sunny Ray" plays piano boogie-woogie for dancers in the kind of girly-show joint where Diana Ross's Billie Holiday started out. (The real Ra left Birmingham for Chicago in 1946.) As in the opening of *Blues in the Night* or *A Man Called Adam*, the hero's music is not to a patron's taste. "I think he sounds like shit," says the Overseer, a sharp-looking black man who comes on like a successful pimp: white suit, fedora, walking stick, female entourage. Ra/Ray doesn't respond, but the emcee has a quiet word with him. When Ra goes into his next number—the dancers wait backstage, unsure when to come in—he starts pounding the keys in dissonant defiance and the vibrations he unleashes manifest themselves as physical forces. Drinking glasses shatter, a mirror ball falls, the room fills with smoke, and folks are blown out the door. It's *Dr. Terror*'s supernatural nightclub scene, except here the musician on stage isn't at the mercy of such forces. He controls them.

In the aftermath, Sunny Ray and the Overseer talk. They appear to be old adversaries. The Overseer challenges him to a game of his choice—craps maybe? Ray chooses "the end of the world" and with the Overseer's gleeful laugh of assent, they are suddenly transported 33 years ahead in time and into the California desert. Sun Ra and the Overseer sit at a card table and play high card for the fate of Earth, using a mock-tarot deck. The first card the Overseer draws is labeled "The World 1976"—the near future when the film was released. The Overseer keeps score, apparently arbitrarily. The rules are murky.

These two move through time as easily as mortals walk across a room. As Ra says, speaking for himself, "We work on the other side of time." The Overseer is satanic—the name says it all—but he's less interested in destroying Sun Ra than discrediting him in the black community. Besides knocking Ra's music, the Overseer tells folks that his philosophical musings are nonsense, that he's just out to sell records, and that he doesn't honor his commitments. When Ra's spaceship appears over Oakland—pointedly passing over the Mt. Wilson observatories on the way—the Overseer grouses he's two minutes late.

Sun Ra's orange spaceship itself looks like two giant carrots united by a crosspiece. Ra and minions emerge from a hatch that opens like an overhead garage door, located between what we might call the ship's thighs—born(e) into a world not their own. The ship is powered by music. Ra's instrument panel includes a stereo amplifier, reel-to-reel tape deck, and synthesizer keyboard. He was indeed a master of such technology, always checking out the latest electronic instruments and discovering each new device's most useful sounds.

There is plenty of Arkestra music to be heard and sometimes we cut away to concert footage for no apparent reason. The music may reinforce the action or atmosphere—Ra's

FIGURE 7.2 Sun Ra pilots a spaceship powered by music in *Space Is the Place*.

keyboard provides the sound of the ship approaching Oakland, fusing the diegetic and nondiegetic—or highlight the film's themes. Interludes of massed hand-drumming put the Afro in Afrofuturism. Ra's synth abstractions suggest an alien aesthetic, just as Louis and Bebe Barron's electronic score for *Forbidden Planet* helped create that film's other-worldly air. As musicologist Ekkehard Jost pointed out, the sometimes thin textures of the Arkestra's collective improvising could suggest the emptiness of the void.[10]

Once on the ground, Ra interacts with the indigenous population. For a mouthpiece, he chooses local radio newsman Jimmy Fey (Christopher Brooks, who also plays the Chicago emcee—a couple of actors from that sequence appear later, as if pulled through time). Sun Ra opens an employment agency where he flummoxes one applicant, ex-NASA engineer Curtis Rockwell, with talk of "multiplicity adjustment, readjustment synthesis, isotope teleportation, transmolecularization, frequency polarization" and such. But then Ra has already told Rockwell he won't hire him because he's white—since white folk already look after their own (and haven't done the planet any favors). From *Space Is the Place*, you'd think Earth had only two continents, Africa and North America, and two races, save for one reference to "the Eurasian Occidental conspiracy."

Ra talks a lot about "alter(ed) destiny"—the idea that fate can be avoided, as if there are many possible, ever-diverging parallel worlds. Indeed, *Space Is the Place* may depict an Earth similar but not identical to our own: there's a NASA and an FBI, but this Oakland is part of Government Sector Five.

Some characters Ra encounters are street-theater stereotypes: a wino, corner boys Bernard and Bubbles (who likes bubblegum), and a big guy named Tiny with a tag line: "What's goin' on, man?" When Jimmy Fey tells Sun Ra there's money to be made, considering all the interest in his arrival, Ra doesn't spurn the offer—business is good for publicity. (In the movie as in life, he records for the Blue Thumb label and makes the cover of *Rolling Stone*.) He and Jimmy Fey cruise around Oakland in a 1940s convertible with Ra in full regalia, to the amusement of real pedestrians and kids on bikes, as Jimmy interviews him for broadcast. Why are black men at the bottom of society? Because their position's inverted; they belong on top.

The savviest scene in *Space Is the Place* gives Sun Ra's philosophy a reality test. It plops him down at an Oakland community center, where a doo-wop quartet rehearses as people talk and play pool or ping-pong. One guy's reading LeRoi Jones's/Amiri Baraka's *Black Music*, open to the middle where Sun Ra is discussed. He looks up in surprise when Ra announces himself: "Greetings, black youth of planet Earth." Said youths are realistically skeptical of this grave gentleman in gold-chain headgear and resplendent gold robes, flanked by aides sporting giant gilt animal heads, when he introduces himself as the ambassador from the Intergalactic Regions of the Council of Outer Space. How do we know you're real, he's derisively asked, and not some old Telegraph Avenue hippie?

"I'm not real, I'm just like you. You don't exist in this society. If you did, your people wouldn't be seeking equal rights. . . . So we're both myths." He continues: "I came from a dream that the black man dreamed long ago. I'm actually a present sent to you by your ancestors"—present also in the temporal sense. (Later, when he dozes off at a rehearsal, Ra dreams of ancient Egypt.) He explains he's here to take a selected few back to the stars with him. And if we won't come? "Then I'm going to have to do you like they did to you in Africa—chain you up, take you with me."

"Are there any whiteys up there?"

"They're walking there today."

His rap wins at least some of the community over. But Ra also attracts the attention of other nemeses: a couple of government agents who've got him under electronic surveillance and who'd assassinate him if they didn't crave his knowledge. A few hours before Ra's big Oakland concert, they abduct him in front of the hall and take him to a warehouse where they play a halfhearted game of Good Cop/Bad Cop. But when their interrogation proves fruitless, they resort to torture: put him in headphones blasting an oompah version of "Dixie."

Luckily, Bernard and Bubbles have witnessed the kidnapping, and with Tiny's help they rescue Sun Ra and take him to the big show, where the agents try to shoot him from the wings; once-skeptical Bubbles selflessly leaps out to block a bullet. Preparing to leave Earth, Ra takes along Bernard, Tiny, a revived Bubbles, and "the black part" of Jimmy Fey—the less mercenary part, presumably. Ra leaves everyone else to take their chances. As he's departing there are fires, earthquakes, collapsing buildings and dams—though it's not clear if he's causing it all or just foresaw the moment when this sick sad world would self-destruct. (There had been four earthquakes around the time he landed.) After his departure, Earth explodes; the last we see of it is a red chunk of crust spinning through space, like a shard of smashed watermelon. We scarcely care: our sympathies are more with Sun Ra than the Earthlings. That explosion plays on the end of *Forbidden Planet*, where Earth's white men, fleeing in their saucer, blow up a world whose technological culture they've deemed too toxic.

But still, there is hope. As the ship takes off from a planet aflame, we hear June Tyson sing, "In some far-off place/Many light years in space/We'll wait for you." And as we've seen, in the opening scene that follows this ending, Ra still intends to bring Earth's black people to their own world, in an alter-destiny enforced migration: a Middle Passage with a happier outcome.

Ever the visionary, with *Space Is the Place* Sun Ra looks ahead: to Parliament's 1975 album *Mothership Connection*, whose cover depicts George Clinton emerging from a flying saucer; to Nathaniel Mackey's series of hallucinogenic novels, full of wordplay and hidden meanings, about a Bay Area improvising collective; to Public Enemy's *Fear of a Black Planet*.

(There are two versions of the film; Ra had insisted on cuts, and the trim 63-minute original release is sleeker and more unified than the 82-minute restoration, in which the Overseer has some sexytime with a couple of nurses, Jimmy Fey is more morally compromised, and there's a visit to a brothel where the government men are revealed as NASA employees and racist brutes. We also get more concert footage and the Overseer's explicit comeuppance, see that a few more Earthlings escape with Ra, and discover that his preconcert rehearsal had been going on for four days, which explains that Egyptian-dream catnap.)

> **Louis Armstrong-Chicago Style** (1976; 115 minutes; director: Lee Philips; writer: James Lee). **Cast includes: Ben Vereen (Louis Armstrong), Red Buttons (Red Cleveland), Margaret Avery (Alma), Janet MacLachlan (Lil Armstrong), Lee de Broux (Jack Cherney), Jerry Fogel (Jack Teagarden), Albert Paulsen (The Man).**
> **—Due to a corrupt manager, Louis Armstrong is framed on a marijuana charge in Los Angeles and leaned on by gangsters in Chicago.**

Louis Armstrong died in 1971—the most famous, film-iliar and imitated jazz musician. There was a time when seemingly every American adult and many kids impersonated his gravel singing voice. Yet his own life had never been brought to the big screen, save where he played a version of himself in *New Orleans* or *Paris Blues*, or was fictionalized as in *Syncopation*.

The TV movie *Louis Armstrong-Chicago Style* isn't a proper childhood-to-stardom bi-opic, but focuses on one sliver of his career. Set in 1931, it deals with his marijuana bust in Los Angeles and a subsequent episode in Chicago where he tangled with gangsters. That bust was actually late in 1930, but the film gets a fair amount right. Armstrong was indeed on a break outside the LA club he was working when the cops pinched him for pot possession—as in life, they're apologetic about it, telling him he'd been informed on (by the owner of a rival club; in the movie the rat is his own manager, trying to force him back to Chicago). Once in Chicago, and under contract at a nightclub, gangsters press him to move to another room that they control. (In life, that was Connie's Inn in New York; here it's a rival Chicago spot run by The Man, a character whose generic name suggests a refugee from *Lady Sings the Blues*.) In addition, Louis is accurately shown to be estranged from wife Lil, a classically trained pianist whose advice he trusts, and looking to get with dancer and sometime domestic Alpha Smith, called Alma Ray here. (Many proper names are altered, even of folks from his distant New Orleans past, as if to appease nervous lawyers. In Los Angeles he plays the Cotillion Club not the New Cotton Club; his crooked manager is Red Crawford, not Johnny Collins.)

Details get fudged, as always. Even Lil and Alma call him Louie, not Louis with a sounded *s*. (He even calls himself Louie, once.) Armstrong sings "When the Saints Go Marching In," often, seven years before he made it an instant standard. And there's premature talk of how the French want to bring him to Paris—he didn't make it till 1934. (The film evokes the cliché, attributed here to a French critic, that "Jazz is the only indigenous American music." "You mean I'm playing indigenous all these years?" Louis asks—a line you could picture Armstrong delivering.) His first racially mixed record date, including trombonist Jack Teagarden, happens here two years too late, in the wrong city. The biggest fabrication: Armstrong, a proselytizer for marijuana and daily smoker for 40 years, declares himself antipot. The smell reminds him of skanky Storyville cribs. When he's busted, he's framed like Gene Krupa.

The film might be better remembered were it not for the low-budget look and mostly pedestrian acting; director Lee Philips worked almost exclusively in TV. Its chief liability is its star, singing, dancing stage and screen personality Ben Vereen, one adult American whose Armstrong impersonation is decidedly lacking. His Louis is no tea-head, but Vereen plays him like he's stoned, often bursting into unmotivated laughter. As much Armstrong as there is on film to study, Vereen absorbed none of his musical or comic timing. When he sings on stage, in a hoarse voice, his melodic variations don't really swing. When he plays, his Louis points his trumpet bell every which way, gyrating and shimmying like some proto-Elvis—making the point Armstrong was a pop star too.

Still, this is not how Pops moved on stage. As his performances in 1933's *København, Kalundborg Og -?* show, much as he may clown verbally, whatever the context, when the horn's in his mouth, Armstrong is all business, pointing the bell slightly upward or straight ahead. Trumpet embouchure is complex and specific; a player can't hold the mouthpiece steady against the lips while leaping around. (His horn is credibly ghosted by Teddy Buckner.) Vereen uses a white handkerchief as a prop, like Armstrong. To his credit, the actor doesn't try to copy Louis's pop-eyed mannerisms, or make him seem obsequious—save when he and manager Red are driving through the Southwest and run into gun-toting rednecks and Louis has to pretend to be the shufflin' chauffeur: a little heartland racism à la *Lady Sings the Blues*.

Much of Armstrong's life story was well-known by 1975—we hear about him delivering coal to Storyville as a kid and getting his first horn at the Waif's Home. The screenplay evidently relies on Max Jones and John Chilton's 1971 biography *Louis*. Many specific incidents from the book turn up, and even some dialogue, almost word for word. When the other prisoners make a fuss, a jailer asks Louis if he's someone special. "No, just one of the cats." Jack Teagarden proposes a racially mixed record date: "You're a spade and I'm an ofay, but so what, man? I mean, we both got the same soul!"[11] (In the movie Louis thinks it's too risky, but makes the record date anyway when he passes the studio while evading some thugs after checking himself into a jail overnight for his own protection— fiction all the way.)

The film's theme is built around one of Armstrong's most notorious comments, found in Jones and Chilton: advice about management he'd received before leaving New Orleans. The film version: "When you get up north, make sure you find yourself a white man who's gonna put his hand on your shoulder and say, 'This heah my nigger.'"[12] The movie is about getting Louis to the point when he tells Red Crawford to take that hand off his shoulder—when he finally stands up for himself, as Lil has urged. And high time too. Late in the film, we discover Red has been getting 50 percent of Louis's take (though in the film's universe, it was Red, not King Oliver, who'd brought Louis north from New Orleans).

So on one level *Louis Armstrong-Chicago Style* follows *Sweet Love, Bitter* in its critique of the black musician's white friend. Red acts like he's Louis's buddy, but he's devious and spineless. He's also a liar. Red tells Louis he has a Chicago job lined up post–Los Angeles, but when the trumpeter gets there, he's out of work. Louis holes up in a rooming house, or roams the streets, eyeing Depression-era soup kitchens. (The real Armstrong went straight into the 3,500-seat Regal Theater. And he temporarily lived with Lil in the house they'd bought together; here she has a third-floor walkup.)

These deviations from fact make room for Louis's more reliable (made-up) white best friend, club owner Jack Cherney, who rescues the trumpeter by putting him in the band at his China Garden. When The Man and his men try to pry Louis away, he and Jack stand fast, out of mutual loyalty. At one point, Jack points out there are better managers than Red out there, like (Louis's soon-to-be real manager) Joe Glaser.

Courageous Jack even takes a stand against gratuitous expository dialogue. The Man sends a couple of trumpeters, one white and one black, down to the China Garden. One after the other they challenge Armstrong with their horns, uninvited, but he brushes them back with eight bars of musical rejoinder in one case and four in the other. (These challengers fold quickly, knowing who they're up against.) At the back of the room, Red says, "Old New Orleans trick—top another musician with your horn, they run you off the turf." Jack, testily: "You don't need to tell me what carving is!"

The whole stand-up-for-yourself storyline is a bit of a cheat; Louis would eventually defer on all business matters to Joe Glaser, who took a very generous cut of the proceeds himself. In reality Armstrong replaced one white hand on his shoulder with another. (There is a far superior 1931 Armstrong impersonation in 2019's *Bolden*.)

Scott Joplin (1977; 95 minutes; director: Jeremy Paul Kagan; writer: Christopher Knopf). **Cast includes: Billy Dee Williams (Scott Joplin), Art Carney (John Stark), Clifton Davis (Louis Chauvin), Margaret Avery (Belle Hayden Joplin), Eubie Blake (Will Williams), Godfrey Cambridge (Tom Turpin), Samuel Fuller (potential backer). New song: "Hangover Blues" (Harold Johnson).**
—At the turn of the twentieth century, Scott Joplin plays excellent ragtime piano but wants to be taken seriously as a composer, eventually writing and striving to stage an opera. But he grows increasingly ill.

There is a wilder cutting contest, and a more ethical white hand on the shoulder, in another TV movie from the following year: *Scott Joplin*, a better, shorter, cheaper, more accurate biopic from *Lady Sings the Blues* producer Berry Gordy and star Billy Dee Williams. (It's billed as "A Motown Production.") A Joplin revival had been brewing throughout the decade, owing to Joshua Rifkin playing the composer's piano rags with admirable fidelity to the scores and stately period tempos, and Gunther Schuller conducting small-group orchestrations of Joplin's works. Those interpretations inspired the Joplin rags that rattled through the 1973 Depression-era caper *The Sting*. Nobody cared that classic ragtime preceded the Depression by 30 years; the music's jaunty defeat of (rhythmic) expectations fit the story's double-fakeout con game. With *The Sting*'s success, the black pianist who'd played in brothels and died of syphilis in 1917 became America's hot new composer. You couldn't walk down the street without hearing "The Entertainer" coming from a radio, piano lesson, or ice-cream truck.

Before the 1970s, Joplin was better remembered as a forerunner of jazz, popularizing African American syncopation and writing the early jazz evergreen "Maple Leaf Rag." The tune had several two-bar breaks, where the accompanying beat would fall silent; negotiating those, improvisers would substitute their own licks for Joplin's fast tremulous ascents. As in the film, the composer preferred his pieces played straight and not too fast. *Scott Joplin* contrasts him with his (real) friend Louis Chauvin, portrayed as a sort of proto-jazz musician: a hotter player and inventive melodist, who left almost no written music behind. Chauvin: "Why you mess around with that note music for? You the only one can read it. My ears tell me everything."

Joplin was a serious composer, and *Scott Joplin* checks off the classical-biopic character traits. He's a virtuoso performer who finds immortality in composing, like Paganini in *The Magic Bow* (1946), and wastes away, like Schubert in *Blossom Time* (1934). His music, like Chopin's (*A Song to Remember*, 1945), reflects his people, and like Johann Strauss's (*The Great Waltz*, 1938) appeals to listeners of diverse classes.[13] As biopics go it's uncommonly accurate. Christopher Knopf's screenplay fudges relatively few dates and invents relatively few details.

The action spans 11 years in Joplin's life, tied to his relationship with music publisher John Stark, our occasional voiceover narrator, from 1899, the year Stark issued "Maple Leaf Rag" in Sedalia, Missouri, to his closing his New York office in 1910, as a failing Joplin was trying to get his opera *Treemonisha* produced. Stark is the composer's advocate in the world and the world of the movie. In life he didn't lobby to have Joplin's music featured at the 1904 St. Louis Exposition, but in the film that lets him defend ragtime as serious music to the city's blue-noses. Comic actor Art Carney, authentically bewhiskered, plays Stark as a somber man with a small chip on his shoulder. Billy Dee Williams is remarkably good as the dedicated, sometimes imperious, and ultimately infirm Joplin. He also looks right, in his starched collar, just as *Scott Joplin* re-creates the waves in Chauvin's hair as seen in photographs. Director Jeremy Paul Kagan makes the most of his low budget, even if Scott's backlot neighborhood doesn't much resemble red-brick Sedalia. (Harder to excuse: the riverboat berthed in this landlocked railroad town.)

Writer Knopf relied on the best study of Joplin at the time, Rudi Blesh and Harriet Janis's *They All Played Ragtime*, first published in 1950. It's the source of myriad story and character details, and even some dialogue. ("Get up from the piano boy—you're hurting its feelings.") The smoking gun is a (lightly tweaked) line of Blesh's about Chauvin, which Joplin (mis)uses to describe one of his own pieces: "legato cantilena in virtuoso tempo"—a phrase so posh Chauvin parrots it. The details harvested from the book include the terms of Joplin's original contract with Stark, and the fact that the musicians' union discouraged its members from playing ragtime. Per the book, Stark has Joplin demonstrate "Maple Leaf Rag" at the piano to boost sales and Scott marries Sedalia widow Belle, a poor student when he tries to teach her violin. (The real Belle was indifferent to his music.) Scott and Belle follow Stark to St. Louis, where the Joplins live in a large house, but the couple break up after the death of their infant daughter. In the film, interviewed by a hostile music critic, Stark compares Joplin's genius to Chopin nocturnes and Bach fugues, and observes that he makes Mississippi water taste like honeydew—paraphrasing the real Stark's promotional prose.[14]

For a TV movie, *Scott Joplin* is disarmingly up front about ragtime pianists working in brothels—it comes up in the first three minutes—and about Joplin contracting syphilis; he exhibits shaky-hand symptoms earlier than in life. As shown, St. Louis pianist Tom Turpin once hosted an evening for visiting madams, including New Orleans' fabled Lulu White, who were scouting for piano talent to hire—although the real Joplin does not seem to have performed that night. (In the movie he does, but hates himself for it.)

The film accurately shows his "Ragtime Dance" being performed on stage; a couple of sheet-music montages tally some of his enduring pieces, and suggest their widespread circulation and influence. (We see women, the main consumers of ragtime scores, buy his music but we don't see any play it.) The film does quietly conflate his two operas, omitting 1903's *A Guest of Honor*, and the real Joplin didn't compose them to compete with gargantuan music like John Philip Sousa's, which (in the movie) had drowned out Scott's piano music at the 1904 St. Louis Fair. You'd never know that Sousa was playing some rags and cakewalks by then. As depicted, Stark moved his operation to New York, only to be undersold by major publishers. He continued to publish Joplin, but declined to back his new opera *Treemonisha*. Stark gets in a meta-dig at movie convention, when he mocks Joplin for wanting the white establishment's recognition: a Carnegie Hall finale.

After Joplin withdrew from the sporting life, other pianists would accuse him of ducking competition. But while this biopic champions the written over the improvised, its finest sequence showcases virtuoso performance: the cutting contest held at Sedalia's Maple Leaf Club on the day Joplin meets his publisher. John Stark may have first heard him there, if under different circumstances such piano jousts were more common in St. Louis. In the film the contest brings Joplin to Sedalia (where he'd lived before, a fact only obliquely referred to when he mentions having studied at George Smith College).

The Maple Leaf battle is adjudicated by surviving rag composer and pianist Eubie Blake, then a spry 90, who'd met Joplin. (Alas, Eubie doesn't play. The film's music director and ghosting pianist is historical-styles expert Dick Hyman.) Two upright pianos stand back to back, and five combatants volley the music and a few razzing comments back and forth; as a defeated contestant vacates a piano stool, the next challenger replaces him. The early lead is taken by a showman (singer Taj Mahal) who plays fat keyboard clusters using his elbows, forearm, rump, and foot; one challenger (Spo-De-Odee) has only one arm, but a mighty left hand. Earlier, Joplin had shown his imperious ways by complaining about the tuning of a mid-keyboard A-flat (the piano tuned, it turns out, by John Stark himself, who was also in the piano business). Before sending him into combat, Eubie's referee instructs Joplin to work in Von Suppé's 1846 *Poet and Peasant* overture—a genuine ragtimers' test piece—in A-flat. He barely touches on it, but Joplin's facility in odd keys flummoxes his opponent. However Scott doesn't mind when he's then bested by the flashier Chauvin, playing "Maple Leaf Rag." They'd agreed to split the proceeds if either won.

As Joplin gets respectable, Chauvin sticks to his showy and whoring ways, and succumbs to an early death—but not before Scott transcribes the opening strains of the lovely "Heliotrope Bouquet" as Chauvin plays them. Joplin will finish the piece himself. That's all straight from life. And as the movie has it, that rag is the main reason we remember Chauvin, who died before getting the chance to record or cut player-piano rolls. (Piano didn't record well, early on, which is why early ragtime on cylinder or disc mostly came from bands or banjos.) *Scott Joplin* sets the table for early jazz; we don't hear any, although late in the film scuffling Chauvin and Joplin sing a generic blues and namecheck Jelly Roll Morton, the New Orleans pianist who moved in some of the same competitive circles. *Scott Joplin* ends on a downer, as the debilitated composer stumbles off into a snowy New York night. But a voiceover (not Stark's) informs us Joplin's day would finally come, in the years just before the film was made.

Jelly Roll Morton is the model for the New Orleans bordello pianist in 1978's **Pretty Baby**, which presents life in 1917 Storyville from a working girl's or woman's perspective. (Its French director Louis Malle's 1958 noir *Elevator to the Gallows* had been elegantly scored by Miles Davis.) In the parlor, the Professor (Antonio Fargas) tickles out, and maybe sings, a few compositions by or associated with Morton—"Buddy Bolden's Blues," "Mamanita," "Winin' Boy"—and by Scott Joplin. (He's ghosted by pianist Bob Greene and vocalist James Booker.) The Professor isn't braggarty like Jelly, but, feeling frisky one evening, he slams out clusters with his left forearm, making the piano roar Morton-style on "Tiger Rag."

When a winds-and-strings sextet joins him on gala brothel evenings, the music is a polite "Heliotrope Bouquet" and suitably sedate "Moonlight Bay," not blasty dixieland. In *Pretty Baby* even the closing of Storyville is subdued. The displaced folk plan ahead, packing and departing at their own pace, during daylight, instead of getting evicted at the stroke of midnight as in *New Orleans*. The Professor, looking as sharp as Jelly Roll himself, declares he's off to Chicago. The real Morton was long gone from New Orleans by then. After three years in Chicago he'd tired of it, and was bound for California.

New York, New York (1977; 1981 re-release, 163 minutes; director: Martin Scorsese; screenplay: Earl Mac Rauch, Mardik Martin, [uncredited] Julia Cameron; story: Rauch). Cast includes: Liza Minnelli (Francine Evans), Robert De Niro (Jimmy Doyle), Georgie Auld (Frankie Harte), Barry Primus (Paul Wilson), Mary Kay Place (Bernice), Leonard Gaines (Artie Kirks), Clarence Clemons (Cecil Powell). New songs: "There Goes the Ball Game," "And the World Goes 'Round," "Happy Endings," "Theme from New York, New York" (words Fred Ebb/music John Kander).
—A sweet singer and sour saxophonist team up at the end of World War II and tour with a failing big band. They drift apart; she goes to Hollywood while he pursues progressive jazz. Could her big New York concert reunite them?

Martin Scorsese isn't very fond of *New York, New York*, but then he made it at a crazy time in his life. He was consuming a lot of cocaine. His wife Julia Cameron (who'd worked on the script) was pregnant and would file for divorce two months after it opened, partly because of his affair with star Liza Minnelli. The film's production ran overlong and over budget, and was the director's first commercial flop when released in truncated form in 1977. (We assess the better received, restored 1981 release.)[15]

It is better than Scorsese thinks, one of the most polished and thematically coherent jazz films—even if jazz "loses" in the end. It merges content and form, juxtaposing naturalistic, improvisational 1960s/1970s acting and the look of late 1940s/early 1950s Technicolor musicals: a clash of styles that complements the plot. On one level *New York, New York* is an independent director's salute to the (already defunct) studio system, shot on MGM's (soon to be dismantled) soundstages and not-quite New York streets—where the curbs are too high, the avenue ends at the corner, there's parking out front, and a lone saxophonist plays under a streetlamp.

But messy human relations play out all too realistically in front of that scenery. The story charts the coming together and apart of Robert De Niro's abrasive tenor saxophonist Jimmy Doyle and Minnelli's sweetly accommodating bandsinger turned Hollywood star Francine Evans: characters representing Art and Entertainment like Gershwin's girlfriends in *Rhapsody in Blue*. The disjunction between the realistic and stylized is often identified as *New York, New York*'s fatal flaw, but the tension between an improvisational aesthetic and showbiz gloss drives the movie on every level. One of Scorsese's early boosters was John Cassavetes, and *New York, New York* like *Too Late Blues* is about the director's own life and work—in this case, his crumbling marriage and competing art-versus-commerce priorities.

It's a period piece, beginning on V-J Day in 1945, and one of its subjects is the collapse of the big bands after World War II. (The score is by one-time big-band arranger Ralph Burns.) But like any period piece, it's also about when it was made: the mid-1970s, when it looked to some folks like jazz itself was on the way out, having gotten too weird for mass consumption. In *New Orleans*, jazz and classical got married. In *New York, New York*, jazz and pop get divorced.

The film was already in the works before Scorsese wanted in. Producer Irwin Winkler had bought Earl Mac Rauch's original story and script, and subsequent rewrites by Mardik Martin (and Cameron) helped guide Scorsese's improvisations with his lead actors during preproduction. As with other films utilizing improvised content, at the rehearsal stage the actors would make up their own lines in an outlined scene, and the cream was then skimmed into the written dialogue. They also improvised a little on camera, using the script as a guide. Scorsese and De Niro had recently worked that way on *Taxi Driver*; Minnelli was game, and a quick study. The stars don't hem and haw like Diana Ross and Billy Dee Williams ad libbing in *Lady Sings the Blues*.

Scorsese's process worked fine until shooting caught up with the script; then the crew might wait around for hours while director and actors pondered or rehearsed their next moves. And because elaborate sets were being constructed and struck throughout the production, sometimes they'd improvise scenes out of chronological order, complicating continuity. Worse, they didn't know how the story would end: didn't know what destination to aim for.

To get everyone in a proper period mood, Scorsese screened his collaborators umpteen Hollywood musicals and films about musicians. As specific inspirations, he regularly mentions 1954's *A Star Is Born* starring Minnelli's mother Judy Garland—whose plot parallels this one right down to a movie within the movie—and eye-popping early 1950s MGM musicals where abstract sets and the color palette were pushed to cartoonish extremes, like *The Band Wagon*, directed by Liza's dad Vincente Minnelli.[16] In *The Band Wagon*, an acclaimed director of dramas stages a revisionist musical with mismatched leads, elaborate sets, and a downer ending. That film was written by Betty Comden and Adolph Green, who wrote the lyrics to the other/original standard "New York, New York."

We can identify elements from some other films rarely mentioned in this context, starting with *Alexander's Ragtime Band*. Production designer Boris Leven had worked on *Alexander* (and *Second Chorus*) four decades earlier. As in *Alexander*, squabbling leads are thrown together at an impromptu joint audition; changes in jazz and pop mark the passing years; estranged lovers reconnect at a big New York concert in a scene that echoes the night they met. There's even a cameo by *Alexander*'s Jack Haley (then Liza's father-in-law), playing a Hollywood elder in the movie within the movie. As in *Stormy Weather*, the romantic leads meet at a victory dance where a famous bandleader plays, and later the heroine follows her own path instead of bending to her man's will. As in 1944's *Sweet and*

Low-Down, a dying orchestra plays to a nearly empty ballroom. And the principals argue over who gets to count off the band—a sign of deeper problems out of *The Fabulous Dorseys*.

One of those battling Dorseys, trombonist Tommy, is depicted as playing the night Jimmy and Francine meet, at midtown Manhattan's Moonlit Terrace, on August 15, 1945, where everyone's celebrating the end of the war. (The band looks and sounds right—right number of players in every section, one black trumpeter, and a plausible repertoire: Dorsey was playing the exotic "Song of India" at the time and had worked up the riff tune "Opus One" for a 1943 movie. But—inside joke?—Tommy was in Hollywood that month.) On the prowl, hitting on any good-looking woman within earshot, Jimmy Doyle eventually zeroes in on Francine Evans, who has no trouble recognizing the insincerity of his come-on, and like any prudent person confronted with a con artist, just keeps saying no, 15 times. Perhaps in homage to Cassavetes's long scenes, this ballroom sequence runs over 16 minutes—and yet this unhurried film moves agreeably well.

Real jazz musicians hitting on women can be just as subtle. De Niro plays pushy creeps with conviction, and there is something about Doyle's relentless attention Francine finds vaguely flattering. Minnelli makes you buy it; you see her thaw a bit despite knowing better.

The next day they share a cab to Brooklyn, where he has an audition (at a below-street-level club with a skylight). Doyle demonstrates his hot tenor saxophone, but the boss wants Maurice Chevalier songs to appeal to returning GIs (as if they're returning from World War I). And just as Doyle's about to argue his way out of the gig, Francine starts singing Chevalier's "You Brought a New Kind of Love to Me" and Jimmy plays obbligatos around her vocal, and they're both hired. They don't take it seriously but they do connect. Her singing (and dance moves and spoofy Jolson jazz hands) help put his playing over by placing it in a palatable context—even if it puts the spotlight on her.

That dynamic holds when she gets him into the big band she tours with that winter, fronted by clarinetist Frankie Harte (swing tenor and Hollywood session man Georgie Auld, who ghosted and coached De Niro and could veto takes where the actor's fingering was too far off). De Niro mimes on saxophone exceptionally well, where other musicians are obviously sidelining—more artifice. Auld had led his own band after the war and had an edgy personality that seeps into Harte's character, and Doyle's. "He blows a barrel full of tenor," Frankie says of Jimmy. "But he's some kind of pain in the ass." Doyle takes every opportunity to blow, cutting in on a solo by pianist Paul Wilson, Francine's loyal sidekick.

The swing era cratered in 1946, with big bands breaking up every month. Eleven years is a good run for any dominant musical style. Now people were staying home and dancing less. Even during the war, pop singers were nudging big bands out of the way. As Frankie Harte's band limps along, forestalling the inevitable, its main asset is Francine, who's good looking and personable and can sing. After Doyle takes over the failing band, and ups the screeching Stan Kenton brass content, she wins over skeptical ballroom owners and any critics who lend an ear. Her likability puts the band over, not his bold ideas.

On impulse, Jimmy had persuaded Francine to marry him, with his usual selfless charm: "I don't want anybody else to be with you." Now it's killing him that she gets more attention, her name above his on the sign out front. That's what leads to their confrontation at a rehearsal over who gets to count off the band. When Francine gets pregnant and returns to New York, over his protests, everything tanks. New singer Bernice (Mary Kay Place, mauling "Blue Moon") is comically inept, and now the crowds really dwindle. Within months Doyle signs the band over to Paul Wilson. When that edition reaches New York, it'll sound worse than ever, with violins added, as Bernice assaults Ellington's "Do Nothing Till You Hear from Me."

Living together back in the city, Francine and Jimmy pursue separate careers that underscore their aesthetic differences. She, very pregnant and ever accommodating, makes demo records in the styles of other singers, hoping to interest them in the songs. (We hear only her spot-on Peggy Lee.) Doyle reconnects with an old friend, black trumpeter Cecil Powell, and starts playing with Powell's bebop combo at the Harlem Club, a subterranean room decked out like an Henri Rousseau jungle. On the job, Doyle, like Francine, pretends to be someone he's not: a bebopper. He can handle the frantic new tempos but (like Georgie Auld) still phrases like a swing musician. He sounds best when he plays a cappella, under that lamppost, when he's missing Francine, or on a rooftop like movie Benny Goodman, alone with his thoughts. (On another level he's practicing in public spaces at night, whereas Sonny Rollins took to the Williamsburg Bridge to avoid disturbing his neighbors.) Doyle's solo musings recall Coleman Hawkins, the swing-era

FIGURE 7.3 Stylized sets, naturalistic acting: Francine (Liza Minnelli) and Jimmy (Robert De Niro) at the subterranean Harlem Club in *New York, New York*.

saxophonist who recorded solo and who could blend with boppers without coming all the way into their camp.

On the road, Francine had been singing the jazzy classics—"Once in Awhile," "Just You, Just Me," "The Man I Love" with its little-heard opening verse—and if she's no solid swinger, she infuses those tunes with personality and showmanship. She comes on like an MGM star, not a team-playing bandsinger; she's bigger than the band. Once out on her own, she does new material: songs by Minnelli's longtime collaborators, composer John Kander and lyricist Fred Ebb. These include the film's celebrated theme and future Sinatra standard "New York, New York." In the story it's a collaboration: Doyle writes the music (for her, he says), which sounds almost dreamy when he plays it on piano or tenor. Francine gives it a title and pens the words, which help clarify the melody's phrasing. But Doyle is lukewarm about her lyric, flagging the phrase "top of the heap." (It's an in-joke; De Niro disliked an earlier version of the song, so Kander and Ebb rewrote it. The revised lyric's defiant tone—look out Gotham here I come—stemmed from Ebb's annoyance with De Niro.)[17]

Decca Records producer Artie Kirks takes a shine to Francine, wants to sign her to the label, and solicits her prickly husband's approval, though he's too prickly himself for them to get along. Once more, Doyle can't handle her greater success. (She makes the cover of *Down Beat* long before he does.) Francine comes up/down to the Harlem Club to discuss the deal with her husband, and when the band goes into "Just You, Just Me," she reads it as an invitation to sit in. (We've just heard that the band can behave behind a singer: Diahnne Abbott on a sultry "Honeysuckle Rose.") But when Francine reaches the bandstand, Doyle cuts her off, switching to a fast riff blues. Things come to a head: after they leave they have a screaming match, she goes into labor, and the next day they part, in the film's most heartfelt scene, at a maternity ward.

For Decca, Francine records the showstopper "But the World Goes 'Round," whose ups-and-downs lyric—"One day it's kicks / Then it's kicks / In the shins"—is a Hollywood remake of Kay Starr's 1952 "Wheel of Fortune." The scene was shot with one camera, in a continuous take, with Minnelli recording the vocal live. Here, more clearly than in *Lady Sings the Blues*, we see how a singer puts personal hurt into a song. As Francine pours her heart into it (over a prerecorded backing track, a sign of changing times), the studio dims and her face is framed in a tight spotlight: a signifier she's not just drawing on her own hard knocks, but on the energy she brings to the stage. When the spot widens, Francine uses some of the same hand gestures she'll use on a live version later.

The tune establishes something else. As Minnelli said of her character, "When the man leaves, it's not her undoing. She has fulfillment in her work."[18] (In that she fares better than Ida Lupino in 1947's *The Man I Love*—another film Scorsese cites as inspiration—where other people's problems disrupt her singing career.) Francine's empowered, but she does whatever material she's handed, no less after she graduates to making movies. *New York, New York*'s great set piece is the Francine Evans Hollywood musical *Happy Endings*.

Throughout *New York, New York*, Scorsese and designer Boris Leven have called our attention to the phoniness of its look: painted trees in a snowy woods, the same indoor-for-outdoor set playing a justice of the peace's street and a motor court. When Doyle hitchhikes down a country road, on the MGM backlot, inappropriate structures in the background are framed into a shot. In a stylized nightclub ridiculously bathed in red neon, Artie Kirks jokes, "If nothing else, we can get a tan here." In the film's most meta-moment, a disc jockey (radio icon Casey Kasem) who uses Doyle's tune as his intro music and makes it a hit, identifies it as the "Theme from *New York, New York*" (its actual title, by the way, at Comden and Green's request). This film is at once a retro homage and a ground-breaking postmodern pastiche, where disjunct styles collide to celebrate (as pomo films are said to do) a "flattened, dehistoricized space."[19]

The plot of film-within-the-film *Happy Endings*, mostly cut from the 1977 release, parallels *New York, New York*. (The inner movie's title song notes the distance between Hollywood romances and real ones.) Like the parent film, it begins with a Manhattan street scene that's really an elaborate fake: a mural on the back wall of a moviehouse. There usherette Peggy Smith is beset by a suitor she tries to put off—although, this being the movies, this persistent fellow will advance not hinder her career. When Peggy (unlike Francine) goes to a nightclub, she's urged to sit in, and she's a smash. As in the host movie, the guy leaves when her success overshadows his, and in the end they meet again back where it all began. *Happy Endings* even has its own musical-within-the-musical, Peggy's stage show *Aces High*, stylized beyond *Happy Endings* to the degree *Happy Endings* exceeds *New York, New York*. This mirrors-in-mirrors, cinematic Droste effect is curiously enter-taining, even as we recognize *Happy Endings* is all glitz, no substance—the kind of mu-sical whose aesthetic would pass soon enough. But it does provide the happy ending the larger film doesn't—which is why the 1981 cut of *New York, New York* works better, and was received better with that sequence restored. (The musical within *The Band Wagon* was a flop too, till they lightened it up.) Robert Altman would play a similar narrative trick later in *The Player*.

Francine moves up in the world with ease—success hasn't changed her (or so she says). Scorsese: "She is a natural. He has to work at it and work at it."[20] She's ever-amenable, turning out fluff, where Doyle's uncompromising nature creates problems. The years polish away some of his abrasiveness, but he keeps his integrity. Doyle's version of "New York, New York," heard only in part, is a slow, sometimes out-of-tempo mood piece for low-moaning tenor over a quintet with vibes—a sort of dreary "Harlem Nocturne." It's not a song you write in search of a hit. But a *Down Beat* column touts it over Charlie Parker's "Mohawk" and Dizzy Gillespie's "She's Gone Again," both from 1950.

Doyle's hit gets him into the gossip columns, and he opens his own improbably swank jazz club. (Georgie Auld briefly had a midtown spot himself.) There Doyle plays his signa-ture tune to end a set, and then the stage revolves to reveal Cecil Powell's two-horn quintet, demonstrating how far jazz has veered from popular music. (The revolving stage reaches back to *Sweet and Low-Down* and *The Benny Goodman Story*.) Scorsese has said it's now 1957.[21] Powell's band sounds like an avant-garde-hater's idea of 1959 Ornette Coleman freebop: recognizably jazzy but gratuitously raucous, with a lot of horn squealing. Even so the crowd starts applauding at an arbitrary moment, as jazz-movie audiences do. The club is named Jimmy Doyle's Major Chord, a callback. A major chord, he'd once told Francine, is when you have the music and the woman you want, and enough money to live comfortably. But he only has two out of three—making the Major Chord one more false front in a movie full of fake New York facades.

When Francine returns to town for one big show in the ballroom where they met, now rebranded the Starlight Terrace, he has the clout to snag a good table on short notice. He arrives just before the show ends and, though he applauds heartily, stays seated while everyone else gives her a standing ovation.

This scene is singled out for Minnelli's amusingly uncanny impersonation of Judy Garland circa 1960; Francine, in a loose blouse hanging over tight shiny pants, thanks the crowd in Minnelli's mother's voice. But the version of "New York, New York" Francine performs as her encore is Minnelli's own. Art and Entertainment have tussled all through the picture, but this bravura performance declares a winner. Pop wins out over jazz: Her pizazzy version is 10 times more electrifying than Jimmy's, starting as it does with that signature, applause-prompting five-note, three-pitch piano hook (not in Doyle's version, as she'll remind him afterwards, and possibly contributed by accompanist Paul Wilson, finally in his element). She's brought a two-beat strut to the melody, which she accents with her hips, inhabiting the role of a small-towner looking to take the city by storm—the life Francine had pictured before Doyle walked into it. She shows how a pop singer can improve on jazz material. In a reaction shot even Jimmy looks impressed.

He comes backstage, greets his son (who looks about nine by now, and seems to be doing fine), and banters with Francine in their old jockeying-for-position way, getting in a dig at *Happy Endings*. "Let's not start all over again now," he joshes, when she pushes back. But after he leaves, he phones her from the street: Come meet me.

Scorsese shot a happy ending, where they stroll off, chatting amiably. Director George Lucas (about to release his own *Star Wars*, which would make this movie seem even more old-fashioned), famously told Scorsese an upbeat finish would pull in an extra $10 million at the box office. But the director's Art side won out. Francine starts heading out to meet Doyle, but thinks better of it and gets back on her elevator to the top. Stood up, he walks off. The last we see of him, his vagabond shoes step out of a low-angle shot, mirroring his two-tone brogues stepping into the frame at the beginning. It's a return to the head, in jazz parlance: ending with the theme you start with.

New York, New York could not end happily. The gulf between Francine's crowd-pleasing act and the increasingly bewildering sound of modern jazz had grown too wide. There's no common ground left to meet on. Jazz, here at least, has lost its mass audience: okay for nightclubs, but no longer filling ballrooms as in Tommy Dorsey's day.

The Cotton Club (1984; 129 minutes; director: Francis Ford Coppola; writers: William Kennedy, Coppola, Mario Puzo). Cast includes: Richard Gere (Dixie Dwyer), Gregory Hines (Sandman Williams), Diane Lane (Vera

Cicero), Lonette McKee (Lila/Angelina); James Remar (Dutch Schultz), Bob Hoskins (Owney Madden), Fred Gwynne (Frenchy DeMange), Maurice Hines (Clay Williams), Nicolas Cage (Vincent Dwyer), Tom Waits (Herman Stark), Ron Karabatsos (Mike Best), Zane Mark (Duke Ellington), Larry Marshall (Cab Calloway), Charles "Honi" Coles (Sugar Coates), Tucker Smallwood (Kid Griffin), Joe Dallesandro (Charlie Luciano).

—In the late 1920s and early 1930s, against the backdrop of Harlem's flashiest nightspot, gangsters battle over turf as cornetist Dixie Dwyer and dancer Sandman Williams rise through the ranks of entertainers and pine for elusive women.

Although released in 1984, in some ways *The Cotton Club* feels like the last 1970s jazz spectacle. Like Martin Scorsese, director Francis Ford Coppola had broken out in that decade, and one might see *Cotton Club*—a double homage to 1930s musicals and gangster sagas—as his *New York, New York*: a glittering period piece that ran way over budget, a lavish backstage melodrama with plenty of jazz whose action marks a time of transition. The story begins with what may be a nod to Scorsese's opening, with shoes on a New York sidewalk.

In 1979, producer Robert Evans optioned James Haskins's 1977 photo/history book *The Cotton Club*. Evans commissioned a script from *Godfather* author Mario Puzo, then hired Coppola to do a rewrite. Deep in debt, partly due to his own quixotic soundstage musical *One from the Heart*, Coppola wound up directing as well. To collaborate on a new script he brought in jazz-and-gangster–literate novelist William Kennedy.[22] Haskins's book would provide a lot of atmosphere and many details; sundry story points were plucked from his narrative and creatively repurposed.

The credits open with Ellington's "The Mooche," where a trio of wailing clarinets slither down a chromatic scale. Its placement here affirms Duke's central role in setting the tone at the venue. ("The Mooche" is being played at the club; at first the white audience claps along on one and three, like squares.) The action starts in 1928, shortly after Ellington's three-year residency began. Duke rose to prominence at that Harlem club, thanks to frequent remote broadcasts and to the character of the music he wrote, keyed to the faux-African theatrical costumes and decor. His "jungle style" relied on wah-wah brass effects, also displayed on "The Mooche," which were already part of his music when he arrived. The place was a chic destination for well-heeled white New Yorkers, who would come up to Lenox Avenue and 142nd Street—100 blocks north of Times Square—to see and hear all-black revues. (Ellington's success there led to the early film appearances recounted in chapter 1.)

The story weaves in a variety of real-world (mostly underworld) figures, among them racketeer Dutch Schultz (a sneering, psycho James Remar, with a fake and variable hooked nose) and more temperate Cotton Club owner Owney Madden and his counselor Frenchy DeMange. As played by short Bob Hoskins and very tall Fred Gwynne, they have the best chemistry in the movie.

Movie stars drop by the club to see and be seen; Harlem's Barefoot Prophet might preach on the sidewalk out front. Backstage, we glimpse Ellington (Zane Mark), running down a chart for his musicians, with throwaway dialogue. ("You come in right here with the vocal.") It's a muted callback to Duke's first screen moment, in *Black and Tan*, rehearsing with Arthur Whetsol. It's also the only time he speaks, though we'll see him briefly on stage, conducting the orchestra or stage-grinning over his shoulder as he and the band play "Ring Dem Bells."

We hear plenty of period Ellington but there should be more of the man himself, if only because he never got a biopic. Jazz and film producer Norman Granz had tried, optioning Ellington's life story in 1965 and hoping to cast Sidney Poitier. But Granz couldn't coax Duke off the road for even three days to discuss the story. Ellington, all graciousness in public, guarded his privacy.[23]

There's enough dramatic potential for a subplot at least: Duke Ellington was dapper and well-spoken, and cultivated eccentric soloists. Separated from his wife, he fell at first sight for Cotton Club dancer Mildred Dixon, who started the same night he did, and successfully wooed her. George Gershwin came by to listen and wanted to collaborate on songs; Duke demurred. A firm believer in mixing social classes, he'd sometimes play cards after hours with white brass like DeMange and stage manager Herman Stark, and sometimes with maître d' Kid Griffin and the black waitstaff. He'd been bumping into criminals in clubs for years already, and though he never discussed it, his contacts were extensive. (Later, when some small-time Chicago thugs gave him grief, a phone call from Madden fixed it.) After crooks started kidnapping prominent New Yorkers—a crime spree that figures in *The Cotton Club*—an Irish hood drove Duke to work in a bulletproof car, machine gun at the ready. And the owners started admitting a few black patrons after

FIGURE 7.4 Duke Ellington (Zane Mark) runs down some music for his players in *The Cotton Club*.

Duke diplomatically pointed out that performers' friends and families might enjoy seeing the shows.[24]

None of that's in the picture, except for those black patrons getting admitted later and a new hire falling instantly in love. That smitten individual is not Ellington but the film's black hero, tap dancer Dalbert "Sandman" Williams (Gregory Hines), part of a brother act that will later break up. Gregory's brother and ex-partner Maurice Hines plays Clay Williams; they re-enact their own strife, though their split and reconciliation pass oddly quickly on screen. The Williams Brothers' duo act suggests the Nicholas Brothers, who were still kids in Philadelphia in 1928 and wouldn't play the club till 1932. Sandman instantly falls for Lila (Lonette McKee), a mixed-race dancer and singer aiming to crack white show business.

The white hero is then-hot Richard Gere as a jazz musician who becomes a movie star, Michael "Dixie" Dwyer. Gere had played trumpet since he was a kid, appearing with the Syracuse Symphony at 16, and he insisted on playing cornet in character, although the Cotton Club didn't hire white musicians.[25] (Gere had script approval.) Dixie's paired with vampy Vera Cicero, lightly based on comedian, singer, and nightclub host Texas Guinan, whose tag line was "Hello suckers." (Vera's variant is "Hello chumps." She's played by Diane Lane, daughter of Cassavetes's acting-workshop associate Burt Lane.) But Vera is still in her teens in 1931, when Guinan turned 47.

Cornet aside, Dwyer is a fictionalized George Raft, a New York dancer who'd done a little driving for the mob during Prohibition. Raft had grown up with Owney Madden and hung out at the Cotton Club before heading to Hollywood, where (like Dixie) he played gangsters modeled on real-life hoods. In a general way, Dixie's plotline remakes the first 40 minutes of 1961's *The George Raft Story*. Both films start in New York in the late 1920s and have a wah-wah main theme ostensibly played by a house jazz band. Musical and terpsichorean interludes punctuate the sometimes romantic, sometimes violent action (much more violent in *The Cotton Club*). Both heroes had danced a bit and done light gigolo work early on, and each has a stormy on-and-off relationship with a singer whose other man is a jealous thug who comes after him. Each hits Manhattan nightspots featuring lavish floor shows and shady customers, and runs errands for gangsters including Frenchy DeMange. In either film there's a minor bit about a razor-cut left ear, an injury the victim dismisses. Ray Danton's Raft crosses paths with Texas Guinan, with whom (off-screen) he leaves for Hollywood to start his movie career at the mob's instigation. (A later episode in the *Raft Story* anticipates Coppola's *The Godfather Part II*—George fronts for the mob at a Havana casino until the Cuban revolution forces them out.)

Gere playing his own horn is like Tom Cruise doing his own stunts: it affirms the maxim that "action is character"—that Dixie's sound will reveal how he feels—and it appeals to a star's vanity. The opening credits announce, "Cornet Solos by Richard Gere." Played by, not improvised by. Jazz cornetist Warren Vaché worked out the solos and taught them to the actor: solos that manage to convey zesty period syncopations without straining nonprofessional chops. Nothing's too fast, and everything's in a comfortable middle register. Dixie's no virtuoso, and his sound isn't so special, but Gere looks right—he breathes properly, and doesn't get hammy fingering the valves. Callow Dixie is never broadly expressive in a jazz-movie way—as if he doesn't feel much for his horn to convey.

We hear Dixie solo a few times, starting in the opening sequence, at Harlem's Bamville Club—the real one was on 129th Street—where the primitivist murals wouldn't look out of place in *New York, New York* and a sign out front advertises "Jam session tonight." Such sessions became public attractions only later, but then this isn't much of one—only Dwyer, just off the road, has come by to sit in. When we first lay eyes on Dixie, he's trading phrases on "How Come You Do Me Like You Do" with an unidentified black cornetist who's part of a slightly old-fashioned sextet, with banjo and tuba, though they have a limber stride pianist. Dixie was raised in Harlem himself, so his nickname isn't a geographic locator; it makes a rhyming link with Bix Beiderbecke, Dix's dominant influence. At the Bamville, his horn catches the ear of Dutch Schultz—"He's not bad for a white kid, huh?" Chatting him up afterwards, Dutch talks the jazz talk, disparaging the other cornet: "He oughta be put away for larceny. He just lifted those riffs from King Oliver." But later Dutch will betray a double standard; he digs Dix's Bixiness and will make him play Beiderbecke's trademark "Singin' the Blues" (on piano, which Bix also played). Later still Schultz will deride Dixie's mimicry after seeing Dwyer's movie *Mob Boss*: All he did was copy my style.

Dixie makes the rounds. At a cafe, with an integrated band and audience, he plays cornet on "Indiana." But seven bars into the melody a gangster interrupts to drag him away on Schultz-related business. (Dutch is not easy to shake off. The real Schultz dug jazz, but his Harlem hangouts were Connie's Inn on 131st and the Swanee Club on 125th.) When Vera gets her own club downtown, Dixie sits in, playing polite obbligatos behind her vocal on "Am I Blue?" And finally, once he's a star, Dwyer is introduced uptown as "the first white musician ever to sit in with the Cotton Club orchestra." "Hi, Cootie," he says, stepping on stage; Cootie Williams played trumpet in Ellington's band, but tonight Cab Calloway is headlining. Dixie plays "Big Butter and Egg Man," which Louis Armstrong had recorded in 1926 but which hadn't yet caught on as a jazz standard. It's an odd pick for 1931, but it lets Dixie show how much Armstrong influenced even Bix disciples. (It's Gere's fanciest solo, with some staccato repeated notes and a couple of fast licks.) In fact Bix and a few white pals had sat in with Duke's Cotton Club band years earlier. Maybe every white guest gets announced as the first, to hype the occasion.[26]

Dixie's jazz is noticeably weak tea compared to the dozen-plus period Ellington pieces that undergird action on and off stage. (They're faithfully re-created by saxophonist Bob Wilber's white repertory orchestra.) Since action defines character, Duke's music speaks to his ability to stylize the blues and frame striking soloists. In the film as in life, in 1931 Ellington is succeeded at the club by gyrating, magnetic shouter Cab Calloway (impersonated by Larry Marshall), foreshadowing the upheaval depicted in *New York, New York* when vocalists replaced bandleaders as pop stars. Inevitably Cab sings "Minnie the Moocher," his career-making Cotton Club hit. (The real Cab was in late-career revival after singing it in *The Blues Brothers*.) We also hear a bawdy double-entendre number, and

Lila sings Harold Arlen and Ted Koehler's very lovely "Ill Wind," the 1934 sequel to their Cotton Club smash "Stormy Weather."

Jazz musicians had been encountering crooks on screen for over 40 years. *The Cotton Club* spells out the complex dynamic: criminals who employ musicians might like what they play and generously reward them for it, but never let them forget who's boss. As in life, Owney Madden doesn't deal with the help, but the violence he traffics in trickles down. Backstage, Herman Stark treats the talent and staff with cool respect; enforcer Mike Best crudely insults them and treats them like chattel (until he gets his comeuppance, his head dunked in a toilet—a detail from Haskins's book, only the dunkee was Lena Horne's stepdad, when teenage Lena broke her contract).[27] The stage area's faithfully re-created plantation motif—with the musicians often playing on the "porch"—underlines the economic realities: this false front is for real. (The exterior facade is pretty accurate too, though the club's on the wrong end of the block and the Lafayette Theater shown next door was eight blocks away.)

Outside this uptown plantation, it's not just Dutch who's out of control. Dixie's reckless brother Vincent (Nicolas Cage, in an early gung-ho performance) is patterned on Schultz flunky-turned-enemy Mad Dog Coll; Vincent's tough-guy patter unconsciously echoes Dixie's Mob Boss. The gangster plot marks a change of epoch—the passing of New York's underworld from Jewish and Irish to Italian control. It takes a late arriving Lucky Luciano to stop Dutch Schultz—which happened some years later than depicted.

The last act brings various events, music, and peckin' dance moves forward by a few years; though the story ends in 1931, various details suggest 1933. The musical anachronisms mount as we approach the finish. Sandman sings "Copper Colored Gal," actually from the 1936 Cotton Club show, by which time the real club had moved to midtown.[28] As the anachronisms abruptly pile up, it's as if the narrative were sliding into a slippery, unanchored, postmodern space.

With many storylines in play, *The Cotton Club* seems both overstuffed and underdeveloped. Like *New Orleans*, it's torn between narratives that compete for screen time—a tommy-gun epic and a celebration of Harlem culture. (Owing to cuts, subplots get reduced to single scenes.) One interlude stands out as pure luxury, doing nothing to advance the story. On little pretext Sandman brings Lila to the back-of-a-poolhall Hoofers Club, where real tap elders show their stuff and cut their younger colleagues; they include Honi Coles, Jimmy Slyde, and early Hines-brothers mentor and the film's tap choreographer Henry LeTang. (The Hoofers Club was real, if less spacious, and Coles was often there.)[29]

Ellington occasionally returned to spell Calloway at the Cotton Club, starting in 1933. Duke's band is back for the film's grand finale, where various threads are tied off in a "jazzy" fantasia suggesting a different, more stylized movie. At Grand Central Station, Sandman and Lila are off on their honeymoon, Dixie and Vera are headed for Hollywood, Dutch's widow escorts his casket out of town, and Frenchy sees off Owney, who's taking a three-month sabbatical at Sing Sing. At the same time—because Coppola loves elaborate cross-cut sequences—we are at the Cotton Club, where a porters-and-passengers Grand

Central dance routine is in progress, with suitcases for props and departure-gate signage. Immediately, the Cotton Club's Grand Central bleeds into the real thing, with dancers doubling as real redcaps; a specialty step might begin on stage and end via match cut on the marble floor of the station, where a couple of passengers play luggage with drum sticks. "This is for your fantasies," Lila helpfully declares, throwing her bridal bouquet. You wish there'd been more like this.

This sequence harks back to the impossible-to-stage train-station production number at the end of 1935's *Sweet Music,* and even more to the 1932 Vitaphone short *Smash Your Baggage*—starring the Small's Entertainers, from rival Harlem nightspot Small's Paradise—in which dancing Grand Central redcaps leap over steamer trunks and shimmy to "Tiger Rag." What really puts over the *Cotton Club* variation is the music: Duke's frantic "Daybreak Express" (1933) based on "Tiger Rag" chords, supplemented by his "High Life" on the same template, and a smidge of "Slippery Horn"—a medley expertly stitched to sound like a single composition. The headlong music gives the picture a supercharged finish. As in *Paris Blues,* we exit at the station, as an unseen Ellington steals the ending with a train tune.

/// 8 /// SUFFERING ARTISTS 1984–1989

At the end of the 1970s, Hollywood execs saw *New York, New York* as a symptom of a wider problem: new star directors being given too much leeway (and money) to pursue arcane visions. By the early 1980s, even as *The Cotton Club* was taking shape, there was a new focus on films designed for easy marketing: "high concept" pictures whose premise could be pitched to producers or ticket buyers in a sentence. Thus, 1981's *Outland* was "*High Noon* in outer space."

The cable channel MTV (Music Television), launched in 1981, created a need for music videos to fill programming time, and commercial films began including dialogue-free montage sequences set to contemporary pop songs: MTV-ready content used to market the music and the movie—not that such cross-promotion was a new idea: *Butch Cassidy and the Sundance Kid* had shoehorned in a nondiegetic "Raindrops Keep Falling on My Head" in 1969.

We mention these trends only to note how little effect they had on 1980s jazz films; MTV wasn't interested in jazz even as the music was coming back into public consciousness, mostly due to the publicity surrounding new star Wynton Marsalis and other young players who came along in his wake. Jazz films in general were by now for a niche audience, even when they had studio money behind them.

Paul Mazursky's 1984 ***Moscow on the Hudson***—about a Russian circus saxophonist who defects in Manhattan to become a typical melting-pot New Yorker—isn't a jazz film, but there's a pertinent subplot. At home in Moscow, Vladimir Ivanoff (Robin Williams) gets a pleasantly Getzy tenor sound, playing a leisurely solo "Take the 'A' Train" in a resonant space. He is sentimental about African Americans, not that he's met any, and idolizes some standard jazz greats. But once Vladimir's in New York, music falls by the wayside for a while. He scuffles through a series of entry-level jobs before buying a (cheap) new tenor.

Friend Lionel (Cleavant Derricks) arranges for Vlad to sit in at a Harlem club with an Ivanoff hero, Wild Bill Hawthorn (tenor saxophonist George Kelly). Hawthorn invites Vladimir up, believably mangling his first and last names, and calls a blues his guest knows. Wild Bill plays a frisky opening chorus: neither intimidating nor patronizing, but full of hard-won authority. When Vladimir takes over he plays a few prefab licks but bobbles a fingering approaching bar four of his solo. Rattled, and hearing his own callowness, he cuts himself off after a chorus. (When he looks like he might dive back in, a cut ends the scene.) Lionel, afterwards: "You don't just pick up soul in two or three months—even if you are a Russian." Vladimir starts seriously woodshedding at home, getting some New York grit into his sound, like he's been digging Michael Brecker. But when the saxophonist reprises his solo "'A' Train" in tribute to his late grandfather, on his East Village fire escape—like something out of a movie—a neighbor yells to knock it off. (Also when he continues indoors.) Vladimir gets mugged, and admits New York frightens him, but he stays, and ends up playing soprano in a Russian showband in Brighton Beach and jazz tenor for spare change at Grand Army Plaza. Whether that's making it in New York is a matter of perspective.

Swing Shift, also from 1984, suffered from the same problems as that year's *Cotton Club*—it pulled in conflicting directions, thwarting new-style marketing. Director Jonathan Demme shot *Swing Shift* as a tribute to Southern California women who built World War II bomber planes. But then star Goldie Hawn ordered rewrites and reshoots that effectively turned it into the story of how she'd fallen in love with costar Kurt Russell during filming. He plays Lucky Lockhart, jazz trumpet player (and factory supervisor) who hits on Hawn's Kay Walsh relentlessly while her husband's off to war. She begins to soften after hearing him play one night. Lucky's cocky trumpet playing mirrors his breezy confidence—more *Kings Go Forth* Tony Curtis than *Cotton Club* Richard Gere.

"Kurt Russell was supposed to be a bastard," Demme lamented later.[1] But even after cuts and reshoots designed to make him more sympathetic, Lucky is not so noble, rebounding into bed with Kay's best friend when the absent husband comes home on leave. The trumpeter does, however, play with more bluesy feeling after Kay gives him up. Exempt from wartime service because of some unspecified heart condition (it's a metaphor—see his last name), Lockhart exits before the story ends. He joins a traveling integrated combo that's heading back east by touring car, but their small-group swing will soon sound out of date as bebop takes hold.

We've seen randy trumpeters before, of course, from *Second Chorus* to *A Man Called Adam*. (*Cotton Club*'s Dixie is a notable exception; he only has eyes for Vera. And women don't hit on him, even after he becomes a movie star.) Lucky Lockhart wouldn't be the last horndog with a horn. Around the time cornetist Warren Vaché composed Richard Gere's *Cotton Club* solos, writer Frank Gilroy approached him between sets at Eddie Condon's in New York to ask if he'd ever done any acting.[2]

> *The Gig* (1985; 92 minutes; director/writer: Frank D. Gilroy). **Cast includes: Wayne Rogers (Marty Flynn), Cleavon Little (Marshall Wilson), Warren Vaché (Gil Macrae), Jerry Matz (Aaron Wohl), Andrew Duncan (Jack Larmon), Daniel Nalbach (Arthur Winslow), Joe Silver (Abe Mitgang), Jay Thomas (Rick Valentine), Susan Egbert (Laura Macrae), Stan Lachow (Georgie). —An amateur dixieland band hires a professional bassist for a two-week gig at a Catskills resort.**

Frank Gilroy's *The Gig* looks at a subset of players who get little serious attention: dixielanders, the modern-day, mostly white players who gravitate to the spirit of early jazz's ragtimey beats and jostling horns. Dixieland as self-consciously rearguard action had established itself by the early 1940s, when some musicians who saw the 1920s as a golden age sneered at regimented swing and (a few years later) wrong-note bebop. There have been dixieland musicians ever since. In the 1980s, there were enough amateur and semipro outfits to stock the catalogs of several specialty labels, and to fill programs at annual festivals from Sacramento to Dresden.

As mentioned in chapter 2, even when played by musicians who'd been around in the 1920s, the self-consciously traditional jazz of the 1940s (and later decades) didn't really sound like actual early jazz. The material was mostly newer, less marchy, and more pop-oriented, and the soloists play one by one, after the collective hubbub of the opening chorus. Such music (sometimes unconsciously) reflected later rhythmic, melodic, and harmonic refinements. Everything is more streamlined.

After bebop became the new thing in the later 1940s, swing and trad musicians got thrown together more and more, in settings that smoothed over stylistic differences. By the 1980s, few younger musicians were celebrated for their loyalty to prebop solo styles. Warren Vaché was among the few. Even Roy Eldridge liked him.

Amateur dixieland musicians vary widely in quality and attitude; for some, it's foremost a social music, not a display of virtuosity. The interweaving of horns—trumpet or cornet playing the melody, trombone sliding up on the next chord change, clarinet sailing over the top—made for companionable, maybe comfortably predictable playing. The old tunes may get better, not staler, with time as the players polish their solos. Some elders did that too.

So it goes with *The Gig*'s nameless sextet, who've been together since 1970: They play one night a week in trombonist Marty's den over a few beers, then break out the sandwiches and chips. Only clarinetist Aaron is in the musicians' union, and he mostly teaches. Drummer Arthur is a dentist, pianist Jack a corporate drone. Marty is a Ford dealer who hawks used cars on TV; he's the leader, if only because they rehearse at his house in some New York suburb. The band's one true talent, cornetist Gil (Warren Vaché), had played professionally for a couple of years before slacking off into real estate by marrying the boss's daughter.

Frank Gilroy had his greatest success as a playwright, and *The Gig* betrays a stagey sense of construction. The dramatic beats and complications arrive on schedule: watching it is like watching a good traditional jazz band, everyone hitting their marks on time.

The band has its tunes down, and Gil takes lovely solos that aren't ostentatious—he's one of the gang, not above them. (Vaché's lowkey cocky acting is likewise just right.) No one speaks of it, but you can picture how playing with Gil would motivate the others; he makes them musically respectable, even if they've never performed in public.

An opportunity to play two weeks at a Catskills resort throws them into crisis. The horn players are all for it, but the dates conflict with Jack's family vacation and Arthur dotes on an aging mom. Then bassist Georgie announces he's facing major surgery, and turns the naysayers around: You guys do so much for others—do this for yourselves. And play one for me.

When they break the news to their women, Gil is surprised wife Laura doesn't object: There'll be girls up there, he tells her, prodding. "And you so dashing, playing your golden horn," she mocks, not caring. The marriage looks rocky, but Laura gives him good advice, even if she yells it. If you really think you've sold out, go back to music for real: look up that bandleader who heard you sitting in at Eddie Condon's.

The men are in high spirits, packing the van for the drive upstate—until the arrival of the professional bassist they'd hired sight-unseen, who bums them out. He negotiates an extra hundred a week and a cash advance before getting in the van, and his bass will ride in the front seat. And no, he won't be wearing one of their sky-blue blazers. The trip is awkward; as the old chums babble about their upcoming adventure, the bassist sits reading Orwell and asks Gil to snuff that cigarette.

This sequence is Gilroy at his deftest, conveying much left unsaid. The friends think Marshall (Cleavon Little) is copping an attitude because he's black and they're white, but it's because he's a professional and they're amateurs. For them it's The Gig, for him just a gig. (Worse, he knows they got hired because they're cheaper than pros; he's accepting less than union scale himself.) The friends stop at a bar to let off steam; Marshall naps in the van—touring musicians know how to pass travel time. When they return, we see it all from his side: he's in black jazzman hell, surrounded by tipsy whites singing "Down by the Riverside" with no self-awareness.

Tension mounts till Marshall has them pull over. He gets out his bass and plays the same piece (which he improbably claims not to know), showing his stuff on improvised breaks—just to remind them why they'd hired him. Marshall's sound will lift them all. Instantly the ice is broken. (He's ghosted by Reggie Johnson and esteemed vet Milt Hinton.)

"Why are you playing with us?"

"I've got a wife and two kids and I haven't worked in a month."

Who've you played with? You name it, he says: Lee Konitz, Charlie Parker, Sonny Rollins, Dizzy Gillespie, Duke Ellington, Lionel Hampton—I did a year with Basie and toured the Far East with Benny Goodman.

This is a suspiciously impressive résumé. We don't learn how old Marshall is—the guys say he looks young—but actor Cleavon Little was 15 when Parker died in 1955, and that Goodman tour began in 1956. Marshall's mood brightens so much at this point, you might deduce he's putting them all on, laughing at these easily snowed dabblers. (Or else the script had sat around a while.) Later, when Aaron pumps him for details, Marshall has soured on this game.

"Must have been a gas playing with Basie."

Flatly: "Yes."

"What's Dizzy Gillespie like?"

With a bland smile: "Good people."

By then they've arrived at Paradise Manor and face new setbacks. Host and emcee Abe Mitgang installs them in a rundown bunkhouse, and their swimming hours are restricted. Rumble-voiced Joe Silver's bravura performance as Mitgang represents the whole Catskills hospitality industry. Gilroy gives him plenty to chew: on- and off-stage blather peppered with Yiddish, a compulsion to badmouth competitors, and cheapness coupled with a need to feel loved. (He may have been observed from life; Gilroy lived in the Catskills.)

As soon as the musicians kick off their first set with "The Saints," there's trouble. The coddled oldsters, used to sedate dance music, are stunned by the racket. Mitgang tells them to stop with the "biff, bam, bang," and the band are ready to walk. Marshall steps in to broker a deal: they'll play nice for one night, for more money. A pro when these amateurs need one, he orchestrates the program on the spot: has Gil play "My Gal Sal" as the other horns fake the harmony, Marshall whispering chord changes to the pianist. Their "Cucaracha," "Hava Nagila," waltz and rumba win over Abe and the customers. Now thinking more like pros themselves, the amateurs press Mitgang for concessions: If we stay we play one jazz tune per set and one dixieland set a night. And we will be ordering off the guest menu.

Daytimes, Marshall leads rehearsals, teaching the guys more tame tunes, but he's frustrated by their limitations. Jack keeps messing up the piano chords, and drummer Arthur's tempos waver (or so Marshall claims: he's finicky in a *Whiplash* way—but we'll get to that later). The band's ghosts include ace pianist Dick Wellstood and clarinetist Kenny Davern, and the amateurs sometimes play improbably well. Clarinetist Aaron squeaks when practicing a scale, but weaves supple lines that sail across the register break on "The Saints." Pianist Jack keeps forgetting to play that added seventh Marshall requests, but breezes through "Maple Leaf Rag." We can chalk up some of this inconsistency to these musicians feeling secure only in their safety zone: They're slick on stuff they've rehearsed for years, shaky on new material. Marty's trombone solos sound canned; Aaron mentions without embarrassment that he's working up a new solo on "Star Dust."

With a little more exposure, the hotel guests warm to the dixieland and ask for more. There are nonmusical developments too; Gil started sweet-talking one of the waitresses as soon as they arrived, and she fixes up a friend with homesick Arthur. (He'll fall for her, only to find out she's married, dallying with him while her husband's in the service—a gender-switch on *Swing Shift*.) Marshall and Marty bond over fishing.

Just when they've settled in, there's a final complication. Their closing weekend, over Labor Day, they're to play three nights with one-time singing star Rick Valentine, who's hoping this gig will help revive his failing career. (It surely won't; it's a last-minute booking with no promotion.) At their first rehearsal, Valentine—who thinks an abrasive attitude and thuggish entourage make him Sinatra—passes out charts most of the band can't play. (Now they really sound like amateurs.) Valentine has them fired on the spot— all but Marshall, who agrees to send to New York for replacements. "For you guys it's a lark," he explains to the angry cohort. "For me it's my bread and butter." He asks Gil to stay on, but the cornetist declines—he'll stick with his buddies, doesn't feel that need to play (or to be the new band's outsider). Aaron would love to be asked but Marshall tells him he doesn't have the chops: "Devotion isn't enough."

On the way home, Aaron rails about Gil. "I who love music more than life am given a second-rate talent, while he is handed a one-in-a-million gift—a one-in-a-million gift—which he shits on." That's playwright speech not jazz talk.

During the ride the guys quarrel, get a flat tire, and call home to learn that while they've been away, Georgie died from complications. They play him a farewell blues by the roadside—callback to Marshall's "Down by the Riverside." Alas, *The Gig* doesn't track Marshall's weekend with pissy Rick Valentine, who's sure to throw a tantrum when the important New Yorkers he invited fail to show. Professional musicians earn those bigger bucks.

> *'Round Midnight* (1986; 131 minutes; director: Bertrand Tavernier; writers: David Rayfiel, Tavernier). Cast includes: Dexter Gordon (Dale Turner), François Cluzet (Francis Borier), Gabrielle Haker (Berangere), Sandra Reaves-Phillips (Buttercup), Bobby Hutcherson (Ace), Herbie Hancock (Eddie), Wayne Shorter (Wes), Lonette McKee (Darcey Leigh), Hart Leroy Bibbs (Hershell), John Berry (Ben), Liliane Rovère (Madame Queen), Martin Scorsese (R. W. Goodley).
> —In 1959 Paris and in a bad way, ailing alcoholic saxophonist Dale Turner is befriended by a devoted French fan. In time he takes Dale back to New York, where life is less rosy.

A few years after *New York, New York*, Martin Scorsese introduced its producer Irwin Winkler to French director Bertrand Tavernier. Over lunch, Tavernier asked whether they'd been happy with how that movie ended. They confessed they hadn't been, and kicked around other possible fates for saxophonist Jimmy Doyle—like having him move to Paris in the 1950s. When Tavernier heard that, he pitched the producer on the spot: We should make a movie about that guy. So began the road to *'Round Midnight*.[3]

Warner Bros. showed some interest in the script by Tavernier and American writer David Rayfiel, but balked at the director's choice for the lead, newly retired saxophonist Dexter Gordon, then in his early sixties. (Tavernier had seen him on film, and seen how the camera loved him.) A nudge from Warners favorite and Tavernier ally Clint Eastwood helped get the studio on board.

Casting Gordon was the master stroke—he's *'Round Midnight*'s raison d'être. Dexter's distinctive slow motion sets the tempo, for better and worse. The rare jazz musician to carry a feature, he'd briefly appeared in a film made at Chino prison when he was an inmate, 1955's *Unchained*—source of the evergreen "Unchained Melody" sung by *Syncopation*'s Todd Duncan. Gordon had also appeared in a West Coast staging of *The Connection*, bringing his expertise on the realities of heroin addiction.

Dexter's character Dale Turner amalgamates his own colorful personality with that of a key personal and musical influence, the aloofly hip, slang-talking Lester Young (nicknamed Pres, for President of the Tenor Saxophone). But Turner's Paris trajectory closely parallels that of pianist Bud Powell, in particular his friendship with fan turned caretaker Francis Paudras. The film is dedicated to Young and Powell; Dexter Gordon had known both. The Dexter, Lester, and Bud strains in Dale's character are tightly braided—a bit like the mashup of Whiteman, Berlin, and Goodman in *Alexander's Ragtime Band*.

A composite character allows for a sweeping story. But the meticulous particularity of real-life incidents restaged in *'Round Midnight* gives the film a tone that's both reverent and disconcerting, especially when all three lives intertwine. In a way, the film justifies its elisions by presenting the action as a remembrance, with all the confabulation memory brings; the story begins and ends in that remembered realm. It fictionalizes Francis Paudras's time with Bud Powell, which was memorialized and codified in Paudras's book *La Danse des Infidèles*, published in 1986. The period when Francis knew Bud (and fictional counterpart Francis Borier knows Dale) defines the film's time frame. Along the way there are brief flash-forwards to Borier's later life, as he and his now-adult daughter Berangere watch grainy home movies of Dale and recall funny things he used to say. The film ends on that warm note.

The action begins with remembering: Francis, off camera, asks Dale, in a New York hotel room in 1964 (in black-and-white, like home movies), if this is where Hershell died—and then without a cut, Dale is in the same room, now in color, visiting bed-ridden Hershell. Dale has come to say goodbye to his old musical sparring partner before leaving for Paris, where Francis will one day do this remembering. And it begins with reconstructing: of incidents like this one, in which Hershell wants to know if Dale is still playing weird chords. ("You drive people wild—they can't follow the tune!" And: "Can't you talk the way th'other folks talk neither?") That remembering/reconstructing frame suits a story where jazz anecdotes are free-floating and repurposed, like vintage riffs at a jam session. It gives the action room to roam between fact and fiction.

The unsettling part, from a jazz perspective, stems from characters who both are and aren't recognizable figures. Hershell (as his name appears in the credits) is plainly based on Herschel Evans, Lester Young's fellow tenor and friendly rival in the 1930s Basie band. Hershell is an older man, while Herschel died of heart disease at 29—in the hospital, not a fleabag hotel—and dug Lester and his playing. Later on there's a singer, Darcey Leigh, an old flame of Dale's who performs with gardenias in her hair, like Lester's old comrade Billie Holiday—who did cross paths with him in Paris 1959, sitting in a few times. But by then Holiday was worn out and near death herself, while Darcey (Lonette McKee) is all dewy freshness, singing "How Long Has This Been Going On" not like Holiday but like herself doing "Ill Wind" in *The Cotton Club*. (In 1986 McKee was also the original star of *Lady Day at Emerson's Bar & Grill*. And credit *'Round Midnight* for at least hinting at the Holiday-Young partnership *Lady Sings the Blues* ignored.)

Turner tells a story about his army experience that blends Lester Young (an officer gave him grief after seeing a photo of his white wife), Bud Powell (he was beaten about the head by the authorities), and Dexter Gordon (while he was incarcerated, a compassionate Jewish doctor helped him). Dale's beating, however, did not permanently damage him the way a 1945 assault by Philadelphia transit cops messed up Powell. Thereafter Bud was in and out of mental institutions, subject to dozens of induced grand-mal seizures.

Lester Young spent two months in Paris early in 1959, his final engagement. Like Dale Turner, he had to be helped to his gig from the Louisiane hotel; and he played the Blue Note, where he tinkered with the lineup of the band, which included bassist Pierre Michelot. As in the movie, the club's real boss was Madame Queen, though her husband Ben was the front man who dealt with the musicians. The locals noted Lester's fondness for Creole food. (He cooked on a hot plate, a trait transferred to Dale's reclusive hotel-hallmate Ace, played by vibraphonist Bobby Hutcherson.) And Lester had a farewell party before returning to New York where he soon died (like fictional Hershell) in the Alvin Hotel. Lester Young used colorful language—once calling Birdland's vexing diminutive emcee Pee Wee Marquette "half a motherfucker." That jibe makes less sense when Dale applies it to (two) taller folks.

Four weeks after Young closed at the Blue Note, Bud Powell came in, with Michelot again on bass. Bud would stay in Paris five and a half years; unlike Dale Turner he also played other clubs in town and toured Western Europe. Like Dale, Bud arrived with his domineering manager and sometime common-law wife, Buttercup, who collected his pay every night. (The film implies but doesn't spell out their backstory.) Like the real one, movie-Buttercup sings a little, and winds up opening a soul-food beanery in Paris. Dale, like Bud, has a drinking problem—an occupational hazard for artists who work in bars—and Blue Note staff try to keep him away from alcohol. When a drunk keels over at the bar one night, Dale (like Bud) quips, I'll have what he had. And Dale, also like Bud, cadges money from fans and sneaks over to the bar across the street.

More crucially, Dale Turner, like Bud Powell, is befriended by a graphic artist named Francis who thinks his idol plays brilliantly even when he doesn't and listens from outside the club when he can't afford to come in. The Dale-Bud parallels mount: Francis wrests him away from Buttercup and moves to a bigger apartment to accommodate his new flatmate. The musician doesn't recognize his own sound when Francis puts on a record. Francis encourages him to compose, shoots home movies of him, and arranges for him to be paid directly every night. (In celebration, Dale, like Bud, cooks a big steak dinner.) Francis looks all over town for his charge when he goes off on a bender, once finding him at a hospital (as shown, on a tip from a biracial charwoman) where the Frenchman eavesdrops on his friend's interview with a psychiatrist. In time Dale, like Bud, tells Francis not to cry for him, he'll quit drinking, but when the musician goes out to a cafe Francis tails him, checking up. Francis takes his friend on a vacation to the beach, where they clown around, pretending to talk on a broken telephone. (In the movie it's a found toy, improving on the real story.)

In Francis Borier's eyes, everything is going great until Dale accepts a homecoming gig in New York—depicted in the film as a grimy, frightening town where a predatory pusher lurks. The jazzman starts to backslide, ultimately standing Francis up at the airport when it's time to return to Paris.

Dexter Gordon was confident he could handle the acting, and loved the idea of representing his heroes on screen, but the script needed work: "The musicians thought and spoke like they were down on the levee. 'Dese, dose'—it was degrading."[4] The final product has much more Dexter in it, his gestures as well as words, if not his happy life trajectory. (Gordon himself had gone to Europe in 1962 and settled in Copenhagen. Like Dale Turner, he had a drinking problem and was sometimes beset by drug dealers. He eventually returned to the States. But Dexter's 1970s homecoming was wildly successful and after a few busy years he happily retired, the year before the filmmakers came calling.) To acknowledge applause at the end of a number, Dale, like Dex, holds his horn before him, horizontally, presenting it to the audience—as if to say, this is what I do, or, I'm just a vehicle for the music that comes out here. Darcey Leigh calls Dale "Long Tall"—a Dexter nickname—and Dale plays Dexter's music: the ballad "Tivoli," the blues "Society Red."

Tavernier was open to input from the musicians, who helped polish the dialogue; Gordon, Hutcherson, drummer Billy Higgins, and record producer Michael Cuscuna offered corrections and suggestions during production. But there are still stabs at insider talk that fall flat. Darcey Leigh: "It was you who taught me to listen to the bass and not the drums." When Dale asks Buttercup to buy him a Rico #3 reed, she acts like it's some exotic thing, not a music-store staple.

The liberal borrowings from the lives of Pres and Bud are complicated by the fact that Lester Young and Bud Powell themselves are referred to and seen in photographs. Dale acknowledges Lester's influence. But he also says, referencing Coleman Hawkins, "I ain't Bean, or anybody else." Should we consider Dale a Lester Young copycat? (There were plenty of real ones, black and white.) Dale, like Lester, calls his male friends Lady so-and-so as an honorific, but Dexter sometimes did that too, in tribute. Still, in manner Dale is far more like Dexter Gordon, with that basso wheeze of a voice, the way his fingers fan out in front of his face like a flower blooming when he talks, the toothy grin, and especially that shambling walk, each limb to its own rhythm like Elvin Jones at the drums. "He is bebop in walking," Tavernier said. "You don't find that in Paul Newman and Sidney Poitier."[5]

That dig makes clear the director set out to top *Paris Blues*; the new film's working title was *Paris/Jazz*. There's some Franco-American rivalry involved, and the (mostly French) notion that jazz is more honored in France than at home. *'Round Midnight* is set in the same period as *Paris Blues*, and its forced-perspective set, recreating the street in front of the cellar jazz club, surpasses the earlier film's rendition; this time there's an alley behind the building and a walk-in bar across the way. (Production designer Alexandre Trauner had art-directed *Paris Blues*.) And here musicians are way too cool to go around sightseeing, even when entertaining a lady visitor.

The movie is admirably serious about the music, a model more films might emulate. Dale's several bands are stocked with excellent musicians, most of whom had history with Dexter Gordon. At the Blue Note, Turner opens with Michelot, Higgins, and guitarist John McLaughlin. The pianist, Eddie, who is married to a French woman and is working on learning the language, is played by Herbie Hancock, who also supervised the film's music. In New York, Dale has Freddie Hubbard on trumpet, Cedar Walton on piano, Ron Carter on bass, and Tony Williams on drums.

'Round Midnight is the rare modern film in which the diegetic jazz was recorded live on set while cameras rolled—the way Dudley Murphy had done it in 1929. There's no sidelining and no synchronization issues. Also unusual, there's very little dialogue over diegetic music, mostly small talk from the bar staff. French nightclub patrons aren't so gauche they'd talk over Dale Turner. (For extras Tavernier used real jazz fans, including pianist Jacky Terrasson and Paudras himself, seen tape-recording Dale's live "'Round Midnight.")

But even here, performances are foreshortened. Dexter Gordon can play a slow ballad like he has all the time in town, but that allows for only one drowsy chorus of "Body and Soul." A blues where he stretches out, "Society Red," runs all of two and a half minutes. One night fellow American tenor Wes (Wayne Shorter) sits in to trade eights with Dale on Bud Powell's tribute to his friend "Una Noche con Francis." On their realistically cordial exchanges, Wes has a more modern conception (even if we can hear the Dale Turner in it), though Dale has a more commanding sound. Even that joust barely tops three minutes.

Musical anachronisms may be inevitable in period pieces, and Hancock didn't fight them: "I didn't want to copy the music from the '50s, because anything that's a copy is by definition not real." So he discreetly reharmonized the older songs Dale plays, using chord voicings that were known but not common at the time—a way to stimulate the improvisers that's historically plausible.[6] Still—as with forged old-master paintings that

FIGURE 8.1 Saxophonist Dale Turner (Dexter Gordon) plays as colleague Wes (Wayne Shorter) listens, in 'Round Midnight, with Pierre Michelot (bass) and Billy Higgins (drums).

only begin to look hinky after decades—some anachronisms are too much of their own time for the creators to notice: notably, a heavily amplified bass sound. (This is hardly the first or last instance.) We also hear a bit of an anachronistic free-jazz record Berangere blasts as an act of rebellion; it recalls Cecil Powell's gratuitously raucous combo late in *New York, New York.*

Home from the club one night, Francis opines that Dale played like a god (à la Paudras re: Powell). But coming out of retirement after more than a year laying off the horn, Dexter Gordon was by definition past his peak, although his foghorn tone was ever arresting. During filming, he could only work a few hours a day and sidestepped learning Hancock's fancy arrangement of "As Time Goes By," arguing that Dale wouldn't have learned it either. (On that one he plays a full chorus, guitar and piano split a half-chorus, then Dale takes the last eight bars.) Tavernier's dealings with an occasionally recalcitrant Gordon might mirror the story on screen.

A little ghoulishly maybe, the director sought to capture his lead actor's dissolution on film. (Tavernier and Rayfiel had already made a film about such unseemly voyeurism, 1980's *Death Watch.*) "Like Lester or Bud, in the last recordings they did, you feel death coming, you felt it there," Tavernier said at the time. "There was an emotion in each note, even while he was fighting with the melody, that was part of the subject of the film."[7] We witness Dale suffering for art. As Ace loftily explains to Francis (in Bobby Hutcherson's own words), "When you have to explore every night, even the most beautiful things that you find can be the most painful."

Movie-style, the dying man provides life lessons for a surviving friend. The biggest change *'Round Midnight* makes to Francis Paudras's story is to swap out his supportive wife for a daughter, Berangere. (Young Gabrielle Haker, in her only film, is remarkable, playing Berangere as a girl of 11 and as a young woman.) When Dale moves in, this trio forms a new family unit, with Francis as the supportive helpmate. One night Dale can't play "Autumn in New York" because he's forgotten the words; like Lester Young, he's influenced by the lyrics. (Knowing them also fosters accurate phrasing.) So Francis recites a verse from memory—presciently, the one where fall in Gotham "is often mingled with pain." And Dale teaches Francis not to neglect Berangere for the music, the way Dale neglected his own daughter (capriciously named Chan, after Charlie Parker's widow). Berangere's estranged mother briefly contemplates returning to husband and daughter, but sees that Francis loves Dale more.

With some trepidation, Francis takes Dale back to New York. Bud Powell had returned to play Birdland, "the Jazz Corner of the World," owned by his longtime manager Oscar Goodstein. Dale returns to play for unctuous R. W. Goodley (Martin Scorsese, representing American jazz movies), who owns the Jazz Corner, a handsome recreation of the actual Birdland, a club that will look gloomier in *Bird* (and every other movie where it's represented). Bud's daughter came down to Birdland one night with her mother and he played his dedication "Celia." The film's Chan comes down to the Jazz Corner alone and Dale plays "Chan's Song," but misremembers her age when introducing it. He tries, but can't connect with her the way he had with Berangere.

Tavernier shot New York exteriors on location without worrying much about anachronistic cars or skyscrapers. (Nor does he fret over period mike stands or mixing boards when Dale records for Dexter's real producer Michael Cuscuna; we also hear Hancock's record "Watermelon Man" a little too early.) Goodley tells Francis, "New York, for me the music is better, 'cause it's tougher"—a real New Yorker's argument. But through Francis's eyes, we mostly see squalor and exploitation. When Francis returns to Paris alone, Dale's death is a foregone conclusion.

There is a coda, set in what appears to be the film's present. At Lyon's packed Roman amphitheater—a jazz festival?—pianist Eddie leads a seven-piece electro-acoustic band. When he announces they'll play a piece by the late great Dale Turner, the audience erupts in applause—they remember! But the septet's tepid, mildly funked-up "Chan's Song" with Wes on soprano wears less well than any other music in the film. So this unconventional jazz movie ends in a familiar way, with a big concert number that's a fizzle. Despite having tried to learn French a quarter century before, Eddie now addresses the Lyon audience in English, suggesting he'd left France himself. But not necessarily. Steve Lacy, after he'd lived there for decades and spoke the language well, still made stage announcements in English, even Anglicizing his French bassist's name—because American musicians have greater cachet.[8]

In 'Round Midnight's Paris, there's almost no hint of racism. (Jazz fans there used to act surprised when American musicians reported instances of it.) But there's one glimmer, easy to miss. At Dale's farewell party, Buttercup sings Bessie Smith's "Put It Right Here," replete with an offensive "Chinaman" verse, highlighted by Eddie's piano pentatonics. Months later, at the exact moment Francis learns Dale has died, Berangere is in the next room singing that Chinaman verse to herself. Americans have no monopoly on cultural blind spots.

Postscript: Dexter Gordon was nominated for an Academy Award for Best Actor. He lost to Paul Newman, in Scorsese's *The Color of Money*.

> ***Bird*** **(1988; 160 minutes; director: Clint Eastwood; writer: Joel Oliansky) Cast includes: Forest Whitaker (Charlie Parker), Diane Venora (Chan Richardson), Michael Zelniker (Red Rodney), Samuel E. Wright (Dizzy Gillespie), Keith David (Buster Franklin), Diane Salinger (Baroness Nica), Michael McGuire (Bernie), Anna Levine (Audrey), Hamilton Camp (Pincus), Bill Cobbs (Kansas City doctor), Tony Cox (Pee Wee Marquette), Damon Whitaker (Charlie as a teen).**
>
> **—In the 1940s, saxophonist Charlie Parker revolutionizes jazz while self-medicating with heroin and alcohol. In the 1950s he makes a family with his last wife Chan.**

Putting in a good word for 'Round Midnight at Warners, Clint Eastwood was laying groundwork for his own jazz project, the biopic of hugely influential bebop-founding genius virtuoso Charlie Parker. A high-minded art movie, *Bird* greatly enhanced the director's reputation. The film features actual Parker solos, letting the character's alto saxophone sing in Bird's own thrilling voice. Eastwood loves an underlit image, and this color film has the richly dark sheen of black-and-white photographs of African American musicians working dim nocturnal rooms.[9]

Bird runs over two and a half hours, and has a stylish scrambled chronology. In the first 20 minutes we touch down in the late 1920s, 1945, 1954, and twice in the mid-1930s. The film's structure plays games with time in a way you can liken to bebop, the revolutionary modern jazz of the 1940s: It may seem haphazard at first, but there's an underlying logic—even if things may get so complicated time gets turned around. Motifs—visual riffs—come back when the narrative needs a jolt. Quick leaps between time frames parallel bebop's veerings out of key. The style's sheer velocity is conveyed more by the Parker solos embedded in the narrative than by *Bird*'s sometimes lugubrious pace.

Most everything depicted is based on something that happened to Charlie Parker. He did ride a pony as a kid, and was known to ride a horse in Manhattan. As a Kansas City teenager, he did have a cymbal tossed at his feet when he played poorly at a jam session—although it didn't haunt him ever after as it does in the movie. ("Everybody's laughing at me now, but just wait and see," he'd told friend Gene Ramey, shrugging it off.)[10] Parker did create a sensation on Fifty-Second Street (in 1945) playing alongside trumpeter Dizzy Gillespie, and not too long after that they did take their bebop to Billy Berg's club in Hollywood, where some listeners found the new music difficult. (But the band didn't get fired, as *Bird* has it.) Parker did stay on in Los Angeles, where, as a heroin addict in a city with an uncertain supply, he did record an infamous, anguished "Lover Man" while strung out. He hated it, but the producer found it worthy of release. (Bird didn't throw his horn through the control-room glass, though, as he does here—that cinematic flourish appeared in Julio Cortázar's Parker-inspired story "The Pursuer.") Subsequently he was sent to Camarillo State Hospital to dry out, and came back to New York looking fit. Before his return, his future wife Chan Richardson did secure him a homecoming Fifty-Second Street gig, which did pay the band $700 a week.

As shown, Bird dug Stravinsky and counseled other musicians to stay off junk. He played Paris, where he ate the petals of a rose presented in tribute and where an expatriate musician friend (pioneer bop drummer Kenny Clarke in real life) tried to convince him to stay. Back home he took an engagement at a new club named for him, Birdland. He started using white trumpeter Red Rodney, who (according to Rodney at least) joined Parker's black band on tour in the South. Race-mixing in the South was taboo, so Red was presented as an African American albino and sang the blues to sell the story. (His singing is woeful; the receptive black audiences depicted can only be cheering the audacity of the deception.) Afterward Bird began fronting a small ensemble with violins, playing standard ballads, and he and Chan slowly became involved and eventually moved in together.

You wouldn't know from *Bird* that after Camarillo State Hospital Parker had married his third wife Doris. But we do see one of his other women, Audrey (based on California sculptor Julie MacDonald), whom he dallies with out west. As shown, he treated Chan's daughter Kim as his own, and he and Chan had two more kids together. They were devastated when, in 1954, sickly daughter Pree died while Charlie was on the West Coast. Parker sent Chan a series of disturbing telegrams instead of hurrying home. (A sign of Eastwood's aversion to retakes: the film's telegrams, seen in inserts, don't quite match what Forest Whitaker dictates.)

In *Bird*, mirroring life, Parker starts drinking heavily—partly to control drug cravings and manage pain from stomach ulcers—and goes into a tailspin. Playing with the strings one night, he began one tune as they began another, and his normally reliable ear failed him—he couldn't make it fit. He was fired, and later that night swallowed iodine in a suicide attempt, subsequently undergoing observation at Bellevue Hospital. After his release, the family moved to the country. Parker came back to New York (he and Chan had separated, though *Bird* omits that), and missed an engagement in Boston. Half dead, he turned up at Baroness Nica De Koenigswarter's pad. (Finally, after *Too Late Blues* and *Sweet Love, Bitter*, a movie shows that friend of musicians some respect, though Diane Salinger plays her as an oddball, breathing heavily as Bird solos.) Nica summoned her doctor, and when he asked Bird if he drank, he really did answer "Sometimes I have a little sherry before dinner." Parker refused to be hospitalized, and died laughing at jugglers on the Dorsey Brothers' TV show. (We see the actual clip.) As depicted, his funeral was held at the Rev. Adam Clayton Powell's church (shot in what is obviously not Harlem).

Once more, we marvel at how much biopics get right while still missing many of their marks. *Bird* falls short because of what it leaves out, and because of a failure of tone. Friends of Parker who disliked the movie would speak of how much fun he was to be around. You get little sense of that from *Bird*. Forest Whitaker catches Parker's way of sliding into different modes of speech for comic effect—elevated diction, or a Gabby Hayes impression. But even when joking, he exudes melancholy, as if doom hovers near. This Bird is rarely airborne. He hunches over his alto like it's weighing him down. Whitaker mimics correct fingering but wiggles his digits madly to signal how much Bird puts into every note. The real Parker barely moved while playing; the seemingly effortless economy is part of his music's elegance.

The movie's dark in more ways than its look. It zeroes in on his grim final months, and the first 20 minutes dwell on the stormy night he drank iodine and its aftermath. Parker fan Joel Oliansky's script had been written years earlier for Richard Pryor. The comedian would not have made a good Parker—economy of movement wasn't itchy Pryor's thing—but he'd have supplied the levity, as in *Lady Sings the Blues*. Comedian Dick Gregory had brought that leavening humor to Eagle in *Sweet Love, Bitter*.

The real Charlie Parker grew up and learned to play in Kansas City's black community, where he was mentored for a spell by altoist Buster Smith. Bird polished his style and found compatible players at Harlem jam sessions. He mostly worked with fellow African Americans, and married two black women. But *Bird* focuses on his relationships with two white consultants on the film: last wife Chan and Red Rodney, his trumpeter from 1949 to 1951. (The black musicians on the film's Albino Red auto tour are always in the back seat.) We've noted this spotlighting of white characters in black stories before, as if white viewers need white characters to identify with. But resorting to that expedient here clashes with bebop's rejection of white show-biz convention.

Bird's best black friend is Dizzy, who leads a responsible, respectable life. As shown, Parker once woke him in the middle of the night to ask him to jot down a new composition—although it wasn't his catchy blues "Now's the Time," so easy to remember it got plagiarized as R&B hit "The Hucklebuck." At their last meeting in *Bird*, Dizzy scolds his friend for his self-destructive ways, but tells him he'll be remembered, and paraphrases a line from Gillespie's 1979 autobiography: "I'm a reformer, you tryin' to be a martyr."[11]

In place of Parker benefactor Buster Smith, *Bird* gives us fictitious Buster Franklin (Keith David), who like Smith is said to have played alto with Bennie Moten and Count Basie. But instead of encouraging Bird, this Buster helped laugh teenage Charlie off the bandstand at that cymbal-toss jam session when the youngster tried to play something new on the blues and couldn't make it fit. The memory of it makes Franklin disparage Parker as the new toast of Fifty-Second Street—until he hears how much horn he's playing now. In response, a shaken Buster drops his own saxophone into a river, off a street-level bridge—but what New York bridge might that be, exactly? *Bird* depicts a nightclub-crammed Fifty-Second Street, re-created on the Warner Bros. lot, but this is one of those Hollywood pictures where characters also roam New York's elusive midtown alleys. Parker spies Birdland from under a stoop across a narrow street; the real Birdland was on Broadway right off Times Square. *Bird* even gets Hollywood wrong; it places Billy Berg's up in the hills, not a corner storefront on Vine near Sunset.

FIGURE 8.2 The look of New York's fabled Swing Street is approximated in *Bird*. Unlike the real Fifty-Second Street, this one ends at the next corner.

Shortly before his death, Bird encounters Buster Franklin again—playing rock-and-roll in a gold lamé jacket at the Paramount and honking for a mindlessly adoring (interracial) crowd. The real Parker's tastes were broad—he dug the doo-wop Clovers, splitting bills with them—but this Bird is horrified, like an antirock 1980s bebop diehard.[12] Never mind that rock honkers usually blow tenor, not alto. Eastwood might have given the scene some teeth by having Buster play "Now's the Time"/"The Hucklebuck." When he's done, Parker acts like he's making off with Franklin's horn—as if Buster ought to discard this one too. Naming this sell-out Buster, like calling that cranky old man in 'Round Midnight Hershell, besmirches a worthy musician.

In *Bird*, Parker's sound is less dynamic than Buster's, because the Parker solos we hear have been extracted from historical recordings. Music director Lennie Niehaus—a jazz altoist himself, and Whitaker's saxophone coach—supervised isolating Parker's sound from that of the original backing musicians, masking their contributions with newly recorded accompaniment and further compromising that fragile alto sound when overtones got stripped away in the process. Parker's new accompanists include such bebop authorities as pianists Barry Harris and Walter Davis Jr., bassist Ray Brown, and trumpeters Red Rodney (ghosting his own character) and Jon Faddis (ghosting Dizzy). They try their best to play in the idiom, as if conversing with jazz's quickest wit—who, obviously, can't respond in kind. Anachronisms (again) include a fat amplified bass sound very different from what you'd hear in a 1945 club or 1936 KC jam session. (It helps mask traces of Parker's original bands.) In the Kansas City scene, John Guerin's bumptious drumming is likewise out of another era. In life it was Basie's sleek swinger Jo Jones who tossed that cymbal at the Reno Club; he had a habit of playfully gonging underperforming musicians off stage, without dire psychological repercussions.

So in *Bird* the murky Parker solos gleaned from home recordings both are and aren't his real sound. You get the headlong pace and fecund imagination, but not the acidic, indelible, supremely communicative tone. His horn loses its bluesy bite, as if stuffed with cotton—or as if he's dead already, his wraithlike sound wafting from the beyond, à la *Three Little Bops*. Here and there, Niehaus or Birdologist Charles McPherson plays fill-in saxophone in character, just before the soundtrack switches to a real Parker solo. The transition can be jarring, as if an image had been knocked out of focus. (Almost the only nondiegetic music is a little atmospheric alto, variations on the signature blues "Parker's Mood." We also hear that tune in King Pleasure's 1953 vocal adaptation, its macabre lyric speaking of Bird as if he's already dead.)

Screenwriter Oliansky drew on Chan Richardson's then-unpublished memoir *My Life in E-Flat*. Many details of their domestic life found their way into *Bird*, along with some dialogue. After he swallows iodine: "That was stupid. Now I'll have to call an ambulance."[13] Chan visited the set and gave Diane Venora line readings—the way Venora brays her conversational placeholder "man" smacks of direct imitation. The script is also informed by Robert Reisner's 1962 oral history *Bird*, where there's brief mention of a horn thrown in a river, and Ross Russell's 1973 biography *Bird Lives!*[14] Russell turns up briefly if anonymously, producing that West Coast "Lover Man" session. (He'd also dreamed up the promotional slogan "Bebop Invades the West," here placarded outside Berg's.) *Bird Lives!* supplied more action and detail than we have room to tally, right down to the book's cinematic death montage of its flying-cymbal callback.

The scrambled chronology may have been suggested by Reisner's book, in which witnesses testify in alphabetical order, so time is jumbled and incidents recur. As mentioned, we hop around in the opening minutes—glimpses of boyhood and his early teens, then a slice of 1945 Swing Street—before we settle into the first extended sequence, the 1954 iodine-and-Bellevue arc. We float away from that after Chan tries to explain her husband to an unsympathetic doctor, sending her into a flashback, prancing down Fifty-Second Street back in the day.

But just over a minute into that outdoor sequence, we abandon Chan to track Pincus (she calls him Pinky), the Street's legendary freelance doorman, as he shills for various clubs and helps folks out of cabs up and down the block. We are well clear of Chan's reverie by the time Pincus runs into Buster Franklin, who then has his own flashback as he recounts (with demonic glee) the long-ago night of the flying cymbal. But even before Chan's motivated flashback, we leap to an episode from Bird's adolescence, wherein a doctor lectures him on the evils of dope. (It's that kind of picture—a narc who plagues Bird later slows the action to a crawl. An explanatory card at the end tells us one-time junkie Red Rodney now leads a drug-free life. But Whitaker's Bird does make Parker's actual observation, that heroin kills his pain better and cheaper than anything his doctors prescribe.)

After Buster's gleeful tale, the pretense of a flashback structure is largely dropped: time is free-floating. But strip out brief modulations to another period, and *Bird* has a familiar in medias res structure. Once we jump from 1954 back to 1945, the story mostly proceeds in chronological order, save for one protracted post-Bellevue detour, where Charlie gets hassled by that narc, until (a half-hour before the ending) an insert of that iodine bottle hitting the bathroom tile signals our return to where we started. From there Parker skids toward his death in March 1955.

There are little whirlpools within the stream, including an extended section, presented as a Parker flashback, where time appears to turn around. While waiting for Birdland to open—as in life he goes to view the exterior with his manager, here named Bernie—Parker takes an engagement in Paris. (He went there in May 1949, seven months before Birdland opened.) At the end of the Paris sequence—where Charlie and his expat friend talk about Birdland like it's already open—a New York waterfront shot establishes Parker's return, and in the next scene, with the opening of Birdland still a month away, Bird is reunited with old acquaintance Red Rodney. On the spot Red hires Bird and band to play a Jewish wedding (at a most un-Brooklyn-looking mansion), a gig that isn't so far-fetched; Parker once sat in with a polka band.[15] Now that they're reacquainted, and while still waiting for Birdland to open, Charlie hires Red for that 10-day southern tour. But making the offer, he talks as if he's just in from Paris—as if the French trip followed, not preceded, the wedding. That would give Bird a very busy month before Birdland opens, squeezing in France and a domestic tour. With such a long run up to its opening, you'd expect Birdland, "the Jazz Corner of the World," to look less shabby inside—it's nothing like 'Round Midnight's accurately sleek Jazz Corner.

Bird's corkscrew structure distracts us from what it leaves out. With all the leaping, you could miss that we barely alight in the nine years between Kansas City humiliation and Fifty-Second Street triumph, which is the heart of the real Charlie Parker story: the years when he forged his revolutionary style. He described his breakthrough moment occurring at a Harlem jam session, where he heard in the top notes of guitarist Biddy Fleet's altered chords the suggestion of a new brand of dissonant but pleasing melody. At other Harlem sessions, he bonded with fellow searchers like Gillespie, who'd arrived at similar ideas through study rather than intuition, though he too practiced obsessively. Pianists, drummers, and bass players all picked up on Bird's phrasing. All of which is barely noted in the film. Bud Powell, who adapted Parker's language to the piano, is never mentioned. We barely visit Harlem at all.

Bird reduces Parker's long search to one made-up anecdote, which he relates late in the film: how he'd suddenly hit on those weird higher intervals one night while backing (fictitious) Violet Welles, who responded, "Don't be playing that shit behind me when I'm trying to *sang*." This purple anecdote replaces Parker's gestation among Harlem's best with an African American musician who dismisses his innovations.

Bird gives us Great Man history writ large—divorcing Parker from his collaborators both on the soundtrack and within the story. Jazz is about musicians working together, as other movies show—like Blues in the Night, briefly alluded to when Charlie plays a snippet of "This Time the Dream's on Me." When he does take wing, this Bird flies alone.

Bird's chronological scramble will echo in a few later biopics, among them Tate Taylor's 2014 James Brown film Get On Up, and others we'll get to. The cult of the isolated jazz musician—and that flying cymbal—will come back with a vengeance, literally, in Whiplash.

> ***Stormy Monday*** **(1988; 93 minutes; director/writer: Mike Figgis. Cast includes: Sean Bean (Brendan), Melanie Griffith (Kate), Tommy Lee Jones (Frank Cosmo), Sting (Mr. Finney), Andrzej Borkowski (Andrzej), People Band: Mel Davis, Terry Day, Ed Deane, Charlie Hart, Paul Jolly, Davey Payne (Krakow Jazz Ensemble).**
> **—During Newcastle's "America Week," a young couple connect, while a pushy Texas developer, angling to acquire choice real estate, encounters pushback from a jazz club owner and a Polish free-jazz band.**

Robert Reisner's book Bird makes its own cameo appearance in another 1988 film, Stormy Monday, English director Mike Figgis's debut feature. We see the book, open to a Charlie Parker photo on page 101, sitting on a table in a still-life that reveals much about our quiet hero, Sean Bean's Brendan, who is about to become a minor player in a civic power struggle. The information in that shot—a couple of books, a typed note—tells us that Brendan is into jazz, has spent time in the States, and is currently house-sitting, new in town. Such narrative efficiency is typical of *Stormy Monday*—every detail feeds the whole.

The action is set during the last three days of America Week in the city of Newcastle in northeast England, and one of *Stormy Monday*'s themes is a perennial pet topic of filmmakers east of the Atlantic: the Americanization of world culture. That theme plays out in the background in myriad ways. Tourist-magnet America Week has brought all manner of cultural coal to Newcastle: American movies, old Detroit sedans, a rodeo, a Sousa concert, a parade with a New Orleans-y jazz band and drum majorettes, a giant Pepsi bottle planted in the middle of an intersection. At an upscale mall, a punk with a Mohawk checks out Plains Indians' music and dance. (The Americanisms include the film's incongruous title, cribbed from bluesman T-Bone Walker. The action's set on a Thursday, Friday, and Saturday.)

Newcastle's Americanization was underway before America Week. Teens play mid-night basketball. A diner is named for New York photographer Weegee and adorned with blow-ups of his crime-scene photos; the place carries American, not English, beers. (Even a pub stocked with Scottish single malts has an American bartender.) At a club called The Precinct, bouncers dress like New York cops.

American culture: love it for its riches, hate it for its overbearing hegemony. Mike Figgis knew that attraction-repulsion response to American culture from his own experience as a musician and as a filmmaker. (He'd soon be working in Hollywood.) In London 20 years earlier, Figgis had played trumpet and guitar with the free-improvising People Band. Groups improvising without any written starter material had sprouted up all over Western Europe in the 1960s in response to Stateside free jazz. Free improvisation's jazz roots were unmissable—all those saxophones and piano-bass-drums rhythm sections made that plain. But the Europeans also put some distance between themselves and American culture, partly in response to the Vietnam War. Swinging was not a priority. Soon, distinct national styles developed; English improvising usually had more (British) reserve than continental versions. The rudely howling People Band were an exception; they claimed to have been booted from an Anarchists' Ball for excessive anarchism.[16]

The players saw political ramifications in their music-making, and aligned themselves with left-wing movements. Personnel was flexible. People Band had a lot of drop-ins, and they'd switch instruments to make things more spontaneous and unrefined. After the band dissolved in 1972, a few of its members worked with friend and proto-punk singer Ian Dury.

Figgis reassembled a six-member People Band, including multi-instrumentalist Terry Day and Dury saxophonist Davey Payne, to improvise and act in *Stormy Monday*. (The director didn't join them, but did compose the film's atmospheric jazzy score.) They appear as the Krakow Jazz Ensemble, a "Polski free-jazz" band whose music has its own stick-it-to-the-man political implications. There were such Eastern-bloc free-jazz bands, some of whom lagged behind their western models. A Polish group that sounded like the People Band of 20 years earlier is entirely plausible.

Stormy Monday is another jazz-and-gangsters picture at heart, with a club owner mediating between worlds, like *The Cotton Club*. One engine behind America Week is shady Texas oil man Frank Cosmo (a quietly scary Tommy Lee Jones), who's moving into waterfront redevelopment under landmark Tyne Bridge. One property he covets is occupied by a jazz club run by a tough local who understands strongarm tactics himself, Mr. Finney (Newcastle's own Sting). When Cosmo sends a couple of London gangsters to threaten him with a blowtorch, Finney gets the upper hand but lets them live, sending them home after confiscating their car and breaking only one arm in retribution: ruffians' professional courtesy.

At his Key Club, Finney thumbs his nose at America Week (as far as any jazz club owner can) by hosting English saxophonist Don Weller on Thursday and bringing the Krakow Jazz Ensemble in on Saturday. The American deejay on the local jazz station gives the KJE some airplay; *Stormy Monday* may be the only film in which free jazz not only gets played on the radio, but goes over with casual listeners, which speaks to Newcastle's sophistication.

The Polish musicians get no dialogue—their manager Andrzej does the talking, in halting English—but the KJE functions as a collective secondary character, making musical comments within the story, like the noise band in 1935's *Sweet Music*. When the Ensemble is detained at the airport till their paperwork's sorted out, they're corralled in a transit lounge. Since there's a spinet in the room, their pianist (Mel Davis) sits down and begins to play something soothing and pastoral, and a few travelers look cautiously appreciative. But when we cut back to the lounge moments later, the other Krakowiaks have joined in, on three saxophones, bass, and electric guitar. Now the listeners look less enchanted; you can hear the band all over the terminal. Coincidentally Cosmo arrives as they're playing; he glances in their direction without betraying annoyance.

FIGURE 8.3 Krakow Jazz Ensemble (People Band) redefine music for airports in *Stormy Monday*.

This improvisation seems to help expedite the ensemble's release: effective practical protest music.

Cosmo will encounter them again, once a day. On Friday, he's throwing a hotel-ballroom luncheon for the mayor and city brass who will signal their support for his big plans, and he endlessly fusses over the details. But the band booked to play the event has had a road accident. (This literal car-wreck of a band is called Transatlantics—that's symbolism for you.) Since the Polish musicians are staying in the same hotel (all the cheaper ones are booked up: Figgis plugs his plot holes) and no one there knows what they sound like, they get drafted as a replacement. Before Cosmo can give his rousing let's-all-make-some-money speech, the band plays "The Star-Spangled Banner" on cue, and the guests rise out of respect—but the tenor saxophonist (Payne) overblows like Albert Ayler, the guitarist (Ed Deane) puts a little Hendrix in it, and the band doesn't really know more than the start of the tune, which devolves into sarcastic blues licks: a middle finger to the USA from behind the iron curtain. The Poles attack the Americans in their own language, rudely.

We see Cosmo give them the beady eye, but he keeps his irritation to himself until a little later, when a conversation-time bossa nova gets spiky. To the event planner: "You shut those motherfuckers out." As luck will have it, when Cosmo goes down to the Key Club Saturday night, making one last bid for Finney's property, they're playing when he walks in. He catches more of their gigs than anyone in town. Cosmo does miss one show. Friday night they make a side appearance at a northside Polish Club, playing for the expatriates, and here the KJE are on very good behavior, doing traditional songs to sing along with or polka to, with the pianist on accordion. (Here People Band act, not react: they become those Poles, bonding with homesick compatriots.)

The ensemble's minder in Newcastle is house-sitting newbie Brendan, who Finney hired on discovering their mutual admiration for drummer Dave Tough. These two jazz fans have commendably broad tastes; they dig Eddie Condon's trad jazz and the way-out Poles. There's also a romance plot: Brendan meets cute with Kate (Melanie Griffith), a waitress from New York whom Cosmo has persuaded to come over to work as a paid escort, a decision she regrets. Kate also waits tables at Weegee; she misses some shifts, but has a marketable American accent.

Cosmo recognizes that violence is bad for his business. (There's only one gun in the movie, though it does go off—killing the picture's only black henchman.) But Cosmo's judgment is clouded when he learns Kate's involved with Finney's flunky, and he tries to wipe out the couple with a car bomb. (Quick joke: the bomb's faceplate has a blue field and red and white stripes.) But Brendan lends the car to Andrzej and his girlfriend who get blown up instead—collateral damage—just down the block from Finney's club. That blast that will prove to be Cosmo's undoing, a step too far. Inside, unaware, the Krakow Jazz Ensemble is just wrapping up a very well-received set. The Key Club's all-ages crowd digs their bracing free music. We are not in Hollywood. But this triumph will bring the musicians no happy memories.

In *Stormy Monday*, the members of People Band have an integral role and improvise in character, and on camera, and get to be as dissonant and high-energy as they please, in a studio picture with Hollywood stars. There's only about six minutes of their free music all told, but dramatically and musically it feels like the right amount. As we saw with *'Round Midnight*, even in prestige pictures, club music is highly compressed and is meted out in small doses. (Sting improvises on camera too; Finney plays an acoustic bass solo when the club's empty, a frustrated musician.)

Mike Figgis did well by his old London scene, getting free music's political implications on screen without preaching. He would play with the old gang again, after *Stormy Monday* prompted People Band to reunite for real.

> **The Fabulous Baker Boys (1989; 114 minutes; director/writer: Steve Kloves).**
> **Cast includes: Jeff Bridges (Jack Baker), Beau Bridges (Frank Baker), Michelle**
> **Pfeiffer (Susie Diamond), Albert Hall (Henry).**
> **—Brothers Frank and Jack Baker's fading two-piano lounge act takes on a singer,**
> **changing the lives of all three, and turning Jack back toward jazz.**

Jazz heroes sometimes sell out and go commercial. Jigger Pine joins a novelty band in *Blues in the Night*. Ghost Wakefield plays lounge piano in *Too Late Blues*. Buster Franklin honks rock-and-roll in *Bird*. Often the sellout comes to regret it. In Steve Kloves's enjoyable date movie *The Fabulous Baker Boys*, it's 15 years since promising jazz talent Jack Baker joined his brother in a two-piano act that plays hotel lounges and tiki bars, and by now Jack's practically numb. Off-hours, he has meaningless sex to complement the meaningless music. At each engagement the Bakers do the same tired tunes the same way—"People," "Girl from Ipanema"—and brother Frank tells the same stale jokes. When a defensive Jack points to the act's achievements, all he can say is that they've never taken day jobs and that they've outlasted most Seattle lounge acts.

But after eons on the circuit the Bakers are aural wallpaper. Bar patrons have stopped listening, as they chat, laugh, and order blender drinks. Lounge managers have tired of the brothers and vice versa, and bookings are getting thin. And though it's never discussed, they have an unsustainable business model. Two brothers sitting behind matching grand pianos look smart, but the Bakers arrange their own instrument rentals. Even if a room already has one grand, they still need another, and in Seattle in 1989, a one-night rental including delivery might run $175. Even allowing for discounts extended to regular customers who sometimes work multinight gigs, overhead's hell on the profit margin. One night's pay envelope looks like it has about $100 in it.

Footloose bachelor Jack plays the fancy runs as Frank lays down the foundation. (Jack is ghosted by Los Angeles jazz pianist and GRP label head Dave Grusin, who also composed the blandly jazzy score: Miles-y muted trumpet over synthesizer.) Family man Frank handles the business, makes up the set lists, and micromanages, getting on Jack's nerves.

Frank and Jack are played by the Bridges brothers, Beau and Jeff, and the film's title salutes another movie where brothers play squabbling brothers, *The Fabulous Dorseys*. The stunt casting of brothers as brothers gives the film part of its charm and dramatic tension. There is something of the Bridges brothers' dynamic in the Bakers. Beau/Frank is the older, doughier-looking one; when a character nicknames him Egghead, it's not because he's smart. Beau makes earnest uptight Frank oddly endearing, but *Baker Boys* is really his brother's story. Jeff/Jack is who the ladies go for, the intense handsome one with the deeper talent; here and there Jack improvises keyboard fills that hint at his dexterity. But he's aloof and emotionally closed off; lest he appear too unsympathetic, he's befriended a neglected kid who lives in his building, and he loves his old dog.

To revitalize the act, Frank suggests adding a singer, cutting her in for 20 percent of the take. In a funny audition montage, successive chanteuses show different ways to murder tunes that need killing—though Jack ungraciously plays "Up, Up and Away" for one in what is plainly not her key. They are ready to give up when Susie Diamond makes a klutzy entrance, way late, popping bubblegum, and tells them she has no entertainment experience, unless you count work as a paid escort. But she wins them over by the time she's sung half a chorus of "More Than You Know." Susie gets deep into a song, becomes someone else as long as it lasts. Then she pops the gum back in.

At first the Bakers treat Susie like hired help; her name's not on the sign out front. Unkindly, they have her debut with "Ten Cents a Dance," about a different kind of lowly escort work. But she's a natural, and learns her stagecraft fast, and begins acting more refined. (The same thing happened to Alice Faye in *Alexander's Ragtime Band*. Michelle Pfeiffer plays Susie a bit broadly at first, but gives her interior life.) Audiences start paying attention, and bookings are up; she's bought the act some time, though now Jack gets to improvise even less. Frank's as controlling as ever, telling her what to wear—gowns not miniskirts. But soon she's dressing the way she wants; it's better for business.

They get a sweet gig for the week after Christmas, at a fancy resort somewhere in hilly country way outside of town: picture *The Shining*'s Overlook Hotel after a corporate makeover. Susie's been with them for weeks now, but has no clue Jack's a gifted pianist. Then she hears him in the ballroom one morning, musing at the keys in a Bill Evans-y vein. (He listens to Evans at home and has his picture on the wall.) Now she hears how all work and no play have made Jack only appear to be a dull boy. Susie's no jazz expert, but has been making an effort to educate herself. At the hotel she blasts Ellington music in their suite—but it's literally the wrong Ellington: not Duke but the posthumous ghost band run by his son Mercer (from GRP's not-so-forthrightly–titled *Digital Duke*: an album a novice might well pick up, not knowing better).

The sexual tension between Susie and Jack has been building—everyone on either side of the screen knows they'll get it on—when Frank is abruptly called back to Seattle. On stage New Year's Eve, Jack and Susie chuck the holiday set list and have musical foreplay. In *Baker Boys*' most famous scene, Susie in a red dress writhes all over the grand piano lid, as she purrs "Makin' Whoopee" like Marilyn Monroe's Sugar Kane. Jack stretches out on piano too, in his way. He spontaneously orchestrates, playing with the time, interacting with her—improvising some life into the act. Of course they're a hit. "You're good, aren't you?" she says after the set. Now she really hears it.

FIGURE 8.4 Susie (Michelle Pfeiffer) discovers Jack (Jeff Bridges) can really play, in *The Fabulous Baker Boys.*

But sleeping with a coworker is often a mistake, as Frank had warned his brother. Back home after the holidays, Jack is sullen and Susie resentful, and Frank is horrified they didn't even play the crowd-pleaser "Feelings," a song Susie disparages. She considers leaving the act; a conventioneer at the hotel has offered her a job singing jingles. Jack gives her good professional advice: Take it. (It's a good career move—a paying gig with a future.) But then he adds, meanly, "There's always another girl."

On stage, still reeling from his coldness, Susie is disgusted to find herself investing "Feelings" with real feeling, and quits that night. She gives Jack some parting advice, based on her escort experience: "Every time you walk into some shitty daiquiri hut, you're selling yourself on the cheap." You tell yourself it doesn't touch you, she says. "But you do it long enough and all you are is empty." Susie makes explicit the parallel between prostitution and playing hack music that *Too Late Blues* hinted at.

Without her, work for the Bakers dries up. Jack angrily quits, and is offered two nights a week at Henry's, a (basement) jazz club on a Pike-Market back alley, where he sometimes sits in and the African American owner believes in his talent. When Jack seeks out Frank at home to make peace with him, they reminisce about an early gig when they were forced to sing, and then perform together one last time—singing the rock evergreen "You're Sixteen" at Frank's twin practice pianos. They sing partly because an instrumental number wouldn't have quite the right oomph, but also (since the actors do their own singing, but not playing) to let the Bridges brothers make actual music together. (Earlier they'd split the introductory verse to "Ten Cents a Dance," to cover for a fumbling Susie.)

In the end Jack looks up Susie too, to apologize for being a jerk and to tell her he'd like to see her again. She doesn't agree, exactly, but for someone as closed off as he is, it's a start. Maybe jazz can put him in touch with his emotions, so he can feel the way he plays.

American Blue Note (1989; 96 minutes; director: Ralph Toporoff; screen-play: Gilbert Girion; story: Girion, Toporoff). Cast includes: Peter MacNicol (Jack Solow), Jonathan Walker (Tommy), Carl Capotorto (Jerry), Tim Guinee (Bobby), Bill Christopher-Myers (Lee), James Puig (Jimmy), Mel Johnson Jr. (Ron), Charlotte d'Amboise (Betina), Eddie Jones (Sean Katz), Zohra Lampert (Jerry's mother). New song: "Blue Midnight" (words Billy Mernit/music Larry Schanker).

—After a year of running a jazz band with dim prospects, saxophonist Jack Solow pulls the plug.

The Baker Boys had a good run before business tanked. The young Jack Solow Quintet in the same year's *American Blue Note* never had a chance. Alto saxophonist Jack has asked the other guys to give it a year, and in that time they've gotten nowhere. Traditional jazz-movie heroes have a musical vision. Jack started with the idea the band would play weddings and small town bars, and somehow graduate to Manhattan jazz clubs.

It hasn't worked out, not least because "When Irish Eyes Are Smiling" and "Come Back to Sorrento" don't inspire musicians, help forge a group aesthetic, or build a jazz repertoire. For all Jack frets over the band's fate, no one steps up to steer. Trumpeter Tommy writes some good tunes but is in no hurry to document them. Only after a year do the players discuss recording a demo, and the guys grouse that'll just mean more rehearsing. The big prize for Jack is to land the band on "Fifty-Two Street," as he insists on calling Fifty-Second—the legendary jazz district long gone by the time this story is set, sometime in the early 1960s. Jack has only one contact there, a club owner who explains he's booked up till the fall. Maybe he's the only one left.

It's hard to pin it down exactly when *American Blue Note* takes place. In the first scene we hear Jack's half of a phone call, as he takes a survey, and his last answer is "Kennedy"—placing the action somewhere around the 1960 election, more or less concurrent with *Paris Blues*. But the period details are casual at best, the atmosphere mostly conveyed by vintage sedans. In one scene, Jack's big old 1950 Plymouth is trailed by a '63 Rambler. There's an ad for a digital camera in a shop window. The period is also elusive because the Solow Quintet exists in a musical vacuum, divorced from the explosive changes of that era. One minor character does mention Coltrane, putting the accent on the wrong syllable. Jack invites a woman out to "my favorite jazz club," but never names it (or follows up).

He apparently lives in New York—he has that state's tags on his car and belongs to musicians' local 802—but his gigs all seem to be in northern New Jersey, where the film was shot. They rehearse at dim, mouth-breathing drummer Bobby's boyhood home, away from town. Jack is the band's business manager, but he's awkward with people, a nervous laugher who makes aggressively long stage announcements to dead rooms. He frets over the band's publicity photo as if that's the problem.

American Blue Note is a low-budget independent by still photographer turned cinematographer turned commercial director Ralph Toporoff, who'd spent time around jazz musicians and film sets while a Paris-based stringer in the 1960s. But save one hard-boppish tune of Tommy's, little of the Solow Quintet's music bears markers of that period. Getting a fix on the band is also difficult because (as in *The Gig*) the players' capabilities vary, according to the needs of the scene. Pianist Jerry has little apparent interest in music—asked to name a favorite player, he changes the subject. He seems to prefer accordion, bringing it to a wedding job. But elsewhere he'll break into limber boogie piano, or deftly shadow a singer on a tune he doesn't know, alighting on the right key and chords by ear. The film's blandly generic title could be a comment on the quintet's vaguely defined music.

Given the decade, the musicians' inexperience and their matching jackets, *American Blue Note* plays like a movie about a fledgling rock band. They even get pushed in that stylistic direction when happy (black) drunk Ron gets nudged onstage on his birthday and he turns out to be terrific, singing the moody "Blue Midnight." Jack is taken with the rueful lyric: "Sometimes you miss the boat." If he'd really been paying attention he'd have hired Ron on the spot. With him they could go places.

There is another elegant sequence, a spontaneous roadside performance for newlyweds, bathed in late afternoon light. But the film is mostly clunky. There are little subplots involving the musicians' families, and two-minute bits for veteran character actors. *American Blue Note* aims for the ensemble camaraderie of Barry Levinson's period comedy *Diner*—there's even a diner scene, depicted on the film's poster—but the depth of characterization and the chemistry aren't there, and it's hard to pull off wistful nostalgia for a period so sketchily evoked. Comic bits mostly fall flat, notably that diner scene, where the boys' hijinks amount to gratuitously harassing the staff. One night when bassist Lee fails to send a sub—they keep using the word "replacement"—they hire a ringer to mime playing bass on detuned strings. And yet a bass part creeps back in on the soundtrack, as if ringer Jimmy had learned to play over the course of the evening. The level of wit: a nasty bar owner is Mr. Joy, and everyone they audition for is named Katz. Those auditions are short because the stakes are so low; mostly bookers just want to know if they have their own transportation.

Credit *American Blue Note* for a metafictional fusion of form and content: The film, like the band, slowly grinds to an end, but there's a bright coda. Jack pulls the plug when Lee (the band's lone African American) gets hired by a (made-up) famous leader. But the quintet has one last gig to play.

Jack has been conducting an awkward courtship with ballet teacher Betina, who's asked the band to play Tchaikovsky's *Nutcracker* for a student recital. The performance is short even by jazz film standards: 83 seconds. After eight bars of "Dance of the Reed Flutes," trumpeter Tommy unexpectedly syncopates his line, nodding to Jack to join him, and the horns slide into spontaneous Brubeck-style jazz counterpoint. (It's the Dorsey boys at Gorman's all over again.) The rhythm section starts swinging along, and the initially perturbed young dancers catch the groove, adjusting their timing to match. The band shares a spontaneously creative moment, enjoying themselves on stage before going separate ways. Here, at last, we have a connection to actual period jazz. Duke Ellington's version of the *Nutcracker Suite* arranged by Billy Strayhorn had been released in November 1960. Even these guys may have heard it.

Earlier someone had asked Jack if he was a professional musician and he'd answered "sort of." Now that the band is finished, he expresses relief. Better to find a job he's better suited for. He can always play on the side, like the hobbyists in *The Gig*.

/// 9 /// YOUNG LIONS AND HISTORICAL FICTIONS 1990–2000

The young generation of musicians who shook up jazz in the 1980s made it to the screen in the following decade. Even underage players show up in movies again, as in the 1940s. Another 1990s trend (which spills over into chapter 10): historical tales with unreliable narrators, a sign that storytelling conventions were loosening up.

> ***Bix: An Interpretation of a Legend*** **(1991; 100 minutes; director: Pupi Avati; writers: Avati, Antonio Avati, Lino Patruno; English dialogue: Fred Chalfy, Mark Wolfson). Cast includes: Bryant Weeks (Bix Beiderbecke), Emile Levisetti (Joe Venuti), Romano Orzari (Hoagy Carmichael), Mark Sovel (Frankie Trumbauer), Michael T. Henderson (Pee Wee Russell), Curtis N. Wollan (Paul Whiteman), Darell Bishop (Andy Secrest), Joe Thingvall (Big Eddie), Mark Collver (Burnie Beiderbecke).**
> **—In the 1920s, cornetist Bix Beiderbecke plays like an angel but drinks too much, maybe because his family doesn't understand him.**

In many ways, this somber Bix Beiderbecke biopic is as stiff as one might expect, given an Italian filmmaker working in the Midwest with a modest budget, an unknown cast, and translated dialogue. Almost none of the actors had prior film experience, star Bryant Weeks included. But that stiffness dissipates whenever period music furthers the story, and there's plenty of such jazz, re-created by Bob Wilber, who'd done similar duty on *The Cotton Club*. (The music was recorded in Rome with American and Italian players.) Then, everyone's speaking the same language.

Beiderbecke is a rich subject, revered and discounted for the same reason: He was an original who sounded different from 1920s black cornet kings Armstrong and King Oliver (not that you couldn't hear their influence). Bix didn't slur or growl, but he had an uncanny ear and a way of stringing phrases together and stringing them out that made for exceptionally coherent solos. And his story lends itself to dramatization, per *Young Man with a Horn*.

Bix declares its historical high-mindedness, shooting at the actual Beiderbecke home at 1934 Grand Avenue in Davenport, Iowa, a mile from the upper Mississippi. (He was born in Davenport in 1903.) As if to verify the story's accuracy, many scenes are stamped with a date and location, documentary-style, even when the scene is made up. Beneath that veneer of authenticity, *Bix* is biopic business as usual, with composite characters, a reshuffled timeline, and invented subplots. But writer/director Pupi Avati leaves himself an out. This is the cornetist's story as told by his friend Joe Venuti to a traveling companion over a long train ride. That device raises the possibility that Joe is an unreliable narrator—that he, not the filmmakers, is responsible for the distortions. *Bix*'s double-giveaway subtitle is *An Interpretation of a Legend*.

The basic facts are sound. As shown, Beiderbecke came from a middle-class family that never warmed to his music or perceived his genius. (In Bix lore, and the movie, they never play the records he mails home.) A poor student, he was sent to Lake Forest Academy outside Chicago to finish high school; he was soon missing classes, drawn to the city's music and sitting in with local bands including (mostly because he kept pestering them) the illustrious New Orleans Rhythm Kings. Expelled from school, and back in Davenport, he briefly worked for his father's business before joining the Wolverines, the first band he'd record with. They opened at New York's Cinderella Ballroom in 1924, around the time Louis Armstrong arrived to join Fletcher Henderson. (Armstrong is mentioned but no black musicians appear in *Bix*; the two cornetists rarely crossed paths but loved each other's playing.) Bix was hired away by Detroit bandleader Jean Goldkette, who employed violinist Joe Venuti, but Bix lost the job owing to poor sight-reading. Subsequently he worked on correcting that and teamed up with saxophonist Frank Trumbauer. Eventually they (like Venuti) were induced to join Paul Whiteman's big busy orchestra. ("With me, you'll work yourselves to death," movie-Whiteman tells them.) But Bix's drinking got bad and his behavior became erratic. He trashed a hotel room, went into rehab, and returned to Whiteman—but not for long. He'd become so unreliable, the bandleader had understudy Andy Secrest on standby. In 1931 Beiderbecke drank himself to death in a low-rent New York room. *Bix* finds room for all that.

Pupi Avati had made an Italian miniseries that dealt with young dixieland musicians, based on his own experience as a clarinetist: 1978's *Jazz Band*. Italian fans are very aware of the contributions made by early Italian-American jazz soloists, such as Bix's early inspiration Nick La Rocca, Rhythm Kings clarinetist Leon Roppolo, guitar virtuoso Eddie Lang (born Salvatore Massaro), and Lang's frequent partner Venuti. In *Bix*, even Indiana's cornfed Hoagy Carmichael (Montreal's Romano Orzari) looks Italian, suave and black-haired. The real Joe Venuti was less photogenic than American actor Emile Levisetti, who has more presence than anyone else here. Venuti was not as close to Beiderbecke as depicted, and was no (guardian) angel, but Joe is *Bix*'s true hero: a mensch.

The real Venuti was an epic practical joker: arranging to have a large number of bass players assemble on a certain streetcorner as he laughed from a high window. One night at a party, it's said, Bix passed out in a bathtub and awoke encased in Jell-O. That was Joe's handiwork—sadly omitted from the film. Joe's trickster side briefly shows itself in the opening scene, where he weaves around a radio boom mic while playing violin and sticks his tongue out at his announcer. But you might also look at the film's whole flashbacky frame story as part of a deadpan practical joke, perpetrated on the Beiderbecke family by Joe and his late friend Bix with the consent of Bix's generally disapproving older brother Burnie.

There's a (made-up) twist in *Bix*'s plot, slowly revealed, and this paragraph is one big spoiler. Bix's mom frets he needs someone to look after him, so to soothe her he invents one: he buys a photo of a woman who looks like mom's ideal and sends it to the family, promising to bring her around sometime. But now that Bix is dead, mom really wants to meet her, so Venuti finds the woman—we never get her name, and I can't even tell you who plays her—and brings her 900 miles west to meet the family, filling her in about Bix on the train. (She wants to break into show business, and Joe's promised her dinner with Bing Crosby—but then he's also told her they'll be headed home from Iowa the following day, despite the 24-hour travel time such a trip required and his assurances he's reserved her a hotel room.)[1] Oddly, this is the second jazz film in which the story of a doomed horn man, initials BB, is told on a train, following *Dr. Terror's House of Horrors*.

The tale Venuti tells her is less Bix's real story than Joe's talking biopic: the streamlined version, with fewer characters. Beiderbecke did indeed meet Carmichael and clarinetist Don Murray early, but they were not his Lake Forest roommates, nor fellow Wolverines, the way Joe tells it; Murray died years later than *Bix* has it, and not as described. (But as shown, Murray sometimes played a metal clarinet.) Bix recorded his piano poem "In a Mist" in 1927. In the movie it's 1931, an item the fading Bix crosses off his bucket list.

Embellishments aside, the order in which Joe tells it all is logical enough. When we talk about our friends, we don't start with their birth. First he tells of how he and Bix met, which is also a story about Beiderbecke's musical strengths and limitations—letting us viewers hear his sound. (He's ghosted by Bix scholar and expert mimic Tom Pletcher.) It's the day Beiderbecke joins Goldkette in November 1924, fresh from the Wolverines; the scene both echoes *Young Man with a Horn* and dramatizes a real incident, when Bix got dissed by jazzphobic recording supervisor Eddie King. When the cornetist starts ad libbing on a rehearsal of "I Didn't Know"—filling in a fetching countermelody on open horn as the other brass buzz along with mutes—belligerent producer Eddie calls a halt. "What is that shit you're playing?" "What everybody else was playing, my version," Bix says mildly. "And you think we spend hundreds of dollars on arrangements so you can wipe your ass with them?"

It takes Bix less time to get fired than young Rick Martin, who got the same lecture. But when the Goldkette band then plays "I Didn't Know" without Bix, you can hear what they're missing; the scene establishes his musical authority even as he loses the job. We will hear his absence again later, when he flubs a solo with Whiteman. Andy Secrest jumps in for the last eight bars: he's got greater facility, but lacks the burnished timbre. (A filmmaker's embellishment: one night the Beiderbeckes do tune in to Whiteman's broadcast and mistake Secrest for Bix.)

For a month after that, Bix slept on my couch, Venuti says, to wrap up the Goldkette story, putting himself in a good light for his comely listener. The second story he tells her sketches in some of Bix's romantic history, namely his shy affair with Ruth from St. Louis (though the real Ruth Shaffner didn't meet him on a blind date arranged by the Trumbauers). Then storytelling Joe skips back to 1917 and from there tells Bix's story mostly in order.

This rock-skipping back in time and then creeping forward mirrors Eastwood's *Bird*, and *Bix* lays bare a practical reason to scramble biopic chronology—it frees the story's emotional arc from the order of actual events. (No new idea: writer/director Preston Sturges had divined as much, devising a similar structure for a biopic released in 1942 as *The Great Moment*. "I believe a biographer has two obligations: he must be true to his subject and he must not bore his public. Since he cannot change the chronology of events, he can only change the order of their presentation."[2] But Paramount straightened out the timeline before releasing it.)

As Bix, Bryant Weeks fingers cornet convincingly, sometimes aping an unorthodox third-valve fingering Beiderbecke used. But tousled sandy-haired Weeks looks nothing like the real Bix, with his moon face and dark hair slicked back. Clarinetist Pee Wee Russell hangs around but you could miss the moment he's named. Actor Michael T. Henderson lacks Russell's hangdog look, but a raspy tag at the end of a clarinet solo confirms his identity to any Pee Wee–phile. (Kenny Davern ghosts him.) The real Russell was brilliant but disorganized; movie Pee Wee is Bix's informal agent, smoothing his way to Goldkette.

FIGURE 9.1 Violinist Joe Venuti (Emile Levisetti) hears Bix Beiderbecke (Bryant Weeks) for the first time, in *Bix*.

(The real Bix returned to Goldkette after being fired. *Bix* gets to the gist of that, by flipping the chronology—showing him getting fired, then hired.) Frank Trumbauer becomes another disappointed father figure who (like Bix's real father) has a big house and more sympathetic wife. He and Bix quarrel over the younger man's drinking before they reunite under Whiteman. (Even Mrs. Trumbauer calls her husband Frankie, his public nickname.)

The acting—how to say it?—is frequently adequate. Doomed genius Beiderbecke is a juicy part for an actor. Weeks gets the cool that Bix brought to the music, but not the fire. He plays Bix's Midwestern reticence to a fault, hinting at the social awkwardness that made his genius easy to miss. The period details are all right; all the old autos are shiny, as if no one ever drove through mud, but that's typical of pictures using collectors' cars. Chicago's Loop doubles for old New York.

The musical recreations are faithful, and soloists play in character—they sound right even if they don't look right. Bob Wilber ghosts Trumbauer's C-melody saxophone solos, and Andy Stein plays Venuti's violin. But at one point faithful music trips things up. There's a St. Louis 1925 sequence set mostly at Trumbauer's house—situated next to a cornfield—where he helps Bix learn to read music well enough to join the union. (The real Beiderbecke had already faked his way through the exam on piano.) Their practice piece is 1920's "Singin' the Blues," and within a few rehearsals they work up the classic, much-imitated version they'd record in 1927, right down to Eddie Lang's guitar arpeggios and Bix's classic solo; they preview it at a picnic. This fixed musical text denies Beiderbecke (or Lang) his genius as an improviser in the moment. It also fetishizes the recording as a platonic ideal, not one possible version that's revered because it's the one that got preserved.

The film is similarly short on spontaneity—a succession of set pieces with little room for the participants to breathe in more life. One aspect of the Beiderbecke legend *Bix* conspicuously skips: that playing in Whiteman's leviathan band demoralized jazzmen who got few openings to improvise. *Bix* pulls its punches; it never goes big. He dies in bed, off camera. We see only his dead feet.

There are a couple of anachronistic sequences, anachronisms with a point. In one, the Wolverines are mobbed by young fans, as if they're the Beatles, and to stave off a riot the already-exhausted band has to go back on stage. That giving till there's nothing left helps explain Bix's drinking.

Late in the film, when our hero tries to struggle through one last (made-up) record date with Hoagy, Andy Secrest tries to introduce Bix to a callow colleague, who's rudely dismissive. "They're all the same, these young kids," Andy grouses. "They think they're hot shit—just because they made it through the conservatory." There were always well-schooled jazz musicians, and such players would soon find employment in swing-era dance bands. But in 1931 no one was talking about a conservatory generation. Such musicians were however much-discussed in the age when *Bix* was made: tradition-minded players sometimes accused of insufficiently valuing Beiderbecke.

Mo' Better Blues (1990; 129 minutes; director/writer: Spike Lee). Cast includes: Denzel Washington (Bleek Gilliam), Wesley Snipes (Shadow Henderson), Giancarlo Esposito (Left Hand Lacey), Bill Nunn (Bottom Hammer), Jeff "Tain" Watts (Rhythm Jones), Spike Lee (Giant), Cynda Williams (Clarke Bentancourt), Joie Lee (Indigo Downes), Dick Anthony Williams (Bleek's father), Abbey Lincoln (Bleek's mother), John Turturro (Moe Flatbush), Nicholas Turturro (Josh Flatbush), Samuel L. Jackson (Madlock), Zakee Howze (Bleek as a boy/Miles Gilliam), Branford Marsalis (himself). New song: "Pop Top 40 R n' B Urban Contemporary Easy Listening Funk Love" (words Spike Lee/music Branford Marsalis).

—For top trumpeter Bleek Gilliam, music comes first, as his two women know well. But he's got an incompetent agent and a rebellious saxophonist to contend with. And when he loses his ability to play, his world crumbles.

Although jazz hadn't really gone away in the 1970s, in the early 1980s the word was that jazz was back, personified by trumpet virtuoso Wynton Marsalis, who dropped out of Juilliard to tour with Art Blakey. The son of a New Orleans jazz pianist, Marsalis championed traditional jazz values—swinging above all—and trashed 1970s electric and free jazz. He was as known for his opinions as his combustible quintet music, patterned on the still-startling sound of mid-1960s Miles Davis.

Soon many younger, mostly African American players who came up in Wynton's wake were dubbed Young Lions. They wore sharp suits, played post-bop music with energy, polish, and conviction, and swung hard. Not all shared Wynton's views. More typical of the new breed was his quintet's saxophonist, brother Branford Marsalis, older by a year. Branford had a similar aesthetic, but didn't reject the pop, funk, and hip-hop also in the air—even if he kept all that separate from his straight jazz work. After leaving Wynton's band, Branford toured with Sting, led a burning jazz quartet, and (in the 1990s) assembled the R&B/hip-hop side project Buckshot LeFonque.

By the mid-1980s, Branford was friends with aspiring Brooklyn filmmaker Spike Lee, also a son of a jazz musician. Both were well established by 1991, when Lee's fourth feature *Mo' Better Blues* brought the Marsalis generation to the screen. Lee had hated the gloom of *'Round Midnight* and *Bird*. The musicians he knew had a good time, made decent money, partied, went to Knicks games, and had girlfriends or families.[3] *Mo' Better Blues* captures that milieu very well, the music included, in telling the story of trumpeter Bleek Gilliam. An established jazz star, with numerous albums on a major label (to judge by the slick album art), Gilliam tours the US and Europe, though at the moment he's in long-term residence at a Manhattan club.[4]

The film's sometimes symphonic, sometimes jazzy score is by Spike's father, bassist Bill Lee, whose title tune Bleek's band plays on stage; it's heard in full, three and a half minutes. Gilliam introduces it as a blues, while going on about the blues, although "Mo' Better Blues" isn't a blues. It's a catchy 16-bar tune (of almost identical 8-bar units) with gospel cadences. That melody aside, the Bleek Quintet owes its aesthetic to Branford

Marsalis, with a crucial assist from trumpeter Terence Blanchard, who coached and ghosted star Denzel Washington. (Blanchard would go on to score Lee's subsequent films.) Washington mimes playing very well, with a little but not too much body English, and in repose he often touches his lips, as some horn players do. Spike Lee knows the look and rhythms of a jazz composer's life; we see how Bleek tunes the world out when he's composing, muttering chord changes to himself. Practicing, he'll sing a solo while fingering it in the air—a way not to be limited to what he knows he can do already. We see him take his horn apart to clean it. At one lonely moment he practices on the walkway of the Brooklyn Bridge, as Sonny Rollins famously did on the Williamsburg Bridge three decades before.

Branford's band ghosts for Bleek's, and the number that introduces their sound is Marsalis's "Say Hey," whose tricky head studded with piano-bass unison figures gives way to headlong swingtime behind the horn solos. These compositions are ostensibly Bleek's, ditto the jazz rap tune he is moved to sing one night, in which he blasts the vapidity of modern love songs—at a time when a few real jazz musicians tried rapping, with comparably sad results.

The old Marsalis gang gave each other schoolyardy nicknames; Wynton was Skain, drummer Jeff Watts was (and is) Tain. Bleek's tenor saxist is Shadow Henderson—that's the name on his American Express card—and Bottom Hammer plays bass. Jeff "Tain" Watts himself portrays Rhythm Jones, so the drumming always looks convincing. Foppish pianist Left Hand Lacey sports an ostentatious earring that dangles like a watchchain. Left dotes on his high-maintenance French girlfriend who invades the band's dressing room and bugs the other guys. *Mo' Better Blues* is the rare jazz film with realistic

FIGURE 9.2 Bleek (Denzel Washington) plays for himself on the Brooklyn Bridge, in *Mo' Better Blues*.

dressing-room banter. A couple of scenes have the right free-flowing combination of trash talk and attempts to conduct actual business. (The actors seem to crack each other up for real.) These are jazz musicians we have not seen on screen before—more authentic, and happier than most. It's a bum note when Bleek utters a little corny jazz dialogue: "It's the wrong key, bringing your lady in here."

Bleek's life is not only about music. He plays catch with his widowed father, and his lifelong pal is his incompetent manager Giant (Spike Lee, in a characteristically prominent supporting role), whose gambling addiction will undo them both. Bleek has two steady girlfriends, grounded schoolteacher Indigo and aspiring singer Clarke, who hopes to sit in with the band one night. Bleek rejects the idea out of hand, as if he thinks she's too pretty to be talented. Indigo and Clarke know about each other, but put up with the situation (Bleek's played by Denzel Washington after all).

Tenor saxist Shadow has numerous (unseen) women himself, but makes his own play for Clarke because she's sexy and he wants her for the band he's getting ready to form—faint echo of 1962's *All Night Long*, where a rebel sideman tries to pry a singer away from the boss. On stage with Bleek, Shadow is in it for himself, playing long frantic solos. (Or so we're told—given jazz-movie bandstand time-compression, the in-your-face solo that demonstrates his self-indulgence runs all of 80 seconds before Bleek reins him in.) He's played by Wesley Snipes, as ready to steal the show as Shadow is.

In conversation at a party, Bleek laments that jazz has lost its African American audience (the mixed crowds at his club gigs notwithstanding). But Shadow turns the complaint back on him: If you played music your people wanted to hear, they'd come out. (This conversation might logically have preceded rather than followed Bleek's onstage rap, "Pop Top 40 R n' B Urban Contemporary Easy Listening Funk Love.") "I have my own voice," Bleek insists. Shadow: "Ain't nobody listenin'." That tension between artistic integrity and commercialism has come up before (and will come up again), and as usual it's a discussion that also applies to artists behind the camera.

Shadow challenges Bleek's dominant role; aesthetics aside, this is also a contest of manliness. Bleek's music can be tender, but it's strong. Late in the film, when we hear Shadow's band with Bleek's old rhythm section, plus Clarke who gets featured billing, she sounds perfectly fine on a radical revamp of W. C. Handy's "Harlem Blues"—his lyric, to a new melody by Raymond Jones. (Cynda Williams prerecorded her vocal, line by line.) But backing her on straight soprano, most phallic of saxes, Shadow sounds emasculated: a black Kenny G.

For phallic trumpets in jazz movies, *Mo' Better* takes a prize. When Clarke interrupts Bleek's practice one day, he winds up nuzzling her breasts with the bell of his horn, as foreplay. (In a later scene, during sex, she reaches over to caress the mouthpiece.) This makes his own later emasculation by brass even more disturbing. Giant's long-unpaid bookie sends a couple of thugs to rough him up, and when Bleek intervenes, one of them (Samuel L. Jackson, pre-stardom) cleaves his lips with two roundhouse swings of Bleek's own horn. (This assault echoes an incident in Chet Baker's life, later staged in *Born to Be Blue*.)

Indigo had once asked him, what would you do if you couldn't play? "Probably roll up in a corner and die." Unmanned, Bleek all but makes good on that prediction, living up to his name. He stops returning calls, or cleaning his apartment, and only gradually picks up the trumpet again—the way Miles Davis dropped out in the 1970s. But after a year in seclusion, when Bleek tries to sit in with Shadow's band (on Bill Lee's ballad "Again, Never"), his playing is painful, both for him and his listeners. Shadow has to slide in to finish his solo, like Andy Secrest covering for Bix. Bleek flees the club, giving his horn away to doorman Giant, and immediately seeks out Indigo, begging her to salvage his life, now that the jazz part appears over. You might commend his judgment, choosing the woman who seemed to love him more. But she's his only option, now that Clarke and Shadow are together (and rightly so—he'd made her a better offer after urging Bleek to give her a hearing).

Indigo takes a chance on him, and in a hectic montage set to the mantra-like first movement of John Coltrane's *A Love Supreme* (built on an ostinato we'd heard Bleek chant earlier, while meditating), they marry and have a son named Miles, who grows by stages till he's about eight. Miles is played by Zakee Howze, who'd played young Bleek in the film's 1969 prologue. Back then, Bleek's mother (Abbey Lincoln, in a brief, thankless role) made her son practice trumpet when he'd rather be playing baseball, and his dad took his side. As on a jazz tune the ending recapitulates the beginning, beat for beat—except this time dad/Bleek wins the argument, and Miles gets to run with his friends.

Just as the 1980s generation of jazz musicians looked back on the mid-1960s as the golden age, when Miles Davis was burning but hadn't yet gone electric, the more fanciful aspects of *Mo' Better*'s look have a retro feel. Production designer Wynn Thomas likened it to "a period film without specifying a period."[5] The band's suits look a little out of time, like Left Hand's cigarette holder. Their world is chronologically unmoored. A poster locates the club Bleek plays, Beneath the Underdog, on Fifty-Second Street, decades after the last of the (rather smaller) jazz clubs there closed. The exteriors were shot on a narrow West Village street, dressed to look like a still thriving jazz district, home to a Blue Mill Tavern, Satin Ballroom, Quarter Note, and one more cinematic Jazz Corner of the World. Hollywood-style, *Mo' Better* places an alley behind the club Bleek plays. Spike Lee imagines his own movieland New York, like Martin Scorsese. Lee said the film presents "a romantic ideal of the jazz world." That mood is reinforced by the cinematography of Ernest Dickerson (another son of a jazz musician), pushing the warm and cool extremes of the color spectrum.

The band's months-long stand in one club is another throwback to decades past. Beneath the Underdog, named for Charles Mingus's autobiographical novel, is an idealized jazz club, with quiet customers, lowkey waitstaff, big tables not too jammed together, good sightlines, a high ceiling and balcony, and a comedian (Robin Harris) to entertain between sets.

But the owners don't match the tablecloths. It's not just that they prefer Elvis as music and always refuse Bleek a raise. They're also stereotypical greedy Jews, the bespectacled brothers Moe and Josh Flatbush, played with unseemly, lipsmacking glee by the Italian-American Turturro brothers. Spike Lee took a lot of flak for the flat evil Flatbushes, and rightly so—they are so gratuitously ugly they strain credibility. Any club owners so tightfisted would have squeezed in twice as many tiny tables and dropped the comedian long ago.

In hindsight, *Mo' Better*'s boyhood bumper segments, with their demanding mom and indulgent dad, are a warm-up for Spike Lee's semi-autobiographical ***Crooklyn*** (1994). It's really the story of Troy (Zelda Harris), the lone girl among five kids living with their parents in a Brooklyn rowhouse on a noisy Bed-Stuy block in the summer of 1973. That summer Troy will turn 10 and do a lot of growing up. (Joie Lee wrote the original story and cowrote the screenplay with brothers Spike and Cinque Lee.) Head of the family Woody Carmichael (Delroy Lindo) is a jazz composer who'd made good money playing music as a sideman—enough to buy their house. Now, like jazz heroes in other movies, he pursues his own vision. With five kids, however, that's a luxury the Carmichaels can ill afford. Since dedicating himself to his own music, Woody literally can't keep the lights on, even with tenants passing the family food stamps and wife Carolyn (Alfre Woodard) taking an outside job. He loves his kids, brings them treats when he can, and wants to provide for them. "But I've got to do it in my own way."

As Woody sits in the basement musing on piano, composing music for a (self-promoted) solo concert he hopes will brighten his prospects, the world passes him by. A jazz snob, Woody puts down even the Chi-Lites' soul classic "Oh Girl," with its jazzy harmonies—but upstairs his kids sing along with TV's whitebread *Partridge Family*, hoping they won't be overheard. Disciplinarian Carolyn implores Woody to come back to the real world, reminding him of the sacrifices she's made, "so you can be a pure musician playing pure music." Do you want me to strap on a guitar and play rock-and-roll? he asks contemptuously. If only. (The director's father, bassist Bill Lee, resisted switching to bass guitar in the rocking 1960s, costing him studio work.)

As his luck would have it, Woody's concert in a modest hall falls on the same night as the final game of the NBA playoffs at Madison Square Garden (at the wrong time of the year, but let it pass). His recital draws fewer than 20 people, none of them influential; even his eldest son skips dad's concert to attend the game. (Bill Lee's eldest son Spike had once done the same.) He didn't miss much from what we hear of Woody's pleasant piano balladry, ghosted in character by Sir Roland Hanna. Not that the composer is discouraged by the turnout; now he's talking about a folk opera. Life will intervene, forcing him to become more responsible, but Woody is something new in jazz movies: the follow-your-dream idealist as selfish jerk.

Giant Steps (1992; 94 minutes; director: Richard Rose; writers: Paul Quarrington, Greg Dummett). Cast includes: Billy Dee Williams (Slate Thompson), Michael Mahonen (Arvo Leek), Ted Dykstra (Graeme Gaines), Ranee Lee (Stella Della), Nicu Branzea (Uldis Leek), Robyn Stevan (Leslie),

Kristina Nicoll (Tara), Julian Richings (band director), Doc Cheatham (Oliver K. Nash).
—**Student trumpeter Arvo clashes with his old-world dad, gets mentored by wiggy jazz pianist Slate Thompson, and gets bad advice from a drummer. Slate, meanwhile, contemplates taking a commercial gig with his on-and-off mate, singer Stella Della.**

Spike Lee had wanted *Mo' Better* to be called *A Love Supreme*, but Coltrane's widow Alice nixed the title. A year later came a little-known Canadian indie set in Toronto, named for an earlier Coltrane classic, *Giant Steps*.

Many young tradition-minded players who came up in the Marsalises' wake turned to jazz's wise elders for guidance, given the opportunity. Some had to settle for whoever they could get. The high-school trumpet player at the heart of *Giant Steps* picks up a good mentor—eccentric pianist Slate Thompson (Billy Dee Williams)—and a bad one: Thompson's macho drummer Graeme.

Giant Steps plays like a jazz After-School Special—a made-for-TV movie about teenagers' problems—save for a little fleeting, gratuitous (male and female) nudity and rude language. Our young hero, Estonian immigrant Arvo Leek, has a harsh, disapproving old-world dad, and is confused by a sexual encounter with artist and free spirit Tara. Arvo's Platonic gal pal Leslie is thinking of cheating on her math final and gets involved in her sleazy adult brother's skeevy business. The school band director tells Arvo to play those charts as written instead of ad libbing. We paid good money for these arrangements, the teacher says, à la *Bix* and *Young Man with a Horn*. (There's another callout to the latter, when Arvo perched at a high window spies on a gig by his mentor-to-be.) But *Giant Steps* references those films only to subvert, like *Crooklyn*, the paradigm of the uncompromising artist.

This is also the story of Slate Thompson at a critical juncture in his own life. His ex-lover and ex-performing partner, jazz and R&B singer Stella Della (Brooklyn-born Montreal jazz singer Ranee Lee), is back, and they make an effort to reconcile personally and professionally. (Swing-era trumpeter Doc Cheatham also turns up for a minute, representing musicians who came up the old hard-knocks reform-school way.) Expat Slate is a free spirit who might wander home from downtown by cutting through backyards and across rooftops and wading through shallow basins. He ranges over the landscape as a pianist too. Slate pummels the keys free jazz–style—Billy Dee has a good time with that—and then calls the ballad "When Sunny Gets Blue," quiet-like. He's a purist, in a way—wants the real sound of a Brazilian cuíca drum, not a digital sample.

Slate bristles at such concessions to commercialism as playing two sets a night that start at certain times and last at least 45 minutes. "What the hell does that have to do with me and music?" His purity has cost him; instead of working steadily at a downtown club, Slate holds sessions at an old factory building where he lives, accompanied by a stutter-toned electric bassist and bashing drummer Graeme who thinks brushes are for "wimp-asses." Graeme's drumming is so unsubtle a successful hair-metal band would hire him, if he didn't look down on them.

Williams gives a funny, hammy performance as Slate, slow talking with a big scratchy voice, like a bear roused from hibernation—a sitcom Thelonious Monk. Slate wears colorful hats, including a spangled Sun Ra cap. He's so deep he's barely on the planet, and given to deep pronouncements. After Arvo crashes his session one night and acquits himself well—Slate calls for bop anthem "Ornithology," as luck would have it the very tune Arvo's been woodshedding—the pianist takes a liking to him. Slate starts giving Arvo practical advice—learn to slap out a different meter with either hand, to master polyrhythms—and shares some Zen wisdom. Fill your mouth with rice grains and then spit out just the right one: because improvising is like that, picking the perfect note over all the others. He's a zany Art Hazzard. Before long, Arvo's sporting his own hat, a grown-up's fedora.

But Slate isn't available to dispense koans all the time, and Arvo also starts hanging out with Graeme, who lets the kid buy him beers and messes with his head because the drummer's been shagging Tara himself. He indoctrinates Arvo in his idiot wisdom: "Music is better than pussy," because the former is always different and the latter always the same. (That says it all about Graeme as sexual partner.) The drummer is so awful, even his boss Slate tells Arvo that Graeme's an asshole. But can Arvo still trust Slate, who's decided to take a high profile gig at the (real) Top o' the Senator—an upstairs room, for once— where he politely backs Stella Della's song stylings?

When Arvo goes to see him at the club and shames Slate by loudly slapping his table in two meters at once—he's finally mastered that—the elder walks out in humiliation. But in the end, everything works out, for the principals at least. (Tara gets quietly dropped from the story once she's filled her function; Leslie flunks the big exam and breaks a leg joyriding.) Slate comes to enjoy playing behind Stella, and they're held over. He's even started going to bed when she tells him. Arvo reconciles with his father Uldis, who used to play horn himself in the old country, though he lacked Arvo's talent. I hear you upstairs, dad says, playing "Ornithology" and "Giant Steps." We do not, in fact, hear Arvo even hint at that Coltrane steeplechase.

After-School Specials have a didactic social-engineering side, and *Giant Steps* runs true to form. Like *Crooklyn* and unlike just about any other jazz film, it presents artistic compromise as the mature, responsible choice. Throughout the picture, Arvo clashes with the joyless band teacher as the school band rehearses the standard "Easy Living." Earlier he'd bristled when Arvo suggested an alternate chord change to the bass player. But in the last scene, at what looks like the senior prom, Arvo in band uniform plays "Easy Living" with only minimal embellishment, doing what's expected of him, as the camera pulls back to reveal his classmates, shuffling inexpressively on the dance floor, molding themselves to social expectations in their own way.

Once more, in the finale, a public performance brings divided parties together—in this case, Arvo's real and symbolic dads. Uldis watches the prom from a narrow balcony, and Slate turns up beside him, ostentatiously grooving. (They've never met.) Hearing Arvo's tasteful melodizing, Slate drawls out, "Ah, that's my boy," and Uldis gives him a look of puzzlement, then pleased recognition, but doesn't introduce himself. It's the film's deftest touch.

> **Lush Life (1993; 106 minutes; director/writer: Michael Elias). Cast includes: Forest Whitaker (Buddy Chester), Jeff Goldblum (Al Gorky), Kathy Baker (Janice), Lois Chiles (Lucy), Don Cheadle (Jack), Charlie Heath (young trumpeter).**
> **—Freelance musicians Buddy and Al live it up, getting paid to play every night. But then Buddy starts getting bad headaches.**

Just as "Giant Steps" goes unheard in *Giant Steps*, Billy Strayhorn's "Lush Life" isn't in 1993's cable-TV movie *Lush Life*. But the story justifies the title. Jazz musicians have a good time in *Mo' Better Blues*, but *Lush Life* ups the ante, glamorizing the lives of New York freelancers who prefer jazz but play any style, as epitomized by trumpeter Buddy Chester (Forest Whitaker, overdoing his fingering, as in *Bird*) and tenor saxophonist Al Gorky (Jeff Goldblum). For these chums life is a blast: an endless succession of jazz-club engagements, record dates, jingle sessions, and sitting around the studio earning good money waiting for stars to arrive. In real life (or even *American Blue Note*), playing weddings is something you do early on and drop as soon as you can afford it—unless the money is ridiculously good. Buddy and Al play a double-scale society wedding at a swank hotel, then the musicians get $1,000 each to play a Park Avenue afterparty—where Al sneaks off the bandstand for a quickie with attractive host Lucy.

Al is a dog, always on the prowl though married to sweet thoughtful Janice, an amateur singer with a day job. Divorced Buddy is more responsible, and the more successful. He's been on the cover of *Down Beat* and shared stages with the greats, but like other successful musicians he chooses to earn better money closer to home. Al is content to play whatever comes his way, knowing he has the reading skills and experience to cut it on any woodwind, whether subbing in a Broadway pit band or playing recorder in a baroque quintet. (He's the guy Tony Curtis aspired to be in *The Rat Race*.) Real jobbing musicians take just such pride in their craft, but (for some at least) random work gets meaningless after a while. They miss working on their own music.

Writer/director Michael Elias is a veteran of New York's Living Theater—he appeared in the 1966 art movie *Who's Crazy?* remembered for its Ornette Coleman score. Elias went on to direct and create TV sitcoms. In tone, *Lush Life* is as far from *The Connection* as a New York jazz film can get. It was shot mostly in Los Angeles and employs many studio pros, on and off screen—Chuck Findley ghosted Buddy's showy trumpet, and cool-jazz veteran Bob Cooper plays Al's muscular tenor. Some exteriors were shot in New York, but California locations unconvincingly fake Long Island's north shore, Woodstock, and the lake in Central Park.

Even where the film gets gritty, it's a self-conscious fantasy. Buddy starts getting headaches and is bothered by high notes. "You and Buddy Bolden," Al helpfully glosses. Turns out Buddy has a brain tumor and just months to live. When Al hears the news he's all denial and bargaining, but Buddy skips ahead to acceptance. He wants to keep his illness a secret—only Al and Janice know—but to go out in style, throwing himself a lavish bon voyage party. So the pals invent a double-scale gig (Park Avenue's Lucy lends them her palatial apartment), for which Al hires all their many musician friends. This leads to a real session-musician's complication; he runs afoul of a contractor who needs players himself that night. (So they hire him on too, and he subcontracts his own gig, making the labor shortage someone else's problem.) Buddy's final months are a time for reflection and some dark moments, but mostly party planning. Will there be enough lox?

On the big night, the musicians find out they're (well paid) guests at their own surprise party, and are invited to jam. What they play sounds less like an informal New York session than an LA big band rehearsal. Everybody's playing charts, as if a party's an excuse to practice. (The music is by saxophonist Lennie Niehaus, who'd worked on *Bird*.) Buddy's secret is safe, and he has a fine night, connecting with a singer he likes. Which is just about where we leave him. The messiness of impending death is demurely sidestepped.

In the run-up to the party Al and Janice have been estranged, owing to his catting around and lack of commitment. She wants them to buy and run a copy shop out in Northport, 40 miles from Times Square, which would seriously hinder his music career (and the catting). Al has resisted, but since dying people in movies exist to give life lessons to survivors, he rethinks it and agrees to give straight life a try. Janice in turn helps Al wrap up a subplot. Buddy has had his eye on a trumpet reputed to have been owned by the great Clifford Brown, which is improbably sitting in a pawnshop at the suspiciously low price of $2,500. When Al goes to buy it for Buddy, he discovers a doctor has bought it for his son—a waste of the instrument, we assume.

But on the night of the big party, Al and Janice track the kid down at a Brooklyn high-school dance, and he turns out to be a self-possessed African American prodigy: a new Bleek Gilliam, or Buddy Chester. They bring him to the party, Buddy gets to play Brownie's horn, with brio, and the kid sits in and makes a good impression. He's the new generation, coming up to replace the greats who've now moved on, to the grave or the photocopy business.

Swing Kids **(1993; 114 minutes; director: Thomas Carter; writer: Jonathan Marc Feldman). Cast includes: Robert Sean Leonard (Peter Müller), Christian Bale (Thomas Berger), Frank Whaley (Arvid), Tushka Bergen (Evey), Kenneth Branagh (Knopp), Barbara Hershey (Frau Müller), David Tom (Willi Müller).**
—In 1939 Hamburg, swing-crazy teen Peter Müller is forced to join the Hitler Youth, but strives to retain his ideals. Meanwhile, guitarist Arvid's left hand gets crushed, but he can still fret with two fingers like his idol Django Reinhardt.

Swing Kids has a classic Hollywood high concept: Hitler Youth versus swing dancers—*Footloose* in jackboots. To be fair, this movie targeted at young people didn't chase a trend as much as accelerate one: a fad among young (mostly white) folk for athletic 1930s African American dance styles accompanied by youthful retro swing bands. The movement was just getting underway in 1993 and would crest five years later.[6] In *Swing Kids'* 1939 Hamburg, German teens move on the dance floor like they're telepathically connected to Lindy Hoppers at Harlem's Savoy Ballroom. (It was shot in Prague. There are no black characters, but the director is African American TV veteran Thomas Carter, experienced with young actors.)

They weren't called Swing Kids—not before the movie anyway—but *Swingjugend* did exist, and Hamburg was their capital. They were mostly upper-class teens who, as depicted, sported umbrellas (as Anglophiles), grew their hair longish, adopted American slang, collected jazz records by Benny Goodman above all, and gathered to dance in music halls in an inevitably charged atmosphere. Commentators are of two minds about what it all meant. Was it teenage rebellion, more about sex than society, or a movement whose political implications were all too plain, celebrating black and Jewish music in Hitler's Germany? As guitarist Arvid asserts, "No one who likes swing can become a Nazi."

Swing Kids tests that premise. It's the story of three teenage friends: hero Peter (Robert Sean Leonard), Arvid, and upper-class, slightly arrogant Thomas (Christian Bale, capitalizing on his dead-behind-the-eyes stare). Peter and Thomas are scene-makers, stepping out at Cafe Bismarck, where they're greeted with a "swing heil" and dance with girls whose moves frequently expose their underwear—as licentious as *Swing Kids* gets. "Go Thomas, you're the king of Harlem!" Peter calls out to the dance floor. (Leonard and Bale, truth to tell, are not great dancers.) The kids' secret signal is to whistle the first five notes of Ellington's "It Don't Mean a Thing (If It Ain't Got That Swing)."

"You can't listen to this and not dance," Peter tells shy schoolmate Evey one day, turning her on to Goodman's "Bugle Call Rag": "He just swings it out!" It's easy to learn to jitterbug, he tells her, and sure enough, her first time out on the floor they're doing unison turns, coordinated handwaves, hand-to-hand Charleston kicks, through-the-legs, and around-the-back and over-the-head aerials, like they'd been working with a choreographer for weeks.

The kids dance to live music at the Bismarck and the Trichter Cafe, and the jazz on the soundtrack (ghosted by LA studio musicians) veers between believable 1939 German swing and improbably faithful recreations of, say, the snarling trumpets on Goodman's "Sing, Sing, Sing." Arvid doesn't hit the dance floor—he has a deformed foot, is always hobbling to catch up—but deeply digs the music.

Like a real 1930s European jazz nerd, Arvid collects rare records, leads an informal Hot Club—in emulation of France's network of jazz appreciation societies—and memorizes discographical details, rattling off the personnel on English trumpeter Teddy Foster's obscure 1936 "Harlem," though he's a year off on the date. He's jazz nerd enough to discuss the pros and cons of Dorsey's (Tommy's, from context) style on trumpet, an instrument that trombonist had played on occasion, years earlier. (Or else actor Frank

Whaley bobbled both that recording date and Dorsey's main instrument.) Peter is the more complete swing aficionado: likes the music for listening and dancing both. For Thomas, jazz is mostly just dance music—he's put off by Arvid's fussing over his precious 78s. Unlike his friends, Arvid makes his own music. He's so taken with the style of guitarist Django Reinhardt, who played brilliantly despite a fire-ravaged fretting hand, that when he solos, Arvid fingers the neck with only two fingers in imitation. He's even got a similar single-cutaway, oval-hole acoustic guitar. (Whaley's obviously not a guitarist.) His friends sometimes call him Djangoman.

Early on, Peter sees a Nazi confiscate a radio from a home being raided, and when it turns up in a local shop, he and Thomas steal it as a present for Arvid. A chase ensues—a market stall is tipped over—accompanied by Goodman's "Swingtime in the Rockies." But when Peter is apprehended, he's forced to join the Hitler Youth, *Hitlerjugend*—HJ, everyone calls it. And in solidarity, Thomas joins as well: We'll be HJ by day and swing kids by night.

The HJs are inundated with propaganda, and Thomas begins to succumb, seduced less by Nazi ideology than the perks and power. Eventually he plays the classic Hitler Youth card and informs on his father. When Thomas disses the Jews, Peter is aghast: "But Benny's Jewish!" Peter is facing a parallel challenge at home. His father was political, and the Nazis killed him around the time Hitler came to power. But now his mother is making nice with the smiling, dimpled face of the Gestapo, Herr Knopp (Kenneth Branagh, blandly mild till his final scene), not above listening to a little jazz himself, if only to be ingratiating.

Peter, like a real European collector, goes down to the docks to buy the latest records from merchant sailors who pick them up abroad. He acquires them improbably quickly. He and his friends go around singing Jimmie Lunceford's "'Tain't What You Do (It's the Way That Cha Do It)," recorded in early January 1939, singing it even before Hitler invaded Czechoslovakia in mid-March of that year.

Arvid has a girlfriend who digs the music, but he's the least virile jazz musician since Jack Haley in *Alexander's Ragtime Band*. Still, his storyline takes us deepest into jazz country. His Django worship makes sense. A European who brought his own sensibility to American songs he swung, Reinhardt was a role model for countless continental jazz musicians. But for the Nazis, a maimed jazz-playing Manouche (gypsy) was triply damnable. Arvid is stopped on the street by some HJs, and when they ask him his name he says, I'm Django Reinhardt, I'm Duke Ellington. He's knocked to the pavement, and one of his attackers, a former swing kid himself, stomps on Arvid's left hand, leaving the last two fingers especially damaged. As we clearly see (later) when he packs up his guitar for the last time, he retains independent use of those two fingers. But when he plays, post-stomping, those injured digits are folded closed and all but glued together, weirdly replicating Django's hand after it was badly burned in a 1928 fire. Arvid has a Sympathetic Django Wound—and maybe a nerve adhesion problem as in *Broken Strings*.

Arvid's breaking point comes when he's playing in a cafe with a Djangoesque string band—Reinhardt fave "Daphne," uptempo—and a polite young Luftwaffe officer digging

FIGURE 9.3 Injured Arvid (Frank Whaley) frets guitar with two fingers like his idol Django Reinhardt, in *Swing Kids*.

the music requests some (unidentified to us) German tune. Arvid spurns the request, then laces into everyone in the room for their quiet complicity with the Nazis: When you go along, or help their morale, you're feeding Hitler's death machine. Soon after, Arvid slits his wrists in the bathtub, using a shard of a shattered 78. (We see him in a tableau of Jacques-Louis David's *Death of Marat*.) The cause of Djangoman's suicide appears to be partly disgust with the Nazis, and partly being the butt of a cosmic joke: a Django imitator who ends up with a Django-like injured hand.

Arvid exits a half hour before the close, but Peter will come around to his no-compromises viewpoint. The seemingly innocuous errands he runs for the HJ turn out to be more sinister than he imagined: delivering boxes of ashes to families whose husbands had been arrested, sadistic death notices. Earlier we'd seen another HJ—a stranger who'd whistled the Ellington recognition code to Peter on the street—with an identical parcel.

Revulsed, Peter rebels, in his way: goes down to the Cafe Bismarck and dances a silent, solo dance of protest, just as *Cotton Club*'s Sandman Williams had been advised to tap out his hate for a racist handler (though Peter is no Sandman). The HJs raid the place, and in the ensuing fracas Thomas almost chokes his best friend before realizing how low he's sunk. As Peter is being shipped off to a work camp on the back of a truck, Thomas—and Peter's little brother Willi, who's just turned up—yell "Swing heil" to him, as Herr Knopp glowers. Even so, James Horner's somber, symphonic closing theme, capping a film heavy with swing classics, implies the ultimate triumph of European culture—in contrast to the Ellington number that ends *Paris Blues*.

Swing Kids doesn't note it, but Django Reinhardt passed through Hamburg in February 1939 en route to Scandinavia. During the German occupation of France—in which tens of thousands of Romani people were sent to concentration camps, and a few joined the Resistance—Django's celebrity protected him. He recorded dozens of sessions, toured France and Belgium, and stocked his pantry with black-market goods. His new tune "Nuages" became a wartime anthem. Two groups of conspicuous fans: the *zazous*—French swing kids—and members of the German military, from whom he took requests for the sentimental "Lili Marleen." In Paris, contra Arvid, a German could like swing and be a Nazi both.[7]

> ***Kansas City*** **(1996, 115 minutes; director: Robert Altman; writers: Altman, Frank Barhydt). Cast includes: Harry Belafonte (Seldom Seen), Jennifer Jason Leigh (Blondie O'Hara), Miranda Richardson (Carolyn Stilton), Michael Murphy (Henry Stilton), Dermot Mulroney (Johnny O'Hara), Albert J. Burnes (Charlie Parker), Jeff Feringa (Addie Parker), Ajia Mignon Johnson (Pearl), Jane Adams (Nettie Bolt), Geri Allen (Mary Lou Williams), Joshua Redman (Lester Young), Craig Handy (Coleman Hawkins), James Carter (Ben Webster), Kevin Mahogany (Joe Turner), Cyrus Chestnut (Bill Basie), Don Byron, Ron Carter, Tyrone Clark, Olu Dara, Jesse Davis, Curtis Fowlkes, Clark Gayton, Victor Lewis, Russell Malone, Christian McBride, David Murray, David Newman, Nicholas Payton, Mark Whitfield, James Zollar (Hey-Hey Club musicians).**
> **—In 1934 Kansas City, a white woman kidnaps a politician's wife. It's a desperate ploy to leverage the release of her own husband from the clutches of an African American gangster—one who runs a jazz club where musicians jam around the clock, as young Charlie Parker looks on.**

Before Francis Ford Coppola had signed on to direct *The Cotton Club*, Robert Altman had expressed interest, and you can see *Kansas City* as his riff on the same concept: an urban 1930s period piece with gangsters, a kidnapper who emulates a movie actor, characters based on real people, and jazz interludes. As in *Bird*, Charlie Parker is a character—albeit at age 13. Like *'Round Midnight*, it includes deliberately modernized music, improvised live on camera, and a fictionalized Lester Young. As in *Stormy Monday*, improvised music is meant to highlight political subtext.

Altman's 1975 *Nashville* had also been set and shot in and named for a music capital, a film in which (as in *Kansas City*) actors created music for their characters and Michael Murphy played a political operative against the backdrop of a big election. (A campaign truck with a loudspeaker in *Kansas City* is a straight shoutout.) But where *Nashville* was about the musicians, in *Kansas City* they're peripheral. They don't get any lines, though they play a lot of music—and during one number the horns heckle a character getting bounced from a club. The Kansas City jazz scene in the mid-1930s was explosively creative, and the film aims to catch that excitement—but as a sideshow.

Kansas City is set in March 1934. Other fictionalized historical figures include gangsters Seldom Seen and John Lazia, and Altman's grandmother Nettie Bolt (portrayed as an ineffectual do-gooder). They're folded into a story indebted to real events: the 1933 kidnapping of a city manager's daughter by amateur criminals; elections rigged by trucking in ringers to vote early and often; and the night in December 1933 when visiting tenor saxophonist Coleman Hawkins squared off against Kansas City's finest at a jam session.

Altman aimed for authenticity, shooting in KC neighborhoods and along commercial strips that looked much as they had 60 years earlier. The production renovated part of then-shuttered but grand Union Station where much of the action takes place. And it built a false-front Eighteenth Street, representing the old jazz district, although for storytelling convenience Seldom Seen's Hey-Hey Club conflates the Sunset Cafe where Joe Turner was the blues-singing bartender, the Reno Club where young Parker hung out in the balcony, and the Cherry Blossom, site of that epic December jam session.[8]

Young Charlie Parker is barely in the story, a bystander. We first encounter him at the train station, where he's just played at a political rally with the band from Lincoln High (where he was a freshman). There he befriends 14-year-old Pearl from Joplin who's come to town to have a baby but missed her contact Nettie when she got off the train. It's refreshing to see an uncomplicated Parker, pre-drugs. As shown, his mother Addie cleaned the local Western Union office at night, freeing up Charlie to go hear music till all hours, and she took in boarders at her house on Olive Street. (But movie-Addie lacks the real one's steely demeanor.)

As the story suggests, Charlie was then just getting interested in girls. Two weeks after the action in *Kansas City*, the real Addie would accept as boarders a family whose daughter Rebecca Ruffin would become Charlie's first serious girlfriend and first wife. Rebecca recalled him getting serious about the saxophone only after they started dating, but whenever he started, the horn rarely left his side. In *Kansas City* he keeps it at the ready, around his neck, as if daring himself to blow in public. In life Charlie would drag Rebecca down to the entertainment district after school to hear what was happening, just as movie-Charlie brings Pearl down to the Hey-Hey, where they plant themselves in the balcony and he soaks up the music.[9]

Altman wanted a muted look suggestive of 1930s black-and-white, to match the period locations and stabs at period snappy patter. But a 1934 feature would have wrapped up *Kansas City*'s machinations in 90 minutes. In *All Night Long* the jam-session segments give you time to digest the plot twists; in *Kansas City* music pads out a threadbare story. Low-level white crook Johnny O'Hara, who's less smart than he thinks (pulling a robbery in blackface), runs afoul of and is taken captive by ruthless black gangster Seldom Seen. Hoping to leverage his freedom, Johnny's wife Blondie—who talks tough in emulation of her screen idol Jean Harlow—kidnaps a politician's woozy laudanum-addict wife, hoping to exchange her for Johnny. Complication: the next day there's a city election—March 27, 1934—and with so much going on, Blondie's demands aren't instantly met.

Early on we see a poster for what's billed as the Hey-Hey's "Battle of Jazz": Lester Young versus Coleman Hawkins, all day and all night Monday. Thirty seconds later Seldom Seen sneeringly reads from a newspaper story describing tomorrow's election as "the actual battle for control of the city"—one, Seldom says, that'll really be decided tonight (as contending groups prepare for the balloting). So Altman sets up a parallel between musical and political contests, but fails to follow through. The political struggle is all about power, not issues. There are casual mentions of KC factions, Goats versus Rabbits, but what those groups represent is immaterial—and Altman never stoops to the kind of expository dialogue where characters tell each other what they'd already know.

That jazz battle had factional aspects too, similarly glossed over—but here the details matter. As Kansas City jam sessions go, the night Coleman Hawkins dropped by the Cherry Blossom—December 18–19, 1933—surpasses the night Jo Jones lobbed a cymbal at Charlie Parker's feet. Hawkins, originally from nearby St. Joseph, Missouri, but based in New York, was jazz's reigning tenor saxophonist, known for his vibrant cello-like sound and improvised melodies that elegantly dissected a song's passing chords. Hawkins influenced almost every other leading tenor player, including KC's Herschel Evans and Ben Webster. But local favorite Lester Young had a different approach—leaner, less imposingly loud, melodically simpler, and less tethered to the harmonies. It was sleeker, swung harder, and sounded more modern. He could swing you to death honking one repeated note.

Hawkins had been in town all week with Fletcher Henderson's band. Closing night Hawk and some confreres visited the Cherry Blossom, where a jam was in progress, and the saxophonist was hectored into fetching his horn. When he returned, the formidable locals started lining up to take a shot at the master. At 4 a.m., pianist Mary Lou Williams was awakened at home by Ben Webster. (This is mostly her version.)[10] Get dressed, he told her. We've got Hawkins on the ropes and all the pianists are worn out. When she got there, Hawkins was down to his undershirt, feeling the heat. He could hold off his disciples, but Lester was something else: he'd start out cool and slowly get hotter and hotter. Some who were there that night would swear local hero Pres got the better of New York's star. The sun was up before Hawkins scooted out of town, racing to catch up to Henderson.

That's all easily dramatizable. Charlie Parker in the balcony, explaining to Pearl who's who below—he points out Lester Young for her benefit (and ours), twice—could have laid out the back story in a few sentences. The music would tell the rest. But Altman's quest for authenticity stalled at the jazz plot—or rather, he chose one form of authenticity over another. Instead of recreating 1930s KC jazz, music supervisor Hal Willner assembled nearly two dozen mostly younger (post-Marsalis) New York players to improvise as the Hey-Hey Club band. (Only a few musicians, such as singer Kevin Mahogany as Joe Turner, were from Kansas City. But then Pres and Basie didn't come from there either.) Some of that music is heard behind dialogue; Seldom Seen (Harry Belafonte) has a cocaine habit, and like Blondie rarely shuts up. Belafonte made up the bulk of his character's monologues; he's another improvising soloist.

Better, Altman and Willner reasoned, to feature genuine spontaneous improvising rather than a simulation. Altman said he just wanted to give an impression of period music. But which approach makes for a better jazz story?

Here is *Kansas City*'s blander version of that fabled jam session. In the first place, as noted it's an advertised event, with Hawkins (and Williams and Webster) slated to appear. Unlike the real thing, or most lockhorn battles, it starts during the day (according to the poster anyway: Hawkins turns up by 9:30 p.m. or so, but the combat doesn't get hot till 4 a.m.). At the Hey-Hey as at some real KC clubs, there's live music around the clock, with players coming and going. Nothing clues us that Hawkins is from out of town, except that he's around less. He is played by the fine tenor saxophonist Craig Handy, and Young by Joshua Redman, who's light-skinned like Pres and sports his trademark porkpie hat. But neither Handy nor Redman makes much of an effort to inhabit his character's style. Handy has a big sound, somewhat like Hawkins. But Redman honks and plays some repeated notes, as if vaguely aware that Young went in for those, but unsure what he actually sounded like. Redman's impression of his style is hectic, and he repeats his ideas—the antithesis of Young's laidback creativity. You get no sense of Young's economy, or the fleet rhythm and relaxation that would inspire Parker. Nor do we get a glimmer of different musical sensibilities clashing, of a new order uprooting an old one. (As Morris Holbrook observes, Handy and Redman sound more like each other than the musicians they portray.)[11]

As the contest grows fierce, Hawkins takes off his suit jacket and loosens two buttons on his vest—that's as close as he gets to his undershirt. After trading phrases awhile, he and Young wind down by mutual agreement, call it a draw, and shake hands as equals. Come morning Hawkins is still around, now one of the gang. He's even taught them his tricky Henderson vehicle "Queer Notions," heard behind dialogue. We have observed before that cutting contests are usually about mutual respect, not animosity. But that night in 1933 the home team was out for blood—as serious as *Kansas City*'s gangsters on that score.

In the 1980s and into the 1990s, some jazz writers stressed how deeply the Young Lions and their ilk revered the masters, but this staged display evinces a shallow understanding. *Kansas City* is similarly careless with the city's musical folkways. As Herbie Hancock had demonstrated arranging music for *'Round Midnight*, one could suggest period style without stifling contemporary players. It would have been easy to convey an impression of classic 1930s Kansas City style without strictly recreating it.

Musicians there loved to play the blues, and to work up propulsive riffs behind solos. While a brass musician improvised, one saxophonist might outline a backing riff, which the other reeds would imitate and harmonize, booting the soloist along. Similarly, brass would back a saxophone. And sometimes a band's massed reed, trumpet, and trombone sections would bat written or improvised phrases back and forth. In the Introduction, we'd noted parallels between cinematic cross-cuts and the dialogue of sections in a swing band. Here was a chance to fuse them.

Seasoned conductor of improvisers Butch Morris was on hand to spontaneously structure loose versions of period music, but it was quickly determined that written arrangements would be needed. (The musicians kept the sheet music out of sight.) They might have given Morris more of a shot. Grabbing a phrase someone improvised and then spontaneously orchestrating it, by cueing in various players—that was Butch 101. It would have been easy for him to set up riffs and crossriffs, while leaving the soloists plenty of elbow room—a truer impression of Kansas City style. When musicians crowd the stage in *Kansas City*, they aren't grouped by instrument but mixed willy-nilly; they couldn't organize by section if they'd wanted to. Altman really gives the game away under the closing credits. As Seldom Seen counts his money and young Bird snoozes upstairs, a combo with two soloing basses (Ron Carter and Christian McBride) plays a blatantly anachronistic version of Ellington's "Solitude," a lifelong Altman favorite. It abandons all pretense that the music represents the 1930s.

At the Hey-Hey the band plays period standards ("Indiana," "I Surrender Dear," "Lullaby of the Leaves") alongside vintage KC material ("Moten Swing," Young's "Tickle Toe," Basie's "Blues in the Dark"). Improbably, that tenor battle is fought on "Yeah Man" from Fletcher Henderson's book, the kind of complex arrangement Kansas Citians generally eschewed. Local players were not always strong readers, and would have been unlikely to master that difficult chart, assuming they'd obtained a copy. (Henderson would share some arrangements with Basie after the latter left town, years in the future.) Hawkins would not have brought charts to a jam session.

The contemporary musicians show varying degrees of commitment to historical style. Alto elder David Fathead Newman brings some Southwestern blues sense. Drummer Victor Lewis swings as himself, not Jo Jones. Mark Whitfield strums like Count Basie's signature guitarist Freddie Green—but Green first crossed paths with Basie three years later, in New York. Pianist Cyrus Chestnut, as Basie, doesn't try to replicate his trademark economy.

The only musician to really commit to character is pianist Geri Allen as Mary Lou Williams. Allen was a longtime student of her music, had lived in her old Pittsburgh

FIGURE 9.4 Geri Allen as Mary Lou Williams in *Kansas City*, with Mark Whitfield (guitar).

neighborhood, and knew some of her surviving family. She captures the rollicking spirit of Williams's style. James Carter, playing tenorist Ben Webster (according to publicity, not internal evidence; he doubles on baritone, unlike Webster), is a student of early jazz saxophone techniques with a big sound inspired by the old masters. He exudes the right kind of confidence on the horn, and would have made a more credible Hawkins.

Kansas City posits a double standard for historical accuracy. There's as close as we can get to the real thing, for the look of it, the political background, and the rhythms of period speech—and then there's close enough, for the jazz. Thought experiment: picture *The Cotton Club*, dispensing with Ellington's music, substituting a vague impression of same. There'd be no jazz appeal left.

Much as *Giant Steps* jazzifies the After School Special, Gary Winick's **The Tic Code** (copyright 1997, released in 2000) plays like a 1980s disease-of-the-week TV movie: A West Village piano prodigy with Tourette's syndrome (Chris Marquette's Miles—the youngest jazz hero since the 1940s) and his shy, divorced jazz-fan mom Laura (Polly Draper) are both drawn to tenor saxophonist Tyrone Pike (Gregory Hines), who also has Tourette's. Tyrone is playing down at the neighborhood bar where Miles practices after school: the famed Village Vanguard, its interior simulated by a red-curtained set. (Draper wrote the script; her husband Michael Wolff, who has Tourette's, ghosted Miles's precocious jazz piano.)

Conscientious parent Laura provides exposition along the way: "He's got a few less inhibitors in his brain, so everything comes out a little freer." As we see, Tourette's may manifest itself more through mild physical tics than stereotypical uninhibited utterances. An oft-cited relationship between the syndrome and creativity is imperfectly understood, and *The Tic Code* resists easy or naive answers. As in life, questions are left hanging. Is Miles's talent (or his habit of mimicking people) a function of Tourette's, or just part of who he is as a bright imaginative person? (Determinism or free will? The film's ambient sound is processed through a flanger for a whooshing effect, as if Tourette's folks hear the world differently.)

Meanwhile, there's a bully at school, and Miles's absentee dad, an image-conscious successful pianist, keeps backing away. Worse, school music teacher Miss Gimpole (Carol Kane) wants Miles back on stabilizing meds that deaden his creativity—and she wants him to play with fingers properly curved, not flat like his idol Thelonious Monk's. (Miles does indeed play flat-fingered, and studies Monk concert footage. But he sounds more conventional than his idol—like a later pianist in *La La Land*.) Miss Gimpole insists Miles needs to adopt proper technique like Rubinstein and Horowitz, not knowing that Horowitz played flat-fingered too. Crisis point: Miles's audible tics disrupt a recording session, when Tyrone has him sit beside him in the studio. Also, Tyrone worries Laura is just a Tourette's groupie. When she speculates that Monk might have had it too, he thinks she's gone too far.

On what appears to be a (rare) multiweek stand at the Vanguard, Tyrone on tenor tempers his 1960s-spiritual Coltrane strain with a raspier, late-night-TV edge. (He's ghosted by Alex Foster.) Tyrone blows one brief shrieky bit that may suggest an uninhibited utterance—inspiring instant applause and catching Laura's ear—but that possibility goes unexplored. The takeaway: as Tyrone tells Miles—we liberally paraphrase—creative types are often eccentric, and jazz is one field that can accommodate quirky individuals like us. He'll be a great stepdad.

> **Sweet and Lowdown (1999; 95 minutes; director/writer: Woody Allen). Cast includes: Sean Penn (Emmet Ray), Samantha Morton (Hattie), Uma Thurman (Blanche Williams), Molly Price (Ann), James Urbaniak (Harry), Anthony LaPaglia (Al Torrio), Michael Sprague (Django Reinhardt), Daniel Okrent (A.J. Pickman), Sally Placksin (Sally Jillian), Ben Duncan, Nat Hentoff, Woody Allen (themselves).**
> **—In the 1930s, Emmet Ray can't stop boasting about his greatness as a guitarist, but something nags at him: Django Reinhardt is even better.**

Odd that in the 1990s, jazz movies would present two 1930s guitarists with Django Reinhardt complexes. Although a dixieland clarinetist himself, Woody Allen had been directing for more than 30 years before making his jazz film *Sweet and Lowdown*. He had proposed making *The Jazz Baby*—a darker version of the same story using the same (his term) "anecdotal hearsay" approach—after his gag-rich breakout film *Take the Money and Run* (1969). But his producers at United Artists had wanted lighter fare.[12]

Given the three decades Allen had to flesh out the story, *Sweet and Lowdown* feels remarkably thin, one or two jokes played out for an hour and a half. It carries itself like a comedy but yields meager laughs. Film chronicler Richard Schickel (among others) dismisses it for making the trite point that great artists can be difficult—a reading that gives its protagonist too much credit and the movie not enough.[13]

Emmet Ray, a title card tells us, is a "little known guitarist who flourished briefly in the 1930s" and cut six sides for RCA Victor: "Ray was considered second only to the great Django Reinhardt and is best known by jazz aficionados." At the top, director Allen himself—one of several talking heads who pop up to inch the story along—attests to the quality of his playing, while allowing Ray was "flamboyant . . . boorish and obnoxious."

As played by Sean Penn, he is definitely all that. Next to him, *New York, New York's* Jimmy Doyle is a charmer. Ray's ego is big even by artist standards. He'll tell you he's one of the world's top two guitarists and top six poker players, and among the country's top two or three pool sharks. Various women are drawn to him if only because he's good-looking and a sharp dresser, but he easily casts them aside: "I can't have my life cluttered. I'm an artist. A truly great artist. I need to be free."

He is not as great as he (or Allen) swears he is, but this is a movie filled with unreliable testimony, staged and filmed as if it's all true. *Sweet and Lowdown* is less about the life of a jazz musician than the tall stories that may sprout up around one. None of the talking-head witnesses had known Emmet, and they tend to hedge the stories the film dramatizes: Now I don't know if this is true, but here's the way I heard it. Commentator

Allen drives the point home toward the end of the film, when he presents three widely different versions of (or improvisations on) the same story, involving Emmet hiding in the back of a gangster's car. One of those versions is attributed to jazz gadfly, guitarist, and memoirist Eddie Condon, "a big embellisher himself," Allen points out. As disc jockey/commenter Ben Duncan allows, "You never know what to believe."

The jazz lore of the 1930s and 1940s is rife with tales of colorful (often white) musicians, tales encrusted with dubious anecdotage. Joe Venuti stories, say, can be hilarious—pushing a friend's piano out a window, to hear what key it crashed in—but if a quarter of them are true, it must have been tiresome to know Joe Venuti sometimes. Emmet Ray's a bit like that: a colorful pain in the ass.

One of the film's testifying experts is noted jazz chronicler Nat Hentoff, not normally given to the kind of gossipy commentary he provides here. But Hentoff did co-edit the classic 1955 book *Hear Me Talkin' to Ya*, which arranges excerpts drawn from myriad musician interviews into a coherent narrative of the music's development—jazz history as oral history. In some period musician's oral history, Emmet Ray might sound like a hoot. It might read something like this:

"Emmet? What a character. He'd come to the gig either late, drunk, or not at all. His idea of fun was going to the dump to shoot rats, or watching trains down at the freight yard, schmoozing with the hoboes. He fancied himself a pimp for a minute, had a couple of girls working for him, and was a bit of a kleptomaniac—you learned to hide the good ashtrays when he came over. You couldn't feed his ego enough, like it had a tapeworm. Once, driving through the sticks, he stopped to compete in an amateur talent contest—you know, where the stiff competition is a guy playing spoons. They liked the way he played 'Twelfth Street Rag,' but of course they ran him off. He took up with a mute laundry woman name of Hattie he met when he was playing out at the Lakeside Hotel on Lake Hopatcong in Jersey. That gig ended when he went to a weed and opium party after hours, and woke up four days later in Stroudsburg, PA. He took a taxi home and tried to borrow $900 from the hotel owner for cab fare. And Stroudsburg's, like, 35 miles away![14]

"He took Hattie out to Hollywood where he was making a short, backing blues singer Helen Minton, and Hattie got cast as the kid sister in *The Tomb of the Mummy*, doing a silent three-scene bit. That took the attention off him, which he hated. After a year he ran out on her in the middle of the night, then married some Chicago writer who found him fascinating, always wondering what made him tick. That lasted about five minutes—she took up with a gangster, asking him all the same what-goes-through-your-mind questions. So Emmet looked up Hattie next time he was in Jersey, which took brass, even for him, but by then she was married with a kid. I heard he smashed his guitar one night when a girl he took out didn't swoon over his playing, and after that he sorta disappeared.

"To be fair, much as he'd go on about how great he was, Emmet was always quick to admit Django Reinhardt was better. It was like a sore spot he couldn't stop scratching. But he was petrified of running into him. Once for a joke his manager told him that Django was sitting out front. Instead of going on, Emmet skipped out over the rooftops, and fell through one into the middle of a counterfeiting operation—criminal masterminds printing $1 bills. The crooks split in a panic, and Emmet used their funny money to buy a car."

That's more or less the story *Sweet and Lowdown* tells. The action surrounds what we're told is the height of the Depression. That would make it 1933, before the start of the swing era; but it must be later, because no one in America had heard of Django then. He broke out in 1934, when he started recording with the Quintet of the Hot Club of France and jammed in Paris with Louis Armstrong.

Emmet says he'd heard Django in Europe and has been in awe of him ever since, and he does listen to his idol's records for hours with rapt admiration. But while Ray might have encountered Reinhardt when he was still unknown, in *Sweet and Lowdown* Django's name comes up all the time, and even his face is familiar. (Emmet's manager pranks him as just described after spotting a Django lookalike in the audience.) According to talking-head Woody's recollection of what Eddie Condon once said—a model of shady sourcing—Emmet and Django crossed paths again, when Django was touring in the States, later in the 1930s. (Emmet, as ever, faints at the sight of him.) But Reinhardt's only trip to the US commenced in 1946.

Django's presence hangs even more heavily than over *Swing Kids*. *Sweet and Lowdown*'s opening theme is the Hot Club quintet's 1937 "When Day Is Done," a crash course in Reinhardt virtues: the cascading runs, the stinging vibrato, the way he picks steel strings with the power of a nail gun. It puts his percussive sound in our ears. Nothing we'll hear Emmet play will stack up to it. And yet the on-screen jazz experts tell us almost as often as Emmet does what a great guitarist he is. Hollywood-style, this white musician has his hipness validated by approving African Americans. In Chicago, black players come by after their own gig for Emmet's midnight show. They take him to a South Side apartment where they jam into the wee hours and where he's welcome back any time—an open invitation he takes up.

Emmet is ghosted by jazz guitar whiz Howard Alden, who doesn't push the Django comparisons too far in creating Ray's sound. "Our styles are just different," Emmet says, and Alden takes the character at his word. Still, Django's aesthetic permeates the Emmet Ray Hot Quintet—even the name is a tell—in which he solos over the chunky sound of a furiously strummed rhythm guitar. He even plays a single-cutaway oval-hole guitar similar to Django's. (Penn doesn't work hard at faking the fingering, and the editors make little effort to sync his sidelining to the prerecorded music.)

"I can make my guitar sound like a train," Emmet says, and we know it's true, having already heard him do it, mimicking the Hot Club quintet's (1937) "Mystery Pacific," where guitar accelerates up to speed like a steam engine. (Emmet makes it his intro to "Limehouse Blues.") "Once you record, everybody can copy your stuff," he laments at one point, explaining why he hasn't yet recorded. "They steal your ideas. Why would I wanna make something beautiful, just to have some jerk copy it?" No wonder he cries whenever listening to Django; down deep he knows he's that jerk. (Even the film's title is recycled, from 1944's *Sweet and Low-Down*.)

The film's running gag is that Emmet compulsively qualifies his boasting: "On guitar, nobody can touch me—except this gypsy in France. But mostly I'm untouchable." However, meeting Blanche, the writer he'll marry, he claims "Eubie Blake thinks I'm the best guitar player in the whole world, bar none—and he knows Django," two doubtful claims. Blake's only opportunity to meet Django by then would have been while passing through Paris in 1926, when Reinhardt was 16. Emmet is just making stuff up.

Even his women point out something's missing from his music. Blanche, trying to analyze him, says, if you let your feelings out, you might play better. You don't sound like Django because "his feelings are richer." This gets to the nub of Emmet's insecurity: he's so emotionally stunted, true greatness is beyond him. In an era when musicians prize originality, Emmet's derivative art dooms him to Django comparisons, but Reinhardt's flamboyant playing carries a greater emotional charge than Ray can muster. "I let my feelings come out in my music," he claims, half-believing it. But later he's more candid: "You let your insides get to you, and you're finished." Temporary girlfriend Ann: "You keep your feelings all locked up, and you can't feel nothing for anybody else." Emmet: "You say that like it's a bad thing."

Significantly, the Emmet Ray music that most moves a listener has least to do with Django. After he hooks up with mute but eager Hattie (Samantha Morton, channeling Harpo Marx), he plays her his set piece, a delicate solo version of 1919's fizzy "I'm Forever Blowing Bubbles" (faint callback to the opening of *Blues in the Night*). We witness her

FIGURE 9.5 Hattie (Samantha Morton) hears Emmet (Sean Penn) get out from under Django's influence in *Sweet and Lowdown*.

reaction, unseen by him: she's transfixed, then aroused. When they're together he talks nonstop to fill her silences. But it's his music that really speaks to her.

Presumably, Woody Allen knew Reinhardt didn't visit the States in the 1930s, having researched the guitarist's life enough to riff on one obscure incident. Appearing with a circus in 1942, Django had plotted a grand entrance, lowered onto stage on a giant luminous star, but in the end he chickened out. In Allen's comic variation, for the same purpose Emmet commissions a large decorated crescent moon, affixed with a chair (thereby providing a memorable image for the film's poster). But his big entrance is a fiasco. As he's being lowered into view, Emmet hangs on for dear life; after he awkwardly dismounts, the contraption falls from above, almost clobbering the band. Were this particular Emmet Ray story true, for once Django would have ripped him off. More likely it's one more yarn that got twisted around in the retelling—one more embellishment of the Ray legend.

Sweet and Lowdown gets the look right—the cars, clothes, movie posters, and myriad other period details. Autumnal colors heighten the bygone air. Allen says musicians have told him it feels authentic: "Guys would get in their cars and go across country and have no money and play a job."[15] But it takes place in a curiously underpopulated 1930s jazz scene where Django is almost the only famous musician ever mentioned. No one brings up Eddie Lang, who also set a clear precedent for Emmet's style. The only indication the swing era existed comes late in the film, when rhythm guitarist Harry makes the throwaway observation that the music business has picked up lately. But Emmet has been working right along.

"I'm Forever Blowing Bubbles" is one of those six tunes that Ray recorded for Victor, and one of a few tunes heard in full—another being "I'll See You in My Dreams," with its on-the-nose title, heard under the closing credits (followed by "Shine," in an Emmet-y arrangement). We also hear, at a studio session, the ending of his ballad "Unfaithful Woman," written in response to Blanche's infidelity—though Emmet wasn't heartbroken, just miffed she preferred someone else.

In the end, suffering over the realization he should've stayed with Hattie, Emmet Ray achieves greatness and finally becomes Django's equal—or so avers (fictional) guitar expert A.J. Pickman. But Ray's very good music is never Django-great. Pickman's endorsement of Ray's transcendence-through-pain is too pat, too easy: jazz-aficionado boasting, telling you someone obscure is the greatest. Ray's subsequent disappearance suggests he didn't have what it takes to go the distance.

Postscript: "If somebody would give me $80 million, $100 million," Woody Allen said in 2006, "I could do a great American jazz movie." It'd be about the early days, focusing on young Sidney Bechet, the great clarinetist and Allen hero. "I feel I could re-create New Orleans and the birth of jazz better than anybody else because I think I'm the only film director around who has that particular passion and knowledge."[16] It sounds a bit like one version of the jazz segment Orson Welles had in mind for *It's All True*.

/// 10 /// THE JAZZ MUSICIAN (AND FAN) AS CHARACTER 1959–2016

In the 1990s, unreliable narrators didn't turn up only in *Bix* and *Sweet and Lowdown*. As the music's early years retreated into the distant past, the testimony of fictional witnesses got wilder and wilder. Jazz's early days became one more colorful storyteller's backdrop, like the Old West. Why limit jazz stories to the plausible? That far back, who's to say what really happened?

A 1993 episode of TV's **The Young Indiana Jones Chronicles**, "Mystery of the Blues" (from a story by George Lucas), presents a yarn told by the adult Indy in 1950 to pass the time in a snowbound cabin. (It's the only episode where Harrison Ford appears, in the opening and closing segments.) In Chicago circa 1920, clarinetist Sidney Bechet (Jeffrey Wright) and friends educate college-man Jones (Sean Patrick Flanery) in jazz rhythm and improvisation, its Caribbean and gospel influences, the value of obsessive practicing, the deep emotional resonance of the blues, and some of the realities of quotidian racism and segregation. It's self-consciously educational, even if the story's total bunk. Along the way Indiana encounters King Oliver (Keith David) and Louie Armstrong (trumpeter Byron Stripling, mimicking Pops), investigates a murder, introduces Al Capone to Elliott Ness and Ernest Hemingway, and delivers the quintessential jazz-movie line: "Hi, Bix." Yes, Beiderbecke also turns up, to jam with Sidney on the blues. (The bunk: the real Bechet had left Chicago for England in 1919, before Louis or not-so-bluesy Bix arrived.) Sidney also lends Indy his newly acquired soprano sax, on which—after heavy woodshedding—Jones anticipates or perhaps influences Bechet's own soprano stylings soon to come. (Young Sidney's clarinet lacks his signature tremolo.) That would make Indiana Jones even more of a hero, but then he's the one telling it. The whole series is a name-dropping tall tale.

The title of a 1998 Italian film in English, Giuseppe Tornatore's **The Legend of 1900**, tips us to take nothing literally. In its frame story, trumpeter Max (Pruitt Taylor Vince) tells us about telling others—a music-shop owner, mostly—of his friend 1900 (Tim Roth), named for the (approximate) year of his birth. A foundling raised on a transatlantic ocean liner, and a natural piano improviser, the adult 1900 plays not his own feelings, but those of passengers he observes aboard ship. Having grown up alongside the Jazz Age, 1900 breaks into hot stride piano—streamlined late-phase ragtime—on sedate dance tunes with the ship's orchestra. He stays au courant without ever going ashore. The classic stay-at-home jazz talent, 1900 resists Max's advice to get off in New York and get noticed.

Yet word of his prowess spreads, until formidable pianist and champion jazz braggart Jelly Roll Morton books himself passage to challenge 1900 to a cutting contest. (Inspired casting: Clarence Williams III, who was raised by his grandparents, bluesy singer Eva Taylor and the original Clarence Williams, a New Orleans composer and Morton's friend.) Williams gets Jelly's iron self-confidence but the script affords him only one sustained outburst of trademark volubility.

Their battle before a betting crowd is the film's centerpiece. Jelly Roll does his best to intimidate 1900 like a proper piano gladiator, and serves up some of his showpieces, which also mark jazz's emergence from ragtime: "Big Fat Ham," "The Crave," "Finger Buster." In his innings, 1900 hangs back out of respect, until Jelly's arrogance ticks him off. What follows—à la *Sweet and Lowdown*—plays like a literal enactment of an oft-told tale: 1900 came back with everything he had. He played like he had five hands (conveyed through a multiple-exposure effect) till the piano strings got so hot he lit a cigarette off them. And then he stuck it in a stunned Jelly's mouth and told him to go smoke it. In truth, Morton's classics (very well played), are far better music than 1900's frantic bumblebee churning. How we know it's a fable: Jelly accepts defeat without a word.

On one level, writer/director Tom Hanks's 1996 ***That Thing You Do!***—about a short-lived mid-sixties rock band, The Wonders—is about how a jazz musician saves the day. Two jazz musicians, actually. Protagonist Guy "Skitch" Patterson (Tom Everett Scott) is an aspiring jazz drummer, a cool cat for Erie, Pennsylvania, despite working at the family appliance store. A veteran, Guy drives a sporty Karmann-Ghia convertible, wears sports jackets, and plays drums along with his fave jazz album: Los Angeles pianist Del Paxton's

FIGURE 10.1 Piano gladiator Jelly Roll Morton (Clarence Williams III) sizes up the competition (Tim Roth) in *The Legend of 1900*.

Time to Blow, on Capitol, the LA label with a select jazz roster. Practicing, Guy minds his fancy fills more than his timekeeping. But his school-band training gives him the skills he needs when he's drafted into an amateur rock group on short notice. On his first gig, he spontaneously boosts the tempo and lays a backbeat on leader Jimmy's sappy ballad "That Thing You Do," and transforms it from blah to boffo.

The Wonders record the tune, acquire management, have a fluke hit, and head out on a national package tour, playing state fairs. (We follow the process step by step; it's all surprisingly watchable.) On the road, the band gets believably tighter, playing their hit over and over. The bass player stops using a pick and starts singing harmony (and starts dating a soul singer from the tour's doo-wop trio, an interracial subplot sliced away in the editing).

The Wonders wind up in Los Angeles, where they're slated to make an album. During a band radio interview, Guy namechecks his inspirations: Del Paxton, any Stan Getz on Verve, the Bill Evans trio, trumpeter Kenny Dorham, and Chicago's less famous Ira Sullivan and John Young, as if Guy had had a teacher from there. It's a perfectly respectable list. In the 1960s (unlike 1950s movies) it was fashionable for rockers to dig jazz; the liner notes to the Byrds' first album, *Mr. Tambourine Man*, spoke of drummer Mike Clark's devotion to Elvin Jones and Joe Morello (not that you could hear it). Curiously, there are no drummers on Guy's list—not even Del's old one, who'd played on that package tour. At a jazz club, Guy meets Del himself, and amuses/embarrasses/bores his idol with tipsy hero worship. Paxton (Bill Cobbs) tells him to keep cool when success gets crazy. "And watch your money, you'll land on your feet."

Good advice. The Wonders' bassist drops out, and Jimmy—who keeps his eye on the music, undistracted by the glitz—balks at the label's creative demands. Jimmy's mostly a jerk, but you can't blame the songwriter for wanting to show what he can do—after all his one hit got (spontaneously) rearranged by a drummer. In an instant, the Wonders break up. Burning off already-booked studio time, Guy plays solo drums on a house kit: his rock beat, with something broader and deeper going on under it. Del Paxton happens by from a session down the hall. "Hey you're good," Del says. "You swing." Del asks if he wants to jam, and they improvise a breezy duet over a medium groove. The pianist tells him he has the chops to make it in LA, and Guy resolves to give it a try.

Once more, a white musician gets a hip black listener's stamp of approval. Paxton's life-changing pep talk might make Del the film's Magic Negro, were it not for the hotel doorman who puts Guy together with Jimmy's jilted girlfriend and ends the movie looking knowingly at the viewer. In the after-titles, we learn that Guy and wife, after his years in LA studios, founded a jazz conservatory on Bainbridge Island across the water from Seattle (echoing Bud Shank, who retired from the studios to Port Townsend). We also find out Jimmy had made a good call, junking the one-hit Wonders. He came back with a more successful band, and learned to protect his material by becoming a producer.

There's a subset of films we haven't noted since *The Strip*, in which jazz stars appear in venues unworthy of their level of success. Sometimes that's because filmmakers want to give musicians the exposure, using any flimsy excuse to put them on-screen. Storywise, though, it raises questions. Why is swing sensation Gene Krupa shilling for a seedy Atlantic City boardwalk wax museum in 1939's *Rhythm Romance* (originally titled *Some Like It Hot*) when his band had been a sensation at the city's Steel Pier only the year before? Why, in the 1943 Sonja Henie vehicle *Wintertime*, has Woody Herman committed his orchestra to playing the whole season at a failing Quebec ski resort? How, in *I Want to Live!*, does a seedy Frisco hookers-hotel bar afford to book a four-horn Gerry Mulligan septet that most patrons ignore? (Mulligan may have had a personal reason for appearing in that 1958 woman-on-death-row picture: the judge who'd sentenced the real Barbara Gordon had also sent him up on a drug charge.)[1]

In 1959, Louis Armstrong passed briefly through Charles Haas's low-budget **The Beat Generation**. Under the credits, Louis (with the All-Stars) performs in a drab coffeehouse, to a crowd that's blasé about everything, including the fact that he's there at all, let alone singing a lyric that insults them to their faces: "You think you're really with it / But you're missing all the best"—presaging a sordid crime story to come, in which the beats come off as oblivious nitwits. But why, in the world of the movie, would good-natured Pops maliciously bait these losers at what amounts to his own expense, when he could be making better bread virtually anywhere else? Even more puzzling, Pops's philippic wins him a return engagement, where he gets a little more attention and a smidgen of dialogue. Making the film was a gig of opportunity for the real Armstrong; he was already in Hollywood to shoot *The Five Pennies*. (In 1960's *The Subterraneans*, Carmen McRae was more gracious to San Francisco's beats, singing the procountercultural "Coffee Time.")

Duke Ellington and Billy Strayhorn scored Otto Preminger's 1959 courtroom drama **Anatomy of a Murder**, shot and set in Michigan's Upper Peninsula. Duke makes a cameo appearance, playing piano in a quintet at a rural roadhouse. Jimmy Stewart's character sits in: four hands at the keyboard, as if Duke needed help. (Extenuating circumstances: when Stewart muses on piano at home, he sounds like Billy Strayhorn, who ghosted him.) But Ellington's not Ellington here, he's "Pie Eye." In that role he gets a couple of (trivial) lines for once—"Hey, you're not splittin' the scene, man? I mean you're not cuttin' out?"—then gives Stewart a leering "Okay!" as he leaves with tarty Lee Remick.

Another jazz fish out of water turns up in John Flynn's hardboiled **The Outfit** (1973). On the trail of mobsters who want him dead, Robert Duvall follows a tip to a dimly lit bar on a commercial strip in Bakersfield, in California's Central Valley. It's mid-day, but there's entertainment. Out of focus, deep in the background as Duvall talks to the barkeep, jazz singer Anita O'Day performs "I Concentrate on You." She's not credited, though her voice is easy to identify. But is this singer supposed to be O'Day? She pretends to accompany herself on piano, which the real Anita didn't do.

That said, the filmography in her autobio *High Times, Hard Times* says she plays herself. The same book tells us that around the time she made *The Outfit*, O'Day was living in a three-dollar hotel room with no phone, not that anyone was trying to call. So that Bakersfield gig makes economic sense for a singer in a slump (she'd soon bounce back), if not for the bar. Only a handful of people are listening, outnumbered by empty chairs. But then Bakersfield is outlaw-country territory.

FIGURE 10.2 Just another roadhouse pianist: Duke Ellington as Pie Eye in *Anatomy of a Murder*, with James Stewart and Lee Remick.

In Steven Spielberg's ***The Terminal*** (2004), one more jazz musician appears in a venue beneath his station. The plot features the rare jazz MacGuffin—the thing the hero's chasing whose identity is immaterial to the main plot. Tom Hanks is Viktor Navorski, an East European tourist caught in Kafkaesque limbo at New York's JFK airport; a coup back in Krakhozhia has left him without a valid visa or way home. He winds up living in the international terminal for many months, wanting only to reach midtown Manhattan on some mysterious mission. It turns out that Viktor's quest is to get an autograph that eluded his late jazz-fan father: tenor saxophonist Benny Golson's. (Dad had been checking off the many jazz stars in Art Kane's famous 1958 Harlem-stoop photo for *Esquire*; luckily for Viktor, Golson was among the few still alive.)

Just before Viktor is abruptly sent home, with help from his airport friends he slips away to Lexington and Thirtieth in midtown. There, improbably, esteemed composer and saxophonist Golson has been stuck in a parallel limbo, working the same Ramada Inn happy-hour gig he had when Viktor landed nearly a year ago. The two chat briefly— Benny has the business sense to put off signing that autograph till after he plays, ensuring at least one butt in a seat. But we hear him perform "Killer Joe" for less than a minute, and we never see him sign. (A silver-tongued speaker in real life—rather like Ellington in that regard—Golson hardly says a thing.) *The Terminal* pays lip service to jazz without investing anything in it. The tipoff: a nonjazz score, by Spielberg regular (and one-time jazz pianist) John Williams. The mysterious Planter's nuts can Viktor carries around turns out to be full of Dad's jazz autographs, but the movie can't even muster a Dizzy Gillespie "Salt Peanuts" joke. In fairness, the real Golson, initially skeptical, loved the experience. His lounge gig after all was in a Spielberg movie.[2]

Another kind of lounge gig—singing the Great American Songbook with a jazzy tinge—is celebrated in Giancarlo Tallarico's slow ballad *Moonlight Serenade*, made in 2005 but released (on DVD) in 2009. In a geographically vague New York (played by Los Angeles) where apartment-building security doors are invariably left unlocked, Wall Street wolf Nate (Alec Newman) relaxes after hours at organist Frank D's jazz club before going back to his apartment to sing wistful standards at the piano, with the window wide open—thanks, neighbor. One night, a woman in the shadows below sweetly sings along. But who can this Cinderella be? She's Chloe (Amy Adams), Frank D's hatcheck whom Nate immediately offends. But then she needs a pianist for that after-hours showcase she's booked across town, so Frank can hear her sing. Frank D (jazz organist Joey DeFrancesco, contributing his own bluesy interludes) might more conveniently have her sit in at his own club, but *Moonlight Serenade* loves a gratuitous complication. For Nate music is a hobby. He's more interested in Chloe than performing in public, but she has an off-and-on boyfriend who's trying to kick drugs. After sharing a heartfelt "You Go to My Head" on the piano bench, the songbirds almost kiss, but she pulls back. It's that kind of picture.

The actors do their own adequate singing (though Adams's Minnie Mouse high notes raise suspicions of a stunt double), phrasing with mildly jazzy rhythmic displacements. When Nate plays at home, he's sometimes joined by a phantom bassist and drummer he can apparently hear, as he phrases his piano around their accents. (He's ghosted by DeFrancesco.) We are meant to see how the lyrics Chloe and Nate sing—"When I Fall in Love," "Love Walked In," "Taking a Chance on Love"—mirror their complex emotions; that's how they imbue those evergreens with feeling. Thus she shows up at his pad, in the wee hours, to request "In the Wee Small Hours of the Morning." But later they just start singing "Fool That I Am" to themselves, in a crosstown boy-girl duet, as in a conventional musical. Even Nate's B-plot assistant (Harriet Sansom Harris) sings "Lover Man (Oh Where Can You Be)" while wandering around the office, after missing her client-crush in the kitchenette. Chloe's showcase is billed as "A Night of Mercer," but no Johnny Mercer songs are heard. Nor is "Moonlight Serenade."

We will skip all the reversals that get us to the last scene, after Nate has left his job rather than compromise newfound principles and Frank D has booked him into the club for one night only. Chloe, who's been AWOL for weeks, turns up, and steps on stage—as someone hastily brings her a microphone—to join Nate on "You Brought a New Kind of Love to Me." Then she goes to the piano bench where they confess their feelings for each other, inches from his live vocal mic, oversharing with the audience: a pee-wee version of the New York reconciliation ending where a concert reunites lovers.

Joel and Ethan Coen's 2014 *Inside Llewyn Davis* follows a struggling early 1960s folk singer about to be eclipsed by Bob Dylan. Halfway through, there's a long, nastily comic sequence in which Davis (Oscar Isaac) shares a snowy ride from New York to Chicago with obnoxious-when-he's-awake junkie jazzman Roland Turner (John Goodman) and his sullen driver. Turner's one of the more vivid jazz musicians to pass through a nonjazz movie, and one of the meanest. His orotund voice and precise diction contrast with Llewyn's proletarian mumble. These two represent the gap between the artistic pretensions of jazz (unheard in the film) and folk music's unpretentious humility. Turner is all about the snotty putdown. When he learns what Llewyn plays: "Folk songs. I thought you said you were a musician." Davis defends his honor (and pushes back) by picking and singing one of his more ragtimey guitar tunes in the car. Turner is unpersuaded: "In jazz, you know, we play all the notes, 12 notes in the scale, dipshit. Not three chords on a ook-a-lele." He threatens Llewyn with a Santería curse he claims he'd learned in New Orleans from Chano Pozo—the celebrated Cuban percussionist who spoke little English, and who in his two years in the States almost certainly never set foot in Louisiana. But Davis gets a muted last laugh, and maybe earns that curse. When their shifty driver gets hauled off by the cops along an Indiana highway, Davis abandons the mostly immobile Turner, passed out in the car.

Chano Pozo himself turns up as a character in the animated Spanish feature *Chico & Rita* (2010), which has just enough English dialogue to justify a mention here. Havana pianist Chico, ghosted by Cuban patriarch Bebo Valdés, relocates to New York in 1948, just in time to meet up with the loudly macho Pozo (who's sitting in with Charlie Parker) the night before his murder. The killing itself, and events leading up to it— Chano getting burned on a pot deal—are faithfully rendered. In the 1950s Chico plays Paris with Dizzy Gillespie, the Palladium with Tito Puente, and the Village Vanguard with a courtly Ben Webster (ghosted by tenor saxophonist Jimmy Heath). The period cityscapes re-created from old photographs are lovely. Webster and Woody Herman are the only Anglophone jazz characters who speak. Early on, Chico subs with Herman's band in Havana, and proves himself by sight-reading Stravinsky's *Ebony Concerto*; Woody helps bridge musical cultures, here as in *New Orleans*. But after a decade in the States, Chico's deported back to postrevolution Cuba, where jazz is now out of favor, considered imperialistic.

We've looked at a few films that depict jazz fans and jazz haters, but Michael Grandage's *Genius* (2016), about the working relationship between editor Maxwell Perkins (Colin Firth) and novelist Thomas Wolfe (Jude Law), presents a demographic underrepresented on screen: the jazz-indifferent. Frustrated by Perkins's aggressive pruning of his florid prose, Wolfe drags his editor up to Harlem. "You can never appreciate the music of my book, the tonality and cadence, without experiencing the dark rhythms that inspire me." They are laboring over Wolfe's novel *Of Time and the River*, which would be published in 1935. "The whole thing about jazz is these fellas are artists," Wolfe explains, who "let the music pour out, riff upon riff, just like I do with words. . . . Be original. Blaze new trails."

But the juke-joint band they hear plays dixieish music like it's still the 1920s: perhaps a comment on how Harlem-savvy Wolfe really is. (The film was shot in England.)

Max doesn't care for music, he confesses without embarrassment. When pressed, he does admit to liking (as the real Perkins did) the hymn "Flow Gently Sweet Afton."[3] So Wolfe has the band play it, because somehow they know that old Scottish air. (Jazz versions only came later—Glenn Miller, Red Nichols, Wilbur De Paris—after Maxine Sullivan swung "Loch Lomond.") At first the jazzmen play it prim and proper—that's Henry James, Thomas explains—and then they swing it: that's Thomas Wolfe, in all his raggedy excessive glory. Max at least pretends to like it, even taps his foot a bit. But the editor leaves Wolfe at the club and goes home to continue cutting that thicket of prose, whole swatches at a time. Hearing jazz hadn't changed a thing.

MOVIES WITHIN MOVIES AND NEW ORLEANS COMES BACK 2008–2019

The Terminal and *Moonlight Serenade* aside, jazz stories went on a short hiatus at the turn of the twenty-first century, as if all the stories had been told. As the jazz film geared back up a few years later, approaching the music's centenary on record, new stories kept harking back to old ones—even very old ones. And one comedy—or more precisely, the jazz movie within a nonjazz movie—would comment on jazz-film conventions.

Be Kind Rewind (2008; 102 minutes; director/writer: Michel Gondry). Cast includes: Yasiin Bey/Mos Def (Mike/Fats Waller), Jack Black (Jerry/Fats's manager), Melonie Diaz (Alma), Danny Glover (Mr. Fletcher/Rev. Waller), Mia Farrow (Mrs. Falewicz).
—A video-store clerk and his friends film cheapo remakes of in-demand movies, then mount an original production: a biopic of singer/pianist/composer Fats Waller.

In Michel Gondry's surreal working-class comedy *Be Kind Rewind*, a trio of knucklehead savants—video-store clerk Mike, junkyard buddy Jerry, and clothes-presser Alma—make entertaining 20-minute knockoffs of rental-shelf favorites, from *RoboCop* to *The Umbrellas of Cherbourg*. Their no-budget practical effects are a hoot, making pivotal use of forced perspective, camera rolls and tilts, stop-motion, and lots of decorated cardboard.

Mike's surrogate dad and employer Mr. Fletcher is a nut for pianist Fats Waller—insists, in fact, he was born right here in Passaic, New Jersey. (He knows Fats is really from Harlem, but thought young Mike needed a local hero.) So when the knuckleheads resolve to make an original film, Mike pays tribute to his mentor. Their *Fats Waller Was Born Here* honors and distorts the life of one of the most formidable pianists, organists, and songwriters of the 1920s, who in the 1930s became a singing star and leader of a jumping small band.

We see only isolated bits of *Fats Waller Was Born Here* (shot in flickering, period black and white through a spinning car-radiator fan) scattered throughout *Be Kind Rewind*, from opening scene to closing credits. (In a way, the outer movie is a long making-of-documentary.) A story meeting identifies sequences we don't see—like Fats interacting with Louis Armstrong. Faced with a fresh subject, the Passaic collective recapitulates jazz-film history in cardboard form. *Fats Waller*'s visual style recalls movies from the era when it's set—like *New York, New York*—and the lead actor is too skinny, à la *Lady Sings the Blues*. (Heftier Jerry would play him, although he's white—he auditions in what we might call sootface, to his friends' dismay.) We see Fats born, echoing a birth scene in *Mo' Better Blues*. Six hands at the keys suggest our hero's dazzling technique, versus five in *Legend of 1900*. There's a fancy floorshow and kids gunned down in the street (*Cotton Club*). Our young hero gets laughed off the bandstand—that would not have happened to the real Fats—but later dazzles them all (*Bird*). There are voiceovers and staged interviews as in *Sweet and Lowdown*.

From what we see of it, *Fats Waller*, like a real biopic, gets much right. Fats as a boy plays harmonium on the street to accompany his preacher father. (No one working on the film knows what a harmonium looks like, and they come up with something snazzier, built on a hotdog cart.) Adult Fats becomes a star on the rent-party circuit, dazzling the competition—including a cigar-chomping pianist in a derby and heavy glasses who looks like Waller friend Willie the Lion Smith. And Fats dies from flu complications on a snowy day as his cross-country (model) train sits outside Kansas City station.

As in other biopics, plenty is invented. The movie changes Fat's hometown (like W. C. Handy's in *St. Louis Blues*—or Waller's own in *Stormy Weather*, where he's a Memphian). And the real Waller didn't play Bach in a Passaic church, let alone make Passaic the jazz capital. His life gets streamlined—out go his older siblings—and sanitized: We see

FIGURE 11.1 Mike (Mos Def), with a little anonymous help, plays Fats Waller in a biopic within the movie *Be Kind Rewind*.

nothing about his chronic drinking or intransigence about paying alimony. There are blatant anachronisms (breakdancing). But we get to hear Waller's actual music—hear why
anyone would care to know about him. And there's some spectacle: a derelict warehouse
missing an exterior wall becomes a cutaway set for an elaborate multifloor rent-party
scene, directed by Alma on a construction crane.

Without realizing it, Mike, Jerry, and Alma become bona fide independents—filming
on the street guerrilla-style, enlisting their friends to work on either side of the camera,
ducking cops and counting pennies. By now they're famous throughout the neighborhood, and address that niche Passaic audience. But the making of *Fats Waller Was Born
Here* also illuminates why so few women get to make (jazz) films. Alma joins Mike and
Jerry on their second picture and quickly becomes a full member of the collective, acting,
directing, and refining their business model. She fights to be recognized as their equal,
but Mike and Jerry rephrase her ideas as if they're their own, and won't cop to it when she
points it out. Surreal elements aside, this is a film where people call each other out on un-
tenable beliefs and build a community. Yet even a note in the end credits refers to "Mike
and Jerry's films." Alma's denied credit like manager turned secretary Ellen Miller at the
end of *Second Chorus*. She deserves better.

That said, Michel Gondry serves up a humbling metacritique of jazz movies and their
familiar modes. Implicit in *Be Kind Rewind*'s singular but oddly familiar biopic, and its
frame, is a need for new forms to tell a new century's jazz stories—long-form television
included. As one film that rose to the challenge would put it in the following decade: if
you're gonna tell a story, come with some attitude.

> ***Treme*** **(TV series, 2010–2013; 36 approximately one-hour episodes; creators/
> producers: David Simon, Eric Overmyer; directors include: Anthony
> Hemingway, Ernest Dickerson, Agnieszka Holland; writers include: Simon,
> Overmyer, George Pelecanos, Lolis Eric Elie, Tom Piazza, David Mills). Cast
> includes: Wendell Pierce (Antoine Batiste), Rob Brown (Delmond Lambreaux),
> Clarke Peters (Albert Lambreaux), Steve Zahn (DJ Davis), Phyllis Montana
> LeBlanc (Desiree), Deacon John Moore (Danny Nelson), Jaron Williams
> (Robert), Jazz Henry (Jennifer), Tatsuo Ichikawa (Koichi Toyama), Ron Carter,
> Donald Harrison, Kidd Jordan, Irwin Mayfield, Mac Rebennack/Dr. John,
> Kermit Ruffins, and dozens more musicians (themselves).**
> **—After Hurricane Katrina hits in 2005, a cross-section of New Orleanians—
> including journeyman trombonist Antoine Batiste and rising trumpet star
> Delmond Lambreaux—get on with their lives, with the city's music in their ears**.

As often as New Orleans turned up in the 1940s, it vanished from jazz movies afterward.
But many other movies were set and shot in the city, and characters often encountered
jazz funeral parades, as if those rites occurred daily.

Jazz movies' diminished interest mirrored jazz's own. New Orleans is ever associated
with the music's origins, and as jazz went through one modernizing wave after another,

the cradle receded farther into the mist. A Crescent City heritage burnished a musician's résumé, but few who left to make it big came back to settle. For Louis Armstrong as for Wynton Marsalis, it was a place to be from: jazz's exotic feeder town. Traditional New Orleans jazz was perceived to be old hat, and the city's modernists were barely noticed at all.

Yet attentive out-of-towners on even a quick visit might marvel at how culturally singular New Orleans is, with myriad influences reflected in its music and cuisine: West African, Native American, French, Spanish, Cuban, Anglo-Caribbean, and the far-side-of-the-swamps white and black Cajun strains with their own French-Canadian roots. In this relatively isolated medium-size city, working musicians play all kinds of gigs in all kinds of styles, among which boundaries are porous. Everything influences everything else.

TV writers/producers David Simon and Eric Overmyer had been discussing a New Orleans series since the 1990s—Overmyer lived there part-time—but lacked a marketable hook. Then came Hurricane Katrina in August 2005, the flooding that resulted from infrastructure failures, and the federal government's feeble response. Now they had their hook. The flood and its aftermath focused attention on the venality and political and police corruption that also distinguish the city, and *Treme* deals with all that at length, in multiple story lines. Dozens of musicians and assorted Orleanians—celebrity chefs, writers, community activists, a city councilman—appear as themselves, and a few interact with characters they inspired.

It was New Orleans culture above all that called refugees back—the music, the food, the *bon temps* spirit; it's at the heart of this sweeping portrait of the city in recovery, played out over four seasons in 36 episodes. In depicting how music is central to a city's life, and how jazz fits into a larger musical mosaic, it's *sui generis*. On one level it's a marathon backstage musical, stuffed with as much diegetic music as the storytelling will bear, with jazz as one element in a broad mix.[1]

Its twin stories about jazz brassmen touch on now-familiar themes, often given a fresh spin: music-making as an integral part of healing social ritual; jazz rubbing up against other musics; kid musicians who want to express themselves whose teachers hold them back; musical conflict between father and son; dramatized recreations of events from musicians' real lives.

Treme's dozen-plus principal characters include three African Americans who draw our particular attention. Freelance trombonist Antoine Batiste (Wendell Pierce, ghosted mostly by the Rebirth Brass Band's Stafford Agee) comes from a long line of musicians, like many peers in a city where music may be a family business. (Antoine's fictional, but the Batistes are real.) Rising jazz trumpeter Delmond Lambreaux (Rob Brown, primarily ghosted by Leon "Kid Chocolate" Brown) has a complicated relationship with his perfectionist father Albert, Big Chief of Guardians of the Flame, a seriously depleted Mardi Gras Indian tribe. Antoine and Delmond get more screen time, by far, than any jazz heroes in cinema history.

In New Orleans we put everything together, explains WWOZ radio's DJ Davis, who functions as *Treme*'s Greek chorus: "We are a Creole Nation, whether you like it or not." In its way the series illustrates the central thesis of Simon's *The Wire*: Everything's connected and all the pieces matter. The action regularly cuts between or among scenes to underscore connections. That cross-cutting also frees up editors to dip into and out of music filmed live on location, documentary style, in place of movie-style foreshortened performances.

The jazz on display cuts across a rainbow of styles from parlor ragtime to jazz-funk—pretty much every vernacular style you'd hear in the city except free improvising. (There is some collective blowing at one jam session, when free-thinking saxophonists Kidd Jordan and Donald Harrison drop by, but they wail on Herbie Hancock's funky "Chameleon" with washboard percussion.) The town can support so much diverse music because, we see, there are so many upscale and downscale places to play, from concert halls to the middle of the street on parade day.

On *Treme*, Mardi Gras Indian culture represents everything unique and not-wholly penetrable about the city's folkways, with its *two-way-pocky-way* linguistic codes (corruptions of French, partly), striking syncretisms (dazzling costumes inspired by West African masking, the longtime intermingling of African Americans with Native Americans, and theatrical Wild West shows), and devotional Mardi Gras and St. Joseph's Day rites, when they take the pageant to the streets after months of preparation. There are many scenes of grown men (and any women and children they can rope in) sewing on deadline.

As an invocation, Indians begin weekly practice sessions or a day out with the chant "Indian Red," first commercially recorded by jazz guitarist Danny Barker around the early 1950s. In *Treme*'s first season especially, "Indian Red" is a marker of the tribes' influence on the city's intermingled musics, jazz very much included. DJ Davis spins Barker's original on radio; singer/pianist Dr. John works up an R&B arrangement for a post-Katrina benefit in New York, with Delmond on trumpet; and Antoine plays it after a funeral service with the Treme Brass Band. And we hear it in situ: as Indians' warm-up number, memorial prayer, and proud boast, as they wind their way through the neighborhoods. Other songs turn up in similarly diverse readings: the very old jazz and pop tune "Li'l Liza Jane," the hymn "I'll Fly Away," the not universally beloved local anthem "Do You Know What It Means to Miss New Orleans?" As local critic John Swenson puts it, musicians treat the New Orleans canon "as a series of tropes that can be morphed into a myriad of musical shapes."[2]

Antoine Batiste is our principal window onto New Orleans music's unity in diversity. No *Lush Life* glamor for this gigging musician. As the self-assessed seventh-best trombonist in town, he's got a good growl and pronounced blues sense, even if the intricacies of bebop are beyond him. But he still has to hustle for work every day, and isn't always punctual, not least because post-Katrina he's been living across the city line without a car.

The trombonist has a jazz pedigree but jazz is only one slice of what he does. In the series' opening scene set in autumn 2005, Antoine Batiste subs with the Rebirth Brass Band on a landmark gig: the first conspicuous post-Katrina second-line, that traveling party that accompanies a brass band parading through town, typically returning from a cemetery. It's one of numerous actual events woven into the narrative.

That sequence quickly establishes the series' sensitivity to musical nuance: We hear how the quality of the band's sound changes as it passes under an elevated highway and bounces off the concrete above. In New Orleans, the sonic environment matters. It's a town where, it's said, you'd hear Buddy Bolden blowing across the flats miles away. Starting with a second line confronts New Orleans clichés first thing. But for once we see one from the inside, not the outside.

Over time, Antoine gets some sympathy gigs from trumpeter Kermit Ruffins, does a short stint playing for strippers on tourist-hell Bourbon Street, leads a brass band that greets travelers at Armstrong airport, and subs in various jazz and funk groups. The ubiquity of three-horn sections in New Orleans rock, funk, and R&B bands marks early jazz's continuing influence (or at least its representation) and keeps players like Antoine fed.

As refugees return, and missing persons turn up dead, Batiste plays one funeral parade and second-line after another, and we witness how such customs bring consolation to survivors. We also see the city's inconsistent/ambivalent attitude toward these ceremonies that help define it. Paperwork or caprice determine whether the cops run players in or give them a respectful escort. *Treme*'s police are even more dysfunctional than *The Wire*'s. When a drunken Antoine grazes his trombone slide against a squad car, the cops knock out his front teeth, arrest him, and then (apparently) pawn his horn.

To remind us the rest of the world rallied to help Katrina survivors, Antoine gets a replacement trombone courtesy of philanthropic Japanese fan Koichi Toyama. After Antoine recovers his pawned horn, he gives the new one to his old teacher Danny Nelson, now wasting away in a FEMA trailer. Antoine tries to get Danny work, visits him in the hospital when he's dying, plays his funeral, and on the Day of the Dead blows Nelson favorite "Buddy Bolden's Blues" over his grave. Antoine also passes that gift trombone to the late man's grandson. Later when Koichi hears about the bequest, he says, very good—very Japanese. And very New Orleans, where continuity and family lines count for a lot.

Danny Nelson the inspiring teacher is based on Danny Barker, who'd recorded "My Indian Red." In the 1970s Barker's Fairview Baptist Church band trained numerous young musicians including Wynton and Branford Marsalis. In TV series that go on for years, writers may quietly rewrite character back stories where convenient; in later seasons, after Danny Nelson's gone, Antoine now talks of Danny Barker's mentorship, giving a real hero his due.

Over the course of the second season, Antoine rises to his level of incompetence, leading an R&B band that falls apart before it gets going. But at the same moment, Antoine Batiste discovers what he is good at: teaching, after his good woman Desiree lands him a day job as assistant band director at fictional Elie Elementary School. David Simon is fascinated by how systems perpetuate themselves—how the next generation of practitioners gets indoctrinated. Going way back, New Orleans owes its musical vitality to its strong pedagogical traditions, glimpsed 70 years earlier in *Syncopation*.

Public school music programs had long fed the city's talent pool. But like so much else in New Orleans, music ed got hobbled during recovery—part of a general pattern of reducing services that benefit the poor in an apparent effort to discourage blacks from returning.

We'd already spied one of Antoine's students, in the first scene of season two, which had rung changes on the beginning of *Mo' Better Blues*. There young Bleek's mother had wanted him to stay home and practice his horn. (Ernest Dickerson, who directed six *Treme* episodes, was *Mo' Better*'s cinematographer.) Here, mom shoos fledgling trumpeter Robert away from the house, because the partial scale he's practicing is driving her bonkers. As he walks around town, working that same ascending five-note phrase, we hear what he's reaching for: the start of "When the Saints Go Marching In."

The progress Antoine's kids make over three school years is slow but believable; some days they're getting somewhere, but then they backslide. His most promising charges are trumpeters Robert and Jennifer; she's got curiosity and natural talent and can read music, although she's illiterate. They eavesdrop outside nightclubs, and like youngsters in *Broken Strings* and *Birth of the Blues*, want to play the way they feel. But there are no instant geniuses. Robert: "I want to be in one of them bands where you could play free." Antoine: "What? Y'all not even up on two feet yet!" Months later, when the band rehearses "Basin Street Blues," Jennifer starts ad libbing but can't quite execute what she has in mind. Antoine compliments her tone but tells her, this isn't the place for that.

"I'm sorry, I just felt it, y'know?"

"Oh, I understand. And when the time comes—you can let that rip."

In time, pressed by Robert, Antoine organizes a kids' street band, like Danny Barker before him. And by Antoine's third year teaching, now as sole band director, his Elie Bobcats are just good enough to play in public on Lundi Gras. In class one day, when he asks who wants to play professionally, everyone raises a hand. But the school axes his program because after-hours activities drive up insurance premiums. The private Roots of Music initiative will scoop a few of his kids into its after-school classes, but the rest are out of luck. Budget cuts all but ensure the musicians pool will shrink.

That same fight over the city's soul ultimately surfaces in *Treme*'s other intergenerational saga, of the Lambreauxs father and son. In his mid-twenties, Delmond is a recognizable type: a modern jazz trumpet player from New Orleans now living in New York, who plays in the aggressively swinging 4/4 groove the Marsalis brothers popularized in the 1980s. *Treme* makes you hear a clear contrast between that tippin' New York beat and New Orleans's Caribbeanized lope. Rhythms tell the tale: talking drums.

After a couple of years up north, Delmond's on the fast track: he's seen Paris; records for a big label; dates a stylish journalist; leads a sleek quintet that plays Dizzy's, the nightclub annex to Jazz at Lincoln Center; and sometimes works with his mentor Donald Harrison, son of a Big Chief who became a Big Chief himself.

Jazz was in the house when Delmond was growing up. His father Albert loves his New Orleans R&B classics too. But for an Orleanian, Albert is oddly committed to policing boundaries. He likes his jazz a certain way. To Delmond, home on a visit:

"But can you swing? Not all you modern jazz cats do, you know."

"You sound like Wynton."

Albert, reverently: "I hope so."

Of course Albert has heard Delmond enough to make his question rhetorical, and his own opinion obvious. Where *Treme's* music usually amplifies the story, it's rarely clear what Albert objects to in Delmond's music. But Albert is hard to please, and isn't happy his son has left town as if too good for the place. Delmond does have his reservations. He resists when Harrison tries to nudge him toward hometown material when they co-headline a national tour after Katrina makes New Orleans temporarily trendy. But hearing New Yorkers pontificate about his hometown makes Delmond reconsider. "That's what I like about your record," a well-meaning fan tells him. "Listening to it I wouldn't know you're from New Orleans."

Slowly, in season two, Delmond turns back toward his roots. He listens to Mississippi Fred McDowell's deep blues, and the 1924 Jelly Roll Morton–King Oliver duets: "I'm hearing something. It's old, it's mean," he says. "It got mud all over it." Back in New Orleans on Mardi Gras day, he has a tidy epiphany: hears a boombox blast Quincy Jones's swinging take on Benny Golson's "Killer Joe," just as the Indians pass by, chanting and smacking tambourines. Now he knows what to do: combine his father's Indian calls with modern jazz.

When Delmond enlists Donald Harrison's help, his drily amused response is, "I wonder why nobody ever thought to do that before." This is *Treme's* biggest in-joke. Harrison had made that record himself in 1991—*Indian Blues*, with his own Big Chief father Donald Sr. on vocals. Like artists everywhere, Delmond reinvents a wheel he didn't know existed. Harrison's quip aside, no one on *Treme* seems to remember *Indian Blues*, not even when Donald helps Delmond rope in Dr. John, who'd played on the original record—like the drummer Delmond hires, Carl Allen. Maybe those musicians just let him think his idea's original. Take the money and stay mum. Albert is typically prickly in the New York studio, lecturing esteemed bassist Ron Carter on how to play proper Indian beats on "Hu-Ta-Nay" (a little milder than on *Indian Blues*). At Albert's insistence, they finish the album in New Orleans, adding conga player Uganda Roberts for extra pepper. Now Albert's happy. Delmond can't hear the difference, but Dr. John can: "New Orleans infect music. It reconstitutionalaise it."

When Delmond's (never named) album is released, the critics are mostly laudatory if not always knowledgeable about the cultural context. They don't remember *Indian Blues* either. As often as Wynton Marsalis is invoked on *Treme*—the first jazz drama to acknowledge that influential musician—he doesn't appear, unlike his father Ellis and brothers Delfeayo and Jason. But Delmond relates that Marsalis had paid the Indian album "one of them Wynton compliments"—that it's "an interesting amalgam: not quite jazz, but intriguing for what it is." That backhanded praise rankles even (intermittently) swing-obsessed Albert: "He don't get the last damn word on what jazz and what ain't. . . . You and me done broke some fresh fucking ground."

FIGURE 11.2 On *Treme*, saxophonist Donald Harrison helps re-create an event from his own life: A Mardi Gras Indian Chief (Clarke Peters) records a hybrid session with his jazz musician son (Rob Brown, on trumpet). Bassist Ron Carter is at left.

Before long Delmond leaves New York, to cut expenses and to look after Albert, who's developed a theatrical cough, foreboding a steep decline in health. The series' last grand memorial service will be his. When Delmond moves back to New Orleans, he loses some of that particular hometown cachet that comes from successfully escaping, and his profile dips elsewhere. But there's an unforeseen upside to coming home, in a storyline that plays out over season three. In the wake of Delmond's album, the Lambreauxs make an attractive face for New Orleans's African American culture, and they're approached to consult on—or front for—a new National Jazz Center in the works. Post-Katrina, there was much talk of building such a jazz welcome center, with Armstrong Park touted as a likely site. On *Treme* its backers are the same rich fixers who've been using insider information to demolish homes and scarf up valuable real estate since the flood. But they're not all bad. Even the main puppet master can hold forth on the topic of proper ragtime tempos.

Delmond's recommendations are sensible: have several venues and diverse programming, à la Jazz at Lincoln Center, the gold standard for corporate-funded jazz. And take down the fence around Armstrong Park, which had been locked up since the storm more than two years before. Everyone seems attentive to his ideas. But in the next mock-up we see, the fence still stands. Soon the Lambreauxs wisely bow out, ceding the go-between role to the actual musician associated with the project, Irwin Mayfield, whose advice to Delmond had been, first get the money, then decide how to spend it. (Some years after *Treme*. Mayfield would face charges of misappropriating public funds.)[3] Delmond returns his hefty consultant's fee, but he'd earned it. The last architects' model we see, the fence is gone. But then, as in life, the project falls through. It doesn't feel like much of a loss, for reasons DJ Davis explains: You can't impose top-down culture on a bottom-up town, where music education starts at street level.

In *Treme*'s endgame, Delmond honors his dying father's request and leads the Indians into the streets as Big Chief one time, for Mardi Gras 2009. The son honors the implacable father by taking up his sacred music, before returning to his own secular style. We know that story: it's *The Jazz Singer*.

In Antoine Batiste's last act, *Treme* gets self-reflexive. The trombonist gets hired as a technical advisor on a jazz movie shooting in town—acknowledging the impact of productions like this one on the local economy. He coaches the very white actor who's playing mixed-race Creole Kid Ory, and then Antoine ghosts Ory's trombone parts live, off to the side of the set, as the actor discreetly spies and mimics his moves. That was a process Wendell Pierce knew well by season four.

Our peek at this fictitious Ory biopic reminds us that jazz movies aren't half so true to life as *Treme* is—for example, the culture-mixing movie that ends with the same song the series finale does: *New Orleans*.

> ***Whiplash*** **(2014; 107 minutes; director/writer: Damien Chazelle). Cast includes: Miles Teller (Andrew Neimann), J.K. Simmons (Terence Fletcher), Paul Reiser (Jim Neimann), Melissa Benoist (Nicole), Damon Gupton (Joe).**
> **—A headstrong student drummer battles, but craves the approval of, an implacable band director. Might a big Carnegie Hall concert resolve their differences?**

Treme dramatizes the high-stakes importance of music education: New Orleans culture and tourism depend on it. The stakes have never seemed lower than in *Whiplash*, a cautionary tale of jazz ed gone awry, tucked inside the inspirational saga of an ambitious conservatory student who earns a demanding teacher's respect. It's a jazz bootcamp movie, combining the uplift of Jack Webb's 1957 *The D.I.*—in which a tough sergeant turns a spoiled recruit into a Marine—and the profane, abusive fury of the drill instructor in Stanley Kubrick's *Full Metal Jacket* (1987). There's a lot of yelling, a few ethnic and homophobic slurs, and some face slapping.

Writer/director Damien Chazelle, a jazz fan and one-time student drummer, based *Whiplash* on his own experience in an intensive high-school jazz program where "enjoyment and appreciation of the art of music was inextricably wrapped up in fear and dread and anxiety"—where messing up a tempo seemed like the end of the world. He'd be elated when his teacher was approving and crushed when he wasn't. *Whiplash*'s climactic sequence is based on a recurring nightmare Chazelle was still having years after making it, in which he's on stage with his school band, unprepared or unable to perform—except the movie gives the nightmare a happy ending.[4]

So *Whiplash* is also an adolescent's empowerment fantasy: I'll show that teacher who underestimated me! Teenage problems get blown up to apocalyptic proportions. Its loner hero Andrew Niemann—he's Andy only to his annoying extended family—is a

New Yorker just out of high school, in his first semester at the Shaffer Conservatory some-where on Manhattan's West Side. Andrew calls it "the best music school in the country," though nothing we see supports that. One telling detail: when the school's flagship stu-dent band has a competition in a college town two hours away, players must provide their own transportation.

Andrew's a drummer who wants to get noticed, practicing in Shaffer's windowless bowels, with the doors to the rehearsal room wide open—a breach of conservatory et-iquette. His drumming summons a demonic presence from the shadows, voodoo-style. We don't learn this wraith's name till much later, but he's Terence Fletcher, feared/revered director of the school's top big band, and the very figure whose attention Andrew seeks. (J.K. Simmons's over-the-top portrayal got him an Oscar for Best Supporting Actor.) Fletcher asks to hear Andrew's double-time swing, but it's apparently not fast enough—a harbinger of conflicts to come.

Fletcher is a one-man Good Cop/Bad Cop—he may step out of a room as one and step back in as the other. He'll ask Andrew concerned questions about his family, and minutes later loudly use what he's learned against him. Fletcher always punches down. He picks on a trombone player because he's fat and tells Andrew to show up at 6 a.m. for a rehearsal that starts three hours later, just because. Dropping by junior band teacher Joe's class—Joe is more easygoing, though his band doesn't crackle or even play very well—Fletcher snorts at their sheet music and insults a young saxophonist (and Joe along with her): "Well you're in the first chair. Let's see if it's just because you're cute." He listens to her play one phrase. "Yep!"

This unnamed altoist does in fact bobble that phrase, so blatantly no moviegoer could miss it, but then Fletcher's pedagogical method isn't designed to bring out players' best. It's meant to unnerve them. His MO: ask a student to play some difficult snippet out of context, then cut them off after a couple of seconds. The drummer in Fletcher's band has alternates/understudies, so the teacher can play them off against each other, some-times three at once. So Fletcher's a drill sergeant who has recruits train their guns on each other. Friendless Andrew doesn't bond with other students. He doesn't jam or talk music with them or make his own contacts outside the classroom, like jazz students everywhere else. He and his drum rivals eye each other with contempt, waiting for the other guy to screw up.

In *Whiplash*'s most notorious/absurd scene, Fletcher keeps micromanaging Andrew's tempo (it's about 160 beats a minute—fairly brisk), interrupting to make him play the same passage in 7/4 time over and over.

Andrew: [not quite 2 bars of drums]
Fletcher: Not, not quite my tempo. . . .
Andrew: [not quite 1 bar]
Fletcher: Downbeat on 18. . . .
Andrew: [not quite 1 bar]. . . .
Fletcher: Not quite my tempo. . . .

Andrew: [1 bar, faster]
Fletcher: You're rushing. . . .
Andrew: [just over 1 bar]
Fletcher: Dragging just a hair. . . .
Andrew: [1 bar]
Fletcher: Rushing. . . .
Andrew: [not quite 1 bar]
Fletcher: Dragging. . . .

Till finally Fletcher just throws a chair at him. This dialogue's deadpan, dead-end loopiness signals social breakdown as in a Beckett play: *Whiplash* as a jazz *What Where*.[5] In jazz, the "right" tempo, as Count Basie knew, is the one that maximizes swing (relaxation). Haggling over 160 versus 159 beats per minute doesn't facilitate that. At least when *The Fabulous Dorseys* argued about tempos, you could hear why they bothered.

Basie drummer Jo Jones was a master of such relaxed deep grooving, but in Fletcher's telling, Jo is on his side: "Charlie Parker became Bird because Jones threw a cymbal at his head. You see what I'm saying?" (Jones, you may recall from discussion of *Bird*, drolly lobbed the cymbal at his feet.) Later Fletcher embellishes further: Jo Jones nearly decapitated him; Parker cried himself to sleep, but came back a year later and played "the best motherfucking solo the world has ever heard." (That's a bit much, but local musicians were in fact struck by how much he'd improved.) Fletcher is one more unreliable narrator, but Andrew believes him and starts repeating the same nonsense instead of checking teacher's facts.

Fletcher is considered a starmaker, but the lone success we hear about is a little-known (within the movie) trumpeter in the Lincoln Center Jazz Orchestra. On a recording, he wah-wahs like a weak Wynton wannabe. Even so, Andrew buys into the tough-love program, gloating when Good Cop praises him and sulking when Bad Cop withholds. He's drawn to the sadism and corrosive hostility his protective father Jim thoughtlessly denies him. Andrew's idol Buddy Rich was a great drummer but a famously abusive bandleader, so he may think all the shouting (like Buddy's old-school drum fireworks) is the norm.

Andrew is tenacious, trying to win Fletcher's respect. He ditches his nice girlfriend Nicole to free up more practice time and seems to forgo all other classes, including any in which he might learn about the interactive aspects of jazz drumming: of blending with, accommodating, and prodding other players; accompanying soloists; and making spontaneous choices—the African-derived, communal side of it.[6] Instead Andrew devotes himself to memorizing the tricky drum part to Hank Levy's 1970s chart "Whiplash" in 7/4, helping the band win a competition. (These contests are more common at the high-school level, by the way.)

As Andrew, Miles Teller plays the drums and looks at ease behind them; the soundtrack musicians are uncredited. The music we hear doesn't closely match what we see, but it scarcely matters once Chazelle and the editors go to work. On the climactic big-band "Caravan," we get overhead views of piano keyboard and drum set; matching dolly shots moving across the brass and reed sections; quick cuts on the beat between long shots; close-ups of drum hardware, trumpet bells, and sheet music; a trombone slide coming at you; the trumpet section seen from below; and (inevitably) whip-pans from one part of the stage to another, for visual call-and-response. You can't say the movie isn't stylish, though it's sometimes underlit, for extra menace.

Andrew is so dedicated to playing first chair, when his rental car is T-boned by a truck he crawls out of the overturned wreck and runs the last two blocks to a big-band competition. (And this after he'd sped back to the rental place where he'd left his drumsticks. The movie's borderline hysterical, like a too-fast drum solo.) But once on stage he's dazed, and drops a stick—with no spares within reach, of course—and wilts before the tune is over, leaving blood on the ride cymbal. When Fletcher disses him to the jury and the audience, Andrew tackles his teacher on stage and gets himself booted from school. At his father's urging, Andrew testifies anonymously against Fletcher—other students are oddly reluctant to speak out—and the ogre gets fired.

The last act takes place the following June. Andrew hears Fletcher sitting in at a jazz club, playing sleepy-samba piano. (The man has layers, and this one is mellow.) They get to talking, and the elder explains his insane what-doesn't-kill-you-might-possibly-make-you-stronger teaching philosophy—one sure to crush gentle souls like, say, Lester Young. And then Good Cop Fletcher offers Andrew the drum chair on his upcoming gig, the opening concert of the JVC Jazz Festival at Carnegie Hall. You'd think the kid would smell a rat. Andrew even invites his ex Nicole to come. She says she might, but any real musician would know she won't—she doesn't ask if he's leaving her free tickets.

Of course it's Bad Cop who conducts at Carnegie. (LA's Orpheum Theater stands in.) Fletcher has known all along who got him fired. So his plan is to embarrass Andrew on stage, by kicking off the set with a complex piece the drummer doesn't know or have sheet music for. And since Andrew has acquired no listening or improvising skills, or ear for form, he does indeed make a mess of it. Applause is tepid and slow in coming. ("I guess you don't have it," Fletcher comes over to tell him, right for once.) Andrew flees the stage, and Fletcher makes a dismissive comment to a remarkably docile house full of New York jazz aficionados. They sit there and take it, like his students; nobody boos or goes to the lobby. But then *Whiplash* is never about the audience.

Not that this revenge plot adds up. Consider: Fletcher has just lost his long-running, presumably well-compensated conservatory post, but gets a chance to rebound with a plum festival slot. Evidently he's using his Carnegie set to advertise for another teaching job, by featuring his college repertoire, including a superfast take on the Ellington-Tizol warhorse "Caravan." Much earlier, the teacher had promised dire consequences for any student who sabotaged a Fletcher ensemble. Now he's going to sabotage his own band and prospects out of spite?

In the wings, coddling dad Jim tries to drag his son home. Instead Andrew walks back on stage—the drums are still vacant, as if the band were going to carry on without—and interrupts Fletcher who's introducing a ballad, crashing in with the "Caravan" drum intro. Andrew blatantly hijacks the gig; his tempo is a hair slower than the one Fletcher prefers—giving the leader the figurative finger. Before it's over Andrew treats himself to a five-minute drum solo, using an accelerando bit he'd been practicing back in the opening scene, and by now he's playing so brilliantly even Fletcher is won over and starts conducting his dynamics, bringing the volume way down before they build to a killer-diller finale. (Andrew spatters a cymbal again, but with sweat, not blood. He's stronger now.) Good Cop smiles his benediction, and Andrew beams. It's the wackiest Carnegie-reconciliation ending yet.

Before the band went on, Fletcher had given his young players a pep talk: A good performance tonight could make you a Blue Note artist—as if that leading jazz label often signed heretofore anonymous big-band musicians. (It doesn't.) From that buildup, a viewer might infer that tonight will make Andrew's reputation. But look at his performance from the audience's viewpoint: he makes a hash of the first number, walks off in disgrace, and then hijacks the second tune to indulge himself at length in a blatant ego display. Only in the movies would that be a triumph.

> **Low Down (2014; 114 minutes; director: Jeff Preiss; writers: Amy-Jo Albany, Topper Lilien, from Albany's memoir Low Down: Junk, Jazz, and Other Fairy Tales from Childhood). Cast includes: John Hawkes (Joe Albany), Elle Fanning (Amy-Jo Albany), Glenn Close (Gram), Flea (Hobbs), Peter Dinklage (Alain), Caleb Landry Jones (Cole), Lena Headey (Sheila Albany), Billy Drago (Lew).**
> **—Amy-Jo Albany grows up on the seedy end of Hollywood in the 1970s and has a close bond with her father, bebop pianist (and heroin addict) Joe Albany.**

Jeff Preiss's downbeat *Low Down* is in color, not grainy black-and-white, but its ambling story and subject matter suggest kinship with 1960s independent jazz films. John Hawkes plays Joe Albany, in actuality one of the first bebop pianists in the 1940s, who'd played with Charlie Parker and recorded with Lester Young. After that Albany hardly worked for 20 years, hamstrung by a succession of heroin busts and jail terms. Like other bebop junkies, he could be as fluid musically as he was awkward in life. At the piano, everything fell into place; he'd improvise with clarity and dexterity, and resourcefulness that kept his style from sounding like a compendium of ready licks. You could see his mastery: hands poised above and parallel to the keys, every digit deployed to make a hornlike spontaneous melody line sing out.

Low Down follows Joe Albany in the 1970s when he languished in Los Angeles trying and often failing to stay off junk—anticipating 2016's cycle of lost-years biopics of Chet Baker, Miles Davis, and Nina Simone. But *Low Down* is less about Albany himself than his daughter Amy-Jo's experience of life with father, in a scuzzy hotel at the wrong end of Hollywood, starting in 1974. So it's also a white West Coast counterpart to *Crooklyn*.

Low Down is based on A. J. Albany's 2003 memoir. Amy-Jo Albany also cowrote the script, which was directed by her friend (and Joe's fan) Jeff Preiss, a commercial director who'd photographed the Chet Baker documentary *Let's Get Lost*. The filmmakers worked hard to get *Low Down*'s tone right, shooting in a real (downtown LA) hotel in decline.

Only a few incidents come straight from the book, yet the film catches its bittersweet flavor and down-and-out milieu very well. Amy really did have a crush on a morphine-addicted dwarf who appeared in art-porn films. (Movie-Amy is shocked to find out what he does, but book-Amy takes it in stride.)

Amy-Jo is played by Elle Fanning, from approximately age 12 to 15, which was Fanning's age while making the film. Almost all the action is seen from Amy-Jo's viewpoint. She had to grow up quickly, given her father's sometimes precarious condition. Amy and Joe clearly love each other, sharing an appreciation for trashy horror films, and she loves to hear him play when he duets in private with his junkie friend Hobbs (Flea of the Red Hot Chili Peppers), who plays bop on an odd rotary-valve cornet; or when Joe lands a rare club date. There he gets to play with bass and drums, in front of some attentive fans and a few loud yahoos—a believable mix.

But paid work is scarce, and Joe has too many hours to fill. Amy knows to feign sleepiness or excuse herself when Dad and his visitors fidget and exchange nervous looks, and knows how to cope when he's suddenly hauled off by probation officers. Her absent mother (icy Lena Headey) is a mean drunk who turns up only long enough to skip out with most of Joe's cash, on Valentine's Day no less—the same day unsentimental cops run him in. Whenever he's off the scene Amy stays with her Gram, Joe's strong, free-thinking, working-class intellectual Sicilian mother, played with gusto by Glenn Close. She too loves her son and knows his value: "I've heard you play Joe when I sincerely think you have been touched by God." When she visits him in lockup her first question is, "Have you had a chance to play at all?"

We see even more clearly than in *The Connection* the dreary realities of junkies' lives: how they flinch at any knock on any door—potential trouble—and endlessly explain why nothing is ever their fault. It's time-consuming drudgery, finding dope to score, then a place to fix, and then a vein to puncture that might get overlooked during a cursory physical exam. And then making amends to the people you let down when you were high.

The movie streamlines history a bit, compressing a whole childhood into a few years. In the 1970s the real Joe Albany decamped to Europe for about six years, finding greater fame and more work and opportunities to record, while returning to the States on occasion. The real Amy would visit him there; she became friendly with Dexter Gordon in Denmark. In the movie Joe rather abruptly expatriates for two years—a hiatus in the story, which picks up on his return. (He's been deported from Europe—the whole continent, apparently—over what he claims is a minor marijuana bust.)

Despite a spate of new European LPs, once back home Joe reverts to old habits, after moving in with Gram and Amy in his mother's cramped overstuffed flat. Joe hasn't changed, but Amy is now a full-fledged teenager, dating an epileptic garage band drummer named Cole. He's a good kid, but she winds up having to look after him, a mirror image of Dad. Joe can't stay off drugs; Cole won't stay on his meds. But when he has a seizure, seen-it-all Joe knows what to do.

Stories about how the 1970s was bad for jazz always come back to diminished opportunities for bebop masters, and now that Joe's back, there's even less work to be had;

he plays an out-of-tune spinet in a fleabag bar. Hobbs has pawned his horn and piano, so they can't even jam any more. *Low Down* catches the frustration of artists who don't get to practice their art, with unhappy consequences. Things keep sliding downhill until Amy has to score for her father from his sleaziest contact. She and Cole get high too—sniffing glue?—and the day comes when she tastes a grain or two of heroin, if only because it's so much a part of her life already: a foretaste of the real Amy-Jo's drug years, before she got straight. As the film makes clear, she's resilient.

John Hawkes brings out the joshing warmth in Joe's relationship with Amy, as well as his creative side, and his many slippages and shortcomings. We see how Gram, Joe, and Amy make a solid family, where each generation's preoccupations influence the next. One true anecdote catches their old-world dynamic. When Joe, in an ugly mood, threatens his mother with violence, Amy yells that she hates him and calls him an asshole. Gram, immediately: "Don't you *ever* talk to your father that way again!"

Hawkes, with his generous nose, noble forehead, and thick flyaway hair, resembles the actual man, as seen in Carole Langer's 1980 documentary *Joe Albany . . . A Jazz Life*—where he tells a story about being fired off the bandstand by Charlie Parker, a story Hawkes's Joe recounts in *Low Down*. Hawkes doesn't try to mimic all of the man's hand-waving and head-bobbing gestures, but he gets his breezy manner and genuine charm.

In the three scenes where Joe performs for listeners, we hear actual Albany recordings—notably Bird's Latin bump "Barbados" for trio and a florid solo "Lush Life." (When Joe and Hobbs jam on "'Round Midnight" and Clifford Brown's "Daahoud," they're ghosted by Jacob Sacks and Russ Johnson.) Hawkes learned to play piano for the role, and does a conscientious job of synching his hands to Albany's elliptical phrases. He looks like a real pianist, albeit one without Joe Albany's gracefully economical poise over the ivories. You don't *see* the poetry when Albany touches the keys.

> ***Bessie*** **(2015; 112 minutes; director: Dee Rees; screenplay: Rees, Christopher Cleveland, Bettina Gilois; story: Rees, Horton Foote). Cast includes: Queen Latifah (Bessie Smith), Michael Kenneth Williams (Jack Gee), Mo'Nique (Ma Rainey), Tika Sumpter (Lucille), Khandi Alexander (Viola), Tory Kittles (Clarence Smith), Charles S. Dutton (Pa Rainey), Bryan Greenberg (John Hammond), Oliver Platt (Carl Van Vechten), Mike Epps (Richard).**
> **—Bessie Smith rises to become the Empress of blues singers in the 1920s. But her personal life gives her the miseries**.

The idea for a Bessie Smith biopic had been kicking around since the early 1970s, when Chris Albertson's biography *Bessie* and the film *Lady Sings the Blues* came out. But Smith may have been too colorful for Hollywood at the time: the boozing, brawling, bisexual who'd taught early jazz musicians how to express the blues, and who died a sensational death; the woman whose 1929 *St. Louis Blues* brought the blues to the movies.

Possible stars mentioned over time included Dionne Warwick, Cicely Tyson, and Roberta Flack, none of whom much resembled the big-framed Smith. (The more substantial Nina Simone, no actor, also lobbied for it.)[7] In 1974, playwright Horton Foote wrote a screenplay based on Albertson's book, and revised it in 1992. Foote, who died in 2009, shares *Bessie* story credit with director Dee Rees, originally brought in to do a rewrite—making this the rare film in this book directed by a woman of color.

Such a film was long overdue. Blues queens like Smith and Ma Rainey rarely get credit for putting jazz on the right footing in the 1920s, when (as we've seen) the music's definition was up for grabs—when Jolson or Vallee might get tagged as jazz artists. So-called classic blues is the only jazz or blues style dominated by (southern/black) women, often accompanied by jazz horn men, who'd play short phrases—obbligatos—to answer a sung line. Mimicking or echoing those singers taught blues feeling and inflection to northern or classically trained black musicians. These women inspired a range of growling, shouting, or otherwise vocalized instrumental conceptions that permeated jazz. You can hear it happening on record.

Queen Latifah had screen-tested for the role in the 1990s, and there are moments late in *Bessie* when she looks very like Smith in Carl Van Vechten's much-reproduced 1936 photographs.[8] Latifah had the musical and acting chops to pull off singing in character, and to suggest Bessie's onstage power. And she holds her own opposite a withering Khandi Alexander as Bessie's cold sister Viola.

As biopic this HBO production is acceptably accurate, though as ever details go astray. As shown, Bessie Smith comes from a poor black Chattanooga neighborhood. Her parents die when she's small, and she and her brothers are raised by Viola (though the film erases a few other siblings). Unable to get chorus-line work because her skin is too dark, with brother Clarence's help she joins a train-traveling minstrel show starring blues singer Ma Rainey. Bessie apprentices with Ma before going out on her own. She meets and ultimately marries Philadelphia security guard Jack Gee; on their first date he's involved in a violent incident (as victim, not perpetrator as the film has it). She drinks a lot, preferring moonshine to store-bought.

As in life, black-owned Black Swan Records auditions her but rejects her in favor of the more prim Ethel Waters. Bessie signs with Columbia, starting at $125 a side, and records "Downhearted Blues" at her first session. She adopts a son, Jack Jr. (a few years earlier than shown). Clarence rejoins her entourage (though not before she hooks up with Jack Gee, as depicted) and suggests that Bessie's troupe should travel in its own train car, though vain Jack claims credit. At a party in Chattanooga, Bessie has an altercation with a man who's been bothering her woman companion; she throws him out, but later, as she's leaving, he leaps out of the shadows and stabs Bessie several times. She's taken to a hospital, but insists on playing her matinee the next day. (This is deftly handled in the film, where she staggers out of the ward and directly onstage.) When some members of the Ku Klux Klan try to torch her tent show in North Carolina, she runs them off (less dramatically than shown—the real crowd didn't even know there was a problem).

Bessie moves her family north to Philadelphia; husband Jack and sister Viola intensely dislike each other. Jack sees his wife's family as freeloaders. Jack and Bessie both have outside lovers, and Jack takes up with a singer named Gertrude (Saunders), financing her appearances with Bessie's money. Jack and Bessie split, and Jack spirits their son, Jack Jr., away from her. Post-peak, after record sales dip, Bessie records some salacious songs. She falls in love with bootlegger Richard Morgan, who becomes her companion for the rest of her days. During the Depression, she starts to look like a has-been. Then producer John Hammond records her with a changing-of-the-guard band including Benny Goodman and Chu Berry.

Bessie covers all that—though somehow she never utters her real-life tag line, "I ain't never *heard* of such shit." Conspicuously missing: the notorious death of Bessie Smith in 1937 after a grisly road accident near Clarksdale, Mississippi, the cradle of the man-with-guitar Delta blues that had supplanted her voice-and-piano kind. Director Rees defended omitting her death: "I wanted to leave her with a win. People that don't know Bessie, the one thing they do know is that she died in a car accident."[9] True enough, though what some people know is wrong. What happened: Richard Morgan was driving Bessie south on a dark narrow road, very very late, when they rear-ended a slow moving truck. Smith was severely injured, one arm partly severed. A doctor soon drove up, and while they waited ages for a summoned ambulance, his car was struck by another vehicle, injuring a white couple. In time two ambulances arrived. Smith was taken to a black hospital, where she died.

Weeks later, in Alabama, writer and jazz kibitzer John Hammond heard a rumor that Smith had bled out because a white hospital refused to admit her. (No Mississippi ambulance driver would waste precious time taking her to one.) Instead of looking into it, Hammond reported the rumor in *Down Beat*, in a just-asking-questions kind of way. A myth was born—and lingered, even after the magazine set the record straight two decades later. The myth would figure in Edward Albee's short 1960 play *The Death of Bessie Smith*, in which she never appears. It focuses on an unpleasant white hospital nurse, ready to turn Bessie away, were she not already dead.

Rees might have clarified matters, sidestepping a tragic ending by starting with the fatal crash à la *Lawrence of Arabia*, but a two-hour film can only do so much. Albertson's biography, not credited as a source, contains enough colorful incidents to fill a whole second movie, like Clarence Williams hiding under his desk from Bessie and Jack, come to collect recording fees he's skimmed.

Bessie does begin *in medias res*, with Smith at her 1927 peak. She has just finished performing, her face shiny and impassive as black marble: an onyx icon, bathed in deep blue light. A star, she barely hears the huzzahs of the crowd or the praise of theater staff as she makes her way to her limo—the diegetic sound fades in and out. She acknowledges no one. But once she's home, her ears are open to the silence. Her big house is dark and lifeless, prompting the first of many fleeting flashbacks to miserable childhood. Bessie's at the top, but has the blues.

Now the story begins in earnest, with the young singer already on the road, Atlanta 1913. *Bessie* isn't about the birth of a music; classic blues as a style and business is already up and running. Of the blues, mentor Ma Rainey tells her, "You done heard them a dozen hundred times from a dozen hundred people"—hyperbole for sure, given the year, but Rainey talks big. When we hear Bessie/Latifah sing the first time—"Young Woman's Blues," which she recorded in 1926—Bessie already has a powerful voice, but no stage-craft, reading lyrics off a cheat sheet and failing to connect with the audience. She needs polishing, and gets it from Rainey, the Mother of the Blues. Mo'Nique plays Rainey like a wise force of nature and a stage dynamo, strutting the boards in a spangled gold gown with a suitcase for a prop—like the real Ma—as she belts out (1927's) "Weepin' Woman Blues." (She lip-syncs to recordings by Pat Bass and Carrie Twillie.)

Ma's got the crowd in her pocket from the jump, as Bessie checks out her act from an aisle seat. Queen Latifah's face is all subtle reactions. She gives Ma a professional's cool appraisal, objectively admiring her craft—Bessie observes how the crowd is rocking, but doesn't join in. And then she leans forward, shakes her head slightly in wonder, and a smile creeps onto her face. She's sucked into Ma's force field like everyone else.

Rainey shows her the ropes—how to conduct business where everyone's looking to chisel you, and how to sell a song: picking out people in the house to focus on, as if this one is the woman who stole your man or that one is the man who stole your money. She's a font of movie wisdom: "The blues is not about people knowing you—it's about you knowing people." And: "If you not riskin' nothing, neither will they." She's salty, though the real Rainey was said to be exceptionally sweet.[10]

As a featured member of Ma's troupe, Bessie develops her signature throaty growl. They share the spotlight in a "Weepin' Woman" duet: women making music together, if not always peaceably. On the night brother Clarence drops by to check out her progress, Bessie shows off, literally upstaging her boss, and that's the abrupt end of her apprenticeship: "I ain't playing second to nobody any more." The women trade harsh words,

FIGURE 11.3 Ma Rainey (Mo'Nique) and protégé Bessie Smith (Queen Latifah) sing together in *Bessie*.

but it's just business: later we'll see Ma digging Bessie's first record, proud of her. Rainey has taught her more than craft; she's also taught her to be comfortable in her own skin, as a woman who loves women. We've already seen Bessie's sexually voracious side—dry-humping a guy behind the theater at night, bedding dancer Lucille by day.

Last time we'll mention it: period pieces are about when they're made as well as when they're set. Latifah's Bessie is less circumspect about bisexuality than the real Smith, but by 2015 a bisexual movie heroine was no big shocker. By laying it all out there, *Bessie* celebrates that cultural shift. Ma has her own mini-harem on the train, and Pa Rainey, who's affectionate with her, doesn't even blink. (The Raineys are real partners, hashing out her touring schedules and tag-teaming crooked promoters.) Before long Ma and Bessie are painting on facial hair, wearing men's suits, and hitting a high-stakes poker game.

After the break with Ma, Bessie and Clarence send for some minstrel musicians from earlier days. They rendezvous at a curiously dinky, rural Baltimore train station—as if the classic blues era was much farther back in time. (The city's block-long marble station dates from 1911.) Clarence gives the musicians all the direction we hear them get: "We're bringing a little South to the North—a little taste of home for all these homesick Yankees." No one talks about the bond between singers and horn players, but you can hear it. Bessie also reconnects with lover Lucille, a stand-in for her protégé Ruby Walker. (With women, Bessie wasn't so monogamous.) When Bessie takes up with Jack Gee, he's pretty lowkey about her bisexuality, except when they're brawling.

Bessie catches the broad outlines of a classic blues singer's working life, playing theaters in cities, and tent shows in the rural South. We don't see much of the vaudeville trappings that stuck to such shows, save for a couple of decorative flats and the elaborate gowns and headgear the blues queens wore—though Smith tells one potential hire that everyone on her show has to know how to sing, dance, and tell a joke. Records are Smith's most lasting legacy, but we see only her first and last recording sessions—and only see her cut her debut "Downhearted Blues": acting a little jittery, just as engineer Frank Walker remembered. We don't get the date where Louis Armstrong tried to upstage her with his horn, on a subtext rich "I Ain't Going to Play No Second Fiddle"—not even after her parting comment to Ma set it up: "I ain't playing second to nobody any more."

There are false notes for jazz folk to flag. In 1921 Bessie auditions for Black Swan sitting at a desk, unaccompanied. (You can tell it'll go badly from how light-skinned and uptight the company's African American execs are. Colorism is pronounced in *Bessie*'s world, and she replies in kind: she won't hire light-skinned dancers.) At her first record date, for piano and voice, horn players sit around idle for some reason, and they're white, but all the players on her earliest sides were African American. Her stage band is always in the background, but we see a cup mute stuck in the trumpet, while hearing an actively manipulated plunger. Such goofs are minor but avoidable. Bessie's world gets movie-glamorized. Her Philly-neighborhood house becomes a country mansion, big enough for her whole reunited family—shades of *Lady Sings the Blues*' East Baltimore. (When Smith brought her people north, she sensibly installed them elsewhere.)

The timeline gets fuzzier as *Bessie* goes on. When her sales tank with the Depression, Clarence plays her Lucille Bogan's obscene "Till the Cows Come Home," telling her that business is good for such "party records," an anachronistic term for X-rated comedy LPs. Hearing the naughty possibilities, Bessie records tamer double-entendre songs like (1929's) "Kitchen Man." But "Till the Cows Come Home" was recorded four years after "Kitchen Man," and went unreleased for decades.

When she meets a very slick John Hammond in 1933, he relays his plans for a Spirituals to Swing concert: "Gonna build a new venue especially for it, called the Café Society, the first integrated nightclub." That club did open, with Hammond as an advisor, the same night as that Carnegie Hall concert, but those events were five years in the future, and he'd only hear about the club shortly before it opened.[11] At what would be her last record date in 1933, producer Hammond grandly introduces her to (a preppy) Benny Goodman, then unknown, ignoring the established Jack Teagarden, anonymous in the background. (Unmentioned: Billie Holiday would record her first session, with Goodman and Hammond, in the same studio three days later.) *Bessie* implies without outright fibbing that this is when she records 1931's "Long Old Road"—we see her looking at the music Hammond has thoughtfully brought along—which is heard under a montage that follows: "It's a long old road / But I'm gonna find the end." Biographer Chris Albertson had used that line for a chapter epigraph. Movie-Hammond also offers to produce Bessie's comeback tour, and as the montage rolls on she's singing "Long Old Road" to a packed theater—whites downstairs, blacks in the balcony. The real Smith had a late-period comeback, and that's the high *Bessie* goes out on.

The last act is all about closure. Before that recording and revival, Clarence takes her south for a healing reunion with Ma Rainey (who retired to Georgia in 1935); they do a happy, casual duet on "Ma Rainey's Black Bottom"—Mo'Nique singing this one herself. They sing together cheerfully now, if only for themselves. Ma also reads to her from a (1926) *Vanity Fair* article on blues singers by Carl Van Vechten, self-satisfied white chronicler of the Harlem arts.

Earlier, Bessie had attended a party thrown by rich patronizing Van Vechten, where (as in life—1928) she'd performed "Work House Blues," misbehaved a bit, and met (a timid) Langston Hughes. In the movie she also throws a drink in her host's face when he utters the title of his novel *Nigger Heaven*—period slang for theater balconies where blacks were permitted. As she storms out he quips, "If Bessie Smith is crude and primitive, she reflects the true folk spirit of her race," quoting from that very *Vanity Fair* article Ma will read from years later, as if it had just arrived in the mail. (Even I don't care she's holding the wrong issue.) She reads the passage where he declares Ethel Waters "superior to any stage singer of her race."[12] Ma comments, very adroitly for the 1930s, " 'Superior': See how they love to instigate, set us up against each other?" She and Bessie are beyond that now.

Although *Bessie* sidesteps her death, there's foreshadowing. In that "Long Old Road" montage, Bessie dedicates a new tombstone for her mother—prompting a rare happy flashback to childhood; it's an allusion to how fans would finance a stone for her own unmarked grave in 1970. In the last scene, Bessie and her man Richard picnic in the idyllic country, sitting in the back of his pick-up: "I do wanna know," she tells him, "what's over that next hill, around the next corner."

"Well let's go."

Under the closing credits, we finally hear the real Bessie Smith, singing the most rousing tune from her final session, "Gimme a Pigfoot and a Bottle of Beer." But it's overlaid with a tacky, tin-eared, modernized swing arrangement—as if to remind us this whole project might have turned out much worse.

> **Miles Ahead (2016; 101 minutes; director: Don Cheadle; screenplay: Cheadle, Steven Baigelman; story: Baigelman, Cheadle, Stephen J. Rivele, Christopher Wilkinson). Cast includes: Don Cheadle (Miles Davis), Ewan McGregor (Dave Braden/interviewer), Emayatzy Corinealdi (Frances Taylor Davis), Lakeith Stanfield (Junior), Michael Stuhlbarg (Harper Hamilton), Ken Early (George Butler), Jeffrey Grover (Gil Evans), Herbie Hancock, Wayne Shorter, Esperanza Spalding, Gary Clark Jr., Antonio Sanchez, Phil Schaap (themselves).**
> **—Circa 1980, on the eve of Miles Davis's comeback after five years in seclusion, the trumpeter trawls New York for a stolen session tape and thinks back on his relationship with dancer Frances Taylor.**

Among the biopics of the mid-teens, Don Cheadle's *Miles Ahead* was especially audacious and genuinely entertaining, with a method self-consciously modeled on Miles Davis's restless search for new modes of expression. As screen Miles says—one of many echoes of the trumpeter's actual pronouncements—"Music don't move on, then it's dead music."

Cheadle had been the Davis family's choice to play the late trumpeter, and the actor took that endorsement seriously. He became the film's chief fundraiser, its director and cowriter, and got deep into character over eight years of prep. On set, he might direct in character, as if channeling the man: "I wanted to do what Miles did, as opposed to just show who he was. I wanted to take on the task of being like Miles."[13] He described the story as something Miles might've wanted to star in, a tall tale rooted in historical fact. *Miles Ahead* deals with the period starting in 1975 when Davis dropped out of making records or touring for five years. Its central plot is pure fiction: a coked-up gun-toting Miles seeks to retrieve a tape of one of his rare period sessions, swiped from his house during a party. The film recasts Miles Davis as blaxploitation hero.

It's a biographical fantasy, but to be fair, (living) subjects of fanciful biopics don't always mind, preferring to keep their real selves off screen. George M. Cohan encouraged the makers of the malarkey-ful *Yankee Doodle Dandy* to take even more liberties. (James Cagney's Cohan is its unreliable narrator, telling his story to Pres. Franklin Roosevelt as momentary diversion from the headaches of leadership.) The very private Jerome Kern signed away the rights to his life on condition the story would be hokum. Cole Porter was fine with being portrayed as heterosexual in 1946's *Night and Day*.[14] "I don't think anybody cares about the facts of my life, about dates and places," Al the character advises the writers of *The Jolson Story*, in its sequel *Jolson Sings Again*. "You juggle them any way you like." (On the other hand, Francis Paudras objected when *'Round Midnight*'s story departed from his own.)

Setting the main action in *Miles Ahead* in a period where Miles Davis was out of the public eye gave the writers extra leeway. As he summed up those years in his nominal autobiography, "I just took a lot of cocaine (about $500 a day at one point) and fucked all the women I could get into my house."[15] He was addicted to pills and drank heavily. His life as depicted in *Miles Ahead* is consistent with details that emerged. Persistent hip trouble gave him a limp, he mostly stayed in, and he painted a bit; his music-making mostly consisted of musing on piano, making chords. An amateur boxer, he'd watch old title bouts on TV; he'd owe drug dealers money, always a bad idea; he called Phil Schaap's jazz radio show to request his own *Sketches of Spain*. His converted church in the middle of a block on West 77th Street was a mess, with trash and newspapers everywhere. And occasionally, his eldest son Gregory wrote, he'd get into druggy escapades out of boredom.

In his own memoir, Gregory Davis says most stories written about his father were "pure bullshit," but that Miles "very often found the fictionalized accounts of his deeds far more interesting than the factual ones."[16] Still, Miles did not seem to harbor aspirations as an actor. A couple of cameos aside, his oeuvre consists of a 1985 *Miami Vice* episode, "Junk Love" (written by Julia Cameron), where he plays Ivory Jones, brothel proprietor turned government snitch. He croaks his lines in a halting cadence, looks cornered and forlorn with a furrowed brow, and exits halfway through, killed off-camera. He didn't care for the role, which gave him little to do. Gregory says Miles didn't like blaxploitation films either (and that he'd found the focus on drugs in *Lady Sings the Blues* and *Bird* distasteful). Even so, Corky McCoy's cover paintings of funky folk for *On the Corner* and other 1970s Miles LPs lined up with *Shaft*'s and *Super Fly*'s streetwise aesthetic.

Miles Ahead is partly an homage to blaxploitation films—stories of urban black men who dominate their women and defeat white fat cats—with a nod to period cop shows where cars plow into piled-up cardboard boxes. But Cheadle's Miles has something few blaxploitation heroes do: a white sidekick. The director was frank about why: they couldn't raise enough money without a bankable white costar. So Ewan McGregor was cast as Dave Braden, a Scot who hopes to write Miles's comeback story for *Rolling Stone* and winds up tagging along with him for two crazy days.[17] (Impossible to say exactly when *Miles Ahead* is set. From dialogue and an outgoing phone message, we know day one is a Tuesday and Yom Kippur falls on day two. The film's publicity says it's 1979— and that missing tape from 1978 is said to be almost a year old—but in the story he's been gone five years, which would make it 1980. Yom Kippur didn't fall on a Wednesday either year.)

But with McGregor on board, Cheadle and cowriter Steven Baigelman—who'd worked on the time-looping James Brown biopic *Get On Up*—nonetheless devised an ingenious white-buddy workaround. Miles was a Gemini, and liked to say he was two people. Many have testified he could be very sweet, or anything but. So the writers fashioned an opposite-twin story line to complement the A plot: the romance between Miles and his favorite of all his women, dancer Frances Taylor Davis. Within the main tale, he's often flashing back to his life with her—not least whenever he sees her face on the cover of his 1961 LP *Someday My Prince Will Come.*

The 1979–80 story is macho and mostly fiction; Miles acts evil and looks frazzled, and interacts mostly with white people. The 1950s–60s story is feminist, and mostly true; Miles is dapper and sensitive (often, anyway), and his social milieu is much blacker. The Frances story is the date movie within the blaxploitation film.

Both stories have a third one wrapped around them: a narrative frame the film begins and nearly ends with. Ewan McGregor plays a (mostly off-camera) TV journalist who may or may not be Braden (different hair), interviewing Miles on the eve of his come-back. (He resumed playing concerts in 1981.) The trumpeter balks at hearing his music called jazz—"It's social music"—and pointedly chides the interviewer for his stodgy introduction: "If you're gonna tell a story, come with some attitude, man." With that, director Cheadle declares his artistic intentions.

The interviewer asks, how did you find your way back to the music? By way of answer, Miles puts his horn to his lips and begins to blow a solo we don't hear—because at that moment we jump into the main story, via a 35-second 1970s-TV–style teaser of a car chase to come. An hour and 26 minutes later, when we return to the interview, Miles is blowing the last note of his apparently brief solo. (The same track from his acid-funk classic *Agartha* is playing in the background, but "rewound" to a passage already heard.) So you might interpret the main story as a flashback, or as a fantasy that flashes through Miles's mind as he improvises. Either way, the main story answers the interviewer's question.

Or perhaps the whole tale is Dave Braden's account of his two days with Miles—the one he has threatened to write just before the film's main action ends. Post-solo, when the interviewer asks, how would you put what you just played into words, Miles responds "You just did." And since (as we're reminded) journalists habitually make stuff up about

FIGURE 11.4 The date movie within the blaxploitation movie: Miles Davis (Don Cheadle) serenades Frances (Emayatzy Corinealdi) in *Miles Ahead.*

him, Braden's version is likely embroidered: unreliable. Like the ambiguous tunes Miles's quintet played in the 1960s, this tale is open to a few interpretations.

Reading the main narrative as Miles's own fantasy opens a window onto his/the character's state of mind, drawing on details from his daily life, and those blaxploitation movies he'd checked out and crime shows on the TV that's always on. That subjective viewpoint also justifies various misremembered or reshuffled dates, skewed details, and even apparent continuity errors. (After the party at his pad, the place immediately reverts to everyday mess, not postparty mess.)

Seeing this urban adventure as Miles's dream is consistent with his sometimes delusional state of mind during his druggy 1970s intermezzo. It may even explain why New York looks like Cincinnati (where it was shot), or why West 77th is a two-way street. In *Miles Ahead*, the Village Vanguard—the basement venue whose small kitchen doubles as dressing room—has a spacious sub-basement containing stacks of firewood, an incongruous David Lynch detail. When Miles is riding in a corporate elevator adorned with album covers including *Someday My Prince Will Come*, he pushes away the back wall and steps onto a concert stage, playing "Miles Ahead" in 1953, on the night he'll meet Frances. Much later, at the film's dramatic climax, Miles goes to a boxing match—where, as in a joke, a fight breaks out—and sometimes it's boxers in the ring, and sometimes it's his quintet, playing "So What": the 1964 *Miles in Berlin* version, with its bobbing and weaving, sting-like-a-bee pugilistic timing.

Not that he's totally delusional. Some details ring true. In *Miles Ahead*, fans can be ghoulish and a producer speculates he might be worth more to his record company dead. A drug dealer ups his price because Miles is the customer. Braden acts like his friend but is plotting to steal that tape everyone's after. (Miles distrusted reporters and most critics—and Dave has been lying since they met). Columbia Records jazz honcho George Butler is looking to replace him with some younger trumpeter the label can groom into the next Miles. (The real Butler did court a couple of young prospects back then, signing Wynton Marsalis in 1980.)

In the movie the upstart taking a meeting at Columbia when Miles drops by is a young funkster (with a dope habit) literally named Junior. On trumpet, both Miles and Junior are ghosted by Keyon Harrold, who sometimes had to dub plausible lines to match actor Cheadle's on-set fingerings. Junior's abusive patron is smiling sleazy independent producer Harper Hamilton, who'd like to gets his mitts on Miles's mystery tape himself. As would George Butler, who's dangling a $20,000 paycheck. They're all in the room, along with Harper's armed muscle, and lying Dave (covertly taping this very conversation), when Miles fires a gun over the shoulder of a bean-counter who's just smugly explained that Columbia really owns that session tape. Miles takes all the man's cash for a little extra humbling—the hero's blaxploitation moment—then looks at them all in disgust: "And I'm the asshole in the room, right?" The scene calls back to the Miles-y *A Man Called Adam*, when Adam humiliates his agent in his office.

The 1979/1980 storyline is all chaos, fueled by Davis's jittery early-1970s wah-wah funk, lifted from the albums *Jack Johnson*, *Dark Magus*, and *Agartha*—music far removed from Miles's poppier 1980s comeback sound. The 1970s superfunk was so unpopular when new that two of those albums weren't issued in the States for 15 years. Its prominence here marks how its reputation grew later. Popular taste had caught up.

Contrasted with that timeline is the world Miles drifts into whenever he thinks of Frances, where nattily besuited Harmon-muted Miles can be utterly charming, and makes this gorgeous, talented woman melt. In Frances-land we see a bit of Miles Davis's real white buddy, orchestral arranger Gil Evans, who helped make the music we hear from *Porgy and Bess* and *Sketches of Spain* so ravishing.

The film restages the recording of *Porgy*'s "Gone," almost as a documentary—a brass section rehearses on camera from the original score. But when the tape starts rolling we discreetly skip straight to the master-take trumpet solo—getting straight to the heart of the number. Cheadle's sidelining to Davis solos is very good; he'd spent years learning trumpet and looks at home with it. The physical gestures are less about touching the lip than things he does with his lips when he's not playing: little flutters that hint at music Miles hears in his head. (In these flashback scenes, he's playing a modern Monette trumpet, with streamlined tubing. Much as this book sweats jazz-historical details, we haven't fretted over anachronistic microphones or incorrect saxophone models. But such details matter where an iconic, much-photographed figure is concerned, like Miles with his Martin Committee trumpet and its rounder curves. His playing the wrong horn is like a movie-Hendrix playing a hollow-body at Woodstock.)

Miles Ahead re-creates with admirable fidelity several scenes involving Miles and Frances, as he or she later recalled them. (She has a co–executive producer credit.) This starts with the moment they met, as told in his autobiography, when he accompanied a friend who was dropping off a package for her and the pair felt an instant attraction. We feel it too. The camera loves Cheadle's and Emayatzy Corinealdi's faces; both actors are even better-looking than the people they play. We see the casual racism Frances endures as a dancer (a couple of suits at an audition joke about "dark meat"), and the blatant racism Miles suffered one night in 1959 outside Birdland (unnamed here). A policeman angered by seeing Davis usher a white woman into a taxi told him to move along, and then two cops beat him up after he replied he had every right to stand outside his workplace. When the cops dump him in a cell, Cheadle looks very like Miles in newspaper photos: two bandages on his head and blood spattered over the right shoulder of his light-colored jacket. And as in life, he's bailed out by an incensed Frances, in no mood to be placated by the authorities.

He loves her, though he cheats on her. When she's at a club, he plays only for her. (For a moment, the rest of the band and audience disappear.) It's very romantic: Miles's beautifully crafted ballad solos are *billet doux*. But he asks a lot—for Frances to play hooky from a successful show to be beside him, and finally, after they're married, to give up dancing altogether. "I know it's a sacrifice," he says, though the look she gives him says he can't begin to know. But she acquiesces. Later we'll see her on the phone, trying to schedule student lessons, a more mundane life than flying off to dance in London or doing *West Side Story* on Broadway.

Frances is with him into the mid-1960s, by which time he's got a new band, rehearsing Wayne Shorter's "Nefertiti." (That would make it 1967, but the couple had broken up by then. The sidelining musicians look little like their real counterparts, even if the pianist wears glasses, like Herbie Hancock.)

The frame-story interviewer had called Frances Miles's muse. It's a difficult role for a mortal. "I gave up everything for you, Miles," she reminds him. "You have never played better a day in your life, and you know it." And truly, in the mid-1960s his sometimes erratic chops were in great shape, the better to keep up with his explosive young band.

We glimpse the years with Frances in discontinuous (but sequential) episodes. As we've seen, narratives that skip around in time can cover a lot of ground while quietly sidestepping conventional biopic business. This Miles has no parents, no kids, no other wives. That elliptical economy—a hallmark of Davis's music too—makes the film a bit fragmentary: a postmodern puzzle-box. That's what movies had become by the 'teens anyway, with the likes of *X–Men: Days of Future Past*—a succession of jagged scenes between which heroes travel through time. *Miles Ahead* speaks the language of the pop (movies) of its era.

In the end, the twin tales swallow each other's tails. The Frances story ends as Miles gets hooked on hip-related painkillers and inches toward the madness of his dark years. As in life, he convinces himself there's someone else in the house—her phantom lover—and he threatens violence. Frances humors him so she can get away. That episode is intercut with the boxing-match climax of the later timeline, which will end with Miles beginning to climb out of his druggy hole. Frances briefly bridges both arcs. We see her, dressed as in the parallel 1960s scene, fleeing the auditorium along with the other fight fans, when Miles punches Harper Hamilton and in the ensuing melee finally retrieves his tape, with help from Dave and from Junior, who's decided to switch allegiances.

At long last, we—and Dave and Junior—hear the mystery tape. (The can is labeled 9–7–78, a date that can be read two ways but matches no known July or September session.) Instead of a new sound to rocket Miles into the next decade—when he played big arenas, worked with hip-hop producers, and covered Michael Jackson and Cyndi Lauper—it's a spare meandering improvisation with a little organ noodling, like a 1970s Sun Ra outtake. It's pointedly unstupendous (and not real Miles).

After a polite interval Dave asks, "When do you come in?"

Miles says that's him on organ.

Dave, incredulous: "The whole time?"

To explain why, Miles picks up his horn: his chops are totally shot, as they often were back then. (The horn talks for him.) You could go back to playing scales, Junior glumly suggests—he's sabotaged his own prospects for this? But as the tape rolls on, and Dave angrily tells Miles he's going to write the true story of this whole sorry episode, hapless Junior comes to the rescue. He starts playing trumpet over the tape, a Milesy kind of Spanish line snaking through modal changes—something he hears in those inchoate organ chords: a melody and harmonic progression to draw out.

Miles: "That ain't in there."

Junior (sounding confident, for the first time): "Yes it is. Lemme show you." He goes to the piano and demonstrates, and Miles comes over and immediately (as he was wont to do with his sidemen's compositions) begins to edit Junior's work: Play this chord instead of that one. And voice this one like so: "It opens it up, makes it a little cooler. You can go anywhere with that." Junior reawakens Miles's interest in music.

As Dave approvingly observes this intergenerational exchange, we hear Miles's words from the opening interview, about telling a story with attitude, and suddenly we're back in the frame story—evidently set some considerable time after the scene just witnessed, since Miles can now play again. And when he abruptly gets up to leave—"I got work to do"—the interviewer steps into the shot to deliver the punchline: "Hey Miles! Are you coming back?"

Then the action steps out of that frame story, into another postmodern box: to Miles looking rather like his 1980 self, playing a concert encore, his vest emblazoned with the very-2016 Twitter hashtag #SOCIALMUSIC, and fronting a multigenerational funk band with real elders Wayne Shorter and Herbie Hancock, hip-hop/jazz pianist Robert Glasper who supervised and contributed to the score, rock/blues guitarist Gary Clark Jr., jazz/pop star Esperanza Spalding on electric bass, and drummer Antonio Sanchez pounding a backbeat. The music—Glasper's (and Cheadle's, say the credits) "What's Wrong With That?"—is the closest thing to 1980s Miles we hear.

In life as in movies, some folks brazenly speak for the dead in confident unprovable assertions: If Charlie Parker were alive today he'd be playing _____ (bebop, fusion, free jazz, hip-hop, easy-listening, classical music). This all-star dream band cheekily declares Miles's posthumous preferences. But he embodied too many contradictions and his legacy is too contested, even within his family, for channeling Cheadle to speak for him with confidence. This out-of-time sequence is meant to remind us of Davis's broad and continuing influence. Lest we miss the point, a legend over the final freeze frame gives his date of birth, but leaves his death date blank—because Miles is forever, you dig? And then there's hip-hop over the final credits. Not jazz. But social music.

> **Born to Be Blue** (2016; 97 minutes; director/writer: Robert Budreau). **Cast includes: Ethan Hawke (Chet Baker), Carmen Ejogo (Jane Azuka/Elaine), Callum Keith Rennie (Dick Bock), Kevin Hanchard (Dizzy Gillespie), Kedar Brown (Miles Davis), Stephen McHattie (Chet's father), Janet-Laine Green (Chet's mother), Kwasi Songui (Birdland emcee), Joe Cobden (actor playing Dick Bock), Tony Nardi (Nick Dean), Tony Nappo (Officer Reid).**
> **—In 1966, trumpeter Chet Baker is playing himself in a biopic, which is canceled when he loses his front teeth in a beating. His costar Jane sticks around to help him recover—as long as he stays off heroin.**

There are striking parallels between *Miles Ahead* and the Chet Baker biopic *Born to Be Blue*, released just weeks earlier, in March 2016. Each focuses on an introspective-sounding trumpeter during a career hiatus, imposing a fantasy narrative on that time. In each, the horn man asks his woman to sacrifice her performing career to his. And each reminds its viewer the story's a fiction: *Miles Ahead* with that unmoored-in-time concert finale; *Born to Be Blue* with an audacious biopic-within-the-biopic, featuring Chet playing himself.

Chet playing Chet: that had almost happened. In 1961, while Baker was locked up on a drug charge in Lucca, Italy, film producer Dino De Laurentiis bought the rights to his life story, intending Baker to play the lead. (He'd already had small roles in the American war movie *Hell's Horizon* and Italian youth comedy *Urlatori alla sbarra*.) Baker was never much of a composer, but while in prison, he wrote some music for the film. By the time he was released months later, however, De Laurentiis had moved on.

Once more, a fictionalized life story incorporates shards of the real thing. *Born to Be Blue* is the first fiction film to take up the 1950s schism between jazz in New York and in Los Angeles—broadly referred to in jazz parlance as East Coast versus West Coast. New York jazz was more intense, even as the Charlie Parker–Dizzy Gillespie bebop of the 1940s morphed into slower, bluesier, distinctly African American hardbop. Los Angeles had boppers too, but the press zeroed in on (mostly) white cool-school musicians influenced by Miles's svelte nonet of 1949 and 1950, whose recordings were collected as *Birth of the Cool*. Baker was the face of West Coast cool; he played in a lyrical laidback Miles-derived style that seemed to go with sunshine and Pacific breezes. He also sang with a choirboy's uninflected purity.

As in life, and as depicted in *Born to Be Blue*—or sometimes in the black-and-white biopic within it (also called *Born to Be Blue*, after a tune Chet recorded in 1964)—a symbolic title bout was arranged at Birdland in 1954. In life, Baker's band split the bill with either Dizzy Gillespie or Miles. In the movie it's Chet versus Dizzy *and* Miles, two against one. Baker did not take New York by storm on that trip, and it rattled him.[18]

As the movie shows, with varying degrees of accuracy, at the instigation of his long-time record producer Dick Bock, Baker made some cheesy Tijuana Brass–knockoff albums (in 1965 and 1966). He had lost one front tooth in a childhood mishap. In 1966, the real Baker lost another, in a mysterious beatdown that may have resulted from a drug connection gone sour. His mouth was so damaged he had the rest of his front uppers extracted and replaced with dentures, and had to learn to play with a new, less stable embouchure. His recovery was slow and fitful, and complicated by drug relapses. He basically stopped recording till 1970. Around that time he was playing in a San Jose pizzeria jam session, trying to get back in shape. With help from Dizzy Gillespie, in 1973 he got a rare New York club date that earned him some renewed attention (along with some lukewarm reviews).

In standard biopic fashion, *Born to Be Blue* compresses the time frame, squeezing the Italy-1961-to-New-York-1973 action into about two years. It pushes his incarceration in Lucca ahead to 1966, mere months before the beating that (in the movie) knocks out all his upper front teeth, the central moment in *Born to Be Blue* as triumphant comeback story.

In 1966, the real Chet Baker had been living outside Los Angeles with third wife Carol, who gave birth to their third child that year. In *Born to Be Blue*, American director

Nick Dean gets Chet released early from Italian prison in 1966 to shoot a Baker biopic in Hollywood, an arrangement that somehow saddles Chet with a California probation officer. Movie-Chet has no wife or family—there are throwaway references to a son and two failed marriages—and he's on the lookout, as the real Baker often was, for a good-looking woman to care for him. He makes a play for his costar, who portrays his wife Elaine, Jane Azuka. (Her surname: "It's African and it means 'Past Glory.'") Jane's wary of Chet, but consents to go on a date with him, if only to find out what women see in this guy who's obviously bad news and not much of an actor. That first date (bowling alley—subtle callout to *Young Man with a Horn*) is going great till three black guys jump him outside and one punitively pistol-whips him: "No more jazz, mother-fucker!" Jane's heart then goes out to him: Chet has nobody else. Even old friend Dick Bock turns away.

Born to Be Blue subjects Baker's story to the usual screen contortions and character compositing. (Bock for instance becomes his manager as well as producer.) But Canadian writer/director Robert Budreau uses the film-within-the-film to highlight such biopic chicanery. After a brief, subjective Lucca prologue—strung-out Chet sees/imagines a tarantula crawling out of his horn—*Born to Be Blue* begins in black-and-white, with Baker at Birdland in 1954, besieged by screaming girls who want his autograph (that used to happen), and getting cold eyes from Miles. Birdland's emcee—a big guy, not diminutive Pee Wee Marquette—gives Chet a warm introduction riddled with inaccuracies: Chet hadn't, in fact, won any *Down Beat* polls as vocalist; *TIME* hadn't claimed he'd invented "West Coast swing," a term which refers to a much later dance style.[19] (Chet's music was dubbed West Coast jazz or West Coast cool.) And no one was calling him "the James Dean of jazz" in 1954, when Dean was a little-known TV actor. After that buildup, Chet goes into "Let's Get Lost," which he hadn't yet recorded.

That same night, Chet injects heroin for the first time (after Miles has put him down)—which is very bad history. But then the actors break character, and on a cut between shots we go from black-and-white to color and discover we've been watching the movie-within-the-movie. Chet complains about how fake everything is: he'd first shot heroin long before. "And if you want it to be realistic there should just be puke everywhere. . . . It wasn't like this at all." We can't put much stock in Nick Dean's fictional biopic: Dick Bock (Callum Keith Rennie) visits the set and tells the actor playing Dick Bock he's doing it wrong—much as Francis Paudras lambasted François Cluzet on the set of *'Round Midnight*. Jane is playing a composite of all Chet's women, and was cast because of her resemblance to (fictitious) ex-wife Elaine.

Born to Be Blue skips around in time, like a proper postmodern biopic, and shifts between color and black-and-white like a 1960s art movie. Dean's picture is weeks into shooting when it's canceled, and later in the parent film, when an image goes to b&w, it is typically footage from that abortive film, filling the flashback function—clever. Yet the lines between inner and outer biopics blur. The same actors play Chet and Miles in both, and Chet's woman still looks like Carmen Ejogo. (Blurring even more, for a moment we see Chet with his postbeating mouth in the Birdland era.) The only sure tells: when Jane is Elaine, she wears bust-enhancing falsies and carries herself like a bigger person. And there are the two Dick Bocks.

By making viewers question exactly what we're looking at, *Born to Be Blue*'s black-and-white segments remind us the whole film is a biopic. The outer, color movie offers reminders too. There's blatantly expository dialogue. "A lot's changed since you left," Dick tells Chet. "Jazz is dying. Dylan went electric." After Chet gets beaten, Jane is struck by how improbably quickly Dean's film gets canceled—highlighting biopic time-compression. Later when Chet lands a special return one-nighter at Birdland, he has to leave for New York the very next day. Not even Manhattan moves that fast.

Budreau keeps faith with one biopic tradition: Invented events reveal some higher truth about a character. The director takes his subject seriously. In 2009 he made an eight-minute short, *The Deaths of Chet Baker*. It has never been explained how the trumpeter was found dead on the pavement below his Amsterdam hotel window in 1988. Budreau's short lays out three possibilities: he nodded out while high and fell; he jumped to his death; he was pushed by some fellow lowlife. (Baker's played by craggy character actor Stephen McHattie, and his killer by Ted Dykstra, who'd bedeviled another trumpeter in *Giant Steps*.)

Budreau and *Born to Be Blue* star Ethan Hawke bring out aspects of the real Baker's personality: his competitiveness, his persuasive ways with women, his need to be cared for. His first two wives were said to look alike—so here he gets involved with an actress who resembles his ex-wife. (Dark-skinned Halema Alli Baker wasn't African American like Jane/Elaine, but the real Baker had at least one black girlfriend.) Even his sexual shortcomings and strengths—as reported by his women, and we'll skip the details—are tastefully dealt with. But Jane helps up his game in bed: "Pretend you're playing me." That slows him down.

We also see Baker the way his fans do, and hear how they justify their love of his strained later work. "Everything came so easily for him musically," Dick says of Chet's early days. "I think that was one of the problems." Bock serves up a little flawed-artist romanticism: "Maybe poor technique will actually give his sound character—like the old Chet, but deeper."

Born to Be Blue likewise romanticizes his trumpet sound. We don't hear any actual Chet Baker—his trumpet parts (like Miles's and Dizzy's) were ghosted by Toronto jazzman Kevin Turcotte, who gets the flavor of his careful, tentative middle-register lyricism, and bathes his lines in an idealized, rosy tone. Not that we hear Chet play so very much, though we see him in the studio more than most jazz heroes—with the Mariachi Brass (wearing sombreros while they record, an absurdity justified by a photographer's presence), or warming up "There's a Small Hotel" and "Over the Rainbow" in quartet, or singing "My Funny Valentine" for invited guests. In concert, the character does jazz-movie–abbreviated tunes and one-tune sets, and might sing more than play even then.

Chet Baker fascinates people partly because of his striking decline. He became a youth idol because he was California good-looking, with high cheekbones and a strong jaw. (He did get called a jazz James Dean, after 1955.) But later in life, after decades of drug use, his face collapsed into a wizened mug out of a Dorothea Lange dustbowl portrait. In the movie, as part of his long road to recovery, Chet takes Jane back to his parents' farm in Yale, Oklahoma, where he spends the winter learning to play again (almost literally woodshedding). As in life, mother dotes on him and father is cold and sarcastic. (Stephen McHattie is perfect as the bitter dad; his weathered face predicts Chet's future. Has any other actor portrayed a jazz musician and his father in different films?) Dad finds Chet's singing effeminate, and his behavior the family's shame. As the trumpeter sits in the yard, trying to build up his lip, Chesney Sr. tosses Chet's old rocking horse on a pyre and sets it ablaze. This Midwest idyll lays bare Baker's roots, and like much in this film it's strikingly photographed. When the real Baker came back from Europe in 1964, he (and his family) did move in with his parents, and after his bustup he did (as shown) work temporarily at a nearby gas station. But the Bakers had left Oklahoma when Chet was 10. His parents lived in Redondo Beach.

Born to Be Blue was mostly filmed in Ontario, but Budreau also shot along the California coast and captures the romance of 1950s West Coast cool as portrayed on sun-and-surf album covers and in William Claxton's photographs of young Chet and beautiful Halema. Chet moves into Jane's (too modern) VW camper, parked among the dunes; Chet hitchhikes to Malibu to beg Dick Bock to give him another chance. (He'll soften when Chet sticks to a methadone-maintenance program.) It's not so much that Budreau (or Nick Dean) quotes classic images as that he provides more of the same: Chet and Elaine in a picnic tableau from the inner biopic, overlooking the ocean, with a surfboard and portable radio for props; Chet blowing horn in the surf. The California and Oklahoma sequences look great and are a pleasure to watch. New York is a different matter—nothing but bad vibrations there. Birdland is a dungeon by comparison.

FIGURE 11.5 Chet Baker (Ethan Hawke) and Jane Azuka (Carmen Ejogo) get iconically Californian in the biopic within the biopic *Born to Be Blue*.

Promoting the film, star Ethan Hawke suggested *Born to Be Blue* is a story you might imagine while listening to Chet Baker. More plausibly, you might read it as Baker's own fantasy version of his life story, a story he'd relate with many variations over the years. (Was it three black guys who jumped him, or five? Why not 50, one friend wondered.) When Chet recounted his life to interviewers and others, details were invented, chronologies shuffled, awkward storylines excised, and nothing was ever his fault. The real Baker was an occasional thief; he abandoned wives and neglected his kids; his girlfriends often developed their own drug problems. But months before he died, he'd say, "I've never done anything to hurt anyone." Movie-Chet says much the same: The only one I've hurt is me.[20]

Born to Be Blue isn't the only film to let Baker off easy. Bruce Weber's creepy 1988 documentary *Let's Get Lost*, filmed in fashion-magazine black-and-white, took distasteful pleasure in getting various women in Chet's life to speak ill of each other, while leaving him above the fray. Baker is more a presence than a character in *Let's Get Lost*, an Easter Island monument draped by young women as he rides around in the back of a convertible. It's a movie about surfaces: about the lunar phases of Chet's face over the years, full to waning. It also became one of the essential jazz films for cineastes and future filmmakers.

Ethan Hawke likes that documentary, and had first considered playing Baker in the late 1990s when he and director Richard Linklater sketched a possible scenario: Chet just before heroin. Hawke brings unshowy intensity to the part, his hair slicked back like Baker later in life. (Chet's 1960s hair was wilder, of its time.) Hawke's face, with its pronounced cheekbones and its own weathering, hints at Baker's early prettiness and at the dissipated Okie to come. The actor approximates Baker's quiet way of speaking, and the moonlit singing voice. (One night in Jane's little blue camper he sings an a cappella "Blue Room" very like Baker's own on the *Let's Get Lost* soundtrack album.) He's believable as Chet struggling to play himself in Nick Dean's movie, where he's told to improvise dialogue and then told he's doing it wrong. But Hawke also makes us see the seductive charm: makes you see the world Chet's way. Even within the narrative he chisels the facts; he later refers to that life-changing beatdown as "the accident." In the movie Chet loses all those front teeth in that beating—just the way he'd sometimes tell it. When his probation officer says, "I've been working with junkie musicians for over 20 years, I have never seen anyone work this hard before," or when surly Miles is moved to applaud him, that sounds like Chet's version.

In the movie as in life, Chet tells uncorroborated stories that make himself look good—like the time dozens of trumpeters turned out to audition for a Charlie Parker gig, and Bird sent them all away when he found out Chet was there. (He did get that job.) Or how Bird warned Dizzy and Miles, "There's a [little] white cat on the coast who's gonna eat you up." (Chet loves that one, repeats it to himself like a prayer.)

Even when he goes back to heroin in the end, it's not really his fault; it's Jane's, because she hasn't come to New York with him, instead staying in LA to try to salvage her own career. (Elsewhere he's more honest: he gets high because he likes it, likes the effect heroin has on his mindset. "Time gets wider. . . . I can get inside every note.") Similarly, in Nick Dean's biopic, Chet starts shooting up because Miles had paid him a snippy compliment on opening night in 1954—a plot point even movie-Chet finds contrived. In the scene in question, Miles tells him he plays "sweet—like candies." (The actual trumpeter who made a candy analogy was Baker's LA friend Jack Sheldon.) New York isn't for you, movie-within-the-movie–Miles tells him: "Come back when you've lived a little."

This hostile New York jazz establishment is seen through Chet's filter (and that's realistic enough for a mid-1960s jazz film; many white musicians reported black colleagues weren't so friendly anymore). At 1954 Birdland, Miles might glare and Dizzy kept his distance, but the mostly black audience gives his first tune a warm reception. Later in *Born to Be Blue*, when Chet is climbing out of his hole in the 1960s, Dizzy comes to hear him at a showcase Dick Bock has arranged and mildly praises his playing. "It's almost flat—but somehow it's still nice." (Though Dizzy still doesn't like the singing.)

In life, in 1973 when Gillespie ran into Chet and found out he was out of work, immediately and unprompted, he called New York and arranged for Baker to play two weeks at the Half Note.[21] In the movie, Dizzy has that same kind of clout—"Everybody respects you; you got the key to the gate," says Chet. As in *Bird*, Gillespie is the voice of the responsible jazz establishment. His endorsement counts, like Paul Whiteman's in 1940s films. The real Dizzy was known for helping other trumpeters, but in *Born to Be Blue*, he's a reluctant benefactor. Chet wants Diz to help him book Birdland. They only do special events now, Diz explains. (That's one way to put it—the club had closed in 1965.) And he doesn't think Chet is up to it: "You can only be ready when your mind is ready." But as Chet reminds him, Miles had said come back after you've lived a little—Chet now confusing his unfinished biopic for his actual life—prompting Dizzy to reluctantly (but instantly) arrange Chet's New York one-nighter. Dizzy will attend that Birdland gig, dragging along a reluctant Miles, sporting a 1960s Nehru jacket.

Throughout Chet's painful recovery Jane has stuck by him, even backing him on piano at that pizza parlor. (The real Baker became involved long term with the drummer on that gig, Diane Vavra.) Jane pledges her support as long as he stays off junk. But in New York without her, out of methadone, and with Miles scowling out front, Chet shoots heroin before going on at Birdland (and, very unjunkie-like, leaves his works lying around the dressing room).

But then Jane shows up after all. When Chet sings "Please excuse this haze I'm in" during "I've Never Been in Love Before"—the first song he ever sang for her, when she started warming to him, just before he lost his teeth—she sees that he's stoned and walks out on him for good (or so we hope for her sake, although she's pregnant). But it's OK. When Chet tells the story of this night later, he'll talk less about losing her than how he played with so much soul, even Miles had to give it up.

Twist ending: at his New York reconciliation concert, the hero and his mate break up.

Nina **(2016; 90 minutes; director/writer: Cynthia Mort). Cast includes: Zoe Saldana (Nina Simone), David Oyelowo (Clifton Henderson), Ronald Guttman (Henri Edwards), Ella Joyce (Clifton's mother), Keith David (Clifton's father), Mike Epps (Richard Pryor).**

—By the late 1990s, tempestuous singer Nina Simone barely works anymore and lives in French exile. But new manager Clifton works to get her back into performing shape, with an eye toward a big New York concert.

"I am not a jazz pianist at all," Nina Simone said in 1983. "African-rooted classical music is what I play. I play jazz and blues, but they are not mine."[22] Pegging her as a jazz musician—because she was a black woman who sang and played piano—was stereotyping. Classically trained from childhood, denied the conservatory scholarship she'd been counting on, she started playing in an Atlantic City bar, where pianists were also obliged to sing. She'd improvise, but with a baroque flavor, as she segued between tunes, and she demanded nightclub audiences be recital-quiet. The songs she wrote put her closer to 1960s singer-songwriters than jazz composers. She borrowed material from folkie Judy Collins as well as Billie Holiday; the British-invasion band the Animals had two hits with songs she sang. Cynthia Mort's 2016 biopic *Nina* rightly places her in that broad context—even if Simone attracted a jazz audience by virtue of playing jazz clubs, concerts, and festivals.

Nina dovetails neatly with *Born to Be Blue* and *Miles Ahead*, both released that same spring: one more tale of a star in a troubled period of eclipse, a tale that skips around in time to cherry-pick from a complicated life, and gets the musician back on stage in the end. Like movie-Miles, Nina pulls a gun on a record company exec who tells her she's owed nothing. There are other echoes. An early sequence—Nina dragged kicking and screaming into a hospital ward—recalls the opening of *Lady Sings the Blues*. (A doctor helpfully recounts her maladies, à la *Bird* at Bellevue.) *Nina* also circles back to familiar story tropes, such as a reconciliatory New York concert finale. The production also evoked the stain of blackface, one more (inadvertent) echo of *The Jazz Singer*.

Nina was embroiled in controversy before shooting began, when lighter-skinned beauty Zoe Saldana was cast as the artist who'd been told "her nose is too big, her lips were too full, and her skin was too dark," per Simone's daughter Lisa. The filmmakers' workaround was to give Saldana a prosthetic, broader nose, and to darken her skin tone. But it's never as dark as the real Simone's; its pigment or texture varies from scene to scene; the nose doesn't always quite match the rest of the face. Makeup meant to fix a problem calls attention to it. (Simone's own fantasy-biopic casting: *High Society*'s very white—and retired—Grace Kelly.)[23]

Saldana does about as well as a miscast actor can. She captures Simone's regal hauteur, the sudden explosive mood swings, the bipolar peaks and troughs, the way she could play the grand lady to get what she wanted, the glare she'd give anyone who dared talk while she held the stage, and the boredom of doing bread-and-butter song "My Baby Just Cares for Me" for the billionth time. (But Saldana surely misspeaks, talking of Nina's early work in Atlanta rather than Atlantic City.)

Simone's great strength as a singer was her intensity, building from a subterranean rumble to shouts with the blunt fury of an expletive. Her most angry and sarcastic lyrics—like the pitiless "Mississippi Goddam"—were acid flung in a tyrant's face. Saldana, who does her own singing, suggests some of that power, doing the slowly building "Wild Is the

Wind" in a French cavern, Nina pulling herself out of a chemical fog to bewitch an audience. Saldana gets the film started with proper energy. Her slamming take on Anthony Newley's "Feeling Good" (ostensibly the Village Gate, 1965) is heard under the film's credits and over a headlines-and-LPs this-is-who-she-is montage.

Not that Zoe Saldana sounds like Nina Simone. When Clifton's admiring mom sings Nina's signature song "Four Women" back to her, she matches the real Simone's tight vibrato better than the star does. Singing a drowsy "Black Is the Color of My True Love's Hair," in what's presented as a black-and-white TV clip, and sporting a bushy circa-1970 Afro, Saldana looks and sounds like she's portraying Roberta Flack.

Nina focuses on the later 1990s, when Simone took on Clifton Henderson as her caretaker and then manager. He'd been a medical aide in the Los Angeles hospital where she'd been detained (because she pulled that gun, in the movie; after an altercation with a neighbor, in life). In *Nina*, Clifton is her entire household staff; the real Simone's entourage was a bit larger. Mostly they live at her place in Bouc-Bel-Air in the south of France, where he tries to keep her off champagne and on her stabilizing meds. (It must be a sign of her addled condition that they fly into Nice, two hours away, instead of nearby Marseilles. *Nina* was filmed in LA, but there's a *soupçon* of Riviera stock footage.)

From her chateau we bounce back to scenes from her earlier life. The real Nina's complex relationships with her sometimes abusive ex-husband and often neglected daughter are reduced to a happier-times montage, as Saldana sings "Brown Baby." Every flashback is dutifully teed up in a way that now seems old-fashioned. The filmic syntax, like Simone's piano, is more classical than jazzy. Clifton finds an old cassette tape, leading us to a flashback of Nina playing "(To Be) Young Gifted and Black" for playwright Lorraine Hansberry who inspired it—although that song written four years after Hansberry died in 1965 was named for a posthumous work.

At 90 minutes, *Nina* is admirably brisk—singing the quadruple-portrait "Four Women," she only has time for three—and the dialogue highlights its themes like a laser pointer. "I lost my family, my people, my country, my money, my dreams—I lost it all." And: "The only time anybody can ever deal with me is when my power's channeled through my music!" And: "I don't want to be stabilized. I want to feel free, really free." To an interviewer: "I'll tell you what freedom means to me: no fear." That last quote at least is authentic.

Her sometime manager Henri doles out the exposition: "She's a fucked-up alcoholic drug addict—but people still pay money to see her." And: "She's in bad shape: physically, financially and mentally." And: "All the promoters think you're a five-star asshole, Nina." It isn't subtle. After she sings "I Put a Spell on You" to Clifton, he asks, "Is that what you think? That you put a spell on me?" Comedian Richard Pryor (Mike Epps), on the phone: "First I lit my shit up with this crack pipe, now this MS shit is fuckin' me up." (Cue flashback to the night young Richard was so nervous Nina had to hug him before he went on.)

As shown, Simone had embraced the Civil Rights movement and began appearing in colorful outfits evoking African garb, and later felt betrayed when, in her view, African

Americans turned away from the good fight and from her as its symbol. In the film's present, David's starstruck mother tells Nina how much her songs had meant in the 1960s. Especially, she tells her in close-up, "the song that kept us marching: 'Mississippi—.'" We cut away to a reaction shot before she finishes naming the incendiary protest song which we never hear, as if someone had lost courage at the editing stage. The excision is unworthy of *Nina*'s subject. (Never mind that "Mississippi Goddam" wasn't exactly a street anthem like "We Shall Overcome.")

In the years before she died in 2003, Simone still performed in the States on occasion, including a couple of brief Carnegie Hall appearances. She'd been playing that venue since the 1960s, including a 1965 concert with orchestra and strings, and her parents and first piano teacher in the house: the kind of triumphant show *St. Louis Blues* or *Lady Sings the Blues* had to invent. But that concert's not here, too early in her career to be dramatically useful.

Instead, Clifton dreams of a free concert Nina will play in Central Park, where she'll see that her people remember her. The film's last 40 minutes is him getting her in shape for that (fictitious) show, where an all-ages interracial audience makes her feel the love and Nina feels so good she reprises "Feeling Good" to take us out. In this book we've encountered grander examples of the reconciliatory New York concert finale, but none with grander implications. This one reunites not lovers, or a family, or two kinds of music, but Nina Simone and America.

> ***La La Land*** **(2016; 128 minutes; director/writer: Damien Chazelle). Cast includes: Ryan Gosling (Sebastian), Emma Stone (Mia), John Legend (Keith), J.K. Simmons (Bill). New Songs: "Another Day of Sun," "Someone in the Crowd," "A Lovely Night," "City of Stars," "Audition" (words Banj Pasek, Justin Paul/ music Justin Hurwitz), "Start a Fire" (John Legend, Marius De Vries, Angelique Cinelu, Hurwitz).**

FIGURE 11.6 Nina Simone (Zoe Saldana) reconciles with America in *Nina*.

> **—Young hopefuls, actor Mia and jazz pianist Sebastian, look to make their mark in Los Angeles, and sometimes burst into song or dance in scenic locations. But can love survive two demanding careers? Also, can he save jazz?**

Damien Chazelle had spent years trying to finance his new-wave musical *La La Land* before the success of *Whiplash* made it possible. It's set in a Los Angeles stocked with artistic young hopefuls yearning to be noticed, strivers personified by actor Mia and jazz pianist Sebastian, whose love of nonmainstream music is part of his prickly who-cares-what-you-think personality. The film is eye-popping, with luminous magic-hour scenery, and shoutouts to *Rebel without a Cause* and color-saturated MGM spectaculars. It also owes a frank debt to Jacques Demy's 1960s French musicals, particularly *The Umbrellas of Cherbourg*. That film's jazz-inflected, romantic Michel Legrand music was a major influence on Justin Hurwitz's score, and on Sebastian's moody piano. Below those homages are deeper echoes of story tropes from all over jazz-movie history—as if by now all the jazz plot points are already out there, awaiting fresh reassembly. As musicians say when a new melody resembles some old one: there are only 12 notes.

In Chazelle's original script, Mia and Sebastian were younger and new in town, just getting oriented.[24] The characters were aged up when Emma Stone and Ryan Gosling were cast—Mia's now been in town six years—but they still have that early-twenties amiable self-absorption, and they still face rookie ordeals. She has three roommates and an out-of-date head shot, parks in a clearly marked towaway zone, and thinks the way to recognition is an autobiographical one-woman show with the name of her sleepy hometown in the title. But her email press release is inept and she books a too-large theater, for only one night. Not even Sebastian can make it. (Shades of *Crooklyn*.)

Sebastian's newbie problems are different. He loves jazz, which doesn't make him happy—it makes him desperate because jazz is dying. "It's dying, Mia. It's dying on the vine! And the world says, let it die. It had its time. Well not on my watch." He wants to put it back on the map he thinks it fell off. In the 1960s the Art Ensemble of Chicago had a comic bit: Is jazz as we know it dead? That depends on what you know. Someone somewhere always thinks it's dying, if not dead already—witness *Syncopation*, *The Cry of Jazz*, *A Man Called Adam*, and *Born to Be Blue*. (Fletcher says it's dying in *Whiplash*, without considering his own poisonous effect.) Its death was predicted as early as 1920.[25] Yet generation after generation of musicians keep coming up to play it and develop it further. No need for the rest of us to panic.

Some of what Sebastian knows about jazz he gets from hard listening. He keeps rewinding/needle-dropping on an obscure Thelonious Monk intro (to 1967's "Japanese Folk Song") until he's mastered its tumbling line and microhesitations. He can go on about what makes jazz special like a Ken Burns talking head. Everybody pitches in with a different idea, and maybe tries to steal the show: "It's conflict and it's compromise. . . . It's brand new every night." But some of what he knows is as fuzzy as *Whiplash*'s take on Jo Jones's flung cymbal: history as hearsay.

Seb and Mia are strolling the Warner Bros. lot in Burbank one afternoon, getting acquainted, when she confesses that she hates jazz—thinks it's wallpaper music. When he hears that, they have to go to a jazz club Right Now: the historic Lighthouse in Hermosa Beach, a locus of cool-jazz activity in the Chet Baker 1950s that's still in operation. (It's a 30-mile drive, over an hour away in late afternoon; we've already seen how bad local traffic can get. Yet they take two cars.)

At the club for an early show, they sit at a table near the bandstand, and he explains the music's origins, like Nick schooling Miralee in *New Orleans*—except Sebastian does it while the band is playing, and his history is shakier: "Jazz was born in a little flophouse in New Orleans, and it—just because people were crammed in there, they spoke five different languages, they couldn't talk to each other, the only way they could communicate was with jazz." (That is a novel theory. Chazelle has said he based Sebastian on his own younger, less enlightened self.) Jazz is life-or-death stuff—the opposite of easy listening: "Sidney Bechet shot somebody because they told him he played a wrong note."

There are conflicting accounts of what motivated an exchange of gunfire that night in Paris in 1928. In one version, Bechet and banjo player Mike McKendrick had disagreed about a tune's correct chords. But the cause may have been someone calling Bechet a cheapskate. In Sidney's own version, Mike shot first and Sidney was only returning fire—missing his target but wounding three bystanders.[26] Sebastian shoots similarly wide. Earlier he'd mentioned the LA club Chick Webb's big band used to play. Chick never toured west of Oklahoma.

But if jazz is dying, what's the cure? Sebastian dreams of his own club, a haven for "pure jazz," whatever that might be. (The music was a mutt from day one. But he makes that comment in a decade when folks were defining jazz very broadly, waving in border-trampling jazz-pop hybrids.) He's even accumulating jazz memorabilia to display, Planet Hollywood–style; he has a piano stool he's convinced Hoagy Carmichael used. How adorable is all that? His devotion is enough to make one convert: Mia comes to like jazz too. Or so she tells him.

For now, he composes a little, in particular the Legrand-like love theme that first catches Mia's attention—the melody that lured her off the sidewalk into a restaurant where he was about to be fired for playing his own music—and the movie's big ballad "City of Stars," which the two will sing together. (Actually for that one he just sets words to a melody lifted from one of his old jazz LPs, heard later.)

But after Sebastian overhears Mia on the phone, lamely defending his feckless ways to her mother, he joins a commercial band led by old music-school acquaintance Keith (singer John Legend), whom Sebastian holds in low regard. Keith plays swinging 1970s George Benson–style guitar and scat-sings to match—music Seb considers less serious than his own (Keith also programs in frothy electronics). On the other hand, he offers Seb a generous deal to go out on tour, with a cut of the merchandising. He also offers some ideological pushback, echoing *Mo' Better Blues*'s Shadow Henderson: "How you gonna save jazz if no one's listening?" You purists are the ones killing it, Keith says. "You're so obsessed with Kenny Clarke and Thelonious Monk. . . . You're holding on to the past. But jazz is about the future."

Fair enough; you don't honor innovators by being a copycat (not that Clarke and Monk leap to mind when Seb plays). But once Keith's band The Messengers is on the road, the leader's concern for jazz fades, as his swingy five-piece band morphs into a rhythm-and-blues stage show with light cues, backup singers, dancers, and a bumping horn section. (Art Blakey's band was The Jazz Messengers—Keith expels the jazz.) Sebastian's arsenal of equipment includes a boutiquey old monophonic keyboard, for a stylishly retro effect that mirrors the movie's own aesthetic.

We see the Messengers' glitzed-up act through Mia's big expressive eyes. She's appalled for Sebastian, who spots her in the crowd and tries to look like he's having a laugh. But she sees what it's costing him—like Jigger's friends witnessing his debasement in *Blues in the Night*. (Except Jigger quit that job like a proper jazz hero. Seb toughs it out—doesn't wilt like frustrated Johnny in *Syncopation*.) The lovers begin to drift apart; he's always on the road, although in time he'll use the money he's raking in to buy that club where he can live out his dream. It's not hard to see how Seb's artistic crisis parallels his creator's, just as Ghost's reversals in *Too Late Blues* recalled Cassavetes. You come up idealistic, then sell out a while to pay the bills—Chazelle pre-*Whiplash* wrote page-turning "rewrites, horror movies and sequels" to stay afloat—and then you try to reclaim that idealism.[27]

Somehow Mia's flop one-woman show lands her the audition of a lifetime, at which she's asked to make up a story on the spot—Emma Stone telling/singing it live, as the room goes dark and the camera dollies in, recalling Liza Minnelli's "But the World Goes 'Round" in *New York, New York*. Mia's improvisation wins her a career-making role.

Spoiler: five years later, Sebastian has a successful club where he can play his own music whenever he likes, and Mia's a Hollywood star, but they're not together—so they end up very like Jimmy Doyle and Francine Evans in *New York, New York*. The parallels with that film are surely deliberate: Keith tells Seb he's a superior player, but a pain in the ass—echoing Frankie Harte assessing Doyle. Even this movie's big opening number "Another Day of Sun"—hopefuls declaring, "Big town here I come"—harks back to the earlier film's defiant theme song. "It's about the period in your life when you're about to make it," the director has said, "but you just don't quite make it, not for another four or five years." That was Scorsese on his movie, with its own echoic locator title.[28]

Since *New York, New York* had an ending audiences hated, Chazelle pulls out one last trick—one that, coincidentally, echoes *Miles Ahead* earlier in 2016: a magical solo that (re)tells the movie's story in some mystical kind of way. One night Mia and her jazz-fan husband drop into Sebastian's club, and when he spies her in the audience he plays a solo piano version of their love theme, the first music she'd ever heard him play. And in playing that doleful, not very jazzy (let alone "pure jazz") slow-arpeggio melody—one so inoffensive he'd apparently recorded a Muzak-y version Mia had once recognized in a restaurant—he creates a vision the ex-lovers share, of another life: an alternate take, where all obstacles are removed. They soar from triumph to triumph and Seb makes it to Paris, like alternate-ending Jimmy Doyle. That happy fantasy sometimes looks like an MGM musical, as did *New York, New York*'s movie within the movie, *Happy Endings*, which filled a similar narrative function. Except in *La La Land* that alternate resolution has been moved to the very end, for cleaner closure and bigger box office.

Chazelle's regular composer Justin Hurwitz is not a jazz musician, though there are jazzy (and Latin) touches in some big-bandy orchestrations. His earwormy melodies are pop songs, and that's okay—it's a pop movie. Even at the Lighthouse, where black musicians on stage sideline to prerecorded white players, there's no whiff of the 1950s cool jazz this venue came to stand for. It's outside Hurwitz's frame of reference. His jazz sequences most always sound like simulacra: the Hollywood version, no more real than the convicts' lament in *Blues in the Night*.

Drummer Peter Erskine, who plays on the soundtrack, tried to persuade Hurwitz to let Sebastian's piano music better reflect his Monk-worship—to help the music reveal his character.[29] But that Monk strain surfaces only on one two-bar break, when Seb gigs at the Lighthouse (where he's the only white bandmember, and the only one spotlit). In this mainstream Hollywood film, having a character hip enough to love Monk is one thing. Having him sound like Monk is another—Thelonious is brilliant enough to name-drop, but too thorny for mass consumption. In *La La Land*, then, "jazz" is more a signifier of a certain kind of hipness than a specific sound—as in *The Jazz Singer* 89 years earlier.

> ***Bolden* (2019; 102 minutes; director: Dan Pritzker; writers: Pritzker, David N. Rothschild). Cast includes: Gary Carr (Buddy Bolden), Erik LaRay Harvey (Bartley), Reno Wilson (Louis Armstrong), Ian McShane (Judge Perry), Robert Ri'chard (George Baquet), Breon Pugh (Willie Warner), Ser'Darius Blain (Willie Cornish), Yaya DaCosta (Nora Bass/Bolden), JoNell Kennedy (Ida Bass), Catherine Russell (bordello singer), Timmy Richardson (Buddy as a child).**
> **—In 1931, prompted by hearing a Louis Armstrong broadcast, asylum inmate Buddy Bolden recalls the days when he played cornet, led a band, and invented a new music.**

We end at the beginning. Jazz had entered its second century on record before we got a biopic of original jazz star Buddy Bolden, who played his last job in 1906. The New Orleans cornetist looms large in jazz lore, the first man with a horn who burned so bright he burned himself out: "a one-man genius that was ahead of 'em all—too good for his time," per Louis Armstrong 1936.[30]

Three years later the book *Jazzmen* expanded on King Bolden's prowess at playing slow blues and limbered-up ragtime with crisscrossing horns: jazz in embryo. *Jazzmen*'s Bolden was a working-class barber who published a scandal-sheet newspaper and played cornet loud enough to be heard for miles. His blunt sound fit the rough, sometimes violent dancehalls he played—but he'd have the band simmer down to listen to dancers' shuffling feet. Buddy could blow sweetly too—even politely, at white ladies' lawn parties. Women fought over him, and he overextended himself on every front. Fed up, the band replaced him on his own gig one night—sent him home when he finally showed. He cracked up while playing a 1906 Labor Day parade, and the following year was sent to an insane asylum upstate where he died late in 1931. That happened before researchers started seeking out the old-timers, whose Bolden mis-memories and fibs got repeated as fact.

The *Jazzmen* narrative is remarkably detailed, considering how little of it could be substantiated later. The legend kept growing, for decades. He wore his shirt open to reveal a blaring red flannel undershirt. He'd jumped out of a hot-air balloon over Lincoln Park to draw attention. One night at home, playing alone, he seesawed between the blues and the hymns he'd grown up with, as if the devil and God were vying for his soul. (Danny Barker, who wrote about New Orleans music as well as making it, spread that one.) Many stories evaporated when biographer Donald Marquis investigated the facts: Bolden had been a plasterer, and hadn't published a scandal sheet or leapt from that balloon. The actual aeronaut was Lincoln Park emcee Buddy Bartley.[31]

Colorful as Bolden was, save for the sandpaper feet on the dance floor in *Syncopation*, no jazz-origins picture of the 1940s paid tribute. He was too rough a figure for screenwriters trying to put the music in a good light. *Bolden* had been over a decade in coming. Billionaire, guitarist, and novice filmmaker Dan Pritzker began shooting what turned out to be a first draft in 2007, but got sidetracked making a silent film in broad silent-serial style, *Louis*: a yarn about young Armstrong's Storyville adventures, in which he gets his first horn, and Bolden (Anthony Mackie), bound for the asylum, passes him the torch. *Louis* wasn't released commercially, though there were a few 2010 screenings with Wynton Marsalis leading a live band. Its balletic fantasias would echo in *Bolden*, which Pritzker would reshoot almost entirely starting in 2014 with a revamped cast, including a new Buddy, English stage and TV actor Gary Carr.[32]

Bolden freely mixes Buddy the man and myth, like movies about, say, Wyatt Earp. Bolden's not a barber (though the band rehearses in a barber's back room), but he does parachute from that hot-air balloon—nudged by Bartley (one name only), who in the movie becomes Bolden's pushy manager. Once more, a brassman's story is told in (partly) jumbled chronological order, and we view it all through an unreliable lens: the older, addled Buddy himself, thinking back on and trying to piece together his glory days, which come back (as memories do) in fragments.

His remembering is prompted by hearing the broadcast played by returning hero Louis Armstrong in June 1931 for a white audience at Suburban Gardens, a fancy roadhouse just outside New Orleans. Louis would later recall that a throng of African Americans listened from a nearby levee, as shown. Also as shown, the white announcer declined to introduce a black man, as he explained on-air in insulting terms; Armstrong brushed off the insult, and addressed the audience directly. (He is expertly impersonated by Reno Wilson—shaming Ben Vereen's 1931 Pops in *Louis Armstrong-Chicago Style*. One tune Louis performs is Irving Berlin's 1927 "Russian Lullaby," which would figure in the elder Armstrong's mis-memories; in 1969 he'd go on about having heard it in 1907.)[33] Pops's growl, wafting through the asylum from a nurse's radio, is one more voice in Bolden's head. His horn calls Buddy home.

So we shunt, often quickly, among Bolden's present, past, and fantasies, and between his 1931 institutional netherworld and Armstrong's bright ballroom. Thanks to virtuoso editing often keyed to the music and stylish visual coding, the shifts are easy to track. Each realm has its own (color-corrected) look—and we jazz-film viewers know such zigzags by now. The sound design is equally ambitious, layering eras and playing with time. (There's a bit of backwards cornet.) *Bolden* looks handsome and mostly moves right along, smartly choreographed.

The Bolden of 1931 usually appears as his younger self—the way 53-year-old Buddy pictures himself in his mind. Musicians were telling and singing stories about him while he was still around, so why mightn't he buy into and embellish such tales himself, with decades of time to fill? So in his memory, to attract listeners, he doesn't blow his horn out a hall's window, but from a peaked roof he's climbed, high above the street.

Some of Buddy's hyperbolic memories are daydreams. He imagines the laundry/sewing shop where his mother worked as a place where seamstresses dance *en pointe*. There young Buddy discovers interlocking rhythms: squeaky flywheels, sewing-machine doubletime, steampress hiss, baskets slapping the floor, linens shaken out. . . . Those shopfloor polyrhythms echo in a later episode when Buddy teaches his musicians to interweave the bumping beats that fuel his conversational music, clapping out each man's pattern in rehearsal. (It's something Pritzker had seen Wynton do. Buddy's on-screen drummer is Justin Faulkner from Branford Marsalis's quartet.) Then we hear those rhythms superimposed on, and implicit in, Louis's radio "Muskrat Ramble": Bolden's legacy in action.

As a promotional stunt, the real Bartley would fly his balloon over a block-square amusement park where bands played indoors, Lincoln Park in New Orleans' Gert Town neighborhood. There was another park directly across Short Street, and Bolden might play either location, blasting his horn through the fence to poach listeners from John Robichaux's rival Creole orchestra next door. In the movie, the day Bolden parachutes from Bartley's balloon, horn in hand, the action has been moved to a wooded grove outside town, where Robichaux is playing the cakewalk "Creole Belles" in a gazebo, for whites. Even before Buddy lands he's sounding his call-the-children-home cornet lick, despoiling Robichaux's stately sound. Bolden's bravura stunt makes the crowd literally come running, some black folk from over the hill included. The pied piper's musicians have pulled up in a dray wagon, and answer his brass call with a shout of "Hey, Buddy Bolden," to promote the brand. Then they strike up the evergreen "Didn't He Ramble" (a tune the real Buddy played) as Robichaux glares. The lineup mirrors Bolden's in a surviving photograph: cornet, Willie Cornish's valve trombone, two clarinets, guitar, and string bass—adding drums, which Bolden used.

We know that Buddy was loud, played slow drags and blues and rubberized ragtime. But since he left no records behind, musicians (and critics) imagine the particulars according to taste. In *Bolden*, Buddy's and Louis's horns are ghosted by their heir Wynton

Marsalis, who also wrote Buddy's band music, with nicely greasy harmony from two clarinets. Wynton's Armstrong solos are lovingly authentic, and his Bolden gets the right earthy rasp. But movie-Buddy is more of a technical player than the real one—more like Wynton. When a cornet upstart—Bunk Johnson?—challenges him one night, Buddy blows him back with sheer technique, even though his mind is already slipping. (He sees his horn's valves wiggle as if alive, a Cronenberg moment.) We hear about Buddy's preternatural volume, but don't really hear that brute force. When he does get loud, his sound breaks up, shrieky. Alas, in no scene do blues and hymns battle for his soul. He's at peace with both, telling future mother-in-law Ida, "I make the church music better."

The day of that parachute jump, his music catches the ear of Robichaux's star clarinetist George Baquet. The real Baquet once sat in with Buddy's sextet, igniting George's own interest in hot music. (He'd mentor young Sidney Bechet, play in the Creole Band that brought jazz to the vaudeville circuit in the 1910s, and record with Jelly Roll Morton.)[34] *Bolden* puts Baquet in Buddy's inner circle. He sits in often, squeezing out Bolden's merely adequate clarinetist and lifelong chum Willie Warner. Buddy tutors the educated Baquet in his new (unnamed) style that doesn't rely on paper. Working class and Creole musicians come together, to give jazz its mix of deep feeling and deft technique. Jamming, Baquet plays Mozart, while Bolden improvises around him. Buddy: "I play my way, every time." But also: "Sometimes it's better to play nothing at all"—like he's a proto-Miles. Baquet asks, if you don't write down your music, how will anyone play it when you're gone?

Recordings preserve unwritten music, of course, and it's rumored Bolden had made a wax-cylinder recording. He does so in *Bolden*, at Bartley's urging, although Buddy's already nervous other musicians will steal his stuff. (His wife Nora's for it too; they need the money, with a baby coming.) We hear it as it's being recorded, and—irony alert—this lost Grail doesn't do the band justice. Buddy tones his sound down for broader appeal, halfway to Robichaux territory, with Baquet on the date. This parlor rag—Marsalis's "Timelessness"—is aimed at whites, who can afford playback machines. Earlier, Bartley had booked the band to play mind-numbing background music for a ladies' tea, where the petit fours and décor were even paler than the patrons. Such compromises make Buddy's jazz even more urgent, playing for dancers and the women who are always around, back home at Funky Butt Hall.

Bartley becomes more of a bully as *Bolden* progresses, and Buddy doesn't push back much. Gary Carr conveys his vulnerability (and he fakes cornet well), but this King is a curiously muted figure. Even his red flannel shirt is toned down, and mostly under wraps. He's overmatched. Bartley is only an underling, ultimately answering to the devil at the top of the racist food chain, imperious, loquacious Judge Perry (a typecast Ian McShane). The judge holds African Americans in contempt; his fixer makes Bartley stage deadly battles royale where black men destroy each other for whites' amusement. (Some too-easy parallels are drawn between those doomed combatants and black musicians—whereas *Miles Ahead* made a benign connection between boxing and jazz rhythm.) The white powers flood the black community with white powder—early for heroin as a street drug, though cocaine and morphine were common. Danny Barker once wrote of the ready availability of hard and soft drugs at Lincoln Park, quoting the brother of "Buddy Bottley."[35]

The real Bolden drank heavily. Movie-Buddy messes with dope, to his detriment, but his mind is already going. After recording that cylinder, listening to the playback, he compulsively pulls the pistons from his horn, as if to silence (or unman) it. On a gig later, Baquet plays a mocking variation on that breakdown, soloing as he takes his clarinet apart section by section from the bottom up, till he's blowing mouthpiece alone—an actual Baquet stunt. When Buddy starts missing jobs, the band replaces him with that upstart challenger. Bolden, now destitute, hears a younger band that copies his style and sings his band's signature "Buddy Bolden's Blues" (whose lyric declares its own unreliability: "I thought I heard Buddy Bolden say . . ."). But the bouncers won't let Buddy into the joint where his praises are sung, just as Bird would be banned from Birdland.

As in life, Bolden's dissolution is fairly abrupt, and the film itself wobbles in the last act. The centerpieces of his famous crack-up—erratic behavior at that 1906 parade, and striking mother-in-law Ida with a pitcher (which had actually happened earlier)—are over in moments. Buddy's real undoing is less mental than political. Judge Perry concludes Buddy's freedom music is giving blacks dangerous ideas. That's the real reason he signs Buddy's commitment papers (and suppresses his recording). This cruel twist takes poetic license pretty far. There's scant evidence white New Orleans noticed King Bolden existed; his music never made the papers. Having him swept aside for political reasons—tying him into a larger discussion about racism and power—aims to make this fable more resonant, for our time. But it turns the King into a pawn in his own biopic. Even so, 1931 Bolden goes out on a high, imagining himself in his prime, trading phrases across space and time with Pops at Suburban Gardens, on Buddy's lost recorded tune, no less: a fantasy duet both corny and endearing.

Bolden has dazzling set pieces and dispensable episodes (muses cavort in an Arcadian setting, playing silver clarinet and strings). If the whole seems a bit stitched together, that's how it is with myths built up over time. Alongside the epic action there are puzzling details and gaps, historical improbabilities, and parts that don't quite fit. Such tales retain their instructive power just the same.

POSTSCRIPT

Print the Legend

Amsterdam drummer Alan Purves sometimes gets very quiet playing jazz or improvised music. He'll make small sounds, on undersized drums using lightweight beaters. Growing up in Edinburgh, he tippy-tapped on buckets with mom's knitting needles. Most of what he knew about jazz came from movies. One formative influence: Gene Krupa playing a matchbox with matchsticks in *Ball of Fire*.

Movies didn't stamp just the musicians who appeared in them. They marked a few who saw them as well. Young drummer Mel Tormé was also inspired by Krupa, and watched *Hollywood Hotel* over and over. Chicago experimentalist Bill Brimfield: "I had seen *Young Man with a Horn* with Kirk Douglas four times and I knew I had to be a trumpet player." Hugh Masekela in South Africa had a similar epiphany, seeing it at 14. For later trumpeters like Bronx-born Bruce Harris, the trigger was *Mo' Better Blues*.[1] Sometimes the movies musicians saw might find their way into their own stories.

Sidney Bechet was given to adorning biographical narratives with borrowed material, riffing like a true improviser. In his autobiography *Treat It Gentle*, he turns the (true) folk tale of runaway slave Bras Coupé into an elaborate fable about his grandfather and the prehistory of jazz. Sidney wasn't a liar, his friend Claude Luter explained. "But when he told a story, he always wanted it to be a *good* story."[2]

Another one from that book: When Sidney was six, Freddie Keppard's band played a surprise party for older brother Leonard Bechet at the family home in New Orleans. Sidney was so taken with the music, he started playing along from the next room. The musicians were mystified by the sound of a phantom clarinet till Sidney was discovered, after which they asked him to join them: "Well, you're awful little, but we heard you, and you were sure playing like hell."[3] Clarinetist George Baquet had Sidney sit right beside him as they all carried on. It's a lovely story that gives an early Bechet mentor his due— and curiously like the opening of 1941's *Birth of the Blues*. I don't know if Bechet ever saw it, but he was living in New York when that film about a fictional New Orleans clarinetist came out. The first reference I've found to Sidney discussing such a party was in a 1951 magazine story. In that version, he was eight at the time. In 1949, Alan Lomax interviewed Leonard Bechet about Sidney's early development. Leonard recalled Baquet's encouragement when Sidney started playing around age 12. He mentioned no parties.[4]

By 1959, Nina Simone, one-time child prodigy who'd played piano at her preacher mother's church, was a rising star. That March, interviewed for the Philadelphia *Evening Bulletin*, she reminisced about her early years, fudging a few details. Simone also touched on her habit of cutting up while playing in church: "I found it hard to resist sneaking in an extra beat in the arrangements now and then, although mother didn't approve."[5] It's a detail she'd leave out of later interviews and her 1991 autobiography. Simone related this 11 months after the release of *St. Louis Blues*, in which Billy Preston's young Will Handy does much the same at the organ, to his preacher father's disapproval. But I can offer no evidence Simone had seen that 1958 film brimming with black entertainers, starring an unclassifiable singing pianist like herself, let alone that she'd drawn on it in her interview.

This last one, I'm on firmer ground. In the early 1990s, when trumpeter Lester Bowie would play "Strange Fruit" with his band Brass Fantasy, he'd introduce it by telling how Billie Holiday had written it while traveling in the South, after coming upon the scene of a lynching.[6] Lester and I were on friendly terms, so after hearing this introduction a couple of times I pointed out to him this was the movie version, from *Lady Sings the Blues*—that Billie hadn't written it, or witnessed a lynching. The next time I saw Brass Fantasy, Lester had added a preamble to his introduction: "Some people say it didn't happen this way, but . . ." The movie version was more compelling than the truth. Those fables have staying power. That realization helped lead to this book.

ACKNOWLEDGMENTS

My mom, Sally Whitehead, pointed out recurring story patterns when we watched soap operas together when I was small. My research and thanks really start there. In Baltimore in the 1980s, Michael Yockel at the *City Paper* and *Baltimore Sun* book editor John Kelly got me writing regularly about film, and Pat Moran gave me open access to a local repertory house where I became a fixture. Back then I often compared notes with fellow scribes Stephen Hunter, Bob Lopez, and George Udel. In 2006, Tom Lorenz at the University of Kansas encouraged me to teach a class on jazz films and fiction; unbidden, my colleague Paul Lim immediately made numerous then-rare films available, and scholars Chuck Berg and Sherrie Tucker graciously shared their considerable knowledge of the field. As this book took shape, my staunchest ally has been film critic, historian, rarity-sleuth, and lifelong friend Chuck Stephens. He read the manuscript with a sharp eye and made many valuable suggestions; Ladd Lanford answered a couple of questions too. Late in the writing, jazz/film scholar Mark Cantor—of the invaluable jazz-on-film.com—kindly fielded various queries. Cantor also read and commented on portions of the manuscript, as did friends/scholars John Corbett and Christopher Robinson. A special thanks to Tad Hershorn and Elizabeth Surles at the Institute of Jazz Studies at Rutgers–Newark for their expertise and hands-on help.

On the jazz side, dozens of musicians, scholars, critics, collectors, interviewers, and fans have offered valuable advice, information, or opinions, tipped me to various films, lent materials, talked of their own experiences with musicians portrayed on screen, offered timely encouragement or bracing skepticism, provided pieces of the puzzle (sometimes, long before this book was conceived), and answered arcane questions—like, what did it cost to rent a grand piano in Seattle in 1989? (I had an answer in twenty minutes.)

The honor roll from all fields includes Jeff Albert, Larry Appelbaum, Dave Ballou, Joey Baron, Steven Bernstein, Bob Blumenthal, Lester Bowie, Anthony Braxton, Dave Cappello, Hope Carr, Allan Chase, Aaron Cohen, John Corbett, Andrew Cyrille, Francis Davis, Paul De Barros, Rev. Arvid "Bud" Dixen, Dominique Eade, Ellery Eskelin, Michael Fitzgerald and the members of the [jazz-research] email list, in particular Ed Green, Guy Kopelowicz, Steven Lasker, Walter van de Leur, Marcello Piras, Peter Vacher, and Scott Wenzel; Michael Formanek, Von Freeman, Lelio Giannetto, Lyubov Ginzburg, Terry Gross, Ethan Iverson, Sheila Jordan, Bob Koester, Art Lange, Bernard Lyons, George

Manning, Francesco Martinelli, Joe McPhee, Bill McQueeney, Misha Mengelberg, Bill Milkowski, Danny Miller, Dan Morgenstern, James Mockoski, Oscar Noriega, Herman Openneer, Huub van Riel, Lloyd Sachs, Bill Shoemaker, Roberta Shorrock, Leslie Stallknecht, Larry Stanley, Jason Stein, Irving Stone, Stephanie Stone, Chad Taylor, Mal Waldron, Kirsten Walsh, Bayard Williams, and the anonymous reviewers of my sample chapters and manuscript.

Some of them are no longer with us, but the debt carries.

And then there's family, often helping more than they know, in particular Carol Koitzsch, Eileen Wernsdorfer, Dennis Whitehead, Mick Whitehead, and Kay Koitzsch. Not forgetting Gabe, Veronica; Zach and Myla; or Lana, Kurt, Wallace, and Conrad Dempsey.

Thanks also to the many hands behind Maryland's interlibrary loan system Marina, and the helpful staffs of the Baltimore County Public Library at Cockeysville and the Enoch Pratt Free Library. Baltimore's Art Seminar Group gave me an early opportunity to present some of this material in a public forum. Editor Suzanne Ryan at Oxford University Press has been in this book's corner from the beginning, and helped bring it into focus. I can't thank her enough.

Early in the writing when progress was fitful, my wife Lesley Ann Wernsdorfer suggested a way to jump-start the process. She is also an excellent copy editor and sounding board, and frequent editorial consultant. Every day I'm thankful she took a chance on me.

NOTES

INTRODUCTION

1. We draw on Stanley Crouch, who noted the cross-cut/call-and-response and solo/close-up parallels in "Jazz Criticism and Its Effect on the Art Form," in David Baker, *New Perspectives on Jazz*, 82.

    1.   On Jolson's Bert Williams influence, see Thomas Postlewait, "The Hieroglyphic Stage: American Theatre and Society, Post-Civil War to 1945" in Wilmeth, Bigsby, and Bigsby, *Cambridge History of American Theatre*, 2:186. For *The Jazz Singer* as story template, see Gabbard, *Jammin' at the Margins*, 35–42, 47–63.

2. Ted Gioia, "Al Jolson: A Megastar Long Buried Under a Layer of Blackface," *New York Times*, Arts Section, October 22, 2000.

CHAPTER 1

1. Bogdanovich, *Who the Devil*, 38.
2. Michael Levin and John S. Wilson, "No Bop Roots In Jazz: Parker," *Down Beat*, September 9, 1949: "His first musical idol, the musician who so moved and inspired him that he went out and bought his first saxophone at the age of 11, was Rudy Vallee."
3. On Vallee and Wiedoeft, see Vallée, *Vagabond Dreams*, 165–186; and *My Time Is Your Time*, 24–27.
4. "1917 comedy," Morgenstern, *Living with Jazz*, 628.
5. For production details, see Delson, *Dudley Murphy*, 88–92; Handy, *Father of the Blues*, 224; and Robertson, *W. C. Handy*, 201–202.
6. On Ellington, Mills, and marketing, see Cohen, *Duke Ellington's America*, 41–89.
7. Delson, *Dudley Murphy*, 97, and 92–99.
8. Ellington, *Music Is My Mistress*, 54.
9. Whiteman and McBride, *Jazz*, 3. For production details, see DeLong, *Pops*, 134–137, 141–145.
10. Ellington, *Music Is My Mistress*, 454.
11. "ambitious suite," Ulanov, *Duke Ellington*, 155; and "concert hall," Hasse, *Beyond Category*, 212.
12. Mark Tucker, *Duke Ellington Reader*, 52–53.
13. Holiday, *Lady Sings the Blues*, 53.
14. "droning airplane," Vallée, *Vagabond Dreams*, 79; "hand signals," 44–45; "two saxes at once," 80.
15. For production details, see Furia, *Irving Berlin*, 137, 183–186; Bergreen, *As Thousands Cheer*, 357–362; Jablonski, *Irving Berlin*, 187–191; Flinn, *Brass Diva*, 94–100; Zanuck, *Memo*, 12–14.
16. Barrios, *Song in the Dark*, 214.
17. Whiteman and McBride, *Jazz*, 32–33.
18. The point about diction and the example (from "Top Hat, White Tie and Tails," not in *Alexander's*) from Furia, *Irving Berlin*, 173.
19. That outtake is an extra on the 2004 20th Century Fox DVD.
20. DeLong, *Pops*, 136.

21. For background and production details, see Levinson, *Puttin' on the Ritz*, 120; Nolan, *Three Chords*, 148; Astaire, *Steps in Time*, 242; Shaw interview in Hall, *Dialogues in Swing*, 136–139.

22. Hayde, *Stan Levey*, 149.

23. Hall, *Dialogues in Swing*, 139.

24. For an extended close reading, see Adam Knee, "Class Swings: Music, Race, and Social Mobility in *Broken Strings*," in Wojcik and Knight, *Soundtrack Available*, 269–2 (269–294) 94.

CHAPTER 2

1. Gabbard, *Jammin' at the Margins*, 110.

2. Ellington, *Music Is My Mistress*, 97.

3. Ramsey and Smith, *Jazzmen*, 13. Bolden quoted by Danny Barker, in Shapiro and Hentoff, *Hear Me Talkin' to Ya*, 20; for Ory, see Armstrong, *In His Own Words*, 134; for Manetta quote, see Brothers, *Louis Armstrong's New Orleans*, 151.

4. "working title," Rimler, *George Gershwin*, 5.

5. Hischak, *Encyclopedia of Film Composers*, 650.

6. Production details, see *Syncopation*'s American Film Institute page at http://www.afi.com/members/catalog/DetailView.aspx?s=&Movie=27493 (page discontinued).

7. Pollack, *George Gershwin*, 52; 76–77; Smith, *Music on My Mind*, 225; on Roberts's credibility, friend Eubie Blake once commented, "Luckey was the biggest liar I've ever known." Waldo, *This Is Ragtime*, 113.

8. Handy at Rhapsody premiere, Robertson, *W. C. Handy*, 197. Handy and Murphy both lived in or near New York when *Blue Monday Blues* premiered, and when Whiteman revived it late in 1925.

9. Levant, *Smattering of Ignorance*, 170: "George, if you had to do it all over, would you fall in love with yourself again?" For Levant, recreating scenes from his own life was a "very Pirandelloish," surreal experience, see Kashner and Schoenberger, *Talent for Genius*, 269–277.

10. For a succinct account of the abortive jazz segment in *It's All True*, see Szwed, *Billie Holiday*, 56–58; for *Syncopation* script in Welles files, see Bret Wood, "The Road to New Orleans," supplemental feature on 2000 Kino Video DVD of *New Orleans*, in which Wood describes the script in detail without recognizing it was produced as *Syncopation*.

11. "Levey ordered rewrites," Tucker, "But This Music Is Mine," in Rustin and Tucker, *Big Ears*, 255.

12. Collier, *Louis Armstrong*, 308; Chilton, *Billie's Blues*, 105; and Bigard, *With Louis and the Duke*, 93; the other film is 1958's *St. Louis Blues*.

13. "12 days late," Bigard, *With Louis and the Duke*, 94. "I was no actress," Holiday, *Lady Sings the Blues*, 121.

14. "feminist reading," Tucker, "But This Music Is Mine," 235–266.

15. "never set foot," Chilton, *Billie's Blues*, 225.

16. Ramsey and Smith, *Jazzmen*, 58.

17. "ghosted by socialite," Tucker, "But This Music Is Mine," 252.

18. Callender and Cohen, *Unfinished Dream*, 62. For early script details and quoted lyric, see Tucker, "But This Music Is Mine," 257.

CHAPTER 3

1. Morton: 1938 Library of Congress interview transcript 1547b, quoted in Reich and Gaines, *Jelly's Blues*, 15; Mezzrow and Wolfe, *Really the Blues*, 4, 13–14; and Cripps, *Slow Fade*, 281.

2. Kazan, *A Life*, 189–190; Schickel, *Elia Kazan*, 88–89.

3. For production details, see Simon, *Glenn Miller*, 295–301.

4. For historical background, see Collier, *Benny Goodman*, 276–277; and Simon, *Big Bands*, 66–68.

5. Haddix, *Kansas City Jazz*, 123–124, 128, 130.

6. Levinson, *Tommy Dorsey*, 199.

7. Levinson, *Tommy Dorsey*, 4–8.

8. "domestic chores," see Erenberg, *Swingin' the Dream*, 87.

9. Levinson, *Tommy Dorsey*, 88–89.

10. O'Day, *High Times*, 221.

11. For production details, see Koenig, *Danny Kaye*, 113–120, 288; McCarthy, *Howard Hawks*, 433–437; and Bogdanovich, *Who the Devil*, 345–346.

12. "absent-minded professor reputation," Lee, *Miss Peggy Lee*, 15.

13. "chaconne and passacaglia," Sergeant, *Jazz*, 157; "*umpateedle*," Sargeant, 72–78; the term comes from Don Knowlton, "The Anatomy of Jazz," *Harper's*, April 1926.

CHAPTER 4

1. Baker, *Young Man with a Horn*, author's note; Ferguson, *In the Spirit of Jazz*, 20.

2. Baker, *Young Man with a Horn*, 173.

3. Baker, *Young Man with a Horn*, 31, 96.

4. For production details, see Robertson, *Casablanca Man*, 102–104; Rode, *Michael Curtiz*, 429–436.

5. Gabbard, *Jammin' at the Margins*, 74; Sudhalter, *Stardust Melody*, 268. Mezzrow and Wolfe, *Really the Blues*, 3.

6. Sudhalter, *Stardust Melody*, 247; Carmichael, *Sometimes I Wonder*, 287.

7. Mezzrow and Wolfe, *Really the Blues*, 200.

8. Dorothy Baker, *Young Man with a Horn*, 61.

9. Douglas, *Ragman's Son*, 168.

10. Condon, *We Called It Music*, 270.

11. Gabbard, *Jammin' at the Margins*, 67–75.

12. Mezzrow and Wolfe, *Really the Blues*, 258–260.

13. Gabbard, *Jammin' at the Margins*, 225.

14. Barnet, *Those Swinging Years*, 91.

15. Simon, *Big Bands*, 350.

16. Simon, *Glenn Miller*, 443.

17. Simon, *Glenn Miller*, 70–72.

18. For production details, see Gavin, *Is That All*, 165–166, 170–175, 178–180. Unaccountably, there is no Jack Webb biography.

19. Lee, *Miss Peggy Lee*, 165.

20. Firestone, *Swing, Swing, Swing*, 384.

21. Goodman and Kolodin, *Kingdom of Swing*, 87, 122; and Crow, *Jazz Anecdotes*, 225.

22. Hammond, *John Hammond on Record*, 324.

23. Clayton and Elliott, *Buck Clayton's Jazz World*, 158.

24. Goodman and Kolodin, *Kingdom of Swing*, 246.

25. Gabbard, *Jammin' at the Margins*, 39, 54–58.

26. Goodman and Kolodin, *Kingdom of Swing*, 242.

27. Epstein, *Nat King Cole*, 274.

28. "22 days," Cripps, *Making Movies Black*, 283.

29. Handy, *Father of the Blues*, 74.

30. Handy, *Father of the Blues*, 76–77.

31. Handy, *Father of the Blues*, 11: "I'd rather follow you to the graveyard than to hear that you had become a musician."

32. Kaminski and Hughes, *Jazz Band*, 50; and Condon, *We Called It Music*, 152.

33. Hedda Hopper, "Looking at Hollywood: Band Leader Red Nichols' Life Story Will Be Filmed," *Chicago Daily Tribune*, November 1, 1954, B18. Nichols biographical details from Evans et al., *Red Nichols Story*; Stroff, *Red Head*; and Nichols clipping files at Institute of Jazz Studies, Rutgers University–Newark.

34. For production details, see Koenig, *Danny Kaye*, 189–194.

35. Personal communication, Nederlands Jazz Archief's Hermann Oppenneer, 1997.

36. Stroff, *Red Head*, iv.

37. For production details, see Klauber, *World of Gene Krupa*, 128–130; Michaud, *Sal Mineo*, 98, 129–134, 140–150. For biographical details, see Crowther, *Gene Krupa*; Klauber, *World of Gene Krupa*; Blesh, *Combo*, 134–160; Korall, *Drummin' Men*, 42–88; and Simon, *Big Bands*, 304–311.

38. Condon, *We Called It Music*, 187–191.

39. Korall, *Drummin' Men*, 78.

CHAPTER 5

1. Pepper and Pepper, *Straight Life*, 138.

2. Boujut, *Louis Armstrong*, 115.

3. "pitched in on the lyric," Wilk, *They're Playing Our Song*, 211.

4. Marc Myers, "Interview: Chico Hamilton (Part 3), JazzWax, posted March 4, 2009, at http://www.jazzwax.com/2009/03/interview-chico-hamilton-part-3.html.

5. Parisian Redheads photo in Dahl, *Stormy Weather*, 46. For more on early women's bands, see Dahl, *Stormy Weather*, 45–58; McGee, *Some Liked It Hot*, 31–49; and Tucker, *Swing Shift*, 5–6, 8, 37–38, 206, 211, 335n4.

6. Gavin, *Deep in a Dream*, 159; Wagner, *Pieces of My Heart*, 127.

7. For *Shadows* and *Staccato* production details, see Cassavetes, *Cassavetes*, 66–90; and Fine, *Accidental Genius*, 112–118.

CHAPTER 6

1. For more on Cassavetes's improvisational aesthetic, and a detailed account of how he used Mingus's music in *Shadows*, see Lipman, "Mingus."

2. See DeeDee Halleck's 1985 "Interview with Shirley Clarke," available at http://davidsonsfiles.org/shirleyclarkeinterview.html.

3. "700 performances," see Kenneth Jones, "Living Theatre Will Revive Its Groundbreaking 1959 Jazz Play, *The Connection*," *Playbill*, December 12, 2008, at http://www.playbill.com/article/living-theatre-will-revive-its-groundbreaking-1959-jazz-play-the-connection-com-156097; McLean quote, Spellman, *Four Lives*, 227; "the images, the voices," Clarke quoted in Mekas, *Movie Journal*, 66. She elaborates: "In *The Connection*, the lines really do not matter. They talk, talk, talk, but really it is not important what they say."

4. Ira Gitler, liner notes to Freddie Redd, *Music from The Connection* (Blue Note 84027, 1960).

5. Brian Case, "Nostalgia in Times Square," *The Wire*, July/summer 1984, 25.

6. Poitier quote in Goudsouzian, *Sidney Poitier*, 193; Ritt quote in *Martin Ritt*, 170. For Flender's novel as source material, see Fry, *Paris Blues*, 3; and O'Meally, Edwards, and Griffin, *Uptown Conversation*, 301–302. For production details, see Jackson, *Picking Up the Tab*, 62–64; Carroll, *Diahann*, 94–96; Ellington, *Duke Ellington in Person*, 183; Godfrey, *Paul Newman*, 100–102; Goudsouzian, *Sidney Poitier*, 188–194, 199; and Hajdu, *Lush Life*, 206–211. Gabbard has written extensively about *Paris Blues*, and our take on Ellington hijacking the ending echoes and expands on his incisive reading in *Jammin' at the Margins*, 192–203, and in O'Meally et al., *Uptown Conversation*, 298–311. Our take is also informed by another admirably close reading in Holbrook, *Music, Movies, Meanings*, 188–199.

7. Taylor, *Notes and Tones*, 259.

8. Hammond, *John Hammond*, 315; and Hershorn, *Norman Granz*, 202.

9. See for example Cohen, *Duke Ellington's America*, 231.

10. Whitehead, *New Dutch Swing*, 101.

11. Cassavetes quote, Cassavetes, *Cassavetes*, 108; "friend Sidney Poitier," Bogdanovich, *Who the Hell's*, 329, 451; for *Too Late Blues* production details, see Cassavetes, 106–117; and Fine, *Accidental Genius*, 129–136.

12. Quoted in Andriessen, *Tetterettet*, 226: "Ik zie niet in waarom je populaire muziek zou moeten subsidiëren."

13. James, *Too Late Blues*, 128.

14. For production details, see Priestley, *Mingus*, 125–128; and Gabbard, *Better Git It*, 239–241.

15. Kenton 1956 telegram to *Down Beat*, in Feather, *Jazz Years*, 122.

16. Dance, *World of Duke Ellington*, 267.

17. Sublette, *Cuba*, 372, citing Carpentier writing in Spanish in 1994.

18. Kelley, *Africa Speaks*, 21, 24.

19. For background and production details, see Early, *Sammy Davis*, 240–243; Fishgall, *Gonna Do Great Things*, 200, 211–213, 216; and Haygood, *In Black and White*, 328, 341, 344–348, 357–359.

20. Early, *Sammy Davis*, 210.

21. Boujut, *Louis Armstrong*, 64.

22. Barker, *Buddy Bolden*, 46.

23. Davis, *Hollywood*, 90; and Gregory, *Callus on My Soul*, 102–109.

24. Reisner, *Bird*, 14, 66, 75, 130, 131.

25. "Mingus grumbled," Kastin, *Nica's Dream*, 88; "only about a year," Kastin, 87.

CHAPTER 7

1. For background and production details, see Clarke, *Billie Holiday*, 399–400, 402–403; Gordy, *To Be Loved*, 308–325; Griffin, *If You Can't Be Free*, 31–32, 56–64; Szwed, *Billie Holiday*, 64–71; Saul, *Becoming Richard Pryor*, 276–280; and Taraborrelli, *Diana Ross*, 242–260.

2. Taraborrelli, *Diana Ross*, 244; and Bob Hope show clip at https://youtu.be/Xrinb2fU_dw.

3. "more blackness," Gordy, *To Be Loved*, 312.

4. Taraborrelli, *Diana Ross*, 249–250; and Sarris, *American Cinema*, 194.

5. Griffin, *If You Can't Be Free*, 60.

6. Taraborrelli, *Diana Ross*, 258.

7. Gordy, *To Be Loved*, 317.

8. For background and production details, see Szwed, *Space Is the Place*, 294–299, 330–333; see also, John Szwed, liner notes to Sun Ra, *Soundtrack to the Film Space Is the Place* (Evidence 22070-2, 1993).

9. Dery, *Flame Wars*, 212. On the film's Afrofuturism, see Namwali Serpell, "Afrofuturism: Everything and Nothing," Public Books, April 1, 2016, http://www.publicbooks.org/fiction/afrofuturism-everything-and-nothing.

10. Jost, *Free Jazz*, 188.

11. Jones and Chilton, *Louis Armstrong Story*, 15, 62.

12. Jones and Chilton, 17.

13. On Paganini, Schubert, Chopin, and Strauss, see Tibbetts, *Composers in the Movies*, 22–26, 33–35, 41–45, 81–101.

14. Blesh and Janis, *They All Played Ragtime*: "Get off that piano stool, you're hurting the piano's feelings" (160); "Among the new St. Louis men Chauvin was almost unique in retaining the legato cantilena with virtuoso tempos" (66); "Chopin nocturnes and Bach fugues," 118; "like honeydew," 53. .

15. For production details, see Scorsese, *Martin Scorsese*, 71–78; Baxter, *De Niro*, 156–168; Biskind, *Easy Riders*, 315, 325–326; Cameron, *Floor Sample*, 57–61; Kelly, *Martin Scorsese*, 98–112; Keyser, *Martin Scorsese*, 85–97; Levy, *De Niro*, 194–202, 206–209; Schickel, *Conversations with Scorsese*, 122–130; and Carrie Rickey and Martin Scorsese, commentary track, 2004 MGM DVD. Our reading is also informed by Friedman, *Cinema*, 88–107.

16. Parallels to *A Star Is Born* include: cityscape under the opening credits; at the top, pandemonium in the streets of an entertainment district sets up a long sequence in which the hero meets and pesters the heroine; a loyal pianist sticks with her through the whole picture, and never warms to the prickly husband, who embarrasses his wife in front of her showbiz friends; she becomes the bigger star, and in the end returns to the venue where the couple had met. We draw on Baxter, *De Niro*, 157.

17. Kander and Ebb, *Colored Lights*, 142–144.

18. McKay, *Robert De Niro*, 73.

19. Woods, *Beginning Postmodernism*, 242.

20. Schickel, *Conversations with Scorsese*, 128.

21. "Georgie Auld briefly," Gitler, *Swing to Bop*, 223; and "now 1957," 2004 MGM DVD commentary track.

22. We skip over the film's acrimonious production; details from Michael Daly, "The Making of *The Cotton Club*, A True Tale of Hollywood," *New York Magazine*, May 7, 1984, 41–62; Schumacher, *Francis Ford Coppola*, 336–368; Cowie, *Coppola*, 169–180; Robert Evans, *Kid Stays*, 327–351; and Kennedy, *Riding the Yellow Trolley*, 390–402.

23. Hershorn, *Norman Granz*, 315.

24. For biographical details, see Ellington, *Music Is My Mistress*, 82, 126; also, Bigard, *Louis and the Duke*, 50; Haskins, *Cotton Club*, 57; Hasse, *Beyond Category*, 148; and Ulanov, *Duke Ellington*, 113–118.

25. Gere as trumpeter, see Davis, *Richard Gere*, 11–12, 20.

26. "Harlem hangouts," Haskins, *Cotton Club*, 59; Sann, *Kill the Dutchman!* 116; "In fact Bix," Sudhalter and Evans, *Bix*, 210.

27. Haskins, *Cotton Club*, 104.

28. Haskins, 116.

29. The published screenplay lays out a slightly longer edit. Hoofer's Club, Stearns and Stearns, *Jazz Dance*, 173–175, 306–307. An expanded director's cut released in 2019, *The Cotton Club Encore*, arrived too late for consideration.

CHAPTER 8

1. Demme, *Jonathan Demme*, 70.

2. Francis Davis, *In the Moment*, 86.

3. Winkler relates this story in *The New York, New York Stories Part Two*, bonus feature with the 2007 MGM *New York, New York* DVD. For Production details from Tavernier and Winkler interviews in studio press kit; Britt, *Dexter Gordon*, 115–124; Gordon, *Sophisticated Giant*, 188–213; and McGilligan, *Clint*, 417–419.

4. Britt, *Dexter Gordon*, 117.

5. Britt, 116.

6. Hancock, *Possibilities*, 256–257.

7. Whitehead, "Paris Blues," *Towson Times*, November 5, 1986, 42.

8. Ake, *Jazz Matters*, 133.

9. For background and production details, see McGilligan, *Clint*, 419–424; Schickel, *Clint Eastwood*, 424–430; Goldman, *Clint Eastwood*, 97, 105, 113, 115, 121–125, 206–207; and Eastwood, *Clint Eastwood*, 153–159. *Bird* was much analyzed by jazz critics; many points here echo Stanley Crouch's and Francis Davis's perceptive/corrosive reviews, reprinted in Gottlieb, *Reading Jazz*, and Kevin Whitehead, "Messy Life, Perfect Art," *Down Beat*, February 1989, 6.

10. Reisner, *Bird*, 186.

11. Gillespie, *To Be*, 402: "Yardbird became a martyr for our music, and I became a reformer."

12. On the Clovers, see Giddins, *Celebrating Bird*, 104; and Amram, *Vibrations*, 101.

13. Parker, *My Life*, 49.

14. "thrown in a river," Reisner, *Bird*, 116.

15. "polka band," Warner, *Text and Drugs*, 90.

16. People Band background mostly drawn from Martin Davidson's liner notes to their *1968* (Emanem 4102, 2004) and Terry Day's to *69/70* (Emanem 5201, 2009).

CHAPTER 9

1. "24-hour travel time," Michael Graham Richard, "How fast could you travel across the U.S. in the 1800s?" *Mother Nature Network*, December 26, 2012, http://www.mnn.com/green-tech/transportation/stories/how-fast-could-you-travel-across-the-us-in-the-1800s.

2. Curtis, *Between Flops*, 172.

3. For production details, see Lee, *That's My Story*, 130–154; and Lee, *Mo' Better Blues*, 31–218.

4. Bleek's LP sleeves were designed in-house at Columbia records: Lee, *Mo' Better Blues*, 214.

5. Lee, *Mo' Better Blues*, 151.

6. "accelerate one," Bobby White, "Swingjugend: The Real Swing Kids," Swungover, July 26, 2013, https://swungover.wordpress.com/2013/07/26/swingjugend-the-real-swing-kids/. On the 1990s swing revival, see Stevens, *Swing Dancing*, 166–172; and Milkowski, *Swing It!* 243–267.

7. Delaunay, *Django Reinhardt*, 96, 99–125; and Dregni, *Django*, 154–187.

8. There was a real Hey-Hay Club, at Fourth and Cherry. The Cherry Blossom on 18th had been converted from the Eblon Theater in 1933, though the Eblon's still open in *Kansas City*. For production details, see Altman, commentary track, 2005 New Line DVD; Michael Bourne, "Goin' to Kansas City and Robert Altman Takes You There!" *Down Beat*, March 1996, 22–27; Altman, *Robert Altman*, 211–214; and Zuckoff, *Robert Altman*, 446–452. For a more sympathetic view, see Gabbard, *Black Magic*, 235–250.

9. For Parker in this period, see Crouch, *Kansas City Lightning*, 48–57; and Haddix, *Bird*, 11–16.

10. Jones, *Talking Jazz*, 192.

11. Holbrook, *Music, Movies, Meanings*, 169. He debates the relative merits of historical-versus-improvisatory realism at length, 164–169.

12. "anecdotal hearsay," Lax, *Conversations*, 130; for production details, see Lax, 128–130, 158–160, 207, 214, 336–337.

13. Schickel, *Woody Allen*, 59.

14. Lake Hopatcong is not specifically identified, but had a lakeside hotel and amusement park, as depicted. Allen has placed this sequence in Atlantic City—140 miles from Stroudsburg—but the resort is clearly not on the ocean. See Lax, *Conversations*, 207.

15. Lax, *Conversations*, 130.

16. Lax, 315–316. See also Allen, *Woody Allen*, 179–183.

CHAPTER 10

1. Gavin, *Deep in a Dream*, 72.

2. Golson and Merod, *Whisper Not*, 227–232.

3. "as the real Perkins did," Berg, *Max Perkins*, 227.

CHAPTER 11

1. For background and production details, see Cook, *Flood of Images*, 309–314; "After 'The Wire,' Taking on New Orleans in 'Treme'" (David Simon and Eric Overmyer interview with Terry Gross), NPR's Fresh Air, April 5, 2010, http://www.npr.org/templates/transcript/transcript.php?storyId=125364838; "David Simon and Clarke Peters on 'Treme'" (interview with Steve Inskeep), NPR's Morning Edition, April 9, 2010, http://www.npr.org/templates/transcript/transcript.php?storyId=125741067; Dave Walker, "'Treme's' [*sic*] Antoine Batiste Gets His Horn Sound from Rebirth's Stafford Agee," *New Orleans Times-Picayune*, December 13, 2013, http://www.nola.com/treme-hbo/index.ssf/2013/12/tremes_antoine_batiste_gets_hi.html (page discontinued).

2. Swenson, *New Atlantis*, 74. Swenson's journalistic account of post-Katrina musical activity in New Orleans is a helpful parallel text to *Treme*.

3. David Hammer and John Simerman, "Indictment: Jazz trumpeter Irvin Mayfield's Alleged Fraud Scheme Began with Loss of Nagin-approved Grants," New Orleans *Advocate*, December 19, 2017, http://www.theadvocate.com/new_orleans/entertainment_life/music/article_d17ea608-e50f-11e7-8135-4b70bebbbdea.html.

4. "'La La Land' Director Aimed To Make A Film Even Musical Skeptics Would Love" (Damien Chazelle interview with Terry Gross), NPR's Fresh Air, January 5, 2017, http://www.npr.org/templates/transcript/transcript.php?storyId=508338063.

5. The "Weird Al" Yankovic parody/remix of this sequence, incorporating actual Fletcher footage, is devastating: https://www.youtube.com/watch?v=mVt_1lGTUcg.

6. For more on this aspect, see Ethan Iverson, "The Drum Thing, or, A Brief History of Whiplash, or, 'I'm Generalizing Here'," Do the Math, March 1, 2015, https://ethaniverson.com/rhythm-and-blues/the-drum-thing-or-a-brief-history-of-whiplash-or-im-generalizing-here/.

7. On the project's early history, see Albertson, *Bessie*, 288–289. On Simone, see Cohodas, *Princess Noire*, 276.

8. Excerpts from Queen Latifah's 1990s screen test appear in the promotional short *Bessie: A Creative Journey*, on the 2015 HBO DVD.

9. Rees, HBO publicity.

10. On Rainey, see Lieb, *Ma Rainey*, 1–48.

11. Hammond, *John Hammond*, 199, 206.

12. Carl Van Vechten, "Negro 'Blues' Singers: An Appreciation of Three Coloured Artists Who Excel in an Unusual and Native Medium," 1926, reprinted in Tracy, *Write Me a Few of Your Lines*, 317.

13. Lanre Bakare, "Don Cheadle: 'I wanted to create a film that Miles Davis would want to star in'," *Guardian*, March 17, 2016, http://www.theguardian.com/film/2016/mar/17/don-cheadle-miles-davis-biopic-miles-ahead-sxsw.

14. Tibbetts, *Composers in the Movies*, 129, 133–134.

15. Davis, *Miles*, 335.

16. Davis, *Dark Magus*, xiv.

17. For production details, see Bakare, "Don Cheadle" (n13); Allen Morrison, "Troubled Genius: Don Cheadle's Gritty Portrayal of a Drug-Addled, Gun-Toting Miles Davis Is the Most Anticipated Jazz Film in Decades," *Down Beat*, April 2016, 22–26; Robert Ito, "Don Cheadle on Becoming Miles Davis," *NY Times*, March 27, 2016, http://www.nytimes.com/2016/03/27/movies/don-cheadle-on-becoming-miles-davis.html. Biographical details from Davis, *Dark Magus*; Szwed, *So What*; Davis, *Miles*; Nisenson, *'Round About Midnight*, 227–235.

18. Gavin, *Deep in a Dream*, 207.

19. Baker profiled in *TIME*: "Listen to Those Zsounds," February 1, 1954.

20. "Hawke suggested," unnamed "making of" featurette on 2016 MPI DVD. For production details, see MPI DVD; and "Ethan Hawke Channels Chet Baker in 'Born To Be Blue'" (Hawke and Robert Budreau interviewed by Shad) CBC's Q, March 29, 2016, https://www.youtube.com/watch?v=X9_3TVPQVzY. Baker biographical details from Gavin, *Deep in a Dream*; Baker quote, Gavin, *Deep in a Dream*, 353.

21. Gavin, *Deep in a Dream*, 236.

22. Cohodas, *Princess Noire*, 319.

23. Lisa's quote, Light, *What Happened*, 32. On casting controversy, see for example Feldstein, *How It Feels*, 193. On Grace Kelly, Al Schackman, "The Person Who Nina Simone Wanted to Play Her in a Biopic Might Surprise You," *Huffington Post*, April 19, 2016, http://www.huffingtonpost.com/al-schackman/nina-simone-the-movie_b_9729078.html.

24. For production details, see "La La Land Director" (n4); Rebecca Ford, "How 'La La Land' Went From First-Screening Stumbles to Hollywood Ending, *Hollywood Reporter*, November 11, 2016, http://www.hollywoodreporter.com/features/la-la-land-unrealistic-hollywood-dream-critical-acclaim-942793.

25. Moore, *Yankee Blues*, 90.

26. Chilton, *Sidney Bechet*, 83–84; and Bechet, *Treat It Gentle*, 152.

27. "La La Land Director."

28. McKay, *Robert De Niro*, 67.

29. Gary Fukushima, "What Do Actual L.A. Jazz Musicians Think of La La Land's Portrayal of L.A. Jazz?," *LA Weekly*, February 21, 2017, http://www.laweekly.com/music/what-do-actual-la-jazz-musicians-think-of-la-la-lands-portrayal-of-la-jazz-7952454.

30. Armstrong, *Swing That Music*, 12.

31. For Bolden lore, see Ramsey and Smith, *Jazzmen*, 10–18; Barker, *Buddy Bolden*, 1–52. For facts versus legends, see Marquis, *In Search of Buddy Bolden*.

32. Production details from press kit and Phillip Lutz, "The Resurrection of Buddy Bolden," *Down Beat*, June 2019, 40–44. On *Louis* and the first draft of *Bolden*, Shaun Brady, "Dan Pritzker's new silent film imagines obscure musician Buddy Bolden's influence on Louis Armstrong," *Philadelphia Daily News*, August 24, 2010, https://www.philly.com/philly/entertainment/20100824_Dan_Pritzker_s_new_silent_film_imagines_obscure_musician_Buddy_Bolden_s_influence_on_Louis_Armstrong.html; and Mike Fleming Jr., "Seven Years After Production Began, Dan Pritzker's 'Bolden' Skeds New Shoot, Sans Star Anthony Mackie," *Deadline*, May 28, 2014, https://deadline.com/2014/05/seven-years-after-production-began-dan-pritzkers-bolden-skeds-new-shoot-sans-star-anthony-mackie-737128/.

33. "Africans Americans listened," Jones and Chilton, *Louis Armstrong Story*, 148. On "Russian Lullaby": "Louis Armstrong + the Jewish Family in New Orleans, LA., the Year of 1907" in Armstrong, *In His Own Words*, 17–18, 30, 33.

34. On Baquet and Bolden, see Gushee, *Pioneers of Jazz*, 39–40; and Marquis, *In Search of Buddy Bolden*, 81, 99.

35. Barker, *Buddy Bolden*, 27.

CHAPTER 12

1. On Purves, Whitehead, *New Dutch Swing*, 200; and author interview, 1998. Torme, *It Wasn't All Velvet*, 17; Lewis, *Power Stronger*, 27; Masekela, *Still Grazing*, 59–60; on Harris, "Inspired by acclaimed director Spike Lee's 'Mo Better Blues,' Harris became enamored with the trumpet and at the age of 13 his musical journey started," https://www.bruceharristrumpet.com/bio.

2. Chilton, *Sidney Bechet*, 292.

3. Bechet, *Treat It Gentle*, 72.

4. Anderson, "Evolution of Jazz," *Down Beat*, March 9, 1951. We surveyed the extensive (but incomplete) Bechet clipping files at Institute of Jazz Studies, Rutgers University–Newark. Alan Lomax interview with Leonard Bechet archived at http://research.culturalequity.org/get-audio-ix.do?ix=recording&id=2900&idType=performerId&sortBy=abc.

5. Cohodas, *Princess Noire*, 92.

6. For example, on Lester Bowie's Brass Fantasy, *The Fire This Time* (In+Out 7019, 1992).

BIBLIOGRAPHY

Ake, David. *Jazz Matters: Sound, Place, and Time Since Bebop.* Berkeley: University of California Press, 2010.

Albany, A. J. *Low Down: Junk, Jazz, and Other Fairy Tales from Childhood.* Portland, OR: Tin House Books, 2003.

Albee, Edward. *The Collected Plays of Edward Albee 1958-65.* New York: Overlook, 2008.

Albertson, Chris. *Bessie.* 2nd ed. New Haven, CT: Yale University Press, 2003.

Allen, Woody. *Woody Allen: Interviews.* Edited by Robert E. Kapsis and Kathie Koblentz. Jackson: University Press of Mississippi, 2006.

Altman, Robert. *Robert Altman: Interviews.* Edited by David Sterritt. Jackson: University Press of Mississippi, 2000.

Amram, David. *Vibrations: The Adventures and Musical Times of David Amram.* New York: Macmillan, 1968.

Andriessen, Bas. *Tetterettet: Interviews met Nederlandse improviserende musici* [Interviews with Dutch improvising musicians]. The Hague: Tandem Felix, 1996.

Armstrong, Louis. *Louis Armstrong in His Own Words: Selected Writings.* Edited by Thomas Brothers. New York: Oxford University Press, 1999.

Armstrong, Louis. *Swing That Music.* 1936. Reprint, New York: Da Capo, 1993.

Astaire, Fred. *Steps in Time.* New York: Harper & Brothers, 1959.

Baker, Chet. *As Though I Had Wings: The Lost Memoir.* New York: St. Martin's Griffin, 1997.

Baker, David, ed. *New Perspectives on Jazz: Report on a National Conference Held at Wingspread, Racine, Wisconsin, September 8-10, 1986.* Washington, DC: Smithsonian Institution, 1990.

Baker, Dorothy. *Young Man with a Horn.* 1938. Reprint, New York: Penguin, 1945.

Barker, Danny. *Buddy Bolden and the Last Days of Storyville.* Edited by Alyn Shipton. New York: Continuum, 1998.

Barker, Danny. *A Life in Jazz.* Edited by Alyn Shipton. New York: Oxford University Press, 1986.

Barnet, Charlie, with Stanley Dance. *Those Swinging Years: The Autobiography of Charlie Barnet.* Baton Rouge: Louisiana State University Press, 1984.

Barrios, Richard. *A Song in the Dark: The Birth of the Musical Film.* New York: Oxford University Press, 1995.

Baxter, John. *De Niro: A Biography.* London: Harper Collins, 2002.

Bechet, Sidney. *Treat It Gentle: An Autobiography.* 1960. Reprint, New York: Da Capo, 1978.

Berg, A. Scott. *Max Perkins: Editor of Genius.* New York: Dutton, 1978.

Bergreen, Laurence. *As Thousands Cheer: The Life of Irving Berlin.* New York: Viking, 1990.

Berrett, Joshua. *Louis Armstrong and Paul Whiteman: Two Kings Of Jazz.* New Haven, CT: Yale University Press, 2004.

Berry, Jason, Jonathan Foose, and Tad Jones. *Up from the Cradle of Jazz: New Orleans Music Since World War II.* Athens: University of Georgia Press, 1986.

Bigard, Barney. *With Louis and the Duke: The Autobiography of a Jazz Clarinetist.* London: Macmillan, 1985.

Bingen, Steven. *Warner Bros. Hollywood's Ultimate Backlot.* Lanham, MD: Taylor Trade Publishing/Rowman & Littlefield, 2014.

Bingen, Steven, Stephen K. Sylvester, and Michael Troyan. *M-G-M: Hollywood's Greatest Backlot.* Solana Beach, CA: Santa Monica Press, 2011.

Biskind, Peter. *Easy Riders, Raging Bulls: How the Sex-Drugs-and-Rock 'n' Roll Generation Saved Hollywood.* New York: Simon & Schuster, 1998.

Blesh, Rudi. *Combo: USA—Eight Lives in Jazz.* Philadelphia: Chilton, 1971.

Blesh, Rudi, and Harriet Janis. *They All Played Ragtime.* 4th ed. New York: Oak Publications, 1971.

Bogdanovich, Peter. *Who the Devil Made It: Conversations with Legendary Film Directors.* New York: Ballantine, 1997.

Bogdanovich, Peter. *Who the Hell's In It: Portraits and Conversations.* New York: Knopf, 2005.

Bogle, Donald. *Toms, Coons, Mulattoes, Mammies, and Bucks: An Interpretive History of Blacks in American Films.* 4th ed. New York: Continuum, 2002.

Booth, Martin. *Cannabis: A History.* New York: Picador, 2003.

Boujut, Michel. *Louis Armstrong.* New York: Rizzoli, 1998.

Britt, Stan. *Dexter Gordon: A Musical Biography.* London: Quartet Books, 1989.

Brothers, Thomas. *Louis Armstrong's New Orleans.* New York: W. W. Norton, 2006.

Brunn, H. O. *The Story of the Original Dixieland Jazz Band.* 1960. Reprint, New York: Da Capo, 1977.

Büchmann-Møller, Frank. *You Just Fight for Your Life: The Story of Lester Young.* New York: Praeger, 1990.

Callender, Red, and Elaine Cohen. *Unfinished Dream: The Musical World of Red Callender.* London: Quartet Books, 1985.

Cameron, Julia. *Floor Sample: A Creative Memoir.* New York: Jeremy P. Tarcher–Penguin, 2006.

Carmichael, Hoagy, with Stephen Longstreet. *Sometimes I Wonder.* New York: Farrar, Straus and Giroux, 1965.

Carroll, Diahann, with Ross Firestone. *Diahann—An Autobiography.* Boston: Little, Brown, 1986.

Cassavetes, John. *Cassavetes on Cassavetes.* Edited by Ray Carney. New York: Faber and Faber, 2001.

Chambers, Jack. *Milestones: The Music and Times of Miles Davis.* Originally in 2 vols., 1983, 1985. Reprint, New York: Quill, 1989.

Chilton, John. *Billie's Blues: The Billie Holiday Story.* New York: Stein and Day, 1975.

Chilton, John. *Sidney Bechet: The Wizard of Jazz.* New York: Oxford University Press, 1987.

Clarke, Donald. *Billie Holiday: Wishing on the Moon.* 2nd ed. New York: Da Capo, 2002.

Clayton, Buck, and Nancy Miller Elliott. *Buck Clayton's Jazz World.* London: Macmillan, 1986.

Cohen, Harvey G. *Duke Ellington's America.* Chicago: University of Chicago Press, 2010.

Cohodas, Nadine. *Princess Noire: The Tumultuous Reign of Nina Simone.* New York: Pantheon, 2010.

Collier, James Lincoln. *Benny Goodman and the Swing Era.* New York: Oxford University Press, 1989.

Collier, James Lincoln. *Louis Armstrong: An American Genius.* New York: Oxford University Press, 1983.

Condon, Eddie. *We Called It Music.* 1947. Reprint, New York: Da Capo, 1992.

Cook, Bernie. *Flood of Images: Media, Memory, and Hurricane Katrina.* Austin: University of Texas Press, 2015.

Coppola, Francis Ford, and William Kennedy. *The Cotton Club* [screenplay]. New York: St. Martin's Press, 1986.

Cortázar, Julio. *Blow Up and Other Stories.* New York: Pantheon, 1985.

Cowie, Peter. *Coppola.* Milwaukee: Applause–Hal Leonard, 2014.

Cripps, Thomas. *Making Movies Black: The Hollywood Message Movie from World War II to the Civil Rights Era.* New York: Oxford University Press, 1993.

Cripps, Thomas. *Slow Fade to Black: The Negro in American Film, 1900–1942.* New York: Oxford University Press, 1977.

Crouch, Stanley. *Kansas City Lightning: The Rise and Times of Charlie Parker.* New York: HarperCollins, 2013.

Crow, Bill. *Jazz Anecdotes: Second Time Around.* New York: Oxford University Press, 2005.

Crowther, Bruce. *Gene Krupa: His Life and Times.* New York: Universe Books, 1987.

Curtis, James. *Between Flops: A Biography of Preston Sturges.* New York: Harcourt Brace Jovanovich, 1982.

Dahl, Linda. *Stormy Weather: The Music and Lives of a Century of Jazzwomen.* 1984. Reprint, New York: Limelight, 1996.

Dance, Stanley. *The World of Duke Ellington.* New York: Charles Scribner's Sons, 1970.

Daniels, Douglas Henry. *Lester Leaps In: The Life and Times of Lester "Pres" Young.* Boston: Beacon Press, 2002.

Davis, Francis. *In the Moment: Jazz in the 1980s.* New York: Oxford University Press, 1986.

Davis, Gregory. *Dark Magus: The Jekyll and Hyde Life of Miles Davis*. San Francisco: Backbeat Books, 2006.

Davis, Judith. *Richard Gere: An Unauthorized Biography*. New York: Signet, 1983.

Davis, Miles, with Quincy Troupe. *Miles: The Autobiography*. New York: Simon & Schuster, 1989.

Davis, Sammy, Jr. *Hollywood in a Suitcase*. New York: William Morrow, 1980.

Delaunay, Charles. *Django Reinhardt*. Translated by Michael James. New York: Da Capo, 1961.

DeLong, Thomas A. *Pops: Paul Whiteman, King of Jazz*. Piscataway, NJ: New Century, 1983.

Delson, Susan. *Dudley Murphy: Hollywood Wild Card*. Minneapolis: University of Minnesota Press, 2006.

Demme, Jonathan. *Jonathan Demme: Interviews*. Edited by Robert E. Kapsis. Jackson: University Press of Mississippi, 2009.

Dery, Mark. *Flame Wars: The Discourse of Cyberculture*. Durham, NC: Duke University Press, 1994.

Douglas, Kirk. *The Ragman's Son: An Autobiography*. New York: Simon & Schuster, 1988.

Dregni, Michael. *Django: The Life and Music of a Gypsy Legend*. New York: Oxford University Press, 2004.

Early, Gerald, ed. *The Sammy Davis, Jr., Reader*. New York: Farrar, Straus and Giroux, 2001.

Eastwood, Clint. *Clint Eastwood: Interviews*. Edited by Robert E. Kapsis and Kathie Koblentz. Jackson: University Press of Mississippi, 1999.

Ellington, Edward Kennedy. *Music Is My Mistress*. Garden City, NY: Doubleday, 1973.

Ellington, Mercer, with Stanley Dance. *Duke Ellington in Person: An Intimate Memoir*. Boston: Houghton Mifflin, 1978.

Epstein, Daniel Mark. *Nat King Cole*. New York: Farrar, Straus and Giroux, 1999.

Erenberg, Lewis A. *Swingin' the Dream: Big Band Jazz and the Rebirth of American Culture*. Chicago: University of Chicago Press, 1998.

Evanier, David. *Roman Candle: The Life of Bobby Darin*. Albany: State University of New York Press, 2010.

Evans, Philip R., Stanley Hester, Stephen Hester, and Linda Evans. *The Red Nichols Story: After Intermission, 1942–1965*. Lanham, MD: Scarecrow, 1997.

Evans, Robert. *The Kid Stays in the Picture*. New York: Hyperion, 1994.

Feather, Leonard. *The Jazz Years: Earwitness to an Era*. New York: Da Capo, 1987.

Feldstein, Ruth. *How It Feels to Be Free: Black Women Entertainers and the Civil Rights Movement*. New York: Oxford University Press, 2013.

Ferguson, Otis. *In the Spirit of Jazz: The Otis Ferguson Reader*. Edited by Dorothy Chamberlain and Robert Wilson. 1982. Reprint, New York: Da Capo, 1997.

Fine, Marshall. *Accidental Genius: How John Cassavetes Invented American Independent Film*. New York: Miramax–Hyperion, 2005.

Firestone, Ross. *Swing, Swing, Swing: The Life & Times of Benny Goodman*. New York: W. W. Norton, 1992.

Fishgall, Gary. *Gonna Do Great Things: The Life of Sammy Davis, Jr.* New York: Lisa Drew–Scribner, 2003.

Flender, Harold. *Paris Blues*. New York: Ballantine, 1957.

Flinn, Caryl. *Brass Diva: The Life and Legends of Ethel Merman*. Berkeley: University of California Press, 2007.

Freedland, Michael. *Fred Astaire: A Biography*. London: W. H. Allen, 1976.

Freedland, Michael. *Irving Berlin*. New York: Stein & Day, 1974.

Freedland, Michael. *Jolson*. New York: Stein & Day, 1972.

Friedman, Lawrence S. *The Cinema of Martin Scorsese*. New York: Continuum, 1997.

Fritts, Ron, and Ken Vail. *Ella Fitzgerald: The Chick Webb Years and Beyond, 1935–1948*. Lanham, MD: Scarecrow, 2003.

Fry, Andy. *Paris Blues: African American Music and French Popular Culture, 1920–1960*. Chicago: University of Chicago Press, 2014.

Furia, Philip. *Irving Berlin: A Life in Song*. New York: Schirmer, 1998.

Furia, Philip. *Skylark: The Life and Times of Johnny Mercer*. New York: St. Martin's, 2003.

Gabbard, Krin. *Better Git It in Your Soul: An Interpretive Biography of Charles Mingus*. Oakland: University of California Press, 2016.

Gabbard, Krin. *Black Magic: White Hollywood and African American Culture*. New Brunswick, NJ: Rutgers University Press, 2004.

Gabbard, Krin. *Jammin' at the Margins: Jazz and the American Cinema*. Chicago: University of Chicago Press, 1996.

Gavin, James. *Deep in a Dream: The Long Night of Chet Baker*. New York: Alfred A. Knopf, 2002.

Gavin, James. *Is That All There Is? The Strange Life of Peggy Lee*. New York: Atria Books, 2014.

Gennari, John. *Blowin' Hot and Cool: Jazz and Its Critics*. Chicago: University of Chicago Press, 2006.

Giddins, Gary. *Celebrating Bird: The Triumph of Charlie Parker*. New York: Beech Tree Books, 1987.

Gillespie, Dizzy, with Al Fraser. *To Be. . . or Not to Bop*. New York: Doubleday, 1979.

Gitler, Ira. *Swing to Bop: An Oral History of the Transition in Jazz in the 1940s*. New York: Oxford University Press, 1985.

Godfrey, Lionel. *Paul Newman, Superstar: A Critical Biography*. New York: St. Martin's, 1978.

Goldman, Michael. *Clint Eastwood: Master Filmmaker at Work*. New York: Abrams, 2012.

Golson, Benny, and Jim Merod. *Whisper Not: The Autobiography of Benny Golson*. Philadelphia: Temple University Press, 2016.

Goodman, Benny, and Irving Kolodin. *The Kingdom of Swing*. New York: Frederick Ungar, 1939.

Gordon, Maxine. *Sophisticated Giant: The Life and Legacy of Dexter Gordon*. Oakland: University of California Press, 2018.

Gordy, Berry. *To Be Loved: The Music, the Magic, the Memories of Motown—An Autobiography*. New York: Warner Books, 1994.

Gottlieb, Robert, ed. *Reading Jazz: A Gathering of Autobiography, Reportage, and Criticism from 1919 to Now*. New York: Pantheon, 1996.

Goudsouzian, Aram. *Sidney Poitier: Man, Actor, Icon*. Chapel Hill: University of North Carolina Press, 2004.

Gourse, Leslie. *Wynton Marsalis: Skain's Domain—A Biography*. New York: Schirmer, 1999.

Gregory, Dick, with Shelia P. Moses. *Callus on My Soul: A Memoir*. Atlanta: Longstreet, 2000.

Griffin, Farah Jasmine. *If You Can't Be Free, Be a Mystery: In Search of Billie Holiday*. New York: Free Press, 2001.

Gushee, Lawrence. *Pioneers of Jazz: The Story of the Creole Band*. New York: Oxford University Press, 2005.

Haddix, Chuck. *Bird: The Life and Music of Charlie Parker*. Urbana: University of Illinois Press, 2013.

Haddix, Chuck. *Kansas City Jazz: From Ragtime to Bebop: A History*. New York: Oxford University Press, 2005.

Hajdu, David. *Lush Life: A Biography of Billy Strayhorn*. New York: Farrar, Straus and Giroux, 1996.

Hall, Fred. *Dialogues in Swing*. Ventura, CA: Pathfinder, 1989.

Hammond, John, with Irving Townsend. *John Hammond on Record: An Autobiography*. New York: Summit Books, 1977.

Hancock, Herbie, with Lisa Dickey. *Possibilities*. New York: Viking, 2014.

Handy, W. C., ed. *The Blues: An Anthology*. 1949. Reprint, New York: Da Capo, 1990.

Handy, W. C. *The Father of the Blues: An Autobiography*. New York: Macmillan, 1941.

Haskins, James. *The Cotton Club*. 1977. Reprint, New York: Plume–New American Library, 1984.

Hasse, John Edward. *Beyond Category: The Life and Genius of Duke Ellington*. New York: Simon & Schuster, 1993.

Hayde, Frank R. *Stan Levey: Jazz Heavyweight*. Solana Beach, CA: Santa Monica Press, 2016.

Haygood, Wil. *In Black and White: The Life and Times of Sammy Davis, Jr.* New York: Alfred A. Knopf, 2003.

Hershorn, Tad. *Norman Granz: The Man Who Used Jazz for Justice*. Berkeley: University of California Press, 2011.

Hischak, Thomas S. *The Encyclopedia of Film Composers*. Lanham, MD: Rowman and Littlefield, 2015.

Holbrook, Morris B. *Music, Movies, Meanings, and Markets: Cinemajazzmatazz*. New York: Routledge, 2011.

Holiday, Billie, with William Dufty. *Lady Sings the Blues*. 1956. Reprint, New York, Penguin, 1992.

Jablonski, Edward. *Irving Berlin: American Troubadour*. New York: Henry Holt, 1999.

Jackson, Carlton. *Picking Up the Tab: The Life and Movies of Martin Ritt*. Bowling Green, OH: Bowling Green State University Popular Press, 1994.

James, Stuart. *Too Late Blues*. New York: Lancer Books, 1962.

Jones, Max. *Talking Jazz*. 1987. Reprint, New York: W. W. Norton, 1988.

Jones, Max, and John Chilton. *The Louis Armstrong Story, 1900–1971*. 1971. Reprint, New York: Da Capo, 1988.

Jost, Ekkehard. *Free Jazz*. 1974. Reprint, New York: Da Capo, 1981.

Kaminski, Max, and V. E. Hughes. *Jazz Band: My Life in Jazz*. New York: Harper & Row, 1963.

Kander, John, and Fred Ebb, with Greg Lawrence. *Colored Lights: Forty Years of Words and Music, Show Biz, Collaboration, and All That Jazz*. New York: Faber and Faber, 2003.

Kashner, Sam, and Nancy Schoenberger. *A Talent for Genius: The Life and Times of Oscar Levant*. New York: Villard, 1994.

Kastin, David. *Nica's Dream: The Life and Legend of the Jazz Baroness*. New York: W. W. Norton, 2011.

Kater, Michael H. *Different Drummers: Jazz in the Culture of Nazi Germany*. New York: Oxford University Press, 1992.

Kazan, Elia. *A Life*. New York: Alfred A. Knopf, 1988.

Kelley, Robin D. G. *Africa Speaks, America Answers: Modern Jazz in Revolutionary Times*. Cambridge, MA: Harvard University Press, 2012.

Kelly, Mary Pat. *Martin Scorsese: A Journey*. New York: Thunder's Mouth Press, 1991.

Kennedy, William. *Riding the Yellow Trolley Car: Selected Nonfiction*. New York: Viking, 1993.

Kenney, William Howland. *Chicago Jazz: A Cultural History, 1904–1930*. New York: Oxford University Press, 1993.

Keyser, Les. *Martin Scorsese*. New York: Twayne, 1992.

Klauber, Bruce H. *The World of Gene Krupa: That Legendary Drummin' Man*. Ventura, CA: Pathfinder Publishing of California, 1990.

Koenig, David. *Danny Kaye: King of Jesters*. Irvine, CA: Bonaventure, 2012.

Korall, Burt. *Drummin' Men: The Heartbeat Of Jazz—The Swing Years*. New York: Schirmer, 1990.

Lait, Jack, and Lee Mortimer. *U.S.A. Confidential*. New York: Crown, 1952.

Lax, Eric. *Conversations with Woody Allen: His Films, the Movies, and Moviemaking*. New York: Alfred A. Knopf, 2007.

Lee, Peggy. *Miss Peggy Lee: An Autobiography*. New York: Donald I. Fine, 1989.

Lee, Spike, as told to Kaleem Aftab. *That's My Story and I'm Sticking to It*. New York: W. W. Norton, 2006.

Lee, Spike, with Lisa Jones. *Mo' Better Blues*. New York: Fireside/Simon & Schuster, 1990.

Levant, Oscar. *A Smattering of Ignorance*. New York: Doubleday, Doran, 1940.

Levinson, Peter J. *Puttin' on the Ritz: Fred Astaire and the Fine Art of Panache: A Biography*. New York: St. Martin's Press, 2009.

Levinson, Peter J. *Tommy Dorsey: Livin' in a Great Big Way*. New York: Da Capo, 2005.

Levy, Shawn. *De Niro: A Life*. New York: Crown–Archetype, 2014.

Lewis, George E. *A Power Stronger than Itself: The AACM and American Experimental Music*. Chicago: University of Chicago Press, 2008.

Lieb, Sandra R. *Ma Rainey: A Study of the Mother of the Blues*. Amherst: University of Massachusetts Press, 1981.

Light, Alan. *What Happened, Miss Simone? A Biography*. New York: Crown Archetype, 2016.

Lipman, Ross. "Mingus, Cassavetes, and the Birth of a Jazz Cinema." *Journal of Film Music* 2, no. 2–4 (Winter 2009): 145–164.

Marquis, Donald. *In Search of Buddy Bolden: First Man of Jazz*. Baton Rouge: Louisiana State University Press, 1978.

Masekela, Hugh, and D. Michael Cheers. *Still Grazing: The Musical Journey of Hugh Masekela*. New York: Crown Archetype, 2004.

McCarthy, Todd. *Howard Hawks: The Grey Fox of Hollywood*. New York: Grove Press, 1997.

McGee, Kristin A. *Some Liked It Hot: Jazz Women in Film and Television, 1928–1959*. Middletown, CT: Wesleyan University Press, 2009.

McGilligan, Patrick. *Clint: The Life and Legend*. New York: St. Martin's, 1999.

McKay, Keith. *Robert De Niro: The Hero Behind the Masks*. New York: St. Martin's, 1986.

Mekas, Jonas. *Movie Journal: The Rise of the New American Cinema 1959–1971*. New York: Macmillan, 1972.

Mercer, Johnny. *The Complete Lyrics of Johnny Mercer*. Edited by Robert Kimball, Barry Day, Miles Krueger, and Eric Davis. New York: Borzoi/Knopf, 2009.

Mercer, Johnny. *Our Huckleberry Friend: The Life, Times, and Lyrics of Johnny Mercer*. Edited by Bob Bach and Ginger Mercer. Secaucus, NJ: Lyle Stuart, 1982.

Mezzrow, Milton "Mezz," and Bernard Wolfe. *Really the Blues*. New York: Random House, 1946.

Michaud, Michael Gregg. *Sal Mineo: A Biography*. New York: Three Rivers Press, 2010.

Milkowski, Bill. *Swing It! An Annotated History of Jive*. New York: Billboard Books, 2001.

Moore, MacDonald Smith. *Yankee Blues: Musical Culture and American Identity*. Bloomington: Indiana University Press, 1985.

Morgenstern, Dan. *Living with Jazz: A Reader*. Edited by Sheldon Meyer. New York: Pantheon, 2004.

Nisenson, Eric. *'Round About Midnight: A Portrait of Miles Davis*. New York: Dial, 1982.

Nolan, Tom. *Three Chords for Beauty's Sake: The Life of Artie Shaw*. New York: W. W. Norton, 2010.

O'Day, Anita, with George Eells. *High Times, Hard Times*. 1981. Reprint, New York: Limelight, 2003.

O'Meally, Robert G., Brent Hayes Edwards, and Farah Jasmine Griffin, eds. *Uptown Conversation: The New Jazz Studies*. New York: Columbia University Press, 2004.

Parker, Chan. *My Life in E-Flat*. Columbia: University of South Carolina Press, 1993.

Pepper, Art, and Laurie Pepper. *Straight Life: The Story of Art Pepper*. New York: Schirmer, 1979.

Pitts, Michael R. *The Rise of the Crooners: Gene Austin, Russ Columbo, Bing Crosby, Nick Lucas, Johnny Marvin, and Rudy Vallee*. Lanham, MD: Scarecrow, 2002.

Pollack, Howard. *George Gershwin: His Life and Work*. Berkeley: University of California Press, 2007.

Priestley, Brian. *Mingus: A Critical Biography*. New York: Quartet Books, 1983.

Pullman, Peter. *Wail: The Life of Bud Powell*. Brooklyn, NY: Bop Changes, 2013.

Ramsey, Frederick, Jr., and Charles Edward Smith, eds. *Jazzmen*. New York: Harcourt Brace, 1939.

Rauch, Earl Mac. *New York, New York*. New York: Pocket Books, 1977.

Reich, Howard, and William Gaines. *Jelly's Blues: The Life, Music, and Redemption of Jelly Roll Morton*. Cambridge, MA: Da Capo, 2003.

Reisner, Robert, ed. *Bird: The Legend of Charlie Parker*. 1962. Reprint, New York: Da Capo, 1977.

Riccardi, Ricky. *What a Wonderful World: The Magic of Louis Armstrong's Later Years*. New York: Pantheon, 2011.

Rimler, Walter. *George Gershwin: An Intimate Portrait*. Urbana: University of Illinois Press, 2009.

Ritt, Martin. *Martin Ritt: Interviews*. Edited by Gabriel Miller. Jackson: University of Mississippi Press, 2002.

Robertson, David. *W. C. Handy: The Life and Times of the Man Who Made the Blues*. New York: Knopf, 2009.

Robertson, James C. *The Casablanca Man: The Cinema of Michael Curtiz*. New York: Routledge, 1993.

Rode, Alan K. *Michael Curtiz: A Life in Film*. Lexington: University Press of Kentucky, 2017.

Russell, Ross. *Bird Lives! The High Life and Hard Times of Charlie Yardbird Parker*. 1993. Reprint, New York: Da Capo, 1996.

Rustin, Nicole T., and Sherrie Tucker, eds. *Big Ears: Listening for Gender in Jazz Studies*. Durham, NC: Duke University Press, 2008.

Sann, Paul. *Kill the Dutchman! The Story of Dutch Schultz*. New Rochelle, NY: Arlington House, 1971.

Sargent, Winthrop. *Jazz: Hot and Hybrid*. 2nd ed. New York: Dutton, 1946.

Sarris, Andrew. *The American Cinema: Directors and Directions, 1929–1968*. New York: Dutton, 1968.

Saul, Scott. *Becoming Richard Pryor*. New York: HarperCollins, 2014.

Saxon, Lyle, Edward Dreyer, and Robert Tallent. *Gumbo Ya-Ya: A Collection of Louisiana Folk Tales*. Boston: Houghton Mifflin, 1945.

Schickel, Richard. *Clint Eastwood*. New York: Knopf, 1996.

Schickel, Richard. *Conversations with Scorsese*. New York: Knopf, 2011.

Schickel, Richard. *Elia Kazan: A Biography*. New York: HarperCollins, 2005.

Schickel, Richard. *Woody Allen: A Life in Film*. Chicago: Ivan R. Dee, 2003.

Schumacher, Michael. *Francis Ford Coppola: A Filmmaker's Life*. New York: Crown, 1999.

Scorsese, Martin. *Martin Scorsese: Interviews*. Edited by Peter Brunette. Jackson: University Press of Mississippi, 1999.

Shapiro, Nat, and Nat Hentoff, eds. *Hear Me Talkin' to Ya: The Story of Jazz as Told by the Men Who Made It*. New York: Dover, 1955.

Shaw, Arnold. *The Street That Never Slept: New York's Fabled 52d Street*. New York: Coward, McCann & Geoghegan, 1971.

Shaw, Artie. *The Trouble with Cinderella: An Outline of Identity*. New York: Da Capo, 1979.

Sikov, Ed. *On Sunset Boulevard: The Life and Times of Billy Wilder*. New York: Hyperion, 1998.

Simon, George T. *The Big Bands*. 4th ed. New York: Schirmer, 1981.

Simon, George T. *Glenn Miller and His Orchestra*. New York: Thomas Y. Crowell, 1974.

Simone, Nina, with Stephen Cleary. *I Put a Spell on You: The Autobiography of Nina Simone*. New York: Pantheon, 1992.

Smith, Willie the Lion, with George Hoefer. *Music on My Mind: The Memoirs of an American Pianist*. New York: Doubleday, 1964.

Spellman, A. B. *Four Lives in the Bebop Business*. 1966. Reprint, New York: Limelight, 1985.

Stearns, Marshall, and Jean Stearns. *Jazz Dance: The Story of American Vernacular Dance*. New York: Macmillan, 1968.

Stevens, Tamara, with Erin Stevens. *Swing Dancing*. Santa Barbara, CA: Greenwood, 2011.

Stroff, Stephen M. *Red Head: A Chronological Survey of "Red" Nichols and His Five Pennies*. Lanham, MD: Scarecrow, 1996.

Sublette, Ned. *Cuba and Its Music: From the First Drums to the Mambo*. Chicago: Chicago Review Press, 2004.

Sudhalter, Richard. *Stardust Melody: The Life and Times of Hoagy Carmichael*. New York: Oxford University Press, 2002.

Sudhalter, Richard, and Philip R. Evans, with William Dean-Myatt. *Bix: Man and Legend*. New Rochelle, NY: Arlington House, 1974.

Swenson, John. *New Atlantis: Musicians Battle for the Survival of New Orleans*. New York: Oxford University Press, 2011.

Szwed, John F. *Billie Holiday: The Musician and the Myth*. New York: Penguin, 2015.

Szwed, John F. *So What: The Life of Miles Davis*. New York: Simon & Schuster, 2002.

Szwed, John F. *Space Is the Place: The Lives and Times of Sun Ra*. 1997. Reprint "with several minor textual emendations," New York: Da Capo, 1998.

Tackley, Catherine. *Benny Goodman's Famous 1938 Carnegie Hall Jazz Concert*. New York: Oxford University Press, 2012.

Taraborrelli, J. Randy. *Diana Ross: An Unauthorized Biography*. New York: Citadel Press/Kensington, 2007.

Taylor, Arthur. *Notes and Tones: Musician-to-Musician Interviews*. 1982. Reprint, New York: Da Capo, 1993.

Tibbetts, John C. *Composers in the Movies: Studies in Musical Biography*. New Haven, CT: Yale University Press, 2005.

Tingen, Paul. *Miles Beyond: The Electric Explorations of Miles Davis, 1967–1991*. New York: Billboard Books, 2001.

Tormé, Mel. *It Wasn't All Velvet: An Autobiography*. New York: Viking, 1998.

Tracy, Steven C., ed. *Write Me a Few of Your Lines: A Blues Reader*. Amherst: University of Massachusetts Press, 1999.

Tucker, Mark, ed. *The Duke Ellington Reader*. New York: Oxford University Press, 1993.

Tucker, Sherrie. *Swing Shift: "All-Girl" Bands of the 1940s*. Durham, NC: Duke University Press, 2000.

Ulanov, Barry. *Duke Ellington*. New York: Creative Age Press, 1946.

Vail, Ken. *Dizzy Gillespie: The Bebop Years 1937–1952*. Cambridge, UK: Vail Publishing, 2000.

Vallée, Rudy. *Vagabond Dreams Come True*. New York: Dutton, 1930.

Vallée, Rudy, with Gil McKean. *My Time Is Your Time: The Story of Rudy Vallee*. New York: Ivan Obolenski, 1962.

Wagner, Robert, with Scott Eyman. *Pieces of My Heart: A Life*. New York: William Morrow, 2008.

Waldo, Terry. *This Is Ragtime*. New York: Da Capo, 1976.

Warner, Simon. *Text and Drugs and Rock 'n' Roll: The Beats and Rock Culture*. New York: Bloomsbury Academic, 2013.

Wein, George, with Nate Chinen. *Myself Among Others*. Cambridge, MA: Da Capo, 2003.

Whitehead, Kevin. *New Dutch Swing*. New York: Billboard Books, 1998.

Whiteman, Paul, and Mary Margaret McBride. *Jazz*. New York: J. H. Sears, 1926.

Wilk, Max. *They're Playing Our Song: From Jerome Kern to Stephen Sondheim—The Stories behind the Words and Music of Two Generations*. New York: Atheneum, 1973.

Williams, John A. *Night Song*. New York: Farrar, Straus and Cudahy, 1961.

Wilmeth, Don B., C. W. E. Bigsby, and Christopher Bigsby, eds. *The Cambridge History of American Theatre*, vol. 2. New York: Cambridge University Press, 1998.

Wojcik, Pamela Robertson, and Arthur Knight, eds. *Soundtrack Available: Essays on Film and Popular Music*. Durham, NC: Duke University Press, 2001.

Woods, Tim. *Beginning Postmodernism*, 2nd ed. Manchester: Manchester University Press, 2009.

Wyatt, Justin. *High Concept: Movies and Marketing in Hollywood*. Austin: University of Texas Press, 1994.

Yablonsky, Lewis. *George Raft*. New York: McGraw-Hill, 1974.

Youngquist, Paul. *A Pure Solar World: Sun Ra and the Birth of Afrofuturism*. Austin: University of Texas Press, 2016.

Zanuck, Daryl F. *Memo from Daryl F. Zanuck: The Golden Years at Twentieth Century–Fox*. Edited by Rudy Behlmer. New York: Grove, 1993.

Zuckoff, Mitchell, ed. *Robert Altman: The Oral Biography*. New York: Alfred A. Knopf, 2009.

INDEX